CHRISTOPHER H. LOVELOCK
CHARLES B. WEINBERG

READINGS IN PUBLIC AND NONPROFIT MARKETING

READINGS IN PUBLIC
AND NONPROFIT
MARKETING
Christopher H. Lovelock
Charles B. Weinberg

Copyright © 1978 by The Scientific Press

Published by The Scientific Press

Library of Congress Catalogue Card Number LC78-59621

ISBN 0-89426-019-7

Cover design by Katherine Steichen
Illustrations by Rogondion & Associates
Typography by The Scientific Press
Printed in the USA

Contents

Preface

Preparation of this book of readings reflects our belief —discussed in some depth in the first chapter—that public and nonprofit marketing has now come of age. We have tried here to show the state of the art in both research and practice, as these apply to marketing among public agencies and nonprofit organizations. To do this, we searched widely to assemble a collection of articles that would stimulate as well as inform, provide relevant case histories as well as conceptual insights, and demonstrate the value of new methodological approaches as well as that of tried and tested managerial policies.

The resulting book comprises a total of forty chapters. These are organized into eight parts, each preceded by a brief overview. Topics include the role and use of marketing, organizing for marketing activities, market structure analysis, developing marketing programs, introducing new services and behavior patterns, keeping existing organizations responsive, and analyzing the environment and evaluating marketing efforts.

The sources of these articles together represent a remarkable cross-section of publications, drawn from both the United States and abroad, and extending far beyond the traditional marketing literature. To us, the availability of such work is evidence of the breadth of interest in marketing outside the circle of professional marketers. It also emphasizes the integrative nature of the marketing discipline.

In our experience, managers in different types of nonbusiness organizations often believe that their field of actitivity is so different and so specialized that they can learn little from studying the operations of organizations in other fields. We suggest that this is a mistaken view. Developing a professional sense of management entails the ability to distinguish the specific from the generalizable; to recognize the value of certain concepts, tools, and strategies for problem-solving across a wide array of situations; and to apply these in ways that recognize the distinctive nature of the specific problem under review.

Accordingly, we have combined articles involving general discussions of marketing's value for nonbusiness organizations with articles covering a broad range of specific applications. These include health care, public transportation, library services, the performing arts, education, and such governmental programs as energy conservation and introduction of currency changes. The textual overview preceding each section tries to highlight the conceptual links between successive chapters. But we also invite readers to compare and contrast the different situations presented, with a view to developing their own conceptual insights and evaluating the transferability of specific marketing strategies and analytical procedures. A concluding note at the end of the book provides suggestions for further study and advice on how to conduct a search of both printed and computerized information bases.

ACKNOWLEDGEMENTS

The readings reprinted here represent the work of 45 authors and coauthors, in addition to ourselves. Their names appear alphabetically in a separate *List of Contributing Authors*. We would like to express our appreciation to all of them for their contributions to the book. Where known, authors' current affiliations appear with their articles. In a few instances, we have had to list the author's affiliation at the time the article was first published.

For the sake of consistency (and with their publishers' permission) chapters that originally appeared in British periodicals are reprinted here using American spelling conventions, although textual quotes within these readings have not been altered. In several other instances, we have made minor editorial additions, deletions, and changes. Of course, those who prepare anthologies are deeply indebted to the original publishers of the works included. In our case, acknowledgements are due to the following organizations and publications:

American College of Hospital Administrators
The American Council for the Arts
The American Hospital Association
American Marketing Association
Association for Consumer Research
Association of College, University & Community
    Arts Administrators
Association of Professional YMCA Directors
College Entrance Examination Board

East-West Center
The Flint Journal
Harvard Business Review
The Institute of Management Sciences
Jossey-Bass, Inc.
Journal of Consumer Research
Journal of The Market Research Society
Macmillan Publishing Co., Inc.
Modern Railways
Online
Operations Research Society of America
The Public Interest
D. Reidel Publishing Company
Scientific American
Seattle-Post Intelligencer
Smithsonian Institution
The Texas Monthly
Transportation Research Forum
Unilever, Ltd.
Urban Mass Transportation Administration
The Wall Street Journal

A number of other people have made specific contributions to this book, for which we are grateful. Several of the articles reprinted here were first brought to our attention by colleagues, students, or friends. The literature search needed to develop this readings book was stimulated by an invitation by Thomas Bonoma and Gerald Zaltman of the University of Pittsburgh to prepare an article for the *Review of Marketing 1978* on the state of the art in public and nonprofit marketing. Not only did this task expand our awareness of the relevant literature, but the resulting paper is also reprinted as the introductory chapter in this book.

We are particularly grateful to Douglas Solomon of the Stanford University Libraries for suggesting numerous references and introducing us to the power of computerized literature searches. The staff of Baker Library, Harvard Business School, have also been most helpful.

Financial support for our work was generously provided at Harvard by the Associates of the Harvard Business School, and at Stanford in part through grants from TRW, Inc., for support of the public management program.

Twenty-three of the articles reprinted here were originally published in 1977 or 1978. This must set some sort of record for fast publishing and is a tribute to the energy and technical skills of our publisher, Paul F. Kelley, and his typographer, Roy Woods, at The Scientific Press.

Finally, we want to say thank you to our secretaries, Emily Feudo and Frances Bertetta, who have cheerfully handled both routine and panic situations; to Karen Lindsey for her eagle-eyed proofreading and helpful editorial advice; and to Katherine Steichen for designing the cover.

Christopher H. Lovelock
Charles B. Weinberg

List of Contributing Authors

Author	Chapter Number(s)	Author	Chapter Number(s)
Michael B. Amspaugh	29	Stanley R. McAnally	12
J. Allison Barnhill	21	J. McDonald	22
Boris W. Becker	7	Jeffrey S. Milstein	39
Edward J. Blakely	6	Michael B. Mokwa	5
Daniel J. Brown	7	Bradley G. Morison	15
Peter F. Drucker	9	Elizabeth Nelson	40
Anders Englund	30	Nicholas Phillips	40
Ben M. Enis	5	Roger Ricklefs	33
Douglas Ferguson	26	Al Ries	17
Kay Fliehr	15	Thomas S. Robertson	27
Roger Ford	24	Everett M. Rogers	25
Howard Geltzer	17	Michael L. Rothschild	8
Peter Harvey	6	Patrick Ryan	3
Douglas B. Herron	36	Adrian B. Ryans	16
Regina Herzlinger	37	Philip B. Schary	7
Richard M. Johnson	18	Howard Schutz	6
Norman Kangun	5	Douglass J. Seaver	32
David N. Kershaw	38	Kenneth M. Shachmut	23
Philip Kotler	2	F. Floyd Shoemaker	25
Sidney J. Levy	2	Lawrence K. Spitz	19
Linda Lewis	35	Charles B. Weinberg	1, 4, 16, 20, 23, 31
Christopher H. Lovelock	1, 4, 10, 14, 28	Yoram Wind	19
Richard K. Manoff	13	Lawrence H. Wortzel	27
William Martin	34		

Chapter Index of Application Areas

Note: Bold-face indicates major coverage, light-face indicates minor coverage.

Chapter Index of Marketing Topics

Chapter Numbers	Marketing Mix	Product Policy	Communications	Pricing	Distribution	Market Segmentation	Competition	Consumer Analysis	Marketing Audit	Marketing Research and Information Systems	Objectives	Marketing Organization	Marketing Strategy	Issues in Transferring Marketing Concepts
1														3
2	2	2						2	1	1				3
3								1		1	1			
4	2									1				3
5								2		1				1
6	2							2		1				3
7						1		2		1				1
8			3					2						1
9										1	3			
10	2	1	1	1	1	2	1						2	
11										1			3	
12			3		1	1		1				1		
13			2		2									
14						3				2			1	2
15			1		1	3								
16				2		2		3		2				
17		2					1	1		1			3	1
18		2				3		2						
19		2	1	1	1	1		2		1				
20	2	1	1	1	1	1	1	1	1	1		1	2	
21		1			1			2		2		2		
22				3				2		2			2	
23		3	1							2			2	
24		1		3			1							
25			3			1		2						
26	1	1	3			1							2	
27			3			1								
28	1	2	2		2	1		2		2	1		2	1
29			2		2			1		2	1			
30			2			1		2		2				
31		3						2			2			
32		3	1		1	1				2			2	1
33		2	2	1									2	
34			3		1		1	2		1			2	1
35			3				1	1		2		1		
36	1	1	1	1	1	1	1	2	3	1	1	2	1	
37										3				
38		2						2		2				
39			1	1				3					2	
40		2	2	1	2	2		3		2			2	

Key: The numbers 1, 2, 3 indicate intensity of coverage of a specific topic in the chapter.
3 = major coverage, 2 = moderate coverage, 1 = minor coverage

Part I
Introduction

The application of marketing tools, concepts, and strategies to the activities of public agencies and nonprofit organizations represents a relatively new field of study for the marketing discipline. Yet significant progress has been made in this area during the past several years.

The three chapters in Part I collectively serve as an introduction for the rest of the book. The first and second chapters were written almost ten years apart. Chapter 1 describes the state of the art of nonbusiness marketing in early 1978, documenting major achievements in many areas and reviewing a wide range of recent publications in the literature. Chapter 2, written in 1968, was an early call for more emphasis on applying marketing tools and concepts to the management of public and nonprofit organizations. Comparing and contrasting these two chapters provides a measure of how far this field has progressed in a relatively short time. But it also shows that many of the marketing basics outlined in the older article remain just as fundamental today, despite advances in marketing theory and technology. Chapter 3, written in 1977, provides a contrast to the previous two chapters on several levels. It is short; it is journalistic rather than academic; and it is written in a tongue-in-cheek style. Yet it demonstrates convincingly that in spite of all the advances made in nonbusiness marketing, the marketing concept is still not understood by many public and nonprofit managers.

Part I seeks, therefore, to highlight the need for a marketing orientation in nonbusiness organizations and to clarify the specific problems faced by such organizations, as well as to evaluate the overall progress that has been made in both conceptual and managerial terms in recent years.

In the opening chapter, "Public and Nonprofit Marketing Comes of Age," Lovelock and Weinberg, review the growth of public and nonprofit marketing during the past decade. The issue is no longer one of "does marketing apply to nonbusiness organizations?" Instead, the question is "how can marketing tools and concepts be employed most effectively in helping nonbusiness organizations to meet their objectives?" Achievements are highlighted in five key areas of application—public transportation, energy conservation, higher education, health care, and the arts. These examples serve to demonstrate the high level of maturity and sophistication achieved in specific nonbusiness marketing programs, but show that there have also been shortcomings and failures, too.

The second chapter, Kotler and Levy's classic 1969 article on "Broadening the Concept of Marketing," was the first serious attempt to introduce the subject of nonbusiness marketing. Although initially somewhat controversial, the basic arguments advanced by these authors are now, of course, well accepted. The chapter presents the principal concepts in the field of marketing, demonstrating their applicability to management of nonbusiness organizations.

It corrects the popular misconception that marketing comprises merely advertising and selling tactics, identifying it instead as a strategic management function that encompasses an understanding of consumer needs, clarification of the organization's capabilities, and the development and delivery of goods and services. Subsequent chapters in the book serve to expand on and illustrate these concepts.

As its title, "Get Rid of the People and the System Runs Fine," suggests, the third and final contribution to this introductory section is somewhat irreverent. Yet its managerial implications are significant. Patrick Ryan aptly demonstrates the conflicts that arise in service organizations between operating efficiency and consumer satisfaction. He also shows how easy it is for a public service organization to lose sight of its real goals.

In short, an important lesson to be drawn from Part I is that while much progress has been made in public and nonprofit marketing, there is no room for complacency among either researchers or managers. Some areas of application undoubtedly show greater marketing sophistication than others. Furthermore, just as in the private sector, some individual organizations are clearly more progressive and more consumer-oriented than others. Once marketing weaknesses are acknowledged, organizations still face problems of diagnosis, analysis, strategy development, implementation, and evaluation of subsequent performance. The remaining seven parts of this book will elaborate upon these and related issues in greater depth, addressing them both from a general marketing perspective and also within the context of specific organizational settings.

Public and Nonprofit Marketing Comes of Age

Christopher H. Lovelock
Charles B. Weinberg

How are marketing theory and practice applied in nonbusiness marketing? This chapter reviews developments in public and nonprofit marketing in recent years, highlighting achievements (and a few failures) across a wide array of application areas. Particular attention is devoted to the role of marketing in the arts, health care, energy conservation, public transportation and higher education.

We believe that public and nonprofit marketing has come of age. Before the late 1960s, applications of marketing theory and practice outside the profit-making private sector were, if not unheard of, certainly very rare. Ten years later, a very different situation prevails.

As evidence of the maturation of nonbusiness marketing, we first review the historical development of the broadened concept of marketing. We show that, in addition to being widely written about, nonbusiness marketing is being taught in both academic and executive development programs. We highlight some of the public and nonprofit areas in which marketing tools and concepts are being actively employed by practicing managers. And, as evidence of nonbusiness marketing's newly adult status, we show how insights developed by researchers and practitioners in nonbusiness marketing contribute usefully to marketing activities in the business sector.

Christopher H. Lovelock is Associate Professor of Business Administration, Harvard University.

Charles B. Weinberg is Associate Professor of Marketing, Stanford University.

HISTORICAL PERSPECTIVE

In 1969, Kotler and Levy [1] published their now classic article "Broadening the Concept of Marketing" in which they criticized the then prevailing view of marketing as "a function peculiar to business firms." They rebuked students of marketing for either ignoring marketing in such nonbusiness areas as politics, higher education, and fund raising, or for treating them cursorily as public relations or publicity activities. Instead, they argued, marketing thought and theory should be expanded to incorporate marketing activities in public and nonprofit organizations.

Their article was intended to be provocative. And, indeed, it stimulated a debate that continued for several years. For instance, Luck [2] argued that the marketing discipline should be confined to market transactions characterized by the sale and purchase of goods and services for money. So long as nonbusiness organizations sold their products, he wrote, they were engaging in marketing. But if there were no established terms of sale, then it was not marketing.

Despite—or perhaps because of—these debates, nonbusiness marketing became integrated into the mainstream of both marketing theory and practice in the 1970s. The dedication of the entire July 1971 issue of the *Journal of Marketing* [3] to marketing's changing social/environmental role was particularly influential. That issue included applications of marketing technology to fund raising, health services, population problems, solid waste recycling, and other aspects of "social marketing."

Shortly thereafter, Kotler [4] developed his "generic concept" of marketing, highlighting the evolution of marketing through several stages of "consciousness." Consciousness One conceived of marketing as essentially a business subject concerned with market transactions. Consciousness Two extended marketing's realm to include all transactions where "one can identify an organization, a client group, and products broadly defined." Finally, Consciousness Three argued that "marketing applies to an organization's attempt to relate to all of its publics, not just its consuming publics."

A survey of marketing educators published in 1974 [5] showed that an overwhelming majority of them agreed that marketing went beyond just economic goods and services and market transactions. Yet some authors still remained skeptical of the broadened concept. For instance, Bartels [6] expressed fears of an "identity crisis in marketing." He perceived several disadvantages in shifting marketing's emphasis from economic to social behavior. These included the diversion of attention from such pressing problems as physical distribution; teaching that emphasizes methodology at the expense of a practical knowledge of products, markets, and specific applications; and a trend toward an abstract, esoteric literature that cannot be understood by practitioners. However, Bartels also conceded some benefits. Among these were the transfer of knowledge to areas where little behavioral research had been done and the cross-fertilization of concepts developed by researchers in dissimilar fields.

We believe that the controversy over broadening the marketing concept is now over. But perhaps it is being replaced by a new debate. In 1976, Hunt [7] proposed a conceptual model of the nature and scope of marketing that included separate categories for the profit and nonprofit sectors. Subsequently, he defended this model against critics who argued that the profit/nonprofit dichotomy was unnecessary [8].

> My own belief [he wrote] is that the *similarities* between marketing in the profit sector versus the nonprofit sector greatly outweigh the *differences*. . . .
> [But] I suggest that the profit–sector/nonprofit–sector dichotomy will be useful until such time as (1) "broadening the concept of marketing" ceases to be controversial, (2) nonprofit sector marketing is completely integrated into all marketing courses (and not treated as a separate subject with separate courses), (3) administrators of nonprofit organizations generally perceive their organizations as having marketing problems, and (4) these administrators hire marketing people and, where appropriate, set up marketing departments.

In following sections, we review recent progress in the field of public and nonprofit marketing, in the academic literature and elsewhere. We first explore the question of whether the differences between business and nonbusiness marketing are meaningful ones, and then examine the literature of nonbusiness marketing, educational activity in this area, and five specific areas of application: the arts, health care, energy conservation, public transportation, and higher education. In the process, we address certain points raised by Hunt: (1) to what extent has nonbusiness marketing been integrated into the mainstream of marketing coursework and literature (rather than being treated separately), and (2) how much progress has been made by different types of nonbusiness organizations in accepting the validity of the marketing concept, employing marketing professionals, and making use of marketing tools and concepts? Future managerial and research needs also are considered. Because of space limitations, we seek to highlight issues rather than be comprehensive. However, the references cited in the footnotes should prove useful to those wishing to explore particular issues in greater depth.

IS PUBLIC AND NONPROFIT MARKETING REALLY DIFFERENT?

What, in fact, are the differences between business and nonbusiness marketing? Are they important, and do they aid or hinder integration? Four key differences are examined: the presence of multiple publics, a nonprofit orientation, a concern with services rather than physical goods, and public scrutiny and nonmarket pressures.

Multiple Publics. Shapiro [9] highlights the separation between resource attraction and resource allocation in the nonprofit organization. In profit-making enterprises, clients pay money for the products received. But in nonprofit organizations, the clients who receive services and the donors or taxpayers who provide funds are often unrelated groups. Thus, fund raising and service delivery may involve separate, but interrelated, marketing activities to two different publics. Although taxation may be thought of as involuntary, initiating new or increased taxes often requires marketing efforts. These marketing efforts involve individual taxpayers directly when the procedure followed includes a referendum on the issue. For example, only after the schools in Toledo, Ohio, had been closed indefinitely did a fifth attempt to pass a referendum for a property tax increase succeed in November 1977 [10].

This notion of two publics can be readily expanded to one of multiple publics including outside suppliers, employees, regulators, and many others [11]. But this concept of multiple publics is not confined to nonprofit organizations. Business firms engage in periodic resource attraction activities—separated from the sale of products—as they seek to sell new stock or bond issues or to negotiate loans from banks. Firms also have suppliers with whom they engage in market transactions. Many industries are increasingly regulated at the federal, state, or local level. In addition to their relationships with consumers, many companies are involved in ongoing relationships—often of an adversary nature—with citizen groups, formalized consumer organizations, and stockholders. Orchestration of the exchange relationships with each of these publics is necessary if a firm is to succeed in its central purpose of selling the goods and services that it produces.

There are, admittedly, differences between business and nonbusiness organizations in the emphasis they place on relating to publics other than consumers. But the concept of multiple publics *is* relevant for business marketers [12]. What is interesting, in relation to developments in marketing theory and practice, is that it was the study of nonbusiness organizations that highlighted the importance of these publics for marketers.

Nonprofit Objective. Because nonbusiness organizations do not normally operate for profit, it has been argued that their success or failure cannot be measured in strictly financial terms [13]. The lack of even a theoretical goal of profit maximization makes it more difficult to choose among strategic and tactical alternatives. This is a fundamental distinction. However, the fact that the bottom line tends to be colored red does not mean that financial performance is a meaningless measure for public and nonprofit marketers. Let us examine two implications of the nonprofit objective.

First, the presence of an operating deficit usually signals that the funds needed to balance operating revenues and expenses are coming from sources other than consumers. When the public treasury funds the deficit, the justification for tax-supported subsidies reflects a belief that the external economies or ''social profit'' resulting from providing a public service exceed its associated financial costs. This notion forces the public sector marketer to review the objectives of the organization, to develop marketing plans for achieving these objectives (within the prevailing financial constraints), and then to devise nonfinancial measures of performance which will allow management to evaluate later how well these objectives have, in fact, been achieved.

The second implication of a nonprofit orientation is actually very businesslike and applies to those public or nonprofit organizations that sell their services at a price. Although deficits may be accepted in such organizations, significant increases in current deficits may not be. When coupled with a distrust of marketing by top management, the possibility of incurring such deficits may make it difficult for nonbusiness marketing managers to enlarge their scope of operations. This problem has led some marketing personnel to adopt a strategy of incremental analysis, isolating the projected costs and revenues of specific actions. Approval for expansion of operations can be gained if costs do not exceed revenues. However, even if costs do exceed revenues, incremental ''social profits'' from the expanded programs that justify a deficit increase may be identified.

Incremental analysis has long been used by business marketers, but the concept of balancing financial profits against ''social profits'' is relatively new to the private sector. Devising appropriate measures—or social indicators—was first raised by Bauer et al [14]. The development of social indicators and their integration with marketing strategy are of concern to both public and private sector marketers [15, 16].

Services Rather than Physical Goods. Most nonbusiness organizations produce services rather than physical goods [13]. One might expect that public and nonprofit marketers could benefit from studying the marketing of consumer services in the private sector. But, in fact, the latter area received relatively little attention from marketing scholars until recently [17, 18].

The lack of private sector analogues has had two effects. First, it has made the successful transfer of the marketing tools, concepts, and strategies that have been developed by consumer goods firms more difficult because two hurdles had to be leaped, from the private to the public/nonprofit sector and from goods to services. Second, it has forced marketing theorists to radically rethink previous conceptions and definitions of marketing in order to make this double jump.

Recent conceptual and empirical research in services marketing is tending to include both business and nonbusiness services and, thus, is leading to a fruitful cross-fertilization between the two sectors [19]. In many service industries, such as higher education, public transportation, and utilities, the public/private and profit/nonprofit distinctions are blurred anyway.

Public Scrutiny and Nonmarket Pressures. Most public agencies are subject, at least in theory, to close public scrutiny because of their role in the provision of public services, an expressed desire for openness in government, and a need to prevent abuses of natural or legislated monopoly power. The review of proposed prices for mail services in the United States by the Postal Rate Commission exemplifies a particularly intensive form of public participation in the strategy formulation process.

Because public and nonprofit organizations do not have profit as an objective, and often are heavily subsidized, they are not constrained by the ''discipline of the marketplace.'' Instead, they may be expected or even required (in the case of some public agencies) to provide services or serve market segments that a profit-making organization would find uneconomic. Political pressures, in particular, may force retention of inefficient services and economically suboptimal strategies. Examples include the requirement that the U.S. Postal Service maintain rural postoffices and that Amtrak provide rail passenger service on routes across thinly populated areas.

However, private firms also may be forced by political and other pressures to keep plants open that they would rather close, or to withdraw from the marketplace such profitable but unsafe or socially undesirable products as noisy machines, dangerous children's toys, and "gas guzzling" cars. Regulation is increasing in the private sector, and marketers in both private and public sectors must learn to work within the constraints that it imposes. Information disclosure requirements, meantime, have eliminated some of the traditional secrecy of private firms.

PUBLICATIONS AND PEDAGOGY IN NONBUSINESS MARKETING

Although relatively little has been published on public and nonprofit marketing in the *Journal of Marketing* since the initial flourish of the early 1970s, publishing activity elsewhere has been at a high level.

General Books and Monographs. Seven books or monographs have been published which cover a broad range of applications: three books of readings [20, 21, 22], two volumes of conference papers [23, 24], one textbook [11], and one casebook [25]. Collectively, these seven publications integrate a wide range of concepts and fields of application, providing a useful set of references for the teacher, researcher, and thoughtful practitioner. However, managers should be cautioned that most tend to be conceptually oriented and contain relatively little pragmatic "how to" advice. Though Gaedeke's readings book [22], and Lovelock and Weinberg's casebook [25] are more applications oriented, obviously neither was designed as a manual for management. In short, a managerially oriented text which embraces a broad cross-section of nonbusiness marketing applications has yet to be written.

Articles and Conference Papers. Articles on applications of consumer research and marketing technology to nonbusiness situations have not been confined to marketing journals. Increasingly, they are also appearing in trade and professional publications directed at specific "industries" or application areas. Rothschild's 1977 bibliography [26] contains more than 600 references relating to marketing for public and nonprofit organizations. A substantial proportion of these appeared in vertical (industry) publications, rather than in horizontal (functional) ones. And although most of the functional publications were primarily marketing oriented, not all of them were.

Conferences have provided an active forum for presentation and discussion of issues relating to nonbusiness marketing. A study of the proceedings and conference agendas of the American Marketing Association (AMA), the Association for Consumer Research (ACR), and the American Institute for Decision Sciences (AIDS) from 1973 to 1977 yield some interesting findings.

Exhibit 1 shows the number of papers devoted to nonbusiness marketing, broadly defined, at conferences of these

---

EXHIBIT 1
AMA, ACR, and AIDS National Conference Proceedings: Incidence of Papers Highlighting Nonbusiness Marketing and Consumer Research Topics Each Year, 1973–1977

Year of Conference	No. of Papers
1973	9
1974	23
1975	12
1976	20
1977	36
	100

Note: Totals in 1976 and 1977 include several workshop and "topic table" papers delivered at AIDS' National Conference, but not published in the "Proceedings."

---

three organizations in each of the five years. Though the emphasis given this area is relatively modest in the context of the 1,500 or so papers presented at these conferences during this period, the total of 100 papers is significant. Any suggestion that nonbusiness marketing is simply an ephemeral "fad" area is contradicted by the sustained number of conference presentations over the years.

Additional insights are provided in Exhibit 2, which shows a breakdown of the topic areas addressed between 1973 and 1977. Papers relating to public transportation appeared with the greatest frequency, followed by papers on health care, energy conservation, other health related areas, politics, education, and the performing arts. Obviously, all are important areas. However, it might be a mistake to equate

---

EXHIBIT 2
Specific Topics in Nonbusiness Marketing Papers at AMA, ACR, and AIDS National Conferences 1973–1977

	AMA	ACR	AIDS[1]	Total
Public Transportation	4	12	6	22
Health care	5	6	3	14
Other health related[2]	4	3	4	11
Energy conservation	5	5	3	13
Politics	3	4	1	8
Education	1	2	4	7
Performing arts	3	0	0	3
Fundraising	1	1	0	2
Highway safety	1	1	0	2
Recycling	1	1	0	2
Religion	0	2	0	2
Miscellaneous applications[3]	6	2	3	11
Conceptual/general	3	0	0	3
Totals	37	39	24	100

[1] AIDs totals include papers presented at the National Conference but not published in the "Proceedings" in 1976–77.

[2] Alcoholism, rehabilitation of the handicapped, blood donation, immunization, drug use, antismoking, and family planning.

[3] Police services, tourism, postal service, volunteer programs, wilderness recreation use, wilderness cause, public TV, city marketing, and environmental responsibility.

this rank ordering with the relative levels of marketing management activity in these fields, for the ranking reflects in part the interests of session coordinators and referees as well as those of authors.

Teaching and Course Development. Although we have not attempted any formal poll of marketing faculty members, there is convincing evidence of interest in teaching new courses in nonbusiness marketing, and also in incorporating nonbusiness materials into present marketing courses.

A growing number of schools are offering elective graduate or undergraduate courses in nonbusiness marketing, under such titles as Marketing in the Public Sector, Marketing in Nonbusiness Organizations, or Marketing for Public Sector and Nonprofit Organizations. At some institutions, marketing courses (or marketing modules in general management courses) are being offered in specific application areas, such as health care or arts administration.

Executive programs, ranging in length from a day to several weeks, are now being offered for practicing managers in many specific fields. Among those in which we have found a significant marketing component are higher education, health care, public broadcasting, arts administration, library management, public transportation, and fund raising. The number of such offerings appears to be increasing.

Teaching materials used in these educational efforts include texts, case materials, and other readings. Examples for class discussion often are drawn from both the public and private sectors.

Of particular significance is the trend toward incorporating materials on public and nonprofit organizations in mainstream courses. From its inception, the introductory marketing course at Yale's School of Organization and Management has included a broad cross-section of nonbusiness materials. In 1977–78, the 25-section course included 10 sessions featuring marketing applications in a public or nonprofit organization, in addition to another two featuring a government regulatory agency. Seven of the 54 sessions in the Harvard MBA program's First Year Marketing course were devoted to cases on public and nonprofit organizations in 1977–78, and a similar percentage was held at Stanford. Significantly, the course heads at each school indicated that incorporation of such materials enhanced student understanding of basic marketing concepts.

Several recent texts and casebooks in general marketing provide evidence of the trend toward integration of public and nonprofit marketing with a traditional business orientation. Marketing texts by Enis [27], Kotler [28], and Heskett [29], and marketing casebooks by Boyd and Davis [30], and Star and others [31] are among those that have moved in this direction. However, all these books still have far to go before one could claim that they have completely integrated nonbusiness marketing.

Perhaps the closest that any general marketing book comes to treating nonbusiness marketing on an equal footing with business marketing—and not as some rarified extension of it—is a newly published introductory text by Nickels [32].

Another measure of the increased emphasis on teaching nonbusiness marketing is provided by development and distribution of individual cases. A comprehensive bibliography of nonbusiness marketing cases, published in July 1977, listed a total of more than 100 cases in this area [33], 40% of which had been entered in the Intercollegiate Case Clearing House (ICCH) within the previous two years. A particularly significant statistic is that 14 of the 157 marketing cases included in ICCH's Spring 1977 "best seller" bibliography had public or nonprofit organizations as their subject [34]. No nonbusiness marketing cases appeared in the previous list of best sellers published in 1975.

MARKETING APPLICATIONS
IN SPECIFIC FIELDS

Efforts to apply marketing and consumer research to nonbusiness organizations first appeared in number during the mid-1960s. They focused on specific areas, notably health, public transportation, and political topics. These efforts provided the necessary base for development of an integrated theory and conceptual organization in the late 1960s and early 1970s.

Most current work in nonbusiness marketing centers on application of marketing concepts and strategies in specific fields. However, as the level of sophistication rises, researchers in public and nonprofit marketing are ceasing simply to borrow and adapt tools and theories developed elsewhere and are themselves contributing to knowledge generation in marketing. In other words, a two-way traffic is emerging.

One example comes from market research involving a review of drop-off delivery techniques for self-administered questionnaires. The consumer surveys in which this methodology was used and progressively refined all had nonbusiness topics—politics, adult education, health behavior, and public transportation [35, 36].

We now review briefly developments in five specific application areas: the arts, health, energy, public transportation, and higher education. It is important to note that each of these fields includes both profit and nonprofit organizations and straddles both the public and the private sectors.

The Arts. The arts have established a good record of both theoretical and practical developments in the use of marketing. Baumol and Bowen's pathbreaking analysis [37] shows that labor intensity in the performing arts and the limited opportunity to substitute capital for labor make it unlikely that the performing arts could exist without subsidy and donation. This analysis has since been used in other public sector areas, such as higher education [38].

Morison and Fliehr's book *In Search of an Audience* [39] shows how a marketing approach helped build an audience for the Tyrone Guthrie Theater in Minneapolis. Many visual and performing arts groups have conducted surveys of their audiences, and some have developed strategies based on the results.

For example, a survey of subscribers to the American Conservatory Theatre (ACT) in San Francisco [40, 41] showed that the 15% price discount (seven tickets for the price of six) was not one of the major benefits sought. The discount was discontinued, yet both renewal and new subscriber acquisition rates remained within the usual bounds. The most frequently cited benefit of subscriptions was to "make me more certain to attend each play." This finding not only provided an interesting perspective on human behavior, but also suggested possible copy strategies to use in subscription campaigns. Attendance behavior before subscribing also was studied. It was found that as many as one-third of new subscribers had not attended an ACT performance in the previous five years. The size of this "sudden subscriber" group was surprising, because it was counter to the conventional wisdom that patrons gradually increase frequency of attendance before deciding to subscribe.

Relatively little work on the arts has appeared in the marketing literature. Some exploratory consumer research and a commentary appeared in the 1974 AMA conference *Proceedings* [42], and the 1977 *Proceedings* contained a summary paper by Laczniak and Murphy [43] on planning and control for performing arts marketing.

However, in personal communications, several colleagues have reported the use of marketing approaches by arts organizations. A December 1977 conference sponsored by the National Endowment for the Arts reviewed achievements in several areas, including marketing and economic analyses, as it sought to identify and stimulate work on specific problems in the arts. An example of a cooperative educational effort across numerous different types of arts organizations is provided by the Metropolitan Cultural Alliance in Boston, which arranges educational sessions in marketing and other areas for its member organizations. Obviously, these examples do not show that arts managers have uniformly adopted a marketing viewpoint and successfully applied such an approach. Nevertheless, the success rate has been high enough to make it worthwhile to speculate on possible reasons.

Most arts organizations are typically small and have relatively few management positions. Thus, bureaucratic procedures are limited and access to management generally implies access to top management. Development and implementation of a computer-assisted performance selection model with the Lively Arts at Stanford program [44] required intensive contact with the entire management structure, but was greatly facilitated by the fact that this structure consisted of only three people.

Many arts managers seem to be more receptive to new and creative approaches than are managers in other fields. "We've never done it that way before" is not often given as a reason for rejecting marketing. However, arts managers are particularly sensitive to the threat of diluting quality standards in order to appeal to mass markets. There may also be a conflict between satisfying artistic needs for creativity and self-expression and appealing to audience tastes. This conflict may necessitate persuasive communications to educate the audience.

Arts organizations have found it easy to undertake consumer research because it is relatively simple to identify a sample of users and to administer a questionnaire to them. A museum can readily interview visitors, and a performing arts organization can send questionnaires to samples selected from its mailing list. However, relatively few arts organizations survey people who do not already have a tie to the organization.

Health Care and Related Areas. Rising medical costs, excess capacity in many hospitals, and the development of new forms of health care delivery, such as health maintenance organizations (HMOs), have served to spur interest in marketing in the field of health care. At the same time, growing attention has been devoted to encouraging changes in behavior patterns which will lead to better health and/or broader societal benefits [45]. This effort was stimulated by the National Consumer Health Information and Health Promotion Act of 1976, which provided for a national program [46]. Areas of application include nutrition, alcohol and drug abuse, birth control, and immunization campaigns. Interest in health behavior marketing appears to predate that in health services marketing; several articles on the former topic appeared during the 1960s [20].

In terms of marketing, health provides an interesting contrast to the arts. The latter are seen by most people as a luxury, and the proportion of the population regularly attending or participating in arts-related activities is very small. Health, however, is of concern to everyone at some point or another, rich and poor alike. Though some people are extremely concerned about health matters, others are afraid to seek health care. The health care marketing task is further complicated by the fact that services often must be marketed in advance of need.

Marketing studies in health care have emphasized not only consumer research and communication, but also distribution systems. Bucklin and Carman [47] applied the theory of vertical market structures to the evaluation of alternative health care delivery systems. Developing alternative ways of delivering health care to provide better service to consumers at lower cost has been an important concern of health care planners in recent years. Marketing activity was greatly stimulated by passage in 1975 of the Health Maintenance Organization and Resources Act; it effectively requires all

HMOs seeking federal certification and funding to give explicit attention to marketing.

HMOs have been instrumental in overturning long-standing professional prohibitions on the use of advertising in the health care field. Research by Richard et al [48] suggests that most HMOs recognize the need for marketing activities to achieve an adequate enrollment base, but marketing responsibilities in such organizations are often dispersed and lack focus. In an effort to develop strategies for diffusion of the HMO concept, Venkatesan [49] applied consumer behavior concepts to marketing this approach to health care delivery. Two applications of management science to marketing health care facilities were published in the 1976 volume of *Operations Research* [50].

Evidence of continued interest in health marketing is provided by academic and professional meetings devoted to this topic. For instance, in 1976, the University of Nebraska sponsored a symposium examining consumer behavior in the health marketplace from a variety of perspectives [51]. Also, many general management development courses for health professionals now include marketing modules.

Other aspects of health marketing have been treated in recent conference papers. The "Patients Bill of Rights" and marketing of blood donorship have been discussed at AMA [52]. Nutritional behavior and preventive medicine, antismoking, and antidrug abuse have been discussed at ACR [53, 54], and HMOs were among the topics discussed at AIDS in 1977 [55].

Marketing management articles are appearing with greater frequency in professional and "trade" health publications, although they are generally introductory in tone. More in-depth treatment was provided in a June 1977 issue of *Hospitals* [56], which devoted six articles and an editorial to hospital marketing. Convincing evidence of the maturation of the field was provided in 1977 by publication of a 300-page text on health care marketing [57].

Energy Conservation. Energy conservation provides a good illustration of the premise that a crisis spurs innovation [58]. Before the crisis resulting from the Arab oil embargo of 1973–74, there had been limited recognition of the need for future energy conservation but minimal action directed toward achieving that end. Although oil prices rose sharply as a result of exporter-initiated price increases and several communication campaigns were launched to promote energy conservation, marketing applications in this field must generally be regarded as a failure in the United States. The greatest achievement to date probably represents a legalistic approach rather than a marketing one, consisting of an effort to enhance vehicle fuel efficiency by legislating rising minimum standards for U.S. produced cars.

Energy has been a popular topic for papers at recent AMA, ACR, and AIDS conferences. Twelve papers were presented in 1976–77, most of them emphasizing consumer attitudes, behavior patterns, and response to information programs [e.g. 59–64]. Yet Montgomery and Leonard-Barton's 1977 review of the literature [65] concluded that "relatively little is known about several major dimensions of importance in the marketing of home energy conservation. Further, what literature exists is diffuse and often inaccessible. . . ." These authors cited no U.S. examples of organizations that employed an articulated marketing program—starting from consumer research and leading to a positioning and marketing mix strategy designed to achieve specific objectives—though they found many consumer and market research studies and some examples of unidimensional use of marketing variables (they did not review in detail the British experience discussed later). Thus, utilities have employed price incentives to discourage consumption, but rarely integrated these with other marketing mix elements. As the authors point out, price is at best a necessary but not a sufficient condition to achieve conservation. For example, many Northern Californians reduced water usage in 1977 without direct price variation in response to general and specific campaigns based on the drought and the consequent need for water conservation.

Why has marketing had such limited impact on energy conservation in the United States? First, general concern with energy conservation probably dates only from the 1973 Mideast War, although several prominent ecologists had foreseen the need for conservation earlier. Second, there are few organizations whose primary purpose is to encourage energy conservation, in contrast to those that have been vitally concerned for many years with such social causes as preservation of the environment (such as the Sierra Club) and family planning (such as Planned Parenthood). Until the establishment of the Department of Energy in 1977, federal attention was spread across many different offices. The Federal Energy Administration employed several people with titles such as "energy conservation marketing specialist," but political pressures confined its consumer marketing efforts to public service advertising involving such vague messages as "Don't Be Fuelish."

Regulated utilities, whose long-term strategy has been to pursue profit growth through increased consumption, are only now beginning to adapt their marketing programs to achieving profits through such strategies as smoothing demand for service on a time-of-day basis.

A third reason lies in the debate about whether the solution to the energy problem lies in technological ("hard") solutions or in changing behavior patterns to conserve and reduce waste ("soft"). Because many technological solutions would be invisible to the user, some writers seem to focus on technology as the sole answer because it would be more convenient. Yet, Montgomery and Leonard-Barton [65] present many examples, especially from industry, in which electrical energy consumption has been dramatically reduced through conservation. A marketing approach would attempt to combine ''hard'' and ''soft'' solutions. For example, adopting solar energy will require identification of the needs of target segments and their responsiveness to alternative solar energy devices.

Fourth, because utilities are regulated profit-seeking companies, the primary focus of their marketing program has been price. But regulatory procedures often make it difficult for utilities to practice differential price strategies and to use price as a promotional device in conjunction with other marketing efforts.

In summary, little has been accomplished in the marketing of energy conservation in the United States. Yet it is a major societal problem that raises a classic public sector marketing challenge: How to maintain a behavior over time? The primary energy conservation problem is not to persuade people to adopt less wasteful behaviors in the midst of a crisis, but to do so continuously. The same problem also occurs, for example, in programs to encourage people to adhere to low cholesterol diets, to obey the 55 mph speed limit, and to stop smoking.

Rather more success in energy conservation has been achieved in Britain, where a 12-point program was introduced by the government in December 1974. It was directed at both individual and industrial users and included incentives, legal compulsion, economic pricing of energy, and a major communication campaign. This campaign, directed by the U.K. Department of Energy and firmly based on consumer research findings, began in January 1975 and continues in a new phase in 1977–78. It seeks to secure both immediate reductions in energy use and the longer term changes in public attitudes and habits needed to secure continuing economies. A wide range of paid media are used, supplemented by exhibitions, syndicated articles, and publicity campaigns by the various fuel industries. The approach has been not only to persuade people of the *need* to save energy, but also to demonstrate specifically *how* to do so (research findings showed that people were ignorant of such approaches as home insulation).

According to Phillips and Nelson [66], regular surveys of public attitudes, claimed behavior, and future intentions show significant gains from the original, precampaign baseline figures. Retail audits of sales of thermal insulation materials provide encouraging confirmation that consumers are acting in accordance with campaign recommendations, not only to insulate but also to use a specific thickness of insulation.

Phillips and Nelson draw some important conclusions about energy conservation marketing from the British experience: (1) price alone will not lead directly to efficient energy saving (although economic pricing is a prerequisite of a credible conservation policy), (2) paid advertising should be supported by other publicity activity, (3) publicity support and cooperation by the fuel industries provides needed credibility to government programs, (4) point-of-sale follow-through is needed to achieve the objective of stimulating

energy-saving durables, and (5) households may differ in their energy-saving priorities according to both household composition and circumstances, and thus a segmented strategy is required.

Public Transportation. Urban transit probably has received more attention from consumer researchers and marketing specialists than any other single public or nonprofit field. The seminal work on transit marketing was published by Schneider [67] in 1965. By the early 1970s, a significant number of research studies and demonstration projects had been undertaken by university researchers and consulting firms, many of them financed by federal agencies. Writing in 1972, Lovelock [68] attempted to coordinate and synthesize this previous work with his own research, and to develop some general strategic marketing recommendations for transit management.

Transit marketing has benefited from strong federal support. Since the early 1970s, a determined effort has been made by the Urban Mass Transportation Administration (UMTA), an agency of the U.S. Department of Transportation, to promote improved management skills in the transit industry. In part, this effort may have been a response to charges that the industry was poorly managed and too operations oriented, and that excessive emphasis was being given to developing new technology at the expense of improving the quality of management.

UMTA has given particular attention to marketing. In 1975, the agency sponsored a National Transit Marketing Conference in conjunction with the American Public Transit Association (APTA), the industry trade organization [69]. Subsequently, UMTA commissioned development of a *Transit Marketing Management Handbook* [70] from several consulting firms. Four volumes had been published by 1977 on the marketing plan, pricing, organization, and transit information aids. UMTA also has sponsored a two-week marketing management program and management courses which include a marketing component for transit personnel. In addition, UMTA has financed university research projects in marketing through its University Research and Training program. The findings of UMTA-financed studies are widely available through the National Technical Information Service, a U.S. Department of Commerce service.

UMTA's major investment in marketing to date has been its sponsorship of the Transit Marketing Project, described as ''the first major commitment at the Federal level to define and demonstrate a basic methodology for transit marketing; to test and upgrade state-of-the-art techniques; and to develop new techniques'' [71]. Initiated in 1975, the project began with consumer research studies in both Baltimore and Nashville. These studies sought to (1) define the consumer groups offering the greatest potential as a source of rider volume and (2) identify the most important benefits people desired from transportation for local trips, as well as their attitudes and behavior patterns in regard to alternative modes of transportation. Subsequently, marketing strategies were developed for both cities to enable their respective transit systems to tailor improved services to target market segments.

Although there is now greater awareness of marketing among transit managers and certain systems are engaged in sophisticated marketing efforts, others remain heavily operations oriented. For the latter group, marketing often is still equated with advertising and community relations. Pricing, scheduling, routing, vehicle design, driver training, and public information services have yet to be widely accepted as elements in an integrated marketing package.

Consumer research in transportation by marketing academics (often closely linked to the work of consulting firms) has extended traditional work by engineers and economists in modal choice modeling. Emphasis has been placed on developing better understanding of the consumer decision process, incorporating attitudinal concepts in modal choice research [72], and on relating transit objectives to market segmentation strategies [73].

A variety of modal choice model forms have been developed recently and several were presented at the 1977 ACR meeting [74]. Other recently published work includes a study of the role of security in transit marketing [75] and development of a procedural marketing planning model for use by transit managers [76].

Higher Education. At a 1972 conference, Kotler and Dubois [77] discussed marketing and the American education "industry" in broad terms. They examined three major problem areas (insufficient funds, lagging innovation, and unmotivated students) at both school and college levels. But nearly all marketing attention since then has focused on improving admissions for individual colleges. Though fund raising has been extremely important for higher education during the past few years, the limited literature on this topic has been directed at fund raising in a general rather than at a specifically educational context.

Interest in marketing has been spurred by the publicity given to noncontrollable demographic trends. Primary demand for a college education from students in traditional age groups is ceasing to grow and will soon start declining because of a fall in the birth rate that began in the 1950s. This change has led to a shift from a sellers' to a buyers' market in higher education. Many traditionally strong institutions now worry about their ability to attract students of the same academic caliber as in the past—a problem exacerbated by the national trend of declining SAT scores. Other institutions worry about their ability to attract sufficient students of almost any caliber. In an "industry" with heavy capital investments, failure to maintain or increase student enrollment levels at a time of rapidly rising costs can lead to a drastic shortfall between revenues and expenses.

As a result, admissions offices have shifted their emphasis from screening to recruitment; marketing has been seized upon—sometimes indiscriminately—as a means of improving a college's competitive position in recruiting students in traditional age groups. To a lesser extent, market and consumer research has been used to identify nontraditional students and develop offerings tailored to their needs.

Some schools have succumbed to the "majority fallacy." These schools, by lowering admissions standards and broadening their range (but not depth) of courses, have failed to appeal to any specific segment and, consequently, have intensified their admissions problems.

Among recent literature in higher education marketing is the proceedings of a 1976 colloquium on marketing and college admissions sponsored by the College Entrance Examination Board [78], which includes papers on analyzing the future market for college education and applications of marketing theory and positioning strategy to college admissions. It is interesting to compare Kotler's model of an applicant's college decision process [79]—a choice process which may extend over more than a year and have lifelong implications—with Lovelock's model of modal choice decision-making in transportation [80]—a frequently repeated and relatively low-risk decision.

Other recent works include an evaluation of the community college transfer market by Leister and MacLachlan [81], and conference papers on modeling college choice [82, 83] and on the marketing of institutions of higher education [84, 85].

Articles on marketing-related topics have been appearing periodically for several years in selected educational publications and seem to be moving beyond the basic introductory stage.

Evidence of educational administrators' perceived interest in marketing is provided by advertisements for marketing workshops and seminars in the *Chronicle of Higher Education*. However, personal experience suggests that many top administrators are not especially interested in, or able to relate to, marketing; they appear to see it as a necessary tool for their fund-raising and admissions offices, but not necessarily as a fundamental concept underlying management of the entire institution. Possibly this disinterest reflects their own pressing involvement in such issues as faculty management, labor relations, and compliance with federal equal opportunity regulations.

WHAT NEXT FOR PUBLIC AND NONPROFIT MARKETING?

Several broad conclusions can be drawn about the state of the art in nonbusiness marketing. No serious controversy remains among academics as to whether or not nonbusiness marketing belongs in the general field of marketing. As with other marketing topics, personal interests, together with institutional priorities, will determine whether or not an individual does research in the area or an institution offers a course in it. The trend toward integration of nonbusiness material in basic texts and courses suggests, however, that this aspect of marketing is being accepted on its own merits.

Further evidence of research interest in nonbusiness marketing is provided by the results of the 1977 AMA Doctoral Dissertation Competition. The first prize winner and one of the five honorable mention winners both wrote dissertations on aspects of health care marketing [86].

It is clear that nonbusiness marketing has progressed beyond the stage of a topic discussed only between academics. Marketing tools and concepts are being widely discussed, written about, and promoted across a broad range of diverse application areas. To an increasing extent, marketing is the subject of articles in "trade" publications, is included in professional development courses, and provides the major topic of workshops and conferences sponsored by practitioner organizations. Marketing activities also are being promoted by government legislation as well as by research contracts and dissemination of findings.

When one looks at the record of marketing in a nonbusiness managerial context, however, the picture appears cloudy and the results have been mixed. As in the private sector, there have been failures in planning and execution,[1] and even outright bungling (as in the case of the $2 bill reissue). But there have been successes, too, in the arts, health care organizations (notably HMOs), public transportation, higher education, and other areas of application. And there is growing recognition that marketing techniques provide a new perspective and powerful new tools for tackling a range of difficult social welfare problems [88].

Successful applications of marketing by nonbusiness organizations also can be found outside the U.S. Several British public agencies have had a marketing orientation longer than their American counterparts. For instance, British Rail, the (British) Post Office, and London Transport all show a high level of sophistication in their use of marketing research and in strategic implementation of such concepts as market segmentation; they have been much studied by representatives of similar organizations in other countries. As a general policy, nonbusiness marketing managers should make a point of seeking insights from related organizations abroad as well as at home.

To further increase acceptance of marketing tools and concepts among public and nonprofit managers will require the *marketing of marketing itself*. The task is twofold. First, it must be demonstrated that marketing is applicable to their specific situations. Second, nonbusiness managers (like their business counterparts) must be educated to recognize the scope and complexity of marketing, and to realize that it extends far beyond just advertising and selling. Initially nonbusiness managers sometimes resist the use of marketing terminology. As a first step, it often helps to explain market-

ing concepts and strategies in terms with which these managers feel comfortable. However, in the long run, development of a professional marketing orientation and cross-fertilization of ideas are impeded if each area of application retains its own terminology.

One practice which represents a double-edged sword is the use of outside marketing consultants. Although consultants can be a valuable educational resource and provide important analytical and strategic insights, any set of recommendations is only as good as the skills of the managers responsible for implementation. Continued use of consultants may deprive "in-house" personnel of the experience of on-the-job training. Consultants should be used as a supplement to, rather than a replacement for, an organization's own staff. If on-the-job training activities are limited, then participation in professional development programs may be valuable for fledging marketing managers.

We see three specific areas in which nonbusiness managers need to develop their skills for the future. The first is the ability to understand and to analyze the impact of marketing variables. Decisions on allocating marketing resources among different variables and orchestrating the marketing mix to achieve desired objectives cannot be made effectively without this understanding and analytical skill.

The second need is for better understanding of consumer decision processes. It is difficult to develop strategies for influencing consumer behavior if one does not understand how consumers make decisions about their behavior patterns in the first place. Public and nonprofit organizations generally lack detailed data bases on which to identify problems and test decision alternatives.

Last, there is a need for a better understanding of marketing and a stronger consumer orientation among non-marketing personnel. This need is especially pressing in service organizations, because services tend to be labor-intensive, there is a high degree of personal contact with consumers, and production and consumption often take place simultaneously. Too often, an operations orientation prevails, and marketing's role is limited to that of a communications appendage.

Future Research Needs. Overall, we see a need to coordinate and consolidate managerial learning, both within the nonbusiness area and between business and nonbusiness marketing. Business and nonbusiness services, in particular, may have much to learn from each other. Taken as a group, neither has historically had a strong marketing orientation, and thus each is developing expertise in marketing concurrently. In another area, computer and model based marketing decision aids, which have had increasing impact in the private sector, have had only limited use in the public sector [89].

More work also is needed on developing a rigorous taxonomy of marketing [90]. One possibility is to consider splitting marketing by government agencies away from marketing by private nonprofit organizations. The rationale for

---

[1] Although the Federal Reserve Board had the benefit of findings from an in-depth research study it had commissioned of bankers, retailers, and consumers, it appeared to make no use of these insights when reintroducing the bill, limiting its efforts to a low-level public relations program [87].

this separation lies in the greater impact of nonmarket factors on the former group. An alternative approach would be to categorize marketing activities by all types of organizations into three major areas, according to the nature of the product being marketed—namely, physical goods, services, and behavior patterns (safe driving, for instance). One problem facing marketers in the third category is maintaining behavior over time (for example, preventing reversion to previous "bad" behavior once people have given up smoking, started to floss their teeth, and begun driving at 55 mph). Relatively little work on this topic is found in the social psychology literature, and marketers need to devote more attention to it.

Another area meriting further study involves the strategic implications of decision-making when profit is not the goal. Public and nonprofit organizations badly need to develop clearly defined and measurable objective functions that are appropriate to their particular missions. Without these, it is hard to formulate marketing strategies and harder still to assess whether or not they have been successful. Also needed is a mechanism to facilitate decisions on tradeoffs among multiple objectives.

A final area meriting research is marketing's role in government. Can marketing technology be brought to bear on transactions between federal and state or local governments? In particular, how should the federal government go about obtaining voluntary compliance with its policies (adoption of high technology waste disposal system, for example) as an alternative to trying to force compliance through legislation?

Even in the area of legislation, marketing insights may prove useful. People will not necessarily obey laws just because they are on the statute books. Consumer research is needed to help legislators frame laws that are realistic in their expectations of human behavior. Moreover, marketing efforts may also facilitate individual understanding of the rationale of new legislation, its impact, and what will be expected of citizens by way of compliance.

CONCLUSION

It is evident that nonbusiness marketing has come a long way in a relatively short period of time. The subject is taken seriously in academia, is having a growing impact on management practice in a diverse range of applications, and is contributing to general advancement of the field of marketing. These facts, we believe, justify our contention that public and nonprofit marketing has come of age. They in no way imply a lack of potential for future growth, improved judgment, or greater sophistication.

REFERENCES

1. Kotler, Philip, and Levy, Sidney J. "Broadening the Concept of Marketing." *Journal of Marketing* 33 (January 1969):10–15.
2. Luck, David J. "Broadening the Concept of Marketing—Too Far." *Journal of Marketing* 33 (July 1969): 53–55.
3. Kotler, Philip, and Zaltman, Gerald. "Social Marketing: An Approach to Planned Social Change." *Journal of Marketing* 35 (July 1971): 3–12.
4. Kotler, Philip. "A Generic Concept of Marketing." *Journal of Marketing* 36 (April 1972):46–54.
5. Nichols, William G. "Conceptual Conflicts in Marketing." *Journal of Economics and Business* 27 (Winter 1974):140–43.
6. Bartels, Robert. "The Identity Crisis in Marketing." *Journal of Marketing* 38 (October 1974):73–76.
7. Hunt, Shelby D. "The Nature and Scope of Marketing." *Journal of Marketing* 40 (July 1976):17–28.
8. Hunt, Shelby D. "The Three Dichotomies Model of Marketing: An Elaboration of Issues." In *Macro-Marketing: Distributive Processes From a Societal Perspective,* edited by Charles C. Slater, pp. 52–56. Boulder: University of Colorado, 1977.
9. Shapiro, Benson P. "Marketing for Nonprofit Organizations." *Harvard Business Review* 51 (September–October 1973):123–32.
10. Stuart, Reginald. "Toledo Students Back in School After Tax is Approved." *The New York Times.* 10 November 1977, p. A-18.
11. Kotler, Philip. *Marketing for Nonprofit Organizations,* Chapter 2. Englewood Cliffs, NJ: Prentice-Hall, 1975.
12. Heskett, James L. *Marketing,* pp. 531–33. New York: Macmillan, 1975.
13. Lovelock, Christopher H., and Weinberg, Charles B. "Contrasting Private and Public Sector Marketing." In *1974 Combined Proceedings,* edited by Ronald C. Curhan, pp. 242–47. Chicago: American Marketing Association, 1975.
14. Bauer, Raymond A., ed. *Social Indicators.* Cambridge: MIT Press, 1966.
15. Clewett, Robert L., and Olson, Jerry C., eds. *Social Indicators and Marketing.* Chicago: American Marketing Association, 1974.
16. Hamburger, Polia Lerner. *Social Indicators—A Marketing Perspective.* Chicago: American Marketing Association, 1974.
17. Rathnell, John M. *Marketing in the Service Sector.* Cambridge, MA: Winthrop, 1974.
18. Lovelock, Christopher H. "Marketing Consumer Services: Insights from the Public and Private Sectors." In *Proceedings. Seminaire de Recherche en Marketing.* Aix-en-Provence, France: Institut d'Administration des Affaires, 1975.
19. Eigler, Pierre; Langeard, Eric; Lovelock, Christopher H.; Bateson, John E. G., and Young, Robert F. "Marketing Consumer Services: New Insights." Marketing Science Institute, Report #77-115, December 1977.
20. Zaltman, Gerald; Kotler, Philip, and Kaufman, Ira. *Creating Social Change.* New York: Holt, Rinehard & Winston, 1972.
21. Lazer, William, and Kelley, Eugene J. *Social Marketing: Perspectives and Viewpoints.* Homewood, IL: Irwin, 1973.
22. Gaedeke, Ralph M. *Marketing in Private and Public Nonprofit Organizations: Perspectives and Illustrations.* Santa Monica, CA: Goodyear, 1977.
23. Sheth, Jagdish, and Wright, Peter L., eds. *Marketing Analysis for Societal Problems.* Urbana: University of Illinois, 1974.
24. Zaltman, Gerald, and Sternthal, Brian, eds. *Broadening the Concept of Consumer Behavior.* The Association for Consumer Research, 1975.
25. Lovelock, Christopher H., and Weinberg, Charles B. *Cases in Public and Nonprofit Marketing.* Palo Alto, CA: The Scientific Press, 1977.
26. Rothschild, Michael L. *An Incomplete Bibliography of Works Relating to Marketing for Public Sector and Nonprofit Organizations.* 2nd edition, #9-577-771. Boston: Intercollegiate Case Clearing House, 1977.
27. Enis, Ben M. *Marketing Principles: The Management Process.* Santa Monica, CA: Goodyear, 1977.
28. Kotler, Philip. *Marketing Management: Planning, Analysis, Control.* 3rd edition. Englewood Cliffs, NJ: Prentice-Hall, 1975.
29. Heskett, James L. *Marketing.* New York: Macmillan, 1976.
30. Boyd, Harper W., Jr., and Davis, Robert T. *Marketing Management Casebook.* Revised edition. Homewood, IL: Irwin, 1976.
31. Star, Steven H.; Davis, Nancy J.; Lovelock, Christopher H., and Shapiro, Benson P. *Problems in Marketing.* 5th edition. New York: McGraw-Hill, 1977.
32. Nickels, William G. *Marketing Principles.* Englewood Cliffs, NJ: Prentice-Hall, 1978.
33. Lovelock, Christopher H., ed. *Nonbusiness Marketing Cases.* 8-378-001. Boston: Intercollegiate Case Clearing House, 1977.

34. Intercollegiate Case Clearing House. *Selected Cases in Administration: Current Best Sellers*, 8-377-190. Boston: Intercollegiate Case Clearing House, 1977.

35. Stover, Robert V., and Stone, Walter J. "Hand Delivery of Self-Administered Questionnaires." *Public Opinion Quarterly* 37 (Summer 1974): 284–87.

36. Lovelock, Christopher H.; Stiff, Ronald; Cullwick, David, and Kaufman, Ira M. "An Evaluation of the Effectiveness of Drop-Off Questionnaire Delivery." *Journal of Marketing Research* 13 (November 1976): 358–64.

37. Baumol, William T., and Bowen, William G. *Performing Arts: The Economic Dilemma*. New York: Twentieth Century Fund, 1966.

38. Massy, William F. "A Dynamic Equilibrium Model for University Budget Planning," *Management Science* 23 (November 1976): 248–56.

39. Morison, Bradley G., and Fliehr, Kay. *In Search of an Audience*. New York: Pitman, 1968.

40. Ryans, Adrian B., and Weinberg, Charles B. "Consumer Dynamics in Nonprofit Organizations." *Journal of Consumer Research*, in press.

41. Weinberg, Charles B. "Building a Marketing Plan for the Performing Arts." *Association of College, University, and Community Arts Administrators Bulletin*, May 1977.

42. Nielson, Richard P., and McQueen, Charles. "Performing Arts Consumer Behavior: An Exploratory Study," pp. 392–95; and Kirpalani, V. H. "Marketing and the Arts: Discussion," pp. 396–98. Both in *1974 Combined Proceedings*, edited by Ronald C. Curhan. Chicago: American Marketing Association, 1974.

43. Laczniak, Gene R., and Murphy, Patrick E. "Planning and Control for Performing Arts Marketing." In *1977 Educators: Proceedings*, edited by Barrett E. Greenberg and Danny E. Bellenger. Chicago: American Marketing Association, 1977.

44. Weinberg, Charles B., and Shachmut, Kenneth M. "ARTS PLAN—A Model Based System for Use in Planning a Performing Arts Series." *Management Science*, February 1978.

45. Mushkin, Selma J., ed. *Consumer Incentives for Health Care*. New York: Prodist, 1974.

46. Somers, Anne R., ed. *Promoting Health: Consumer Education and National Policy*. Germantown, MD: Aspen Systems Corporation, 1976.

47. Bucklin, Louis P., and Carman, James M. "Vertical Market Structure and the Health Care Delivery System," pp. 7–41. In *Marketing Analysis for Social Problems*, edited by Jagdish Sheth and Peter L. Wright, pp. 7–41. Urbana, IL: University of Illinois, 1974.

48. Richard, Lawrence; Becherer, Richard, and George, William R. "The Development of Marketing Management Technology in a Health Care Setting: The Health Maintenance Organization Experience." In *1976 Educators' Proceedings*, edited by Kenneth L. Bernhardt. Chicago: American Marketing Association, 1976.

49. Venkatesan, M. "Marketing of Health Maintenance Organizations: Consumer Behavior Perspectives," pp. 45–69. In *Broadening the Concept of Consumer Behavior*, edited by Gerald Zaltman and Brian Sternthal. The Association for Consumer Research, 1975.

50. Wind, Yoram and Spitz, Lawrence K. "Analytical Approach to Marketing Decisions in Health-Care Organizations;" and Parker, Bennett R., and Srinivasan, V. "A Consumer Preference Approach to the Planning of Rural Primary Health-Care Facilities." Both in *Operations Research* 24 (October–November 1976): 973–90, 991–1025.

51. Newman, Ian M., ed. *Consumer Behavior in the Health Marketplace: A Symposium Proceedings*. Lincoln, NE: Nebraska Center for Health Education, University of Nebraska, 1977.

52. Densmore, Max L., and Klippel, R. Eugene. "Marketing Management: A New Contributor to Health Care Management," pp. 135–38; and Henion, Karl E., and Batsell, Richard R., "Marketing of Blood Donorship, Helping Behavior, and Psychological Reactance," pp. 652–56. Both in *1976 Educators' Proceedings*. Edited by K. L. Bernhardt. Chicago: American Marketing Association, 1976.

53. Venkatesan, M. "Consumer Behavior and Nutrition: Preventive Health Perspectives," pp. 518–20; Wortzel, Lawrence H., and Clarke, Roberta N., "Environmental Protection for the Non-Smoker: Consumer Behavior Aspects of Encouraging Non-Smoking," pp. 521–24; Robertson, Thomas S., and Wortzel, Lawrence H., "Consumer Behavior and Health Care Change: The Role of Mass Media," pp. 525–27. All in *Advances in Consumer Research*, Vol. 5, Association for Consumer Research, 1978.

54. Ray, Michael L.; Ward, Scott, and Reed, Jerome B. "Pretesting of Anti-Drug Abuse Education and Information Campaigns." In *Communication Research and Drug Education*, edited by R. E. Ostman. Beverly Hills, CA: Sage Publications, 1975.

55. Moriarty, Mark M., and Venkatesan, M. "Adoption of an HMO as an Innovation." *Proceedings. American Institute for Decision Sciences:* 9th Annual Conference, 1977.

56. American Hospital Association. Editorial and section on "Taking Health Care to Market." *Hospitals: Journal of the American Hospital Association* 51 (June 1977):51–72.

57. MacStravic, Robin E. *Marketing Health Care*. Germantown, MD: Aspen Systems Corporation, 1977.

58. Rogers, Everett M., and Shoemaker, F. Floyd. *Communication of Innovations: A Cross-Cultural Approach*, pp. 138–39. New York: The Free Press, 1971.

59. Reizenstein, Richard C., and Barnaby, David J., "An Analysis of Selected Consumer Energy-Environment Trade-Off Segments," pp. 522–26; Becker, Helmut, and Fritzche, David J., "Energy Consumption and Marketing: A Comparison of German and American Lifestyles," pp. 527–32. Both in *1976 Educators' Proceedings*, American Marketing Association.

60. Craig, C. Samuel, and McCann, John M., "Communicating Energy Conservation Information to Consumers: A Field Experiment," pp. 432–36; Russo, J. Edward, "A Proposal to Increase Energy Conservation Through Provision of Consumer and Cost Information to Consumers," pp. 437–42. Both in *1977 Educators' Proceedings*. American Marketing Association.

61. Reizenstein, Richard C., and Barnaby, David J., "The Consumer and the Energy Shortage: A Post-Embargo Assessment," pp. 308–14; Milstein, Jeffrey S., "Attitudes, Knowledge and Behavior of American Consumers Regarding Energy Conservation with Some Implications for Governmental Action," pp. 315–21. Both in *Advances in Consumer Research;* Volume 4, Association for Consumer Research, 1977.

62. Milstein, Jeffrey S., "Energy Conservation and Travel Behavior," pp. 422–25; Cunningham, William H., and Joseph, Brondel, "Energy Conservation: Price Increases and Payback Periods," pp. 201–05. Both in *Advances in Consumer Research*. Volume 5, 1978.

63. Rothe, James T.; Oberg, Kenneth H., and Kerin, Roger A. "Synchromarketing of Electrical Energy: Consumer Receptivity and Marketing Tasks." *Proceedings.* pp. 238–40. American Institute for Decision Sciences: 8th Annual Conference, 1976.

64. Tankersley, Clint B. "Concern Over the Energy Crisis: Some Social Psychological Correlates." *Proceedings.* American Institute for Decision Sciences: 9th Annual Conference, 1977.

65. Montgomery, David B., and Leonard-Barton, Dorothy. "Toward Strategies for Marketing Home Energy Conservation." Stanford University, Graduate School of Business: Research Paper No. 372, June 1977.

66. Phillips, Nicolas, and Nelson, Elizabeth. "Energy Savings in Private Households—An Integrated Research Programme." *Journal of the Market Research Society* 18 (October 1976): 180–200.

67. Schneider, Lewis M. *Marketing Urban Mass Transit—A Comparative Study of Management Strategies*. Boston: Division of Research, Harvard Graduate School of Business Administration, 1965.

68. Lovelock, Christopher H. *Consumer Oriented Approaches to Marketing Urban Transit*. Ph.D. dissertation, Stanford University. Springfield, Virginia: National Technical Information Service, PB 220781, 1973.

69. U.S. Department of Transportation. *National Transit Marketing Conference Proceedings*. Washington, D.C.: Urban Mass Transportation Administration and American Public Transit Association, 1975.

70. U.S. Department of Transportation. *Transit Marketing Management Handbook*, "Marketing Plan," "Pricing," "Organization," "Transit Information Aids" Washington, D.C.: Office of Transit Management, Urban Mass Transportation Administration, 1976, 1977.

71. U.S. Department of Transportation. *The Transit Marketing Project: Summary of Consumer Research, Baltimore MTA and Nashville MTA*. Washington, D.C.: Office of Transit Management, Urban Mass Transportation Administration, June 1976.

72. Gilbert, Gorman, and Foerster, James. "The Importance of Attitudes in the Decision to Use Mass Transit." *Transportation* 6 (December 1977): 321–32.

73. Lovelock, Christopher H. "A Market Segmentation Approach to Transit Planning, Modeling and Management." *Proceedings*. The Transportation Research Forum: 16th Annual Meeting, 1975.

74. Tybout, Alice M.; Hauser, John R., and Koppelman, Frank S. "Consumer Oriented Transportation Planning: An Integrated Methodology for Modeling Consumer Perceptions, Preference, and Behavior," pp. 426–34; Tischer, Mary Lynn, and Shey, Carl G. "Attitude-Behavior Changes in a Before-After Mode Choice Situation," pp. 456–64. Both in *Advances in Consumer Research,* Volume 5, Association for Consumer Research, 1978.

75. Feldman, Laurence P., and Vallenga, David B. "The Role of Security in Marketing Urban Mass Transportation." *High Speed Ground Transportation Journal,* Summer 1977, pp. 157–72.

76. Vanier, Dinoo J., and Wotruba, Thomas R. "Mass Transit: Devising a Research Based Marketing Plan." *Transportation Research* 11 (1977): 245–53.

77. Kotler, Philip, and Dubois, Bernard. "Education Problems and Marketing," pp. 186–206. In *Marketing Analysis for Social Problems,* edited by Jagdish Sheth and Peter L. Wright. Urbana, IL: University of Illinois, 1974.

78. College Entrance Examination Board. *A Role for Marketing in College Admissions.* Princeton, NJ: 1976.

79. Kotler, Philip. "Applying Marketing Theory to College Admissions," pp. 54–72. In College Entrance Examination Board. *A Role for Marketing in College Admissions.* Princeton, NJ: 1976.

80. Lovelock, Christopher H. "Researching and Modeling Consumer Choice Behavior in Urban Transportation." In *Advances in Consumer Research,* Volume 2, edited by M. J. Schlinger. Association for Consumer Research, 1975.

81. Leister, Douglas V., and MacLachlan, Douglas L. "Assessing the Community College Transfer Market: A Metamarketing Application." *Journal of Higher Education* 47 (November–December 1976):661–80.

82. Vaughn, Ronald; Pitlik, Joseph, and Hansotia, Behram. "Understanding University Choice: A Multiattribute Approach," pp. 26–31. *Advances in Consumer Research,* Volume 5. Association for Consumer Research, 1978.

83. Heinlein, Albert C., and Krampf, Robert F. "Identification of Attitudinal Differences Between Attendees and Non-Attendees at a Major University." *Proceedings.* American Institute for Decision Sciences: 9th Annual Conference, 1977.

84. Cook, Robert W.; Krampf, Robert F., and Shimp, Terence A. "A Nonmetric Multidimensional Approach to the Marketing of Higher Educational Institutions." *Proceedings.* American Institute for Decision Sciences: 9th Annual Conference, 1977.

85. Hise, Richard T., and Smith, Ephraim P. "Using Cognitive Dissonance Theory to Reduce the Back-Out Rate in School of Business Applications." *Decision Sciences* 8 (January 1977):300–10.

86. "AMA Honors 6, Parker First in Doctoral Dissertation Competition," *Marketing News,* July 29, 1977, pp. 1, 12.

87. Intercollegiate Case Clearing House. "Department of the Treasury: Reissue of the $2 Bill." 9-576-102. Boston: 1975.

88. Zaltman, Gerald, and Jacobs, Pol. "Social Marketing and a Consumer-Based Theory of Marketing." In *Consumer and Industrial Buying Behavior,* pp. 399–408. Edited by Arch G. Woodside, Jagdish N. Sheth, and Peter D. Bennett. New York: North Holland, 1977.

89. Montgomery, David B. and Weinberg, Charles B. "Modeling Marketing Phenomena: A Managerial Perspective." *Journal of Contemporary Business,* Autumn 1973, pp. 17–43.

90. Sokal, Robert B. "Numerical Taxonomy." *Scientific American* 215 (December 1966):106–16.

2
Broadening the Concept of Marketing

Philip Kotler
Sidney J. Levy

Marketing is a pervasive societal activity that goes considerably beyond the selling of toothpaste, soap, and steel. The authors interpret the meaning of marketing for nonbusiness organizations and the nature of marketing functions such as product improvement, pricing, distribution, and communication in such organizations. The question considered is whether traditional marketing principles are transferable to the marketing of organizations, persons, and ideas.

The term "marketing" connotes to most people a function peculiar to business firms. Marketing is seen as the task of finding and stimulating buyers for the firm's output. It involves product development, pricing, distribution, and communication; and in the more progressive firms, continuous attention to the changing needs of customers and the development of new products, with product modifications and services to meet these needs. But whether marketing is viewed in the old sense of "pushing" products or in the new sense of "customer satisfaction engineering," it is almost always viewed and discussed as a business activity.

It is the authors' contention that marketing is a pervasive societal activity that goes considerably beyond the selling of toothpaste, soap, and steel. Political contests remind

Philip Kotler is the Harold T. Martin Professor of Marketing, Northwestern University.

Sidney J. Levy is Professor of Behaviorial Science, Northwestern University.

us that candidates are marketed as well as soap; student recruitment by colleges reminds us that higher education is marketed; and fund raising reminds us that "causes" are marketed. Yet these areas of marketing are typically ignored by the student of marketing. Or they are treated cursorily as public relations or publicity activities. No attempt is made to incorporate these phenomena in the body proper of marketing thought and theory. No attempt is made to redefine the meaning of product development, pricing, distribution, and communication in these newer contexts to see if they have a useful meaning. No attempt is made to examine whether the principles of "good" marketing in traditional product areas are transferable to the marketing of services, persons, and ideas.

The authors see a great opportunity for marketing people to expand their thinking and to apply their skills to an increasingly interesting range of social activity. The challenge depends on the attention given to it; marketing will either take on a broader social meaning or remain a narrowly defined business activity.

THE RISE OF ORGANIZATIONAL MARKETING

One of the most striking trends in the United States is the increasing amount of society's work being performed by organizations other than business firms. As a society moves beyond the stage where shortages of food, clothing, and shelter are the major problems, it begins to organize to meet other social needs that formerly had been put aside. Business enterprises remain a dominant type of organization, but other types of organizations gain in conspicuousness and in influence. Many of these organizations become enormous and require the same rarefied management skills as traditional business organizations. Managing the United Auto Workers, Defense Department, Ford Foundation, World Bank, Catholic Church, University of California has become every bit as challenging as managing Procter and Gamble, General Motors, General Electric. These non-business organizations have an increasing range of influence, affect as many livelihoods, and occupy as much media prominence as major business firms.

All of these organizations perform the classic business functions. Every organization must perform a financial function insofar as money must be raised, managed and budgeted according to sound business principles. Every organization must perform a production function in that it must conceive of the best way of arranging inputs to produce the outputs of the organization. Every organization must perform a personnel function in that people must be hired, trained, assigned, and promoted in the course of the organization's work. Every organization must perform a purchasing function in that it must acquire materials in an efficient way through comparing and selecting sources of supply.

When we come to the marketing function, it is also clear that every organization performs marketing-like activities whether or not they are recognized as such. Several examples can be given.

The police department of a major U.S. city, concerned with the poor image it has among an important segment of its population, developed a campaign to "win friends and influence people." One highlight of this campaign is a "visit your police station" day in which tours are conducted to show citizens the daily operations of the police department, including the crime laboratories, police lineups, and cells. The police department also sends officers to speak at public schools and carries out a number of other activities to improve its community relations.

Most museum directors interpret their primary responsibility as "the proper preservation of an artistic heritage for posterity." [1] As a result, for many people museums are cold marble mausoleums that house miles of relics that soon give way to yawns and tired feet. Although museum attendance in the United States advances each year, a large number of citizens are uninterested in museums. Is this indifference due to failure in the manner of presenting what museums have to offer? This nagging question led the new director of the Metropolitan Museum of Art to broaden the museum's appeal through sponsoring contemporary art shows and "happenings." His marketing philosophy of museum management led to substantial increases in the Met's attendance.

The public school system in Oklahoma City sorely needed more public support and funds to prevent a deterioration of facilities and exodus of teachers. It recently resorted to television programming to dramatize the work the public schools were doing to fight the high school dropout problem, to develop new teaching techniques, and to enrich the children. Although an expensive medium, television quickly reached large numbers of parents whose response and interest were tremendous.

Nations also resort to international marketing campaigns to get across important points about themselves to the citizens of other countries. The junta of Greek colonels who seized power in Greece in 1967 found the international publicity surrounding their cause to be extremely unfavorable and potentially disruptive of international recognition. They hired a major New York public relations firm and soon full-page newspaper ads appeared carrying the headline "Greece Was Saved From Communism," detailing in small print why the takeover was necessary for the stability of Greece and the world.[2]

An anti-cigarette group in Canada is trying to press the Canadian Parliament to ban cigarettes on the grounds that they are harmful to health. There is widespread support for this cause but the organization's funds are limited, particularly measured against the huge advertising resources of the cigarette industry. The group's problem is to find effective ways to make a little money go a long way in persuading influential legislators of the need for discouraging cigarette consumption. This group has come up with several ideas for marketing anti-smoking to Canadians, including television spots, a paperback book featuring pictures of cancer and heart disease patients, and legal research on company liability for the smoker's loss of health.

What concepts are common to these and many other possible illustrations of organizational marketing? All of these organizations are concerned about their "product" in the eyes of certain "consumers" and are seeking to find "tools" for furthering their acceptance. Let us consider each of these concepts in general organizational terms.

Products. Every organization produces a "product" of at least one of the following types:

---

[1] This is the view of Sherman Lee, Director of the Cleveland Museum, quoted in *Newsweek*, April 1, 1968, p. 55.

[2] "PR for the Colonels," *Newsweek*, March 18, 1968, p. 70.

Physical products. "Product" first brings to mind everyday items like soap, clothes, and food, and extends to cover millions of *tangible* items that have a market value and are available for purchases.

Services. Services are *intangible* goods that are subject to market transaction such as tours, insurance, consultation, hairdos, and banking.

Persons. Personal marketing is an endemic *human* activity, from the employee trying to impress his boss to the statesman trying to win the support of the public. With the advent of mass communications, the marketing of persons has been turned over to professionals. Hollywood stars have their press agents, political candidates their advertising agencies, and so on.

Organizations. Many organizations spend a great deal of time marketing themselves. The Republican Party has invested considerable thought and resources in trying to develop a modern look. The American Medical Association decided recently that it needed to launch a campaign to improve the image of the American doctor.[3] Many charitable organizations and universities see selling their *organization* as their primary responsibility.

Ideas. Many organizations are mainly in the business of selling *ideas* to the larger society. Population organizations are trying to sell the idea of birth control, and the Women's Christian Temperance Union is still trying to sell the idea of prohibition.

Thus the "product" can take many forms, and this is the first crucial point in the case for broadening the concept of marketing.

Consumers. The second crucial point is that organizations must deal with many groups that are interested in their products and can make a difference in its success. It is vitally important to the organization's success that it be sensitive to, serve, and satisfy these groups. One set of groups can be called the *suppliers*. *Suppliers* are those who provide the management group with the inputs necessary to perform its work and develop its product effectively. Suppliers include employees, vendors of the materials, banks, advertising agencies, and consultants.

The other set of groups are the *consumers* of the organization's product, of which four sub-groups can be distinguished. The *clients* are those who are the immediate consumers of the organization's product. The clients of a business firm are its buyers and potential buyers; of a service organization those receiving the services, such as the needy (from the Salvation Army) or the sick (from County Hospital); and of a protective or a primary organization, the members themselves. The second group is the *trustees* or *directors,* those who are vested with the legal authority and responsibility for the organization, oversee the management, and enjoy a variety of benefits form the "product." The third group is the active *publics* that take a specific interest in the organization. For a business firm, the active publics include consumer rating groups, governmental agencies, and pressure groups of various kinds. For a university, the active publics include alumni and friends of the university, foundations, and city fathers. Finally, the fourth consumer group is the *general public*. These are all the people who might de-

velop attitudes toward the organization that might affect its conduct in some way. Organizational marketing concerns the programs designed by management to create satisfactions and favorable attitudes in the organization's four consuming groups; clients, trustees, active publics, and general public.

Marketing Tools. Students of business firms spend much time studying the various tools under the firm's control that affect product acceptance: product improvement, pricing, distribution, and communication. All of these tools have counterpart applications to nonbusiness organizational activity.

Nonbusiness organizations to various degrees engage in product improvement, especially when they recognize the competition they face from other organizations. Thus, over the years churches have added a host of nonreligious activities to their basic religious activities to satisfy members seeking other bases of human fellowship. Universities keep updating their curricula and adding new student services in an attempt to make the educational experience relevant to the students. Where they have failed to do this, students have sometimes organized their own courses and publications, or have expressed their dissatisfaction in organized protest. Government agencies such as license bureaus, police forces, and taxing bodies are often not responsive to the public because of monopoly status; but even here citizens have shown an increasing readiness to protest mediocre services, and more alert bureaucracies have shown a growing interest in reading the user's needs and developing the required product services.

All organizations face the problem of pricing their products and services so that they cover costs. Churches charge dues, universities charge tuition, governmental agencies charge fees, fund-raising organizations send out bills. Very often specific product charges are not sufficient to meet the organization's budget, and it must rely on gifts and surcharges to make up the difference. Opinions vary as to how much the users should be charged for the individual services and how much should be made up through general collection. If the university increases its tuition, it will have to face losing some students and putting more students on scholarship. If the hospital raises its charges to cover rising costs and additional services, it may provoke a reaction from the community. All organizations face complex pricing issues although not all of them understand good pricing practice.

Distribution is a central concern to the manufacturer seeking to make his goods conveniently accessible to buyers. Distribution also can be an important marketing decision area for nonbusiness organizations. A city's public library has to consider the best means of making its books available to the public. Should it establish one large library with an extensive collection of books, or several neighborhood branch libraries with duplication of books? Should it use bookmobiles that bring the books to the customers instead of relying exclusively on the customers coming to the books? Should it distribute through school libraries? Similarly the police de-

[3] "Doctors Try an Image Transplant," *Business Week,* June 22, 1968, p. 64.

partment of a city must think through the problem of distributing its protective services efficiently through the community. It has to determine how much protective service to allocate to different neighborhoods; the respective merits of squad cars, motorcycles, and foot patrolmen; and the positioning of emergency phones.

Customer communication is an essential activity of all organizations although many nonmarketing organizations often fail to accord it the importance it deserves. Managements of many organizations think they have fully met their communication responsibilities by setting up advertising and/or public relations departments. They fail to realize that *everything about an organization talks*. Customers form impressions of an organization from its physical facilities, employees, officers, stationery, and a hundred other company surrogates. Only when this is appreciated do the members of the organization recognize that they all are in marketing, whatever else they do. With this understanding they can assess realistically the impact of their activities on the consumers.

CONCEPTS FOR EFFECTIVE MARKETING MANAGEMENT IN NONBUSINESS ORGANIZATIONS

Although all organizations have products, markets, and marketing tools, the art and science of effective marketing management have reached their highest state of development in the business type of organization. Business organizations depend on customer goodwill for survival and have generally learned how to sense and cater to their needs effectively. As other types of organizations recognize their marketing roles, they will turn increasingly to the body of marketing principles worked out by business organizations and adapt them to their own situations.

What are the main principles of effective marketing management as they appear in most forward looking business organizations? Nine concepts stand out as crucial in guiding the marketing effort of a business organization.

Generic Product Definition. Business organizations have increasingly recognized the value of placing a broad definition on their products, one that emphasizes the basic customer need(s) being served. A modern soap company recognizes that its basic product is cleaning, not soap; a cosmetics company sees its basic product as beauty or hope, not lipsticks and makeup; a publishing company sees its basic product as information, not books.

The same need for a broader definition of its business is incumbent upon nonbusiness organizations if they are to survive and grow. Churches at one time tended to define their product narrowly as that of producing religious services for members. Recently, most churchmen have decided that their basic product is human fellowship. There was a time when educators said that their product was the three R's. Now most of them define their product as education for the whole man.

They try to serve the social, emotional, and political needs of young people in addition to intellectual needs.

Target Groups Definition. A generic product definition usually results in defining a very wide market, and it is then necessary for the organization, because of limited resources, to limit its product offering to certain clearly defined groups within the market. Although the generic product of an automobile company is transportation, the company typically sticks to cars, trucks, and buses, and stays away from bicycles, airplanes, and steamships. Furthermore, the manufacturer does not produce every size and shape of car but concentrates on producing a few major types to satisfy certain substantial and specific parts of the market.

In the same way, nonbusiness organizations have to define their target groups carefully. For example, in Chicago the YMCA defines its target groups as men, women and children who want recreational opportunities and are willing to pay $20 or more a year for them. The Chicago Boys Club, on the other hand, defines its target group as poorer boys within the city boundaries who are in want of recreational facilities and can pay $1 a year.

Differentiated Marketing. When a business organization sets out to serve more than one target group, it will be maximally effective by differentiating its product offerings and communications. This is also true for nonbusiness organizations. Fundraising organizations have recognized the advantage of treating clients, trustees, and various publics in different ways. These groups require differentiated appeals and frequency of solicitation. Labor unions find that they must address different messages to different parties rather than one message to all parties. To the company they may seem unyielding, to the conciliator they may appear willing to compromise, and to the public they seek to appear economically exploited.

Customer Behavior Analysis. Business organizations are increasingly recognizing that customer needs and behavior are not obvious without formal research and analysis; they cannot rely on impressionistic evidence. Soap companies spend hundreds of thousands of dollars each year researching how Mrs. Housewife feels about her laundry, how, when, and where she does her laundry, and what she desires of a detergent.

Fund raising illustrates how an industry has benefited by replacing stereotypes of donors with studies of why people contribute to causes. Fund raisers have learned that people give because they are getting something. Many give to community chests to relieve a sense of guilt because of their elevated state compared to the needy. Many give to medical charities to relieve a sense of fear that they may be struck by a disease whose cure has not yet been found. Some give to feel pride. Fund raisers have stressed the importance of identifying the motives operating in the marketplace of givers as a basis for planning drives.

Differential Advantages. In considering different ways of reaching target groups, an organization is advised to think in terms of seeking a differential advantage. It should consider what elements in its reputation or resources can be exploited to create a special value in the minds of its potential customers. In the same way Zenith has built a reputation for quality and International Harvester a reputation for service, a nonbusiness organization should base its case on some dramatic values that competitive organizations lack. The small island of Nassau can compete against Miami for the tourist trade by advertising the greater dependability of its weather; the Heart Association can compete for funds against the Cancer Society by advertising the amazing strides made in heart research.

Multiple Marketing Tools. The modern business firm relies on a multitude of tools to sell its product, including product improvement, consumer and dealer advertising, salesman incentive programs, sales promotions, contests, multiple-size offerings, and so forth. Likewise nonbusiness organizations also can reach their audiences in a variety of ways. A church can sustain the interest of its members through discussion groups, newsletters, news releases, campaign drives, annual reports, and retreats. Its "salesmen" include the religious head, the board members, and the present members in terms of attracting potential members. Its advertising includes announcements of weddings, births and deaths, religious pronouncements, and newsworthy developments.

Integrated Marketing Planning. The multiplicity of available marketing tools suggests the desirability of overall coordination so that these tools do not work at cross purposes. Over time, business firms have placed under a marketing vice-president activities that were previously managed in a semi-autonomous fashion, such as sales, advertising, and marketing research. Nonbusiness organizations typically have not integrated their marketing activities. Thus, no single officer in the typical university is given total responsibility for studying the needs and attitudes of clients, trustees, and publics, and undertaking the necessary product development and communication programs to serve these groups. The university administration instead includes a variety of "marketing" positions such as dean of students, director of alumni affairs, director of public relations, and director of development; coordination is often poor.

Continuous Marketing Feedback. Business organizations gather continuous information about changes in the environment and about their own performance. They use their salesmen, research department, specialized research services, and other means to check on the movement of goods, actions of competitors, and feelings of customers to make sure they are progressing along satisfactory lines. Nonbusiness organizations typically are more casual about collecting vital information on how they are doing and what is happening in the

marketplace. Universities have been caught off guard by underestimating the magnitude of student grievance and unrest, and so have major cities underestimated the degree to which they were failing to meet the needs of important minority constituencies.

Marketing Audit. Change is a fact of life, although it may proceed almost invisibly on a day-to-day basis. Over a long stretch of time it might be so fundamental as to threaten organizations that have not provided for periodic reexaminations of their purposes. Organizations can grow set in their ways and unresponsive to new opportunities or problems. Some great American companies are no longer with us because they did not change definitions of their businesses, and their products lost relevance in a changing world. Political parties become unresponsive after they enjoy power for a while and every so often experience a major upset. Many union leaders grow insensitive to new needs and problems until one day they find themselves out of office. For an organization to remain viable, its management must provide for periodic audits of its objectives, resources, and opportunities. It must reexamine its basic business, target groups, differential advantage, communication channels, and messages in the light of current trends and needs. It might recognize when change is needed and make it before it is too late.

IS ORGANIZATIONAL MARKETING A SOCIALLY USEFUL ACTIVITY?

Modern marketing has two different meanings in the minds of people who use the term. One meaning of marketing conjures up the terms selling, influencing, persuading. Marketing is seen as a huge and increasingly dangerous technology, making it possible to sell persons on buying things, propositions, and causes they either do not want or which are bad for them. This was the indictment in Vance Packard's *Hidden Persuaders* and numerous other social criticisms, with the net effect that a large number of persons think of marketing as immoral or entirely self-seeking in its fundamental premises. They can be counted on to resist the idea of organizational marketing as so much "Madison Avenue."

The other meaning of marketing unfortunately is weaker in the public mind; it is the concept of sensitively *serving and satisfying human needs*. This was the great contribution of the marketing concept that was promulgated in the 1950s, and that concept now counts many business firms as its practitioners. The marketing concept holds that the problem of all business firms in an age of abundance is to develop customer loyalties and satisfaction, and the key to this problem is to focus on the customer's needs.[4] Perhaps the short-run problem of business firms is to sell people on buying the existing products, but the long-run problem is

---

[4] Theodore Levitt, "Marketing Myopia," *Harvard Business Review,* July–August, 1960, pp. 45–56.

clearly to create the products that people need. By this recognition that effective marketing requires a consumer orientation instead of a product orientation, marketing has taken a new lease on life and tied its economic activity to a higher social purpose.

It is this second side of marketing that provides a useful concept for all organizations. All organizations are formed to serve the interest of particular groups; hospitals serve the sick, schools serve the students, governments serve the citizens, and labor unions serve the members. In the course of evolving, many organizations lose sight of their original mandate, grow hard, and become self-serving. The bureaucritic mentality begins to dominate the original service mentality. Hospitals may become perfunctory in their handling of patients, schools treat their students as nuisances, city bureaucrats behave like petty tyrants toward the citizens, and labor unions try to run instead of serve their members. All of these actions tend to build frustration in the consuming groups. As a result some withdraw meekly from these organizations, accept frustration as part of their condition, and find their satisfactions elsewhere. This used to be the common reaction of ghetto Negroes and college students in the face of indifferent city and university bureaucracies. But new possibilities have arisen, and now the same consumers refuse to withdraw so readily. Organized dissent and protest are seen to be an answer, and many organizations thinking of themselves as responsible have been stunned into recognizing that they have lost touch with their constituencies. They had grown unresponsive.

Where does marketing fit into this picture? Marketing is that function of the organization that can keep in constant touch with the organization's consumers, read their needs, develop ''products'' that meet these needs, and build a program of communications to express the organization's purposes. Certainly selling and influencing will be large parts of organizational marketing; but, properly seen, selling follows rather than precedes the organization's drive to create products to satisfy its consumers.

CONCLUSION

It has been argued here that the modern marketing concept serves very naturally to describe an important facet of all organizational activity. All organizations must develop appropriate products to serve their sundry consuming groups and must use modern tools of communication to reach their consuming publics. The business heritage of marketing provides a useful set of concepts for guiding all organizations.

The choice facing those who manage nonbusiness organizations is not whether to market or not to market, for no organization can avoid marketing. The choice is whether to do it well or poorly, and on this necessity the case for organizational marketing is basically founded.

3
Get Rid of the People and the System Runs Fine

Patrick Ryan

Operations and marketing managers sometimes seem to be on a collision course in service organizations. Each may see the "product" of the organization in very different ways: the former tends to worry about efficiency, the latter about serving consumer needs. This author takes a look at the consequences of an operations orientation, which is at once both lighthearted and sobering.

Until Theseus terminated his fell career, Procrustes, the legendary Attic brigand, used to measure his captives on an iron bed. If they were longer than the bed, he chopped off their surplus parts; if they were shorter, he stretched them till they fitted. Some revival of this Procrustean precept that the people should be made to fit the system can be detected these days.

Note this newspaper report from the Midlands of England: "Complaints from passengers wishing to use the Bagnall to Greenfields bus service that 'the drivers were speeding past queues of up to 30 people with a smile and a wave of a hand' have been met by a statement pointing out that 'it is impossible for the drivers to keep their timetable if they have to stop for passengers'."

It will thus be seen that the official function of a bus service is not, as popularly misconceived, to carry people from A to B, but to meet its timetables. The sacred schedules must be maintained, even if the bus has to run empty. Therefore, ultimate efficiency of bus services can be achieved only if passengers are banned altogether. Such a prohibition would have the ancillary advantages of extending clutch and brake longevity and markedly reducing the wear and tear on the upholstery. Much the same attitude can be observed in the facial expressions of the staff at any airport as they handle your tickets, while longing for the day when they can be left to run the place like clockwork with their TV screens and admonitory announcements, without all those blasted, disorganized air-travel passengers milling about all over the place.

On the stationary side, John Cleese, the skyscraping British comic of Monty Python fame, runs a television series in Britain in which he plays a manic and domineering hotel proprietor. He said that he got the idea from actually staying at a West of England hotel "where there was this wonderfully rude owner who maintained that the guests stopped him from running his hotel. . . . It was the first time we'd come across

Patrick Ryan is a freelance writer who frequently contributes to the *Smithsonian*.

such a situation—now I know that it happens all round the world.''

And all round the world, hoteliers painstakingly display their monastic rules and detailed eating routine on that card on the bedroom door. Only if all prisoners obey its timely regulations can the establishment's system be operated harmoniously. The virtue most in request, as Emerson once bemoaned, is conformity. It is ill-trained guests like you and me, who forget the feeding orders and lie abed to unhinge the cleaning rota, who are the monkey wrenches in the hospitable works—thus driving hotel managers to dream of that perfect Grand Hotel which runs with daily, clockwork precision, where all meals are completed on time, all rooms are cleaned to split-second schedule, and the bartenders can keep their glasses eternally polished to perfection—because the place steadfastly refuses to take in any guests at all.

An occupational psychologist employed as a consultant to a Middle Eastern air force recently reported an unusual method of fitting people to prevailing constraints. There was a local supply difficulty in obtaining irregular sizes of uniform shoes for airmen. So, in philosophical compromise, the recruiting board selected successful candidates on the regular proportions and commonplace dimensions of their feet.

A popular weapon of bureaucrats bent upon keeping people subservient to their system is the regular demand that they categorize their lives on meaningless forms and unnecessary returns. I have long admired the ploy that George A. Birmingham, the novelist and essayist, adopted in retaliation. In his nonliterary life he was a clergyman in Ireland and, as such, he was pestered by bishops and other authorities to fill in recurring questionnaires. He took particular umbrage against the annual demand from the education office to report the dimensions of his village schoolroom. In the first and second years, he duly filled in the required figures. On the third year, he replied that the schoolroom was still the same size as before. Schoolrooms are not trees, he observed, they do not grow. The education office badgered him with reminders until Birmingham finally filled in the figures.

But he didn't put in the same figures as before. He doubled the dimensions of his schoolroom. Nobody queried it. So he went on doubling the measurements until ''in the course of five or six years that schoolroom became a great deal larger than St. Paul's Cathedral.'' But nobody at the education office was at all concerned. So, the next year, the Canon suddenly reduced the dimensions of his colossal classroom ''to the size of an American tourist trunk. . . . It would have been impossible to get three children, without a teacher, in that schoolroom.'' And nobody took the slightest notice, for nobody needed the information. But the system did, and the system had to be satisfied. So why not try the George A. Birmingham treatment next time they send you a form to fill out?

Part II
The Role and Use of Marketing

The purpose of this part of the book is to show that marketing plays many different roles, depending on the nature of the problem and the organizational context. The next five chapters show that marketing may provide a new conceptual framework for examining an organization, as well as offering its managers powerful strategic and tactical tools.

Marketing is fundamentally concerned with identifying and satisfying the needs of prospective consumers. For government agencies, this translates to understanding and meeting citizen needs. In contrast to other approaches to "needs assessment" used by planners and public managers, marketing is distinguished by its emphasis on a managerial approach. However, concerns have been expressed about possible abuses of marketing in the public arena, notably the use of heavily financed communications efforts to shape citizen opinion towards political issues or candidates. In addressing this issue, the last chapter in Part II stresses the importance of avoiding gross generalizations, showing how the impact of marketing efforts is likely to vary according to the nature of the specific situation.

"Contrasting Private and Public Sector Marketing," by Lovelock and Weinberg, focuses on ways in which the institutional context influences and constrains the use of marketing by public agencies and nonprofit organizations. It shows that marketing tools and strategies developed in the private sector cannot be applied in identical fashion to nonbusiness organizations, but must be adapted to differing environments. This article also evaluates the factors that motivate organizations to adopt a marketing orientation in the first place, raising the question of what public managers can and should expect to accomplish through use of marketing efforts.

In "Public Policy Development: A Marketing Perspective," Enis, Kangun, and Mokwa extend the use of marketing tools to a role in the policy making area. They argue that marketing's consumer orientation and strategic perspective will lead to selection of better policies and more effective implementation.

What does marketing have to offer that other community development programs do not? "Public Marketing: Policy Planning for Community Development in the City," highlights the distinctive characteristics of marketing versus alternative means of needs assessment. Blakely, Schutz, and Harvey argue that a public marketing approach leads to strategies that are more responsive to community concerns, as well as to more accurate evaluations of potential and actual programs.

One approach to making government agencies more responsive is to encourage citizen participation in planning and in public decision-making. However, Brown, Schary, and Becker show that in reality most citizen participation programs generate unrepresentative, biased samples of community opinions. Their article, "Marketing Down the Road: The Role of Marketing

Analysis in Transportation Planning," goes on to evaluate the contribution made by marketing research to development of a transportation plan that accurately reflects the concerns and viewpoints of the community for which it is being designed.

From marketing's role in planning at the local level, the discussion turns to an in-depth review of a highly contentious issue, the use—some would say misuse—of marketing communications in the electoral process. In "Political Advertising: A Neglected Policy Issue in Marketing," Michael L. Rothschild undertakes a major review of the extensive literature on political advertising. His thesis is that instead of making a broadside attack on political advertising expenditure levels, policymakers need to make a reasoned evaluation of the specific effects of such advertising in different situations. He then constructs a paradigm for predicting the types of effects that communication campaigns can have.

In summary, these five chapters show that while marketing can play a significant role in a variety of public and nonprofit organizations, its impact is likely to be highly variable and dependent on the particular organizational setting.

4

Contrasting Private and Public Sector Marketing

Christopher H. Lovelock
Charles B. Weinberg

The main issue in public sector marketing is how skills, techniques, and concepts developed originally in business can be transferred to nonbusiness organizations. In evaluating the extent and nature of the transfer, we identify four characteristics common to most public sector organizations and show how they influence and constrain the use of marketing in nonprofit organizations. We also identify three dimensions: (1) motivation for adopting marketing, (2) prior history of marketing activities, and (3) the nature of ownership of the public sector—all three of which influence the choice of marketing strategies.

There is growing interest in applying management techniques in public sector agencies and not-for-profit organizations. Marketing tools and strategies, in particular, are now finding increasing application outside the realm of profit-oriented private business, where they were originally developed.

As the role of the public sector continues to grow in the U.S. economy (and also in most other Western nations), pressures are mounting for more effective administration of both new and traditional government activities. Meanwhile, numerous not-for-profit institutions—such as hospitals, universities, libraries, and symphony orchestras—are finding that application of managerial skills may be essential to

success, and even to survival. That marketing skills are transferable from the private to the public sector is no longer in doubt, as has been shown by several authors in this field [3, 4, 5, 8, 9]. The real issue now confronting marketers is the *extent* to which these skills are transferable.

CHARACTERIZATION OF THE PUBLIC SECTOR

The term "public sector" usually is used to denote that area of economic activity which is in public ownership. However, it is not always entirely clear where the public sector ends and the private sector begins. For instance, some agencies, such as Amtrak or Comsat, are semi-public corporations that are both publicly and privately financed. In certain fields of endeavor—such as universities, libraries, hospitals, museums, and public utilities—some institutions are in private hands while others are publicly owned. Sometimes,

Christopher H. Lovelock is Associate Professor of Business Administration, Harvard University.

Charles B. Weinberg is Associate Professor of Marketing, Stanford University.

as is the case with a number of public transit services in the U.S., a publicly owned facility may be managed and operated by a privately owned contractor.

In many instances where actual ownership is in private hands, it is generally true that such institutions are particularly close to the public sector, being either closely regulated and/or receiving special tax-exemptions on account of their non-profit status.

Differences Between Private and Public Sector Organizations. What common threads run through this broad group of agencies and organizations? First of all, public sector agencies and organizations are almost exclusively *service operations*. Thus, although the U.S. federal government has market-related ''sales'' of goods and services of almost 70 billion dollars, only ten percent of these sales are for goods [7]. And this ten percent is largely composed of sales by military retail establishments to military personnel and the sale of stockpiled or surplus military hardware and agricultural commodities. In a number of instances, public agencies do not even market a service; rather they are in the business of marketing ideas and behavior patterns—such as the use of metric weights and measures, the adoption of new agricultural methods, or the practice of safer driving habits.

Second, the majority are *non-profit operations*, often incurring substantial deficits and thus requiring government subsidies or private benefactions. As a result, success or failure cannot be measured in strictly financial terms. In some instances—such as postal services and public transportation—the service typically is offered for sale at a price, while in others—such as city parks and police services—it may be provided free of charge to users.

Third, although the services provided by public sector organizations tend to be regarded as *essential or socially desirable, their benefits and costs usually are distributed across the population unequally*. As a result, some public sector services are of direct use or immediate interest to only a limited segment of the population. For example, although there are many arguments for giving public money to the arts, less than five percent of the U.S. population attends a live performance of any of the professional performing arts (dance, symphony, orchestra, drama or opera) in a year [2]. A difficult question facing performing arts managers is whether to increase the number of performances targeted at current audience members, or to attempt to broaden public attendance at artistic performances.

The fourth common thread is that public sector organizations tend to be more *subject to public review, regulations, and criticism* than most private firms. Business practices which are tolerated in the private sector may be regarded as unacceptable or inappropriate for a public sector organization, on account of the involvement of public funds and/or the special nature of the services rendered.

MARKETING IMPLICATIONS OF THE CHARACTERISTICS OF PUBLIC SECTOR ORGANIZATIONS

To what extent do these differences between private and public sector organizations affect the transfer of marketing tools and strategies? It is helpful to consider each of five key marketing elements in turn.

The Product. Because most public sector organizations market services, ideas, or behavior patterns rather than physical goods, useful insights into public sector marketing problems are more likely to be obtained from a study of service marketing than from marketing physical products. Unfortunately, however, the marketing of services in the private sector is less well developed than the marketing of products on both a theoretical and operational level. This makes it harder to identify appropriate analogs. It is also more difficult to communicate and sell intangible services or concepts than it is to market physical products.

Distribution. The distribution problems facing service marketers differ from those faced by goods marketers. When developing a distribution strategy for services, marketers rarely are confronted by problems of physical distribution and only seldom need to make use of more than one level of middlemen. What is important is the seller's or agent's location relative to the potential market. Proximity of customers to the source of a service can affect both demand for the service and the degree of satisfaction with it. Consumer analysis has often led to the relocation of sources of services closer to users' locations. For example, government agencies providing social and welfare services used primarily by low income or elderly groups are increasingly thinking in terms of locating their offices in or near the neighborhoods where these people live, rather than locating downtown. Bus routes that were established years ago are now being rerouted to take into account new travel patterns resulting from changing home, shopping, and employment locations.

Pricing. The fact that most public sector agencies are nonprofit in nature and operate at a deficit changes the role of price in the marketing mix. Some public sector agencies provide services at no charge at all to the user, while most others do so at prices which are not expected to cover all expenses of the operation. The objective is seen as providing a public service whose availability free or at a low price will be beneficial to the entire community. In other instances, while it may be reasonable to make at least some charge, the price elasticity of demand is such that it is not feasible to set price at a level which will yield revenues sufficient to cover all costs. Consequently, pricing schemes must be evaluated relative to the objectives of the organization as well as to their ability to earn funds. Particular problems are faced when formerly free services must henceforth be charged for, a problem for which there are few private sector analogues. In organizations where no price at all is charged, but utilization is still disappointing, managers are beginning to examine possible psychic costs which restrict or discourage usage; location, hours of opening, and a remote or intimidating image.

Communications. Another problem in the transfer of marketing is that many public sector organizations have a strong aversion to spending money on communications campaigns. Many public organizations seem to believe that "if the public needs our services, they will come and see us." Moreover, public officials historically have been loathe to invest public funds in promotional activities that they may have viewed as crass commercialism inappropriate to a public agency, or simply as an expenditure whose usefulness was hard to measure and therefore could not easily be justified to financial supporters. Fortunately, however, as marketing matures and its applicability becomes more widely recognized, and as more public organizations are run by professionally trained managers, this reluctance to use advertising and other elements in the communications mix is breaking down. Above all, there is growing official recognition of the public's need for information.

Nevertheless, since public agencies are highly visible and more subject to criticism than business firms, the content of all communications messages has to be closely monitored. Where a public sector agency is managing an activity that competes in any way with that of some private business, elected officials usually are very sensitive to the risk of offending the electorate by appearing to condone so-called "unfair competition." For example, heavy promotion of the use of a state university's dormitory space and classroom for conferences during vacations might be perceived as undermining the business of the local hotel and motel industry.

This risk is compounded when the public sector organization in question is making use of free "public service" advertising, in that the medium carrying such advertising may be reluctant to risk offending its paying advertisers. In order to give themselves greater freedom of expression and also to gain control over the location, size, and timing of messages than is possible with public service advertising, many government agencies now use paid advertising for all but the most innocuous messages. By 1972 the federal government had become the 22nd largest advertiser in the United States [1].

Market Research. Conducting marketing research efforts designed to monitor the progress and effectiveness of public sector organizations poses particular difficulties on account of their non-profit characteristics. The one common measure of success or failure for all commercial businesses is finan-

cial; by contrast, the ability to break even or even to minimize the size of the deficit does not necessarily connote success for a public organization, which, within certain financial constraints primarily, is in business to maximize social welfare. Nowadays, the objectives of public programs are being spelled out in much clearer terms than previously, which makes it possible to establish certain non-financial measures of performance. Thus, in the San Francisco area, a major long-term study is now under way to evaluate the impact which the recently-inaugurated Bay Area Rapid Transit system is having upon travel patterns, personal lifestyles, shopping habits, employment, urban development, pollution and other variables. Measurement of such social indicators, however, is still in its infancy.

INTERNAL DISTINCTIONS WITHIN THE PUBLIC SECTOR

In addition to the basic differences between the public and private sectors, there are also three significant dimensions on which public sector organizations differ among themselves which may influence the type of marketing transfer to be made.

Motivation for Adopting Marketing. The first dimension concerns the motivation for adopting marketing. Often this reflects *financial pressure*. For example, there are limits as to how far universities can hope to increase revenues simply by raising tuition fees, since many schools are finding themselves moving from a seller's to a buyer's market. The answer to this problem for some institutions has been to undertake a market-oriented redesign of their service offerings (notably the curriculum), followed by a recruiting campaign targeted on specific market segments of the prospective students [5]. In an effort to increase net revenues, many educational and cultural organizations are seeking to maximize the use of their facilities and personnel—which frequently operate well below capacity in summertime—by adding newly designed and often heavily promoted vacation courses or summer festivals.

Organizations which adopt marketing largely because of financial pressures present a special problem. On the one hand, they may have considerable difficulty in setting objectives—especially since closing down is often the most cost-effective tactic. On the other hand, financial pressures and time constraints may discourage the use of marketing variables, such as advertising and market research, whose immediate value is uncertain. In such cases, marketing plans are sharply circumscribed by both the finances available and the time horizon used to judge effectiveness.

Another incentive for introducing marketing strategies is sometimes politically inspired and comes from *pressures to maximize the effectiveness of publicly financed programs*. For instance, government investments in public transportation are designed with such objectives in mind as reducing pollution, congestion and energy consumption and also improving mobility for non-car-owners and non-drivers. However, it is insufficient just to invest in new equipment, for services must be widely used if the desired objectives are to be achieved. A marketing orientation is needed so that services are designed, priced and promoted to appeal to certain key market segments within the population. When marketing is adopted to help an organization become more effective, market research may be difficult to undertake because people are either "turned off" by the service in question or else find it hard to separate out the organization's current image and past performance from future proposals.

The third motivation for employing marketing in public sector organizations comes from *changing technological and social environments which necessitate changes in people's behavior patterns*. Thus, growing population pressures in the world are leading governments and voluntary organizations to set up population planning agencies to promote birth control. Most countries that are not yet on the metric system of weights and measures are now in the process of adopting it or planning how to do so. Another example of "change" marketing is the efforts by numerous bodies to encourage more efficient use of energy. Unfortunately, planning appropriate marketing strategies in such situations is often difficult due to the absence of close analogues. Market research is likely to be complicated by the fact that the new program may require unfamiliar behavior patterns which consumers find hard to envisage from a personal standpoint.

Prior History of Marketing Activities. A second differentiating dimension concerns the organization's prior history of marketing activities. Many public sector organizations have been carrying on marketing-like activities for years, but often at a low level of sophistication and without attempting to explore marketing's true potential. Organizations can be categorized into three groups on the basis of their prior histories. One consists of those *institutions and agencies in which marketing practices were once prominent, but then were dropped* during a period of decline, and are now being restored following injection of public funds and/or public takeover. For example, the privately-owned intercity railroads used to market their passenger services aggressively, but slowly discarded such efforts as the business became less and less profitable. Because of social and environmental priorities, most long-distance passenger train services were taken over by Amtrak in 1971, and marketing practices are now being re-employed.

Another group consists of those *organizations that have made limited use of marketing for years*. For instance, the U.S. Postal Service has long been in the business of selling various types of postal services, offered at different prices, and distributed through retail outlets strategically deployed in virtually all towns and cities throughout the United States. For many years it has engaged periodically in small-scale public service advertising campaigns directed at users with messages such as "Mail early for Christmas" or "Use ZIP codes." It is only recently, however, that this agency has started to operate in terms of the marketing concept, thinking of its users as consumers, evaluating the nature and profitability of its "product line," and preparing large-scale paid advertising and promotional campaigns [6].

In addition to existing organizations, there is a third group—namely, *new agencies and organizations that have been instituted in response to specific problems or tasks*. Among these can be included birth control clinics and population planning agencies, organizations promoting causes such as highway safety, and temporary government agencies charged with organizing and facilitating "one-time" change. Examples of the latter include the Swedish agency, which oversaw the 1967 switch from left to right-hand traffic in Sweden, and the British Decimal Currency Board, which operated from 1966–1971. Since these organizations are concerned with achieving changes in people's behavior (and often in their value systems), their operations tend to place heavy emphasis on the use of marketing communications.

An organization's prior history of marketing activities is important on account of the historical precedents set in terms of the services offered, the commitments made to users of the agency's services, the skills possessed by management, and the managerial strategies considered acceptable. Organizations that have been offering a set of services for many years are often reluctant to discontinue these even when there is little demand for them and/or they consume a disproportionate share of the organization's resources. In addition, management may be reluctant to change its orientation and methods of operation. Most public managers have little or no training in business or marketing [9]; hence, mutual understanding and skills must be built up carefully over time if a meaningful application of marketing strategies is to be made.

An extreme example of what is considered acceptable can be found in the field of health care. Most doctors consider it unethical to advertise and state medical societies often prohibit advertising. This institutional prohibition has made it extremely difficult for Health Maintenance Organizations (HMOs)—which are frequently seen as a very efficient means of distributing medical care—to undertake the marketing communications program needed to achieve economically viable enrollment levels.

Nature of Ownership. The final dimension differentiating public sector organizations is the nature of ownership. The organization in question may either be *government-owned* or belong to a *non-profit corporation*. As will be discussed below, government ownership is especially significant in that it tends to subject an organization to a unique set of political pressures, may limit organizational and managerial alternatives, and often constrains the set of services to be offered.

In any deficit operation, long-term survival depends, at least financially, on people or organizations other than the actual or potential users of the services offered. In non-profit corporations, this often means that the services offered must appeal to the donors' intuitive appraisals of client needs and may limit the range of services provided. Management practices in government agencies, meantime, must be acceptable to at least a majority of legislators voting the necessary funding and are, consequently, subject to political pressures.

This situation contrasts sharply with that prevailing among most commercial organizations, which generally prosper if they can satisfy consumer needs better than competitors. The survival of an organization is dependent upon attracting sufficient resources, but effectiveness depends upon defining and meeting consumer needs. Public sector marketing policies are complex because they simultaneously must attract resources from and satisfy the needs of different groups [8].

STRATEGY CONSTRAINTS FOR GOVERNMENT AGENCIES

The justification for deficit financing of government agencies is generally that they are pursuing socially desirable goals which might not be financially self-supporting in a free market economy. With a few exceptions (such as welfare agencies), *publicly funded organizations are typically expected to serve the entire community;* consequently, it becomes difficult to practice market segmentation. Although a marketing organization can often satisfy consumer needs better and be more effective when it focuses its attention upon carefully defined market segments, it may be politically infeasible for a public agency to deliberately focus its attention on one group and ignore the interest of others covered by its operating responsibilities.

On the other hand, although public agencies may be required to service a broadly defined market, *the charter or operating scope of such agencies is often very narrowly defined*. This situation contrasts sharply with that in most business firms, which usually are free to define the scope of their operations as broadly or as narrowly as they wish, subject only to the constraints imposed by financial, technical, and managerial resources. They have relative freedom of movement to diversify into new areas, introduce new products and services, or acquire other organizations. Most government organizations lack this freedom of movement. For instance, a public library may define its business as information storage and provision, or perhaps as education, but be expressly forbidden from moving into use of audio-visual materials, computerization, or development of teaching materials. A welfare agency may feel that it could usefully expand its "product line" by offering psychiatric treatment, but be restrained from doing so because this activity is restricted by statute to a health agency. In addition to such restrictions on new service offerings, government agencies are often mandated to perform certain services which cannot be abandoned, even in circumstances where the agency is no longer suited to providing them or public demand has largely ceased. In short, the scope of operations is typically narrowly delineated, even though this may act to the disadvantage of the agency and the detriment of consumers.

Another consideration with significant implications from a marketing standpoint is that public ownership or financing of an organization implies *public accountability*. As a result, the degree of disclosure required for a publicly financed agency is greater than for a private firm, thus providing a competitive edge to any private operations which are in the business of marketing a similar or substitute service. Public accountability may also subject an organization to public and political pressures which can have a detrimental impact on the objective function of public sector organizations. In particular, there is a risk that short-term objectives may be emphasized to demonstrate "action" and "results," with resultant failure to develop and implement strategies having long-term pay-offs.

A final and perhaps key constraint on the effective use of marketing strategies in the public sector concerns the *orientation of management and personnel*. Typically, employment in a public agency is more likely to represent a lifetime career commitment than is common in business. The reward and punishment structure is more tightly constrained: it is usually difficult to dismiss incompetents and also hard to build in incentives (such as salary bonuses or rapid promotion) as rewards for achievement. Consequently, there is only a limited relationship between market success (or failure) and an individual's progress and remuneration. This is particularly troublesome in attempting to motivate the public sector equivalent of a "sales force" to achieve specific goals. Private organizations, on the other hand, often rely on short-term incentives which are precluded in the government.

CONCLUSION

There is considerable evidence that the tools of marketing management and research can be transferred from the private to the public sector. Indeed the large number of academics, consulting firms, and executives who are working in this area, as well as the increasing number of "success stories," testifies to this. However, the transfer is not an easy process because public and private sector organizations differ in significant ways. Effective marketing programs developed by public sector organizations must be sensitive to these differences.

REFERENCES

1. "Advertising Marketing Reports on the 100 Top National Advertisers." *Advertising Age,* August 27, 1973, p. 159.
2. Baumol, William, and Bowen, William, *The Performing Arts: The Economic Dilemma,* p. 96. Cambridge: The M.I.T. Press, 1966.
3. El-Ansary A., and Kramer, O. E., Jr. "Social Marketing: The Family Planning Experience." *Journal of Marketing* 37 (July 1973):1–7.

4. Kotler, P., and Levy, S. J. "Broadening the Concept of Marketing." *Journal of Marketing* 33 (January 1969):10–15.

5. Meeth, L. Richard. "Innovative Admissions Practices for the Liberal Arts College." *Journal of Higher Education* 41 (October 1970):535–46.

6. "The Postal Service Tries the Hard Sell." *Business Week,* October 21, 1972, pp. 38–39.

7. Rathmell, John M. "Marketing by the Federal Government." *MSU Business Topics* (Summer 1973):21–28.

8. Shapiro, B. P., "Marketing For Nonprofit Organizations," *Harvard Business Review* 51 (September–October 1973):123–32.

9. Wilkie, William L., and Gardner, David M. "The Role of Market Research in Public Policy Decision Making." *Journal of Marketing* 38 (January 1974):38–47.

5

Public Policy Development: A Marketing Perspective

Ben M. Enis
Norman Kangun
Michael P. Mokwa

If governments used marketing concepts and techniques to supplement the present advocacy approach to public policy development, then the formulation of public policy and the implementation of laws and regulations would be improved. Marketing itself can offer some explanation for public policy shortcomings and suggest specific procedures for improvement.

The current government approach to conflict mediation is advocacy-oriented public policy development. Each stage of the process is affected by advocacy—discussion, debate, and reconciliation of competing viewpoints, whether through lobbying, congressional or other testimony, influence peddling, provision of information, court appearances, etc.

Although this approach is deeply embedded in our socioeconomic and political structure, it seldom functions as smoothly as depicted in civics textbooks and often produces policies that don't really serve the public interest. Marketers would attribute this poor performance at least partially to the failure of public policy-makers to view citizens as "consumers" of public policy.

Ben M. Enis is Bailey K. Howard World Book Professor of Marketing, University of Missouri, Columbia.

Norman Kangun is Professor of Marketing, University of Houston.

Michael P. Mokwa is Assistant Professor of Marketing, University of Wisconsin, Madison.

The advocacy approach doesn't take this perspective. With it, public policy is developed and then "sold" to citizens.

PUBLIC POLICY DEVELOPMENT

The reality of public policy development deviates from the ideal in several ways. Four major ones are: Vague mandates, hidden policy formation, agency capture, and industry capture.

Vague Mandates. Regulatory legislation is almost always passed to accomplish a multipurpose, "public-interest" objective which can accommodate advocates with diverse perspectives. Within the enabling legislation, there is no overall view of the potential impact of a policy upon the total system.

Moreover, most agency mandates lack operational objectives, priorities for action, and performance criteria. Furthermore, most agencies resist attempts to define objectives and specify performance criteria, because such definitions and measurements can limit their discretionary power.

For example, the Federal Trade Commission (FTC) is charged with the responsibility of protecting consumers from unfair and deceptive business practices. This mandate has not been operationally defined, and the agency has not established priorities to guide its use of scarce resources in enforcing this mandate.

In addition, an agency is able to develop its power through interpretation and procedural discretion. Consider, for example, the Environmental Protection Agency (EPA), which insists it can veto inner city construction of shopping centers, housing projects, etc., when, in its judgments, air quality would be adversely affected. (This ruling is being appealed, but the appeal burden rests upon the affected group.) Thus, the EPA effectively controls regional economic development, a power considerably beyond its original mandate of protecting the environment from pollution.

Hidden Policy Formation. A second complaint is that much of the development of public policy is not in the view of the affected publics. Agency procedures, even in this day of open information, often make it difficult, if not impossible, to obtain explicit and comprehensible information about the agency's activities. For example, the FTC has subpoenaed the marketing research materials which the six major tobacco companies have gathered for the past twelve years. When corporate executives ask the Commission's reason for this action, FTC officials state that they are trying to find out why people smoke. Tobacco industry executives complain that the FTC is merely on a "fishing expedition." Similarly, agency processes and activities are frequently complex, decentralized and dispersed. Welfare policies, for example, are administered at federal, state, and local levels. There are hundreds of programs, employing over 300,000 people; these programs cost more than $60 billion in 1976.

Agency Capture. Another shortcoming of public policy development is regulatory-body capture by the affected industry. This issue, a favorite of contemporary social critics, is that regulatory agencies serve not the public interests, but the industries they were created to regulate. This occurs because most regulatory issues are of deep interest only to the regulated industries; frequently, substantial amounts of revenue may be at stake. Air emission standards for automobiles, for example, have been extended by the EPA. The interest of the general public in this case may, in the aggregate, be quite high, but the public's concern is likely to be diffused among a large number of unorganized groups and individuals.

Other examples abound. The Federal Communications Commission (FCC) has delayed, at the behest of the three television networks, the development of cable and subscription television, to the detriment of the general public. The Civil Aeronautics Board (CAB) has not certified a new Interstate Carrier since World War II, so competition is limited and fares are high. Meanwhile, intrastate airlines like Pacific Southwest in California and Southwest Airlines in Texas have shown that profitable operations can result from lowering fares.

Industry Capture by the Regulating Agency. An equally valid criticism, the converse of agency capture, is that some industries are at the mercy of the regulators, again to the detriment of the public interest.

For example, the Interstate Commerce Commission (ICC), once dominated by railroads, now attempts to preserve part of many markets for each mode of transportation. To do so, it frequently sets prices at roughly the cost of the most expensive transportation alternative. The result: Railroads can't lower prices to the level of their incremental costs, thereby taking much of the long-distance shipping business from trucks. Consequently, regulation prevents realization of benefits of a low-cost technology by consumers (in the form of lower prices) and by the low-cost competitor in the form of new business.

We could present many other examples. Perhaps these are sufficient to demonstrate the point that the advocacy approach to public policy development, while deeply embedded in our socio-economic and political structure, seldom produces policies that really serve the public interest. Students of marketing would attribute this poor performance at least partially to the failure of public policy makers to view citizens as "consumers" of public policy. The advocacy approach does not take this perspective. Instead public policy is promulgated through the advocacy approach and then "sold" to citizens. Let us see how the advocacy approach might be supplemented by a marketing approach to public policy.

A MARKETING APPROACH TO PUBLIC POLICY

The basic philosophy of marketing management is embodied in the *marketing concept:* first determine customers' wants and desires, then provide products that satisfy them. In homely words, find a need and fill it. In looking at the development of public policy, the marketing concept would suggest four specific stages: basing public policy on "consumer" research, performing cost/benefit analyses on proposed policies, "test marketing" proposed policies, and evaluating policies that have been put into effect.

Consumer Research. Marketing scholars and practitioners have learned much about how and why consumers behave. For example, information processing studies concern ways in which consumers use information in making choices. Several regulations, mandating both the kind and form of information to be made available, have been adopted to assist consumers in making more intelligent choices: Auto price stickers, open dating and unit pricing on food, fabric care labeling, truth-in-lending, and light bulb lumen life. However, none was based upon empirical consumer research. They were drafted by lawyers steeped in the advocacy approach.

Use of existing knowledge from the consumer information processing field might have prevented or at least alleviated shortcomings inherent in most current information-disclosure programs. The marketing literature suggests that information effectiveness is a function of accessibility, comprehensibility, and relevance:

First, the closer information display is to the point of decision in a form that permits easy comparison, the greater the effectiveness of the information. Yet, the procedure provided by truth-in-lending legislation ignores this point, since it permits effective disclosure only after an agreement is concluded. Similarly, automobile performance data (information on braking power, tire wear, etc.) is contained in a sealed envelope in the glove compartment of each new car. Even the auto salesman may be unaware of its existence.

Second, information availability does not necessarily result in comprehension. Most public policy efforts do not recognize the potential for misinterpretation. For example, a number of possible interpretations exist with respect to open dating. Is the date on the product package the pull date, expiration date, or the display date? Unit pricing information is available, but its form and display cues often do not facilitate comprehension. Some research has been done on the relative effectiveness of different modes of display. Tentative evidence suggests that unit prices in list format, arrayed in descending order, are more effective than shelf tag display, and that unit prices in higher common units (pounds, quarts) are more effective than smaller units such as ounces.

Information effectiveness is also a function of relevance. Attributes relevant to a particular product purchase are determined by the consumer—not the marketer, or the policy maker. Ingredient labeling of packaged foods or detergents is of little relevance, for example, to consumers not possessing degrees in chemistry. Perhaps some consumers would prefer recipes on the label.

Our point is that consumer research techniques could indicate information desires. Or perhaps research would show that consumers would prefer the cost savings that would result from the elimination of disclosure programs.

Matching Costs and Benefits. Marketers realize that *all* the needs and desires of *all* consumers cannot *always* be served. Abraham Lincoln had the right idea when he said, ". . . you may fool all of the people some of the time; you can even fool some of the people all the time; but you can't fool all the people all the time." We suggest substituting "satisfy" for "fool."

However, public policy lacks a coherent hierarchy of objectives. While public policy goals may be neither as clear-cut nor as easy to enunciate as sales goals, at least some of the more important public policy trade-offs of proposed programs could be explicitly considered.

Consider first a straightforward cost/benefit analysis. In general, benefit provision is an increasing cost function.

Improving water purity from 90% to 100% may be four times as expensive as improving water quality from 80% to 90%. In fact, no body of water in its natural state is 100% pure; thus, this 1972 Clean Water Act standard is unattainable at any cost.

Second, there are trade-offs among competing types of benefits. Automobiles should be safe (according to the Department of Transportation), energy-efficient (Department of Energy), and non-polluting (EPA). Regulations promulgated by these agencies are mutually contradictory. Safety, by and large, is a direct function of automobile weight. But weight is the enemy of fuel efficiency. Emission control equipment also adds weight, and emits dangerous levels of nitrous oxides.

Marketing professionals face trade-off questions daily. They routinely use procedures such as consumer surveys, engineering feasibility reports, discounted cash flows, and trend analyses to resolve them.

Such procedures don't always result in optimal answers, but often they improve the odds for success. The social utility of public programs likewise could be enhanced through the use of formalized research and development procedures to balance benefits and costs.

Test Marketing. Some questions about proposed programs can be answered only by implementation. The new product must be offered to consumers in the marketplace even if only on a small scale so that the components of the program can be analyzed before implementing it nationwide.

For public policy development, three types of test markets could provide useful information. First, laboratory tests could be performed. This type of test is conducted on-premises under rather controlled conditions. Evaluation by consumers in the laboratory of the Uniform Product Code, for example, might have revealed such faults as the lack of price information—before every U.S. manufacturer of packaged goods was required to redesign its labels.

Second, the program might be introduced in just a few cities and consumer reaction evaluated before going nationwide with it. Tests of citizen reaction to the $2 bill in a few cities might have demonstrated problems such as consumer desire to hold the bill as a souvenir, retailer resistance to it, and so on before the Treasury Department spent $15 million on manufacturing the bills.

Third, elements of a proposed program might be varied to determine the relative effectiveness of each. This can be done for advertisements, promotions, or the programs themselves.

Test marketing, of course, doesn't guarantee the success of a new product. Many products fail to meet market share, profit, or other objectives and never go into national distribution. The record in the public policy sector, however, is worse; and, without objectives and testing, the programs "go national" with often disastrous results.

Consumer research should be conducted among the citizenry in general and affected groups in particular. Such research can be used to design public policies and to "test market" them before nationwide introduction. Or if test results are poor, such programs should be abandoned so that resources can be reallocated to more promising programs.

Program Monitoring and Evaluation. Marketing programs are monitored continuously and corrective actions are taken as necessary. On the other hand, most public policies after implementation are seldom systematically evaluated. Those evaluations that do occur are generally critiques (often not followed with corrective action) or postmortem examinations of failures.

Thus, agencies go on year after year, expanding budgets and using resources although their programs' usefulness has not been demonstrated or may even have been clearly shown to be nonexistent (for example, many welfare programs). Too often, attempts to improve failure programs are put forward in a crisis atmosphere.

In short, public policies should be evaluated systematically, comprehensively, and in a manner understandable to administrators and voters. This would involve impartial auditing of programs, analysis in cost/benefit terms, and public access to results.

Specifically, we suggest a marketing-oriented approach to public policy-making, starting with an explicit statement of the purpose of the policy—specific mandate, performance criteria, etc. Perhaps an economic impact statement analogous to the currently required environmental impact statement would be a good model to follow. This then should be followed with consumer research, test marketing, and continuous evaluation.

6

Public Marketing: Policy Planning for Community Development in the City

Edward J. Blakely
Howard Schutz
Peter Harvey

We are witnessing a profound and long term redirection of federal program strategies in the area of social welfare and economic development from planning and program design at the national level toward a model that places the city at the center of the development process. Community development is becoming an increasingly important methodology in this transfer of authority from the federal to the local level. However, integrating current community development methods into the policy process of local government has not been fully thought out by academicians or practitioners. This paper suggests that a public marketing model provides a potential framework for accomplishing this integration.

INTRODUCTION

Techniques for assessing community needs and translating this information into social policy form the core of the community development discipline. However, in spite of the proliferation of community analysis techniques and technologies there is a somewhat ominous feeling detected both

Edward J. Blakely is Associate Professor of Community Studies and Development, University of California, Davis, and Associate Dean of the College of Agriculture.

Howard Schutz is Professor of Consumer Sciences, University of California, Davis.

Peter Harvey is City Administrator of Yuba City, California.

in the current literature and at professional meetings that existing methods are either inefficient, unworkable or unreliable [1]. This issue is becoming critical since both local city jurisdictions and the federal government are adopting the community development model or its rhetoric as the basis for current social indicators, and in the evaluation of economic and social impact of federal programs [2]. In essence community development is replacing other social welfare methodologies such as economic development and social planning as the cornerstone of the public policy formulation process [3]. However, at this juncture in the history of the Community Development profession there is no codified or structured methodology for easy presentation to public policy makers. This paper is an attempt to explore a systematic diagnostic and policy formulation strategy applicable to local city government.

HISTORIC COMMUNITY DEVELOPMENT MODELS

Organizing the various community analyses methods into discrete categories or models is somewhat difficult and hazardous since there is so much overlap among them. However, before we discuss integrative policy approaches, an inspection of the relevant literature is in order to examine some of the broad divisions in community development thought as it relates to the policy formulation process.

The Community Inventory Technique. This by far the oldest and most widely accepted method of determining community problems and assessing the existing resources to meet local needs. The technique pioneered by Poston, Biddle, Warren, and others involves citizen assessment of local conditions using some form of check list or inventory document [4]. Roland Warren's excellent work *Studying Your Community* [5] remains the classic model using this approach. More recently local governments have made adaptations of Warren's methods for use of local administrative and elected officials [6].

Unfortunately in highly complex urban environments this method appears too overwhelming (particularly following Warren's outline) to local officials since there is such a plethora of community facilities and programs.

The Reconnaissance Approach. This approach resembles its name in that it describes a means of obtaining an overview or snapshot of a locale. Edward Alchin suggests this method as a means to obtain significant amounts of data on a community or area quickly and relatively easily [7]. The basic strategy in this method is to obtain key information from key citizens or interest groups by using a small sample of persons from each group. This data is compared with observations, secondary sources and related information to formulate a fairly accurate picture of community needs and priorities.

While this method provides good data on the community social system, it requires professional competence to be used effectively. Further this method is subject to professional bias, does not have an easily identifiable measurement or social indicator component, and it is not usually integrated with the existing community policy structure.

Delphi or Group Diagnosis Method. The Delphi process and modifications of it are currently very popular in community problem solving. The basic technique developed by Rand Corporation is a *process* survey method for predicting alternative futures. Individual surveys or interviews are conducted of a relatively small but well selected group. This data is used to shape consensus toward common goals and policies. There is a substantial body of literature on this method and its many variations [8].

The basic liability of this method is that it is "expert" centered. That is, the persons providing the information—the input—to this system are preselected. In some cases such persons may not reflect total local concerns and interest.

Macro Structural Models. Frank and Ruth Young have popularized a method of research communities using unobtrusive measures [9]. The Youngs and others propose that an examination of physical and social institutions, or "institution tracking" as MacCannell labels it, in a given community predicts social dimensions, i.e. political cohesion, etc. [10]. The methodology involved requires the collection of large quantities of secondary data on relevant social, political, and commercial enterprise and scaling (usually Guttman scales) for comparative analysis.

While this method is extremely useful in larger scale analyses, e.g., countries, states and counties, it is deficient as a policy tool for local neighborhoods and city governments, and it does not provide for local citizen involvement in the analytical process.

Opinion or Attitude Surveys. Sampling public opinion by questionnaire or interview is a widely used and accepted technique to ascertain community needs. This method is usually and best employed when specific data is required related to a particular program or service. It is easier to measure the degree of satisfaction or dissatisfaction in a survey than to determine individual or group needs. Surveys are enormously useful and feasible for community development diagnoses as demonstrated by James Christensen's work in North Carolina [11] and Don Dilman's related work in Washington [12] where massive amounts of information in citizen attitudes and desires were identified.

Translating surveys into policy is a somewhat touchy process and monitoring the impacts of the policy using survey exclusively may not be entirely feasible for economic reasons.

The approaches discussed above offer only a brief analysis of the major current community diagnostic and policy processes. Each of these methods has assets and liabilities. The major limitation of these approaches for the current city context is that most of them (a) have limited capacity for linkage with the existing governmental and related policy process; (b) do not offer a means to develop social indicators, benchmarks or monitoring systems; (c) require the assembly of data difficult to interpret by local decision makers; or (d) lack direct citizen involvement.

It is our view that the community development *process* for cities must be firmly anchored in a theoretical paradigm that provides policy guidance and yields an accountability standard with the city as both a geographic and policy entity. However, the authors believe the existing methodologies as combined in the social marketing model meet many of the above requirements and build on as well as integrate earlier efforts into a coherent useful strategy.

THE CONCEPT AND MODEL

We Americans are not at ease with the notion of marketing public goods and services to our communities, cities, and states. Only recently have state and local economic development commissions been able to use tax dollars to advertise the virtues of certain locations to attract business to areas to expand local job opportunities and improve local tax bases. While the idea of state and local tax supported industrial development is still struggling to gain public acceptance it is becoming apparent that the city itself and its related taxing authorities, e.g., school districts, etc., must become more conscious of their own marketing capacities and responsibilities. However, we have grown accustomed to politicians packaging themselves, their campaigns and political promises. In fact, Maginnes in *The Selling of the President* [13] and Teddy White in his *Making of a President* suggest that we anticipate politicians to be good products marketed well [14]!

The advent of inner city blight and urban flight indicates further that the city, both large urban and small rural, must become involved in a widened marketing strategy if it is to survive [15]. As Milton Kotler so aptly notes,

> The process of city administration is invisible to the citizen who sees little evidence of its human components but feels the sharp pain of taxation. With increasingly poor public services, his desires are more insistently expressed. Yet his expression of needs seems to issue into thin air for government does not appear to be attentive to his needs [16].

Very little research has examined cities as marketing entities to address the issues cited by Kotler. Shapiro discusses nonprofit organizations which resemble cities in some respects. The city has several unique functions in that it provides service (fire, sewer, health, etc.) while it has regulatory and control responsibilities (zoning, licensing, taxing, and police). Shapiro, however, relegates marketing in government organizations to politics and political science [17]. In spite of his reservations, Shapiro suggests that there is some potential for applying marketing thinking to most nonprofit situations, including government.

It is our view that changes that have taken place both internal and external to the city have made it mandatory for the growth and stability of the city to utilize some of the thinking and methodology which is currently applied in the commercial marketing sector to the delivery of public goods and services. Kotler's broad definition of marketing is that it is a "set of human activities directed at facilitating and consumating exchanges" [18]. Our definition of public marketing is a modification of the American Marketing Association's language which discusses marketing as "the performance of (public) activities that direct the flow of goods and services from producer to consumer or user" [19].

First, let us examine some of the factors we believe contribute to the appropriate application of marketing principles to communities. First, there is the advent of the national New Federalism policy which transfers much of the responsibility for community development from the federal level of the state, county, and the individual communities. Local governments are using Revenue Sharing funds from the new Housing and Community Development Act (H/CD) to begin to restructure their institutions for economic, social and physical planning. The greatest current need cities face is to determine the appropriate allocation of their resources based on locally assessed needs and priorities rather than merely engaging in police activities, e.g., issuing permits, maintaining streets, etc. Another related factor is the increased sophistication of the community resident that has taken place through the media, consumer organizations, and greater involvement of the individual resident in community affairs at every level. Attendant to this last factor is the increased concern, in fact militancy, of certain segments of the community in influencing the allocation of community resources. Such groups at the aged, economic and ethnic minorities, youth groups, and so on are now much more highly organized and vocal and vie effectively for attention and funds from the city treasury. The majority of communities utilize a city manager system which tends to be relatively independent of politics. This may allow for a more independent, rational, and continuous set of programs.

Lastly, citizens increasingly have found the polling place with its attendant political campaigns more and more a way of communicating their needs and concerns about their community. Recently, concerns for ecological consideration as well as the energy crisis have served to increase the complexity involved in satisfying the community's needs.

All of the above factors have served as an impetus for comprehensive planning for community economic and social development by cities themselves rather than waiting for counties or states to do it for them. Typically community development efforts that have been mounted have been ones which use more traditional or short term methods dealing with a narrow range of physical development or economic problems. Our view is that if one considers the city as a source of goods and services and both the residents and business/industry sectors as consumers of these goods and services, that much practical value can be gained from analyzing the community within a marketing model, and that meaningful changes can be made to produce efficient community development utilizing marketing methods.

Before we look at the specific applications of marketing techniques to community development activities let us examine the general character of the community in relation to the business and private nonprofit organization (See Exhibit 1). Business firms once operational receive their funds from the sale of goods and services to customers. Whereas in private, nonprofit organizations, funds for operation are primarily received from donors rather than from some type of customer. The city represents a much more complex model in that funds for operation come directly from the consumers in the form of property taxes, sales taxes, special bond assessments etc. However, the community also receives redistributed funds from the county and state level as well as

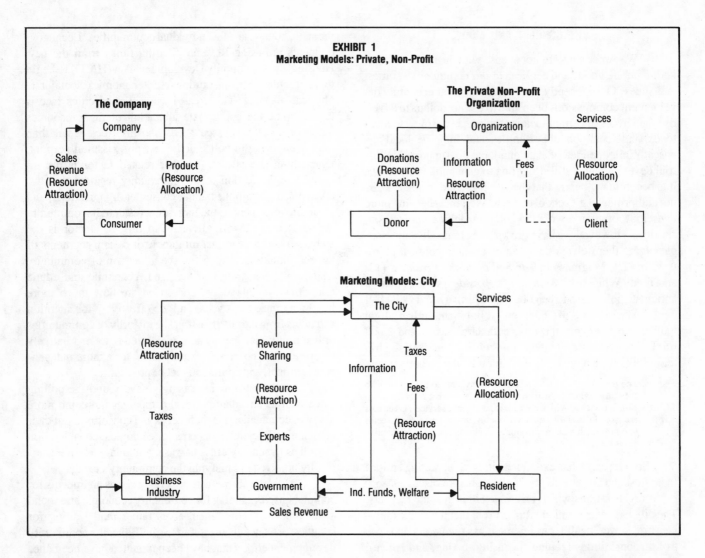

EXHIBIT 1
Marketing Models: Private, Non-Profit

federal funds which although derived ultimately from tax revenue are not under the direct control of the resident consumer. In some instances state and federal funds must be obtained on a competitive basis. The customer in the commercial market place has a variety of choices to select from as far as the types of goods and services that are available and particular brands and sizes within brands. The commercial consumer also is usually quite mobile and can select from local sources, may travel to communities other than his own and by using the mail can purchase goods from throughout the world. On the other hand, within the community the consumer is more a captive; their homes, school, parks, recreation facilities, health facilities, their police and fire protection, are such that they ordinarily do not allow choice to operate. To the extent that children as they leave high school move away and do not return to the community, or the adult residents move to other communities in order to satisfy their needs, the revenue supplied by these individuals is lost to the city. On a more fundamental level, the city or community can be said to have *failed* in the provision of goods and services that satisfy their consumer residents, particularly when consumers are in fact a heterogenous population.

In the past the failure to satisfy the resident in a meaningful way has been viewed, except for rare exceptions in some urban areas, as a minor consequence. Today, as was pointed out earlier, these are becoming of major consequence. The events leading up to the problems of such major cities as New York, San Francisco, and Boston point out vividly what can happen if a relatively captive resident is continually led down the path of dissatisfaction. As Blacks, Chicanos, women and others aspire to achieve equal benefits from the political system this unleashes active, often hostile, forces within the social fabric. In essence the city is no longer made up of superficially homogenous groups (ghettoized) but heterogenous components whose interests become the focal point of the total city political process.

Just as the marketing task for profit making organizations includes the basic marketing function of facilitating and consumating exchanges, the community as a marketing organization has a similar responsibility. This includes viewing consumers rather than as one homogeneous group, as made up of various segments. The city must then know its segments, their needs, and demands. Another factor, however, that operates in the community is not only that it must market goods to the consumer and industry/business sectors, but must in addition market the community to the state and federal organizations so as to increase the likelihood of receiving funds which will help the community achieve its broader mission. Communities no longer can meet the demands of their residents only with locally produced resources. It is mandatory, then, that the various state and federal resources be tapped in order to provide high cost items such as capital improvements. Naturally these resources are also limited and thus the community must present their needs to the funding agencies in such a way that enhances the likelihood of receiving funds in a competitive marketplace as highly as possible.

Another difference between private concerns and cities is that a company is judged in terms of the profit which it makes for its stockholders, whereas in the community the criteria for success should be the satisfaction of the consumer. It would be fair to say that many or most of the residents in a community are not aware of the complex relationships between the goods and services that the city offers and the sources of revenue available to fund those goods and services. It is much more likely that they respond to very personal feelings about community management or service management, as represented by members of the city council and school superintendents. Since the citizen is both a consumer and manager of stockholder he has the right and desire to voice his opinions on the ultimate product as well as the mode of delivery. Let's consider the complex marketing model of the city as illustrated in Exhibit 2.

PUBLIC MARKETING COMPONENTS

Shapiro points out that the basic marketing task can be divided up into three major components, resource attraction, resource allocation and persuasion. The resource attraction activity in profit making firms is a financial one in which funds may be attracted from banking sources but are primarily related to the monies generated by the sale of goods and services. The resource allocation function on the profit making firm involves all those decisions which result in various advertising, capital, research development, and related decisions. In the city, resource attraction sources, as pointed out earlier, come from both the funds received from consumer residents and businesses through taxes as well as the attraction of funds from state, county, and federal agencies. Resource allocation in the community would involve all those decisions concerned with the various goods and services that are potentially offered by a community. In contrast in a profit making organization there is a direct feedback mechanism from the consumer with regard to resource allocation and resource attraction. However, the basic marketing concept which stresses the importance of satisfying consumer needs would certainly seem to apply in both instances.

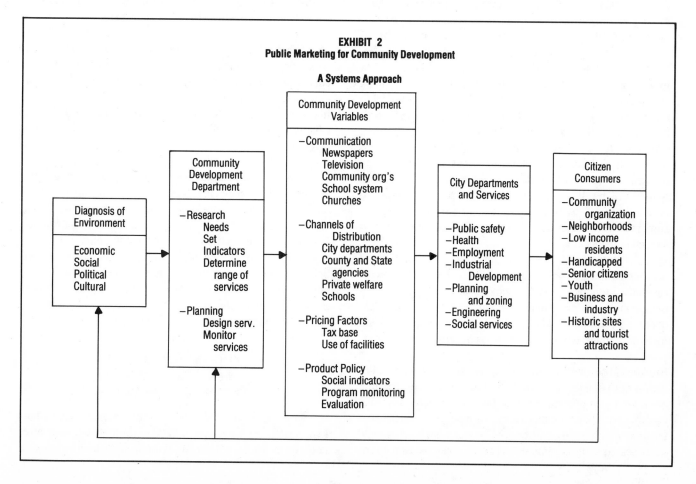

EXHIBIT 2
Public Marketing for Community Development

A Systems Approach

The use of the market model in public decision making is well grounded in the theory of interaction and exchange as suggested by Robert Presthus,

> Interaction theory rests essentially upon two well established principles from psychology and economics. The psychological principle is that all behavior is determined by differential reinforcement. . . . Economic theory contributes the assumption that individuals bring to personal relationships a more-or-less rational calculus which ensures that a given interaction will be continued only if the sum total of benefits received equals or preferably outweighs the cost of time, energy and commitment expended in all such activities. A cost-benefit equilibrium is sought [20].

Max Weber's work further amplifies this conceptual framework and places it in the context of the city when he offers,

> We wish to speak of a "city" only in cases where the local inhabitants satisfy an economically substantial part of their daily wants in the local market [21].

The Weber market assumes a supply of public goods and services as well as private exchanges.

In the following sections we attempt to explore the Presthus/Weber paradigm as it relates to community development methods.

Resource Attraction. The community must attract its resources in several ways. People themselves represent a resource in the sense that the occupation of a residence within the community ordinarily automatically results in certain benefits available to the community. These include the ones mentioned earlier in the paper such as property tax and other levies that occur when the consumer chooses to be a resident in a particular community. In addition, sources are attracted from county, state and federal agencies through such mechanisms as a standard formula based on population size, need, and occasionally through application involving competitive proposals for particular community development projects.

The attraction of these resources in a community utilizes the standard marketing techniques of persuasion which will be discussed in more detail later in the paper. However, it is obvious that successful persuasion of consumers to vote themselves increased taxes has not met with spectacular success.

Another critical area for resource attraction is retail businesses and industrial activities. These sectors help via tax revenues and jobs to establish a more subjective sense of accomplishment or pride in the community such as what might occur if a community adds a favorable image retail establishment or perhaps avoids one which has negative connotations.

Resource Allocation. The first basic decision in resource allocation is to determine what is the function of the particular community. In other words, what are the objectives for that community. Then after this decision is made, one can then determine which goods and services, and at what level, should be allocated to the community. The decision must be made as

to whether or not these goods or services should be available to all neighborhoods to the same degree, or should individual segments of the population receive special goods and services such as youth, the aged, economically deprived, ethnic groups, etc. For the city this is obviously a very complex task since the city provides a wide variety of goods and services that involve different types of individuals, equipment and facilities in order to effectively deliver such goods and services. As C. H. Sandage points out, in our economy these decisions are usually reached based on psychological factors rather than an assessment of physiological need [22]. Therefore psychological assessment and motivation play a key role in the distribution of goods and the response to citizen request for services.

Persuasion. Persuasion is a third marketing function for the community which includes two major components. The first is persuading extramural sources such as state and federal organizations to supply funds and/or expert help in order to accomplish community objectives. The second type of persuasion function is the one involved in persuading the consumer residents to take some action with regard to the community. Paul Lazersfeld and Robert Merton in one of their earliest papers on social organization in 1958 describe this process in a manner that remains true nearly two decades later: such things as volunteer activity for the health, school and other sectors, participation in the voting process, attraction of people from outlying areas to the city proper, as well as persuading people to maintain residence in the community are examples of such a persuasion function [23]. It is interesting to note that almost the only effort that cities and communities make to persuade individuals to come to a particular area involve the attraction for business of tourists during the area's tourist season. It is remarkable how little is done to communicate the values for more permanent residency in a community.

Other areas in which the persuasion function operates for a community include convincing people to change their attitudes and practices in the use of limited resources such as energy, anti-litter campaigns, utilization of community facilities such as parks, swimming pools, and the contribution to other voluntary activities within the community.

Much persuasion effort whether successful or not has been directed toward increasing utilization of downtown core areas by residents. Perhaps the lack of success of these programs is partly due to the fact that appropriate marketing techniques have not been utilized or only partially used.

PUBLIC MARKETING TOOLS
WHICH CAN BE UTILIZED
FOR COMMUNITY DEVELOPMENT

Philip Kotler and Gerald Zaltman suggested that marketing strategies could be utilized to promote social change [24]. Borrowing from the Kotler and Zaltman model as well as the early work of Shapiro and others the following techniques appear to be applicable in the current context.

Communications. The members of a community have a wide variety of communication techniques available for use in carrying out its marketing functions. Most communities have one or more newspapers which can be utilized by the city management as a method of delivering information to its citizens. In some areas a local radio station or cable television can be used for presentations to the city council meetings and other special activities. In addition, annual reports and other special brochures can be developed and distributed to all the members of the community. The various city departments can themselves have techniques for communicating their functions, such as the practice of having police and fire personnel give informative lectures in the schools, as well as use of the more recent technique of having students accompany police officers on their daily rounds. Also, some communities encourage students to play various roles within the community management structure in order to better understand the operation of a city.

It would appear mandatory that if resource attraction from residents is to occur, the managers of the city must communicate what they want to do, the alternatives, and how they expect the residents' contribution to occur, and do this in a meaningful way in order to expect any degree of cooperation.

Obviously communication plays a critical role in the persuasion function. However, the community also may use communications in resource attraction and allocation. In the areas of attraction, certainly communications concerning how funds are utilized and their source can be useful in attracting revenue from the resident. Also, communications via specialized brochures and proposals to state and federal organizations can be critical in the attraction of funds to the community. In resource allocation more efficient utilization of the allocated resources can take place if the residents are fully aware of the variety of facilities and activities that the community has to offer.

Channels of Distribution. For the profit making organization, channels of distribution include the standard wholesale distributor, banker, and retail organization. However, for the community channels of distribution that go directly into individual households are water, electricity, and gas. Other services are provided to the consumer at locations, such as in parks, hospitals, and schools. Some services are distributed primarily on the basis of unique events such as fires and police activities and others such as welfare require the individual to report to certain offices at certain times. Many of these activities have as a common characteristic, that of location. Thus, the degree of satisfaction a consumer can receive will depend to a great extent on the availability of the goods and services. This may include in addition to physical location, the days and/or times of the day in which the particular good or service is made available. Certainly basic decisions with regard to the location of shopping centers, whether in a core downtown section, or in suburban locations, will have direct effects on the satisfaction of the residents of a community. Utilization of various school and health services will depend to a great extent on the propinquity and ease of use of such services. In some cases language and/or cultural barriers may act as a deterrent to the utilization of some goods and services.

Pricing. Pricing as a marketing tool is directly related to the ability to attract resources. Obviously, insofar as a private firm can maintain sales volume and increase prices it will make more profit. However in the community pricing is a more complex activity. Some things naturally are a direct matter of exchange of money for services such as the price for use of a municipal pool, tennis court, and so on. For other areas pricing is a function which may be outside the realm of the community, such as the price for energy resources, gasoline, electricity, and natural gas. The indirect pricing activities, where price in a sense represents the tax assessment for particular activities such as schools, are not as amenable to a simple analysis. However, there should be a relationship between the price, that is the amount of taxes that are paid, and the quality of the product that is received by the resident. When this does not occur and there is a discrepancy or apparent discrepancy between quality and service and the perceived price that the consumer pays, the dissatisfaction which results can lead to many unpleasant consequences. For example, the next tax levy vote, although absolutely essential for maintenance of an activity, may not be approved. In many cases since consumer residents are not charged directly for the use of certain goods and services, it is very difficult to make the connection between the types and levels of goods and services available and what monies are required to support such activities. Clearly the role of communication is one which would be essential in order to improve upon this lack of understanding. When price changes are required it would appear to be essential that information concerning the alternatives and reasons underlying the change of price be communicated in an effective fashion to the consumer resident.

In another area the community prices their proposals for funds and services that they desire from extramural sources. No doubt the relationship between what the community proposes to do and the level of funding and type of expert services they think is necessary to accomplish it, could be a significant factor in the attraction of extramural resources to the community.

It may not seem apparent but the price that one charges for the use of tennis courts, swimming pools, etc., and the level of utilization by the consumer resident is really not much different from what occurs when a consumer makes a choice among various canned soup products in the supermarket. However, in the community situation not only will the consumer perhaps go outside the community to have these needs satisfied but in addition the dissatisfaction with the community will have its effect on the future willingness of that resident to support a voluntary activity or vote for increased taxes. Another more subjective price that is paid by residents is what they have to give up in order to maintain residency in a particular community. Consumer residents pay a price in the sense that living in a particular community may make it inconvenient for them to enjoy a symphony, opera, sports, and a variety of other activities which are not available in the community. Also the price may be in terms of the time and effort they volunteer for community activities. What is returned in value for this price is the other goods and services that are offered by the community to the individual. The question is whether or not these are of sufficient magnitude to justify being a resident and making a contribution to a particular community.

Product Policy. Product policy basically is the determination of which goods and services are made available to the consumer. In the community the definition of product and services is unquestionably the most critical aspect of the marketing process. The wide diversity of goods and services, as well as the variety of segments in the population for which various goods and services are appropriate, makes product policy aspects of the community one of the most important and difficult areas. In addition to offering a product or service to the resident, the community also has in a sense a policy with regard to what types of extramural funding and expertise it decides that it needs and attempts to acquire.

There are many product policy decisions which are critical for the community. Should the community attempt to offer services or goods which will be attractive to the unemployed, to ethnic minorities, to the senior citizen? To do so obviously means the attraction of these types of individual to the community. What are the trade offs among various services which the community might offer and how would revenue sources be made available to support such activities? If the assortment, type, and quality of products and services which are available to the community are not satisfactory, then one can be certain that eventually the resource attraction process will be severely hampered either from the loss of residents themselves to other communities or the unwillingness of the community to assess themselves for the cost of such services, or to volunteer their own time and effort on their behalf.

Marketing Research. An area in which communities have been the least sensitive and active is that of marketing research. If one is to satisfy the consumer as a basic objective, then one must know what the consumer feels, thinks and does with regard to community offerings both present and future. Certainly the techniques utilized by private firms in determining such information from various segments of the consuming population are available for use by investigators in the community development area. From such research community development investigators can get a picture of

how the present goods and services are used or in many cases not used. The degree of satisfaction with these goods and services and some idea of what types of goods and services would be desired by the population can also be determined. In addition, by analyzing the results for various geographical, ethnic, income, or other relevant segments of the population, some of the differences and similarities among these gropus can be ascertained. Thus product policy decision makers can have a much better grasp of the trade offs that might be involved in satisfying particular needs for products and services.

Utilizing marketing research techniques is an important initial activity in the marketing of a community. Such techniques can be used by the city or community to determine attitudes toward proposed changes in the goods or services which have recently been initiated. It may be appropriate in some cases to build in standard feedback mechanisms for individual departments of the city, such as police, park and recreation. One of the values of research of this type is to provide guidelines in the resource allocation process, but in addition, research results can be fed back through communications to the consumer residents along with appropriate educational material. Thus through the use of persuasion techniques different attitudes and/or utilization of goods and services may result.

Certainly resource attraction in the area of retail and industrial establishments could benefit considerably from the results of marketing research activities. It is very likely that many of the dissatisfactions, goals and desires of retail and industrial sectors of a community may well be in opposition to those of the residents and thus require careful analysis of a community's total objectives in order to develop an appropriate trade-off model.

Marketing research, in addition to determining what various segments in a community have or do not have in common, can serve another very important end, in that through careful analysis of marketing research data, segments can be identified and characterized which may not have been visible before the study was conducted. Thus, what on the surface might appear to be a reasonable segmentation in terms of geographical location might well turn out to be more importantly a segmentation based on income or ethnic background. It is clear that unless the homogeneous segments in the community are appropriately identified resource allocation can only be partially successful.

CONCLUSIONS

The previous discussion illustrates that the marketing model can supply insights into the operation of the community. More importantly it can provide tools by which the community can more efficiently determine and implement the goals for its constituents.

The application of this frame of reference is even more critical for the community than it is for the private organization since the private organization has feedback mechanisms which have much shorter time lags and are much more direct. If the private company is not meeting the needs of its customers, it will shortly fail as a profit maker. However, unfortunately for the community, the time lag is much longer and the feedback much less direct. Thus inappropriate decisions are made both on the part of those who are managers and administrators within the community, as well as by the consumer residents and business sectors of the community. It is imperative then, that the various components of the community have a means of more clearly defining the objectives, tradeoffs, and resources of a community and in addition be able to do this as quickly as is feasible. The result of not accomplishing these objectives, although it may not occur as quickly as it does in the private sector, just as certainly does occur, and when it does the retrieval activities must be heroic. In the aftermath of such a failure the spirit of a community can be essentially lost. Unfortunately, there are sufficient examples of cities which have arrived at this state.

We believe it is entirely within the realm of possibility to both analyze a community utilizing the resource attraction, resource allocation and persuasion functions as well as those methods of communication, distribution, pricing, product policy and marketing research in providing an effective array of activities to bring about vital and successful community development programs. Further the paradigm we suggest offers a means of integrating the disparate and sometimes confusing methods and techniques of community development into a system that relates to the realities of modern city government.

REFERENCES

1. Sargeant, Charles, "Decision Making Systems and Planned Change," *J. Comm. Develop. Soc.* 4 (1973), 115.
2. Eberts, Paul R., "A Multi-Level Policy Research Paradigm: Implications for Rural and Regional Development," A paper presented at the Annual Meetings of the Rural Sociological Society, San Francisco, 1975.
3. Blakely, E. J., *The New Federalism: Implications for Community Development in Non-Metropolitan Areas*, Davis: University of California Community Development Research Service, July 1975.
4. Batten, T. R., *Communities and Their Development*, London: Oxford University Press, 1957. See also Poston, Richard W., *Democracy Speaks Many Tongues*, New York: Harper and Row, 1962, and U.N. publications *Social Progress Through Community Development*, U.N., 1959.
5. Warren, Roland, *Studying Your Community*, New York: The Free Press, 1968, second edition.
6. Webb, Kenneth, and Harry Hatry, *Obtaining Citizen Feedback: The Application of Citizen Surveys to Local Government*, Washington, D.C.: The Urban Institute, 1973.
7. Alchin, Edward W., *A Reconnaisance Research Plan for Community Development*, A Technical Bulletin, B–49, The Institute for Community Development and Services, Michigan State.
8. Johnston, A. P., and Mureen Wilson, "From Private to Public Sector Planning: Missing Values and the Need for Adaptation," *Educ. Planning* 1 (2), (1974).
9. Young, Frank, "A Structural Approach to Development," *J. Develop. Areas* 2 (1968), 363–376.
10. MacCannell, Dean, and Ruth Young, "Predicting Quality of Life in the United States," A paper presented at the Annual Meeting of the Rural Sociological Society, 1974.
11. Christensen, James, *Through Our Eyes*, Vol. 1, 2 and 4, Raleigh, N.C.: Agricultural Extension Service, North Carolina State University, 1974.
12. Dilman, Don A., and Russell Dobash, *Preferences for Community Living and Their Implications for Population Redistribution*, Pullmon, Washington: Washington State Agricultural Experiment Station, November 1972.
13. Maginnes, Joe, *The Selling of the President*, New York: Trident Press, 1969.
14. White, Theodore, *The Making of the President*, A series 1960, 1964, 1968, and 1972, Harper and Row.
15. Clewett, Robert L., and Jerry Olson, *Social Indicators and Marketing*, New York: American Marketing Association, 1974.
16. Kotler, Milton, *Community Forum*, Unpublished and undated.
17. Shapiro, Benson, "Marketing in Non-Profit Organizations," *J. Voluntary Action Res.* 3 (1975), 1–16.
18. Kotler, Phillip, "A Generic Concept of Marketing," *J. Marketing* 35 (1973), 46–54.
19. American Marketing Association, *Marketing Definitions: A Glossary of Marketing Terms*, Chicago: American Marketing Association, 1960.
20. Presthus, Robert, *Elites in the Policy Process*, London: Cambridge University Press, 1974.
21. Weber, Max, "The Nature of the City," in Warren: *Perspectives on the American Community*, New York: Rand McNally, 1966.
22. Sandage, C. H., and Vernon Fryburger, *The Role of Advertising: A Book of Readings*, Homewood, IL: Richard D. Irwin, Inc., 1960, pp. 257–65.
23. Lazersfeld, Paul F., and Robert Merton, "Mass Communication, Popular Taste and Organized Social Action," in Wilbur Schromm (ed.), *Mass Communication*, Urbana, IL: Univ. of Illinois Press, 1960.
24. Kotler, Phillip, and Gerald Zaltman, "Social Marketing: An Approach to Planned Social Change," *J. Marketing* 35 (1973), 3–12.

7

Marketing Down the Road: The Role of Marketing Analysis In Transportation Planning

Daniel J. Brown
Philip B. Schary
Boris W. Becker

Public involvement (citizen participation) is becoming increasingly important in government planning. People feel better about the governmental agencies which serve them, but both procedural and substantive problems have arisen. Public inputs have limited usefulness, they are not representative, and they create conflicts. The article shows how marketing analysis may help to alleviate these problems.

INTRODUCTION

In recent years, transportation planners have been required to incorporate broadly based public input into the transportation planning process [18]. This requirement has created difficulties, both in completing particular projects and in developing acceptable participation procedures.

Since there are important parallels between the relationship of public planners to the public and the relationship of marketers to their markets, a number of marketing scholars have investigated the role of marketing research in public policy [4, 12, 19]. This paper goes beyond previously pub-

Daniel J. Brown is Assistant Professor of Marketing, Oregon State University.

Philip B. Schary is Associate Professor of Marketing, Oregon State University.

Boris W. Becker is Associate Professor of Marketing, Oregon State University.

lished reports in addressing the role of marketing research in an increasingly important aspect of public planning. It will focus on three topics that are central to the application of marketing concepts to this problem, and each will constitute a major subdivision of the paper. First is the experience with public inputs in transportation planning. Second is a comparison of the task of marketing managers in the private sector with the job of their public planner counterparts. Third is a marketing strategy for planners to employ in incorporating public involvement into the planning process. The overall purpose of the paper is to identify how marketing can make public inputs more effective.

THE PROBLEM OF PUBLIC INVOLVEMENT

Before they were required to incorporate broad public inputs, transportation planners were free to exercise personal judgment, based on available data combined with their own understanding and convictions about specific aspects of their plan. Before the decision, public inputs were confined to the advice of local governments and agencies about scope and general direction. After the decision, the same agencies provided the scrutiny of formal review and approval. The planner served as expert, approaching specific problems with a set of alternative solutions, serving the public without direct consultation.

As the work of planners became more visible through the implementation of their plans, conflicts arose between planners and public. Some citizens perceived planners to be antagonistic toward public desires. Freeways, in particular, became a battleground as the cost-benefit ratios of additional construction turned negative in the public eye [11]. That planners were appointed technicians rather than elected officials did not help; opponents often viewed them as partisan to business interests or entirely incompetent [16].

In an effort to make projects more attuned to public desires, Congress forced government agencies to include public inputs in planning almost all transportation projects which involved Federal funds—virtually all transportation projects. Voluntary public meetings and citizens' advisory groups became the most common vehicles for eliciting this input. Such groups have played the role of mediator between the public-at-large and the planning agency.

The public, acting through these intermediary institutions, has manifested enough power to force planners to modify their plans or even to stop projects entirely [2, 11, 15, 16]. In concept, the role of these new institutions was to give a voice to the public. Their intervention, however, has created new problems: (1) public inputs have become predominantly negative and, therefore, not very useful, (2) these inputs are not representative of the entire populations, and (3) these inputs incite conflict not only between the public and the planner but also among various partisan groups within the community.

The first problem is that voluntary public meetings or citizens' advisory groups demonstrate what the public does not want. They rarely identify preferred options that can then be used to meet the transportation needs of the public. Participation has demonstrated, on the part of the public, both a lack of technical knowledge and a lack of long-range vision, particularly in the context of unfamiliar technological environments.

A second problem is that "public" inputs do not necessarily represent the public as a whole. While the public consists of multiple clusters of individuals holding pluralistic points of view, only a few of the most vocal and partisan actually become involved in public meetings or advisory boards [2, 8, 11, 14]. Evidence indicates that participation is self-selecting and biased in favor of certain interests and against others [1]. Groups such as the elderly, who have a vital stake in the outcome, are seldom heard at all.

Third, the public forum for participation becomes an arena for conflict among different groups, each espousing

its own cause [17]. Often the result of this conflict is either a nullification of the input or a paralysis of the entire planning process [11].

The degree of conflict and the amount of externality created by the project are closely related. If you proposed a freeway through my neighborhood so that you can drive to work, I may not accept willingly the degradation of my environment for your convenience. If my advocacy is successful, I may force you to choose a different route or abandon the idea altogether.

Thus, the old problem has given way to new problems and, to date, no approach has been devised to solve them. For the transportation planner, the question is whether or not marketing, which deals with similar problems, can help. For the professional marketer the question is to apply the most effective combination of marketing concepts and methodology.

PUBLIC INPUTS IN MARKETING MANAGEMENT TERMS

The magnitude of the problems explored in the last section is sufficient to compel an evaluation of public inputs in marketing management terms. The discussion that follows will employ a view of the public participation arena suggested by Exhibit 1.

Even though one is concerned with private goods purchased by individual customers and the other is concerned with public goods purchased collectively by society, there are several parallel elements between marketing and planning.

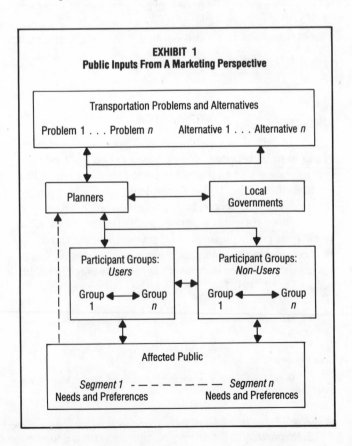

EXHIBIT 1
Public Inputs From A Marketing Perspective

1. Both are responsible for providing ''products'' to a consuming public that decides whether or not the products are acceptable. The transportation product task involves not only the mechanical aspects of making the product available, but also the more important determination of the configuration of the system to be offered. For the transportation planner, the system might include road beds, transit services or bicycle paths. These are shown in Exhibit 1 as alternatives $1, \ldots, n$.

   Both are concerned with product attribute preferences on the part of customers. In order to design products which incorporate appropriate characteristics or features, the planner must be able to identify preference structures. Successful systems must possess those characteristics which customers deem to be both important and attractive.

   Marketing in the public sector means more than ''selling'' the public on existing or conceived systems as some would assume [9, 10]. Even in the private sector, marketing is ineffective in getting customers to purchase products which are not attractive on their own merits [6].

2. Although planners sometimes prefer to deal with a ''consensus'' of the public as a whole [11, 17], segmentation is as necessary in transportation planning as it is in marketing management. Both face segmented markets, different groups of customers with unique and specialized needs which are expressed through product choices. The mass transit market, for example, has been characterized as consisting of five consumer segments: managerial/professional, clerical occupations, inner city residents, the elderly, and suburban housewives [9].

   It is important to note, however, that segmentation has three unique aspects in the context of transportation planning. All are shown diagrammatically in Exhibit 1. First, the planner should use segmentation at both the market and participant level. Failure to match participant segments with their corresponding market segments and failure to make sure that all market segments are represented will insure an unrepresentative set of inputs. Second, ''horizontal'' conflict is relatively unknown in private sector marketing. Third, nonuser segments, which often can be ignored in the case of private sector marketing, are extremely important in the case of a public transportation system. For many projects, the nonusers must pay a financial subsidy on behalf of the users. In other projects, nonusers must bear nonpecuniary externalities, such as higher noise levels (as in the case of air traffic) or pollution. As the effect of these externalities becomes larger and larger, the voice of the nonuser is heard through the public input process.

3. Both operate in environments where customers are free to choose among alternate products. In transportation, this might reflect modal preferences such as taking the bus or driving a car. On the other hand, planners have a monopoly over the transportation system as a whole, so they are able to manage all options available to the public. The only major check on this power is the resistance of the public itself.

   The market operates differently in the world of transportation planning in other ways as well. First, there are extensive time lags between commitment and use. Consumers can vote with their patronage only after the public has paid for the system with taxes or indebtedness. Second, resources may be immobile. Transportation systems of questionable conception cannot be transferred to other uses. Those justified on nonmarket grounds, such as the Bay Area Rapid Transit (BART), may become financial liabilities requiring public subsidies [20]. Marketing may thus be even more important in the public sector than it is in the private sector!

4. The mechanism for public inputs is more formal and inflexible than in the case of the private decision maker. In the private sector, failure to take public input into account may merely mean marketing failure. A similar omission in transportation planning also becomes a violation of the law.

WHAT CAN MARKETING CONTRIBUTE?

The premise of this discussion is that the concepts embodied in modern marketing have an unique and positive contribution to make in providing public inputs for transportation planning. The framework for specifying potential contributions is the ''marketing concept,'' which declares a consumer orientation the principle means of satisfying organizational goals. However, along with lacking a true consumer orientation, transportation planning often fails to formulate any specific operational goals [7, 9].

Transportation planning in the public sector does not ordinarily have objectives as clearly defined as those of profit-seeking firms in the private sector. The marketing concept suggests a surrogate measure: system utilization. Simple use of the system is a necessary, but not sufficient, condition for success. In the face of adequate utilization, success is determined by the actual external costs imposed upon nonusers, relative to their willingness to absorb such costs. Given a standard of utilization and expressed constraints, marketing strategy can be used to help achieve the target goal.

A fundamental characteristic of a consumer orientation is the use of marketing research to provide useful information about the needs and preferences of consumers. Not only are preferences important, but also the strengths of such preferences must be measured.

If some attribute of the system is considered undesirable, it may be possible to combine that negative characteristic with some positive characteristic from another part of the system in order to create a ''bundle of attributes'' which is desirable in light of the needs of other segments. The use of trade-off techniques such as conjoint analysis holds promise in this area. At the minimum, this approach might result in ''sweetening the pot'' for those who might otherwise oppose the system.

A second advantage of a consumer orientation is that planners become sensitive to different demands of a factionalized public consisting of users and affected nonusers. The use of marketing research to segment the market will provide information about different needs, such as motivations for travel, specific physical requirements and differing attitudes toward the use of public facilities. Marketing research can also identify how many people have what sorts of needs and what the characteristics of these people are.

Such information about different segments is necessary to insure that public participation is representative at the level of the voluntary public meeting or citizens' advisory council. Representatives of all segments might be solicited to participate in formal input procedures, or a direct communication link between underrepresented segments and planners might be established through marketing research survey techniques using representative random samples. Such a channel of communication is shown by the broken line at the left of Exhibit 1, that bypasses and supplements the ordinary participation process. A more radical suggestion would be to replace the voluntary meetings and citizens' advisory groups entirely with representative survey information.

At a pragmatic level, it is important to provide consumer advocacy where it can shape the direction of the system in order to achieve higher levels of utilization. At a more abstract level, representation is associated with the working of the democratic process and could increase public confidence that planning and spending done in their name is truly affected by them.

Under current conditions, much of the public input which reaches the planner cannot be expected to represent the public interest. Those who select themselves to serve on advisory boards or to appear at public meetings provide inputs which should not be taken at face value. Yet, without efforts to determine the desires of the public, the planner has no basis for evaluating what is said at meetings or to argue contrary positions.

The third advantage of a consumer orientation can be seen in a potential for conflict resolution among different user groups and between user groups and nonuser groups. The discipline of marketing has no expertise in the case of intractable conflict, such as a zero-sum game. Fortunately, true zero-sum situations are rare in transportation planning. One can often increase the payoff of the game through compromise and comprehensive planning that looks beyond a single transportation project. Bargainable situations then arise, leading to a system which, in total, may improve the position of several, perhaps even all, of the segments involved.

Marketing research can define the preference functions and trade-offs that would be acceptable to different segments. Some pioneering work has been done in this direction by the New York State Department of Transportation [3, 5]. Using this information planners could define bargaining positions and then attempt to negotiate between groups.

DISCUSSION

We began this discussion by examining the process by which public input has become a part of transportation planning. Then we looked at the role of marketing analysis in making public input more effective. The primary contributions are three-fold: first, application of the marketing concept—a public orientation to meet organizational goals; second, segmentation as a means of understanding the public and the participation process; third, utilization of marketing research as a channel of communication with both user and nonuser groups.

Although we have discussed public input in the context of transportation planning, the application of the discussion is much broader. Inclusion of public inputs is becoming popular in other areas of government planning, for example electrical power and mental health facilities. In some cases, it has even spread into the sphere of governmentally regulated monopolies, such as television cable service. Over time, more and more governmental agencies and private companies can expect to become involved. Optimistically, a marketing perspective can help newcomers to the public participation arena avoid some of the problems transportation planners have encountered.

REFERENCES

1. Brown, Daniel J., and Schary, Philip B. "Consumer Participants in Transportation Planning: The Elderly, the Poor, and Special Interests," in William D. Perreault, ed., *Advances in Consumer Research*, 4 (1977), 138–41.
2. Cupps, D. Stephen. "Emerging Problems of Citizen Participation," *Public Administration Review*, 37 (September/October 1977), 478–87.
3. Donnelly, E. P., Howe, S. M., and DesChamps, J. A. "Trade-Off Analysis: Theory and Applications to Transportation Policy Planning," *High Speed Ground Transportation Journal*, 11 (Spring 1977), 93–110.
4. Dyer, Robert F., and Shimp, Terence A. "Enhancing the Role of Marketing Research in Public Policy Decision Making," *Journal of Marketing*, 41 (January 1977), 63–67.
5. Eberts, Patricia M., and Koeppel, K.-W. Peter. "The Trade-Off Model: Empirical and Structural Findings," *Preliminary Research Report No. 123*, (Albany, NY: State Department of Transportation Planning Research Unit, 1977).
6. Hartley, Robert F. *Marketing Mistakes*, (Columbus, OH: Grid, Inc., 1976).
7. Houston, Franklin S., and Homans, Richard E. "Public Agency Marketing: Pitfalls and Problems," *MSU Business Topics*, 25 (Summer 1977), 36–40.
8. Jackson, John S., III, and Shade, William L. "Citizen Participation, Democratic Representation and Survey Research," *Urban Affairs Quarterly*, 9 (September 1973) 57–89.
9. Kangun, Norman, and Staples, William A. "Selling Urban Transit," *Business Horizons*, 18 (February 1975), 57–66.
10. Murin, William J. "Urban Transportation Planning, Politics and Policy Making," *Public Administration Review*, 37 (January/February 1977), 89–97.
11. Park, Ki Suh. "Achieving Positive Community Participation in the Freeway Planning Process," *Highway Research Record*, 380 (1972), 14–21.
12. Ritchie, J. R. Brent, and LaBreque, Roger J. "Marketing Research and Public Policy: A Functional Perspective," *Journal of Marketing*, 39 (July 1975), 12–19.
13. Schary, Philip B.; Brown, Daniel J., and Becker, Boris W. "Consumers as Participants in Transportation Planning," *Transportation*, 6 (July 1977), 135–48.
14. Shermer, Julie Hetrick. "Interest Group Impact Assessment in Transportation Planning," *Traffic Quarterly*, 29 (January 1975), 29–49.
15. Sloan, Allan K. *Citizen Participation in Transportation Planning: The Boston Experience*. (Cambridge, MA: Ballinger Publishing Co., 1974).
16. Taebel, Delbert A. "Citizens Groups, Public Policy, and Urban Transportation," *Traffic Quarterly*, 27 (October 1973), 503–15.
17. Travis, Kenneth M., and Plog, Stanley C. "Community Involvement in Transportation Planning: A New Approach," *Highway Research Record*, 380 (1972), 8–13.
18. U.S. Department of Transportation. *Effective Citizen Participation in Transportation Planning*, (Washington, D.C.: U.S. Department of Transportation, 1976).
19. Wilkie, William L., and Gardner, David M. "The Role of Marketing Research in Public Policy Decision Making," *Journal of Marketing*, 38 (January 1974), 38–47.
20. Zwerling, Stephen. *Mass Transit and the Politics of Technology: A Study of BART and the San Francisco Bay Area*. (New York: Praeger, 1974).

8
Political Advertising: A Neglected Policy Issue in Marketing

Michael L. Rothschild

The use of marketing, especially advertising, for political purposes has become increasingly prevalent and controversial. This article carefully reviews the theories that have been advanced to explain how advertising works in the political arena. The article then develops a framework for understanding the several types of effects that advertising can have and postulates situational contingencies that specify when the different effects will occur. Experimental and survey data are utilized to test the validity of the hypotheses offered.

Over the years, the implicit ties between marketing and the political process have become ever more explicit. Marketing's role and impact now need to be examined closely. Major changes in the political marketplace in the past 30 years relate specifically to (1) the influx of television as an advertising and information disseminating mechanism and to (2) the rapid escalation of campaign costs (in large part to support the use of television). During the latter part of this period, consideration of these changes has lagged dramatically in the political science literature. Two major discrepancies are (1) the use of survey versus experimental and econometric techniques and (2) the examination of presiden-

tial versus all other political races. The author first considers these major marketplace changes and the concurrent research shortfall. Then an integrative model for considering recent political advertising effects is presented, as well as recent data collected in a variety of settings by a variety of methods which support the model. Finally, potential policy implications are considered.

Television: A Catalyst for Change. The use of television has probably been the greatest catalyst in changing the marketing/political relationship from implicit to explicit. This changing relationship can be considered in terms of three time periods.

Pre-1952. Television, although technologically available from approximately 1930, was not a medium for mass transmission of messages during this period. The political communication process during this time was limited primar-

Michael L. Rothschild is Assistant Professor, Graduate School of Business, University of Wisconsin-Madison.

The author thanks Gil Churchill, Michael Houston, Gay Leslie, and the *JMR* Reviewers and editor for their helpful comments on a draft.

ily to print media and, after 1926, radio.[1] The latter was used to transmit speeches and marathon fund raising/interest raising programs after 1926, but there were few, if any, short commercials. The notion of selective exposure [22, 35, 62] developed during this time as an explanation of how voters dealt with political messages. If such a notion were ever valid, it would have been at this time and in this situation, where communications were brought forth in relatively large blocks of time which were relatively easy to receive or avoid.

1952–1967. The general public, political scientists, and legislators did not, in large numbers, recognize the use of marketing as a political technique until the 1952 presidential elections when Dwight Eisenhower used television advertising as a campaign device (for interesting anecdotal work, see [20, 36]). During the next 15 years, the use of television escalated as politicians experimented with and refined its use, although the marketing techniques still were behind the "state of the art" in the private sector.

Post-1967. Campaign expenditures by this time had reached very high levels, mainly because of the sophisticated use of commercial television through the purchase of large numbers of short (30- to 60-second) blocks of broadcast time. This increase, plus a broadened marketing concept, has led to a more detailed examination of the area by some marketers.

CAMPAIGN COSTS ESCALATE

The evolution of political campaigns also can be considered in terms of the changes in the cost of running for office. In 1846, Abraham Lincoln spent $.75 toward his election to Congress; in 1956, Dwight Eisenhower spent about $8 million for re-election to the presidency; in 1972, Richard Nixon spent more than $60 million to achieve the same goal. (Because the $60 million was spent during roughly one quarter of the year, this figure is comparable to an annual promotions budget of $240 million. In 1973, General Motors spent $229 million and was the nation's second largest advertiser).

It has been noted [59] that during the period 1952–74, while the voting-age population increased 40% and the cost of living went up approximately 100%, all political expenditures increased 290%, political broadcast expenditures increased 600%, and presidential campaign expenditures increased 690%. Although some proportion of this increase in spending could be attributed to "keeping up with the opposition" and some to inflation, there must also have been some belief in campaign effectiveness behind these expenditures.

At least in terms of dollars spent, advertising has become a dominant force in the political marketplace during the past 25 years. During this time, both traditional campaign practices and traditional voter response patterns have changed

dramatically. Dreyer [16], for example, notes a steady decline since 1952 in the capacity of party identification to predict voting behavior in presidential elections. It is possible that television and its characteristic short-term information flows have led to this greater volatility; as party ties have lost their salience, the power of the media may have increased in importance.

These recent changes have led to a set of policy questions relating to political marketing: Does political marketing have the potential to affect the political process in a way which, although beneficial to the candidate, may be dysfunctional to society in general? What are the impacts of the various marketing tools and techniques on voter behavior? Is enough known about these impacts to determine whether political marketing regulation is necessary and, if so, how that regulation should be manifested?

A Need to Reassess Earlier Work. The radical transformations in the political process require reassessment of the earlier work and also of the general findings which emerged. The major model of political communications effects to arise during the period 1945–65 was predicated on research which showed great stability in the political process; this model has come to be known as the "limited effects" model [4]. The body of research responsible for this model originated in work by Lazarsfeld [3, 35] and Campbell [8–11]; its findings have been replicated and re-reported many times [2, 5, 27, 32, 42, 55, 61, 67]. For example Lazarsfeld [35] found that the effects of the media were very limited. The media only reached interested people, and these people already were committed. The study further concluded that little attitude change occurred during the campaign; the media in general activated latent predispositions. The magnitude of the collective works as a well respected body of literature certainly established a feeling of reliability of inferences; no doubt, such a body of literature could exert considerable influence in both legislative and judicial decision making.

Hypothetically, there are at least four states of the world with which one should be concerned in evaluating the effects of advertising on voting behavior: high or low level elections, and high or low levels of expenditures. One could argue that in the early stages of political communications research only the low expenditure condition existed and that only the high level election, low expenditure state was examined. To understand the full range of media effects, research should cover all four states. The "limited effects" findings probably were due in part to limited situation exploration. In defense, it should be noted that without high levels of expenditures as an incentive, there was no clear-cut need to enlarge the scope of the investigation. It also should be noted that, though a high level of expenditures is not synonymous with a high level of message repetition, the two variables seem to be highly correlated.

In addition to considering a broader variety of situations, modern investigators also must consider using a wider

---

[1] Calvin Coolidge made the first political radio broadcast in 1926. The author is indebted to Frederick D. Sturdivant for sharing this information. Professor Sturdivant was made privy to this fact when he received a free Wendy's Hamburger Bicentennial Drinking Glass upon which was inscribed this historical note.

variety of methods. When research first was done in this area before the advent of massive political advertising, the media possibly had only a limited effect on the electorate. But modern advertising has added a new dimension—one that has subtle and situation-specific effects. The investigators, as a result, must turn to more subtle and situation-specific methods.

To separate and evaluate methods, one first must consider what the relevant problem is. For studying *existing* cognitive, affective, or conative development, introspective responses common to survey methods might produce the desired information. In contrast, if one were studying *the effects of communication* on cognitive, affective, or conative development, it would be preferable to use some sort of experimental design to separate the effects of the key independent variables(s) and to eliminate contamination from other elements of the environment. The latter task is more relevant to the development of the field of political communications, and the study of political advertising. Much of the early work in the field was concerned with the first of the two problems and appropriately employed survey methods; any attempt to look at the second problem by survey/interview methods would have only limited chance for success. The author contends that the lack of concern for political marketing in the United States is due at least in part to the lack of effects reported in the literature. By re-examining the influence of advertising techniques by different methods and in more situations, perhaps new insights can be developed.

In the past few years, a new body of literature has begun to emerge which casts considerable doubt on the current validity of the limited effects model. This new literature examines three aspects of political marketing.

1. Differential effects of communications as a function of the level of the electoral race and the interest of the voter.
2. Changes in the state of the world due primarily to the more sophisticated and extensive use of the broadcast media and especially the use of television.
3. The inability of survey instruments to measure accurately the effects of communications.

A MODEL OF INVOLVEMENT AND POLITICAL ADVERTISING EFFECTS

Involvement is a hypothetical construct which has received much attention recently [7, 15, 21, 25, 30, 33, 56, 68]. This construct is related to the receipt and use of information by individuals as a function of how much the individuals care about the decision they ultimately will make.

In private sector marketing, one can consider, for example, the case of many low priced, frequently purchased, essentially commodity, consumer convenience goods. In such a case, the consumer is somewhat concerned with the purchase because the product is needed at some basic level (for example, soap is needed to keep one's body odor within some range of societal tolerances), but the consumer may not be concerned enough to evaluate brand choices carefully. This scenario is presented as an alternative to the more traditional consumer behavior models which suggest a more explicit evaluation of alternative choices.

The same low involvement model may hold in many electoral situations. Though there may be some basic need to *perform* (e.g., it is one's civic duty to vote), there is no need to *evaluate* the choices carefully before behaving. Such a model is now made explicit; it considers decision-making styles, the impact of advertising, and the relationship between attitude and behavior for high and low involvement cases.

The Concept of Involvement. The involvement construct, as an operationalization of one dimension of attitude, has been found in the social psychology and marketing literatures for more than 30 years [17–19, 24, 31, 39, 43, 51, 52, 54, 64–66]. Two definitions of involvement from this literature are helpful in constructing a basic model. Festinger [17] defines involvement as *concern with the issue*. This definition implies a *low level of involvement* and represents concern with the general issue or process. Such involvement could possibly lead to action on the issue without taking a stand. Freedman [18] defines involvement *as commitment to a position or concern with a specific stand on an issue*. This definition seems to be a more restrictive one, or, rather, a way of describing a person with *high involvement*. Action would be based on the stand taken on the issue. High involvement would go beyond concern with the issue to include taking a specific stand. This stand can be a result of information seeking and evaluation, or a result of brand or party loyalty. The most common form of high involvement is probably due to loyalty.

The involvement definition more common to marketing relates affective and conative development over time. Attitude strength, or level of development, is considered in a temporal sense in that it can crystallize before, during, or after behavior takes place. This temporal attitude-behavior relationship has been considered most frequently in marketing in connection with the hierarchy of effects paradigm [14, 34, 50].

During the past several years, a limited literature has begun to support the notion of a low involvement hierarchy of effects and to contrast this hierarchy to the more traditional one which marketers have used as a planning tool for perhaps 40 years. The notion of two hierarchies of effects was first specifically proposed by Ray et al. [50]. Their high involvement hierarchy (termed "learning hierarchy") was similar to that traditionally proposed [14, 34, for example]; the low involvement hierarchy stemmed from theoretical work by Krugman [31] and data-based support by Rothschild [59]. These two hierarchies are presented in Exhibit 1. The major difference between the two is in whether affective development (attitude) precedes or follows conative development (behavior).

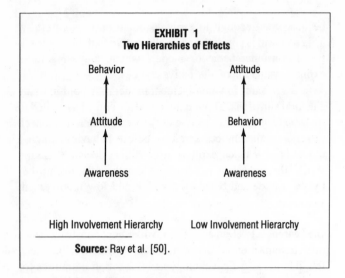

EXHIBIT 1
Two Hierarchies of Effects

High Involvement Hierarchy: Awareness → Attitude → Behavior

Low Involvement Hierarchy: Awareness → Behavior → Attitude

Source: Ray et al. [50].

In the low involvement case, there is no or little attitudinal development specifically toward the candidates prior to behavior, although there is a positive attitude toward the general notion of voting in the particular electoral race. With high involvement, however, there are attitudes toward the candidates themselves. As a result, very different types of pre-behavioral processess are developing, even though they may not be outwardly apparent to the layperson.

The model becomes most relevant to the issue of political advertising effects when one considers the impact of communications on high involvement versus low involvement individuals, or in high and low involvement situations. Because of the pervasiveness of advertising, most individuals will receive messages; the quality of reception will differ greatly, though, as a function of involvement level. At one extreme is the type of reception posited by Krugman [31] where no perceptual defenses are erected to screen the messages because there is concern only with the issue and not with the objects or positions. At the other extreme, messages are sought out and evaluated carefully to arrive at a stand.

The low involvement individual receives messages, does not evaluate them, does not develop a stand, but does behave. Such a person may develop an attitude after behaving. This individual is committed to behaving but not to a stand. Because he or she does not evaluate the messages which have been received (or their sources), one should examine the effect of these messages on the actions which follow.

Persons who are loyal enter the campaign with a preconceived attitude or stand. Although these loyal individuals may receive messages in the sense that they are exposed to and cannot avoid them, they do not find a need to evaluate, and their attitude prior to behavior reflects their early stand. Their behavior also reflects this stand. This is one form of high involvement behavior.

The information seeker also receives messages, but this person evaluates them and may incorporate some of them into the stand that is developed prior to behavior. In the loyal and information seeking cases, a stand is taken prior to action; this is a major difference from the low involvement case.

The development of involvement, as described, is a composite of enduring and situation involvement. *Enduring involvement* reflects the past cognitive, affective, and conative interaction which the individual has had with the underlying process or issue (in this case the political process). *Situation involvement* reflects the specific decision-making instance currently at hand (in this case, the specific electoral race—tempered, perhaps, by other races on the same ballot).

Because of the interaction of enduring and situation involvement, any individual may respond very differently to several specific but different races. For example, in some races the voter may make specific and detailed candidate evaluations which lead to an attitude which precedes behavior. In other cases, the voter does not make these evaluations, but votes on the basis of party loyalty. In still other cases, the vote is cast because the individual is voting in another race and decides to complete the ballot. Finally, in some cases, the voter decides to stay at home.

It seems that the involvement model is potentially very situation-bound. It is this situation specificity that allows one to make *a priori* generalizations about the involvedness of electoral races. Three generalizations are made [in part based on 23];

1. National races are more involving than local races, whereas state races have the lowest level of involvement.
2. Close races are more involving than one-side races.
3. Volatile issues and candidates tend to make races more involving.

In sum, the involvement model postulates that neither all voters nor all voting situations are alike. Highly involved voters will not be greatly affected by a stream of messages, because they will put up perceptual defenses either to evaluate or screen out these messages. Less involved voters will be more easily influences by a stream of messages, because they may be more concerned with the behavior itself than with developing a stand.

The involvement model seems intuitively plausible and relates directly to the issue of political advertising effects. If the model were valid, it would support the findings of the limited effects model previously discussed, for both models predict that the media will have little impact in a high level (highly involving) race such as the presidential race. The involvement model additionally predicts positive effects of advertising in low level (less involving) races such as a state assembly race, whereas the limited effects model makes the same limited prediction for all races, even though little data have been collected in the lower level races.

RELEVANT REPORTED RESEARCH

A limited set of works is now emerging which presents data counter to the limited effects model. In some cases the data implicitly support the involvement model; in other cases, the relationship is more explicit. It should be noted that the studies were conducted and/or first reported within a very short period of time of one another. In addition to these studies, a collection of independent papers further disparages the limited effects model from several different directions [13].

Implicit Examination of the Involvement Model. Three sets of data are described in this section which cast doubt on the limited effects model. In addition, the studies contribute implicitly to the furtherance of the involvement model.

Patterson and McClure [46] collected data by a four-wave panel of 626 respondents in Onondaga County, NY, during the 1972 presidential campaign. The data show that voters received more information from political advertising than they did from television news. "In fact, the evidence clearly shows that televised network evening newscasts contribute almost nothing to the low interest voter's election information . . . [while] Televised advertising not only reaches low interest voters, but also teaches them useful, accurate, issue information" [46, p. 88].

The limited effects model was formulated at a time when broadcast media messages consisted of newscasts, speeches, and marathon types of programs. Patterson and McClure, in effect, concur with this model, that the impact of newscasts is slight and would have limited effect, but they also find that advertising has a very different effect. This finding, though, does not apply to the involvement model because it pertains more to the issue of message quality than to message quantity. The involvement model is concerned only with message quantity.

Patterson and McClure speculate that voters receive more information from advertising than from news because it is in the candidate's best interest to provide information to voters, whereas this is not necessarily so for a news show. In advertising, the candidate has the opportunity to present himself as he wishes, with no outside editing. Though his message is naturally biased it still attempts to provide information which the voter can assimilate.

The news show may have a greater interest in its own ratings than in the dissemination of information; therefore it will show the candidate shaking hands, riding in a motorcade, or kissing a baby because this "action" story is believed to hold the viewer's interest better than 30 or 60 seconds of the candidate making a major policy statement.

Patterson and McClure present data to show that moderate television viewers show gains in information from advertising about the candidates equal to the gains of viewers with heavy exposure. From this finding they conclude that more moderate budgets would be sufficient to inform the electorate, and discrepancies in "spending between candidates do not—within limits—appreciably disadvantage the candidate spending less money." [46, p. 96] This finding of an asymptotic response function is consistent with data from the Stanford advertising laboratory [50] where such a response function often has been noted, especially for high

involvement products and low level types of responses such as awareness.

Elsewhere [37], Patterson and McClure report that heavy television viewers' attitudes changed more than those of light viewers. In addition, viewers with low interest had a greater attitude change than viewers with high interest. Greatest attitude change took place among heavy viewers with low interest. In all cases attitude change was greater in response to televised advertising than to televised news. These findings are in keeping with the involvement model which would predict greater change in attitude among low involvement voters and among those receiving the greatest number of message repetitions. The model does not deal with news versus advertising effects.

These data imply that knowledge and attitude seem to change as a function of repetition of advertising messages and involvement of the message recipient. It is unfortunate that Patterson and McClure did not include a behavioral measure and did not collect data in any lower level elections where the involvement model would posit even more striking results. In any case, there does seem to be an impact of the media on recipients in excess of that postulated by the limited effects model.

A second set of data comes from Palda [44, 45], who studied the relationship between voting behavior and several independent variables: (1) mass media advertising by the candidate and by the opponent, (2) other campaign expenses of the candidate and the opponent, (3) incumbency of candidate's party in the riding (district), (4) urban-rural nature of the riding, (5) past party history in the riding, (6) success of the candidate at the top of the party ticket being considered. The studies were econometric analyses of published official electoral reports for the 108 Quebec electoral districts for 1966 and 1970, and 53 Manitoba districts for 1973. Their value is enhanced by the fact that they are two of very few studies which have *actual* voting behavior (as opposed to voting intention) as a dependent variable.

Palda reports that in 1966 "advertising" was the second most important variable behind "other expenses" in affecting voting behavior; in 1970 it was third most important behind "other expenses" and "party incumbency." In both cases, advertising had a significant positive effect on behavior such that each incremental dollar spent on advertising returned one-third of a vote for that candidate.

A second finding of note is that "at least for Quebec, . . . the higher the total campaign outlays in a riding, the higher the rate of participation" [14, p. 769]. This means that not only selective demand but also primary demand is influenced by advertising. These findings are especially important because Palda's are the only studies based on actual behavior, and, therefore, lend credence to other studies which use voting intention as the dependent variable.

The econometric analysis conducted by Palda seems to offer strong support that political advertising does have an effect on voting behavior. One would posit (based on [23]) that the riding race generally would be of low involvement, and, thus, behavior would be more susceptible to advertising.

Doubt also has been cast on the limited effects model by Kline [29] who presents a review and reanalysis of data from several national and local election field survey studies. Relevant here is Kline's conclusion that there were two types of elections: (1) *presidential elections,* which affected people of different involvement levels in similar ways and where voting was generally very predictable and relatively unaffected by the media, and (2) *party elections* (any below the presidential level), which were very unstable for the low involvement voter. In party elections, low involvement voters relied on simple presentations and deviated from party identification as a result. Because they did not have enough information to make an informed decision, they relied on their recall of images, and, consequently, the predominant image received the vote (in Kline's scenario). This finding is consistent with the involvement model and is also consistent with Dreyer's finding that party ties have lost some of their salience.

Kline writes that highly involved voters cast their vote in a more stable manner than less involved voters and that involvement interacts with complexity of information used in decision making. Type of information is found to be more important in a presidential context than in any other election, and for uninvolved voters the broadcast media have the greatest effect on perceived political affiliation. Kline's analysis relates closely to the involvement model because it contributed to the development of the model; it therefore cannot be included as an explicit test, but it certainly supports the model.

The studies by Patterson and McClure, Palda, and Kline give implicit support to the involvement model and explicit support to the notion that the mass media affect voting behavior. In the next section, three studies are presented which explicitly test the model.

Explicit Test of the Involvement Model. The explicit tests of the involvement model [57, 59, 60] have consisted of a laboratory experiment, a panel study, and a series of field surveys. Over the course of the three studies, four electoral settings and 11 races have been examined by a variety of research methods.

Laboratory experiment. The laboratory experiment was a 5 × 3 posttest-only control group factorial design. The independent vairables were, respectively, number of repetitions of advertising (0, 1, 2, 4, 6) and types of election (presidential, congressional, state assembly). Dependent variables were measures of cognitive, affective, and conative development toward candidates in each of the three races.

The experiment took place in a large shopping mall during mid-September 1972. Its purpose was to observe changes in recall, attitude formation, and voting intention in subjects in a controlled environment by varying the exposure which the subject would have to the messages of political candidates. Candidates used in the experiment were those running at the time for president, and for congress and state assembly in the district of the shopping mall location.

The subjects were assigned randomly to one of six presentation sequences so that each sequence was seen by 23 to 31 subjects. Each sequence was a constrained random ordering of 49–53 slides showing messages for two products/candidates in each of six consumer product classes and three election races. In any particular sequence, messages for a product/candidate might be seen zero to six times and messages for the direct competitor could also be seen zero to six times. The cover story related to "shopping of the future," as used successfully in the Stanford advertising laboratory on other occasions [50]. After viewing a sequence of messages, subjects completed a questionnaire which asked for opinions of the system demonstrated and, then, unaided recall of the messages, attitudes toward the sponsors, purchase/voting intentions, and demographic factors.

Exhibit 2 shows the effect of political advertising on voting behavior in the low involvement and high involvement situations. The state assembly race was believed, *a priori,* to be of low involvement; the other two races were considered to be of high involvement. The *a priori* judgments were based on [23] and on the foregoing discussion of the model. The data support these judgments.

There was no significant change in voting intention in the high involvement races as a function of advertising level (presidential: $F = .16$, d.f. $= 1, 3$, n.s.; congressional: $F = .03$, d.f. $= 1, 3$, n.s.). In the state assembly race, level of advertising did have a significant effect on voting intention ($F = 322.6$, d.f. $= 1, 3, p < .001$). The interaction of situation and repetition level was also significant ($F = 56.4$, d.f. $= 1, 8, p < .001$).

Furthermore, subjects responded in accordance with the appropriate hierarchy of effects notion in that there was a greater change for attitude than for behavior in the high involvement situation; the reverse held in the low involvement situation (method of Stouffer; $Z = 1.45, p = .07$, one-tailed test [40, p. 329]).

Finally, there was some confirmation of Palda's finding that advertising level affected primary demand, or voter turnout. In the experiment, primary demand tended to be affected positively in the low level race (although not to a statistically significant degree), whereas there was no apparent change in the high level races. There was a significant difference in voter turnout between high and low level races in the no-advertising situation ($\chi^2 = 6.96$, d.f. $= 1, p < .01$), but there was virtually no difference in the situations where advertising levels were high.

The experiment showed that political advertising can have an effect and that this effect is dependent on the involvement of the race. Political advertising had a strong positive effect on voting intention in the low involvement race, but not in the high involvement races. In addition, in the low in-

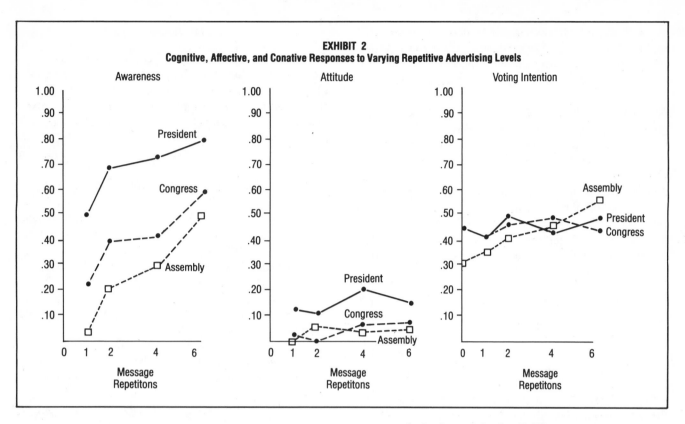

EXHIBIT 2
Cognitive, Affective, and Conative Responses to Varying Repetitive Advertising Levels

volvement situation, it was possible to cause a change in behavioral intent without affecting attitude formation to the same degree. The data indicated a low involvement hierarchy wherein an individual might behave without developing a prior attitude.

Field Panel Study. The field panel study was conducted in a midwestern state from August to November 1972. Data were collected by a political research firm in conjunction with its work for one of the candidates in the race being studied—a race for a U.S. Senate seat. These data then were used by the researcher to test the involvement model.

The panel study consisted of three waves: pre-, during, and postcampaign. These were executed in August, October, and November (shortly after election), respectively.

Information sought from respondents was related to involvement toward the political process, awareness of the candidates and issues, attitudes concerning the candidates and issues, behavior toward the candidates (how will you vote, how did you vote), voting history and party loyalty, demographic factors, and exposure to news and advertising. The panel study basically was an attempt to examine in a natural environment the same relationships as were studied in a controlled environment in the laboratory experiment.

1. There was no significant change in intended behavior toward the candidates during the period of the campaign. The race examined was a higher order involvement situation (senatorial race), and, therefore, the lack of change was predicted by the model.

2. Changes over time in cognitive, affective, and conative development were consistent with what one would predict for a higher

order involvement situation. Stability was greatest in conative development and least in cognitive development.

3. The panel data also were examined in more detail in that respondents were categorized according to their personal involvement with the political process *per se*. The data show that persons with a low level of political involvement were late deciders (and therefore perhaps more susceptible to communications effects) and those with a higher level of involvement were predominantly early deciders ($\chi^2 = 3.42$, d.f. = 1, $p < .1$).

California Poll Data. The data used in this study were a subset of those collected by the California Poll during the 1972 election campaigns. One thousand to 1,500 potential voters responded in one of three polls during the course of the 1972 campaign and gave opinions about seven propositions on the California ballot. Data concerned voting intentions (direction of vote and concreteness of intent) with regard to the propositions.

In addition to these data, supplementary information was gathered from two sources.

1. Archival data were collected by a review of several California newspapers during the period in question.

2. Several experts on California politics were interviewed for subjective data on involvement of voters toward the propositions. The combination of archival and expert witness data allowed *post hoc* evaluation of involvement as well as advertising levels for and against the propositions. This data set then allowed for analysis of the interaction of involvement level of the situation and level of advertising.

The study considered the stability of voting intentions overtime as the dependent variable, which changed as a function of advertising level and involvement level. The data show a significant effect due to advertising level ($F = 2916$, d.f. = 1, 1, $p < .001$), a slight effect due to involvement of the situation ($F = 49$, d.f. = 1 1, $p < .1$) and no interaction effect. These findings are not an overpowering confirmation of the involvement model, but do tend in the right direction.

Summary of the Evidence.   The limited effects model does not seem to be incorrect, but rather it seems to be incomplete. One can see from the use of data sets involving multiple methods and multiple settings that a consistent set of findings is emerging which shows political advertising to have potentially powerful, although situation-specific, effects.

The author has presented data from several studies of the impact of political advertising on either behavioral intent [29, 37, 46, 57, 59, 60] or actual behavior [44, 45]. The studies are summarized in Exhibit 3. The most important findings are:

1. Political advertising seems to affect both primary and selective demand.

2. The effects seem to relate to a hierarchy of effects notion.

3. The effects seem to differ as a function of the involvedness of the situation.

This set of findings is more complex than the larger set of findings which let to the limited effects model. The findings are consistent, though, with Katz's observation [26] that low involvement, low loyalty, and a high probability of exposure to election communications "has become a more probable combination in the era of television than ever before" [p. 307]. Although some of the data are weak, the findings of all the studies tend in the same direction and therefore become more credible as a group (in the spirit of a multiple methodology philosophy) [12, 49, 58].

DISCUSSION

A growing set of data indicates that a major shift in communications and communications effects may be occurring. Therefore, it is crucial to consider the potential effect of such a shift on the democratic processes, on current legislation, and on possible future legislation. Given the model and the data presented, what statements can be made for evaluating present and future campaign legislation and campaign strategy?

The data have shown that political advertising has a strong direct effect on voting behavior in certain situations. If the data and the model have external validity, then there is certainly a potential societal danger present in the unrestricted use of marketing techniques and tools. Among the potential dangers would be (1) that votes could be "bought" indirectly through large advertising expenditures and (2) that this "buying process" would be most effective when voters were encouraged to perform their civic duty without being encouraged to evaluate information.

Proposals have been made at various times to control the nature and amount of political advertising in this country. Proponents of such plans point to the controls imposed in various Western European nations and in Japan. These controls generally provide some or all of the following features:

1. All broadcast advertising time is paid for by the government, so there is no need for candidates to generate revenues to buy time.

2. All major party candidates seeking a high office receive equal amounts of broadcast time; minor party candidates receive lesser amounts of time; candidates for lower level offices receive lesser amounts of time.

3. Candidates can use their allotted time in any way they see fit, but there is some control over the minimum length of a message (usu-

---

EXHIBIT 3
A Summary of the Evidence

Source	Level of race	Method	Major findings
Patterson and McClure [37, 46]	Presidential (high involvement)	Panel	Advertising has a greater impact on awareness and attitude than does news; the impact of advertising reaches an asymptotic level somewhere below actual spending levels.
Kline [29]	Presidential (high involvement)	Reexamination of existing data	Behavior is relatively unaffected by the media, and therefore predictable.
Rothschild [59, 60]	Presidential (high involvement)	Experimental	Advertising has some effect on awareness, little effect on attitude, no effect on behavior.
Rothschild [59, 60]	Congressional (high involvement)	Experimental	Same as above.
Rothschild [57, 59]	Senatorial (high involvement)	Panel	During the campaign, there was some increase in awareness, little change in attitude, and virtually no change in behavior.
Rothschild [57, 59]	Referendum (some high and some low involvement)	Series of surveys	During the campaign, voting intention was strongly related to advertising level and mildly related to involvement level of referendum.
Palda [44, 45]	Canadian electoral district (low involvement)	Econometric analysis	Advertising level of candidate affects number of votes received by candidate; advertising level of race affects total number of votes cast in race.
Kline [36]	Other than presidential (low involvement)	Reexamination of existing data	Behavior is less stable, more image oriented, and more affected by the media.
Rothschild [59, 60]	State assembly (low involvement)	Experimental	Advertising has strong effect on awareness, moderate effect on behavior, and very little effect on attitude.

ally a five minute minimum). Given a finite amount of broadcast time, this policy limits frequency. It also attempts to force a meaningful transfer of information, under the assumption that it is more difficult to say nothing for long periods of time than it is for short periods of time.

4. A candidate using allotted time has simultaneous access to all broadcast media in the relevant geographic area whenever he chooses to use the media. This theoretically insures maximum reach of the message [6, 38].

In the following sections, these controls are discussed and their impact is considered in terms of the involvement model and the data presented. The discussion concludes with an examination of recent legislation in the United States and its impact from a marketing communications viewpoint.

Government Subsidization of Candidates. Two basic questions are: (1) Should the government subsidize election campaigns? (2) If so, at what level should the subsidy be set?

At least three researchers have written in favor of government subsidies for candidates. Adamany [1] and Welch [69] favor substantial subsidies because they find the marginal value of dollars spent decreases rapidly with increased expenditures. If the government subsidizes campaigns well into the area of diminishing returns, the value of dollars contributed by special interest groups becomes diminished. In such a case, candidates would have less incentive to accept such money. This scernario suggests that subsidies could alleviate the problem of campaign fund collections, although the problems related to expenditures (the repetition of advertising) would still remain. If, though, the levels of subsidies were lower and private contributions also were controlled, total spending and repetition levels would diminish. This pattern occurred in the 1976 Presidential campaigns. The data seemed to indicate that it may be important to control level of expenditure as well as level of collection.

Patterson and McClure [46] suggest that the government subsidize candidates by forcing free broadcast time. They believe that free television advertising time would hold down campaign spending, equalize candidate opportunity, and increase the information available to the American electorate. All of these objectives seem desirable, as it is becoming clearer that the sheer volume of advertising transmissions may be affecting voter behavior.

The involvement model is relevant to a discussion of government subsidization of campaigns because subsidies generally carry upper limits. The notion of an upper limit to either spending or some other measure of message units can be examined within the context of the model. It is unclear, though, what those limits should be because variables such as the involvedness of the race and the incumbency/past popularity of the candidates would influence such limits. Though Patterson and McClure believe that subsidies would equalize candidate opportunity, it seems that such a plan would require very complex situation analysis and would need to be followed by complex formulation of unequal subsidies to create equality.

The next section concerns incumbency as an independent variable in such a formulation. Several potential strategies for efficiency-maximizing variables which would also complicate any equalizing plan used by the government are discussed subsequently.

The Advantage of Incumbency. An interesting research question is raised by the second part of the European controls wherein all major party candidates are given equal amounts of broadcast time. This approach provides a great advantage to the incumbent who begins the campaign with a higher level of awareness; in many campaigns, this advantage can never be overcome. Welch [69] points out that incumbency has two advantages. First, because incumbency leads to greater recognition, it gives a direct advantage in attracting votes. The awareness level resulting from at least two years in public office is very difficult to overcome in a two month campaign.

Second, incumbency has the additional advantage of providing ease of campaign fund collection, which may account at least in part for the fact that incumbents generally have more money to spend. Palda posits a lag effect in that past popularity leads to past election. This leads to ease of collecting present dollars and, as shown in his work, dollars spent have a direct positive effect on the number of votes received. So although the nonincumbent needs *extra* funds to overcome the advantages of incumbency, he generally has *fewer* funds.

Whether or not Welch's advantages are indeed the reasons for incumbency being correlated with success, the fact remains that only two incumbent presidents in the past 100 years have not been reelected when seeking that office; in addition, 80% of all members of congress seeking reelection in that period also have been successful.

The hierarchy of effects notion would postulate that the combination of higher early awareness and greater funds could have a tremendous impact on an election outcome. The model would predict that the impact would be greatest in a low involvement race. Indeed, the lower the level of the race, the greater the probability of reelection, both in theory and in fact.

Length of Message, Reach, and Frequency. The value of long versus short messages in political campaigns is discussed by at least two sets of writers. Patterson and McClure [46] argue that though long messages may be theoretically desirable, in practice voters would have little interest in such messages. Conversely, they feel that voters will, and do, sit through a series of short messages and that both the informed and uninformed receive information which is valuable. In addition, they posit that candidates would more readily use short blocks of time and that the television industry would more readily agree to provide free time in short blocks than in long blocks.

Napolitan [41] presents a similar set of arguments on the pragmatic aspects of short messages. He believes that television stations will not sell long (five minutes) blocks of time to candidates during prime time. Therefore these longer messages can only be shown when few people are watching, and this would defeat their purpose.

If Patterson and McClure and Napolitan are correct in their pragmatic assessments, then strategies will certainly tend toward shorter messages. Along with such a strategy will come a higher level of repetition if budgets are kept constant.

Patterson and McClure suggest that greater repetition is not necessary. From their findings, they conclude that "candidates can cut spending on televised ads somewhat and still get their messages across" [46, p. 96]. If this were the case, then repetition could be controlled in such a way as to lessen the impact on voting behavior, yet still adequately transmit information.

Rothschild [59] also suggests advantages to limiting the number of spots. He concludes from his data that high repetition levels have the potential to influence behavior without affecting attitude development in the low involvement situation, even though in the high involvement situation there is no evidence that his problem exists. Patterson and McClure and Napolitan are concerned primarily with presidential elections, but given Palda's and Rothschild's data, one can question the efficacy of their suggestions if they were to be implemented in the lower level elections where repetition may breed liking [31, 71] and where elections are more numerous.

A point not discussed in the current literature is related to the fourth feature of the European controls. To properly disseminate information to an electorate, one should be more concerned with reach than with frequency, yet most of the discussion has been on frequency. Regardless of the length of the message, provisions could be made for simultaneous broadcast of messages on all media (e.g., a 60-second at 8:59 p.m. each night for one of the major party candidates) to insure high reach. If one were concerned with maximizing reach and information dissemination, the simultaneous use of all broadcast vehicles would be a much better strategy than one of using high levels of frequency (or repetition).

The concepts of message length, reach, and frequency are closely related. Given a finite budget, long messages imply less reach and/or frequency; short messages imply greater reach and/or frequency. Given a finite budget there is an additional tradeoff between reach and frequency. If provisions were made for simultaneous broadcast of messages on all media, a very high level of reach would be obtained. If one were concerned with educating the electorate, this high reach would offset the need for the high levels of frequency now used.

The Rational Voter and Maximum Voter Turnout. Two cornerstones of democracy are the notions of rational voting and maximum voter turnout for elections. An important question to consider is whether political marketing induces "rational"

voting behavior. If rational behavior is defined operationally as any behavior which has a concurrent attitudinal development (as in the involvement model), then the data show that in certain cases this notion has broken down.

In the laboratory experiment it was shown that for the low involvement race attitudinal development was not consistent with behavioral development. The attitudinal measure was a very weak one: the respondent had merely to make a positive or negative statement about the candidate in response to the question, "What went through your mind when you saw the message?" For alternative discussions of the concept of rational political man, see [53, 63]. These discussions also center on cognitive, affective, and conative development.

Data from Palda and from Rothschild show that the level of voter turnout for a particular political race is related positively to the level of advertising in low involvement races. Palda suggests that these two variables may be independent but a function of a third variable, closeness of race. However, Rothschild has shown a more direct relationship in the laboratory where closeness of race is not a consideration.

Both researchers also show a positive relationship between level of advertising for a candidate and selective demand. This relationship is a more burdensome one for it suggests that dollars spent influence votes received in a direct manner.

Should an attempt be made to maximize voter turnout for any election? Consider the case of freedom of political advertising and a subset of voters in the electorate who are not involved with the political process. As the society approaches a maximum level of turnout, a higher percentage of disinterested participants will be included. These voters have been shown to be easier to influence. Perhaps society is best served by those voters who conscientiously participate without being persuaded to do so, and perhaps others should not be induced to join them. A political education perhaps should be emphasized. Simplistic slogans which urge the populace to exercise their franchise may be counterproductive.

Legislation and Judicial Rulings. In this decade, Congress has made two attempts to legislate controls over political campaigns. The 1974 amendment (Public Law 93-443) to the 1971 Campaign Act attempted to impose ceilings on expenditures. In January 1976, the Supreme Court held that many of these limitations were unconstitutional. What insight can marketing research provide into the value of past legislation and judicial rulings and the direction of future legislation?

Several inconsistencies are apparent in the examination of potential legislation. The involvement model and data indicate the need for closer examination of lower level electoral races. Present federal legislation covers only higher level races; states cannot impose controls over the broadcast media to attempt to regulate lower level races because the broadcast media report to the Federal Communications Commission, an arm of the federal government. However, candidates in low level elections rarely have the funding to execute a high repetition campaign.

The 1974 amendments provided a limit on dollar expenditures in House, Senate, and presidential races. For the House, the figures were constant regardless of the population density of the district. For the Senate, the limit varied as a function of the voting-age population but also had a ceiling [47]. What is the impact of such legislation on the marketing efforts of candidates in districts of different population density?

A candidate for the office of representative may spend up to $70,000. The law did not consider the equality of that sum for a candidate whose district comprises a small portion of a large urban area, versus a candidate in a district covering a large rural area, versus a candidate whose district is a medium-sized urban area. In the first case, mass media would deliver the message to many people outside the district but the high media vehicle costs incurred would reflect the overall reach of the medium throughout the urban area. In the second case, there is no wasted reach and the cost is low, but no individual vehicles typically would reach the entire district. In the third case, the range of the vehicle covers roughly the same geographic area as the congressional district. As can be seen in Exhibit 4, the volume of print or broadcast messages available would vary greatly among these three cases and so also would the wasted resources. In Chicago, the cost would inhibit the use of a high repetition campaign, whereas in South Dakota there are inefficiencies even with the low cost. The arbitrary limits can become very important to a nonincumbent who must generate awareness at the start of the campaign despite a limited ceiling.

The key argument in the Supreme Court ruling against the 1974 amendments concerned violation of First Amendment freedoms. It has been established that, to override the First Amendment guarantees, there must be a "clear and present danger." For example, in the case of cigarette advertising, the court believed that the advertising contributed to such a danger to the health of citizens. In the recent rulings against the 1974 amendments, the court held that no such danger existed.

At this time there is little direct evidence of a "clear and present danger" (although one might argue that there is more evidence than in the recent past). However, additional research is needed to determine that such a danger does exist. Though proof is a very tenuous matter in social science research, the involvment model and supporting data make the point that the *potential* for danger exists.

Future Research Needs. The reader undoubtedly has thought of several potential research projects which would refute or support some of the points raised in the discussion. Passing judgment on these points would certainly be premature, but it would be appropriate to pursue some of the researchable questions that have been raised.

In proposing research, one should recall the epistemological issues which in part contributed to the limited effects model. If these research pitfalls are to be avoided, any proposed work should employ both multiple methods and multiple situations. In the research presented here, the data which most clearly imply a political advertising effect came from nonsurvey types of designs (specifically experimental and econometric methods.)

An additional epistemological issue is the use of *actual behavior* as opposed to *behavioral intent* as a dependent variable. Most of the reported research has employed the latter, though the former is certainly a more desirable measure. In the spirit of Ray's [48] research sequence, it would be more efficient to begin a stream of research with laboratory experiments. These experiments *do not* deal with actual behavior, but they *do* allow easy testing of hypotheses. Future research then should replicate these laboratory experiments in field work where the dependent variable is actual behavior. Such a stream would be ideal but not pragmatic because few politicians would allow experimentation during a relatively short campaign in which loss of "market share" could mean removal from office.

EXHIBIT 4
Comparative Returns of Campaign Expenditures: Three Examples

	7th Congressional District Illinois (Chicago)	2nd Congressional District Wisconsin (Madison)	1st Congressional District South Dakota (Eastern SD)
Repetitions of 30-second prime time TV spots on NBC affiliate for $70,000	13	400	333
Repetitions of full-page newspaper ads for $70,000	8	43	64
Repetitions of 1-minute drive time radio spots on leading local stations for $70,000	287	3,333	4,375
Comments:	All mass media give wasted reach due to concentrated population and small geographic area of congressional district. Money is inefficiently spent.	Range of mass media closely corresponds to area of congressional district. Therefore, media use is relatively efficient.	Range of any medium falls short of geographic area of congressional district. It is therefore difficult to reach all voters via mass media.

Research is needed in several specific areas. The basic finding that political advertising affects voting behavior needs to be replicated. Is it indeed true that the number of votes cast for a candidate is related directly to the number of dollars spent by that candidate? Is it also true that there are easily definable situations in which voting behavior is not accompanied by attitudinal development? These important questions need to be carefully researched and then replicated. We in marketing have the tools and techniques to answer these questions and have an obligation to contribute to this area.

Lawmakers have shown a great reluctance in the past to accept data-based statements in the development of legislation. If we are to contribute, our work must be validated, replicated, and subjected to sensitivity analysis.

More specifically, several areas will need to be examined in the spirit of sensitivity analysis to establish what might be termed the bounds of reliability. Following are some questions which should be considered:

1. Are there differential effects of advertising in different levels of electoral races?
2. Are there differential effects of advertising and news (beginning with the trivial case where the messages used are identical)?
3. Are there differential effects given a qualitative message difference?
4. Are there differential effects given varying degrees of closeness of races?

These are not difficult questions in a research sense because we as marketers work with similar ones daily in marketing private-sector goods. There is, though, a great need to have answers to the questions in this neglected policy area.

CONCLUSIONS

Researchers, philosophers, and legislators have considered the topic of political campaign expenditures in the past. Generally, their concerns have been with the control of revenue sources and size of contribution. This emphasis implies that the impact of expenditures on voting behavior is less important which in turn implies that a large number of candidates may be wasting inordinate amounts of money on campaign expenditures. Can marketers help to resolve this seeming inconsistancy? Is there an impact which should be systematically observed and reported? Or is there no impact, and should this not also be reported?

The author has presented several views supporting the notion that political advertising is a public policy problem of concern to marketers. Questions are raised about the limited knowledge in this neglected area. The model presented is one attempt to systematize the search for the necessary underlying data. More work is needed; the importance of this work should be self-evident.

REFERENCES

1. Adamany, D. *Campain Finance in America*. North Scituate, MA: Duxbury, 1972.

2. Benham, T. W. "Polling for a Presidential Candidate: Some Observations on the 1964 Campaign," *Public Opinion Quarterly* 29 (Summer 1965):185–99.

3. Berelson, B. R.; Lazarsfeld, P. F., and McPhee, W. N. *Voting: A Study of Opinion Formation in a Presidential Election*. Chicago: University of Chicago Press, 1954.

4. Blumler, J. G., and McLeod, J. M. "Communication and Voter Turnout in Britain." Paper presented to the Theory and Methodology Division of the Association for Education in Journalism, Fort Collins, Colorado, August 19–22, 1973.

5. ———, and McQuail, D. *Television and Politics: Its Uses and Influence*. Chicago: University of Chicago Press, 1969.

6. British Broadcasting Corporation. *BBC Handbook*. London: White Friars Press, 1974.

7. Calder, B. "When Attitudes Follow Behavior—A Self Perception/Dissonance Interpretation of Low Involvement." Paper presented at American Marketing Association, Attitude Research Conference, Las Vegas, Nevada, March 6–10, 1977.

8. Campbell, A. *Elections and the Political Order*. New York: Wiley, 1966.

9. ———; Converse, P. E.; Miller, W. E., and Stokes, D. E. *The American Voter*. New York: Wiley, 1960.

10. ———, and Cooper, H. C. *Group Differences in Attitude and Votes: A Study of the 1954 Congressional Election*. Ann Arbor: Survey Research Center, Institute for Social Research, University of Michigan, 1956.

11. ———; Gurin, G., and Miller, W. E. *The Voter Decides*. Evanston, IL: Row, Peterson, 1954.

12. Campbell, D., and Fiske, D. "Convergent and Discriminant Validation by the Multitrait-Multimethod Matrix," *Psychology Bulletin* 56 (March 1959):81–105.

13. Chaffee, S. *Political Communication: Issues and Strategies for Research*. Beverly Hills, CA: Sage Publications, 1975.

14. Colley, R. *Defining Advertising Goals for Measured Advertising Results*. New York: Association of National Advertisers, 1961.

15. DeBruicker, F. S., and Robertson, T. S. "An Appraisal of Low Involvement Consumer Information Processing." Paper presented at American Marketing Association, Attitude Research Conference, Las Vegas, Nevada, March 6–10, 1977.

16. Dreyer, E. C. "Media Use and Electoral Choices: Some Political Consequences of Information Exposure." *Public Opinion Quarterly* 35 (Winter 1971–72):545–53.

17. Festinger, L. *A Theory of Cognitive Dissonance*. Evanston, IL: Row, Peterson, 1957.

18. Freedman, J. L. "Involvement, Discrepancy and Change," *Journal of Abnormal and Social Psychology* 69 (September 1964):290–95.

19. Greenwald, H. S. "The Involvement Controversy in Persuasion Research." Unpublished manuscript, Columbia University, 1965.

20. Griese, N. L. "Rosser Reeves and the 1952 Eisenhower TV Spot Blitz." *Journal of Advertising* 4 (1975):34–39.

21. Harrell, G. D. "Involvement in Product Class and Confidence in Beliefs About Brands as Potential Determinants of Attitudes—Behavioral Interest Relationships." Paper presented at American Marketing Association, Attitude Research Conference, Las Vegas, Nevada, March 6–10, 1977.

22. Hyman, H. H., and Sheatsley, P. B. "Some Reasons Why Information Campaigns Fail." *Public Opinion Quarterly* 11 (Fall 1947):413–23.

23. Jennings, M. K., and Ziegler, H. "The Salience of American State Politics." *American Political Science Review* 64 (June 1970):523–35.

24. Johnson, H. H., and Scileppi, J. A. "Effects of Ego-Involvement Conditions on Attitude Change to High and Low Credibility Communicators." *Journal of Personality and Social Psychology* 13 (September 1969):31–36.

25. Kassarjian, H. H., and Kassarjian, W. M. "Attiudes Under Low Involvement Conditions." Paper presented at American Marketing Association, Attitude Research Conference, Las Vegas, Nevada, March 6–10, 1977.

26. Katz, E. "Platforms and Windows: Reflections on the Role of Broadcasting in Election Campaigns." *Journalism Quarterly* 48 (Summer, 1971):304–14.

27. Key, V. O., Jr. *The Responsible electorate*. Cambridge, MA: Harvard University Press, 1966.

28. Klapper, J. T. *The Effects of Mass Communications*. Glencoe, IL: Free Press, 1960.

29. Kline, F. G. "Mass Media and the General Election Process: Evidence

and Speculation." Paper presented at the Syracuse University Conference on Mass Media and American Politics, Syracuse, New York, November 16–18, 1972.

30. Krugman, H. E. "Low Involvement Theory in the Light of New Brain Research." Paper presented at American Marketing Association, Attitude Research Conference, Las Vegas, Nevada, March–10, 1977.

31. ———. "The Impact of Television Advertising: Learning Without Involvement." *Public Opinion Quarterly* 29 (Fall 1965):349–56.

32. Lang, K., and Lang, G. E. "The Mass Media and Voting," In *American Voting Behavior,* edited by E. Burdick and A. J. Brodbeck. Glencoe, IL: Free Press, 1962.

33. Lastovicka, J. L., and Gardner, D. M. "Components of Involvement." Paper presented at American Marketing Association, attitude Research Conference, Las Vegas, Nevada, March 6–10, 1977.

34. Lavidge, R., and Steiner, G. A. "A Model for Predictive Measurements of Advertising Effectiveness." *Journal of Marketing* 25 (October 1961): 59–62.

35. Lazarsfeld, P. F., Berelson, B. R., and Gaudet, H. *The People's Choice.* 2nd ed. New York: Columbia University Press, 1948.

36. Mayer. M. *Madison Avenue, U.S.A.* New York: Harper, 1958.

37. McClure, R. D., and Patterson, T. E. "Television News and Political Advertising: The Impact of Exposure on Voter Beliefs." *Communication Research* 1 (January 1974):3–31.

38. Mickelson, S. *The Electric Mirror.* New York: Dodd, Mead, 1972.

39. Miller, N. "Involvement and Dogmatism as Inhibitors of Attitude Change." *Journal of Experimental Social Psychology* 1 (May 1965): 121–32.

40. Mosteller, F., and Bush, R. "Selected Quantitative Techniques." In *Handbook of Social Psychology,* edited by G. Lindzey. Vol. 1. Reading, MA: Addison-Wesley, 1954, 289–335.

41. Napolitan, J. "Media Costs and Effects in Political Campaigns." *The Annals of the American Academy of Political and Social Science.* 427 (September 1976):114–24.

42. Nimmo, D. *The Political Persuaders.* Englewood Cliffs, NJ: Prentice Hall, 1970.

43. Ostrom, T. M., and Brock, T. C. "A Cognitive Model of Attitudinal Involvement." In *Theories of Cognitive Consistency: A Sourcebook,* edited by R. P. Abelson, et al. Chicago: Rand McNally, 1968.

44. Palda, K. S. "The Effect of Expenditure on Political Success." *Journal of Law and Economics,* December 1975, 745–71.

45. ———. "The Marketing of Political Candidates: An Econometric Exploration of Two Quebec Elections," In *American Marketing Association Combined Conference Proceedings,* edited by T. V. Greer. Chicago: American Marketing Association, 1973.

46. Patterson, T. W., and McClure, R. D. "Television and the Less-Interested Voter: The Costs of an Informed Electorate." *The Annals of the American Academy of Political and Social Science* 425 (May 1976): 88–97.

47. Public Law 93-443; 88 Stat. 1263. Federal Election Campaign Act Amendments of 1974. *Congressional and Administrative News, Vol 1, 93rd Congress, Second Session.* St. Paul, Minnesota: West Publishing, 1974, 1436–86.

48. Ray, M. L. "A Proposal for Validating Measures and Models for Highly Competitive Situations." In *Dynamic Marketing in a Changing World,* edited by B. W. Becker, and H. Becker. Chicago: American Market Association, 1973.

49. ———, and Heeler, R. M. "The Use of the Multitrait and Multimethod Matrix for Trait Development: Cluster Analysis and Nonmetric Scaling Alternatives." Graduate School of Business, Stanford University, 1971.

50. ———; Sawyer, A. G.; Rothschild, M. L.; Heeler, R. M.; Strong, E. C., and Reed, J. B. "Marketing Communication and Hierarchy of Effects." In *New Models for Mass Communication Research, Vol. II. Sage Annual Reviews of Communication Research,* edited by P. Clarke. Beverly Hills: Sage Publications, 1973.

51. Rhine, R. J. and Polowniak, W. A. "Attitude Change, Commitment, and Ego Involvement." *Journal of Personality and Social Psychology* 19 (1971):247–50.

52. ———, and Severence, L. J. "Ego Involvement, Discrepancy, Source Credibility, and Attitude Change." *Journal of Personality and Social Psychology* 16 (October 1970):175–90.

53. Riker, W., and Ordeshook, P. *An Introduction to Positive Political Theory.* Englewood Cliffs, NJ: Prentice Hall, 1973.

54. Rosenberg, J. J. "Cognitive Structure and Attitudinal Affect." *Journal of Abnormal and Social Psychology* 53 (November 1956):367–72.

55. Rossi, P. H. "Trends in Voting Behavior Research: 1933–1963," In *Political Opinion and Electoral Behavior,* edited by E. C. Dreyer and W. A. Rosenbaum. Belmont, CA: Wadsworth Publishing Company, 1966, 67–78.

56. Rothschild, M. L. "Advertising Strategies for High and Low Involvement Situations." Paper presented at American Marketing Association, Attitude Research Conference, Las Vegas, Nevada, March 6–10, 1977.

57. ———. "Involvement as a Determinant of Decision Making Styles." *1975 Combined Proceedings American Marketing Association.* Chicago: American Marketing Association, 1975.

58. ———. "On the Use of Multiple Methods and Multiple Situations in Political Communications Research." In *Political Communication: Issues and Strategies,* edited by S. Chaffee. Beverly Hills, CA: Sage Publications, 1975.

59. ———. "The Effects of Political Advertising on the Voting Behavior of a Low Involvement Electorate." Unpublished Ph.D. dissertation, Stanford University, 1974.

60. ———, and Ray, M. L. "Involvement and Political Advertising Effect: An Exploratory Experiment," *Communications Research* I (July 1974): 264–85.

61. Sears, D. O. "Political Behavior." In *The Handbook of Social Psychology,* Vol. 5, 2nd Ed., edited by G. Lindzey and E. Aronson. Reading, MA: Addison-Wesley, 1969, 315–458.

62. ———, and Freedman, J. L. "Selective Exposure to Information: A Critical Review." *Public Opinion Quarterly* 31 (Summer 1967):194–213.

63. Shapiro, M. J. "Rational Political Man: A Synthesis of Economic and Social-Psychological Perspectives." *American Political Science Review* 63 (September 1969): 1106–19.

64. Sherif, M., and Cantril, H. *The Psychology of Ego Involvement.* New York: Wiley, 1947.

65. ———, and Hovland, C. E. *Social Judgment.* New Haven, CT: Yale University Press, 1964.

66. ———, Sherif, M., and Nebergall, R. W. *Attitude and Attitude Change.* Philadelphia: Saunders, 1965.

67. Trenaman, J., and McQuail, D. *Television and the Political Image.* London: Metheun, 1971.

68. Tyebjee, T. T. "Refinement of the Involvement Concept: An Advertising Planning Point of View." Paper presented at American Marketing Association, Attitude Research Conference, Las Vegas, Nevada, March 6–10, 1977.

69. Welch, W. P. "The Effectiveness of Expenditures in State Legislative Races." *American Politics Quarterly* 4 (July 1976):333–56.

Part III
Organizing for
Marketing Activities

The five chapters in Part III develop a framework for examining public and
nonprofit organizations from a marketing management perspective. Collectively, these readings
demonstrate the need for a market orientation, show how marketing tools and concepts can be used
to develop realistic strategies, and clarify how managers should organize marketing efforts.

The opening chapter provides an overview of the issues involved in managing
a broad cross-section of public service institutions, but subsequent readings focus on such specific
areas as health care, public transportation, fund raising, and family planning. Although specificity is
often necessary to develop a program beyond the conceptual stage, many of the conceptual and
strategic insights gained from examing one type of organization are transferable to other settings.

Chapter 9, "Managing the Public Service Institution," by Peter F. Drucker,
emphasizes that administrators should be attuned to market needs as they seek to define their
institutions' specific functions, purposes, and missions. From such a definition can be derived clear
objectives and goals, a set of priorities, measures of performance and feedback mechanisms. Also
needed are procedures for auditing both objectives and results so that unproductive activities can
be revised or discontinued.

In "Concepts and Strategies for Health Marketers," Christopher H. Lovelock
picks up on the themes developed by Drucker and, in Chapter 2, by Kotler and Levy. Using health
care as an example, this chapter looks at the specific tools and concepts of marketing and at how
they can help managers develop carefully targeted marketing strategies. Misconceptions such
as the idea that marketing consists solely of advertising and selling are quickly dispelled; the
discussion of the marketing mix clearly establishes that marketing extends beyond
communications to include design of the goods or services offered, pricing policies, and delivery of
the resulting product to consumers. Also introduced is the concept of market segmentation, which
is discussed in greater depth in Part IV, "Market Structure Analysis."

It is not enough merely to develop a marketing strategy. Effective implementation
of strategy requires a marketing organization that is attuned to the characteristics of the agency in
question, to the objectives with which it is charged, and to the needs of prospective consumers.
"Organizing the Marketing Function for Transit Authorities" looks at this issue from the perspective of
a public transit operation, but the insights developed by this chapter apply readily to other types of
service organizations. The discussion links back to earlier reviews of the elements of the marketing
mix (Chapters 2, 4 and 6) and to the development of implementation strategies that involve each of

these elements (Chapter 10). A particularly useful contribution of this particular chapter is that it clarifies the job responsibilities assigned to different types of marketing personnel, including product managers, advertising directors, and marketing researchers.

As emphasized earlier by several chapters in Part II, marketing needs to be concerned with resource attraction as well as with the subsequent allocation of resources. Private firms usually seek to finance their activities primarily by selling at a profit the goods and services they produce. The operations of public agencies, by contrast, are financed directly or indirectly through tax revenues. Securing such revenues is hard enough, but the resource attraction task is even more difficult for a nonprofit organization which depends for a substantial proportion of its funding on charitable giving. Obtaining donations is an important marketing activity which has become increasingly sophisticated in recent years. Stanley R. McAnally's chapter, "Fund Raising: Development of an Annual Giving Program" highlights the steps required to organize an effective annual fundraising program. Although the specific context of this chapter is charitable giving to colleges and universities, many of the basic principles apply equally to fundraising for other types of nonprofit organizations. This reading provides important insights into such issues as timing considerations, tailoring of efforts to different market segments, and coordination of volunteer efforts.

The final chapter in Part III is concerned with relationships between a specific agency and the other institutions that are involved in development of its marketing efforts. The specific thrust of Richard K. Manoff's article, "The Mass Media Family Planning Campaign for the United States," is the constraints imposed upon preparation and implementation of a major advertising campaign designed to promote family planning. This chapter demonstrates the types of disputes that may arise over matters of taste or conscience, the roadblocks that can be thrown up, and the relatively weak position held by nonprofit organizations when negotiating with the media for free public-service advertising.

9
Managing the Public Service Institution

Peter F. Drucker

Service institutions are an increasingly important part of our society. Schools and universities; research laboratories; public utilities; hospitals and other health-care institutions; professional, industry, and trade associations; and many others—all these are as much "institutions" as is the business firm, and, therefore, are equally in need of management.[1] They all have people who are designated to exercise the management function and who are paid for doing the management job—even though they may not be called "managers," but "administrators," "directors," "executives," or some other such title.

These "public service" institutions—to give them a generic name—are the real growth sector of a modern society. Indeed, what we have now is a "multi-institutional" society rather than a "business" society. The traditional title of the American college course still tends to read "Business and Government." But this is an anachronism. It should read "Business, Government, and Many Others."

All public service institutions are being paid for out of the economic surplus produced by economic activity. The growth of the service institutions in this century is thus the best testimonial to the success of business in discharging its economic task. Yet unlike, say, the early 19th-century university, the service institutions are not mere "luxury" or "ornament." They are, so to speak, main pillars of a modern society, load-bearing members of the main structure. They *have* to perform if society and economy are to function. It is not only that these service institutions are a major expense of a modern society; half of the personal income of the United States (and of most of the other developed countries) is spent on public service institutions (including those operated by the government). Compared to these "public service" institutions, both the "private sector" (i.e., the economy of goods) and the traditional government functions of law, defense, and public order, account for a smaller share of the total income flow of today's developed societies than they did around 1900 —despite the cancerous growth of military spending.

Every citizen in the developed, industrialized, urbanized societies depends for his very survival on the performance of the public service institutions. These institutions also

---

[1] Government agencies and bureaus are also "service institutions," of course, and have management problems which are comparable to those of the institutions I have mentioned. But because they also partake of a general "governmental" purpose, not usefully defined in management terms, I shall not be dealing with them in this article. I shall feel free, however, to include such quasi-governmental organizations as the TVA or the post office in my discussion.

Peter F. Drucker is Clarke Professor of Social Sciences, Claremont Graduate School.

Reprinted by permission of *The Public Interest,* No. 33 (Fall 1973):43–60. Copyright © 1973 by National Affairs, Inc. This article is condensed from several chapters of *Management: Tasks; Responsibilities; Practices* (New York: Harper & Row, 1974). No part of this article may be reproduced in any form without prior written permission from the publisher.

embody the values of developed societies. For it is in the form of education and health care, knowledge and mobility —rather than primarily in the form of more "food, clothing, and shelter"—that our society obtains the fruits of its increased economic capacities and productivity.

Yet the evidence for performance in the service institutions is not impressive, let alone overwhelming. Schools, hospitals, universities are all big today beyond the imagination of an earlier generation. They all dispose of astronomical budgets. Yet everywhere they are "in crisis." A generation or two ago, their performance was taken for granted. Today, they are being attacked on all sides for lack of performance. Services which the 19th century managed with aplomb and aparently with little effort—the postal service, for instance —are deeply in the red, require enormous and ever-growing subsidies, and yet give poorer service everywhere. In every country the citizen complains ever more loudly of "bureauracy" and mismanagement in the institutions that are supposed to serve him.

ARE SERVICE INSTITUTIONS MANAGEABLE?

The response of the service institutions to this criticism has been to become "management conscious." They increasingly turn to business to learn "management." In all service institutions, "manager development," "management by objectives," and many other concepts and tools of business management are becoming increasingly popular. This is a healthy sign—but no more than that. It does not mean that the service institutions understand the problems of managing themselves. It only means that they have begun to realize that, at present, they are not being managed.

Yet, though "performance" in the public service institutions is the exception rather than the rule, the exceptions do prove that service institutions can perform. Among American public service agencies of the last 40 years, for instance, there is the Tennessee Valley Authority (TVA), the big regional electric-power and irrigation project in the Southeastern United States. (TVA's performance was especially notable during its early years, in the 1930's and 1940's, when it was headed by David Lilienthal.) While a great many— perhaps most—schools in the inner-city, black ghettos of America deserve all the strictures of the "deschooling" movement, a few schools in the very worst ghettos (e.g., in New York's South Bronx) have shown high capacity to make the most "disadvantaged" children acquire the basic skills of literacy.

What is it that the few successful service institutions do (or eschew) that makes them capable of performance? This is the question to ask. And it is a *management* question —of a special kind. In most respects, the service institution is not very different from a business exterprise. It faces similar—if not precisely the same—challenges in seeking to make work productive. It does not differ significantly from a business in its "social responsibility." Nor does the service

institution differ very much from business enterprise in respect to the manager's work and job, in respect to organizational design and structure, or even in respect to the job and structure of top management. *Internally,* the differences tend to be differences in terminology rather than in substance.

But the service institution is in a fundamentally different "business" from business. It is different in its purpose. It has different values. It needs different objectives. And it makes a different contribution to society. "Performance and results" are quite different in a service institution from what they are in a business. "Managing for performance" is the one area in which the service institution differs significantly from a business.

WHY SERVICE INSTITUTIONS DO NOT PERFORM

There are three popular explanations for the common failure of service institutions to perform:

1. Their managers aren't "businesslike";
2. They need "better people";
3. Their objectives and results are "intangible."

All three are alibis rather than explanations.

"BUSINESSLIKE" MANAGERS

The service institution will perform, it is said again and again, if only it is managed in a "businesslike" manner. Colbert, the great minister of Louis XIV, was the first to blame the performance difficulties of the non-business, the service institution, on this lack of "businesslike" management. Colbert, who created the first "modern" public service in the West, never ceased to exhort his officials to be "businesslike." The cry is still being repeated every day—by chambers of commerce, by presidential and royal commissions, by ministers in the Communist countries, and so on. If only, they all say, their administrators were to behave in a "businesslike" way, service institutions would perform. And of course, this belief also underlies, in large measure, today's "management boom" in the service institutions.

But it is the wrong diagnosis; and being "businesslike" is the wrong prescription for the ills of the service institution. The service institution has performance trouble precisely because it is *not* a business. What being "businesslike" usually means in a service institution is little more than control of cost. What characterizes a business, however, is focus on results—return on capital, share of market, and so on.

To be sure, there is a need for efficiency in all institutions. Because there is usually no competition in the service field, there is no outward and imposed cost control on service institutions as there is on business in a competitive (and even an oligopolistic) market. But the basic problem of service institutions is not high cost but lack of effectiveness. They may be very efficient—some are. But they then tend not to do the right things.

The belief that the public service institution will perform if only it is put on a "businesslike" basis underlies the numerous attempts to set up many government services as separate "public corporations"—again an attempt that dates back to Colbert and his establishment of "Crown monopolies." There may be beneficial side effects, such as freedom from petty civil service regulation. But the intended main effect, performance, is seldom achieved. Costs may go down (though not always; setting up London Transport and the British Post Office as separate "businesslike" corporations, and thereby making them defenseless against labor union pressures, has led to skyrocketing costs). But services essential to the fulfillment of the institution's purpose may be slighted or lopped off in the name of "efficiency."

The best and worst example of the "businesslike" approach in the public service institution may well be the Port of New York Authority, set up in the 1920's to manage automobile and truck traffic throughout the two-state area (New York and New Jersey) of the Port of New York. The Port Authority has, from the beginning, been "businesslike" with a vengeance. The engineering of its bridges, tunnels, docks, silos, and airports has been outstanding. Its construction costs have been low and under control. Its financial standing has been extremely high, so that it could always borrow at most advantageous rates of interest. It made being "businesslike"—as measured, above all, by its standing with the banks—its goal and purpose. As a result, it did not concern itself with transportation policy in the New York metropolitan area, even though its bridges, tunnels, and airports generate much of the traffic in New York's streets. It did not ask: "Who are our constituents?" Instead it resisted any such question as "political" and "unbusinesslike." Consequently, it has come to be seen as the villain of the New York traffic and transportation problem. And when it needed support (e.g., in finding a place to put New York's badly needed fourth airport), it found itself without a single backer, except the bankers. As a result the Port Authority may well become "politicized"; that is, denuded of its efficiency without gaining anything in effectiveness.

"BETTER PEOPLE"

The cry for "better people" is even older than Colbert. In fact, it can be found in the earliest Chinese texts on government. In particular, it has been the constant demand of all American "reformers," from Henry Adams shortly after the Civil War, to Ralph Nader today. They all have believed that the one thing lacking in the government agency is "better people."

But service institutions cannot, any more than business, depend on "supermen" to staff their managerial and executive positions. There are far too many institutions to be staffed. If service institutions cannot be run and managed by men of normal—or even fairly low—endowment, if, in other words, we cannot organize the task so that it will be done on a satisfactory level by men who only try hard, it cannot be done at all. Moreover, there is no reason to believe that the people who staff the managerial and professional positions in our "service" institutions are any less qualified, any less competent or honest, or any less hard-working than the men who manage businesses. By the same token, there is no reason to believe that business managers, put in control of service institutions, would do better than the "bureaucrats." Indeed, we know that they immediately become "bureaucrats" themselves.

One example of this was the American experience during World War II, when large numbers of business executives who had performed very well in their own companies moved into government positions. Many rapidly became "bureaucrats." The men did not change. But whereas in business they had been capable of obtaining performance and results, in government they found themselves producing primarily procedures and red tape—and deeply frustrated by the experience.

Similarly, effective businessmen who are promoted to head a "service staff" within a business (e.g., the hard-hitting sales manager who gets to be "Vice President—marketing services") tend to become "bureaucrats" almost overnight. Indeed, the "service institutions" within business—R&D departments, personnel staffs, marketing or manufacturing service staffs, and the like—apparently find it just as hard to perform as the public service institutions of society at large, which businessmen often criticize as being "unbusinesslike" and run by "bureaucrats."

"INTANGIBLE" OBJECTIVES

The most sophisticated and, at first glance, the most plausible explanation for the non-performance of service institutions is the last one: The objectives of service institutions are "intangible," and so are their results. This is at best a half-truth.

The definition of what "our business is" is always "intangible," in a business as well as in a service institution. Surely, to say, as Sears Roebuck does, "Our business is to be the informed buyer for the American family," is "intangible." And to say, as Bell Telephone does, "Our business is service to the customers," may sound like a pious and empty platitude. At first glance, these statements would seem to defy any attempt at translation into operational, let alone quantitative, terms. To say, "Our business is electronic entertainment," as Sony of Japan does, is equally "intangible," as is IBM's definition of its business as "data processing." Yet, as these businesses have clearly demonstrated it is not exceedingly difficult to derive concrete and measurable goals and targets from "intangible" definitions like those cited above.

"Saving souls," as the definition of the objectives of a church is, indeed, "intangible." At least the bookkeeping is not of this world. But church attendance is measurable. And so is "getting the young people back into the church."

"The development of the whole personality" as the objective of the school is, indeed, "intangible." But "teaching a child to read by the time he has finished third grade" is by no means intangible; it can be measured easily and with considerable precision.

"Abolishing racial discrimination" is equally unamenable to clear operational definition, let alone measurement. But to increase the number of black apprentices in the building trades is a quantifiable goal, the attainment of which can be measured.

Achievement is never possible except against specific, limited, clearly defined targets, in business as well as in a service institution. Only if targets are defined can resources be allocated to their attainment, priorities and deadlines be set, and somebody be held accountable for results. But the starting point for effective work is a definition of the purpose and mission of the institution—which is almost always "intangible," but nevertheless need not be vacuous.

It is often said that service institutions differ from businesses in that they have a plurality of constituencies. And it is indeed the case that service institutions have a great many "constitutents." The school is of vital concern not only to children and their parents, but also to teachers, to taxpayers, and to the community at large. Similarly, the hospital has to satisfy the patient, but also the doctors, the nurses, the technicians, the patient's family—as well as taxpayers or, as in the U.S., employers and labor unions who through their insurance contributions provide the bulk of the support of most hospitals. But business also has a plurality of constituencies. Every business has at least two different customers, and often a good many more. And employers, investors, and the community at large—and even management itself—are also "constituencies."

MISDIRECTION BY BUDGET

The one basic difference between a service institution and a business is the way the service institution is paid. Businesses (other than monopolies) are paid for satisfying the customer. They are only paid when they produce what the customer wants and what he is willing to exchange his purchasing power for. Satisfaction of the customer is, therefore, the basis for performance and results in a business.

Service institutions, by contrast, are typically paid out of a budget allocation. Their revenues are allocated from a general revenue stream that is not tied to what they are doing, but is obtained by tax, levy, or tribute. Furthermore, the typical service institution is endowed with monopoly powers; the intended beneficiary usually has no choice.

Being paid out of a budget allocation changes what is meant by "performance" or "results." *"Results" in the budget-based institution means a larger budget. "Performance" is the ability to maintain or to increase one's budget.*

The first test of a budget-based institution and the first requirement for its survival is to obtain the budget. And the budget is, by definition, related not to the achievement of any goals, but to the *intention* of achieving those goals.

This means, first, that efficiency and cost control, however much they are being preached, are not really considered virtues in the budget-based institution. The importance of a budget-based institution is measured essentially by the size of its budget and the size of its staff. To achieve results with a smaller budget or a smaller staff is, therefore, not "performance." It might actually endanger the institution. Not to spend the budget to the hilt will only convince the budget-maker—whether a legislature or a budget committee—that the budget for the next fiscal period can safely be cut.

Thirty or 40 years ago, it was considered characteristic of Russian planning, and one of its major weaknesses, that Soviet managers, towards the end of the plan period, engaged in a frantic effort to spend all the money allocated to them, which usually resulted in total waste. Today, the disease has become universal, as budget-based institutions have become dominant everywhere. And "buying-in"—that is, getting approval for a new program or project by grossly underestimating its total cost—is also built into the budget-based institution.

"Parkinson's Law" lampooned the British Admiralty and the British Colonial Office for increasing their staffs and their budgets as fast as the British Navy and the British Empire went down. "Parkinson's Law" attributed this to inborn human perversity. But it is perfectly rational behavior for someone on a budget, since it is the budget, after all, that measures "performance" and "importance."

It is obviously not compatible with *efficiency* that the acid test of performance should be to obtain the budget. But *effectiveness* is even more endangered by reliance on the budget allocation. It makes it risky to raise the question of what the "business" of the institution should be. That question is always "controversial"; such controversy is likely to alienate support and will therefore be shunned by the budget-based institution. As a result, it is likely to wind up deceiving both the public and itself.

Take an instance from government: The U.S. Department of Agriculture has never been willing to ask whether its goal should be "farm productivity" or "support of the small family farm." It has known for decades that these two objectives are not identical as had originally been assumed, and that they are, indeed, becoming increasingly incompatible. To admit this, however, would have created controversy that might have endangered the Department's budget. As a result, American farm policy has frittered away an enormous amount of money and human resources on what can only (and charitably) be called a public relations campaign, that is, on a show of support for the small family farmer. The effective activities, however—and they have been very effective indeed—have been directed toward eliminating the small family farmer and replacing him by the far more productive "agribusinesses," that is, highly capitalized and highly mechanized farms, run as a business and not as a "way of life." This may well have been the right thing to do. But it certainly was not what the Department was founded to do, nor what the Congress, in approving the Department's budget, expected it to do.

Take a non-governmental example, the American community hospital, which is "private" though "non-profit." Everywhere it suffers from a growing confusion of missions and objectives, and the resulting impairment of its effectiveness and performance. Should a hospital be, in effect, a "physician's facility"—as most older American physicians still maintain? Should it focus on the major health needs of a community? Or should it try to do everything and be "abreast of every medical advance," no matter what the cost and no matter how rarely certain facilities will be used? Should it devote resources to preventive medicine and health education? Or should it, like the hospital under the British health service, confine itself strictly to repair of major health damage after it has occurred?

Every one of these definitions of the "business" of the hospital can be defended. Every one deserves a hearing. The effective American hospital will be a multi-purpose institution and strike a balance between various objectives. What most hospitals do, however, is pretend that there are no basic question to be decided. The result, predictably, is confusion and impairment of the hospital's capacity to serve any function and to carry out any mission.

PLEASING EVERYONE AND ACHIEVING NOTHING

Dependence on a budget allocation militates against setting priorities and concentrating efforts. Yet nothing is ever accomplished unless scarce resources are concentrated on a small number of priorities. A shoe manufacturer who has 22 percent of the market for work shoes may have a profitable business. If he succeeds in raising his market share to 30 percent, especially if the market for his kind of footwear is expanding, he is doing very well indeed. He need not concern himself too much with the 78 percent of the users of work shoes who buy from somebody else. And the customers for ladies' fashion shoes are of no concern to him at all.

Contrast this with the situation of an institution on a budget. To obtain its budget, it needs the approval, or at least the acquiescence, of practically everybody who remotely could be considered a "constituent." Where a market share of 22 percent might be perfectly satisfactory to a business, a "rejection" by 78 percent of its "constituents"—or even by a much smaller proportion—would be fatal to a budget-based institution. And this means that the service institution finds it difficult to set priorities; it must instead try to placate everyone by doing a little bit of everything—which, in effect, means achieving nothing.

Finally, being budget-based makes it even more difficult to abandon the wrong things, the old, the obsolete.

As a result, service institutions are even more encrusted than businesses with the barnacles of inherently unproductive efforts.

No institution likes to abandon anything it does. Business is no exception. But in an institution that is being paid for its performance and results, the unproductive, the obsolete, will sooner or later be killed off by the customers. In a budget-based institution no such discipline is being enforced. The temptation is great, therefore, to respond to lack of results by redoubling efforts. The temptation is great to double the budget, precisely *because* there is no performance.

Human beings will behave as they are rewarded for behaving—whether the reward be money and promotion, a medal, an autographed picture of the boss, or a pat on the back. This is one lesson the behavioral psychologist has taught us during the last 50 years (not that it was unknown before). A business, or any institution that is paid for its results and performance in such a way that the dissatisfied or disinterested customer need not pay, has to "earn" its income. An institution that is financed by a budget—or that enjoys a monopoly which the customer cannot escape—is rewarded for what it "deserves" rather than for what it "earns." It is paid for good intentions and for "programs." It is paid for not alienating important constituents rather than for satisfying any one group. It is misdirected, by the way it is paid, into defining "performance" and "results" as what will maintain or increase its budget.

WHAT WORKS

The exception, the comparatively rare service institution that achieves effectiveness, is more instructive than the great majority that achieves only "programs." It shows that effectiveness in the service institution is achievable—though by no means easy. It shows what different kinds of service institutions can do and need to do. It shows limitations and pitfalls. But it also shows that the service institution manager can do unpopular and highly "controversial" things if only he makes the risk-taking decision to set priorities and allocate resources.

The first and perhaps simplest example is that of the Bell Telephone System. A telephone system is a "natural" monopoly. Within a given area, one supplier of telephone service must have exclusive rights. The one thing any subscriber to a public telephone service requires is access to all other subscribers, which means territorial exclusivity for one monopolistic service. And as a whole country or continent becomes, in effect, one telephone system, this monopoly has to be extended over larger and larger areas.

An individual may be able to do without a telephone—though in today's society only at prohibitive inconvenience. But a professional man, a tradesman, an office, or a business *must* have a telephone. Residential phone service may still be an "option." Business phone service is compulsory. Theodore Vail, the first head of the organization, saw this in the early years of this century. He also saw clearly that the American telephone system, like the telephone systems in all other industrially developed nations, could easily be taken over by government. To prevent this, Vail thought through what the telephone company's business was and should be, and came up with his famous definition: "Our business is service."[2] This totally "intangible" statement of the telephone company's "business" then enabled Vail to set specific goals and objectives and to develop measurements of performance and results. His "customer satisfaction" standards and "service satisfaction" standards created nationwide competition between telephone managers in various areas, and became the criteria by which the managers were judged and rewarded. These standards measured performance as defined by the customer, e.g., waiting time before an operator came on the line, or time between application for telephone service and its installation. They were meant to direct managers' attention to results.

Vail also thought through who his "constituents" were. This led to his conclusion—even more shocking to the conventional wisdom of 1900 than his "service" objectives —that it was the telephone company's task to make the public utility commissions of the individual states capable of effective rate regulation. Vail argued that a national monopoly in a crucial area could expect to escape nationalization only by being regulated. Helping to convert the wretchedly ineffectual, corrupt, and bumbling public utility commissions of late 19th-century populism into effective, respected, and informed adversaries was in the telephone company's own survival interest.

Finally, Vail realized that a telephone system depends on its ability to obtain capital. Each dollar of telephone revenue requires a prior investment of three to four dollars. Therefore, the investor too had to be considered a "constituent," and the telephone company had to design financial instruments and a financial policy that focused on the needs and expectations of the investor, and that made telephone company securities, whether bonds or shares, a distinct and preferred financial "product."

THE AMERICAN UNIVERSITY

The building of the American university from 1860 to World War I also illustrates how service institutions can be made to perform. The American university as it emerged during that era was primarily the work of a small number of men: Andrew D. White (President of Cornell, 1868–85); Charles W. Eliot (President of Harvard, 1869–1909); Daniel Coit Gilman (President of Johns Hopkins, 1876–1901); David Starr Jordan (President of Stanford, 1891–1913); William

Rainey Harper (President of Chicago, 1892–1904); and Nicholas Murray Butler (President of Columbia, 1902–1945).

These men all had in common one basic insight: The traditional "college"—essentially an 18th-century seminary to train preachers—had become totally obsolete, sterile, and unproductive. Indeed, it was dying fast; America in 1860 had far fewer college students than it had had 40 years earlier with a much smaller population. The men who built the new universities shared a common objective: to create a new institution, a true "university." And they all realized that while European examples, especially Oxford and Cambridge and the German university, had much to offer, these new universities had to be distinctively American institutions.

Beyond these shared beliefs, however, they differed sharply on what a university should be and what its purpose and mission were. Eliot, at Harvard, saw the purpose of the university as that of educating a leadership group with a distinct "style." His Harvard was to be a "national" institution rather than the parochial preserve of the "proper Bostonian" that Harvard College had been. But it also was to restore to Boston—and to New England generally—the dominant position of a moral elite, such as in earlier times had been held by the "Elect," the Puritan divines, and their successors, the Federalist leaders in the early days of the Republic. Butler, at Columbia—and, to a lesser degree, Harper at Chicago—saw the function of the university as the systematic application of rational thought and analysis to the basic problems of a modern society, from education to economics, and from domestic government to foreign affairs. Gilman, at Johns Hopkins, saw the university as the producer of advanced knowledge; indeed, originally Johns Hopkins was to confine itself to advanced research and was to give no undergraduate instruction. White, at Cornell, aimed at producing an "educated public."

Each of these men knew that he had to make compromises. Each knew that he had to saisfy a number of "constituencies" and "publics," each of whom looked at the university quite differently. Both Eliot and Butler, for instance, had to build their new university on an old foundation (the others could build from the ground up) and had to satisfy —or at least to placate—existing alumni and faculty. They all had to be exceedingly conscious of the need to attract and hold financial support. It was Eliot, for instance, with all his insistence on "moral leadership," who invented the first "placement office" and set out to find well-paying jobs for Harvard graduates, especially in business. It was Butler, conscious that Columbia was a late-comer and that the millionaire philanthropists of his day had already been snared by his competitors (e.g., Rockefeller by Chicago), who invented the first "public relations" office in a university, designed—and most successfully—to reach the merely well-to-do and get their money.

These founders' definitions did not outlive them. Even during the lifetime of Eliot and Butler, for instance, their in-

---

[2] This was so heretical that the directors of the telephone company fired Vail when he first propounded his thesis in 1897—only to rehire him 10 years later when the absence of clear performance objectives had created widespread public demand for telephone nationalization even among such non-radicals as the Progressive wing of the Republican Party.

stitutions escaped their control, began to diffuse objectives and to confuse priorities. In the course of this century, all these universities—and many others, like the University of California and other major state universities—have converged towards a common type. Today, it is hard to tell one "multiversity" from another. Yet the imprint of the founders has still not been totally erased. It is hardly an accident that the New Deal picked faculty members primarily from Columbia and Chicago to be high-level advisors and policy makers; for the New Deal was, of course, committed to the application of rational thought and analysis to public policies and problems. And 30 years later, when the Kennedy Administration came in with an underlying belief in the "style" of an "elite," it naturally turned to Harvard. For while each of the founding fathers of the modern American university made compromises and adapted to a multitude of constituencies, each had an objective and a definition of the university to which he gave priority and against which he measured performance. Clearly, the job the founders did almost a century ago will have to be done again for today's "multiversity," if it is not to choke on its own services.

SCHOOLS, HOSPITALS, AND THE TVA

The English "open classroom" is another example of a successful service institution. It is being promoted in this country as the "child-centered" approach to schooling, but its origin was in the concern with performance, and that is also the secret of its success. The English "open classroom" demands that each child—or at least each normal child—acquire the same measurable proficiency in the basic skills of literacy at roughly the same time. It is then the teacher's task to think through the learning path best suited to lead each child to a common and pre-set goal. The objectives are perfectly clear: the learning of specific skills, especially reading, writing, and figuring. They are identical for all children, measurable, and measured. Everything else is, in effect, considered irrelevant. Such elementary schools as have performed in the urban slums of this country—and there are more of them than the current "crisis in the classroom" syndrome acknowledges—have done exactly the same thing. The performing schools in black or Puerto Rican neighborhoods in New York, for instance, are those that have defined one clear objective—usually to teach reading—have eliminated or subordinated everything else, and then have measured themselves against a standard of clearly set performance goals.

The solution to the problem of the hospital, as is becoming increasingly clear, will similarly lie in thinking through objectives and priorities. The most promising approach may well be one worked out by the Hospital Consulting Group at Westinghouse Electric Corporation, which recognizes that the American hospital has a multiplicity of functions, but organizes each as an autonomous "decentralized" division with its own facilities, its own staff, and

its own objectives. There would thus be a traditional care hospital for the fairly small number of truly sick people who require what today's "full-time" hospital offers; an "ambulatory" medical hospital for diagnosis and out-patient work; an "ambulatory" surgical hospital for the large number of surgical patients—actually the majority—who, like patients after cataract surgery, a tonsilectomy, or most orthopedic surgery, are not "sick" and need no medical and little nursing care, but need a bed (and a bedpan) till the stitches are firm or the cast dries; a psychiatric unit—mostly for outpatient or overnight care; and a convalescent unit that would hardly differ from a good motel (e.g., for the healthy mother of a healthy baby). All these would have common services. But each would be a separate health care facility with different objectives, different priorities, and different standards of performance.

But the most instructive example of an effective service institution may be that of the early Tennessee Valley Authority. Built mainly during the New Deal, the TVA today is no longer "controversial." It is just another large power company, except for being owned by the government rather than by private investors. But in its early days, 40 years ago, the TVA was a slogan, a battle cry, a symbol. Some, friends and enemies alike, saw in it the opening wedge of the nationalization of electric energy in the United States. Others saw in it the vehicle for a return to Jeffersonian agrarianism, based on cheap power, government paternalism, and free fertilizer. Still others were primarily interested in flood control and navigation. Indeed, there was such a wealth of conflicting expectations that TVA's first head, Arthur Morgan, a distinguished engineer and economist, completely floundered. Unable to think through what the business of the TVA should be and how varying objectives might be balanced, Morgan accomplished nothing. Finally, President Roosevelt replaced him with an almost totally unknown young lawyer, David Lilienthal, who had little previous experience as an administrator.

Lilenthal faced up to the need to define the TVA's business. He concluded that the first objective was to build truly efficient electric plants and to supply an energy-starved region with plentiful and cheap power. All the rest, he decided, hinged on the attainment of this first need, which then became his operational priority. The TVA of today has accomplished a good many other objectives as well, from flood control and navigation to fertilizer production and, indeed, even balanced community development. But it was Lilienthal's insistence on a clear definition of the TVA's business and on setting priorities that explains why today's TVA is taken for granted, even by the very same people who, 40 years ago, were among its implacable enemies.

THE REQUIREMENTS FOR SUCCESS

Service institutions are a most diverse lot. The one and only thing they all have in common is that, for one reason or another, they cannot be organized under a competitive market test.[3] But however diverse the various kinds of "service institutions" may be, all of them need first to impose on themselves the discipline practiced by the managers and leaders of the institutions in the examples presented above.

1. They need to answer the question, *"What is our business and what should it be?"* They need to bring out into the open alternative definitions and to think them through carefully, perhaps even to work out (as did the presidents of the emerging American universities) the balance of different and sometimes conflicting definitions. What service institutions need is not to be more "businesslike." They need to be more "hospital-like," "university-like," "government-like," and so on. They need to be subjected to a performance test—if only to that of "socialist competition"—as much as possible. In other words, they need to think through their own specific function, purpose, and mission.

2. Service institutions need to derive *clear objectives and goals* from their definition of function and mission. What they need is not "better people," but people who do the management job systematically and who focus themselves and their institutions purposefully on performance and results. They do need efficiency—that is, control of costs. But, above all, they need effectiveness—that is, emphasis on the right results.

3. They then have to think through *priorities* of concentration which enable them to select targets; to set standards of accomplishment and performance (that is, to define the minimum acceptable results); to set deadlines; to go to work on results; and to make someone accountable for results.

4. They need to define *measurements of performance*—the "customer satisfaction" measurements of the telephone company, or the figures on reading performance by which the English "open classroom" measures its accomplishments.

5. They need to use these measurements to *"feed back"* on their efforts—that is, *they must build self-control from results into their system*.

---

[3] This may no longer be necessarily true for the postal service. At last an independent postal company in the U.S. is trying to organize a business in competition to the government's postal monopoly. Should this work out, it might do more to restore performance to the mails than the recent setting up of a postal monopoly as a separate "public corporation" which is on a "businesslike" basis.

6. Finally, they need an organized audit of *objectives and results,* so as to identify those objectives that no longer serve a useful purpose or have proven unattainable. They need to identify unsatisfactory performance, and activities which are obsolete, unproductive, or both. And they need a mechanism for *sloughing off* such activities rather than wasting their money and their energies where the results are not.

This last requirement may be the most important one. The absence of a market test removes from the service institution the discipline that forces a business eventually to abandon yesterday's products—or else go bankrupt. Yet this requirement is the least understood.

No success lasts "forever." Yet it is even more difficult to abandon yesterday's success than it is to reappraise failure. Success breeds its own *hubris*. It creates emotional attachments, habits of thought and action, and, above all, false self-confidence. A success that has outlived its usefulness may, in the end, be more damaging than failure. Especially in a service institution, yesterday's success becomes "policy," "virtue," "conviction," if not indeed "Holy Writ," unless the institution imposes on itself the discipline of thinking through its mission, its objectives, and its priorities, and of building in feedback control from results over policies, priorities, and action. We are in such a "welfare mess" today in the United States largely because the welfare program of the New Deal had been such a success in the 1930's that we could not abandon it, and instead misapplied it to the radically different problem of the black migrants to the cities in the 1950's and 1960's.

To make service institutions perform, it should by now be clear, does not require "great men." It requires instead a system. The essentials of this system may not be too different from the essentials of performance in a business enterprise, as the present "management boom" in the service institutions assumes. But the application will be quite different. For the service institutions are not businesses; "performance" means something quite different for them.

Few service institutions today suffer from having too few administrators; most of them are over-administered, and suffer from a surplus of procedures, organization charts, and "management techniques." What now has to be learned—it is still largely lacking—is to manage service institutions for performance. This may well be the biggest and most important management task for the remainder of this century.

10

Concepts and Strategies for Health Marketers

Christopher H. Lovelock

Professionals in the health care field are coming to recognize the value of marketing concepts and strategies in helping them do a more effective job of designing and delivering health care services and of developing and implementing health education programs. But despite the interest in marketing, it is often misperceived and misused. Clarification of key marketing concepts and their strategic implications may provide helpful guidelines for health care marketers.

Many people mistakenly equate marketing with advertising and selling, but in practice, the field is much broader. It is often divided into four major elements known as the *Marketing Mix,* namely (1) Product, (2) Price, (3) Distribution, and (4) Communications. As will be seen, advertising, selling, and public relations are simply part of the communications element of the mix.

THE CONCEPTS OF PRODUCT AND EXCHANGE

Marketers use the word product in a generic sense to denote what is being offered in the marketplace. It could be a physical good such as toothpaste or a new drug, or a service such as a haircut, X-ray, or eye-refraction. Alternatively, it might be something as intangible as a politician offering a political platform, a college offering an education, or an agency holding out the promise of better health through improved nutrition.

Central to marketing is the concept of exchange—consumers giving something in exchange for the product. While money is the most common quid pro quo, time and other personal variables may also constitute part of the exchange transaction.

PRICING CONSIDERATIONS

In those situations where products are sold rather than given away, and there is a dollar price attached, purchasing decisions may be influenced not only by the level of price charged, in dollars and cents, but also by how the price may be paid: Are all transactions strictly cash or are checks and credit cards accepted? Are credit terms offered and, if so, what are they?

However, there may be other sorts of costs incurred by the individual in addition to financial ones; these may include

Christopher H. Lovelock is Associate Professor of Business Administration, Harvard University.

time and inconvenience as well as the psychic cost associated with changing established values and behavior patterns with which the individual feels comfortable—overcoming personal fears or risking social disapproval by others. Sometimes people are reluctant to use a product or service that is offered free of charge or to adopt new behavior patterns because the non-dollar costs outweigh the apparent benefits.

DISTRIBUTION

The selection of a distribution strategy—the place where the product is available—may be a very significant factor in determining a marketer's success or failure. Often consumers can obtain similar products or services from a variety of different retail outlets. The choice of a particular retail outlet may be made as much on the basis of the convenience of the location, the appearance and atmosphere of the facility, and the helpfulness and expertise of the sales staff, as on the extent, quality, and value of the merchandise or services sold there.

Proximity of customers to the source of a service can affect both demand for the service and the degree of satisfaction with it. Consumer analysis has often led to the relocation of sources of services closer to users' locations. For example, government agencies providing social and welfare services utilized primarily by low income or elderly groups are increasingly thinking in terms of locating their offices in or near the neighborhood in which these people live rather than downtown. Bus routes established years ago are now being re-routed to take into account new travel patterns resulting from changing home, shopping, and employment locations.

Hospitals, especially older ones, are often located in deteriorating central city locations with limited parking. This may serve to discourage use by middle income people who have moved out to the suburbs where newer, more attractive and more conveniently located competitors may be found. Since it may not be desirable or feasible to move the building, marketing strategies for dealing with this situation might include developing outside clinics in locations near target consumers, provision of improved access (such as the institution of a shuttle bus service from a suitable parking lot elsewhere), or construction of parking facilities providing safe, direct access to the hospital buildings.

THE ROLE OF COMMUNICATIONS

Communications policy is a critical ingredient in virtually all marketing programs. Even a well-designed product or service intended to satisfy a demonstrable consumer need is unlikely to achieve much success unless target consumers (1) are aware that it exists, (2) understand what it is supposed to do for them, and (3) have at least some idea of where and how to obtain and use it.

Note that I have described communications as "a critical ingredient" in marketing. All too many times, nonbusiness marketers take product, price, and place as given,

viewing advertising, personal communications, and various publicity activities as the only ingredients in a marketing program. Let me suggest a set of questions which those responsible for marketing communications ought to be asking themselves so that a consistent overall marketing program can be developed, using each element of the marketing mix:

Questions for marketers

What are we marketing? In other words, what is our product and what does it offer various segments of the population? Is the nature of the present product appropriate and, if not, how might it be changed?

To whom are we marketing it? Sometimes a product is intended for one and all. Alternatively, certain segments of the population are targeted for special attention. Does the product meet the needs of those groups to whom it is primarily directed? Are some important groups being overlooked?

How are we marketing it? What role (if any) does pricing play in the marketing program and how was a price arrived at? Does it take into account the price-sensitivities of target consumer groups? Additionally, what communications are we using to inform people of the product and to encourage them to use it? Are the messages employed appropriate for these target groups? Are efforts made to reduce psychic costs?

Where are we marketing it? This speaks to distribution issues, notably physical location and how convenient it is for the target segment(s). However, it can also include concerns relating to the physical characteristics of the facilities themselves. Are they comfortable, cheerful, properly heated and cooled? The same question can also extend to the locations in which communications messages are distributed—are these locations where the target consumers are likely to hear or see them?

When are we marketing it? Is the product or service available on a 24-hour basis, seven days a week, or only for limited periods? If the latter, are these likely to be the most appropriate times of the day/week for the target segments? A weekday morning clinic is probably less convenient for working men and women than an evening or weekend one would be, unless it is easy for them to get time off work without loss of pay. Timing considerations are also significant in scheduling messages in the broadcast and print media, with a view to maximizing the chance of reaching target consumers at a time when they are not only likely to be exposed to the message, but also attentive towards it.

Health care marketers are often placed in a difficult position in that decisions relating to the nature and quality of services offered, when and where these are offered, and how pricing policy is set, are not always perceived as being within the province of marketing. Again, this suggests a very narrow view of what marketing's role really is.

This leads to a final question that may seem obvious but often isn't. Why are we marketing this product? In the business sector, the long-run objective inevitably centers around profitability. For nonprofit and public organizations, where profits are not the name of the game, the mission or objectives are likely to vary widely. Unless this mission is properly articulated and appropriate measures of performance developed, it is very difficult to formulate a marketing strategy; strategy requires clearly established objectives and a means of subsequently measuring how well these objectives have been met.

THE NOTION OF COMPETITION

Marketing activities are usually concerned with people's behavior, either seeking to change it or reinforce it. One toothpaste manufacturer may urge us to buy his brand, while another may seek to woo us away from established brands by introducing a new brand with yet another miracle ingredient. It's easy to recognize the presence and implications of competition in such a situation.

Hospitals or clinics may be reluctant to admit that they are in competition with one another, but within certain limits they often are, offering similar services at similar prices to the same range of prospective patients who might as readily travel to Hospital X as to Hospital Y.

It may be harder to conceptualize the nature of competition for public health education. However, it does exist and failure to recognize the fact may result in an ineffectual marketing campaign.

Such competition may take several forms. The most obvious is a direct, frontal attack by an opposing organization on the program being marketed. Anti-fluoridation, anti-abortion, and anti-birth control campaigns are an example. Sometimes campaigns of this ilk are undertaken for sincere reasons by groups with strong beliefs and values; sometimes there are sound medical reasons for questioning the use of particular medications (birth control pills) or health practices. Programs of opposition may represent expressions of political beliefs or simply the views of the "lunatic fringe."

It is a moot point when to counter competing communications of this nature and when to ignore them rather than drawing further attention to them. Sometimes, opposition reflects genuine defects in the position (product) advocated by the public health agency (in which case it should be corrected forthwith); alternatively, opponents may simply misunderstand the product, in which case new communications may be needed to correct these misperceptions. In both instances, some marketing research at the outset might have yielded a better initial marketing program which avoided such problems.

COUNTERING THE COMPETITION

A major problem arises when health programs advocating a change in behavior, such as anti-smoking, anti-alcoholism, and anti-drug abuse, must compete with the promotional activities of tobacco, liquor, and barbiturate manufacturers or the personal urgings of friends, acquaintances, and professional "pushers." In such situations, lobbying for legislative controls or "equal time" may be an appropriate strategy.

Perhaps the most subtle form of competition to health education programs designed to change behavior lies within individuals themselves. It is easier to reinforce existing behavior than to change it. Change may be disruptive of present habits or it may simply be an effort for the individual. Here we return to the notion of non-financial costs—time, inconvenience, and psychic costs. Woe betide the marketer who overlooks them!

Flossing one's teeth properly is time-consuming and a nuisance; so is fastening safety-belts, which may connote a sissy image as well as restricting freedom of movement within the vehicle. Nutritious food may, especially initially, look and taste less attractive than so-called "junk foods." Giving up smoking or drinking may induce withdrawal pangs. Taking more exercise is tiring and time-consuming —and initially may make you feel awful; much pleasanter by far to relax with a six-pack in front of the television. Going for hypertension screening may seem scary to some, take time, and involve travel and expense; the immediate outcome may be that you learn something unpleasant about your health at the end of it all. Inoculations are painful, sometimes costly, and also take time and effort.

Proper use of medications requires a level of precision and regularity that conflicts with some people's vague, easygoing lifestyles. Some authorities believe that self breast examination is suffused with fear and emotion for some women. Practicing birth control is contrary to many people's values. The list is almost endless, since matters of health and safety are so intimately related to how we live our daily lives.

WHAT THE NEW BEHAVIOR COSTS

In every instance, there is a perceived "cost" associated with the recommended new behavior that outweighs the benefits (if any) which the individual anticipates receiving as a result. The need for public health marketers to understand the nature and origin of such costs cannot be overemphasized. This may necessitate consumer research.

In many instances, marketing strategies can be developed to neutralize, or at least minimize, the impact of such competitive forces. Clinical treatments can be made less threatening by conducting them in a relaxed, friendly environment; mobile units can reduce the need for travel to a central location; new inoculation techniques (or simply better training of those who inoculate) may make such experiences almost painless; substitute approaches, such as use of air-bags, may achieve safety belts' benefits at less bother to the consumer; improved communications may clarify benefits, simplify required changes in behavior, and perhaps reiterate possible negative outcomes of noncompliance in ways that are meaningful to the consumer and provide added motivation for change.

However, different groups of people require different approaches. Individuals differ from one another in both physical and mental characteristics, they live in different places and are exposed to different media. So-called mass communication campaigns designed to appeal to all often end by influencing no one. Instead of thinking of mass markets, public health marketers need to consider the opportunities for market segmentation.

MARKET SEGMENTATION

In evaluating a market and developing appropriate programs, one of three broad alternative strategies can be followed. The first is *market aggregation*, in which all consumers are treated alike and a single marketing program is developed for everyone. Many broad-based public health programs fall into this category. While such an approach promises considerable economies of scale, it often loses effectiveness as a result of its failure to recognize the varying needs, concerns and behavior patterns of different groups within the population.

At the opposite end of the scale is total *market disaggregation,* where each consumer is treated uniquely. In the last analysis, each individual may be thought of as a separate market segment on the grounds that each person is slightly different from everybody else in personal characteristics, behavior patterns, needs, values, and attitudes. Good personal medical care may fall into this second category, with the practitioner developing a tailored program of treatment for each patient, offering personal advice and instructions, possibly charging according to ability to pay and, in the "good old days," often being willing to make house calls rather than insisting that patients come to the doctor's office.

When developing educational programs for health, however, complete individualization may be too time-consuming and costly. This is where the third approach, *market segmentation,* has much to offer. This calls for grouping consumers with certain definable characteristics in common. Marketing programs can then be developed which are tailored to each group.

The concept of market segmentation is based upon the propositions that (1) consumers are different; (2) differences in consumers are related to differences in market behavior; and (3) segments of consumers can be isolated within the overall market. A number of benefits may result from adopting a segmentation approach, including:

> a more precise definition of the market in terms of the needs of specific groups, why they behave as they do, and possible ways of influencing behavior;

> a better ability to identify competitive strengths and weaknesses, and opportunities for winning specific segments from the competition;

> more efficient allocation of limited resources to development of programs which will satisfy the needs of target segments;

> clarification of objectives and definition of performance standards.

The basic problem is to select segmentation variables that are likely to prove useful in a specific operational context. Three criteria must be satisfied if meaningful market segments are to be developed:

1. *Measurability:* it must be possible to obtain information on the specific characteristics of interest.
2. *Accessibility:* management must be able to identify chosen segments within the overall market and effectively focus marketing efforts on these segments.
3. *Substantiality:* the segments must be large enough (and/or sufficiently important) to merit the time and cost of separate attention.

SEGMENTING THE MARKET FOR HEALTH EDUCATION

Three basic categories of market segmentation are usually proposed in marketing, each capable of subdivision into a variety of separate variables: geographic, demographic, and psychographic.

1. *Geographic* segmentation groups people by the locations where they live, work, or regularly visit. There is generally a limit to how far most people will travel for non-specialist, ambulatory health care and marketing programs should realistically be focused on that segment of the population which enjoys easy access to the facility. Emphasizing the word *access* implies that time and ease of travel is often more significant than actual mileage. In a broader context, such as a national or statewide public health program, it is important to recognize differences in health needs by region, reflecting variables such as climate, pollution levels, quality of water supplies, etc. Communications programs should take into account the coverage of different media—billboards are obviously very location-specific, but there are also geographic limits to the circulation of particular newspapers and to the transmission range of radio and TV stations.
2. *Demographics* are probably the most commonly used set of segmentation variables for health care marketing. Age and sex are obviously related to health care needs, as may be such readily identifiable physical characteristics as height and weight. Some ethnic groups are more prone to certain health problems than others (sickle-cell anemia, for example); other implications of ethnicity may include dietary habits and difficulty in understanding English; some religions have dietary prescriptions and strongly influence attitudes towards certain health-related practices. Differences in income levels often have implications for nutrition as well as for ability to pay for medical care. Educational level—sometimes highly correlated with income—is often associated with understanding hygiene, attitude towards medical treatment, and ability to understand the need for specific behavioral changes. Frequently, demographic characteristics such as income, ethnicity, age, and education are closely associated with geographic location, reflecting the tendency of different demographic groups to form homogeneous clusters in clearly defined neighborhoods. Census data can often be valuable in clarifying the demographic characteristics of areas as small as a city block.
3. *Psychographic* segmentation refers to the lifestyle, attitudes and behavior patterns of individuals. People within the same demographic group often exhibit vast differences in these characteristics. Lifestyles, eating and drinking habits, working conditions, awareness of and attitudes towards health issues, past medical history, current state of health, self-image, personal beliefs, fears, and emotions—each of these can play a significant role in determining an individual's needs for health care, receptiveness to health-related communications, willingness to adopt new behavior patterns, and specific benefits sought.

After reviewing several studies, one researcher concluded that consumer behavior in the health care field was shaped more closely by psychographic factors than by demographic ones.[1] Unfortunately, psychographic variables are often the hardest to identify, making it difficult to seek out and reach such segments with services and messages tailored to their specific situations.

It is more difficult to practice market segmentation strategies when the target segment is not clearly identifiable within the general population. For instance, a health care program may be developed to treat hypertension, clinics sited in what are believed to be appropriate locations, and a flexible pricing policy established. However, informing those who could benefit from the treatment in question and

---

[1] Lawrence H. Wortzel. "The Behavior of the Health Care Consumer: A Selective Review." In *Advances in Consumer Research*. Vol. III. Edited by B. B. Anderson. Association for Consumer Research, 1976.

persuading them to use it may be difficult. In such instances, it may be necessary to use wide-area media targeted toward the segment for whom it is intended. Additionally, referral strategies can be developed whereby the message is passed down through intermediaries, such as employers, who may even be able to provide screening facilities.

CONCLUSION

It is very important to recognize that advertising, public relations, and personal communications constitute only one category within the broader marketing mix. Each of the other elements in this mix plays a role in determining the success or failure of the overall program. It's not merely a matter of looking at all the elements in the mix, but also of ensuring that they mutually reinforce each other to produce an internally consistent program.

Success is also a function of the marketer's ability to understand the different needs, attitudes, characteristics, and behavior patterns of the various segments that make up the mass market, and then develop programs tailored to these segments. In many instances, this will pose a need for market research, both as an input to planning and as a means of monitoring subsequent performance so that appropriate modifications can be made for the future.

What I want to argue for strongly is involvement of marketing specialists from the outset in formulation of any health program directed at educating or caring for members of the public. All too often, it is only after a program or service has already been developed that someone with marketing skills is called in and instructed to ''tell people about this,'' or ''urge them to do such and such.'' In many instances, even that is frowned upon in the health care field. Indeed, it is only recently that certain institutional taboos against advertising in the medical profession have begun to be challenged.

Even though such prohibitions may not apply to the field of public health education, institutional prejudices die hard and there may still be resistance to giving marketing professionals any significant responsibilities outside a limited and strictly reactive communications role.

What this suggests is *a need to market marketing itself to health care professionals,* highlighting the discipline's responsiveness to consumers and clearly defining what it can and cannot do. Just as undesirable as blind resistance to marketing is the unrealistic expectation that marketing can be the salvation of the health care industry.

11

Organizing the Marketing Function for Transit Authorities

Transit Marketing Management Handbook

How should marketing efforts be administered? What is the most effective way of organizing the marketing function in nonbusiness organizations? This article highlights the difference between a consumer orientation and an operations orientation with special reference to the management of public transportation systems. It summarizes four alternative ways of organizing marketing activities commonly used in the private sector, and then suggests an approach for a large transit system.

Marketing in the transit industry is at a critical state of development and acceptance. Only within recent years have the need for and value of marketing been recognized by the more progressive transit managers. At this juncture, the failure of transit marketing programs, for whatever reason, could encourage the skeptics to "write off" marketing as merely a passing fad. Of course, it is true that very few systems have rejected marketing completely or are likely to do so in the future. But fewer still have adopted a total marketing point of view. And even systems which have committed considerable resources to marketing have experienced mixed results.

A healthy transit marketing function is dependent upon many factors: a capable marketing team, a high-quality non-marketing management team, a favorable political atmosphere within the system, a reasonable marketing budget, correct organizational structure, and acceptance of marketing within the system as a legitimate transit function. But without exception, a successful marketing function is never found in systems which lack either genuine support from top management or a *consumer orientation*. Of these two critical

factors, the latter is by far the more difficult to conceptualize and, consequently, to develop within a transit system.

A CONSUMER ORIENTATION VERSUS AN OPERATIONS ORIENTATION

A transit system which is consumer-oriented will investigate the wants and needs of individual transit consumers, accumulate the individual wants and needs over the total marketplace, determine the effectiveness of the transit system in satisfying consumers, and change the manner in which transit services are offered to the consumer in order to improve the effectiveness of the transit system. At the other end of the transit management spectrum is the operations orientation, which seeks the most efficient use of the capital and labor resources available to the transit system. Both viewpoints should be represented in a transit system; ideally, the system should be both effective and efficient. But at present, many transit systems have too much of an operations outlook at the expense of a healthy consumer orientation. As an example, the general manager of a medium-sized, West

Coast transit system told the study team of an incident which occurred during his first few days on the job. He had noticed that the bus schedules printed for the public showed times which were three minutes earlier than those on the drivers' schedule paddles. The general manager asked his scheduling department for an explanation and was told that it had always been done that way because the transit system didn't want riders holding up the buses; the riders could wait but the buses couldn't. From an operations point of view, the practice was perfectly logical. But the new general manager knew that he had his work cut out for him in turning the system around from an operations to a consumer orientation.

To achieve a consumer orientation, a transit system must look outside of itself; this is what distinguishes a consumer-oriented system from its operations-oriented counterpart. The staff of a consumer-oriented transit system understands that the system is a service organization which can be effective only if it meets the needs of current and potential customers. While the operations people in a consumer-oriented system do their best to see that transit service fulfills the current needs of present customers, the marketing and planing people try both to understand the needs of potential customers and to keep current with the changing needs of present customers. The entire system participates in a continuous process of modifying transit service to meet new and changing needs so as to attract new customers while maintaining current customers.

Service modifications may take the form of new or revised routes and schedules, new equipment and facilities, improved rider information, altered pricing schemes, improved safety features, or any number of other changes and combinations of changes. Some changes will be major but most will be small and localized. The ability to accept and thrive on such changes is another characteristic of a consumer orientation in the transit industry. The opposite is true of an operations-oriented system; a bias toward standardization and a reluctance to tamper with the service as provided are dominant in such systems. An operations orientation can be characterized as a belief that, if the transit system is well run according to internally generated performance standards, customers will use it. Stated more simply, an operations-oriented system deals with the customer on a take-it-or-leave-it basis, with little recognition of the fact that public transit faces direct competition from other transportation modes.

One of the most serious mistakes which can be made in operating a transit system is to associate a consumer orientation strictly with the marketing department. In actuality, if the transit marketing staff are the only people with a consumer orientation, both the marketing function and the transit system as a whole are in trouble. It is essential that the consumer approach be an integral part of every organizational unit within the system. And, because the point of view of transit leadership invariably determines the point of view of the entire system, *a total commitment to the consumer must begin at the top of the management structure.* This relationship provided the opening question for the study of marketing functions in transit organizational structures: does the chief executive (and, therefore, the transit system) have a consumer orientation?

TYPICAL ORGANIZATIONAL MODELS

Organization of the transit marketing function takes many forms throughout the industry. Rarely are all transit marketing activities found in one organizational unit. The service development and public relations activities, for example, are most frequently found outside transit marketing departments. Service development, the key activity for improving transit effectiveness in the marketplace, is usually an adjunct to an operations unit or a planning group. In larger systems, public relations is often linked to a legislative affairs or governmental relations activity and operates directly under or within the general manager's office. Market research, the keystone of all marketing activities, is as likely to be found in a planning unit as in a marketing group. The only marketing activities which are more or less consistently found in a marketing department are promotion and customer services.

The scattering of the marketing function throughout the system usually results in a total marketing effort which is both inefficient and ineffective. However, the dispersal of marketing activities throughout the system is not usually the result of a conscious decision on the part of transit management; rather, transit marketing activities have been developed in piecemeal fashion in various departments and have assumed their present niches as a result of many factors, all of which may be associated with expediency. The inefficiencies caused by a less-than-ideal organizational structure can be overcome by an unusually capable marketing staff or management team, but an inefficient organization will always make a difficult job even more difficult.

MARKETING STRUCTURE ALTERNATIVES

A marketing unit may be organized in four basic ways: by product or service, by market-territory, by market-customer, and by function. These four approaches are described below.

A *product organization* for marketing is usually employed where the products or services produced are not homogeneous. Product managers oversee all marketing activities concerning their particular product and are supported by staff units for research, promotion, and sales. A typical product organization is shown in Exhibit 1. This type of organization is most frequently found in the consumer goods industries.[1]

---

[1] The role of the product manager has recently been discussed in Victor P. Buell, "The Changing Role of the Product Manager," *Journal of Marketing* (July 1975), pp. 3–11.

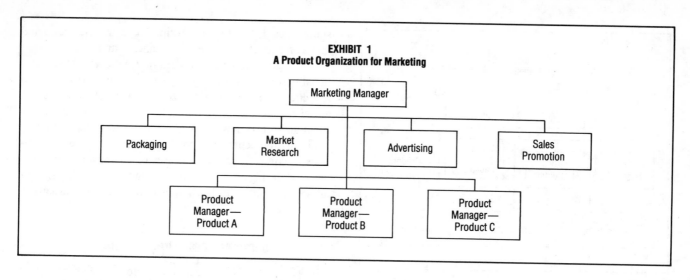

EXHIBIT 1
A Product Organization for Marketing

A *market-territory organization* for marketing is widely used where the product/service line and the market are both relatively homogeneous but the market is so large that it must be geographically segmented for management purposes. If the market segments are large enough, the territory units may have their own support staffs; usually, however, the support staffs are centralized. Large national and international firms with homogeneous products such as insurance and basic materials (steel, aluminum, etc.) are generally organized along the lines of the market-territory model depicted in Exhibit 2.

A *market-customer organization* for marketing is commonly used where the products or services are relatively homogeneous but the customers fall into natural classes or segments. The segmentation might be by industry or by some other real criterion such as government and military markets. The market-customer units are supported by staff functions as shown in Exhibit 3. Marketing functions within the computer industry are frequently organized around the market-

customer model, as are those of some industrial products firms.[2]

A *functional organization* for marketing is the simplest, most common, and, usually, most effective structure. It is also the most easily controlled structure. A functional organization is used where the products or services and the market are relatively homogeneous. Staff members of such an organization are encouraged to become specialists in the important marketing activities of market research, promotion, sales, etc. This specialization almost always results in improved effectiveness and efficiency for the overall marketing effort. Also, because of the easily defined areas of responsibility and functional activity, organizational conflicts are reduced. Exhibit 4 depicts a typical functional marketing organization.

_____

[2] An extensive discussion of the advantages of this approach may be found in Mark Hanan, "Reorganize Your Company Around Its Markets," *Harvard Business Review* (November–December, 1974), pp. 63–74.

EXHIBIT 2
A Market-territory Organization for Marketing

EXHIBIT 3
A Market-customer Organization for Marketing

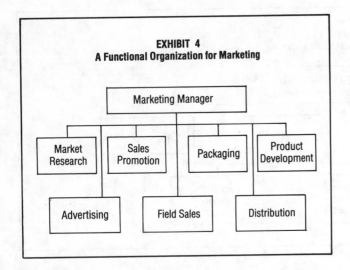

EXHIBIT 4
A Functional Organization for Marketing

The functional organization is the most appropriate structure for the transit marketing function. Transit services are homogeneous, the transit market is relatively localized, and transit marketing resources are limited; these three conditions call for a simple and responsive organizational structure which the functional model can best provide.

The recommended transit marketing organization depicted in Exhibit 5 is strictly a line structure. The decision-making flow for transit marketing proceeds clearly upward from each functional area through the marketing manager to the general manager. Each major activity area within the marketing unit has a well-defined function to perform, thus preventing fragmentation of the marketing effort while minimizing conflicts between groups.

Within service development, there is a natural and logical division between *analysis and planning* activities and *service change implementation*. Similarly, the promotion activity may be broken down into its *advertising* and *public relations* components. Customer services can be divided into *rider information, customer and community relations,* and *special sales*.

Marketing Organizations for Smaller Systems. Smaller transit systems may not have the resources to support the staff requirements of the recommended marketing organization shown in Exhibit 5. The solution is to consolidate the recommended structure by merging different functions. The most appropriate organization will depend upon the resources of the organization and the scope of its marketing program. A large organization is shown to illustrate the diversity of marketing functions.

MARKETING UNIT FUNCTIONAL DESCRIPTIONS

Functional descriptions of organizational units are useful tools for management in that they constitute documentation of the specific authorities and responsibilities of various functions within the organizational structure. More simply stated, functional descriptions define the scope and limits of activity for major organizational units.

A set of functional descriptions follows. These functional descriptions can easily be expanded or condensed to reflect a larger, more specialized or a smaller, more generalized transit marketing unit. The reader is encouraged to adapt and refine these management aids to fit the organizational environment of the specific transit system. Such conditions as strengths and weaknesses of incumbents, resource levels, differing program priorities, and political climate will influence the ultimate distribution of functions within a given transit system.

FUNCTIONAL DESCRIPTION: MARKETING

The marketing function is performed within a major line organizational unit of the transit system; the Marketing Manager reports directly to the General Manager. The general responsibilities of the marketing function include the performance of market research, service development, promotion, and customer service activities. The marketing function represents the customer's point of view in all major transit system decisions on routes, fare structure, and frequency of service.

1. Leads the development and maintenance of a market or consumer orientation throughout the transit system.
2. Performs market research activities, including assessment of the nature of the marketplace, evaluation of the effectiveness of current transit services in fulfilling specific market needs, and other research studies as required.
3. Coordinates service development activities by interpreting market research findings and developing, in cooperation with the operations unit, fare-structures and services to fulfill clearly recognized needs.
4. Performs the mass-market promotional activities of advertising and public relations to inform current and potential customers of transit service benefits and to persuade them to use the transit system.
5. Performs individual customer service activities, including rider information dissemination, telephone inquiry response, direct and special sales, community relations efforts, and coordination of in-house sales training.
6. Establishes well defined goals for the various marketing activities and monitors their achievement.
7. Subject to the approval of the General Manager and other authorities, coordinates the development of an integrated marketing program plan and budget.
8. Monitors the organization of the marketing function and recommends structural revisions to the General Manager as required.
9. Coordinates and integrates the implementation and operation of the various marketing programs within the transit system.
10. Continuously evaluates the performance of all marketing activities, programs, and projects.

FUNCTIONAL DESCRIPTION: MARKET RESEARCH

The market research activity is performed as a line function within the marketing unit and is responsible for the description and measurement of various markets for transit services. The overall responsibilities of the market research activity include (1) generalized data collection, (2) measurement and analysis of specific markets and market segments, and (3) forecasting of market potentials for transit services.

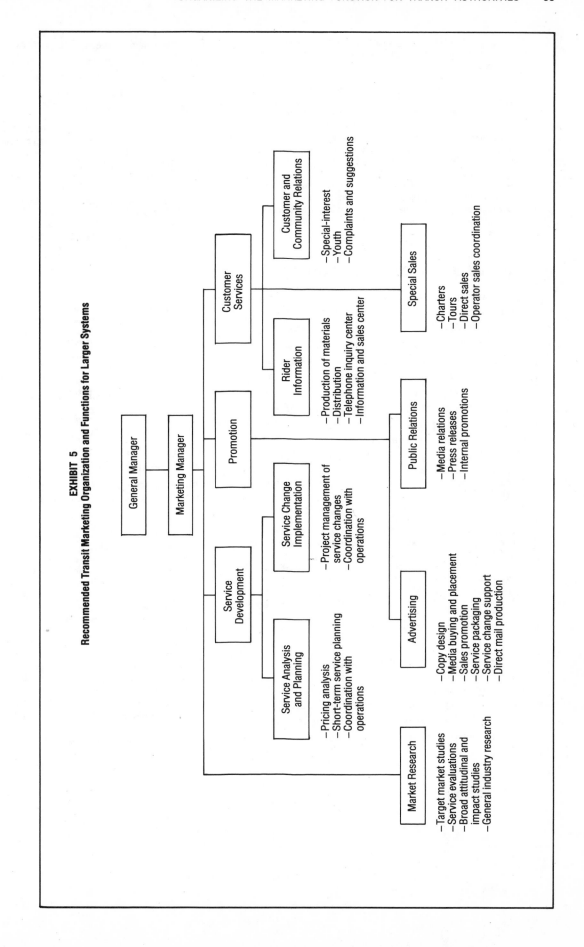

EXHIBIT 5
Recommended Transit Marketing Organization and Functions for Larger Systems

1. Develops and performs target market studies of limited scope to measure and assess the need for transit services within specific market segments.
2. Develops and performs studies of limited scope to evaluate the acceptance and effectiveness of specific transit services (routes, fare structures, express service, etc.) in the marketplace.
3. Periodically designs and manages major market research studies to determine marketplace attitudes toward mass transit and the image and impact of the transit system in the market.
4. Periodically develops and performs studies to determine the effectiveness of specific transit advertising campaigns and themes in the marketplace.
5. Periodically performs projections of market characteristics and trends to support planning and service development.
6. Occasionally performs special studies of a research nature as required by the marketing unit, General Manager, or Board of Directors.

FUNCTIONAL DESCRIPTION: SERVICE DEVELOPMENT

The service development activity is performed as a line function within the marketing unit and is responsible for the planning, development, and initial implementation of changes to transit services. Such changes will improve the ability of the transit system to meet transit consumer needs which have been identified in the marketplace. The service development activity serves as the primary liaison between the marketing and operations functions; service development coordinates all development proposals with the operations function to insure their feasibility and practicality.

1. Performs continuing analysis of transit pricing structures in terms of the trade-off between increased ridership and profitability.
2. Interprets the findings and conclusions of the market research activity in terms of their impact on transit services.
3. Performs planning activities for transit service changes over the short-term planning horizon of one year.
4. Maintains continuing close coordination with the operations function to insure that service change recommendations are feasible and practical.
5. Develops individual service changes by coordination of all aspects of routing, fare structure, service scheduling, operating personnel training, promotion, and rider information.
6. Manages the initiation and testing of service changes throughout the transit system by close coordination between other marketing activities and the operations function.

FUNCTIONAL DESCRIPTION: PROMOTION

The promotion activity is performed as a line function within the marketing unit and is responsible for all advertising, public relations, and mass communications programs within the transit system. The promotion activity serves to within the transit system. The promotion activity serves to inform the market of existing mass transit services and to encourage their use by potential customers. Promotion also supports the introduction of new transit services into the marketplace.

1. Coordinates the development of advertising programs to achieve well defined goals based on market research findings.
2. Performs all design, media-selection, and time-buying activities for both paid and public service advertising programs.
3. Directs the performance of any advertising or public relations agency which may be retained by the transit system.
4. Performs public relations activities, including media relations efforts and distribution of press releases on all transit services.
5. Supports the introduction of new transit services by developing promotional programs and materials tailored to target markets.
6. Develops special sales promotion materials and direct mail campaigns.
7. Supports the customer service activity by assisting in the design of rider information materials to insure compatibility with promotional criteria.
8. Supports the customer service activity by designing promotional materials for direct and special sales activities.
9. Assists the operations function in developing design motifs for bus exteriors and rider facilities which are compatible with the transit system's overall public image.

FUNCTIONAL DESCRIPTION: CUSTOMER SERVICES

The customer service activity is performed as a line function within the marketing unit and is responsible for all rider information, direct and special sales, community and customer relations, and transit sales coordination programs within the transit system. The customer service activity deals with individual customers and small groups in a direct information and sales capacity.

1. Produces, distributes, and maintains inventories of rider information materials, including schedules and route maps.
2. Operates the telephone inquiry response center to provide timely and accurate responses to rider inquiries.
3. Operates the customer information and sales center for distribution of tokens, special passes, discount fare tickets, etc.
4. Performs special sales activities relating to charters and tours and conducts direct sales of regular transit services to companies and other groups.
5. Performs customer relations activities, including the quick and responsive handling of customer complaints and suggestions, to maintain goodwill on the part of present customers.
6. Develops and implements community relations activities which encourage use of transit services by affinity groups based on schools, neighborhoods, religions, national origins, etc.
7. Coordinates the development of a sales consciousness in vehicle operators by assisting the personnel and operations functions in operator training programs.

12

Fund Raising: Development of an Annual Giving Program

Stanley R. McAnally

Public and nonprofit organizations often run operating deficits since their costs frequently exceed operating income. While public agencies can often rely on tax revenues to make up their deficits, nonprofit organizations must look to charitable giving. Effective fundraising involves a good understanding of marketing, including identification of target segments, selection of communications appeals and media, and management of volunteer "salespeople." This article focuses on development of annual fundraising campaigns for colleges and universities, but the strategies and techniques discussed are readily adaptable for use by other types of nonprofit organizations.

Annual giving is based on the theory that people give to people. We are taught from birth that it is more blessed to give than to receive. The giver who has satisfied the basic urge to share feels a deeper sense of commitment and involvement. People want the happy experience that giving to others provides. Their nature demands that they give, their commitment commands that they give, and it remains only to ask that they give. Asking is the function of the annual-giving program.

Developing an annual fund is no easy task. It demands time, effort, commitment, and money, and there are no short-cuts. There is an ever-widening gap between income and expense for most educational institutions. A strong annual program not only helps bridge the gap between essential needs and available money but also produces other

advantages for the institution. With an effective annual-giving program, the following inevitably occur:

1. A greater awareness on the part of alumni and others of the institution's position in the educational world, and an intensified desire to help the institution meet its needs and strengthen its purposes.
2. The creation of a partnership between donors and the institution, in which the donors become better informed about the physical and financial needs of the institution and develop an awareness of the problems of admissions, the difficulty in recruiting and retaining an outstanding faculty in the face of mounting financial pressure, the need to provide more student aid, and so forth.
3. A more sympathetic understanding of the merits of an organized program of annual gift support.
4. The creation of a base of regular annual contributors for future capital campaign efforts.

For most schools and colleges, the annual fund is generally organized around the alumni constituency; but some institutions direct special efforts toward nonalumni parents, other friends, and corporations. The alumni constituency, however, should be the nucleus of the annual fund organization. The key leaders and campaign workers should,

Stanley R. McAnally is Associate Vice President, The University of Tennessee System.

therefore, be alumni and the largest group of prospective donors is the alumni constituency.

Planning. In structuring an annual fund, the basic ingredient is effective planning. But even before you begin to plan, you should think about your institution—its past and its future, and the qualities it has that build a case for private gift support. Consider also why people give, the nature of your alumni constituency, and your own interest and dedication. Think about the time and effort that will be required to make the annual fund a success. Prepare yourself mentally to undergo a rigorous round of letters, reports, acknowledgments, kick-off meetings, and constant efforts to maintain the enthusiasm of your volunteer leadership.

Planning and scheduling are keys to the timing of the fund campaign—the actual length of time of the campaign and when the campaign should be conducted. Individual factors at each institution will determine the length of time that an annual fund takes out of a given year. A short campaign of four, five, or six months duration is often very effective, but, in many cases, this is not the best approach. Many institutions carry on continuous annual-giving campaigns, stretching them out for a full twelve months. There are valid arguments against a long campaign: it is tiring on the staff and on the workers, it creates problems in keeping volunteers' enthusiasm at a high level, and it creates problems with alumni who wonder whether the campaign will ever end.

Regardless of the duration of the fund drive, the November-December-January months should be included in the campaign. In the fall season, education is on the minds of alumni, and a football tradition (if your institution has one) adds to the spirit. The month of December seems to create a generous mood and people are more receptive to an appeal. Perhaps the greatest incentive for including the December–January connection is that you can offer either of two taxable years for an alumnus to make a gift. This is especially important in advance solicitation for large gift prospects. Some institutions use commencement time as a particularly effective ending date for the campaign. Basically, you have to evaluate your own situation, your own constituency, and the history of past campaigns, and then structure your fund campaign accordingly.

After the campaign has been planned, schedules have been prepared, and the people involved have been informed of the details, then these plans and schedules should be organized into a cohesive and effective annual fund campaign. Many institutions use a class agent organization and use it extremely well. Others, for various reasons, use a regional organization, and a number of institutions use alumni clubs as their basic geographic organization.

In organizing for geographic solicitation, it is extremely important that you obtain the best person available as regional agent. You must have an enthusiastic, responsive volunteer who has the time to give and will give it whether you conduct personal, face-to-face solicitation or telephone

campaigns on a regional basis. This person must be your man or woman on the scene and must be briefed on the campaign, the techniques, the objectives, the reasons for the campaign, and the case. It is your responsibility to make this person a part of the team.

The annual-giving program should be geared primarily to the staff director, who, in a sense, acts as a general, plotting the strategy of the war effort. The director plans the mailings, the meetings, and the organization and follows these plans to effective completion. The staff director must be informed, honest, and dedicated to the purposes and goals of the institution. He or she must have an absolute belief in the ability of the annual fund to help meet the objectives of the institution. The director must operate at a level of energy, imagination, efficiency, and purpose that will inspire more people to give and to give more.

Direct Mail Solicitation. In most annual funds, direct mail is the basic system, often grounded in personal solicitation of large gift prospects and telephone calls as a follow-up. In this context, we define direct mail as a means of communication with the total alumni constituency through the use of printed materials mailed on a mass basis.

There are four basic types of direct mail programs used for fund raising. In the first type, appeals are sent through the mails to all prospects, and gifts are returned by mail. The second type of program uses direct mail to supplement other types of fund raising. The basic program, for example, may involve extensive personal contact, with direct mail used to cover areas where volunteers are not available or where it is otherwise impractical to make personal contacts. It may be necessary to use direct mail appeals to follow through in those cases where personal contacts were not accomplished. Many organizations use a third type of fund-raising direct mail—the advance mail contact. In such programs, mailings are used to inform prospective donors about the case and to build an interest in advance of personal contacts. The fourth type of fund-raising direct mail is for supplementary appeals. The most common application is to upgrade previous donors to a higher level. In other cases, mail solicitations are made to cover special emergencies or for audiences with special interests.

Direct mail as a *consistent, effective* communication with alumni, parents, and others will lead to success in the fund campaign. Effective direct mail requires the same thoughtful, thorough research, planning, and scheduling as the most involved personal solicitation campaign.

While direct mail cannot compete with personal or telephone solicitation, its advantages include the following:

1. *Good control.* The staff person can determine schedules and copy deadlines with the printer and mail room. This eliminates some of the personal problems that may beset even the most dedicated volunteer.
2. *Wide coverage.* Direct mail can reach every corner of the world. Personal solicitation depends on the availability of volunteers and the size of the constituency.

3. *Cost control.* Actual costs can be pinpointed and predicted. There are fewer hidden costs, such as extensive telephone charges, meals, transportation.
4. *Built-in records.* Return envelope flaps can be designed so that they can be completed and returned by the donor.
5. *Staff savings.* Direct mail can be done with fewer staff members.

In planning a direct mail campaign, you must first determine its objective and what is to be accomplished with the campaign. Unquestionably, the primary objective of a direct mail campaign is to raise money. Educational fund raising competes with many other interests for the individual's gift dollars. Whether the gift received is a considered portion of the donor's available funds or a token contribution will be determined in large measure by the planning that goes into the fund appeal.

Beautifully designed mailing pieces with lots of color, excellent photographs, and provocative copy are valueless unless they are opened and read. This brings up the question of type of mailing: first class or third class. Not long ago there would have been an easy answer to this question: printed letters sent third class. It saved time and money. Now, however, with the considerable advances in automated equipment for letter writing, a first-class mailing of individually typed letters can be done without a great investment of time or money.

An individually typed letter, addressed to a specific person, and using a personal salutation, has great advantage over a printed form letter addressed to "Dear Alumnus." The first objective with any direct mail effort is to get the letter opened. Very few people can resist opening a first-class letter, in an individually typed envelope. It is even more difficult to resist reading a personally addressed message. Consequently, by the use of first-class personal letters, you almost guarantee that your appeal will be opened and read. When you have accomplished that, you are halfway home. Even though it is a form letter, the recipient gets only one and it is personalized.

In addition to fund appeals, the automatic typewriters can be used to acknowledge gifts personally. How you acknowledge gifts and how *quickly* you acknowledge them are extremely important. A thoughtful, sincere thank you from the national chairperson or the fund office, received by the donor a few days after the gift was made, can be the best direct mail solicitation you do for the following year's campaign.

Once your letter is read, the content determines whether you reach the third goal—getting a gift. Good design, first-class printing, and readable copy are all desirable and necessary for any effective direct mail campaign. But the presentation of the case is probably the single most important element of your letter. You must have a reason for your alumni to want to give to your institution, and you have to present it in such a way that they will give. Far too often, fund raisers insult the intelligence of their alumni in a direct mail appeal.

On the other hand, the now famous Ludgin letters are among the classics of outstanding direct mail. Written by Earle Ludgin, they presented the case for the 1955–56 University of Chicago Campaign with wit and imagination. Not only did the letters produce $4.5 million in gifts, but they also won the 1956 Time-Life Award as "The Outstanding Direct Mail Effort of the Year," in a competition organized by the American Alumni Council.

One paragraph from a typical Ludgin letter illustrates this point:

> Instead of looking to the past with pride, let us look to the future with hope. We who have cause to be proud of the University have the means to implement and increase that pride by giving to the Alumni Fund, giving as generously as our means permit. May I say that this is not an obligation? But if we had asked you in time, would you have sent a thousand dollars to Newton, Galileo or Madam Curie? . . .
> We say a thousand dollars only wishfully. We are really very grateful for the checks of five, ten or twenty-five dollars. . . . [AAC, 1960, p. 17].

Whether you use printed or personal letters in direct mail, the copy is the most important factor. Once, I wrote down this advice from a direct mail expert: "*Bad* direct mail is not poorly printed direct mail; *good* direct mail is not colorful, expensive literature. Bad direct mail *is* a stupid, boring, sterile, unimaginative piece of promotion—no matter how expensively it is produced. Good direct mail *is* an interesting, appropriate piece of correspondence, worthy of the time that must be spent in opening and looking at it." Letters should be friendly, personal, persuasive. They should make the recipient feel important. The letter should do three things: *Get the reader's attention*—the first sentence can make or break the whole appeal; *Get to the point*—do not lose the prospect's attention by beating around the bush for three paragraphs; *Create a sense of urgency* with a strong case— suggest a course of action, never leave the reader wondering what to do next but tell him or her, ask for the gift. In writing effective appeals letters, the following rules of style might be helpful.

Be friendly. Convey a sense of warmth and personal regard for the reader. Friendliness and sincerity are as important in letters as they are in personal solicitation. A word of caution: friendliness should never be confused with disrespect, presumption, effusiveness, or overenthusiasm.

Be clear. The letter you have been laboring over for days is clear to you, but will it be clear to the recipient? Remember that your letter must carry the load in presenting the case. Use short words, reasonably short sentences, and paragraphs of six lines or less. An excellent precaution is to have someone else read the letter before it is printed. This gives you the benefit of a typical first impression and can reveal any serious confusion or misconception.

Be straightforward. Do not adopt a phony "literary" style. Write as though you were talking to the reader.

Be concise. This does not necessarily mean "be short." No letter is too long if it tells the whole story and only that. Remember that the appeal letter has to present the case to the entire constituency; it must cover the reasons the prospect should give. Some of the best direct mail pieces have been three pages long, others less than a page. The letter must *sell* the prospect, not just please him or her by being agreeably short.

Now that you have established what you are trying to accomplish and what type of mailing you will use, a number of smaller problems command attention, such as selection of paper stock for stationery, envelopes, pledge cards, brochures; use of color; selective mailings for previous contributors and chronic noncontributors; determination of mailing schedules, and coordination of schedules with printers. Although relatively minor in themselves, collectively these details can mean the difference between success and failure in direct mail.

In summary, here are some ''do's'' and ''dont's'' in the use of direct mail:

1. *Do* present a sound and interesting case. Offer your reader a reason for giving.
2. *Do* devote time and effort to your direct mail, so that it is interesting, readable, action-getting.
3. *Do* vary your approach. Use some humor occasionally.
4. *Do* try to put yourself in the place of the alumnus and write the type of letter you would respond to.
5. *Do* make occasional special first-class mailings, at least to previous contributors.
6. *Do* change your pace occasionally in letterhead, enclosures, acknowledgments.
7. *Do* use color effectively to make your envelope stand out in a stack of white ones.
8. *Do* remember that every alumnus is a potential contributor. Make your nondonor mailings as interesting and exciting as those to your regular contributors.
9. *Don't* sell the word ''planning'' short. In every phase of your direct mail campaign, do some very careful research and planning.
10. *Don't* assume that an alumnus is going to open every piece of mail from the institution. Make your mailings interesting and attractive.
11. *Don't* use an envelope and stationery so cheap that it implies that what you have to say could not possibly be important.
12. *Don't* neglect your chronic noncontributors. Perhaps your very next appeal will be the motivating factor in getting an affirmative response.

The class agent organization is the nucleus of many direct mail efforts. Again, thorough planning, research, and organization are necessary in the use of class agents as they are in every other phase of the effort. The agents must be selected with care. They must be trained. They must be aware of the case and must have a strong commitment to the institution. A class agent organization can be highly effective if the agent has a manageable number of class members to write. Many institutions permit the class agents to write their own letters, on their own letterhead. But be careful if you do this. Not every doctor, lawyer, and Indian chief can write a sound, convincing fund appeal. Ideally, the letters should be prepared by the annual fund office and sent to the class agents for mailing. The agents can then write personal notes on each letter, and that technique can bolster the effectiveness of the appeal. For institutions with large alumni constituencies, the class agent system can work well with the professional schools where the classes tend to be smaller. The class agent

organization is not a tool for all institutions, but it can be used to some degree in almost every type and size of annual giving programs.

Telephone Solicitation. Telephone campaigns have become integral parts of successful annual funds in colleges, universities, and independent schools throughout the country. The telephone campaign provides the ability to contact large numbers of alumni in a brief time span, low cost, high productivity, limited effort on the part of volunteer workers, and excellent control by the annual fund office. They are used primarily for three purposes: to make advance calls on special gift club prospects, to follow up the direct mail efforts, and to lead off special campaign appeals. If 70 percent or more of your institution's alumni reside within the immediate area of the institution, one telethon conducted locally is probably in order. This effort will take several nights of calling and will require carefully coordinated teamwork with volunteer captains to recruit workers for each night. A local telethon can very easily use class chairpersons, with specific nights designated for calling specific classes. Some competition can be generated between the classes.

Regional telethons are best if the alumni constituency is scattered. The fund office must conduct some demographic research to determine which cities have a sufficient number of alumni to justify a telethon.

Telephone campaigns are personal in nature, although not as much as personal solicitation. They allow the volunteer worker to explain the case for the annual fund and permit the prospective donor to ask questions and air gripes about the institution. Telethons can be conducted at relatively low cost, since the calling locations will be obtained by the volunteer chairpersons. The location is extremely important. There must be enough outside trunk lines to assure all the workers access to a telephone. Good locations for telethons include telephone company business offices, banks, brokerage houses, large law offices, and insurance company offices. The volunteer chairperson can make these arrangements locally.

The annual fund office has the responsibility of preparing the prospect cards and conducting a training session for the workers. The prospect cards should contain the name, address, degree, and class year of the prospect. Some institutions include past giving records.

Telephone campaigns are productive. They use large numbers of volunteer workers who can complete their assignments in the evening. They reach a greater number of noncontributors than could be contacted in face-to-face personal solicitation. An important by-product of the telethon is the number of address changes and other information that is obtained by the workers during the calling sessions.

Important steps in a successful telethon include the following:

1. Begin planning early. The area telephone chairpersons should be selected early, and every effort should be made to have the best leadership available from your alumni constituency in each area.

2. Follow up to make sure the area chairperson has scheduled the telethon for the appropriate date, made the arrangements for the location, and contacted the workers.

3. Prepare the materials (prospect cards, information sheet, envelopes) for the telethon workers in advance.

4. Outline specific points the workers should get across to prospects during the telethon. Let the workers develop their own presentation. A prepared text is not as effective, because the workers will read it to prospects; this limits their enthusiasm.

5. Be enthusiastic in your training session with the workers, so that they in turn will be enthusiastic when talking to prospects on the telephone.

6. Obtain telephone numbers in advance and put them on the prospect cards.

7. Separate cards by class and college for large areas; this gives the worker an opportunity to call people in his or her class or college.

8. Code cards by contributor and noncontributor. Previous contributors will be easy first calls.

9. Provide follow-up material to be sent to all alumni who give any type of affirmative response.

10. Provide a printed form on the back of the prospect cards for address changes, whether or not the prospect will contribute, worker's name, comments.

11. The day after the telethon write a personal letter to all workers expressing appreciation for their time and effort.

12. Make every effort to give each worker a few prospect cards of previous year's contributors. A few easy calls first will build their confidence.

13. Do not make instructions too complicated; this will only confuse the workers. Keep the training session as simple as possible, but convey all necessary information.

14. Do not let the workers ask for only a *dollar*—they might get only that!

15. Do not assume that all workers understand all instructions. Check with them throughout the telethon to answer questions and handle problems.

16. Do not let the workers talk too long to any one prospect. Each worker should complete at least fifteen calls an hour—that is, actually talk to fifteen alumni about the annual fund.

Volunteers. One of the most important elements in the annual giving program is the volunteer worker. Volunteers come in all shapes and sizes, and they volunteer for different reasons. Some people truly volunteer, some are drafted, and some reluctantly agree to serve out of a spirit of obligation. How do you recruit volunteers? The same way porcupines make love—very carefully! It is not difficult to recruit people to work for the annual fund. The problem is getting the right people working the right way for the right reasons. Who are these people? They are your alumni and other friends who are truly committed to the goals and objectives of the institution and who believe that you and your colleagues can achieve those goals with their help.

The right volunteers must be identified before they can be recruited. The annual-giving office has several sources for this important information. Among the lists of possibilities for key leadership positions are contributors of long standing, members of special gift clubs, community leaders, recent graduates who were members of an undergraduate alumni council, and recommendations from current volunteer leadership. The top volunteer leadership should be brought up through the ranks whenever possible. Recruit from among alumni chapter officers, from previous workers in telethons and other projects, from among class agents who have been especially effective.

In recruiting the top volunteers, look for belief in the importance of education; demonstrated commitment to the institution; an understanding of the purposes, mission, and goals of the institution; the willingness to give personal time, effort, and resources; ability to plan and organize; and ability to work with other volunteers and with staff.

In turn, the volunteer has the right to expect the following from the staff of the annual fund: (1) information about the objectives of the institution and facts about its operation; (2) a concise statement of the role and scope of the institution and the importance of annual giving to the successful attainment of the institution's goals; (3) a clear definition of the volunteer's role in the annual fund; (4) the tools that he or she needs to do the job—good schedules, accurate prospect lists, timely progress reports; (5) effective use of his or her time, advance notice of meetings, advance preparation of materials needed to handle meetings; (6) recognition of his or her time, effort, and service through appropriate expressions of appreciation from the president, invitations to special events on campus, an appropriate plaque or certificate when the volunteer's role has been completed.

Special Gift Clubs. For a number of years, special gift clubs of one kind or another have been appearing on the scene. The Century Clubs, in which the minimum gift necessary for membership was $100, became very popular. Other special donor societies with minimum gifts of $250 or $500 have been established by various institutions around the country.

The purpose of a major gift club is, of course, to raise money for the institution. As a general rule, these programs are carried on at a fairly sophisticated level, involving a selected list of prospects. The special gift club is, in effect, a minicapital campaign in which top prospects are considered to be candidates for large annual gifts. Probably the most important aspect of the special gift clubs is that they generally provide unrestricted money which can be used where the needs are greatest. In many institutions, special gift clubs are the best method of securing substantial additional amounts of unrestricted giving while increasing the involvement and participation of alumni and other individuals.

Arthur J. Horton, director of special projects at Princeton University (AAC, 1970, pp. 51–53), has pointed out negative aspects of special gift clubs:

1. There is a tendency for the floor, as represented by the kinds of gifts necessary for membership, to become, in effect, the ceiling. A donor who gives $1,000 to be a member of the club (which admittedly at the time of the gift may well represent a nice increase in his habitual giving), after two or three years is still giving $1,000 because $1,000 is what he looks upon as being his dues, so to speak, for membership in the club.

2. What do you do for an encore? After your donor has paid up his membership, what do you say to him? Do you then announce that the club has a special back room which he may enter by contributing $5,000 a year? The exclusivity of being "in" loses its appeal after exposure over a period of time.

3. Does the special gift club idea become too much of a gimmick? The constituencies involved in annual giving should not need gim-

micks. If the case to potential donors is built on the basic problem of need, this should be sufficient.

4. There is a problem of uneasiness about publicly treating one segment of your annual-giving constituency differently than another; that is, with special parties, preferred seats to football games and other attractions, special mailings and invitations to campus events. By emphasizing the size of gift and making it the only thing of importance, there is the risk of offending the person who is successful by other measurements or who serves well as a worker, or the fellow who really sacrifices—as some do—to come up with a twenty-five dollar gift.

Unquestionably, special gift clubs raise some problems, but the total effect on annual giving is positive. In many institutions, special gift clubs are the best technique available for upgrading annual giving.

In Summary. The whole concept of annual giving can be summarized in four words: attention, interest, involvement, commitment. Before anything can be accomplished, you must have the attention of your various constituencies. This should be done through an effective program of reunions, seminars, continuing education, magazines, and newsletters. Once you have the attention of your alumni and other friends, build their interest. This is the primary function of the case statement, which should be a simple summary of the aims, objectives, and needs of the institution that can be realized through the annual fund. Build your case carefully. Your people are entitled to know why you are asking for money and what you intend to do with it. You must give them a reason to want to give to your institution, and you must present it in such a way that it will precipitate affirmative action.

Three specific ways in which interest in the annual fund may be generated are the following:

1. Continually inform and educate the alumni constituency regarding the annual fund. Tell them what it is and why it exists.
2. Present a case that is interesting, readable, based on careful study and evaluation, and one which embodies the most important characteristics of a case for annual giving—simplicity and universality. The message must be simple and must be universal enough to apply to your entire constituency.
3. Recruit the best leadership possible. The key to successful solicitation is effective volunteer leadership.

Involvement should be a continual process within the total program, and not just encouraged when fund raising is in progress. Involvement of class agents, geographic agents, fund chairpersons for alumni clubs, telephone workers, workers in a personal solicitation campaign—all these lead to greater interest in the annual fund itself and in the institution. They also provide a reservoir of leadership for future campaigns. From such involvement, interest, and participation will come gifts not only to the annual fund but corporate gifts, foundation gifts, special gifts, and deferred gifts.

The last element of annual giving is commitment. Everything done up to now to attract attention, create interest, and foster involvement in the annual fund becomes academic if it does not precipitate affirmative action. Commitment is the end result of the total strategy. If the program has been sound, if a good case has been presented, then the end result is a successful annual fund. People give because their nature demands it. They give because they are asked.

13
The Mass Media Family Planning Campaign for the United States

Richard K. Manoff

Family planning is a major societal issue throughout the world. This article summarizes the Planned Parenthood mass media campaign in the United States in the early 1970's. In particular it discusses the interactions with the Advertising Council, which coordinates much of the public service advertising in the United States.

We were asked by the Advertising Council to appraise the Planned Parenthood Federation project in two steps, the first of which was to explore the practicability of such a campaign. Several members of the board of the Advertising Council did not believe that the problem could be handled through advertising. This may have been a euphemistic way of indicating some of the latent opposition to the idea. In the second step, if we concluded that the campaign was practicable, we were asked to indicate how it could be dealt with in advertising.

Our eventual report was that first, yes, the campaign was practicable and, second, it could be handled by dealing with the problem in terms of the quality of life in America; that is, conditions in our country are such —the high cost of raising children, the crowded conditions of our cities, etc.—

Richard K. Manoff is President, Manoff International, Inc., and Chairman, Richard K. Manoff Inc.

as to make childbearing and childrearing far more difficult than before. Our campaign would sensitize people to think and carefully plan the having of children in the context of these conditions. While the conditions are not themselves the direct result of a rising population, the presence of more people in our society does have an exacerbating effect on them.

There are other justifications for a family planning campaign in the United States, in our opinion. The U.S. is the world's biggest consumer of raw materials. Our concern with the pollution of the world's atmosphere and the depletion of its natural resources must lead us to the conclusion that the prevention of the birth of an American child is more significant than of a Chinese child whose per capita consumption of the world's materials will be one-twentieth as much.

In terms of motivation to action, we knew that self-interest would have to be the primary incentive; that there was not much to be derived from appeals to social respon-

Reprinted by permission of the author, from *Using Commercial Resources In Family Planning Programs: The International Experience* (Honolulu: East-West Center, 1973):113–18. No part of this article may be reproduced in any form without prior written permission from the publisher.

sibility or benefit. Our experience instructs us that broad, socially abstract appeals of this kind usually invite the individual to defer to his neighbor: "Let the other fellow do it, not me." In all my years in communications I have known few efforts and no successes that were persuasively themed in this fashion. On the other hand, I know of many efforts that owe their success to a demonstration of how social benefit and self-interest are interdependent.

We presented our case to the Ad Council. It was persuaded that it could be carried out, and so gave us the task. Had I known in advance what we were in for, I would have had a less sanguine attitude toward our assignment. But the effort has been most stimulating and instructive. I have learned much about human nature and political maneuvering and about my ignorance in both areas.

It took two years to get our campaign approved. Whenever our campaign was presented to a reviewing committee (and we had more reviewing committees than I could possibly remember), some surgical action was always inevitable. We went through amputations, transplants, and radical organ excisions. In our final presentation I was constrained to remind the group that it had taken us two years to obtain their approval and in that period some eight million American children were born. I also ventured the guess that this campaign would go down in history as the one with the longest gestation period.

You will assume from this account that our campaign falls a good deal short of the objectives that Planned Parenthood had hoped for and that I, as a communications man, knew we should have strived for. But compromise is a fact of life, and it is also essential because it makes eventual action possible. Without compromise our campaign would never have been approved.

We had three target populations. The first was made up of opinion leaders. In the United States we have specific magazines whose readership generally is made up of those whose positions in society give their opinions a measure of influence over their fellow men. Such magazines as Harper's and Atlantic are cases in point.

Our second target is made up of young couples entering into the period of family formation. Actually, they are difficult to distinguish from the general populace in terms of media selection. So, in effect, in seeking to reach them we had to reach out for everyone.

Also, since all Ad Council campaigns depend on the beneficence of the media, we did not have the control of media selection to begin with.

Our third target was the young adult population.

These three target groups are not particularly clearly discerned in the print advertisements, although they are in the radio and television messages. Radio in the United States, for the most part, is a young adult medium. It is extensively programmed for music and we use it primarily to reach young adults.

Our creative strategy was, as I have indicated, to motivate self-interest: *family planning is good for you.* Our media strategy was to depend on the generosity of the media. This has never been a wise strategy and it hasn't turned out differently this time. But we had no choice.

The audience attitudes we had to deal with involved differences in religious views about conception, contraception, and birth control in general; political philosophies, such as the feeling on the part of some militant blacks that population control is basically genocidal; and the social philosophy of the population "hawks," who hold that the total answer to pollution and environmental degradation is birth control and almost ignore the central role of modern industrial technology in causing these problems.

We had to deal with all these points of view because at one time or another those who held them asked for special emphases in our messages. We protected our copy, by keeping our ultimate consumers in mind and convincing our review committees that the only important consideration was the proper incentive to motivate them. Our position was that the campaign would be severely reduced in impact if social appeals were allowed to overwhelm the appeals to self-interest.

However, we were forced to accept a very limited objective: To raise the question of family planning and to increase awareness of it. We were not allowed to use such terms as "birth control" or "contraceptives."

Our injunction was limited to an offer of literature. We could not say: "Come to a family planning clinic," or "Visit a family planning clinic to get advice." All we could say was, simply, "Planned Parenthood. Write for Information."

Not even our offered booklets were permitted to be specific in describing birth control devices and services.

Despite all the restrictions, however, I do believe our campaign has had its effect on the attitude of Americans toward family planning. I must refer once again to my philosophy of incremental improvement. What really matters is improvement, no matter how little may take place. In time, that effort accumulates increasing impact both from the multiplier effect of its exposure and from the growing liberalization of attitudes.

The issue of family planning gives rise to many fascinating contradictions. One of the more colorful has to do with the radically different attitudes expressed among media. For example, the April 2, 1971 issue of Life Magazine devoted its cover and major article to the problem of high school pregnancy in the United States. According to Life Magazine, the question of high school pregnancy and the pregnant bride is morally and socially acceptable for public discussion. It is also socially acceptable in Seventeen, a teenage magazine, which ran an article on "Questions you ask most about birth control." But unfortunately, when you get to television and radio, you enter a somewhat different world. For when we proposed a message for television on the same subject we were summarily turned down. As a matter of fact, the Columbia Broadcasting System at first rejected all our television messages, although the National Broadcasting Company and the American Broadcasting Company accepted them.

This kind of contradiction among our media did not simplify our task. We had to make further accommodations in an already over-accommodated campaign in order to get it to the public.

A sample of our advertisements directed at opinion leaders is shown in Exhibit 1. At the bottom of the advertisement is a description of Planned Parenthood. The need for this was revealed in our research: Planned Parenthood was not well known nor was its name obvious enough.

We developed advertisements such as those shown in Exhibits 2 and 3 for the general public. The objective of these ads is to legitimize the concept of family planning and to add it to the social and ethical vocabulary of the United States.

For our young adult audience, we had to employ a different sensibility. In dealing with young people, we knew that we could treat our message with a bit of humor and whimsy in order to achieve the right *tonality*. By tonality we mean the emotional environment of the message. Proper tonality is achieved through the use of terms and expressions that are engaging for our target audience. Some of our advertisements for young people are shown in Exhibits 4 and 5.

It might be of interest for you to see the headlines used in two proposed advertisements that did not run.

> "One thing about the population problem, you don't have to get out of bed to fight it."

> "Darien, Connecticut, is doing its best to contribute to our population growth."

The latter was a deliberate effort to point out that the major increase in population in the United States is coming from middle and upper income families, which is contrary to popular understanding. Lower socio-economic groups do tend to have more children per family, but since they are outnumbered by middle and upper income families, the latter are producing more children in the aggregate. We thought that this was an important piece of attitude education for the

EXHIBIT 1

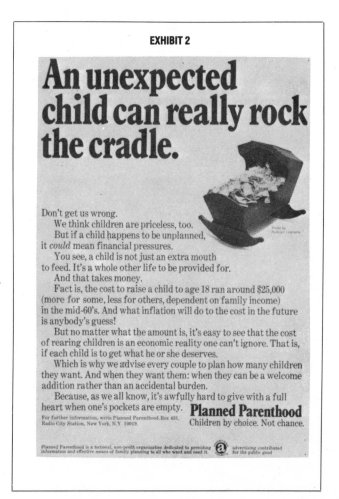

EXHIBIT 2

American people, who labor under the misguided opinion that only the poor people are breeding us into disaster.

For television, we produced two messages which are shown in storyboard form in Exhibits 6 and 7. We had both sixty- and thirty-second versions of each message.

We also prepared one other television message, referred to earlier, which was not produced because the networks would not approve it.

This message has a lovely church setting where a wedding is about to start. Everybody eagerly awaits the bride. Our camera moves close in on the people in the pews who fidget and stare at the rear of the church waiting for the bride to appear.

Then our camera cuts to the minister who finally signals by a slight nod of the head that the ceremony is ready to begin.

We cut to the nervous groom who runs his finger under his collar, and to the best man, who is trying to look relaxed. They too face the rear of the chapel.

Finally the organ sounds and then our camera shifts to the rear of the chapel to pick up the bride as she steps through the double door on the arm of her father. She is beautiful. She is radiant. She is also quite pregnant.

Then for the first time we hear the words of the announcer who says, as the bride and her father glide slowly down the aisle:

"The purpose of this message is not to shock you. It's just to point out one out of five brides in this country is pregnant before the ceremony. We think there is only one time to have a child: when you really want one."

We close on: "Planned Parenthood. Children by Choice. Not by Chance."

That message never saw the light of day. Nobody would approve it. But its time will come.

Materials for radio included recorded messages (and scripts for live presentation) of ten-, thirty-, and sixty-second spot announcements. Here are two of the sixty-second recorded announcements:

"GET TO KNOW THE TWO OF YOU"

OPEN WITH PP THEME MUSIC, THEN UNDER.

Girl: What sign were you born under?
Boy: Do you really think rock has had it?
Girl: How do you like your coffee in the morning?
Boy: Do you like to sleep late on weekends?
Girl: Can a wife work and be a mother at the same time?
Boy: Should a husband help with the housework?
Girl: Where would you like to live—city or country?
Boy: Should we spend a couple of years in Europe?
Girl: How often should we have relatives over?
Boy: Do we take our parents in when they get old?
Girl: How many children do you want?
Boy: How many children do **you** want?

MUSIC UP, THEN UNDER.

Announcer: Before a couple can decide how many children they want, there are a lot of questions that have to be answered: what you're both really like . . . what you both really want out of life. Only time can give you the answers. But an unexpected pregnancy can rob you of that time. And the fact is that more than half of all the pregnancies each year **are** unexpected. (BEAT) Get to know the two of you before you become the three of you.

For more information, write Planned Parenthood, Box 898, Radio City Station, New York 10019. That's Box 898, Radio City Station, New York 10019. Planned Parenthood. Children by choice. Not chance.

Girl: How well do you think you **know** me?
Boy: How well do you think you know **me?**

"THE FUTURE"

OPEN WITH DOCUMENTARY-TYPE SOUND MONTAGE OF STUDENTS TALKING ABOUT THEIR HOPES AND THEIR DREAMS OF THE FUTURE.

Boy 1: Tomorrow? Wow. Like, well . . . I want to be doing something positive . . . like maybe, uh . . . social work . . .
Boy 2: . . . medical research. That's where it's going for me . . . such things can be done . . .
Girl 1: . . . probably wind up in the suburbs with my husband . . . doing the things everybody does . . . but they can't take my education away!
Boy 3: . . . figure, then, with an M.A. from Harvard Business, my wife and I can take my old man's car franchise and really break the bank!
Girl 2: . . . not to be a great actress! But if I can teach the feeling to children . . .
Girl 3: . . . a different lawyer than my father-in-law. Get it down to the people.
Boy 4: . . . know the film business is rough . . . but if you don't make it, well, you can always do commercials!
Announcer: No matter what your plans for the future—an unexpected pregnancy can change them. And the fact is—more than half the pregnancies each year **are** unexpected. So if you want your future to be what you planned—don't take a chance with it. For more information, write Planned Parenthood, Box 898, Radio City Station, New York 10019, That's Box 898, Radio City Station, New York 10019. Planned Parenthood. Children by choice. Not chance.

From these examples, it will be seen how easily the same material transfers from print to television to radio. We always strive for this consistency of language and tonality from medium to medium. It is not always possible, but it should always be an objective.

Part IV
Market Structure Analysis

Development of a successful program requires that the manager have a good understanding of the market to be served. This involves structuring the market into segments that reflect different consumer needs, resources, and purchasing patterns. Some of these segments will inevitably be more important to the marketer than others. Others, while historically of little interest, may represent important potential for the future.

Competing offerings must be identified and an evaluation made of their relative appeal to different market segments. It is essential that the marketer understand the extent to which the specific attributes of a given product appeal to different market segments, since the relative importance of different attributes may vary from one segment to another.

Part IV comprises six chapters, each of which addresses the issues relating to market segmentation and market analysis from the perspective of a different application area or methodology. By comparing and contrasting the problems described in these chapters, the reader will come to realize the fundamental contribution made to managerial thinking and strategy by the concept of market segmentation.

Christopher H. Lovelock's article, "A Market Segmentation Approach to Transit Planning, Modeling, and Management," relates market segmentation strategies to achievement of specific objectives in a transportation context. He shows how to develop an understanding of consumer behavior and of the ways in which travel needs and behavior are influenced by individuals' personal characteristics. An important question in market structure analysis concerns the most appropriate ways of dividing up a mass market into managerially useful segments. This chapter discusses alternative bases for segmenting the urban travel market and relates these to identification of market opportunities and development of strategic efforts.

"In Search of an Audience" applies segmentation concepts somewhat more informally to audiences for the performing arts, specifically live theater. Morison and Fliehr show how market segmentation was used as a means of setting audience development priorities for a new theater and how, in turn, distinct marketing programs were developed for these segments.

In "Consumer Dynamics in Nonprofit Organizations," Ryans and Weinberg emphasize the role of consumer research in developing marketing programs and demonstrate how management decisions may follow directly from market research findings. For example, a survey of subscribers to one repertory theater found that a price discount was not, as previously believed, one of the major benefits sought. Information on what benefits were sought by subscribers and on their attendance patterns before becoming subscribers proved very useful to management in planning strategy.

Market structure analysis goes beyond consumer research to include an analysis of the organization's offerings and how they compare with those of competing institutions. Competition may be either direct or indirect in nature, representing both similar alternatives and sharply different substitutes on which potential consumers might wish to spend their time and money. For instance, a potential theater-goer might face a choice between attending one of two plays or instead spending the evening relaxing at home with a book. Similarly, a high-school student might have to choose between enrolling at one of several colleges versus taking a full time job.

In "The Positioning Era: A Marketing Strategy for College Admissions in the 1980s," Geltzer and Ries raise the issue of positioning an organization against competitors offering somewhat similar alternatives. The authors argue that it is not enough to look at the market in terms of consumer demand patterns. One must also look at how competing organizations are meeting the needs of different market segments, with a view to identifying opportunities for repositioning one's own organization. This might take the form of appealing to segments which are not well served at present, or of focusing on the needs of those segments that offer greatest potential for growth.

The issue of positioning is further explored in Richard M. Johnson's classic article, "Market Segmentation: A Strategic Management Tool." The areas of application illustrated here include both the public and private sectors, with the former focusing on the competition between candidates for political office in elections. Johnson demonstrates how two-dimensional maps can be used to evaluate the relative positions of competing products on key attributes, and to identify how well consumer needs are being met by existing offerings.

Finally, in an "Analytical Approach to Marketing Decisions in Health-Care Organizations," Wind and Spitz introduce a new and powerful approach to help assess the relative importance of a product's attributes to a consumer. For example, would a prospective patient for elective surgery prefer to stay in a nearby, non-teaching, community hospital that has average facilities or in a very modern teaching hospital located downtown? Would the preference change if the recuperative stay were to be a long one? The answers to such questions, and the relative size of the segments expressing different preferences, are important to managers—not only for designing products and choosing markets in which to participate, but also for developing marketing communication strategies.

14

A Market Segmentation Approach to Transit Planning, Modeling, and Management

Christopher H. Lovelock

Services which are developed, priced, distributed, and promoted to appeal to a "mass market" may fall short of their potential because people's needs and behavior patterns often differ sharply. By segmenting the market into different groups, based upon such factors as individual characteristics, attitudes, behavior, and location, important insights can often be obtained into market dynamics. This makes is possible to develop services which are closely tailored to the needs of specific segments. This article examines alternative ways of segmenting the market for public transportation services and considers the implications for marketing strategy.

The importance of marketing for public transportation has received increasing attention in the ten years since Schneider's seminal work on this issue was first published [23]. Recently, it has provided the topic of an entire Transit Marketing Conference, co-sponsored by the Urban Mass Transportation Administration and the American Public Transit Association.

There is a risk that marketing may be seen simply as a managerial activity designed to maximize transit ridership, and as having little relevance for transportation planners and researchers. As emphasized by Kotler, marketing involves analysis, planning, implementation, and control, manifesting itself in carefully formulated programs designed to achieve specific objectives [14]. In most instances, it involves the careful selection of a limited number of target markets, rather than a quixotic attempt to win every market and be all things to all people. As part of this process, marketing requires understanding the needs of each different target market and developing products or services which attempt to meet these needs.

This article will focus on a key marketing concept, market segmentation, and discuss its relevance for planning and modeling as well as for management. First, it looks at

Christopher H. Lovelock is Associate Professor of Business Administration, Harvard University.

what is implied by the concept of market segmentation, at the potential value of dividing a mass market into smaller groups, and at the criteria which must be satisfied if meaningful segments are to be developed for use in a specific operational context.

Alternative methods of segmenting the transit market are then evaluated in the context of relating modal choice behavior to both the characteristics of individual travelers and the types of trip that they make.

Finally, findings are presented from a survey of a specific sub-segment, namely, adults in middle-income, suburban, car-owning households, located within a short distance of local transit routes. This study showed that nontransit users perceived public transportation very differently from regular users and were also less well informed about the specifics of local services.

SEGMENTING THE MARKET FOR "MASS TRANSIT"

It is sometimes observed that the term "mass transit" is an unfortunate one, since it implies a mass market with undifferentiated needs and characteristics [24]. In practice, as will be shown, the demand for public transportation is made up of many submarkets (or market segments) representing people of different ages, sexes, occupations, and income levels, traveling for various purposes, with varying degrees of frequency, at different times of day, and between different locations. Certain segments may be much more important than others from the standpoint of defining and achieving transit objectives.

Although every transit operation is likely to have somewhat different priorities, the objectives for transit tend to fall into two broad categories. The first concerns the diversion of travelers from private automobiles, with a view to achieving such goals as reducing traffic congestion, noise and air pollution, energy consumption, and traffic accidents, as well as avoiding the need for new highways and parking facilities. The second is concerned with improving mobility for those who presently lack access to adequate transportation, either because they do not own a car or lack access to one on a regular basis, or else are unable to drive.

If these goals are to be achieved, it is immediately apparent that planners must set objectives for managers of planned or existing transit systems in terms of encouraging ridership among specific segments of the population, rather than in vague terms of "maximizing ridership" for the overall system.

Various researchers, including Smerk, Lovelock, Reed, and Watson and Stopher, have emphasized the importance of developing transit services which are responsible to the needs of different market segments [25, 16, 22, 30]. This is especially necessary when attempting to encourage a modal shift from autos to transit. Failure to take these varying needs into account and failure to adopt communications and pricing strategies which are tailored to the characteristics of specific segments can only weaken transit's prospects for competing successfully against private automobiles.

Transportation models, too, need to reflect the structure of the market. If transportation objectives focus on specific segments of the travel market, then it is important that models be developed which can predict (and perhaps explain) the behavior of these segments.

Pointing to the limited explanatory power of highly aggregative models based upon economic analysis, a number of transportation researchers have stressed the need to develop a better understanding of the ways in which consumers arrive at modal choice decisions. [26, 15, 12]. Particular interest has been shown in learning more about how behavioral variables such as attitudes relate to modal choice [11, 1].

DEFINING MARKET SEGMENTATION

In the context of the private firm, market segmentation may be defined as the two-stage process of, first dividing the consumer market into meaningful buyer groups, and then creating specific marketing programs for each group such that financial profits will be maximized. In the case of urban public transportation (which has largely ceased to be profitable financially), the objective function theoretically centers, on attaining specified social goals (e.g., helping achieve new air pollution standards) which can justify a defined level of deficit spending on transit. Unfortunately, transit's success or failure is all too often measured simply in terms of gross ridership statistics.

In evaluating a market and developing appropriate programs, one of three broad alternative strategies can be followed. The first is *market aggregation,* treating all consumers as similar and offering a standard product for everyone. Historically, "mass transit" has tended to fall into this category.

At the opposite end of the scale is *total market disaggregation,* where each consumer is treated uniquely. In the last analysis, each individual may be thought of as a separate market segment, on the grounds that each person is slightly different from everybody else in personal characteristics, behavior patterns, needs, values, and attitudes [29]. Total disaggregation of the population has particular appeal for the modeler, in as much as it can be argued that the best way to develop an understanding of how travel decisions are made and how they may be influenced is to study individual consumers.

Recognizing the dangers inherent in taking an undifferentiated, mass market approach to transportation planning and management, interest has been shown in developing disaggregative behavioral models of modal choice [28]. I believe that understanding the behavior of individual travelers can yield valuable insights for model builders, and also assist transit managers in developing strategies for influencing modal choice decisions. However, there are limits as to how far disaggregation can be carried. Planners have to develop transportation systems for populations which may run into the millions, total disaggregation can quickly become a complex and expensive procedure when running large simulation models, and there are limits to the ability of transit managers to provide personalized service in buses designed to seat fifty people and trains which may carry as many as fifteen hundred at a time.

Obviously, there has to be a happy medium between complete aggregation of the population on the one hand and total disaggregation on the other. This is where the third strategy, that of *market segmentation,* promises to be of value. It calls for grouping consumers into segments on the basis of intra-group similarities and inter-group differences. Wilkie notes that market segmentation may be viewed as a descriptive process, in that it recognizes both individual differences and group similarities [31]. Segments can be developed either by dividing a large, amorphous group into smaller groups with certain characteristics in common, or "built from the ground up" by assigning individuals to one of several groups according to certain specific characteristics which each person possesses.

The concept of market segmentation is based upon the propositions that (1) consumers are different, (2) differences in consumers are related to differences in market behavior, and (3) segments of consumers can be isolated within the overall market. Engel, Fiorillo and Cayley summarize a number of benefits which may be expected to result from a segmentation approach [8], including:

1. a more precise definition of the market in terms of the needs of specific groups, why they behave as they do, and possible ways of influencing behavior;
2. a better ability to identify competitive strengths and weaknesses, and opportunities for winning specific segments from the competition;
3. more efficient allocation of limited resources to the development of programs that will satisfy the needs of target segments;
4. clarification of objectives and definition of performance standards.

The basic problem is to select segmentation variables which are likely to prove useful in a specific operational context. Kotler proposes three criteria [13], each of which must be satisfied if meaningful market segments are to be developed:

> *Measurability:* it must be possible to obtain information on the specific characteristics of interest.
> *Accessibility:* management must be able to identify chosen segments within the overall market and effectively focus marketing efforts on these segments.
> *Substantiality:* the segments must be large enough (and/or sufficiently important) to merit the time and cost of separate attention.

Wilkie stresses the importance of choosing segmentation variables which are useful as correlates of behavior and can be related to strategic considerations [31]. He also argues that the best segments are those which display "homogeneity within and heterogeneity between groups"; in other words,

there should be minimal within-group variation and maximal between-group variation.

SELECTION OF SEGMENTATION VARIABLES

How can the transportation market be segmented, and which variables are likely to yield *useful* segmenting descriptors? In order to see how segmentation variables relate to modal choice decisions (and, perhaps, influence the outcome of such decisions), a flowchart of the decision process is shown in Exhibit 1. This illustrates the stages through which an individual traveler is posited to go in selecting a mode for a specific trip and is based upon an earlier, more complex model to which explicit segmentation variables have been added [16, 17].

This diagram helps us categorize *who* is traveling, and also *why, when, where,* and *how* they are making a trip. It serves to indicate some of the many ways in which the travel market can be segmented, as well as providing insights into modal choice behavior patterns and how they may be influenced. The traveler is seen as specifying the modal attributes desired for a particular trip, then evaluating alternative modes to see which is perceived as providing the best "match" for this trip, choosing that which is perceived as the optimal mode, and then making the trip.

Two broad categories of potential segmentation variables are represented here: (1) traveler-related variables and (2) trip-related variables.

As shown in Exhibit 1, travelers can be described according to demographic characteristics, such as age, income, sex, etc., which, in turn, may be related to certain lifestyle characteristics such as car ownership and ability to drive. They can also be segmented by locational variables, such as where they live, work, shop, and so forth; by their actual travel behavior patterns; and, finally, by various psychological variables, which may be linked to such behavior as attitudes and values, or perceptions and knowledge of alternative modes.

Trip-related variables are shown as being categorized in four basic ways: the purpose for which they are made; the size of the party making a particular trip; the length and nature of the route linking origins, destinations and any intermediary points; and the time of day, week, month, or season at which the trip is made.

It is immediately evident that many of these variables are inter-related. Thus, car ownership and ability to drive are in large measure a function of age and income characteristics. Other demographic characteristics may be related to home and work locations, as well as to trip making behavior.

Certain personal characteristics are obviously linked to the type of trips made. People in most full-time jobs have to commute to and from work each weekday, while students have to go to school or college each day during the school year. With a few exceptions (such as traveling salespeople) these journeys are repetitive in nature, being made at approx-

EXHIBIT 1
Relationship of Segmentation Variables
to Modal Choice Decisions

A PARTICULAR INDIVIDUAL
· with specified demographic characteristics
· having/not having a car generally available and able/unable to drive
· living in/working in/frequenting defined geographic locations
· having defined behavior patterns in terms of modal usage and travel frequency on different types of trip

· with certain attitudes and value sets
· with certain levels of knowledge of alternative travel modes
· and with certain perceptions of the characteristics of alternative modes

↓

DECIDES TO MAKE A TRIP
· for a particular purpose
· alone or with others
· between two or more locations
· at a given point in time

↓

HE/SHE SPECIFIES THE MODAL ATTRIBUTES DESIRED FOR THIS TRIP SETTING CERTAIN THRESHOLD STANDARDS OF ACCEPTABILITY

↓

IDENTIFIES ONE OR MORE ALTERNATIVE MODES WHICH MIGHT SATISFY THESE NEEDS AND FORMS PERCEPTIONS OF THE ATTRIBUTES OF EACH

↓

OBTAINS ANY ADDITIONAL INFORMATION DESIRED (AND AVAILABLE) ABOUT THESE ALTERNATIVES AND CHANGES PERCEPTIONS ACCORDINGLY

↓

MATCHES THE PERCEIVED ATTRIBUTES OF ALTERNATIVE MODES AGAINST THE NEEDS SPECIFIED EARLIER

↓

AND SELECTS THAT MODE WHICH IS PERCEIVED TO BEST MATCH HIS/HER NEEDS*

↓

MAKES THE TRIP

↓

AND UPDATES PERSONAL KNOWLEDGE AND PERCEPTIONS OF MODAL ATTRIBUTES ON THE BASIS OF THIS EXPERIENCE

---

* If no acceptable match results, the traveler posited to either change the nature of the trip itself, after his/her requirements or else not make the trip at all.

imately the same time each day and between the same two points. In short, they are ''committed'' trips. Other types of trips, such as shopping or recreational, may be said to be ''discretionary'' in nature, in that there is usually some flexibility in timing and/or the locations visited.

Exhibit 2 shows the distribution of trip purposes by time of day and week experienced by the GO Transit rail service in Toronto, highlighting variations in the nature and timing of travel demands among existing transit users. The study found that travelers at off-peak and weekend periods were less frequent users of the system and that the proportion of the two sexes varied by time of day and week.

Which of all these numerous segmentation variables is likely to prove useful to planners, modelers, and managers? Let's first evaluate them from the standpoint of defining objectives for public transportation.

RELATING TRANSIT OBJECTIVES TO SEGMENTATION VARIABLES

Improving Mobility. It is immediately apparent that objectives relating to improvement of personal mobility tend to be keyed to the needs of specific demographic segments who do not own a car or may not be able to drive one. These groups usually include the elderly, young people, handicapped persons, and low-income groups.

Frequently, transit-related legislation specifically singles out these segments for special attention. Even though some of these segments may be relatively very small (the handicapped, for example), transit planners and managers must still cater to their needs. Ideally, this requires identifying the home origins of as many as possible, the destinations they most need to visit, evaluating their ability to pay, and assessing the extent to which it is necessary and/or feasible to modify vehicle characteristics, promotional strategies and operating policies to meet their special needs. For example see [4].

Modal Shift. Objectives relating to modal shift are concerned with getting people out of their cars and into public transportation. Here the target may at first appear to be simply the four-fifths of all American households which own automobiles. However, when looking at specific objectives, it becomes apparent that priorities need to be set. For instance, if our concern is with reducing energy consumption, then we might usefully attempt to group consumers according to quantity of gasoline they consume annually (presumably a function of miles driven, frequency of trips, and ownership of cars yielding poor gas mileage). If relieving congestion is our concern, then it makes sense to focus on people driving along specific routes during defined periods of the day or week.

Planners and researchers can play an important role here in seeking to identify key groups. However, identification is not enough; it is also important to evaluate the factors motivating the choice of automobiles over other modes

EXHIBIT 2
Trip Purpose of Peak, Off-Peak, Saturday and Sunday Riders

Trip Purpose	Weekdays		Saturdays	Sundays
	Peak	Off-Peak		
Work	♟♟♟♟♟♟♟♟ ♟♟♟♟♟♟♟♟♟	♟♟♟♟♟♟♟♟	♟♟♟♟♟	♟♟
Business	♟♟♟	♟♟♟	♟♟	♟
Shopping	♟♟♟	♟♟♟♟♟	♟♟♟♟♟♟	
School	♟♟♟♟♟♟♟♟	♟♟♟♟♟♟♟	♟	♟
Entertainment	♟	♟♟♟♟	♟♟♟♟♟	♟♟
Social	♟	♟♟♟	♟♟♟	♟♟♟♟♟♟
Personal	♟♟		♟	
Recreation			♟♟	♟♟♟
Other		♟	♟♟♟♟♟	♟♟♟

♟ Represents 1,000 trips, ♟ Represents 100 trips

Source: Government of Ontario (1969).

for individuals within these groups, as well as to discover how susceptible various subcategories of individuals are to switching to public transportation. This is where the consumer research and the model builder may be able to develop useful insights for transit management.

INSIGHTS FROM PAST RESEARCH

Location. Many studies highlight the importance of location as a segmentation variable, indicating that transit's share of the travel market is a function of the accessibility of origins and destinations from stopping points on the transit route.[1] For interurban rail or bus transit, accessibility is perhaps best measured in terms of travel time. A study of the GO Transit rail service in Toronto showed that GO's market share of all "in scope" trips declined from a high of 41.2 percent, when both origin and destination were within ten minutes' walk of the station, to a mere 1.8 percent of trips originating ten to fifteen minutes' drive from the suburban station and terminating fifteen to twenty minutes' transit ride-plus-walk from the downtown station (Exhibit 3). On the basis of other transit research in Toronto, Bonsall has suggested that the effective catchment area (or "transit envelope") for local bus service is about one thousand feet [2].

The implications of location as a segmentation variable are twofold. First, if planners want people living or working in a particular geographic location to use transit, they must ensure that transit service provides acceptable access levels to both their origin and principal destination locations. Second, transit marketers are wasting time and money if they try to market their service for trips whose origins and/or destinations lie outside the transit envelope. For this reason, geographically specific media such as direct mail or billboards may be a more cost-effective means of communicating with potential riders than wide-area media such as

TV and radio. Another advantage of direct mail is that it can tailor information on routes, fares, and schedules to the needs of a specific location (residents of a local area or employees at a specific plant, for example).

Demographics. How useful are demographic variables (other than geographical location) as a means of segmenting that

EXHIBIT 3
GO Transit Market Share by Origin/Destination Zones

Origin*	Destination Zones**	GO Transit Market Share
Suburbs	Central Toronto	
XX2	002	41.2%
XX4	002	39.8%
XX2	004	22.4%
XX4	004	15.8%
XX2	005	12.7%
XX2	006	9.2%
XX6	002	10.5%
XX4	005	6.7%
XX4	006	5.3%
XX6	004	6.5%
XX6	005	2.6%
XX6	006	1.8%
		14.5%

* **Origin zones** in the two suburban corridors were defined as follows:
XX2: Less than 10 minutes walk from the station (innermost zone)
XX4: 5–10 minutes drive from the station (excluding 10 min. walk area)
XX6: 10–15 minutes drive from the station

** **Destination zones** within the Central Toronto area were defined as:
002: Less than 10 minutes walk from Union Station (innermost zone)
004: Up to 10 minutes transit ride plus walk (excluding innermost zone)
005: 10–15 minutes transit ride plus walk
006: 15–20 minutes ride plus walk.

Source: [18].

---

[1] Summarized in [16], Appendix B.

great bulk of the American population which travels by car? It is known that demographic variables may influence the modal attributes desired by consumers and the relative importance they attach to them. Golob *et al.*, Stopher and Lavender, Dobson and Nicolaidis, and Watson and Stopher have all conducted research which indicates that groups with different socioeconomic variables display different preferences for transportation mode attributes [9, 27, 6, 30]. Often the group which stands out most prominently from the others is the elderly.

However, it is worth noting that business marketers consider demographics as only one of several possible methods of segmentation and not necessarily the most useful at that. Haley cites a number of studies which suggest that demographic variables are, in general, poor predictors of behavior and less than optimum bases for segmentation strategies [10].

Trip Characteristics. A number of researchers have found that people's needs differ according to the type of trip they are making. For instance, Paine, Nash, Hille and Brunner identified the relative importance given to various modal attributes for both work and non-work trips [21]. Their study showed that speed, punctuality, and timing considerations were significantly more important for work trips than for non-work trips. However, for non-work journeys, travelers were noticeably more price sensitive and more concerned about weather protection while waiting and having to walk more than one block; they also placed greater emphasis on clean, comfortable vehicles, on availability of package and baggage space, and on the ability to take along family and friends. Domencich and Kraft, too, have found that demand for shopping trips is much more price elastic than that for work trips [7].

MULTIDIMENSIONAL SEGMENTATION

Thus far, segmentation has been discussed primarily from a unidimensional standpoint. In practice, classification may be more useful if it is undertaken along two or more dimensions simultaneously, to yield a variety of subsegments.

It is my belief that transportation researchers and modelers should be taking a matrix approach to segmentation, with meaningful traveler characteristics along one axis and trip characteristics along the other. In such an approach, each cell would represent a separate sub-segment. It might be hypothesized that each sub-segment would have somewhat different modal attribute preferences and might therefore be expected to show variations in modal choice behavior from other cells. Moreover, such an analysis could well yield insights into preference and behavior differences that are presently obscured by segmentation along a single dimension.

Little research is known to have been conducted along such lines, although Bucklin found marked differences in modal choice behavior among shoppers according to (1)

the size and composition of the shopping party, (2) the shopper's marital status and stage in life-cycle, and (3) the time of day and/or week at which the shopping was done [3, pp. 59–61].

Whether or not a sub-segment merits separate analysis will depend primarily on its size. Some cells will contain insufficient travelers. However, by use of multidimensional scaling and cluster analysis, it should then be possible to group modal attribute requirements for different cells according to their similarities to one another, thus collapsing many small cells into a limited number of larger groups, which will satisfy Wilkie's criterion of minimizing differences within groups and maximizing them between groups.

In a number of urban areas, large-scale transportation censuses have been conducted which correlate travel behavior (including modal choice) with data on personal characteristics. Such censuses can provide the basis for an understanding of the size of different traveler/trip cells as outlined above, and the nature of the data available may in itself help determine which bases of segmentation should be employed.

Transportation and population censuses are also valuable in yielding demographic data by geographic area, enabling transportation researchers and managers to identify both the size and geographic location of the segments. Information may be available for population units as small as a city block. This approach has particular value for marketing urban transit services in that these provide transportation along predefined routes which can be related to the characteristics of populations within the surrounding transit envelope.

AN EXAMPLE OF SEGMENTATION IN TRANSIT RESEARCH

Although transportation censuses may describe modal choice behavior, they cannot necessarily *explain* it. By breaking the market down into a series of progressively smaller groupings, it may be possible for researchers to develop new hypotheses into the behavior of specific subsegments.

Such an approach may be particularly useful when seeking to explain differences in model choice behavior among individuals who are realistically in a position to choose between either car or transit for specific journeys, and who appear to have similar demographic characteristics. As suggested in Exhibit 1, personal values, attitudes, perceptions, and knowledge of alternatives may all contribute to determining the outcome of modal choice decisions.

To improve our understanding of the different cells in the segmentation matrix described earlier, therefore, it may be necessary to conduct additional research into (1) the modal requirements of specific subsegments, (2) their perceptions of the various attributes of different modes, and (3) the extent of their knowledge of alternative modes. In this way, it may be possible to relate "soft" characteristics like personal preferences to more readily identifiable personal characteristics such as demographics and behavior patterns.

San Francisco Area Study. With a view to determining the relationship between modal choice behavior and travel perceptions and knowledge, a large scale consumer survey was made in the San Francisco Area of a carefully defined subsegment of the population [16]. The sample was confined to adults aged 18 to 65 years in middle income, car-owning households situated in suburban cities 20–30 miles from San Francisco and located within a quarter-mile of a local transit route and one mile of a trunk-line interurban transit route. Various controls were used to exclude any respondents who might be captive transit users, due to inability to drive or lack of access to an automobile.

Using several measures of reported behavior, the 1,328 remaining respondents could be assigned to one of four categories of transit user behavior:

1. Non user—had never used transit (13.6%)
2. Non-user—but had used transit in the past (49.5%)
3. Occasional transit user (30.1%)
4. Regular transit user by choice (6.9%)

To find out how respondents perceived the characteristics of car, bus, and commuter train travel, they were asked to rate the three modes separately on each of twelve attributes, using a seven-point semantic differential scale keyed to polar opposite descriptors. For instance, on the characteristic of punctuality, the favorable pole was labeled "on-time arrivals" and the unfavorable pole "late arrivals." The results are shown in Exhibit 4 and indicate distinctly different profiles for each of the three modes.

When respondents were segmented according to their transit usage category, there was often a significant difference in their perceptions of the characteristics of the three modes (Exhibit 5). As a broad generalization, the more often people used public transportation, the more favorable their ratings of bus and train travel; by contrast, regular transit users tended to rate car travel somewhat less favorably on most characteristics (despite the fact that they were car owners and drivers themselves).

The findings for bus travel are highlighted graphically in Exhibit 6, showing the difference in ratings for non-users and regular users (for clarity, the two non-user groups have ben combined and occasional users excluded). As can be seen, the differences are largest for convenience, simplicity ('simple to use"–"complicated to use"), enjoyableness, and comfort. With the exception of cost, non-commute speed, safety and punctuality, all differences in ratings between users and non-users are statistically significant at the $p < .05$ level or better. How should we interpret these findings? Can we infer that one explanation for non-users' failure to ride transit lies in the fact that they perceive transit service as much less competitive with the automobile on many attributes than do regular transit users?

Essentially, this begs the question of whether attitudes cause behavior or vice-versa. Behavioral scientists are divided on this point. A majority hold the view that attitudes (of which perceptions are a subset) are intervening variables

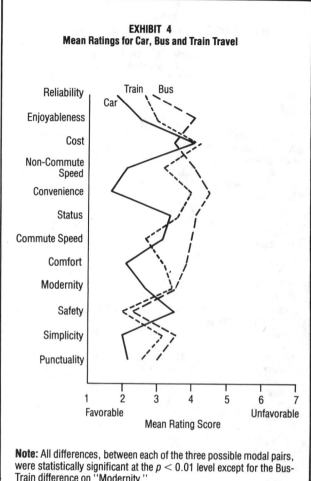

EXHIBIT 4
Mean Ratings for Car, Bus and Train Travel

Reliability
Enjoyableness
Cost
Non-Commute Speed
Convenience
Status
Commute Speed
Comfort
Modernity
Safety
Simplicity
Punctuality

1   2   3   4   5   6   7
Favorable   Unfavorable
Mean Rating Score

Note: All differences, between each of the three possible modal pairs, were statistically significant at the $p < 0.01$ level except for the Bus-Train difference on "Modernity."

which account for behavioral differences. Others, however, argue that attitudes often represent a rationalization for behavior.[2]

I incline towards the view that perceptions are both a cause and an effect of modal choice behavior, with the former the more significant. It is noteworthy that when respondents were asked how confident they were about the ratings they had made of bus travel, non-users showed significantly less confidence in their judgements than users (Exhibit 7).

One of the problems in encouraging car travelers to make use of transit is that many of them are basically unfamiliar with this mode. In the survey, respondents were asked a series of questions designed to test their knowledge of bus services from their community to San Francisco (these questions were phrased in terms of providing information to a new neighbor who had asked for assistance). As can be seen in Exhibit 8, the less respondents used transit, the more ignorant they were about the specifics of the service.

---

[2] For an overview of this controversy, see [5].

EXHIBIT 5
Consumer Ratings of Car, Bus and Train Travel, by Transit Usage Class

	Never Used	Past User (not now)	Occasional User	Regular User (by choice)
N	181	656	399	92
Car Travel				
Reliability	1.70	1.76	1.86	1.92*
Cost	4.04	4.02	4.19	4.51
Enjoyableness	2.51	2.54	2.69	2.57
Non-Commute Speed	2.29	2.10	2.10	2.02
Convenience	1.49	1.52	1.66	1.77*
Status	3.12	3.33	3.36	3.14*
Commute Speed	3.12	3.03	3.23	3.49*
Comfort	2.08	2.11	2.27	2.25
Modernity	2.57	2.52	2.75	2.76
Safety	3.30	3.51	3.79	3.69
Simplicity	1.95	1.96	2.16	2.12
Punctuality	2.14	2.01	2.24	2.44*
Bus Travel				
Reliability	2.92	2.81	2.73	2.25
Cost	3.65	3.65	3.68	3.35
Enjoyableness	4.37	4.28	4.05	3.41*
Non-Commute Speed	4.26	4.17	4.15	3.75
Convenience	4.74	4.70	4.39	3.17*
Status	4.13	4.10	4.12	3.79*
Commute Speed	4.17	4.00	3.81	3.51
Comfort	3.96	3.98	3.86	3.20*
Modernity	3.60	3.64	3.49	3.07*
Safety	2.35	2.35	2.33	2.02
Simplicity	3.79	3.64	3.55	2.58*
Punctuality	3.31	3.11	3.02	2.72
Train Travel				
Reliability	2.82	2.55	2.55	2.15
Cost	4.04	4.19	4.30	4.33
Enjoyability	3.40	3.12	2.99	2.63
Non-Commute Speed	3.33	3.26	3.09	3.09
Convenience	4.31	3.86	3.86	2.91*
Status	3.59	3.54	3.50	3.13*
Commute Speed	2.95	2.74	2.78	2.34*
Comfort	3.37	3.33	3.30	2.81*
Modernity	3.71	3.55	3.60	2.81*
Safety	2.12	2.08	2.04	1.97
Simplicity	3.59	3.07	3.06	2.57*
Punctuality	2.84	2.63	2.64	2.12

* Differences are statistically significant at $p < .05$ level.

Note: Ratings could range from 1 to 7, with a low number constituting a very favorable rating and a high number a very unfavorable one.

EXHIBIT 6
Ratings of Bus Travel by Non-Transit Users and Regular Transit Users

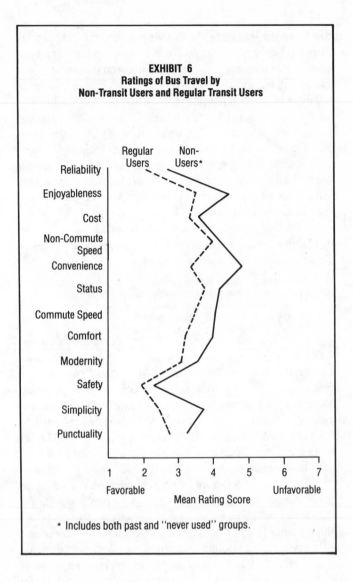

* Includes both past and "never used" groups.

EXHIBIT 7
Confidence in Judgements of Bus Travel by Transit Usage Class

	Usage Class				
Degree of Confidence	(A) Never Used	(B) Used in Past, But Not Now	(C) Occasional User	(D) Regular User	Total
Extremely	3.7%	6.7%	3.9%	30.5%	7.1%
Very	16.7	30.2	39.4	43.9	32.1
Somewhat	49.4	40.9	45.2	23.2	42.1
Only slightly	22.2	19.8	11.0	2.4	16.3
Not at all	8.0	2.5	0.6	0.0	2.5
	100.0	100.0	100.0	100.0	100.0

Measure of Association	γ	signif.
All usage classes	−.322	<.001
(A) + (B) and (D) only	−.677	<.001

It is entirely possible that two individuals may have the same modal attribute requirements for a given trip, but perceive competing modes in different ways. Essentially, then, it is not the "real" or engineering attributes of a mode which may determine success or failure in attracting travelers, but the *perceived* attributes. An obvious corollary is that a person cannot be expected to use a mode of which he or she is largely ignorant. For these reasons, perceptions of specific attributes and the extent of overall knowledge may constitute important variables in modal choice decision-making.

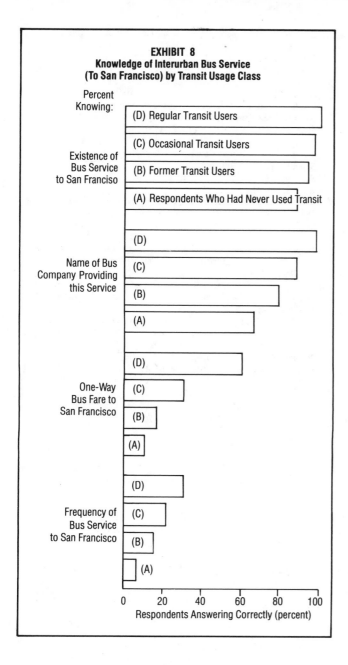

EXHIBIT 8
Knowledge of Interurban Bus Service
(To San Francisco) by Transit Usage Class

transit service areas are deterred from using public transportation because they are either ignorant of the availability and specifics of service or else perceive transit attributes in an unfavorable light, then marketing communications programs designed to correct misperceptions and provide needed information may be able to influence modal choice behavior in many instances.

However, for such an approach to prove effective, it would be most important to tailor the content of the communications to those target segments whom research had shown to be the most likely to change their behavior as a result of (a) obtaining specific needed information and (b) changing their perceptions of specific attributes. A broad based campaign along the lines of "Ride the Bus, It's Nicer than You Think" is unlikely to achieve much.

CONCLUSIONS

This paper has attempted to emphasize both the importance and the benefits of taking a segmentation approach to transportation planning, modeling, and management.

Various bases of segmentation were discussed, including geographic location, other demographic variables, and trip characteristics. It was argued that greater emphasis should be placed on multidimensional segmentation, as opposed to categorizing consumers along only one dimension at a time. By focusing on specific subsegments of the population, it may be possible to obtain new insights into the modal choice behavior of certain groups which have particular significance in terms of achieving transportation objectives.

Although the emphasis in this paper has been directed towards segmentation's application for public transportation, it should be stressed that it is also a potentially valuable concept for a broad range of urban transport services. Issues such as toll road pricing, ramp metering, preferential freeway lanes, parking supply management, and highway safety campaigns all have behavioral implications. Decisions in these areas may benefit from research and analysis which yield a better understanding of the needs and behavior patterns of different highway user segments.

The findings presented from the San Francisco area study suggest a strong link between perceptions of modal attributes and modal choice behavior, but longitudinal studies are needed to test the hypothesis that perceptions and knowledge levels explain behavior, rather than the other way around. If it can be shown that they do, then an attempt should be made to incorporate these variables in future modal choice models, especially when focusing on subsegments of the population which are prime candidates for switching from auto to transit.

Managerial Implications. Clear evidence that perceptions and knowledge levels do influence modal choice behavior among defined segments of the population would have important implications for transit management. If non-users located in

BIBLIOGRAPHY

1. Allen, W. Bruce, and Isserman, Andrew. "Behavior Modal Split." *High Speed Ground Transportation Journal* (Summer 1972):179–99.
2. Bonsall, J. A. *Dial-A-Bus: The Bay Ridges Experiment.* Toronto: Ontario Department of Transportation and Communications, August 1971.
3. Bucklin, Louis P. *Shopping Patterns in an Urban Area.* Berkeley: Institute of Business and Economic Research, University of California, 1967.
4. Cantelli, Edmund J. et al. *Transportation and Aging: Selected Issues,* Washington, DC: Supt. of Documents, Stock #1762-0042, 1970.
5. Day, George S. "Theories of Attitude Structure and Change." In *Consumer Behavior: Theoretical Sources,* edited by S. Ward, and T. S. Robertson. Englewood Cliffs, NJ: Prentice-Hall, 1973.
6. Dobson, Richardo, and Nicolaidis, Gregory C. "Preferences for Transit Service by Homogeneous Groups of Individuals." *Proceedings,* Transportation Research Forum, 1974.

7. Domencich, Thomas A., and Kraft, Gerald. *Free Transit*. Lexington, MA: Lexington Books, 1970.

8. Engel, James F., Fiorillo, Henry F., and Cayley, Murray A. (eds.). *Market Segmentation: Concepts and Applications*. New York: Holt, Rinehart and Winston, 1972.

9. Golob, Thomas F.; Canty, Eugene T.; Gustafson, Richard L., and Vitt, Joseph E. "An Analysis of Consumer Preferences for a Public Transportation System." *Transportation Research* 6 (March 1972):81–102.

10. Haley, Russell I. "Benefit Segmentation." *Journal of Marketing* 32 (July 1968):30–5.

11. Hartgen, David T., and Tanner, George H. "Investigations of the Effect of Traveler Attitudes in a Model of Modal Choice Behavior." *Highway Research Record*, no. 396 1971, 1–14.

12. Horton, Frank E. "Behavioral Models in Transportation Planning." *Transportation Engineering Journal*, Proceedings of the ASCE, May 1972, 411–20.

13. Kotler, Philip. *Marketing Management*. Englewood Cliffs, NJ: Prentice-Hall, second ed., 1972 (See especially chapter 6).

14. Kotler, Philip. *Marketing for Nonprofit Organizations*. Englewood Cliffs, NJ: Prentice-Hall, 1975.

15. Le Boulanger, H. "Research Into the Urban Traveller's Behaviour." *Transportation Research* 5 (1971):113–25.

16. Lovelock, Christopher H. *Consumer Oriented Approaches to Marketing Urban Transit*. Ph.D. dissertation, Stanford University. Springfield, VA: National Technical Information Service, #PB-220 781, 1973.

17. Lovelock, Christopher H. "Modeling the Modal Choice Decision Process." *Transportation* 4 (1975).

18. Metropolitan Toronto and Region Transportation Survey (MTARTS). *GO Transit Commuter Rail Project*. Special Report No. 9 (Second Household Survey, 1968).

19. Oi, Walter Y., and Shuldiner, Paul W. *An Analysis of Urban Travel Demands*. Evanston, IL: Northwestern University Press, 1962.

20. Ontario, Government of, *People on the GO*. Report C4. Toronto, Ont.: Department of Highways, June 1969.

21. Paine, Frank T., Nash, Allen N., Hille, Stanley J., and Brunner, G. Allen. "Consumer Attitudes Towards Auto vs. Public Transit Alternatives," *Journal of Applied Psychology*. November–December 1969, pp. 472–80.

22. Reed, Richard R. *Market Segmentation Development for Public Transportation*. Stanford University, 1973. Springfield, VA: National Technical Information Service, #PB-227 178/AS.

23. Schneider, Lewis M. *Marketing Urban Mass Transit—A Comparative Study of Management Strategies*. Boston, MA: Harvard Business School Division of Research, 1965.

24. Schneider, Lewis M. "Marketing Urban Transit." Highway Research Record, No. 318, 1970, 16–19.

25. Smerk, George M. "Mass Transit Management." *Business Horizons*, December 1971, 5–16.

26. Sommers, Alexis J. "Towards a Theory of Traveler Mode Choice." *High Speed Ground Transportation Journal* (January 1970):1–8.

27. Stopher, Peter R., and Lavender, J. P. "Disaggregate Behavioral Travel Demand Models: Empirical Tests of Three Hypotheses." Transportation Research Forum *Proceedings*, 1972.

28. Stopher, Peter R., Lisco, Thomas E. "Modelling Travel Demand: A Disaggregate Approach, Issues and Applications." Transportation Research Forum *Proceedings*, 1970.

29. Twedt, Dik Warren, "The Concept of Market Segmentation." In *Handbook of Modern Marketing*, edited by V. P. Buell. New York: McGraw-Hill, 1970.

30. Watson, Peter L., and Stopher, Peter R. "The Effects of Income on the Usage and Valuation of Transport Modes." Transportation Research Forum *Proceedings*, 1974.

31. Wilkie, William L. *An Empirical Analysis of Alternative Bases of Market Segmentation*. Unpublished Ph.D. dissertation, Graduate School of Business, Stanford University, 1971.

15

In Search of an Audience

Bradley G. Morison
Kay Fliehr

Successful marketing strategies invariably depend upon the segments to which an organization chooses to market and the program it offers those segments. Rarely does one marketing program appeal to all, and consequently the manager must look at different bases by which to categorize a market. Socioeconomic and demographic data such as age, income, education, and occupation are often helpful segmentation criteria in establishing the broad groups to which the organization may expect to have any appeal at all, but each of these groups must often be subdivided further on the basis of attitudinal, behavioral, and other characteristics. In this excerpt from a book published in 1968 about the first four years of audience development efforts at the Guthrie Theater in Minneapolis, potential theater goers are subdivided into three groups based on their attitudes toward the theater, and different programs are then developed accordingly.

A city sight-seeing bus turned away from the sunstreaked green of Minneapolis' Loring Park and headed west past a carefully groomed park garden. Mrs. Lucia Lewis, travel editor for the Chicago Daily News, was doing a feature on the Twin Cities and had joined the bus-load of tourists for a narrated tour that summer of 1964. The driver's voice rasped over the public address system.

"On your left, across the beautiful formal garden, you see the Walker Art Center. Next to it is the Tyrone Guthrie Theater, opened just about a year ago. It is built so that no seat is more than 50 feet from the stage."

There was no further comment. It could have been a movie house or any ordinary theater. Finally, a curious tourist asked who Tyrone Guthrie was.

"Well," said the driver, "I don't exactly remember whether he was a lumber tycoon or one of our railroad pioneers. Now on your right. . . ."

After a year and a half of performances and nearly three years of rather extraordinary amounts of publicity, a

Bradley G. Morison is Senior Associate and Vice President, Arts Development Associates Inc.

Kay Fliehr is an Arts Consultant.

sight-seeing bus driver in Minneapolis was still confusing one of the most distinguished directors in English-speaking theater with T. B. Walker, a lumber tycoon whose foundation had contributed land and $500,000 to the Guthrie Theater. Nor was the driver alone in his confusion and lack of knowledge. It was evident from research, observation, and conversations in back-street cafes and suburban country clubs that the vast majority of the population in the theater's primary area cared little about the Guthrie Theater Company and knew less. (It should be noted, however, that shortly after Mrs. Lewis reported the above incident in her newspaper, the sight-seeing bus drivers of the Twin Cities were invited for a performance, a backstage tour, and a brief lecture on the history of the theater, complete with biographical notes on Sir Tyrone.)

The bus driver and his thousands of compatriots who have found even reading about the Guthrie Theater uninteresting were one of three major segments into which area residents were classified—people without an interest in the classical theater. In the next section, we discuss the development and utilization of market segmentation strategies.

SEGMENTING THEATER PROSPECTS

One segmentation basis was to identify geographic areas of prime potential based on the proximity of the area to the theater and also the socioeconomic characteristics of the people living in those areas. However, it was necessary to know not only *where* the prospects lived so they could be reached, but *what they thought* about theater so the right approach could be used. Unfortunately, there was no existing knowledge or research on which to draw for the psychological analysis. Nevertheless, the following three segments were defined:

> Type #1—People who *know* they like classical theater and culture for its own sake, or because their attendance at such events gives them intellectual and/or social status.
>
> Type #2—People who are uncertain about whether they like or would like classical theater or things on a so-called "cultural level" and are not driven by the social status urge.
>
> Type #3—People who are quite positive that they do not and will not like classical theater or anything which has to do with culture or art.

These types were termed the Yeses, Maybes, and Noes. Their identification served as a basis for the theater's general selling and promotion strategy. In 1962 we knew little about these groups with respect either to the *numbers* in which they existed in the area or what *kind* of people demographically comprised each group. Subsequently, we learned more about them, and formulated some interesting theories, which may be helpful to those developing audiences for the arts.

The major portion of Yeses is probably made up of people who buy season tickets. In 1963, the theater's season-ticket total represented about 1.5 percent of the total population in the primary geographic area. (Group I, a 100 mile radius.) In 1966, it was exactly 1 percent. Taking into account those who had bought season tickets only once or twice, it would be safe to figure that the Yeses in the theater's Group I population of one and a half million probably number about 3 percent.

The Maybes cannot be estimated as accurately. In 1966 the Guthrie Theater Company played to a total number of different people from Group I representing about 4 percent of that population. Eliminating the 1 percent who were season-ticket holders, or Yeses, 3 percent of the Group I population saw one or more plays on a single-ticket basis. This 3 percent is part, but not all, of the Maybe population. Over four years, the company played to a total number of different people on a single-ticket basis representing about 5 percent of the Group I population. Add to this the season ticket holders and it appears from 7 to 8 percent of the total Group I population had attended the theater at least once. The Minneapolis *Star* Metro-Poll, taken in the Twin Cities metropolitan area in 1965, showed that 9 percent of those interviewed had attended the Guthrie Theater. This would tend to corroborate our figure, since attendance from Minneapolis and its suburbs was higher than that from the rest of the Group I area.

But how big actually is the total number of Maybes in the population? How large is the group which is "uncertain" as opposed to "committed" or "turned off"? We must assume that it is larger than the 5 percent of the population which the theater had attracted; that we had simply failed to communicate well with the rest. Two sets of figures helped us to estimate the total number of Maybes. The same *Star* Metro-Poll found that one of five (20 percent) of those interviewed had seen a stage play during the past year. This included road companies, community theaters, and, presumably, high-school class plays. This, we theorized, could be taken as the outside limit of the Yeses and Maybes combined, since going to see Cousin Julia perform in *Seven Keys to Baldpate* at West Bluff Senior High School is not necessarily indicative of serious theater-going. For corroborating evidence we looked to the readership figures of the Minneapolis *Sunday Tribune*. What percentage of the population was interested enough in theater to *read* articles about it in the newspaper?

Of six major stories on theater events in two different issues of the newspaper (1964 and 1965), the "Read Any" figures ranged from a low of 5 percent on a United Press International feature by Jack Gaver about a new Broadway comedy, to a high of 19 percent on a story about the extension of Theater St. Paul's production of *Three-Penny Opera* given at the Guthrie Theater.

The figures seemed to corroborate each other. We concluded that a maximum of one-fifth of the population had any interest whatsoever in live theater. These were the Maybes plus the Yeses. Theoretically, the four-fifths of the population are Noes. But assuming that about 30 percent are either too young, too old, or economically unable to be considered as prospects, out theoretical breakdown came out like this:

Yeses	3 percent
Maybes	17 percent
Noes	50 percent
Ineligible	30 percent

Profiling the Segments. The next job was to determine the type of people who make up each of these groups. And here the waters tend to muddy.

Initially it was assumed that the Yeses, Maybes, and Noes could be separated accurately on the basis of socioeconomic and educational-occupational characteristics. The happy theory was that if the Maybes, who constitute the best immediate potential for audience development, could accurately be identified demographically, they could be reached effectively by selective promotional efforts. It was suggested that the Yeses were "people of higher educational levels particularly in the liberal arts field, plus those whose earning power or family background had placed them in the higher strata of society.'' The Maybes, were ''people generally on a white collar level including businessmen and professional specialists (engineers, doctors, etc.) whose education has not necessarily brought them into close proximity with the arts.'' And the Noes were ''people quite often on the blue collar level whose comparatively limited education has not allowed them to be introduced to the arts.''

It turns out to be more complex. The Yeses, Maybes, and Noes cannot be defined very accurately by demographic characteristics. The only thing that can be stated unequivocally is that a person with a college education earning a relatively high income in the professional or business world *is more likely* to be a Yes or a Maybe than a No. But these characteristics do not prevent a person from having a totally negative attitude toward the arts. From both statistics and the personal experience of the staff, we know that there are large numbers of college-educated, professional men and businessmen earning substantial incomes who simply will not even sample theater and the arts. We have encountered many who have said quite frankly that they *know* theater is not their cup of tea. Engineers are educated and earning reasonable incomes. Yet audience-analysis reports from a number of theaters indicate that engineers typically are not interested in theater. They are Noes. However, they are not automatically and always Noes. There are enthusiastic, theater-going engineers among the Yeses. We have come to believe that something far beyond just economic-educational-occupational characteristics affects a person's attitude toward theater and the arts—psychological factors as yet undefined—and there seems to be no existing research on the subject to help to clarify the problem.

Lacking data we had to operate on certain speculative conclusions. The matter of the Maybes and our conclusions and questions will be considered below. Here, let us present our premise and questions about the half of the population who are Noes.

Perhaps the strongest characteristic which the Noes share is a deep-rooted psychological barrier against the arts —a kind of cultural curtain fabricated independently of socioeconomic or educational-occupational characteristics. The curtain shuts out any association with cultural activities, making people blind and deaf to normal forms of communication about artistic activity, as indicated by the newspaper-readership figures.

Is there validity to this cultural curtain premise? If so, what are the roots of the psychological barrier? Is it possible that they lie almost entirely in the background of class prejudices and fears stemming from this country's seeming tradition of ''art for the wealthy few''? Is it necessary or desirable to penetrate this cultural curtain? Can it be done without more extensive knowledge concerning the reasons for its existence? Could this be the time for cultural institutions to conduct a national motivational study regarding attitudes toward the arts?

A THREE-POINT STRATEGY FOR MARKETING TO THE YESES AND MAYBES

Rex Partington sat in his backstage office, listmaking—a compulsive preoccupation of production stage managers. A September performance of the 1965 revival of *The Miser* was just underway, and the opening lines of dialogue crackled over the loudspeaker. Suddenly Partington cocked an ear and frowned. A line usually good for a rolling laugh had just died. He went back to listmaking but listened intently for the next laugh. It didn't come either.

An actor on his way to an entrance stuck his head in the office and asked ''What's the matter, don't we have anyone out there tonight?'' Partington assured him the house was full, but he sat back and listened carefully. A few nervous guffaws began to come, then a light, sweeping titter, and finally a great, full-throated downpour of laughter drenched the house.

Partington smiled and reached for the phone. He recognized now the symptoms of an audience which had never been to the new Guthrie Theater before—the first hesitancy to react, then the nervous beginnings, and finally, complete relaxation and enjoyment.

''House manager!'' Archie Sarazin's voice rattled at the other end of the line. Was there anything unusual about tonight's audience, Partington wanted to know.

''I'll say there is,'' Sarazin replied. ''They all came in on books of Gift House Stamps.''

The National Food Stores' Gift House Stamp promotion had brought a house full of Maybes into the theater for the first time, offering further evidence of the validity of the three-point strategy for attracting them. After defining the Yeses, Maybes, and Noes, the Maybes were isolated as ''the type of person most susceptible to promotion and publicity. This is where the potential lies that must be cultivated and sold.''

About the Yeses, the strategy statement had said: ''We will get them as regular customers. They will come. We cannot ignore them, but we must not overdo the emphasis and effort we place against them.'' The Noes were virtually dismissed: ''We cannot afford to waste time and money on them at this stage. They are a harder sale. They may be long-range prospects, but it is too difficult to sell them in the immediate future.''

All three opinions were destined to change by varying degrees in the course of four years.

The Maybes were the prime target. The major problem was defined this way: ''How to convince the Maybes that the Guthrie Theater is *not* so highbrow, cultural, classic, intellectual and socially oriented that they cannot enjoy it, *without* destroying the highbrow, cultural, classic, intellectual and social appeal that is necessary to keep the Yeses in the fold.'' The problem, it turns out, is universal with American artistic institutions. It is still a problem for the Guthrie Theater.

The three-point general strategy for selling the theater to the Maybes and the Yeses was the following:

1. Communicate an image of the Guthrie Theater as one which puts entertainment and excitement into great drama.
2. The satisfied audiences and admirers of this theater constitute our best advertising. Use personal recommendation as a primary selling tool.

3. This theater is not so important to our customers that we can spare any effort to make buying tickets and attending the theater as easy and pleasant as humanly possible.

Regarding the matter of image, the theme of all promotion and advertising would center around the concept that Guthrie, his company and theater together, are uniquely capable of bringing out the inherent excitement and entertainment in classic theater without detracting from its philosophic content and pure classicism.

With respect to point two of the strategy, the strategy acknowledged the exceptional power of word-of-mouth in theater, and then continued:

> We will recognize and take advantage of this by:
> Creating a hard core of devoted personal salesmen for the Guthrie Theater *within* the primary potential areas in the form of women's organizations, advisory groups, etc.
> Developing and exploiting comment and recommendations from important people from *outside* the immediate area. People are always impressed with the opinions of outside authorities about things that are going on in their own backyard . . . often more impressed than they are with opinions of people they know. This should be the primary goal of national publicity efforts.
> Developing and exploiting comment, endorsements and testimonial material from among local people who attend the theater. This should be one of the prime goals of regional publicity.

Finally, regarding point three:

> Because the Maybes are not sure of themselves in the area of theater, because there is so much competition for entertainment dollars, because entertainment decisions are often impulse, and because people are becoming used to extreme convenience in all phases of living, there must be developed a spirit of service on the part of all Guthrie Theater employees which brings them to do *anything* to make purchasing of tickets and attending the theater both easy and pleasant.

Though our wide-eyed naïveté has been dulled by the facts of theatrical life, our egos bruised by a thousand and one failures, and our enthusiasm frustrated by lack of time, money, and energy, we remain convinced of the basic validity of this three-point strategy for audience development. Experience has modified our emphasis and methods of execution, but there is overwhelming evidence that these are the key points.

Even in the example of National Food Stores' Gift House Stamp promotion one can find solid evidence. Here was a houseful of Maybes coming for the first time. What attracted them when two and one half years of previous effort had not? Could it have been that the idea of a food chain offering tickets to a Molière play for a book of stamps had communicated a nonhighbrow image which had not previously reached them? Could it have been that their neighborhood grocery store, participating in a promotion involving the Guthrie Theater, constituted a kind of personal endorsement? Could it have been that picking up tickets at the store when they did their weekend marketing was so easy and convenient that it overcame previous inertia? We think it was all three reasons.

Though we remain convinced that much of the original basic direction was sound, our experience has led us to many changes of opinion. We now believe that it is absolutely vital in any audience-development effort *not* to ignore the Noes as first suggested. Work must go on simultaneously on the problems of the Yeses, Maybes, and Noes. Attempts must be made to upgrade continually both the loyalty and the degree of critical knowledge of the Yeses so that they will stick with the theater in troubled times and continue to challenge it artistically. Yeses must be created from Maybes, and Maybes from Noes.

We are further convinced that, not only is it possible to make some headway in piercing the Cultural Curtain that barricades theater from the Noes, but that *it is absolutely essential to the health of theater that it be done*.

We now believe also that the single most important tool in audience development was hinted at in point two of the three point strategy: "Create a hard core of personal salesmen." Our experience tells us that primary emphasis for any artistic institution should be on creating ever-widening circles of enthusiastic, dedicated, and evangelistic friends.

16

Consumer Dynamics in Nonprofit Organizations

Adrian B. Ryans
Charles B. Weinberg

The study of consumer dynamics, that is, behavior patterns over time, can lead to a better understanding of users of a product or service than can a static analysis. In this study, the attendance behavior of current subscribers to a major repertory theater over a five-year period is examined by means of an extensive subscriber survey. The implications of the survey results, both for attracting subscribers and obtaining contributors, are explored in this article. The results reported here have helped management in making several significant policy changes.

Public and nonprofit organizations are increasingly recognizing the utility of consumer research in their planning activities and in the operation of their organizations (Lovelock and Weinberg 1978). For example, DiMaggio, Useem, and Brown (1977) have recently compiled a list of 270 audience studies conducted by visual and performing arts organizations. However, these studies have been basically static ones (e.g., Kaali-Nagy and Garrison 1972; Nielson and

McQueen 1974; Heitman and Crocker 1976). Relatively little attention has been paid to how the audience is acquired, how the audience's degree of involvement changes over time, and the factors influencing these processes.

For an organization to exist successfully over time, it must be concerned with (1) acquiring new users, (2) maintaining and changing usage patterns of current users, and (3) regaining former users for whom the product or service being offered is still relevant. In successfully dealing with these groups, the organization must be aware of, and adapt to, changing consumer needs, competitive activities, and environmental conditions. One of the most serious errors an organization can make is to assume that the strategy that launched the organization will remain appropriate over time. This is particularly true for governmental programs which often are launched with a wave of publicity and strong commitments from talented and motivated people. For example, when the Peace Corps was launched in 1962, a major problem was how to cope with the excess demand of Americans

Adrian B. Ryans is Assistant Professor of Marketing, Stanford University.

Charles B. Weinberg is Associate Professor of Marketing, Stanford University.

The authors gratefully acknowledge the cooperation and assistance of Charles Dillingham, General Manager, and Patricia Quinn, Assistant General Manager, of the American Conservatory Theatre, San Francisco. The authors also wish to thank Susan Berman, Imran Currim, David Garvin, Elizabeth Leichliter, Mildred McAlister, and Shelby McIntyre for research assistance, and Professor David B. Montgomery for useful comments on an earlier draft of this article.

wanting to be volunteers and host countries who wanted volunteers. By the end of the 1960's, the Peace Corps had difficulty filling its quotas and getting countries to accept volunteers. It received little mention in the press, and the Advertising Council no longer considered the Peace Corps to be a priority account (Star 1970).

Many of the major problems facing managers in the public sector involve how consumers can be induced to maintain socially desirable behaviors. For example, the key problem in such activities as using mass transit, fastening seat belts, stopping smoking, and conserving energy is not establishing the behavior at the time of a crisis but maintaining the behavior when a crisis is not imminent. Similarly, social services agencies (e.g., libraries, community centers, and arts organizations) are not so much interested in one time usage but in usage patterns over time. In this paper, we seek to demonstrate the importance of consumer dynamics and its utilization in the development of a strategy for a performing arts organization.

This study examines the behavior, over a five-year period, of subscribers to a repertory theater. Michaelis (1976) has suggested that the *entry pattern* of subscribers can be divided into stages: (a) starting as a single ticket buyer, then (b) purchasing tickets to several performances in a season, and finally (c) becoming a season ticket buyer or subscriber. Michaelis claims that customers are unlikely to skip stages in this sequence. Further, it is argued that only after a person becomes a season ticket holder does he/she become a contributor.

This hypothezied entry pattern appears to be a logical one, but is it the predominant one? Even if this pattern is predominant, do other important segments of the audience exhibit different entry patterns? The research reported in this paper examines the entry and attendance patterns of subscribers to one major theater. For the patterns observed, the question then arises whether these different patterns are a possible basis for segmentation—that is, are there identifiable behavioral correlates associated with these patterns and can these differences be employed in the development of an audience building and retention strategy? In addition, the relationship between entry pattern and contributing behavior and future subscribing behavior was investigated.

RESEARCH DESIGN

The American Conservatory Theatre (ACT), a major repertory theater located in San Francisco, draws its audience from most parts of the San Francisco Bay Area. In May 1976 when the study described here was conducted, the theater was completing its tenth season. As an aid to planning, management decided to conduct a major research study, including a survey of ACT's approximately 9,000 season subscribers. A mail questionnaire was developed and sent to each subscribing unit, addressed to the person in whose name the subscription was held. (A family that purchased tickets

together was considered to be one unit). The questionnaire was sent to all subscribing units since theater management believed that the survey would also have some promotional and public relations value. Over 40 percent of the subscribing units responded and a random sample of 982 of these were coded, keypunched, and used in the analysis. Economic considerations militated against the use of all returned questionnaires.

One of the dangers in a survey of this type is that the subscriber respondents may not be representative of the subscriber population. To examine this possibility, two key behavioral variables were examined: renewal rate and contribution rate. The theater management knew that 70 to 75 percent of all subscribers renew each year, and that about 20 percent of all subscribers contribute in any given year. As discussed later, 78 percent of respondents indicated they definitely or probably would renew their subscription, and 22 percent indicated that they had contributed in the most recent year. Thus, we concluded that, at least on these two dimensions, our respondent sample seemed representative of the subscriber population, although slightly more likely to say they would resubscribe and had contributed than the historical record for the total subscriber population would suggest.

The questionnaire covered a wide range of subjects including socioeconomic, demographic, and attitudinal data, as well as information on the respondent's participation in other cultural activities, the respondent's media habits, and a detailed history of the respondent's attendance at ACT. Because the history could be as long as ten years, a list of ACT's productions in each of the nine previous seasons was provided to assist the subscriber in remembering his or her past involvement.

RESULTS

Entry Patterns. In categorizing entry patterns of ACT subscribers, the focus was placed on the most recent five seasons, seasons six to ten, for two reasons:

1. The subscriber's recall of the most recent five-year period is likely to be more accurate than that for all ten years.
2. The last five years is likely to be more representative of the ongoing theater operation (and hence the next few years), since the early years included the start-up period during which ACT tried different programming than it employed at the time of the survey.

All but 19 of the 982 respondents included in the analysis provided sufficiently complete data on their involvement in each of the five years to be categorized in the following manner:

- No involvement—the respondent attended no ACT performance in the season.
- Some involvement—the respondent attended one or more ACT performances but was not a subscriber.
- Subscriber—the respondent was a subscriber for that season.

It was then possible to examine the switching patterns of each respondent (3^4, or 81, since all respondents were

EXHIBIT 1
Subscriber Groups Discriminant Analysis

Variable	Mean scores (centroids)			F	Standardized discriminant weights	
	Continual	Gradual	Sudden		Function 1	Function 2
Years resident (1 to 5 scale)	4.32	3.68	3.53	27.9*	0.60	−0.18
Age (1 to 5 scale)	3.34	2.74	2.86	27.7*	0.52	0.50
Income (1 to 4 scale)	2.54	2.39	2.38	2.4	0.23	0.03
Cultural activities (0 to 6 scale)	2.84	2.95	2.08	14.3*	0.30	−0.79
Twenty hours of TV (0–1 dummy variable)	0.31	0.26	0.38	2.4	−0.08	0.28
Group Mean—Discriminant function 1	0.46	−0.19	−0.37	—	—	—
Group Mean—Discriminant function 2	0.05	−0.24	0.30	—	—	—

* Indicates significance at the .01 level.

subscribers in the tenth season). The 81 possible patterns could be summarized in terms of the following three basic patterns and one miscellaneous pattern:

1. *Continual Subscriber* (32 percent of respondents). These respondents were subscribers in all five seasons.
2. *Gradual Subscriber* (no involvement → some involvement → subscriber, 31 percent of respondents). These respondents followed the pattern hypothesized by Michaelis (1976).
3. *Sudden Subscriber* (no involvement → subscriber, 21 percent of respondents). These respondents subscribed toACT without prior attendance at an ACT performance in the five-year period.
4. Miscellaneous patterns (16 percent of respondents).

The presence of such a large sudden subscriber segment was particularly surprising to the management of ACT. As a cross-check, the analysis was repeated using only the new subscribers in the 1975–76 season, the most recent group of new subscribers. It was found that 40 and 33 percent of these subscribers were gradual and sudden subscribers, respectively.

Identification of Characteristics of Subscriber Segments. The next step was to attempt to identify characteristics of the continual, gradual, and sudden subscriber groups that might be of use in understanding the differences between the segments and as inputs for developing audience building and retention programs. Of the available data, five variables appeared to have potential usefulness in this regard:

1. Years resident in the San Francisco Bay Area, measured on a scale ranging from 1 = two years or less, to 5 = more than 20 years.
2. Age of subscriber, measured on a scale ranging from 1 = 25 years old or less, to 5 = more than 65 years old.
3. Household annual income before taxes, measured on a scale ranging from 1 = $15,000 per year or less, to 4 = more than $50,000 per year.
4. Whether the subscriber spent more than 20 hours a week watching TV, measured as a dummy variable, 1 if yes, 0 if no.
5. Attendance at six other cultural institutions in San Francisco (i.e., Ballet, Civic Light Opera, DeYoung Museum, Museum of Modern Art, Opera, and Symphony). The attendance score is the number of the six different activities attended at least once in the previous year.

One way to compare the characteristics of the three subscriber groups would be to cross-tabulate group member-

ship with each of the five variables. However, such an approach would be much less informative and useful than a three-way linear discriminant analysis which would help to discover interrelationships among the five subscriber characteristics. Use of this multivariate technique allows one to test the significance of any differences among the average profiles of the three groups, to find the linear combinations of independent variables that discriminate best among the three groups, and to determine which variables (in a multivariate setting) account most for any observed intergroup differences.[1]

Complete data on the five variables were available for 651 of the 807 subscribing units in the continual, gradual, and sudden subscriber groups. Subscribing units with one or more pieces of data missing were found to be distributed almost proportionately among the three subscriber groups.

The results of the discriminant analysis are reported in Exhibit 1. Comparing the means (centroids) of the three subscriber groups, it is seen that the continual subscriber group has been resident in the Bay Area significantly longer and is significantly older than the gradual and sudden subscriber groups, which are not significantly different from each other. However, analysis of the frequency counts showed that few subscribers, even members of the sudden group, are new residents.

Income does not differ significantly across the three subscriber groups. Yet, the median household income of almost $25,000 for all the respondents is substantially higher than the San Francisco Bay Area median household income. It is interesting to note that the sudden subscribers participate

[1] Some caution must be used in interpreting the linear discriminant results because not all the required statistical assumptions are met. The assumptions are most stringent with respect to testing for significant differences between the average profiles of the groups, when the multivariate normality assumption must be invoked. This use of discriminant analysis is not the major focus in the study. Here we are primarily interested in the second and third uses of discriminant analyses, where we need only assume that within-group dispersions are equal across groups. (Green and Tull 1975, pp. 442–44.) Furthermore, discriminant analysis is usually considered to be robust with regard to the assumption of equality of within-group covariances. (Cooley and Lohnes 1971, p. 24.)

in significantly fewer cultural activities than either the continual or gradual subscribers. Finally, TV watching is not significantly different across the three groups.

Two discriminant functions were estimated, the first accounting for 74 percent of the total variation explained. Both discriminant functions, as indicated by Wilk's λ's (Cooley and Lohnes 1971) of .83 and .95, were statistically significant at the .01 level. The confusion matrix based on using these discriminant functions (Exhibit 2) indicates that these functions were successful in correctly assigning 51 percent of the subjects to the three subscriber segments. This figure compares with 35 and 39 percent correctly assigned, which would be expected with the proportional chance criterion and the maximum chance criterion (by predicting all gradual subscribers), respectively (Morrison 1969). The 51 percent correctly assigned is significantly different (at the .01 level) from the percentage computed using the maximum chance criterion.

EXHIBIT 2
Confusion Matrix for Five Variables Assuming Prior Probabilities

Actual group membership	Predicted group membership*			
	Continual	Gradual	Sudden	Total
Continual	144	79	14	237
Gradual	84	152	21	257
Sudden	57	61	39	157
Total	285	292	74	651

* Predicted group membership was based on the discriminant functions reported in Exhibit 1, adjusted for the prior probabilities of group membership.

Note: Total correct predictions = 335, percentage correct predictions = 51 percent (= 335/651) (significantly different from the maximum chance prediction at the .01 level), and maximum chance prediction = 39 percent (= 257/651).

These results were validated using a double crossover-validation procedure. The sample was divided into approximately equal subsamples, termed Samples A and B. A three-way discriminant analysis was then conducted on the Sample A data. The results of this analysis were used to classify the respondents in Sample B. The procedure was then reversed with the results of a discriminant analysis conducted on Sample B being used to classify the respondents in Sample A. When the results of these cross-validations were combined, it was found that 51 percent of the subscribers had been correctly classified—the same percentage as in the original analysis on the entire sample.

The group means for the first discriminant function shown in Exhibit 1 suggest that this discriminant function distinguishes primarily between continual subscribers and gradual and sudden subscribers (.46 versus −.19 and −.37, respectively). Interpreting the absolute values of the standardized discriminant coefficients as relative importance weights, the main contributors to group separation along the

first discriminant function are the demographic and socio-economic factors of years of residence in the Bay Area and age, high scores on these scales resulting in high scores on the first discriminant function.

On the other hand, the second discriminant function distinguishes primarily between gradual and sudden subscribers, with the main contributors to group separation along this function being the number of cultural activities attended and, secondarily, age. Low scores on the number of cultural activities attended and high scores on age result in high scores on this discriminant function.

These results can be summarized in an impressionistic manner. All subscriber groups are in the high income categories, and can be distinguished from the general population in this way.[2] Although both the continual and gradual groups take part in other cultural activities, the continual group's higher age bracket perhaps suggests that as the family reaches a more mature stage in the life cycle more time is available for cultural activities. On the other hand, the gradual subscribers tend to be somewhat younger and find themselves with limited time and having to choose among many cultural (and, presumably, other) activities.

In contrast, the sudden subscribers participate in fewer cultural activities, and the ACT subscription often may be their introduction to the performing arts. Because of their high income they can afford to subscribe, without the need for a gradual introduction over a period of years. It is possible that precipitating events, such as changes in income or marital-status, may have been contributing factors to the decision to subscribe. In summary, ACT's major competition in the gradual subscribers' segment is probably other cultural activities, whereas the major competition in the sudden subscriber segment is presumably "noncultural" activities or simply spending the evening at home.[3]

Benefits Sought. Each respondent was asked to indicate from a list of eight which two benefits were the best reasons for purchasing a subscription (Exhibit 3). The benefits included subscription price discount (ACT offered subscribers seven plays for the price of six), ease of ordering, and priority seating. The overall χ^2 was statistically significant ($p < .05$), but the differences among the three subscriber groups were relatively minor. All groups cited the benefit "more certain to attend," most frequently. The major differences among the three groups are an increasing emphasis on "ease of ordering" and "more certain to attend," but a decreasing emphasis on "support of ACT" as one moves from continuous to sudden subscribers. The differences between the gradual and

---

[2] It was also found, as has been observed in other studies (DiMaggio, Useem, and Brown 1977), that the subscribers were highly educated. In all three groups, more than half of the respondents had post-graduate schooling.

[3] Another hypothesis is that some portion of the sudden group view an ACT subscription as a status symbol. For this subsegment the nature of the market in which ACT competes would obviously be different.

EXHIBIT 3
Benefits Obtained by Subscribing to ACT

Subscriber group	Benefit*								Total mentions
	Ease of ordering	Guaranteed ticket	Price discount	Priority seating	Discount on special plays	More certain to attend	New play series	Support for ACT	
Continual subscriber	7.5%	16.4%	12.4%	22.0%	1.1%	25.9%	2.9%	11.8%	549
Gradual subscriber	8.2	16.5	12.5	22.2	1.1	28.5	3.0	7.9	558
Sudden subscriber	11.0	13.9	10.4	25.7	1.6	30.7	1.6	5.1	374

* Each respondent could check a maximum of two benefits. Percentages are based on total number of benefits checked.

Note: $\chi^2 = 23.90$, 14 degrees of freedom, ($p < .05$).

sudden subscribers in the number of respondents citing each benefit was not significant at the .05 level.

Most interestingly, the subscription price discount of 15 percent ("seven plays for six") was checked by less than 25 percent of the respondents as one of the two main benefits, even though a subscription to seven performances could cost almost $50.[4] It was checked less than half as often as the most frequently cited benefit for each group. The offering of price discounts is a particularly important issue for performing arts managers. If a discount is a significant factor in converting occasional attenders into subscribers, then its use may be economically justified. On the other hand, if subscribers are primarily the most enthusiastic theater goers, offering a discount may essentially be a price reduction for those who would attend in any case. Although it might be expected that the price discount would be particularly important for sudden subscribers, as just noted, this was not the case.

Contributing Behavior. All respondents were asked whether they had contributed to ACT, and, if so, in what years. Overall, 45 percent of those sampled had contributed at some time, with 22 percent of the respondents contributing in the most recent year. Also, 20 percent of the new subscribers in 1975–76 had contributed in that year. Some subscribers had contributed in every year they had been subscribers. However, an analysis to determine whether a person became a regular (annual) contributor after making one or two contributions produced no interpretable patterns of repeat behavior.

Overall, 64 percent of the continuous, 39 percent of the gradual, and 29 percent of the sudden subscribers had contributed to ACT. However, this effect is due more to the numbers of years of involvement with ACT than to the entry pattern. When a stepwise discriminant analysis was run with the classification variable being whether the subscribing unit

had contributed, and the independent variables being number of years it had attended an ACT performance and its subscriber category (one dummy variable representing the continual and another the gradual group), years attendance was the only variable significant at the .05 level or better. Of course, years of attendance and entry pattern are interrelated.

Intentions to Resubscribe. The subscribers indicated their intention to resubscribe the next year on a five-point scale. Using the Kolmogorov-Smirnov two-sample test, the continual subscriber group was found to be significantly more positive at the .01 level than either the sudden or gradual subscriber groups about their intentions to resubscribe (Exhibit 4). While the gradual subscribers were more positive about their resubscribing intention than were the sudden subscribers, this difference was *not* significant at the .05 level.

PREVAILING BELIEFS, RESULTS AND IMPLICATIONS

A number of the findings in this study appear to run counter to the prevailing beliefs of performing arts managers. In this section, these conflicts and their implications are discussed.

Sudden Subscribers. The presence and size of the sudden subscriber segment and the differences between this group and the gradual subscriber group suggests that different strategies should be considered. The results suggest that the customer benefits ACT should emphasize in its advertising and promotion may very well be different for the two groups. Furthermore, ACT can direct communications to the gradual group by handouts and promotional material in the theater and by direct mail to address lists maintained by itself and other cultural organizations. Much of the sudden group will not be reached by these media: thus, mass media and "upscale" mailing lists can be employed so that the potential sudden subscriber can be reached. As a result of this study, ACT has placed increased emphasis on obtaining, and mailing to, the charge card lists of prestige stores in the San Francisco Bay Area.

---

[4] Caution is needed in generalizing these results. For example, the results do not suggest that ACT can charge a price premium. In addition, generalizations to other areas of operations must be made carefully. For example, another question in the survey asked, when attending a performance, whether a free brochure about the play or an elaborate brochure costing 25¢ was preferred. The same respondents who had not rated the subscription price discount highly opted for the free brochure by a four to one margin.

EXHIBIT 4
Intention to Resubscribe Next Year

Group*	Intention to subscribe					
	Definitely will	Probably will	Not sure	Probably not	Definitely not	Total
Continual subscribers	203	67	21	6	5	302
Percent	67.2%	22.2%	7.0%	2.0%	1.7%	
Gradual subscribers	143	97	30	17	11	298
Percent	48.0%	32.6%	10.1%	5.7%	3.7%	
Sudden subscribers	96	52	24	12	19	203
Percent	47.2%	25.6%	11.8%	5.9%	9.4%	

* The chi-squared statistics are: $\chi^2_{continual-gradual} = 22.12$ ($p < .01$) $\chi^2_{continual-sudden} = 19.42$ ($p < .01$) $\chi^2_{gradual-sudden} = 2.94$ (not significant at the .05 level).

Note: Large sample Kolmogorov-Smirnov one-tailed test $\chi^2 = 4(D^2)n_1 n_2/(n_1 + n_2)$, where D = maximum difference between the cumulative proportions in the two samples under consideration, n_1 = sample size in sample 1, and n_2 = sample size in sample 2.

Whether other performing arts activities also have sudden subscribers is debatable at this point, because theater is in many ways more similar to film and television than are dance, opera, and symphony.[5] In a certain sense, theater may be an entry to the performing arts for the sudden group. Nevertheless, without the study of consumer dynamics, it is difficult to predict the different types of entry patterns that may exist in other art forms and, in particular, whether they too have a current or potential group of sudden patrons.

Price Discounts. The "seven plays for six" price discount not being cited as a major reason for subscribing was not entirely unexpected by ACT—most subscription performances are sold out, the subscribers were believed to be from the higher income brackets, and ACT has an excellent reputation. Those who are price sensitive may purchase cheaper weekday subscriptions.

Based on the preliminary results of this survey and management's prior judgments, starting with the 1976–77 season, subscription price discounts were discontinued. Percentages of subscriptions renewed stayed within the historical bounds for both the 1976–77 and 1977–78 seasons. Total subscription sales were also apparently unaffected.

As discussed earlier, it is vitally important to know what conditions are required for a price discount to be an important benefit. Arts administrations are aware of studies indicating that people feel costs are a dominant factor in preventing them from participating more actively in the arts. (National Committee for Cultural Resources 1975, p. 30). Furthermore, Newman (1977), a well known audience development consultant, has argued that "the discount factor is a formidable one in the promotion of subscription" (p.

111). Although ACT had been in financial difficulty and had had a considerable number of unsold seats in the early 1970's, by 1976 the theater was well established and, as noted earlier, most subscription nights were sold out. Without these conditions, benefits such as priority seating and guaranteed tickets for each play may not be salient and price discount may be a major benefit for all but the most avid theater fan.

Newman has also suggested that as subscription sales approach capacity the promotional emphasis should switch from price discounts to priority seating (Morison and Fliehr 1968, p. 169). Nevertheless, for ACT, the most frequently mentioned benefit, "more certain to attend each play," presents an interesting perspective on personal behavior. In addition, it suggests that being sold out may not be a necessary precondition for not offering a price discount. Finally the benefits cited by the segments suggest copy themes that could be used in soliciting subscriptions.

Contributing Behavior. An extension of the gradual involvement hypothesis is that subscribers do not become contributors until several years after first becoming subscribers. Yet, the data indicate that new subscribers are almost as likely as other subscribers to contribute in a given year. Some subscribers are loyal yearly contributors. However, there does not seem to be a general loyalty pattern of annual giving by subscribers who have become contributors.

That many people are "in and out" contributors suggests that the creative theme and copy of the individual annual appeals are of substantial importance in the contribution decision. Many subscribers do not seem to make a long-term commitment to support ACT but rather make a separate decision each year.

FUTURE RESEARCH

If an organization is to prosper over time, the dynamics of consumer behavior and the factors influencing

---

[5] In a survey carried out at the Krannert Center at the University of Illinois at Urbana-Champaign, Nielsen and McQueen (1974) collected self-report data on annual attendance at 19 types of performing arts events. Three factors—Modern Music and Dance, Classical Music and Dance, and Theater—explained 54 percent of the attendance variance.

these dynamics need to be understood. Thus, the results reported here included a number of unexpected results, though they must be viewed as tentative for various reasons. The study was conducted by a very successful repertory theater in the San Francisco Bay Area, which, given the variety of cultural institutions in the area and the socioeconomic characteristic of the population base, may not be representative of the United States. In addition, greater understanding of consumer dynamics requires a more complete and higher quality data set, e.g., some of the variables employed in the discriminant analysis were coarse measures. Nevertheless, these results do raise questions about the validity of current theories about subscriber entry patterns, the role of price discounts, and contributing behavior. They also clearly imply that managers should consider subscriber entry patterns as a possible segmentation base. The current study focused on subscribers; future work will examine other segments of the ACT audience.

The dynamics of attending, subscribing, and contributing behavior for other performing arts organizations, e.g., dance, opera, and symphony, also need to be examined to ascertain prevalent patterns and develop data on which strategies can be built. More generally, both public and private organizations which seek to establish a continuing relationship with their customers, clients, patients, users, donors, and constituents need to develop marketing programs based on an understanding of consumer dynamics.

REFERENCES

Cooley, William W., and Lohnes, Paul R. (1971), *Multivariate Data Analysis,* New York: John Wiley & Sons, Inc.

DiMaggio, Paul; Useem, Michael, and Brown, Paula (1977), "The American Arts Audience: Its Study and Its Character." unpublished working paper. Cambridge, Mass.: Center for the Study of Public Policy.

Green, Paul E., and Tull, Donald S. (1975). *Research for Marketing Decisions.* Englewood Cliffs: Prentice-Hall, Inc.

Heitman, George, and Crocker, W. E. (1976). "Theatre Audience Composition, Preferences, and Perceptions," *California Management Review.* 19 (Winter), 85–90.

Kaali-Nagy, Christina, and Garrison, Lee C. (1972). "Profiles of Users and Nonusers of the Los Angeles Music Center." *California Management Review,* 15, 133–43.

Lovelock, Christopher H., and Weinberg, Charles B. (1978). "Public and Nonprofit Marketing Comes of Age," in *Review of Marketing 1978.* Eds. G. Zaltman and T. Bonoma. Chicago: American Marketing Association.

Michaelis, Donald (1976). Untitled paper. *Association of College, University and Community Arts Administrators Bulletin,* 48.

Morison, Bradley G., and Fliehr, Kay. (1968). *In Search of an Audience.* New York: Pitman Publishing Corp.

Morrison, Donald G. (1969). "On the Interpretation of Discriminant Analysis." *Journal of Marketing Research,* 6, 156–63.

National Committee for Cultural Resources. (1975). *Americans and the Arts.* New York: Associated Councils of the Arts.

Newman, Danny. (1977). *Subscribe Now!* New York: Theatre Communications Group, Inc.

Nielsen, Richard P., and McQueen, Charles. (1974). "Performing Arts Consumer Behavior: An Exploratory Study." In *American Marketing Association Procedings,* ed. Ronald C. Curhan. Chicago: American Marketing Association, 392–95.

Star, Steven H. (1970). "The Peace Corps." Boston: Intercollegiate Case Clearing House.

17

The Positioning Era: A Marketing Strategy for College Admissions in the 1980s

Howard Geltzer
Al Ries

If colleges and universities were mass-produced consumer products, developing a marketing approach would be a relatively simple task. Analyses would indicate that the market is declining, costs are rising, and other alternatives to the product have been introduced. The marketing experts would undoubtedly commandeer all possible marketing resources and would probably engineer new ways to expand the market, usually through modification of the product.

When peanut butter was first introduced, it was marketed as a gourmet food product. And when it faced failure, the fate of 75 to 90 percent of all new products introduced each year, the marketing experts reintroduced peanut butter as a snack for everyone. The product was repackaged, readvertised, and redirected to a mass market.

A few years ago, Johnson & Johnson looked at a problem that faces colleges today—the declining birthrate—and pondered the fate of one of their most successful products, baby shampoo. Their experts simply created a rationale for a new market, adults, by promoting the shampoo as "gen-

tle enough to use every day." The result has been a resurgence of sales of the product to new heights.

The problems of colleges and universities are certainly much more complex than peanut butter or baby shampoo, because the options available are fewer. Colleges are limited to their service function and do not have staff trained in marketing. In addition, the concept of marketing has been, and we suspect still is, alien and suspect in the college community. We have discovered few colleges or universities that have translated the need for sophisticated marketing thinking into the necessary action required to tackle the new problem of attracting qualified applicants. And yet there is a remarkable abundance of statistics and up-to-date research—far more advanced than for most products and services—avail-

Howard Geltzer is President, Ries & Geltzer. airman of Ries &
Al Ries is Chairman, Ries & Geltzer.

able to colleges to assist in marketing. There is also an effective definition and isolation of the market, and there exists the capability to generate promotional and informational materials describing every aspect of every college in incredible detail.

Hanging overhead like a growing storm cloud is the intelligence that the number of high school graduates will continue to decline and that the available graduates may select alternatives other than, say, four-year colleges. To compound the crisis, there is the agonizing pincer of rising tuition and related costs on the one hand, and a decline in available financial resources from parents and funding organizations on the other.

To dramatize these problems, articles appear in the general press with headlines like:

> "Private colleges in peril"
> "Small private colleges create group to win sympathy and public funds"
> "Princeton, like other universities, is prodding its alumni harder for money as funding falls"
> "Education's big boom is ending, but studies to get more diverse—that cloudy crystal ball"
> "Rise in remedial work taxing colleges"

and even, incredibly, a cover story:

> "Harvard on the way down"

There is no question that the urgency of the problem has been recognized. What does not exist is strategic marketing thinking or the type of marketing strategy essential to deal with the marketing problem that has been defined.

The word "positioning" may not be foreign to you. You may have seen it used and misused countless times in papers and articles discussing marketing. We will discuss positioning as a marketing strategy and communications strategy, relating it to areas in business where it has been implemented and indicate how it can be applied by colleges and universities to help solve their enrollment problems.

POSITIONING

Positioning can best be explained by asking you to ask yourself some simple questions: Who was the first person to fly solo across the North Atlantic? And don't think it couldn't be Charles Lindbergh, because it was. Now, ask yourself, who was the *second* person to fly solo across the North Atlantic. Not so easy to answer.

What is the name of the highest mountain in the world? Mount Everest in the Himalayas, right? What is the name of the second highest mountain?

Who was the first person you dated in college? What about the second? The first person, the first mountain, the first company, the first college to occupy the position in the prospect's mind is going to be awfully hard to dislodge: IBM in computers, Hertz in rental cars, Harvard and Yale in law schools, Northwestern in journalism.

If your name is not IBM or Hertz or Harvard, you must find a way to position your product or school in relation to the leader, the one that exists in the mind first. This is the essence of positioning, a concept that has rapidly become preeminent in marketing.

Positioning had its formal beginning back in 1969 when Jack Trout, president of the advertising agency Ries Cappiello Colwell, wrote in an article in *Industrial Marketing* a remarkably prophetic prediction: "A company has no hope to make progress head-on against the position that IBM has established."

How *do* you market against a company like IBM? As the article pointed out, a second front must be opened. Because RCA is a leader in communications, "If RCA positioned a computer line that related to their business in communications, they could take advantage of their own position."

Trout's article raised a few eyebrows at the time. How could anyone say that powerful, multibillion-dollar companies could not succeed in the computer business if they so desired? Nonetheless, RCA did not succeed, and its incredible story unfolded in the business press: "RCA fires a broadside at No. 1," said the headline of an article in *Business Week;* "RCA goes head to head with IBM," said the headline of a news item in *Fortune;* and "RCA computer push is head-on slash at IBM," said the headline of a story in *Advertising Age*. Less than a year later, the roof fell in. "The 250-million-dollar disaster that hit RCA," said the headline of a story in *Business Week*. That's a lot of money.

Nineteen seventy-one was a bad year for more than one computer manufacturer. Not only RCA, but also General Electric threw in the computer towel. Why did they not succeed? Maybe they did not understand the natural consequences of attacking the leader where it is strong rather than weak.

Subsequently, the positioning concept began to attract attention. *The Wall Street Journal* ran a front-page story on positioning in advertising, saying "It's part of the latest trend on Madison Avenue." *The New York Times* called it "The new password in marketing." Conferences on positioning have been presented in Brazil, the Netherlands, England, Ireland, and Norway. We average a speech a week on the subject, and more than 50,000 people have requested a booklet that is a reprint of articles on the subject.

What is this thing called "positioning"? Why has it become so big in product marketing, and will it succeed in college marketing? One reason why we reply a resounding "yes" to this last question is that we have become an overcommunicated society. There are too many products, too many colleges and universities—in general, too much marketing noise.

Over $100 a year per man, woman, and child is spent on advertising to bombard the mind of the U.S. consumer each year. We estimate that a comparable amount of money is spent by colleges and universities on eligible high school seniors.

Penetrating Prospects' Minds. Although we will not question for now the college's financial ability to turn out advertising material, there is some question about your consumers' mental ability to take it all in. And make no mistake about it, the mind is the battleground. The marketing war takes place between six inches of gray matter. The battle is rough, with no holds barred and no quarter given.

To better understand what each college is up against, consider the mind as a memory bank. Like a memory bank, the mind has a slot or a position for each bit of information it retains. The mind is selective, and as a defense mechanism against the volume of today's communications, the mind screens and rejects most of the information offered it. In general, the mind accepts only that new information that relates to its prior knowledge or experience. It filters out everything else.

For example, when RCA developed marketing programs that said, "RCA computers are best," the prospect said, "No, IBM computers are best." The computer "position" in the minds of most people is filled by IBM. To obtain a favorable position, the competitive manufacturer must either dislodge IBM (an impossible task) or somehow relate the company to IBM's position.

Said another way, the best college or the one with the most beautiful campus or the finest science department is already occupied in your prospect's mind. And, if there is any one statement that can summarize the hundreds of brochures and information about colleges that we have reviewed, it is that they are all saying the same thing: we are outstanding; our campus is beautiful; our science department is terrific.

Evolution of Marketing Strategy. Until recently, it was acceptable for all colleges to claim many attributes. In most respects, we relate this past college marketing environment to the product era in consumer marketing, which existed in the 1950s. Those were the good old days when the "better" mousetrap and enough money to promote it were all that were needed. Like consumer marketing in the 1950s, colleges and universities are currently operating as though in the product era. Their attention is focused only on the features and attributes of their own school.

When technology and competition began to eliminate the unique features and competitive advantages of one product over another in business in the late fifties, the product era ended. And now that the "seller's market" in postsecondary education has ended, colleges must develop communication strategy more effective than simply relating the attributes of their institutions.

Consumer marketing in the 1960s went through the image era. Marketing strategy focused on reputation or image rather than on the product or any of its specific features. The architect of this era was David Ogilvy, who said, "every advertisement (or brochure, mailing piece, etc.) is a long-term investment in the image of a brand." And he proved the validity of his ideas with programs for Hathaway shirts, Rolls-Royce, Schweppes, and others.

The end of the image era came with an avalanche of corporate or institutional image programs. As every company tried to establish a reputation for itself, the noise level became so high that relatively few companies succeeded in being heard.

For the most part, colleges have avoided the image phase of marketing. It was the needs of the marketplace, punctuated by the problems brought by the recession, that brought business to where it is today and have brought education to the threshold of the positioning era. This is an era that recognizes both the importance of the product and the importance of the image. But more than anything else, it stresses the need to create a "position" in the prospect's mind.

In creating a position, your competitor's image is as important as your own. Sometimes, it is more important.

Examples of Positioning Success and Failure. We would like to relate a few examples of positioning success and failure and to discuss how effective positioning can be developed.

The famous Avis marketing program was a classic case of establishing the "against" position, a position against the leader. To understand why this approach was so successful, let us look into the mind of the prospect. For each category or need, there seems to be a product ladder. On each rung is a brand name, in this case, Hertz, Avis, and National at the top. Hertz was already foremost in prospects' minds, so Avis acknowledged this fact and turned their own position as number two into an attractive one to prospective customers: Because we're number two, "we try harder."

Another way to get your message through is by accepting a position that no one else wants. For example, Volkswagen was able to establish the ugly position by default. The strength of this position is that is communicates reliability in a powerful way. "The 1970 VW will stay ugly longer" acknowledges the negative, and when you admit the negative, your prospect is inclined to give you the positive.

Another classic example of positioning strategy is the "uncola" position established by Seven-Up. The brilliance of this idea can only be appreciated when you realize that 63 percent of the soft drinks consumed in the U.S. are cola drinks. By linking its product to cola products, Seven-Up has established itself as an automatic alternative to Coke and Pepsi. No product features, no customer benefits, no company image—only the mental leverage factor of one word, "uncola." Yet, this word more than doubled Seven-Up sales. Today it is the third largest company in the soft-drink industry.

By achieving a clear position that related to what was already in the mind, Avis and Seven-Up were able to attract prospects they never would have because of lack of clear focus.

One alternative to good positioning is the "everybody trap," which, judging from their information material, has caught many colleges and universities today. American Motors fell into the everybody trap when it tried to appeal to a wide range of car buyers in marketing the Hornet. But the buyer who wanted to spend $3500 for a car did not buy the Hornet because that buyer did not want his or her friends and associates thinking it was a $1900 car. And the buyer who wanted to spend $1900 did not want to buy a $3500 car stripped of $1600 worth of accessories. If you try to appeal to everyone, you wind up appealing to no one.

An even more appropriate example of the everybody trap is the case of Protein 21 shampoo. Several years ago, the Mennen Company introduced a combination shampoo and conditioner called Protein 21, which rapidly carved out a 13 percent share of the shampoo market. Then Mennen was lured into extending their product line. In rapid succession, the company introduced Protein 21 hairspray in regular and extra hold, scented and unscented, Protein 21 conditioner in two formulas, and Protein 21 concentrate. To make sure that nobody can keep their products straight, Mennen also markets the Protein 29 line for men. No wonder Protein 21's share of the shampoo market has fallen from 13 percent to 11 to 9 to 7 to 5½ percent. And the decline is bound to continue.

REQUIREMENTS OF SUCCESSFUL POSITIONING

Consistency.   More than anything else, successful positioning requires consistency. You must keep at it, year after year. So often after a company or institution has executed brilliant marketing strategy, the first impulse is to change it. Perhaps it is the lust of the conqueror after new conquests, or more likely, the marketing expert is simply bored working on the same strategy day after day. (The Anacin marketing strategists have stuck with "fights headaches three ways" strategy for almost four decades with great success, while their competitors switch from an animated speedy character, to spicy meatballs, to product line extensions.)

Organizations are susceptible to the "forgot what made them successful" trap. The "Avis is only No. 2 in rent-a-cars" program turned Avis from a loser into a winner. The "Avis is going to be No. 1" program does just the opposite. The older program not only related number two, Avis, to the leader, Hertz, it also exploited the natural sympathy people have for the underdog. The newer campaign is just conventional brag-and-boast advertising.

Another company that seems to have forgotten its successful position is Volkswagen. Their "think small" theme represents probably the most famous advertisement of the sixties. But the program that announced a new kind of Volks-wagen, a big Volkswagen, is confusing to buyers. Does the company want us to think small or think big?

What does your university want its prospects to think about it? That its program is the most well-rounded? That its campus is the most beautiful? That its residence facilities are the most comfortable? That the social life is the most extensive? That its alumni have attained the greatest success in their fields? That the student can develop his or her own curriculum? The fact is that virtually every institution would like every prospect to think all of these things and more, and this desire is reflected in their communications. Is it any wonder that prospects are confused? Or that they tune out your message because it looks and sounds like everyone else's?

Research.   The French have a marketing expression that sums up the concept of positioning. *Cherchez le créneau.* Look for the hole. Like IBM, the first company or college to build a strong position has an enormous advantage. You have to find a position that nobody else owns. Realize that it is the first company or school to build the mental position that has the upper hand, not the first one to make the product. IBM did not invent the computer, Sperry Rand did. But IBM was the first to take that position in the prospect's mind.

Today, however, a would-be leader is confronted with the fact that créneaux are getting harder and harder to find. Did you know that the average supermarket in the United States has some 10,000 individual products or brands on display? And that there are nearly as many post-secondary institutions? Compare that with the fact that the average high school graduate has a speaking vocabulary of less than 8,000 words. With a plethora of colleges and products, how does a company or college find an effective positioning approach?

The best way to begin is with research. Research is the tool with which you chart a positioning map of the prospect's mind. When we have a map of the mind, what are we looking for? We are looking for a hole, a créneau, that does not belong to someone else. To discover this opening, we utilize many well-established research techniques such as semantic differential and perceptual mapping. The research is neither esoteric nor inconsiderate of your time and resources. There is no reason, in fact, why it cannot be accomplished by your own organization.

In conducting positioning research, we violate one old research rule and start with some preconceived ideas. In other words, we work out one or more positioning strategies before we start the research.

Borrowing this idea from the oil industry, we sink test bores in the mind of the prospect. The oil analogy is apropos. If you want to find oil, you do not drill holes all over the landscape. You get out your geological maps and do your homework. Then, if the conditions are right, you sink a test bore and find out if what is down there matches your preconceived ideas. If it does, you get out your wallet and start to drill.

The following is an example of this type of research conducted by Ries Cappiello Colwell, advertising agency, that in our opinion can be adapted for any college and university with new and productive results in terms of marketing and communications strategy.

This example of positioning research concerns commercial banking in the most competitive market of all, New York City. The research was conducted to explore the possibility of a new or alternate strategy for Chase Manhattan Bank. Our preconceived idea based on the marketplace was that fast service would be the most important available position to secure.

Using positioning research, the agency tried to find out first what was already in the mind of the target bank prospect. In this study, we selected the five largest banks in the metropolitan area and we decided to "grade" them on friendliness, variety of services, speed of service, convenience of branch locations, and size of capital. We asked prospective banking customers to rank the strength of each attribute for each bank on a scale of zero to 100. Four of these represent fairly standard banking qualities. Exhibit 1 shows the ratings received by the five banks in each of the five selected categories. This is not conventional research. We were not looking for absolute strength or weakness. Nor were we trying to profile Chase Manhattan Bank. What we were looking for was an available position for Chase Manhattan Bank in the prospect's mind. Unquestionably, with the geographic diversity of your prospective students, it will not be possible to include in your own research every single institution that competes with your college.

EXHIBIT 1
Ratings of the Attributes of Banks in New York City

	First National City Bank	Bankers Trust Company	Chase Manhattan Bank	Chemical Bank	Manufacturer Hanover Trust Co.
Friendliness	38	21	25	26	31
Variety of services	63	40	46	37	38
Speed of service	20	25	29	22	13
Convenience of branch locations	37	20	27	28	17
Size of capital	69	36	59	42	39

The next step in positioning research is to consider how the banks compare in each of the five categories. If you live in New York, you probably know that one bank has been communicating the friendliness idea for five years. "You have a friend at Chase," say their outdoor signs, print ads, and television ads. You would think that Chase Manhattan has preempted the friendly position, but this research indicated they were in fourth place. Over the years, Chase Manhattan invested millions in promoting itself as the friendly bank, with its theme, "You have a friend at Chase Manhattan." What went wrong and ultimately forced a change? It is not enough for an organization to communicate an idea. The

idea must be believed by the prospect. Without proof of friendliness (a difficult, if not impossible, task), the leader tends to inherit this idea by having more friendly people waiting on customers.

The leader is usually ahead in all areas. First National City Bank, now called Citibank, leads the others in friendliness, variety of service, convenience of branch locations, and size of capital, but not in speed of service. In speed of service, Chase Manhattan is the leader, and First National is buried in fourth place.

Fast service, as it happens, was also our preconceived idea of the best available position. Interestingly, this concept could benefit either Chase or Citibank. It would give Chase a viable strategy to use against the leader, Citibank. First National City Bank, on the other hand, could use this speed of service to block their major competitor from the only viable strategy available to them.

The banking business, like other industries, usually revolves around finding an effective strategy against the leader. What is interesting, however, is that positioning research usually does turn up one or more viable options for an underdog. And those options are usually based on the leader's weakness rather than the underdog's strength. This is why it is just as important to measure the positions of your competitors as well as your own in the minds of your prospects.

There is no reason why a college or university could not benefit from a similarly structured positioning research survey. Your research techniques and analysis of your university are far more sophisticated than comparable business organizations. You probably know more about your institution than most businesses know about their products. And, unquestionably, you have some good preconceived ideas about the strengths of your school. If you are ready to try a strategy other than being everything to everybody, you can begin by testing one or more of your preconceived ideas.

Include the attributes that you know are important to your prospects. The ones that we notice emphasized in the college admissions literature that we have reviewed include quality of residences, quality of placement and career counseling program, campus appearance, location, faculty credentials, and student satisfaction. Then include your own preconceived ideas.

Developing Strategy. Research is only part of the positioning job. After you have the research completed, you must then develop the best strategy based on the research. If you are now motivated to apply positioning thinking to your own situation, there are three questions you can ask yourself.

1. What position, if any, do you already own in the prospect's mind? Before starting any program, it is important to prepare a positioning map that outlines in detail who the prospect is and what he or she knows not only about your school, but your prime competition as well.
2. What position do you want to own? You want to choose the best position from a long-term point of view.

3. What institutions must be outgunned if you are to establish that position? Find a way to *reposition* your competition. For example, Volkswagen not only developed the ugly position, it repositioned its U.S. competitors as gas guzzlers.

Marketing battles are today more and more like war. As a matter of fact, the best book on marketing ever written may have been *On War* by Clausewitz. In this masterpiece of military strategy, Clausewitz outlines some strategic factors that are just as important today as they were in Napoleon's time.

The first important factor is *timing*. We are the first generation of management people to face what Alvin Toffler called "future shock": If we do not become future-oriented, we will not survive. Sensing the future in the present can be very profitable for the astute marketing person. It used to be that we had to wait around for years to see the effect of a new marketing idea. You will not have to wait very long for anything any more. Modern technology and communication have speeded up the process. New ideas can be put to use and succeed almost instantaneously.

Another factor as important in marketing as it is in war is *objectivity*. You must be able to see yourself as you are, not as you want to be. To be successful in today's marketplace, you must be brutally frank with yourself. You must try to eliminate all ego from the decision-making process. One of the critical aspects of positioning is being able to evaluate objectively your university and how you are viewed by your students and prospective students.

The third factor important to success in marketing is *consistency*. You have got to reinforce your position month after month, year after year.

In the 1980s, a college or university must think more strategically than it ever did before. Changing the direction of a school is like trying to turn an aircraft carrier. It takes a mile before anything happens. And if it was a wrong turn, getting back on course takes even longer.

Today, strategy and timing are the Himalayas. Everything else is the Catskills.

18
Market Segmentation: A Strategic Management Tool

Richard M. Johnson

In developing market segmentation strategies, it is important for managers to know how consumers perceive alternative, competing products on each of their various attributes. This article demonstrates how two-dimensional maps can be used to evaluate the relative positions of competing products on key attributes, and to identify how well consumer needs are being met by current offerings. The areas of application illustrated here come from both the public and private sectors, with the former focusing on competition in elections between candidates for political office.

Like motivation research in the late 1950s, market segmentation is receiving much attention in research circles. Although this term evokes the idea of cutting up a market into little pieces, the real role of such research is more basic and potentially more valuable. In this discussion *market segmentation analysis* refers to examination of the structure of a market as perceived by consumers, preferably using a geometric spatial model, and to forecasting the intensity of demand for a potential product positioned anywhere in the space.

The purpose of such a study, as seen by a marketing manager, might be:

1. To learn how the brands or products in a class are perceived with respect to strengths, weaknesses, similarities, etc.
2. To learn about consumers' desires, and how these are satisfied or unsatisfied by the current market.
3. To integrate these findings strategically, determining the greatest opportunities for new brands or products and how a product or its image should be modified to produce the greatest sales gain.

From the position of a marketing research technician, each of these three goals translates into a separate technical problem:

1. To construct a product space, a geometric representation of consumers' perceptions of products or brands in a category.
2. To obtain a density distribution by positioning consumers' ideal points in the same space.
3. To construct a model which predicts preferences of groups of consumers toward new or modified products.

This discussion will focus on each of these three problems in turn, suggesting solutions now available. Solutions to the first two problems can be illustrated with actual data, although currently solutions for the third problem are more tentative. This will not be an exhaustive catalog of techniques, nor is this the only way of structuring the general problem of forecasting consumer demand for new or modified products.

CONSTRUCTING THE PRODUCT SPACE

A spatial representation, or map, of a product category provides the foundation on which other aspects of the solution are built. Many equally useful techniques are available for constructing product spaces which require different assumptions and possess different properties. The following is a list of useful properties of product spaces which may be used to evaluate alternative techniques:

6   Richard M. Johnson is President, John Morton Company.

1. *Metric:* distances between products in space should relate to perceived similarity between them.
2. *Identification:* directions in the space should correspond to identified product attributes.
3. *Uniqueness/reliability:* similar procedures applied to similar data should yield similar answers.
4. *Robustness/foolproofness:* procedures should work every time. It should not be necessary to switch techniques or make basic changes in order to cope with each new set of data.
5. *Freedom from improper assumptions:* other things being equal, a procedure that requires fewer assumptions is preferred.

One basic distinction has to do with the kinds of data to be analyzed. Three kinds of data are frequently used.

Similarity/Dissimilarity Data. Here a respondent is not concerned in any obvious way with dimensions or attributes that describe the products judged. He makes global judgments of relative similarity among products, with the theoretical advantage that there is no burden on the researcher to determine in advance the important attributes or dimensions within a product category. Examples of such data might be: (1) to present triples of products and ask which two are most or least similar, (2) to present pairs of products and ask which pair is more similar, or (3) to rank order k-1 products in terms of similarity with the kth.

Preference Data. Preference data can be used to construct a product space, given assumptions relating preference to distances. For instance, a frequent assumption is that an individual has ideal points in the same space and that product preference is related in some systematic way to distances from his ideal points to his perception of products' locations. As with similarity/dissimilarity data, preference data place no burden on the researcher to determine salient product attributes in advance. Examples of preference data which might lead to a product space are: (1) paired comparison data, (2) rank orders of preference, or (3) generalized overall ratings (as on a 1 to 9 scale).

Attribute Data. If the researcher knows in advance the important product attributes by which consumers discriminate among products, or with which they form preferences, then he may ask respondents to describe products on scales relating to each attribute. For instance, they may use rating scales describing brands of beer with respect to price vs. quality, heaviness vs. lightness, or smoothness vs. bitterness.

In addition to these three kinds of data, *procedures* can be *metric* or *nonmetric*. Metric procedures make assumptions about the properties of data, as when in computing a mean one assumes that the difference between ratings of values one and two is the same as that between two and three, etc. Nonmetric procedures make fewer assumptions about the nature of the data; these are usually techniques in which the only operations on data are comparisons such as "greater than" or "less than." Nonmetric procedures are typically used with data from rank order or paired comparison methods.

Another issue is whether or not a *single produce space* will adequately represent all respondents' perceptions. At the extreme, each respondent might require a unique product space to account for aspects of his perceptions. However, one of the main reasons for product spaces' utility is that they summarize a large amount of information in unusually tangible and compact form. Allowing a totally different product space for each respondent would certainly destroy much of the illustrative value of the result. A compromise would be to recognize that respondents might fall naturally into a relatively small number of subgroups with different product perceptions. In this case, a separate product space could be constructed for each subgroup.

Frequently a single product space is assumed to be adequate to account for important aspects of all respondents' *perceptions*. Differences in *preference* are then taken into account by considering each respondent's ideal product to have a unique location in the common product space, and by recognizing that different respondents may weight dimensions uniquely. This was the approach taken in the examples to follow.

Techniques which have received a great deal of use in constructing product spaces include nonmetric multidimensional scaling [3, 7, 8, 12], factor analysis [11], and multiple discriminant analysis [4]. Factor analysis has been available for this purpose for many years, and multidimensional scaling was discussed as early as 1938 [13]. Nonmetric multidimensional scaling, a comparatively recent development, has achieved great popularity because of the invention of ingenious computing methods requiring only the most minimal assumptions regarding the nature of the data. Discriminant analysis requires assumptions about the metric properties of data, but it appears to be particularly robust and foolproof in application.

These techniques produce similar results in most practical applications. The technique of multiple discriminant analysis will be illustrated here.

EXAMPLES OF PRODUCT SPACES

Imagine settling on a number of attributes which together account for all of the important ways in which products in a set are seen to differ from each other. Suppose that each product has been rated on each attribute by several people, although each person has not necessarily described more than one product.

Given such data, multiple discriminant analysis is a powerful technique for constructing a spatial model of the product category. First, it finds the weighted combination of attributes which discriminates most among products, maximizing an F-ratio of between-product to within-product variance. Then, second and subsequent weighted combinations are found which discriminate maximally among products, within the constraint that they all be uncorrelated with one another. Having determined as many discriminating dimensions as possible, average scores can be used to plot products on each dimension. Distances between pairs of products in this space reflect the amount of discrimination between them.[1]

Exhibit 1 shows such a space for the Chicago beer market as perceived by members of Market Facts' Consumer Mail Panels in a pilot study, September 1968. Approximately 500 male beer drinkers described 8 brands of beer on each of 35 attributes. The data indicated that a third sizable dimension also existed, but the two dimensions pictured here accounted for approximately 90% of discrimination among images of these 8 products.

The location of each brand is indicated on these two major dimensions. The horizontal dimension contrasts premium quality on the right with popular price on the left. The vertical dimension reflects relative lightness. In addition, the mean rating of each product on each of the attributes is shown by relative position on each attribute vector. For instance, Miler is perceived as being most popular with women, followed by Budweiser, Schlitz, Hamms, and four unnamed, popularly priced beers.

As a second example, the same technique was applied to political data. During the weeks immediately preceding the 1968 presidential election, a questionnaire was sent to 1,000 Consumer Mail Panels households. Respondents were

---

[1] McKeon [10] has shown that multiple discriminant analysis produces the same results as classic (metric) multidimensional scaling of Mahalanobis' distances based on the same data.

asked to agree or disagree with each of 35 political statements on a four-point scale. Topics were Vietnam, law and order, welfare, and other issues felt to be germane to current politics. Respondents also described two preselected political figures, acording to their perceptions of each figure's stand on each issue. Discriminant analysis indicated two major dimensions accounting for 86% of the discrimination among 14 political figures.

The liberal vs. conservative dimension is apparent in the data, as shown in Exhibit 2. The remaining dimension apparently reflects perceived favorability of attitude toward government involvement in domestic and international matters. As in the beer space, it is only necessary to erect perpendiculars to each vector to observe each political figure's relative position on each of the 35 issues. Additional details are in [5].

Multiple discriminant analysis is a major competitor of nonmetric multidimensional scaling in constructing product spaces. The principal assumptions that the former requires are that (1) perceptions be homogeneous across respondents, (2) attribute data be sealed at the interval level (equal intervals on rating scales), (3) attributes be linearly related to one another, and (4) amount of disagreement (error covariance matrix) be the same for each product.

Only the first of these assumptions is required by most nonmetric methods, and some even relax that assumption. However, the space provided by multiple discriminant analysis has the following useful properties:

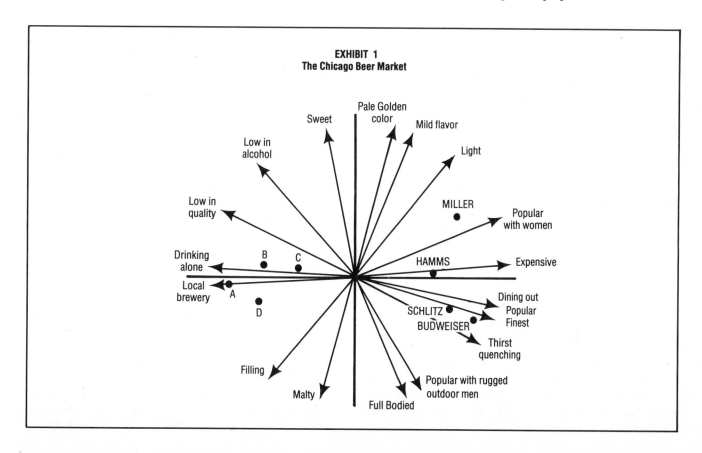

EXHIBIT 1
The Chicago Beer Market

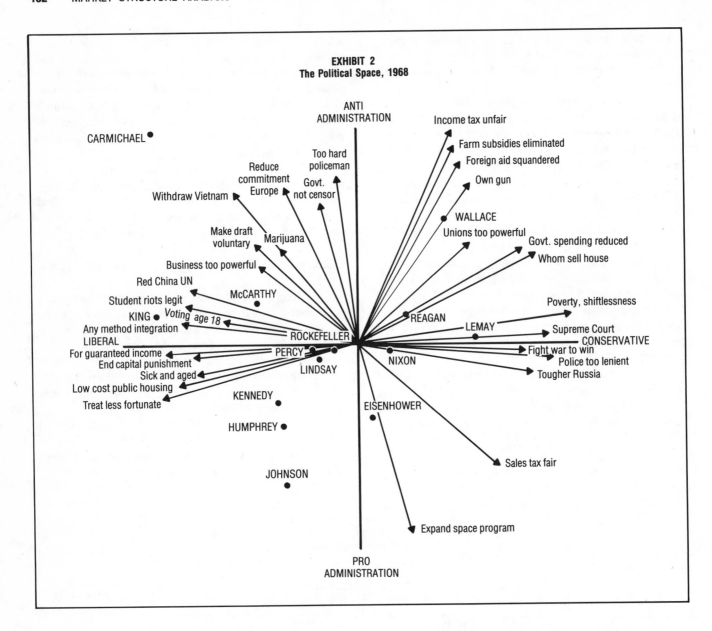

EXHIBIT 2
The Political Space, 1968

1. Given customary assumptions of multivariate normality, there is a test of significance for distance (dissimilarity) between any two products.
2. Unlike nonmetric procedures, distances estimated among a collection of products do not depend upon whether or not additional products are included in the analysis. Any of the brands of beer or political figures could have been deleted from the examples and the remaining object locations would have had the same relationships to one another and to the attribute vectors.
3. The technique is reliable and well known, and solutions are unique, since the technique cannot be misled by any local optimum.

OBTAINING THE DISTRIBUTION OF CONSUMERS' IDEAL POINTS

After constructing a product space, the next concern is estimating consumer demand for a product located at any particular point. The demand function over such a space is desired and can be approximated by one of several general approaches.

The first is to locate each person's ideal point in the region of the space implied by his rank ordered preferences. His ideal point would be closest to the product he likes best, second closest to the product he likes second best, etc. There are several procedures which show promise using this approach [2, 3, 7, 8, 12], although difficulties remain in practical execution. This approach has trouble dealing with individuals who behave in a manner contrary to the basic assumptions of the model, as when one chooses products first on the far left side of the space, second on the far right side, and third in the center. Most individuals giving rank orders of preference do display such nonmonotonicity to some extent, understandably producing problems for the application of these techniques.

The second approach involves deducing the number of ideal points at each region in space by using data on whether a product has too much or too little of each attribute.

This procedure has not yet been fully explored, but, at present, seems to be appropriate to the multidimensional case only when strong assumptions about the shape of the ideal point distribution are given.

The third approach is to have each person describe his ideal product, with the same attributes and rating scales as for existing products. ~~If multiple discriminant scales as for existing products.~~ If multiple discriminant analysis has been used to obtain a product space, each person's ideal product can then be inserted in the same space.

There are considerable differences between an ideal point location inferred from a rank order of preference and one obtained directly from an attribute rating. To clarify matters, consider a single dimension, heaviness vs. lightness in beer. If a previous mapping has shown that Brands A, B, C, and D are equally spaced on this one dimension, and if a respondent ranks his preferences as B, C, A, and D, then his ideal must lie closer to B than to A or C and closer to C than to A. This narrows the feasible region for his ideal point down to the area indicated in Exhibit 3. Had he stated a preference for A, with D second, there would be no logically corresponding position for his ideal point in the space.

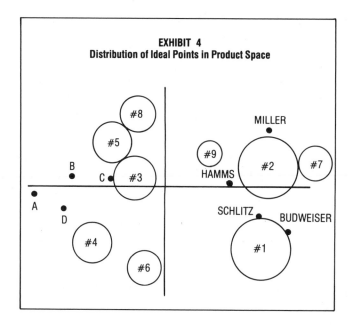

EXHIBIT 4
Distribution of Ideal Points in Product Space

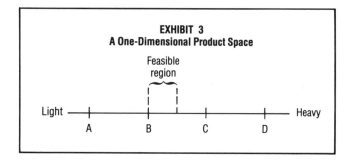

EXHIBIT 3
A One-Dimensional Product Space

However, suppose these products have already been given the following scale positions on a heavy/light dimension: A = 1.0, B = 2.0, C = 3.0, and D = 4.0. If a respondent unambiguously specifies his ideal on this scale at 2.25, his ideal can be put directly on the scale with no complexities. Of course, it does not follow, necessarily, that his stated rank order of preference will be predictable from the location of his ideal point.

There is no logical reason why individuals must be clustered into market segments. Mathematically, one can cope with the case where hundreds or thousands of individual ideal points are each located in the space. However, it is much easier to approximate such distributions by clustering respondents into groups. Cluster analysis [6] has been used with the present data to put individuals into a few groups with relatively similar product desires (beer) or points of view (politics).

Exhibit 4 shows an approximation to the density distribution of consumers' ideal points in the Chicago beer market, a "poor man's contour map." Ideal points tended

somewhat to group themselves (circles) into clusters. It is not implied that all ideal points lie within the circles, since they are really distributed to some extent throughout the entire space. Circle sizes indicate the relative sizes of clusters, and the center of each is located at the center of its circle.

A representation such as this contains much potentially useful marketing information. For instance, if people can be assumed to prefer products closer to their ideal points, there may be a ready market for a new brand on the lower or "heavy" side of the space, approximately neutral in price/quality. Likewise, there may be opportunities for new brands in the upper middle region, decidedly light and neutral in price/quality. Perhaps popularly priced Brand A will have marketing problems, since this brand is closest to no cluster.

Exhibit 5 shows a similar representation for the political space, where circles represent concentrations of voters' points. These are not ideal points, but rather personally held positions on political issues. Clusters on the left side of the space intended to vote mostly for Humphrey and those on the right for Nixon in the 1968 election. Throughout the space, the percentage voting Republican increases generally from left to right.

It may be surprising that the center of the ideal points lies considerably to the right of that of the political figures. One possible explanation is that this study dealt solely with positions on *issues*, so matters of style or personality did not enter the definition of the space. It is entirely possible that members of clusters one and eight, the most liberal, found Nixon's position on issues approximately as attractive as Humphrey's, but they voted for Humphrey on the basis of preference for style, personality, or political party. Likewise, members of cluster two might have voted strongly for Wallace, given his position, but he received only 14% of this cluster's vote. He may have been rejected on the basis of other qualities. The clusters are described in more detail in [5].

A small experiment was undertaken to test the validity of this model. Responses from a class of sociology students in a western state university showed them to be more liberal and more for decreasing government involvement internationally than any of the eight voter clusters. Their position is close to McCarthy's, indicated by an "S."

STRATEGIC INTEGRATION OF FINDINGS

Having determined the position of products in a space and seen where consumer ideal points are located, how can such findings be integrated to determine appropriate product strategy? A product's market share should be increased by repositioning (1) closer to ideal points of sizable segments of the market, (2) farther from other products with which it must compete, and (3) on dimensions weighted heavily in consumers' preferences. Even these broad guidelines provide some basis for marketing strategy. For instance, in Exhibit 4, Brand A is clearly farthest from all clusters and should be repositioned.

In Exhibit 5, Humphrey, Kennedy, and Johnson could have increased their acceptance with this respondent sample by moving upwards and to the right, modifying their perceived position. Presumably, endorsement of any issue in the upper right quadrant or a negative position on any issue in the lower left quadrant of Exhibit 2 would have helped move Humphrey closer to the concentration of voters' ideal points.

Although the broad outlines of marketing strategy are suggested by spaces such as these, it would be desirable to make more precise quantitative forecasts of the effect of modifying a product's position. Unfortunately, the problem of constructing a model to explain product choice behavior based on locations of ideal points and products in a multi-dimensional space has not yet been completely solved, although some useful approaches are currently available.

As the first step, it is useful to concentrate on the behavior of clusters of respondents rather than that of individuals, especially if clusters are truly homogeneous. Data predicting behavior of groups are much smoother and results for a few groups are far more communicable to marketing management than findings stated in terms of large numbers of individual respondents.

If preference data are available for a collection of products, one can analyze the extent to which respondents' preferences are related to distances in the space. Using regression analysis, one can estimate a set of importance weights for each cluster or, if desired, for each respondent,

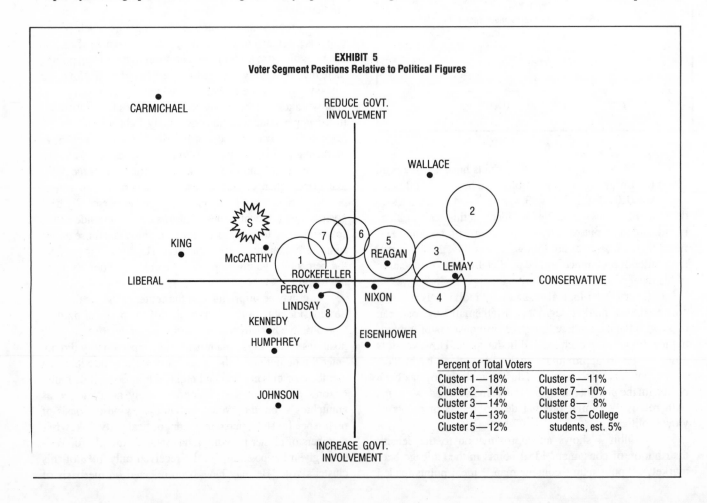

EXHIBIT 5
Voter Segment Positions Relative to Political Figures

Percent of Total Voters

Cluster 1—18%	Cluster 6—11%
Cluster 2—14%	Cluster 7—10%
Cluster 3—14%	Cluster 8— 8%
Cluster 4—13%	Cluster S—College
Cluster 5—12%	students, est. 5%

to be applied to the dimensions of the product space. Weights would be chosen providing the best explanation of cluster or individual respondent preferences in terms of weighted distances between ideal points and each product's perceived location. If clusters, rather than individuals, are used, it may be desirable to first calculate preference scale values or utilities for each cluster [1, 9]. Importance weights can then be obtained using multiple regression to predict these values from distances. If explanations of product preference can be made for *existing products,* which depend only on locations in space, then the same approach should permit *predictions* of preference levels for new or modified products to be positioned at specific locations in the space.

Models of choice behavior clearly deserve more attention. Although the problem of constructing the product space has received much attention, we are denied the full potential of these powerful solutions unless we are able to quantify relationships between distances in such a space and consumer choice behavior.

SUMMARY

Market segmentation studies can produce results that indicate desirable marketing action. Techniques that are presently available can (1) construct a product space, (2) discover the shape of the distribution of consumers' ideal points throughout such a space, and (3) identify likely opportunities for new or modified products.

In the past, marketing research has often been restricted to such *tactical* questions as package design or pricing levels. However, with the advent of new techniques, marketing research can contribute directly to the development of *strategic* alternatives to current product marketing plans. There remains a need for improved technology, particularly in the development of models for explaining and predicting preferential choice behavior. The general problem has great practical significance, and provides a wealth of opportunity for development of new techniques and models.

REFERENCES

1. Bradley, M. E. and Terry, R. A. "Rank Analysis of Incomplete Block Designs: The Method of Paired Comparisons." *Biometrika* 39 (1952): 324–45.
2. Carroll, J. D. "Individual Differences and Multidimensional Scaling." Murray Hill, NJ: Bell Telephone Laboratories, 1969.
3. Guttman, Louis. "A General Nonmetric Technique for Finding the Smallest Space for a Configuration of Points." *Psychometrika* 33 (December 1968):469–506.
4. Johnson, Richard M. "Multiple Discriminant Analysis." Unpublished paper. Workshop on Multivariate Methods in Marketing. University of Chicago, 1970.
5. ———. "Political Segmentation." Paper presented at Spring Conference on Research Methodology, American Marketing Association, New York, 1969.
6. Johnson, Stephen C. "Hierarchical Clustering Schemes." *Psychometrika* 32 (September 1967):241–54.
7. Kruskal, Joseph B. "Multidimensional Scaling by Optimizing Goodness of Fit to a Nonmetric Hypothesis." *Psychometrika* 29 (March 1964):1–27.
8. ———. "Nonmetric Multidimensional Scaling: A Numerical Method." *Psychometrika* 29 (June 1964):115–29.
9. Luce, R. D. "A Choice Theory Analysis of Similarity Judgments." *Psychometrika* 26 (September 1961):325–32.
10. McKeon, James J. "Canonical Analysis." *Psychometric Monographs* 13.
11. Tucker, Ledyard. "Dimensions of Preference." Research Memorandum RM-60-7, Princeton, NJ: Educational Testing Service, 1960.
12. Young, F. W. "TORSCA, An IBM Program for Nonmetric Multidimensional Scaling." *Journal of Marketing Research* 5 (August 1968): 319–21.
13. Young, G., and Householder, A. S. "Discussion of a Set of Points in Terms of Their Mutual Distances." *Psychometrika* 3 (March 1938): 19–22.

19
Analytical Approach to Marketing Decisions in Health-Care Organizations

Yoram Wind
Lawrence K. Spitz

An important component in the design or modification of health-care facilities such as hospitals is understanding the preferences of potential users for different types of facilities. Management would like to know the relative influence of doctors and patients in choosing a hospital, the attributes (such as proximity and price) that are important to each group, and how influential different levels of each attribute are in forming a preference. For example, would a prospective patient for elective surgery prefer to stay in a nearby non-teaching community hospital that has average facilities or a very modern teaching hospital located in a downtown area? Would the preference change if the recuperative stay were to be a long one? This article discusses recently developed approaches to help answer questions about the nature of and variation in users' preferences.

Marketing in nonprofit organizations has emerged as a popular topic in the recent marketing literature [12, 13]. The two basic implicit premises of these efforts are that (a) the survival and growth of nonprofit organizations require the adoption of a marketing orientation and (b) the implementation of the marketing orientation calls for the use of appropriate marketing concepts, approaches, and techniques (including marketing research and marketing applications of the management and behavioral sciences).

Yoram Wind is Professor of Marketing, The Wharton School, University of Pennsylvania.

Lawrence K. Spitz is with the University of Pennsylvania Hospital.

Given these premises and the large repertoire of marketing techniques, one of the questions facing managers of nonprofit organizations is which specific marketing approaches and techniques they should use. Although no single technique can be appropriate for all marketing decisions, it is hoped that the experience gained in the application of marketing research and management science to the solution of marketing problems (and guidance of marketing decisions) in profit-oriented firms could be of some help to the marketing managers of nonprofit organizations.

Thus our objective is to propose, as a research tool for guiding marketing decisions of health care organizations, the use of a relatively new analytical approach to the quantification of utilities (for multi-attribute alternatives).

In particular, we focus on the potential applicability of *conjoint measurement* procedures to the marketing decisions of health care organizations. After a brief discussion of this analytical procedure we describe an illustrative application to the hospital selection decision. The paper concludes with some suggestions for future use of conjoint measurement and related techniques in marketing studies for health care organizations.

ON MEASUREMENT OF MULTI-ATTRIBUTE ALTERNATIVES

The approach we suggest for quantifying the utilities of multi-attribute alternatives differs considerably from traditional attitude measurement procedures. It is based on recent developments in mathematical psychology concerning *conjoint measurement* techniques, which have been applied to such diverse areas as psychiatric diagnosis [5], common stock appraisals [15], job performance [3], a number of marketing problems including product and package design [9], retail discount card evaluations [6], benefit segmentation [10], and one health-care related study on physician selection of a clinical laboratory [17].

As the name suggests, conjoint measurement is concerned with measuring the joint effect of two or more independent variables (such as product attributes) on the ordering of a single response (dependent) variable or a categorical response variable. In a prototypic experiment a respondent is presented with a set of multi-attribute alternatives and is asked to make an overall judgment about the relative value of various combinations of attributes. By evaluating (e.g., ranking or rating) combinations of attributes on some desired dependent variable (preference, liking, intention to buy, etc.), the respondent is not asked to indicate directly the relative importance of each attribute (as in the case of the traditional attitude measurement approaches) but rather to provide his overall evaluation of a "product"—a combination of various attributes. This more realistic task provides insights into the respondent's trade-off among the various attributes, and supplies the input data for the conjoint measurement algorithm.

Conjoint measurement provides a model and scaling procedure for constructing, from these data, utility functions whose arguments are represented by stimulus dimensions. Using a variety of algorithms (such as those in [1] or [14]) the overall evaluations of a set of multi-attribute alternatives are "decomposed" into derived utilities (interval scale values) of the various factors—the components of the multicomponent alternatives—and levels. This "decomposition" of the respondents' overall evaluations into separate compatible utility scales enables the researcher to reconstruct the original global judgments or predict the respondent's evaluation of new combinations of attributes.

These utilities provide unbiased information about the relative importance of the various attributes, the value of various levels of each of the attributes, and an estimate of the

psychological trade-offs respondents make when they evaluate several attributes together. (For further discussion of conjoint measurement see [7–9].)

One of the simplest and most commonly used conjoint measurement models is the additive main effect model. This model, in an illustrative case of a stimulus set composed of three attributes (factors) each at three levels, is:

$$U(X) = F(X) = \beta_0 + \beta_1(X_{21}) + \beta_2(X_{31}) + \beta_3(X_{22}) \\ + \beta_4(X_{32}) + \beta_5(X_{23}) + \beta_6(X_{33}) + e,$$

where β_0 is the contribution to overall utility in which each of the three factors is at its first (lowest) level; $\beta_1, \beta_2, \ldots, \beta_6$ are the incremental contribution of level i ($i = 2, 3$) of factor j ($j = 1, 2, 3$); $F(X)$ is a monotonic increasing function of X; and e is the error term.

Conjoint measurement algorithms, such as Kruskal's MONANOVA [14] establish scale values—utilities—(β_{ij}) for the independent variables whose ranking of the additive utilities of each combination best preserves the respondent's original ranking of the stimulus combination.

ILLUSTRATIVE APPLICATION OF CONJOINT MEASUREMENT TO HOSPITAL SELECTION PROBLEM

The specific pilot application we consider here is the use of conjoint measurement in marketing problems of health care organizations. The problem setting is the hospital selection decision of individuals. A recent study on the referral chain of an urban hospital [2] suggests that more than 50 percent of the admissions to a hospital were based on the patient's decision or the recommendations of a friend (as distinct from physician referral). This finding suggests that hospital administrators should try to understand the factors that determine the consumer's hospital selection decision. Current research approaches to the problem (primarily open-ended direct questioning or simple importance rating of various attributes) were viewed by a number of hospital administrators as unacceptable. Open-ended approaches, although useful for identifying the relevant factors, could not provide insight into the relative importance of the various attributes. Traditional attitude measurement approaches tended to stress price, while indicating that other factors are also very important.

Given the multi-attribute nature of the problem, which involves trade-offs among various cost/benefit options, the conjoint measurement model was viewed as most apropriate for the analysis of the hospital selection problem.

Study Objectives.   The objectives of the study can be stated in terms of the following research questions:

1. What factors do consumers consider in selecting a hospital?
2. What is the relative importance of the various hospital characteristics in the hospital selection decision?
3. To what extent is the relative importance of the various hospital characteristics a function of the type and length of hospitalization required?

4. Do the age, sex, and hospitalization history of consumers affect their evaluation of the various hospital characteristics?

Personal in-home interviews were conducted with a convenient quota sample of 56 respondents from the Philadelphia suburban area. The sample was drawn from a relatively homogeneous socioeconomic area following a balanced factorial design based on age, sex, and hospitalization history. The sample composition is summarized in Exhibit 1.

EXHIBIT 1
Sample Composition

Hospitalization history	Respondent				
	Under 35		Over 35		
	Male	Female	Male	Female	Total
Previously hospitalized	7	7	7	7	28
Never hospitalized	7	7	7	7	28
Total	14	14	14	14	56

Stimulus Set and Respondents' Tasks. An exploratory study among physicians and hospital administrators suggested six factors as possible determinants of the hospital selection decision—the type of hospital affiliation, the physical appearance of the hospital, the proximity of the hospital to the patient's home, the reputation of the attending physician, the familiarity with the attending physician, and the cost per day. The six factors and their corresponding levels are summarized in Exhibit 2.

EXHIBIT 2
Stimulus Set

A. Type of hospital
1. Teaching hospital affiliated with a medical school of a major university.
2. Teaching hospital not associated with a medical school.
3. Non-teaching community hospital.

B. Physical appearance of hospital
1. Very modern.
2. Average facilities.
3. Poor condition, old.

C. Proximity
1. Downtown area—easy parking and access.
2. Downtown area—difficult access and parking.
3. In your neighborhood.

D. Assignment of physician
1. A physician recommended by your doctor.
2. A physician recommended by a friend.
3. A physician assigned to you by the hospital.

E. Prestige of physician
1. World-renowned.
2. Highly respected in his field.
3. A specialist.

F. Price of room per day
1. $60.
2. $90.
3. $120.

A fractional factorial design [5] was developed for the 3^6 design involving 27 profiles (of the 729 possible combinations) of hypothetical hospitals. The 27 combinations are presented in Exhibit 3.

Each stimulus of a hypothetical hospital was presented as a card describing different levels of all six factors. Exhibit 4 presents one of the stimuli. This verbal description seemed appropriate in this case, although at least one of the factors— physical appearance of the hospital—could have been presented pictorially. Cost considerations, however, precluded the development of color photographs of the three levels involved. The description of the hypothetical hospitals as various combinations of levels of all six factors is only one of the possible ways of presenting the stimuli. The alternative two-factors-at-a-time approach [11] does not control for the frame of reference used by the respondents in the evaluation of each pair of factors. Given this limitation of the two-factors-at-a time approach and our favorable experience with the "total-combination" approach (see [6–10, 19]), we decided to use the latter one.

In addition, two scenarios were identified on the basis of the type and length of hospitalization. One was a simple surgery with expected rapid recovery, while the other was serious surgery and an expected longer hospitalization. Each respondent was asked to carefully examine the stimulus set of 27 descriptions of the hypothetical hospitals and, assum-

---

EXHIBIT 3
Fractional Factorial Design For 3^6 Stimulus Set

Stimulus combination	Factor					
	A	B	C	D	E	F
1	1	3	3	3	1	2
2	1	1	3	3	3	1
3	2	1	1	3	3	3
4	1	2	1	1	3	3
5	2	1	2	1	1	3
6	3	2	1	2	1	1
7	2	3	2	1	2	1
8	2	2	3	2	1	2
9	3	2	2	3	2	1
10	1	3	2	2	3	2
11	2	1	3	2	2	3
12	2	2	1	3	2	2
13	2	2	2	1	3	2
14	1	2	2	2	1	3
15	1	1	2	2	2	1
16	3	1	1	2	2	2
17	1	3	1	1	2	2
18	3	1	3	1	1	2
19	2	3	1	3	1	1
20	3	2	3	1	3	1
21	3	3	2	3	1	3
22	2	3	3	2	3	1
23	1	2	3	3	2	3
24	3	1	2	3	2	2
25	3	3	1	2	3	3
26	3	3	3	1	2	3
27	1	1	1	1	1	1

EXHIBIT 4
Illustrative Stimulus Card

A. Type of hospital
   Teaching hospital affiliated with a major university
B. Physical appearance of hospital
   Poor condition, old
C. Proximity
   In your neighborhood
D. Attending physician
   A physician assigned to you by the hospital
E. Prestige of physician
   World renowned
F. Price per day
   $90

---

ing that he (she) were to go through a surgery with a rapid recovery period (Scenario 1) and had to choose a hospital, evaluate the various hospitals and assign them to four categories: "definitely would select it," "probably would select it," "probably would not select it," and "definitely would not select it." Once this task was completed, the respondent was asked to repeat it with respect to the second scenario—going to a hospital for a more severe surgery that requires a long hospitalization period.

These two tasks provided the major thrust of the study and the required input for the conjoint measurement analysis. In addition, each respondent was asked to indicate (at the beginning of the interview) his major considerations in selecting a hospital. This open-ended task was designed to ensure that the relevant factors were included in the subsequent conjoint measurement tasks. In addition, the subjects responded to a short battery of demographic questions and repeated the conjoint measurement task under Scenario 1 for eight additional combinations. These new stimulus combinations were selected at random and screened to exclude all clearly dominant combinations. It provided the basis for testing the predictive power of the conjoint measurement procedure.

Plan of Analysis. The major analytical technique used in this study was Kruskal's MONANOVA algorithm. To test whether the additive main effect model underlying this algorithm does hold in this study, the utilities were developed at the individual level and the stress (badness of fit) measures examined. All respondents had relatively low stress (which is analogous to high correlation between the raw data and the calculated utilities), suggesting the appropriateness of the additive main effect conjoint measurement for the study of the hospital selection decision by this group of respondents.

The specific plan of analysis followed the four key research questions and included the following steps:

1. To establish the factors consumers use in the hospital selection decision, a content analysis was conducted on reasons given by the respondents for selecting a hospital.
2. To determine the relative importance of the various hospital characteristics, conjoint measurement analysis using the MONANOVA algorithm was conducted (separately for each scenario) on the total sample data.

3. To determine the effect of the type of hospitalization required on the evaluation of the six hospital characteristics, the results of the two conjoint measurement analysis (under Scenarios 1 and 2) were compared.
4. To assess the effect of consumers' age, sex, and hospitalization history on their evaluation of the six hospital characteristics, the individual utility scores for respondents in each of the 8 cells (of the $2 \times 2 \times 2$ design—Exhibit 1) were submitted to the BMD 12V-Multivariate Analysis of Variance—MANOVA—program.

In addition, we established the predictive power and validity of the additive conjoint measurement model by comparing the respondent's actual evaluation of the eight validation stimuli (which were not used in the calculation of the utilities) with their predicted position based on the utility scores derived from the conjoint measurement analysis.

Results. The discussion of the results follow the four research questions that motivated this study.

1. *Factors considered in consumers' hospital selection decision.* The analysis of the free response data suggests that the six factors included in the stimulus set are the major characteristics considered in selecting a hospital. The only additional factor (not included in our stimulus set) is nursing care—quality and speed—which was mentioned by all groups but somewhat more frequently by those who have been hospitalized before.

2. *Relative importance of six hospital characteristics in consumers' hospital selection decision.* Exhibit 5 presents the results of the conjoint measurement analysis for the total sample (under both scenarios). An examination of these results suggests the following order of importance for the six factors (determined by the range of utilities for each factor, i.e., the larger the range the more important the factor). Under both scenarios proximity of the hospital is the most important factor (26 percent for Scenario 1 and 24 percent for Scenario 2), followed by prestige of physician (21 and 22 percent), physical appearance of the hospital (17 and 16 percent), price per day (14 percent for both scenarios), type of hospital affiliation (13 and 11 percent). Least important under Scenario 1 and second to last under Scenario 2 is who recommended or assigned the attending physician (9 percent for Scenario 1 and 13 percent for Scenario 2).

3. *Impact of type of required hospitalization on respondents' evaluation of hospital characteristics.* An examination of Exhibit 5 suggests little difference between the utility scores under the two hospitalization scenarios. Under Scenario 2 the respondents have a slightly higher utility for physicians who are recommended by their doctor. Yet this difference is not statistically significant.

4. *Effect of sex, age, and hospitalization on respondents' utility scores.* To examine the differences in evaluation of the six hospital characteristics among the age, sex, and hospitalization experience groups, the individual utilities were an-

EXHIBIT 5
Utility Scores for the Six Hospital Characteristics Under the Two Scenarios:
Total Sample

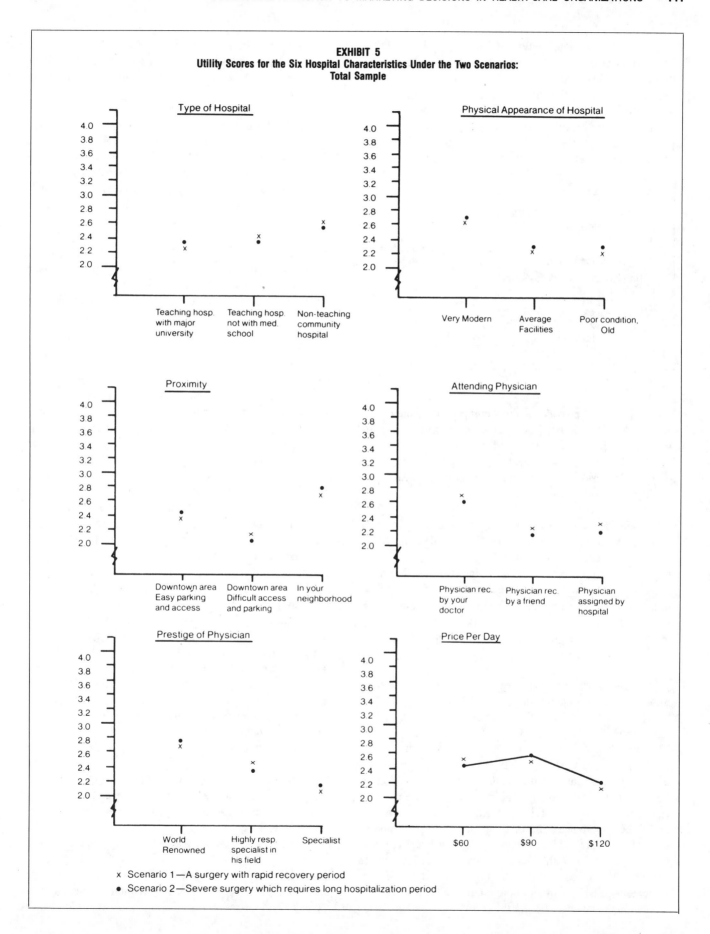

x Scenario 1—A surgery with rapid recovery period

• Scenario 2—Severe surgery which requires long hospitalization period

alyzed via multivariate analysis of variance procedure [18]. The results of this analysis, presented in Exhibit 6, suggest that the age, sex, and hospitalization history had no statistically significant effect on consumers' utilities for the six hospital characteristics. Hospitalization history, although not statistically significant, is the most important factor in explaining the respondents' utility scores (higher omega square value) and is therefore subjected to further analysis.

EXHIBIT 6
Summary of Multivariate Analysis of Variance

Source of variation	Approximate F statistic
A. Hospitalization vs. non-hospitalization history	1.69
B. Male vs. female	0.71
C. Over 35 vs. under 35	1.24
Interaction AB	1.52
AC	0.97
BC	1.49
ABC	0.67

Exhibit 7 provides a direct comparison of the utility scores of the previously hospitalized respondents and those who have never been hospitalized. (Given the similarity in responses across the two scenarios, the results are presented only for Scenario 1.) An examination of this exhibit suggests the following conclusions:

i. Respondents with no prior hospitalization tend to have greater utility for all the factors associated with hospital selection. For the non-hospitalized group the range of the utilities for the six factors is from a high of 0.69 (27 percent important) to a low of 0.24 (9 percent important), compared to a 0.41 to 0.12 range (23 to 7 percent important) for the respondents with prior hospitalization experience. This may reflect a somewhat greater anxiety on the part of the non-hospitalized respondents.

ii. The most important hospital characteristic for both groups is the geographical proximity of the hospital—23 percent (range of 0.41 out of total range of 1.78) for the hospitalized group and 27 percent for the non-hospitalized group. This finding is consistent with a number of previous studies that emphasized the desirability of minimizing the travel distance or time traveled to a health-care facility. Yet, despite its importance, the geographical proximity of the hospital is only one of a number of relevant factors. For the hospitalized group the importance of the other factors is: physical appearance of hospital (22 percent), prestige of physicians (21 percent), familiarity with attending physician (16 percent), price per day (11 percent), and the type of hospital affiliation (7 percent). The rank order of importance of the five remaining hospital characteristics for the non-hospitalized group is:

prestige of physician (21 percent), physical appearance of hospital (19 percent), type of hospital affiliation (11 percent), price per day (13 percent), and the familiarity with the attending physician (9 percent).

iii. The hospital with the highest likelihood of being selected is the same for both groups. The total utility for this "best" hospital is 15.20 for the previously hospitalized group and 16.37 for the non-hospitalized group. The specific characteristics of such a hospital are shown in Exhibit 8. Concerning the cost per day, it seems that both respondent groups are not price sensitive. For both groups price is among the least important factors (reflecting perhaps the respondents' hospital/medical insurance). The respondents are almost indifferent between $60 and $90 a day, and when the price increases to $120 a day the loss in utility is only 0.20 for the hospitalized group and 0.35 for the non-hospitalized group. (This loss in utility can easily be recovered by shifting most other factors from a less preferred to the most preferred position.)

Validation. In the use of conjoint measurement or any other analytical procedure for assessing consumers' responses to a set of attributes, the key question is "How valid is the procedure?" Ideally, one would like to compare the predictions of the conjoint measurement study with the respondent's subsequent behavior, i.e., the actual choice of a specific hospital. Given the obvious difficulties (with respect to cost and time) involved in collecting such data, the validation procedure chosen in this study was based on a comparison between consumers' responses to a validation set of hypothetical hospital profiles (this set included the eight additional randomly selected combinations that were not included in the computation of the utility scores) and the calculated scores for these combinations (based on the results of the conjoint measurement analysis).

The comparison was conducted at both the aggregate and individual levels and included at the aggregate level a comparison of the rank order of the eight stimuli based on the actual and predicted results. The rank order was quite similar, as can be seen in the left-hand panel of Exhibit 9. A more detailed analysis of the relations among all possible pairs of the eight new items was also undertaken and is reported in the right-hand panel of Exhibit 9. An examination of the actual vs. predicted pair-wise relationships indicates a high degree of agreement between the two (86 percent of the cases were correctly predicted), suggesting relatively high validity for the conjoint measurement model. An examination at the individual level suggested that for over 90 percent of the respondents 85 percent or better of the predicted relations between all pairs of the validation set were correct.

Discussion. The hospital selection study was presented not for its immediate implications for hospital management but rather as an illustration for an application of conjoint mea-

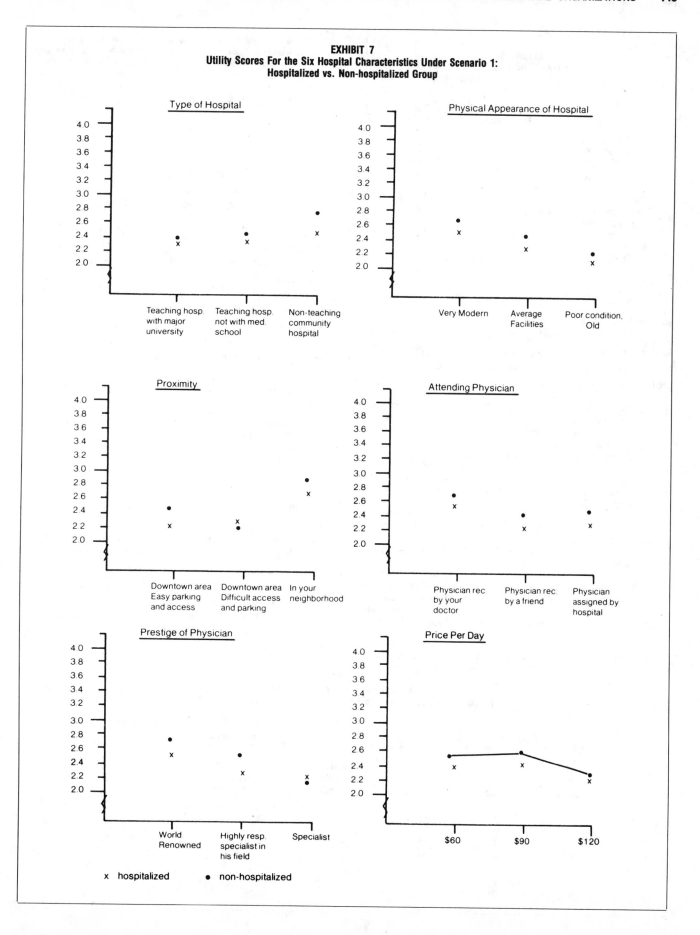

EXHIBIT 7
Utility Scores For the Six Hospital Characteristics Under Scenario 1:
Hospitalized vs. Non-hospitalized Group

EXHIBIT 8
Characteristics (and Their Associated Utilities) of "Best" Hospital for Two Respondents Groups

	Utility score for	
Factor	Hospitalized	Non-hospitalized
Hospital characteristic		
A neighborhood hospital	2.64	2.90
Very modern appearance	2.56	2.71
Non-teaching community hospital	2.44	2.77
Physician		
A world renowned physician	2.59	2.74
Recommended by your doctor	2.56	2.60
Cost		
$60 or $90 a day	2.41	2.60

surement to the study of a health care marketing problem. Given the small size and the non-probability nature of the sample, no substantive implications can be suggested from this exploratory study. Yet a number of conclusions and suggestions for future research can be drawn:

1. The hospital selection problem (and other similar health care problems) can be approached as a marketing problem using standard marketing research techniques.
2. The additive conjoint measurement model seems to be a good descriptor of consumers' choices among various hospital characteristics. More complex interactive models do not seem to be required, although any subsequent study utilizing conjoint measurement should test, for each respondent, whether the additive model holds.
3. This research approach to health-care problems can be extended to cover other respondents, such as physicians or even hospital administrators.
4. In designing conjoint measurement or other studies of the hospital selection decision, other attributes should not be ignored. New factors (e.g., nursing care) and new levels for the existing six factors (e.g., higher prices than the $120 per day) should be examined by management and, if relevant, included in the stimulus set.
5. The descriptive stimulus (Exhibit 4) and respondents task (rating on an "intention to select" scale) were easily comprehended by

the respondents and easy to administer. Yet, in future hospital selection and other health-care studies, attention should be given to alternative mode of stimulus definition (e.g., pictorial presentation) and respondent's task (e.g., "preference" or some other evaluative dimension instead of "intentions to select") and strict ranking or a combination of rating and ranking instead of the rating scale used here.

SOME FURTHER APPLICATIONS OF CONJOINT MEASUREMENT IN MARKETING STUDIES OF HEALTH-CARE ORGANIZATIONS

Most marketing decisions of health-care organizations are multi-attribute in nature, requiring trade-offs between cost, efficiency, political expediency, and consumer and provider satisfaction without sacrificing the fundamental quality of health care. As such, conjoint measurement and its related techniques provide an extremely useful analytical approach to marketing decision in health care organizations.

More specifically, conjoint measurement can be applied to three major decision areas:

1. Determining the objectives, criteria, and decision rules [9] for various health care decisions.
2. Selecting target markets [10] for the given health care organization.
3. Determining the most appropriate marketing strategy [9]—what product/service mix to offer, what price to charge, how to select an appropriate location, what distribution system to employ, and how to communicate with the relevant audience.

Specific illustrative examples of multi-attribute decisions in each of these areas for each of the relevant health care organizations—hospitals, HMO's, physicians (private and group practice), health related organizations (e.g., pharmaceutical companies) and government and other regulatory agencies—are presented in Exhibit 10.

These and similar decisions lend themselves to conjoint measurement study, which can provide management with quantifiable information on the relevant audience utili-

EXHIBIT 9
Comparison of Actual Evaluation of New Hypothetical Hospitals with Predicted Evaluation Based on Additive Conjoint Measurement Results

Rank order analysis			Pair comparisons of actual vs. predicted dominance (at the aggregate level)			
Rank position	Stimulus		Actual evaluation of pairs of 8 new stimuli	Predicted evaluation of pairs of 8 new stimuli		
	Actual	Predicted				
1st	2	2		$i > j$	$i < j$	
2	8	8				
3	5	1				
4	1	6	$i > j$	86%	14%	28 = 100%
5	6	5				
6	4	4	$i < j$	14%	86%	28 = 100%
7	7	3				
8	3	7				

ties for various options. These studies can be supplemented by a computer simulation model that provides management with share of choices information (similar to brand switching matrices) for various alternative strategies. Such simulations have been developed for a number of companies (see [9 and 19]) and can be used by health-care organizations.

In addition to these marketing problems, a number of non-marketing health care problems, such as the understanding of physician's clinical judgments, can benefit from research using conjoint measurement procedures (see [16]).

EXHIBIT 10
Illustrative Set of Multi-attribute Decision Problems of Various Health-Care Organizations

Decision	Health-care organizations					
	Hospital	Health Maintenance Organization (HMO)	Private physician and group practice	Health related organizations	Medical schools and basic research organizations	Government and regulatory organizations
Establishing decision criteria.	How to allocate resources among competing objectives —profits vs. expansion vs. staffing pattern vs. prestige vs. social consideration.	Criteria for ordering, screening, and diagnostic procedures; cost vs. utility for various age groups.	Establishing criteria for type and nature of practice— profits vs. social considerations vs. research etc.	Objectives for new product— profits vs. market share vs. growth vs. cash flow, etc.	Criteria for funding—short vs. long run benefits; applied vs. basic research.	Degree and type of government financing and regulating.
Selecting target markets.	What patient groups to select —poor vs. paying patients, etc.	What target markets and physicians should the HMO try to attract?	What target market to appeal to?	What target groups of physicians and patients to appeal to?— different benefit segments.	Who should be funded?	Who should be regulated and who should receive the benefits?
Determining product/ service mix.	What departments and services should the hospital offer?	What should be the services offered by HMO?	What mix of specialties to offer?	What product benefits should a product offer?	What type of training and research programs should be established?	What central mechanism should be established to assure quality and appropriateness of health care?
Establishing pricing strategy.	How much should the hospital charge for various services?	What should be the prepayment charge?	What should the fee be?	What should the price of the products be?	What incentive system can be designed to attract the "right" type of researchers?	What price controls and guidelines to establish?
Determining distribution/ location mix.	Where should a hospital be located and what transportation system should be offered?	Should an HMO establish peripheral clinics?	Where to locate?	How to distribute the products— Detail men vs. direct selling; drugstores vs. supermarkets; etc.	Where to locate?	How to redistribute health care services geographically and by subspecialty.
Determining the communication mix.	How and what to "advertise" without using advertising.	How to "sell" the HMO concept	How to "advertise" without advertising.	How and what to advertise— physician vs. patient advertising.	How to improve the flow of information among researchers.	How to communicate effectively preventive health campaigns (smoking, cancer).
Other (non-marketing areas).	How to design attractive subspecialty training programs.		How does a physician make a clinical decision?			Establish testing procedures for physicians on realistic, multiattribute patient characteristics.

CONCLUSIONS

Most marketing problems of health care and other nonprofit organizations are basically multi-attribute in nature. As such, conjoint measurement analysis may be an extremely useful analytical procedure for the quantification of respondents' utilities for various multi-attribute alternatives.

Although this paper illustrated the applicability of conjoint measurement techniques to a pilot study of consumers' hospital selection decision and speculated on a number of other possible applications, the study of the marketing problems of nonprofit organizations in general, and of health-care organizations in particular, should not be limited to the use of this procedure. Other choice models at both the individual and group level should be developed and tested. Similarly, other data analytical procedures and especially multi-variate statistical techniques and multi-dimensional scaling procedures can and should be considered, when appropriate, among the tools available to the marketing researcher of nonprofit organizations.

REFERENCES

1. Carroll, J. D. "Categorical Conjoint Measurement," Meeting of Mathematical Psychology, Ann Arbor, MI, August 1968.
2. Creditor, C., and Creditor, V. K. "The Ecology of An Urban Voluntary Hospital, the Referral Chain," *Med. Care* 10, 88–92 (1972).
3. Ford, D. L.; Huber, G. P., and Gustafson, D. H. "Predicting Job Choices with Models that Contain Subjective Probability Judgments: An Empirical Comparison of Five Models," *Organizational Behav. Hum. Performance* 7, 397–416 (1972).
4. Goldberg, L. R. "Man Versus Model of Man: A Rationale Plus Some Evidence for a Method of Improving on Clinical Inferences," *Psychol. Bull* 73, 422–432 (1970).
5. Green, Paul E. "On the Design of Choice Experiments Involving Multifactor Alternatives," *J. Consumer Res.* 1, 61–68 (1974).
6. Green, Paul E.; Carmone, Frank J., and Wind, Yoram. "Subjective Evaluation Models and Conjoint Measurement," *Behav. Sci.* 17, 288–299 (1972).
7. Green, Paul E., and Rao, Vithala R. "Conjoint Measurement for Quantifying Judgmental Data," *J. Marketing Res.* 8, 355–363 (1971).
8. Green, Paul E., and Wind, Yoram. *Multi-Attribute Decisions in Marketing: A Measurement Approach,* The Dryden Press, New York, 1973.
9. Green, Paul E., and Wind, Yoram. "New Way to Measure Consumers' Judgment," *Harvard Business Rev.* 53, 107–117 (1975).
10. Green, Paul E.; Wind, Yoram, and Jain, Arun K. "Benefit Bundle Analysis," *J. Advertising Res.* 12, 31–36 (1972).
11. Johnson, Richard M. "Trade-Off Analysis of Consumer Values," *J. Marketing Res.* 11, 121–127 (1974).
12. Kotler, Philip. *Marketing for Nonprofit Organizations,* Prentice Hall, Englewood Cliffs, NJ, 1975.
13. Kotler, Philip, and Levy, Sidney J. "Broadening the Concept of Marketing," *J. Marketing* 33, 10–15 (1969).
14. Kruskal, Joseph B. "Analysis of Factorial Experiments by Estimating Monotone Transformations of the Data," *J. Roy. Statistical Soc. B.* 27, 251–63 (1965).
15. Slovic, Paul; Fleissner, D., and Bauman, W. S. "Analyzing the Use of Information in Investment Decision Making: A Methodological Proposal," *J. Business* 45, 283–301 (1972).
16. Spitz, Lawrence; Daniele, Ronald, and Wind, Yoram. "Multivariate Decision Making in the Settling of Pulmonary Outpatient Clinic," paper presented at the American College of Physicians, San Francisco, April 1975.
17. Wind, Yoram. "Recent Approaches to the Study of Organizational Buying Behavior," in T. V. Greer (Ed.), *Combined Proceedings of the 1973 American Marketing Association Conferences,* pp. 203–206, Chicago, 1974.
18. Wind, Yoram, and Denny, Joseph, "Multivariate Analysis of Variance in Research on the Effectiveness of TV Commercials," *J. Marketing Res.* 11, 136–42 (1974).
19. Wind, Yoram; Jolly, Stuart, and O'Connor, Arthur. "Concept Testing as Input to Strategic Marketing Simulations," in E. Mazzie (Ed.) *Proceedings of the 58th International AMA Conference,* pp. 120–124, Chicago, 1975.

Part V
Developing Marketing Programs

This part of the book is concerned with the steps to be taken when management reaches the point of developing a marketing program that addresses specific objectives. As in previous parts, the chapters here highlight particular applications. In this instance, the areas discussed include the performing arts, postal service, telephone service, and passenger rail operations.

In these readings, we have tried to highlight situations where management is seeking to break with traditional procedures and start anew. Much can be said for a "zero-based" approach to marketing planning, involving a fresh look at market dynamics, competitive trends, and consumer behavior. In several of the instances reported here, management has succeeded in developing a responsive new program, despite administrative red tape or the forces of tradition and inertia.

Charles B. Weinberg's chapter, "Building a Marketing Plan for the Performing Arts," provides a framework for a zero-based approach to program development. It lays out a format for structuring an annual plan for the organization. The format itself builds from some of the issues outlined in Chapter 9 and also incorporates many of the specific recommendations made in Chapters 2 and 10. This task involves preparing a situational analysis, identifying problems and opportunities, and developing marketing program goals. With goals established, the next steps are to develop appropriate strategies for attaining the desired goals, to set the marketing budget, and to establish a specific marketing action plan that comprises a detailed breakdown of activities. Lastly comes the important task of developing a monitoring system to allow for measurement and evaluation of subsequent performance.

"Developing a Marketing Orientation— A Case Study of the Canada Post Office" concerns a large, long-established public agency which was called upon to look carefully at how it might better serve the public. J. Allison Barnhill's chapter describes the early stages of developing a situation analysis for building a marketing plan. It raises the question of what roles the Canada Post Office should play in a modern market economy and highlights the insights gained from segmentation of mail markets into meaningful categories. Also discussed are the studies which made up the detailed environmental analysis conducted by the Post Office; these studies involved evaluations of projected technological developments and of changing economic, social, and business conditions.

Sometimes public agencies and nonprofit organizations find themselves faced with more demand for a specific service than they can (or wish to) handle. In such an instance, the objective may be to develop a program to *demarket* use of the service. J. McDonald's article, "Pricing Policies for Directory Assistance Service," is concerned with reducing demand for telephone information service in the Bell System. Although some readers may raise their eyebrows at the inclusion of a private company in this book of readings, they should note that telephone service is a key public utility which, because of its natural monopoly status, is heavily regulated by government agencies in the United States and has been nationalized in most other industrialized countries. This chapter starts with discovery of a problem—the rapidly increasing use of the 411 information service. The approach taken involved first trying to understand the components of the situation, and then developing and evaluating alternative strategies for reducing demand. McDonald shows how this was done through careful analysis, including use of economic and consumer behavior models. The concept of demarketing will be revisited later in Chapters 39 and 40, both of which look at the issue of energy conservation.

Another examination of successful use of modeling in developing a marketing program is provided by Weinberg and Shachmut's chapter, "ARTS PLAN: A Model Based System for Use in Planning a Performing Arts Series." The authors note that the programming problems faced by arts managers are analogous to those of other managers at organizations where a series of events or activities is presented over a period of time—for example, "Y's," community centers, adult education centers, or athletic and recreation organizations.

The specific model described here helps the arts manager decide on what events to include when planning a season, or what events to promote in an existing program series. It enables manages to evaluate alternative program schedules by predicting the attendance at different types of performances.

The last chapter in Part V looks at the pricing dimension of marketing program development. In 1968, British Rail abandoned its traditional mass-market approach and successfully adopted new and more flexible strategies. Roger Ford reviews this innovative step in "Pricing a Ticket to Ride," and demonstrates that pricing strategies cannot be developed in a vacuum—they must reflect the nature of the competition and the strength of the market; they must be based on constantly updated information; and they must include effective communications to prospective consumers.

These five chapters, along with those in Part IV, "Market Structure Analysis," collectively show that modern marketing management depends on a careful and rigorous study of markets, followed by development of appropriate strategy and tactics. This is not to deny the important role of creativity in marketing: it is a vital component. But a thorough understanding of the market provides fertile insights to creative thinking, and careful analysis is required to determine which of several creative solutions to a problem is most appropriate for the organization and its publics.

20
Building a Marketing Plan for the Performing Arts

Charles B. Weinberg

In recent years, the management of performing arts organizations has become more sophisticated. One managerial function that a few organizations have started to utilize successfully is marketing. This article shows that marketing can have an important role in the management of performing arts organizations and other public and nonprofit organizations. It then demonstrates the link between consumer or market research and marketing, and provides a framework in which to develop a marketing plan.

Marketing concepts are increasingly being thought of as being applicable in areas outside the private business sector. To illustrate marketing's potential usefulness, two widely known public sector programs, the swine flu innoculation program of 1976–77 and the reintroduction of the $2 bill in April 1976, will be briefly examined from a marketing perspective. Both of these new programs were intended for almost 100 percent support by the American public; however, less than 25 percent of the public (perhaps wisely) had swine flu shots; and, in the words of the *Wall Street Journal*, "the deuce is a dud" [1].

Charles B. Weinberg is Associate Professor of Marketing, Stanford University.

The author gratefully acknowledges helpful inputs for this article from J. Thomas Bacchetti of the Tennessee Arts Commission, Lynn Bonde of the Office of Public Events, Stanford University, Charles Dillingham of the American Conservatory Theater, Christopher Lovelock of Harvard Business School, and Adrian Ryans of Stanford University Graduate School of Business.

In marketing new consumer products, two conceptually different strategies can be used to introduce a product. With a "push" strategy, the manager tries to motivate the retailers to stock the product and display it prominently, so that a shopper may see the product and decide to buy it. In a "pull" strategy, advertising is targeted directly at the customer, who, if the advertising is successful, requests that the store stock the product and in a sense pulls the product through the channels.

The government introduced the $2 bill to save printing costs. A dollar bill has an average life span of 18 months. If two one dollar bills can be replaced with one two dollar bill, printing and other costs of about 5 to 10 million dollars a year could be saved. The $2 bill appears to have used neither a push nor a pull strategy. Upon receiving a $2 bill, a store cashier usually lifts up the cash drawer and places the $2 bill underneath. The stores and banks did not push the $2 bill, and there was no major communication campaign directed at consumers.

It is interesting to contrast the introduction of the $2 bill to the introduction of decimalized currency in Britain, where push and pull strategies were used extensively. In February 1971, the United Kingdom changed from a system of 12 pennies to the shilling and 20 shillings to the pound to a currency with 100 pence to the pound. The British government realized that the conversion to this new type of money would be a very complicated process and established a Decimal Currency Board (DCB) to market the new money. Early on, the banks became convinced that it was their obligation to help introduce this new money and, accordingly, developed extensive educational programs to get people adjusted to it. The DCB also realized that one of the major problems was going to be the retailers. Several years before the changeover, the DCB helped organize the "year of the retailer" in order to focus on the retailer's problems, one of which happened to be how to convert to this new money. The DCB worked with retailers in an open and helpful manner, trying to educate the retailer about how to handle the changeover and how to handle the needs of his clients. Through this push strategy, the DCB built a distribution system. An extensive consumer strategy was also developed. Although the newspapers had predicted a large amount of chaos beforehand, the changeover went smoothly and received minimal news coverage; it was a nonevent. Decimalization in Britain exemplifies the effective use of communication and other marketing notions in the introduction of new programs [2].

Another interesting contrast to the introduction of the $2 bill, which had almost no marketing campaign, was the swine flu inoculation program, which had a massive campaign. Although the vaccine was offered at no charge and intensively distributed in mass clinics, few people were inoculated. From a marketing point of view the program did not work. Neither the push to doctors nor the pull from the public created a clear enough perception of the specific benefits that would be received or of the costs that would be incurred.

MARKET RESEARCH AND MARKETING

Until approximately ten years ago, marketing was largely confined to business. In the past few years, however, there has been increasing recognition that marketing applies to a wide range of non-profit organizations and government agencies. Because advertising is the most visible and intrusive form of marketing, many people equate the two. However, advertising is only a part of marketing. Marketing is primarily concerned with the process by which people adopt and maintain attitudes and behavior patterns. The starting point for marketing management is understanding the potential user or consumer who may interact with the particular set of activities being studied. For example, answering such questions as how does a person decide to go to a theater, what is the relative importance of social, educational, and financial factors in the choice of a play to attend, and how often does he or she go to a theater represents the starting point for a consumer analysis.

EXHIBIT 1

Definition of Marketing. Marketing is fundamentally concerned with the process by which people adopt and maintain attitudes and behavior patterns. Marketing management is a system of interrelated activities that seeks (1) to understand present and potential users and usage systems in detail, (2) to develop products and services that are appropriate from the standpoint of users, funders, and the resources of the organization, and (3) to determine and implement price, distribution, and communication strategies. It is a characteristic function of almost all business organizations and has recently begun to emerge in public and nonprofit sector organizations as well.

The public sector marketing manager needs to develop the products and services which are appropriate from the viewpoint of the user, the provider of funds, and the organization. If an organization produces performances of classical music, an approach which says "rock will sell a lot more tickets" is not a very useful marketing approach. Because most public sector organizations operate at a deficit—because the users of the organization do not pay its full costs—the organization's activities must satisfy the private and/or governmental benefactors who support it. For that reason, social service organizations have often complained of not only having to satisfy client needs, but, also, of having to satisfy the funding agencies' concept of clients' need.

Once the user and benefactor needs are understood, and a product line and service policy have been established, the next stage is to develop the implementation strategy—price, distribution, and communication (e.g., advertising, personal selling etc.). Finally, because user needs are dynamic, the environment changes, and competitors enter and leave, the marketing strategy needs to be continually monitored. The Peace Corps, for example, found that the young, relatively untrained volunteers it provided to host countries in 1962 were no longer wanted by the end of the 1960's. Host countries then demanded highly trained individuals with a specific set of skills [3].

The key to achieving an understanding of the user and the needs the product or service will fulfill obviously lies with market research. The work done by the American Conservatory Theatre (ACT) in San Francisco illustrates the relationship between market research and marketing [4]. Interestingly, ACT has been willing to adopt a marketing approach while it is doing well. Most public sector organizations, such as theater groups, turn to marketing when they are in trouble and seem to say "we don't have much of an audience, the organization's survival is in doubt—anything could help, maybe even marketing." ACT, however, is very close to being sold out, yet still seeks to use marketing to help determine how it can continue to be sold out and to raise funds from its community.

The research reported here was done in April 1976. A questionnaire was mailed to ACT subscribers and a 45 percent response rate was obtained—without paying return postage. In order to examine issues of concern to other actual or potential audience segments, future plans call for surveys of people who have attended ACT performances but don't subscribe, people who contribute but don't subscribe, former subscribers, and the general population. Only a few of the results from the questionnaire will be discussed here.

The issue of why people subscribe to ACT was addressed through a question about benefits people might obtain from subscribing. One possible benefit is the subscribers' price through discount of seven plays for the price of six. Another reason why people might buy a subscription is that it makes them more certain to attend. If a person has tickets to see a play Saturday night, that person will see it. If, on the other hand, a decision to buy tickets has to be made on Saturday afternoon, the person might not go. Still other reasons include priority seating and a guarantee of obtaining a ticket. One of the interesting findings is that price discount was not one of the major benefits that people sought. (This does not imply that ACT can charge subscribers a price premium.) As a result of preliminary findings from this survey, which supported management's prior beliefs and a number of other factors as well, ACT decided to no longer offer subscribers the "7 for 6" price discount. The renewal rate remained within the usual bounds.

Care needs to be taken in generalizing from this result to other pricing strategies. ACT distributed to its audience a glossy, lavish program which described the play and current cultural events in San Francisco. The printing costs of this brochure were increasing, and ACT found that the only way it could afford to continue the brochure (even with advertising) would be to charge 25¢ a copy. ACT asked its subscribers whether they wanted to pay 25¢ a copy, or whether they preferred a less elaborate brochure. Despite the $50+ cost per subscription ticket and the price discount results, 80 percent of the respondents said "no" to the 25¢ charge. Maybe the audience was saying "charge what you want for the subscription, but I want to enjoy my night out, and I don't want to be bothered searching for a quarter when I get to the theater." ACT consequently now prints its own programs and cancelled a contract with the printer of the 25¢ brochure, which many San Francisco theaters still use. Good research leads to marketing action; it is not research that is put into a file for background. Marketing plans based on knowledge of people's preferences and behavior are invariably more successful than those that are not.

Many arts organizations carry out market research projects. For example, a recent review compiled a list of 270 audience studies conducted by visual and performing arts organizations [6]. Unfortunately, the reviewers found that only a minority of the organizations actually used the marketing research in making management decisions.

MARKETING PLAN

The marketing plan is a systematic way of organizing an analysis of a market, an organization's position in that market, and a program for future marketing activities. Marketing strategies should be conditional to the information learned by analyzing the organization's present situation and future goals. The elements of a marketing plan are not discrete components; they are interrelated, so that development of a marketing plan may involve cycling through the elements several times before a satisfactory plan is achieved.

The following outline will amplify portions of the format for a marketing plan for the arts presented in Exhibit 1.

Situational Analysis. Situational analysis, the first component in a marketing plan, examines the organization in terms of its external and internal environment. An in depth procedure for conducting a situational analysis is a "marketing audit" [5].

Environment. In the external environment, the acronym PRESTO represents political and regulatory, economic, social, technical, and other environments. How does the external environment affect the marketing operation? For example, WNET in New York has developed a video technology that allows events at Lincoln Center to be videotaped in an unobtrusive manner. What are the implications for the Metropolitan Opera or for a theater outside one of the big cities; and how do these implications change when the possibility of home video cassettes is factored in as well?

Audience. Earlier, this article discussed market research to understand the potential audience—understanding how people become an audience, understanding the current audience, and even understanding the former audience. Do people who do not come back represent normal "churn," or a signal about the service being offered? Of course, one wants to know the size of the current and potential audience, possible segmentation bases, and awareness of and attitudes toward the organization and its offerings.

Performers. Performers and unions are a part of the environment and have a significant impact on marketing programs.

Funders. Just as consumers needed to be understood, so do funding sources. Familiar marketing concepts involved in understanding users usually can be applied to the funders as well. For example, university fund raisers claim that a trial and repeat pattern exists, that donors of small amounts after graduation are a likely source of substantial donations at a later date. The existence of brand loyalty is suggested by the success of the March of Dimes (the National Foundation) and the American Lung Association (formerly concerned primarily with tuberculosis) who hold the third and fourth leading positions in fund raising for national health organizations—

even after changing their original focus. Government agencies often need to develop strategies to secure funds from four hundred and thirty-five Congressmen and one hundred Senators who have a complex set of personal and organizational needs.

Competition. There are usually many and varied competitors for a person's time. For people who are frequent attenders of arts events, the competition is probably going to be the other cultural activities in the area. For people who infrequently attend arts events, the competition is probably TV or inertia. They are two very different types of competitors, probably posing different types of problems and opportunities and requiring different marketing programs.

Internal. Analysis of the internal environment is critical as well. What are the objectives? What does the organization want to achieve? Overall, what are the strengths and weaknesses, honestly appraised? What key factors are there that distinguish this organization from others that will allow it to succeed in meeting user needs in the face of competition and a possibly hostile environment?

Problems and Opportunities. This analysis of the external and internal environment should lead to the specification of a set of problems and opportunities. It has been said that "we are all continually faced with a series of great opportunities brilliantly disguised as unsolvable problems."

Momentum Forecast. A momentum forecast of year end position can be constructed based on an analysis of the external and internal environment, assuming that the organization is operated as usual. The momentum forecast is then compared with the organization's desired year-end position, wherein the gaps between the momentum forecast and the desired position are identified. This provides a challenge for the organization in order to close the gaps and to help to stimulate the creation of marketing program goals and strategies and motivate the people in the organization.

Marketing Program Goals. The goals should meet a set of guidelines. First, the goals should be specific and quantifiable. It is very hard to use a goal such as increasing the audience as a motivating device, because it is not known when it has been achieved. A goal expressed as "to increase awareness of the programs offered in the community" raises a number of questions. Is it to increase the awareness of students, senior citizens, or new residents, and by how much? A more meaningful goal is that 40 percent of the new residents know that the program exists. The goals should be realistic and tailored to the situation. An organization should need to work to achieve its goals. The goals should not be so easy that attainment of them is boring. On the other hand, the goals should not be set so high that they cannot be achieved.

EXHIBIT 2
Marketing Plan Format

Situational Analysis (Where are we now?)

A. External
   Environment (PRESTO).
   Political and regulatory, economic, social, technical, and other.
   Audience
   Funders
   Performers
   Competition

B. Internal
   Objectives
   Strengths and weaknesses

Problems and Opportunities

   Momentum forecast
   Identify gaps

Marketing Program Goals (Where do we want to go?)

   Specific (quantifiable)
   Realistic (attainable)
   Important
   Prioritized

Marketing Strategies (How are we going to get there?) *

   Positioning
      Target segments
      Competitive stance
      Usage Incentive

   Marketing mix
      Product
      Price
      Distribution
      Marketing communication

   Contingency strategies

Marketing budget (How much and where?) *

   Resources
      Money
      People
      Time

   Amount and allocation

Marketing action plan *

   Detailed breakdown of activities for each goal/strategy
   Responsibility by name
   Activity schedule in milestone format
   Tangible and intangible results expected from each activity

Monitoring system

---

   * Separate but interrelated strategies may be needed for consumers and funding sources.

There should be a few, select prioritized goals which are important to the organization. If the goals are achieved, the organization can feel happy about it; if they are not achieved, then, at least, there should be a way of determining why—which should be useful in determining goals and setting plans for the next year.

Marketing Strategy. Marketing strategy is the means by which the organization achieves its marketing goals. Of course, in building a marketing plan, several different strategies usually must be constructed before the most effective and efficient one is chosen. There are a number of different ways to try to achieve goals. For example, two different strategies were discussed earlier for the $2 bill: a "push" strategy directed at stores and banks and a "pull" strategy directed at "consumers." Either strategy might have been the most appropriate, the problem was that the Treasury did not appear to have any active strategy. Because public sector organizations often need to raise money from people and organizations who do not use the service, two distinct but interrelated marketing strategies may be needed, one for fund raising and one for user services.

Positioning. Positioning, the fundamental statement of what the organization and its services represent and what they provide to whom, involves three factors. First, who are the target segments; that is, to which groups is the organization striving to appeal? The organization may try to appeal to more than one group at a time. ACT, for example, might try to develop one program for people who attend but do not subscribe, another for current subscribers, and a third one for lost subscribers—although problems of coordinating the efforts to reach each group needs to be considered as well. In each of the target segments, the manager needs to set the organization's competitive stance. Depending on the segment, the competition can vary considerably, as was discussed earlier. The next step in positioning is to establish the usage incentive. What are the primary benefits that the organization is going to offer its current and potential users? The positioning strategy is vital not only in terms of the consumers, but also for the organization's management; it provides a focus for management efforts and is a key element, therefore, in channeling the efforts of the organization.

Marketing Mix. The marketing mix (product/service, price, distribution, and communications) is a convenient way of summarizing a set of marketing activities. These marketing activities support the marketing goals of the organization; the execution of these activities is just one part of marketing. Those new to marketing often consider these activities, especially advertising, to be all of marketing.

Product. "Product" is a generic term that includes both goods and services. The product must be considered from the audience's point of view and is best conceptualized as a collection of attributes which provide a set of tangible and intangible benefits. In the performing arts, the product can be categorized in at least four ways. One is the year-after-year product that the organization is providing to its community. A second is a particular year or season; the set of performances being offered—the variety, the quality level, the timing, etc. With the large number of alternatives available, the

problem of which performances to book can be a very complex one. A third level is the series of plays packaged together such as a "choose your own series," a set of soloists, or a mix of types of performers. A fourth level of product classification is the individual performance itself. In most cases, the individual offering needs to fit the perception of a day or evening out. In terms of ACT, for example, the market research indicated that there are very few people who just go to ACT; that is, leave their house to go to ACT and come back home immediately afterwards. Many obtain the benefits of an evening out or a social experience—they may have dinner before, go for a drink after, and drive to and from the theater with some other people.

The offering has to meet the audience's perceptions. Advertising should not promise benefits the product cannot deliver. If an organization tells people "You can have the most exciting evening of your life when you come to one of our performances," and people come and do not have the most exciting evening of their lives, that can be disastrous. The offering has to meet the needs of the audience segments.

One of the real problems in providing performing arts services is reliability. If a performer has an off night or if a third of the audience has colds one night and is sneezing, the quality suffers. Generally, a service organization in which the production of services occurs simultanously with the consumption of services has problems of quality control and of maintaining reliability. One service organization regularly surveys its own and its competitors' customers with regard to customer satisfaction with the performance of services. Both positive and negative results are reported to managers and the employees as a means of motivating and rewarding quality service.

Price. Pricing is obviously a very important factor, even in deficit operations such as is the case for most performing arts organizations, where box office revenues do not cover the full operating costs. In most cases price sensitivity is conditioned on a number of factors, including the overall marketing strategy. Even the offering of free tickets does not ensure that the hall will be filled to capacity. There is also a set of pricing issues with regard to series versus individual tickets, (as in our earlier discussion of the "7 for 6" price discount), student "rush" or last-minute discount tickets versus general student discount, charge card versus cash or check only, as well as setting the overall price for performances. Although not all these issues can be discussed, the student rush versus student discount issue will be discussed to illustrate some marketing concepts.

In one survey of students, it was found that many did not know what student rush tickets were. Student rush offers a discount to students who are willing to buy tickets in the last half hour before a performance starts, and take the risk of there not being any rush tickets available. A student who wants to buy a ticket three weeks in advance does not get the discount. One university performing arts series was selling at

60 percent of capacity and said, in essence, to the students that if they paid at the last minute they were almost sure to get tickets. However, this strategy added a risk element to the price that a student, especially one with a date, might not be willing to pay. With attendance at 60 percent of capacity, the organization then decided to offer student discounts ahead of time and not fall into the "airline trap" of constructing an elaborate and confusing price structure to insure that a business traveler who is willing to pay full fare will do so. The consumer effects of complex discount systems need to be carefully examined, especially when there is substantial excess capacity and readily identifiable segments.

Another problem arises because of deficit operations. One method of reducing losses is to raise prices. But if the price is raised, fewer people attend the organization's events. Thus, a cycle is established. An organization raises the price, and fewer people attend; therefore, the organization reduces the number of performances. But then, fewer people attend, and more money is lost. The conclusion is unfortunately obvious. The marketing approach tries to take a more optimistic view and suggests that an organization does not automatically need to resort to a strategy which appeals to narrower segments of either the wealthy or those people who really desire the service and have no alternative. Rather, a marketing approach suggests that an organization examine the various types of audiences that may attend and try to develop a marketing mix that minimizes the shrinkage.

Distribution. Distribution is of critical importance, if most audience members come from near the auditorium. For example, at Stanford about 75 percent of the audience comes either from Stanford or the adjacent communities. This suggests the need for considering branching strategies if such an alternative is feasible. If it is not feasible for the performance to be offered at more than one location, at least the reservation process can be dispersed geographically. An interesting marketing question is the need for a branch ticket (or voucher) to specify a seat location so that it is perceived as being the same as a box office ticket.

Marketing Communication. Marketing communication has been frequently discussed and will be mentioned here only briefly [7]. Communication includes a whole range of activities such as advertising, personal selling (by volunteers or paid staff), publicity, word-of-mouth, and the performance itself. Communication programs need to be aimed at specific target audiences, with clear objectives set with regard to what informational, persuasive, attitudinal, and behavioral goals are to be reached in conjunction with other elements of the marketing strategy.

Contingency Strategies. A marketing plan should include contingency strategies. Because it is difficult to predict the future precisely, the manager should anticipate what the major surprises might be and, consequently, be prepared beforehand, in case such contingencies occur. One theater group has three plans for the second half of the year, the critical factors being attendance revenues in the first half of the year. One major company has a policy which says that it does not accept unanticipated surprises as an excuse by a manager for annual plan goals that are missed. The plan can include contingencies, but if a manager says, "I never expected that to happen and as a result my sales are down by 20 percent," senior management replies that "if you are a good manager you should at least know what the possible surprises are going to be." Knowing the possible surprises provides a big advantage, because well thought out and timely alternative strategies can be available beforehand.

Marketing Budget. The next step in the marketing plan is the marketing budget. There are three critical resources in running an organization: money, people, and time. The budgeting question is usually how to utilize or allocate these resources, because most non-profit organizations do not have enough money, people, or time. These resources can be increased by a contribution program—a contribution not only of money but also of volunteer time. However, many diverse organizations are increasing their fund-raising efforts so that the market is extremely competitive. Fund-raising is a difficult process and can divert key organizational members from other activities without commensurate return. In allocating resources it is critical to consider the interrelationships among marketing elements and have a clear notion of effectiveness and efficiency.

Marketing Action Plan. Finally, the marketing action plan is a detailed breakdown of the activities that achieve each of the goals and strategies and an assignment of responsibilities by name of individual or office. The activity schedule should be in milestone form. For example, if the goal is to increase the attendance from 60 percent of capacity to 75 percent of capacity at the end of the year, then attendance should be 65 percent of capacity at the end of two months. Or, if a new fund-raising program is to be developed a year from now, it means that three months from now some specified activities should be completed.

SUMMARY

Most performing arts organizations carry out some of the elements of a marketing plan. However, there is a distinct advantage to conducting a thorough and systematic analysis of the organization's marketing situation and using that analysis as the basis for establishing a coherent marketing strategy. Building a marketing plan can take a considerable amount of effort, and each organization must decide how detailed and complex its plan should be and how many resources to devote to the research foundation on which the plan is built, to the creation and evaluation of strategies, and to the construction of the final plan. An organization's first attempt at building a marketing plan is going to be more costly than when the process is repeated. The benefits of building a marketing plan are not limited to those connected with developing an approach to the market; they also include the use of the plan as a form of communication within the organization and as a means to coordinate and focus efforts.

REFERENCES

1. Pappas, Vasil. "The Deuce is a Dud." *Wall Street Journal,* January 5, 1977, page 1.
2. Lovelock, Christopher H. "Decimalization of the Currency in Great Britain," 9-575-101. Boston: Intercollegiate Case Clearing House, 1975.
3. Star, Steven H. "The Peace Corps," 9-571-035. Boston: Intercollegiate Case Clearing House, 1970.
4. Ryans, Adrian B., and Weinberg, Charles B. "Consumer Dynamics." *Journal of Consumer Research* (September 1978).
5. Kotler, Philip. *Marketing for Nonprofit Organizations,* pp. 55–75. Englewood Cliffs, NJ: Prentice Hall, 1975.
6. DiMaggio, Paul, Useem, Michael, and Brown, Paula (1977), "The American Arts Audience: Its Study and Its Character," unpublished working paper, Cambridge, Mass.: Center for the Study of Public Policy.
7. Ray, Michael L. "A Decision Sequence Analysis of Developments in Marketing Communication." *Journal of Marketing* (January 1973): 29–38.

21
Developing a Marketing Orientation—A Case Study of the Canada Post Office

J. Allison Barnhill

This case study provides insights into the managerial approaches used in developing contemporary concepts of marketing (for example, marketing systems and roles, market segments, and environment surveillance) and their application to the formulation of marketing strategies for the Canada Post Office.

The marketing concept has been widely accepted among progressive business organizations. However, adopting a marketing orientation in the public or the governmental sector typically has been viewed as being inapplicable by civil servants. Until the late '60s, some 20 years after the marketing concept had been formulated and implemented at General Electric by Ralph Cordiner, a marketing orientation was unheard of for departments of government. It was as if governments did not have any publics, any consumers or any markets to serve.

During the five years previous to 1969, the Post Office had faced increasing criticism. It had experienced two bitter national strikes and run up major annual deficits. Fluctuating standards of service, rising costs and adverse public reaction to postal rate increases were indicative of the problems facing the Post Office. In addition, there was a mounting annual deficit, which by 1980, could have exceeded $500 million dollars.

In July 1968 a new Minister was appointed to head the Post Office Department and, in September 1968, a series of studies were commissioned. Between November 1968 and July 1969, fifteen studies were conducted by six different consulting organizations. A major conclusion of the investigations was the lack of a marketing orientation in the operations of the Post Office. The report of one eminent management consulting company stated:

> Officers in the Department lack the marketing orientation essential for an efficient service. They see the market as users of mail rather than of communications, transportation and banking services. The services that the Department is permitted to provide under the Post Office Act have been interpreted precisely and have been offered in an administrative and unimaginative manner.

From this juncture in 1969, we are able to trace the evolution of the Canada Post Office's marketing orientation

J. Allison Barnhill was formerly Senior Consultant, Bureau of Management Consulting, Ottawa, Ontario.

which, in 1974, is using some of the most advanced marketing approaches and techniques available. Suffice it to say, marketing alone is not a panacea for all problems of an organization of such magnitude and complexity. However, it does offer a number of ways in which the level of postal service can be improved. When one considers the situation faced by the Canada Post Office in 1969, the need for improvement was imperative. The relatively rapid evolution of these improvements merits closer examination.

THE POST OFFICE IN THE MARKET ECONOMY

One of the 15 commissioned studies was undertaken by a Marketing Task Force headed by Professor Stanley Shapiro. Three career employees of the Canada Post Office and three academics from Canadian schools of business comprised the Task Force. Their landmark report had three main streams of analysis and recommendations, which also provides an outline for this paper. These were:

1. The Post Office as a marketing system;
2. Preparation for marketing; and
3. Marketing strategies for the Post Office.

In its simplest terms, the Post Office marketing system is viewed by the Task Force as having three fundamental sub-systems: an input, a process and an output.

The input sub-system. This sub-system is viewed as undeveloped. In general, the customer must go to the postal system to make an input. The postal system does not go to the customer as it does for delivery, or as competing services do, or as is desired by customers (actual or potential).

The process sub-systems. From the Task Force's perspective, the process focuses predominantly on the services provided by the network of 11,000 retail stations. These services are grouped into mail support (i.e., postage, writing documents, and special mail services) and tangential services such as money order sales, distribution of government forms, and government publicity.

The output sub-system. The output or delivery sub-system is substantially better developed. An extensive network of personnel, facilities, and equipment delivers 5 billion pieces of mail to nearly 5 million locations dispersed in a nation of 3½ million square miles. Various delivery modes being used in 1969 included more than 8,000 letter carriers, 5,600 rural route carriers, and parcel and mobile delivery services.

Roles of the Post Office. From its investigations, the Task Force formulated three conceptual roles for the Post Office. An understanding of these roles was deemed to be a basic prerequisite for the analysis leading to the formulation of a marketing strategy. Furthermore, by focusing on roles, the Task Force was able to broaden the organizational concept of the Post Office from that of handlers of mail and purveyors of other passive services to an organizational concept encompassing operating, communications, and customer responsibilities and functions. The Task Force formulated the following roles for the Canada Post Office.

The operating role. Traditionally, a common view of the Post Office has been ''to carry letters.'' The Task Force broadened this operating role by stating, ''. . . the Post Office is in the business of aggregating, transporting, diffusing, and delivery to the door, through one distribution network, small, individual items of any kind.''

The communications role. In formulating this new role, the Task Force viewed the Post Office as a communications medium; a pipeline of documented information with an input aggregator and an output diffuser. Its main competition in this regard consists of media which transmit messages from one individual to another, e.g., telephone, telex and telegraph. From an analysis of the advantages and disadvantages of the postal system, the Task Force stated that the communication role of the Post Office was to be ''. . . in the business of transmitting documented messages between any individuals, slowly and with inconsistent speed, at low transmission cost but high transformation cost.''

The customer role. The Marketing Task Force considered the Post Office to be in the business of serving four categories of customers: businesses, professional mailers, governments and rural and urban householders. The major flow of mail is from businesses to householders, although important uses are made of the Post Office service by each of the customer groups.

Business uses are the most extensive. Postal services are vital to the survival of most businesses. Predominant business uses include conveying financial and contractual correspondence, and transmitting reference data and documents. Professional mailers use the Post Office to distribute promotional material to the most promising prospects in a more personal manner than can be provided by mass media, i.e., radio, television, magazines and newspapers. Governments use the Post Office for political and administrative purposes. The Post Office provides a basic means of linking all people and regions into a nation. This national purpose continues to be manifested by the uniform postal rate used throughout the country, regardless of the distance and cost of delivery. Householders are the main recipients of mail from the three previously mentioned users. In addition, householders use the Post Office for personal written messages, financial transactions, institutional contacts and mail orders.

MAJOR MAIL MARKETS

Segmenting mail markets into meaningful categories enables marketing strategies to be created and adjusted in response to market demands. The Task Force discerned that mail markets can be segmented based on a number of factors, of which two of the most important are by customer and by content.

Segmenting Mail Markets by Customer. Post Office customers can be categorized in a number of ways, e.g., by type of institution or user, by geographical location, or by size. For purposes of developing marketing strategies, distinguishing between large and small customers is very useful. The Marketing Task Force developed a list of Canadian customers generating more than $50,000 of mail volume per year. This list contained 380 customers which, in total, accounted for approximately one-third of all Post Office revenue (that is, 30% of first class mail revenue, two-thirds of second class mail revenue, half of the income from third class mail, and

23% of fourth class mail revenues). The 100 largest customers accounted for 25% of total Post Office revenue. When derived mail is considered (i.e., mail generated in response to other mail), the 380 largest customers were estimated to account for 45 percent of all postal revenues. Thus, large customers represent an important and special market segment to the Post Office, and special marketing consideration must be given to them.

Segmenting Mail Markets by Content. The four class mail system presently used is one way to segment markets. Classes of mail tend to reflect contents. To illustrate this point, individual letters or personal transactions are generally first class, news publications are second class, other printed materials are generally third class, and parcels are fourth class mail. The Task Force formulated fourteen categories of mail content, each distinct in terms of its potential for market development. These categories included financial transactions, legal transactions, business correspondence, government correspondence, personal correspondence, greeting business correspondence, government correspondence, personal correspondence, greeting cards, news periodicals, special purpose periodicals, documents, national advertising by mail, local advertising by mail, mail order, direct mail sales, and parcels.

To aid in analyzing market segments, certain kinds of data would be needed. These data would include proportions of total sales revenue, sales growth, derivative sales, profitability, number and location of major senders and major receivers, time requirements, price sensitivity, and Post Office market share. These data were not available.

PREPARATION FOR MARKETING

Surveilling the Environment. Realizing that the constantly changing, essentially uncontrollable environment has a considerable impact on the effectiveness of marketing campaigns, the Post office has undertaken various formal investigations of environmental conditions since 1969. These environmental investigations can be reviewed in terms of technological, economic, business, and social conditions.

Technological Developments. Probably no environmental factor poses such a threat to the Post Office as technological developments. Post Office managers must keep abreast of technological developments affecting markets in which they are or could be competing. They must also be aware of the marketing implications of technological advances affecting the processing of mail. Technological trends are an integral part of the planning of marketing strategies. One of the major technological trends having an immediate or expected impact on postal service is electronic mailing.[1]

Interest in electronic mailing is not new. In the United States, the postal service has been intermittently involved in consideration of electronic mail for almost 130 years.

The essential features of electronic mailing, e.g., a telecommunications system, is comprised of three distinct subsystems: input, transmission and output.[2] (These same three basic components were outlined as the three fundamental components of the Post Office as a marketing system in 1969 by the Marketing Task Force.) Viewed from the telecommunications perspective, not unlike that of a postal marketing system, the electronic mail system can be explained briefly as follows.

> *Input.* Collection is the process of bringing order to the variety of mail having potential for electronic transmission. Variety in mail includes the nature of the message, time of receipt, urgency, format, recording medium, and method by which it is generated.
>
> In general, for other than computer generated mail, some input transformation will be required to convert the message from its original form into electronic signals for transmission. For example, for letters originated on paper the two most likely options for transformation appear to be either conversion of alpha-numeric text, character by character, into digital signals or rastertype scanning with a degree of resolution of the original pattern (whether alpha-numeric, diagrammatic or cursive script.)
>
> *Transmission.* Following input transformation, transmission of the electronic signals can take place by well proven, reliable telecommunications techniques.
>
> *Output.* Output from the telecommunications system is crucial both to the economics and customer acceptance of electronic mail. There exist a variety of options, each of which is likely to have appeal to various classes of message recipient. Identification of these options and of the number, size and location of potential customers are factors which must be resolved. Further study of these marketing aspects is likely to be time consuming and expensive.
>
> As an extension of the output process, the Post Office could offer a unique type of delivery service for those messages which are required in hard copy and are received from the telecommunications system at a point separate from the ultimate destination.

Although there are several other forms of electronic mailings (e.g., facsimile transmission, telex-microwave and on-line computer transmission), the telecommunications system outlined above is fundamental to most electronic mailings. At a time when more than two billion pieces of first and third class mail are amenable to electronic mail, the potential for such a technological development by the Canada Post Office is a very attractive marketing prospect.

Economic Conditions. Buoyant economic trends are expected to create more jobs, larger labor forces, bigger payrolls, more sales, and increased business activity generally. The rising income of Canadians is expected to increase the labor costs of Post Office operations. At the same time, the generally increasing affluence of Canadians is expected to result in consumer demands for greater accessibility and convenience in shopping and, as a result, careful consideration needs to be given to the design and location of Post Office "retail

---

[1] Jackson, Charles L. *Electronic Mail*. Cambridge MA: Center for Space Research, Massachusetts Institute of Technology, April, 1973, p. 7.

[2] Department of Communications. "Telecommission." *Postal Services & Telecommications*. Ottawa, 1972, p. 2.

outlets.'' Several, related factors enter into these decision making deliberations. The continuing trend to urbanization will lead to an expected decline in the number of postal stations. More widespread automobile ownership allows for an increase in the distance criterion between Post Offices. The combination of increasing real estate values and spiralling labor costs gives impetus to Post Office consideration for providing a large amount of its retailing effort through self-service outlets.

Business Conditions. Business trends of specific interest to the Post office include funds transfer systems, direct mail advertising trends, developments in the publishing industry, and competitive positions of the communications industry. Changes now taking place in the banking industry indicate that between now and 1985 the system of financial transactions will be less check and cash oriented. Banks are developing and installing on-line systems that are considered to be the beginning of a data transmission network through which funds may be transferred without any paper movement at all. Branch banks are being linked to central computers. Banking transactions are automatically recorded and processed by computers that maintain and update individual accounts. By the end of the 1970s, all banks in Canada are expected to have developed individual computer networks. Interconnection of computerized data transmission between banks is forecasted to begin later in the 1970s and is expected to be completed by 1985. On-line systems, once sufficiently developed, will simplify and expedite the clearing of checks considerably. When consideration is given to the fact that bills, checks and financial statements received or sent by households comprise more than 800 million pieces of mail annually or 30 percent of the first class mail in Canada during 1971, the potential impact of electronic mail on the postal service becomes increasingly apparent.

Social Conditions. Forecasts indicate that, by 1985, 22 million of the 26 million Canadians will live in cities, with more than 17 million expected to inhabit the urbanized region stretching from Windsor to Quebec City, the main concentrations being in Toronto and Montreal. As city environments provide greater opportunity for personal contact, the demand for information, communication, and goods in urban areas will grow at faster rates than in the past. Urban areas are now the most costly to service because of the high labor input, so these urbanizing trends will continue to increase Post Office operational costs if there is no change in the present system of delivery.

In an age of electronics and telecommunications, there has been a concomitant increase in the expectations of Canadians particularly in the business sphere, toward greater speed and reliability of mail services. The exposure of the population to sophisticated communications technologies in the home, at work, or in school is making people less overwhelmed by, and more expectant of, changes in communications.

Changing social conditions are likely to result in a rapid growth in market potential. Because the public expects fast-acting information and communications systems, additional demands will be put on the services that the Post Office offers. Although the Post Office provides the lowest cost information transfer service, the public's real or perceived need for rapid information transmission indicates that people will willingly pay a higher price for a faster service, especially if it is reliable. These conditions will intensify the pressures on the Post Office in its efforts to compete in information transfer and communications markets. Developing marketing strategies to meet these competitive pressures and environmental conditions is a foremost task for Post Office management.

MARKETING STRATEGY FOR THE POST OFFICE

Underlying the development of marketing strategies for the Post Office is the realization by top management that greater consideration of marketing is needed in Post Office planning. One of the first Marketing Plans developed by the Post Office states, in part, the challenge of marketing in the future of the postal system.

> To a large extent therefore, the challenge of the future for the Post Office is a *Marketing* challenge. The need to provide services and products which meet with customer acceptance and which contribute to the overall profit is obvious. The ability to deal effectively with customers and explain how the Post Office can meet their service needs will be of increasing importance in an environment of growing competitiveness.
> Lastly, the quality of innovative thinking which must permeate the entire Post Office is nowhere more urgently required than in the field of Marketing.

Marketing Objectives. In 1970, a statement of marketing policy was approved by the Post Office. This statement was:

> It is the policy of the Canada Post Office to become marketing oriented, through development of a marketing capability and organization, comparable to the best examples in private industry. In our view, the Post Office exists to serve the people of Canada, in pursuit of their social and economic objectives.
> Marketing orientation therefore means an organized concern for the needs of our customers, and a recognition that we exist to serve them. Services must be planned, and priced so as to meet the greatest degree of customer need, while achieving a much more satisfactory financial result. The aim is to bring every service provided by the Post Office as close as possible to financial self-sufficiency, thereby relieving the burden on all other services, and on the tax-paying public.

On the strength of this policy statement, six basic marketing objectives were formulated. These objectives deal with the principal areas of Post Office marketing activity. Briefly stated, the objectives are:

1. Maintain a direct and continuous channel of communication with major customers, to ensure servicing of their total needs in the most profitable way and to provide essential customer contact.
2. Maintain a comprehensive appreciation of all factors having a significant effect on present or future market conditions, including

customer needs, competition, technological changes, mailing and distribution patterns and business trends.
3. Investigate, evaluate and develop product and pricing changes or new service concepts which may enhance the profitability of existing services or identify new lines of profitable endeavor for the Canada Post Office.
4. Simplify and refine methods of doing business to the mutual advantage of both customers and the Post Office.
5. Develop a selling capability which will ensure achievement of full market potential for each product and service of the Canada Post Office.
6. Improve and maintain Post Office public offices to the best contemporary standards of appearance and decor, and recruit, train and motivate counter sales and service staffs to serve customers in the most efficient and friendly way.

Based on the direction provided by these objectives, Canada Post Office marketers proceeded to conduct an analysis of 11 major problems and 8 major opportunities it anticipated in the future. From this analysis was developed a Marketing Plan that indicated a set of market and product strategies. In outlined form, these strategies were aimed at:

1. Correspondence and communications
   a. provide services allied to the electronic communications segment so as to take advantage of this swiftly expanding area of communications.
   b. provide convenience items such as mailgrams and pre-stamped memos, to retain the attractiveness of this means of communication.
2. Machine generated mail
   a. pricing flexibility to retain business of large volume users.
   b. provide services allied to the electronic communications segment to take advantage of this swiftly expanding area of communication.
3. Direct mail advertising and sales
   a. work with the industry to stimulate the whole direct advertising business.
   b. provide service and price packages to complete with private distributors.
4. Parcel Distribution
   a. provide attractive urban delivery services to take advantage of the very large potential in both business and householder areas.
   b. provide links between centers (senders and receivers).
   c. provide rational (competitive) pricing structures.
5. Premium Mail
   a. direct sales effort to selected identifiable targets, e.g., Telex subscribers.
   b. stress the speed and reliability of hard copy.
   c. use of advertising and direct mail promotion in selective trade journals and periodicals.
6. Assured Mail
   a. improve awareness of general public through householder mail, T.V. advertising, etc.

   b. direct sales contact with large volume mailers stressing cost savings in using Assured Mail as a communications media, e.g., sell against the use of the telephone for long distance communications.
   c. publish performance figures.
7. Standard Mail (householders, catalogues, etc.)
   a. maintain close contact with Canadian Direct Mail Association and Direct Mail Advertisers Association.
   b. direct sales effort with large Direct Mail and retail houses.
   c. advertising in trade magazines and journals.
8. Standard Mail (parcels and Postpak)
   a. apply direct sales effort to large volume users.
   b. stress business to business, i.e., intra-urban and inter-city services.
   c. advertise to create an awareness of Canada Post Office as a merchandise distribution service.

In addition to these objectives, competitive analyses and strategies have been undertaken, and a continuing program of marketing research and development is being pursued. At present, a series of fourteen case studies of major mail using industries are being conducted by the Bureau of Management Consulting. These studies are aimed at providing in-depth information regarding the major business segments of the mail to determine: (1) present mailing, information transmission and communications policies and practices; (2) the changes expected in these policies and practices; and (3) the implications for Post Office marketing of these present and future policies and practices.

SUMMARY AND CONCLUSIONS

In five years, the Canada Post Office has come a long way in developing a modern and competitive marketing orientation. From its position of steadily deteriorating services and growing deficits, it has developed into an organization that has a dramatically changed and positive orientation toward its customers, products, services, promotion and public image. Changing the orientation of a large organization, private or public, is not an easy undertaking. Problems of deficits ($90.0 million in 1973), performance and image continue to plague the Canada Post Office. Offsetting these continuing deficiencies have been many, more numerous gains that justify and provide impetus for the continuous development of a marketing orientation in the Canada Post Office.

22
Pricing Policies for Directory Assistance Service

J. McDonald

This paper presents a case study describing how management science techniques assisted a large corporation in making a decision that may ultimately affect almost everyone in the United States. It was AT&T's decision to recommend to its Operating Companies that they request approval from their public utility commissions to charge customers for using directory assistance service. Directory assistance is the system by which a telephone operator provides telephone numbers to customers on a real-time basis.

The article outlines the structure of the telecommunications industry, describes how directory assistance service is provided and indicates how customer use of the service has grown. Then, the analytical techniques that were used to assist in making the decision are described. These include: the development of quantifiable objectives, the determination of how customers currently use the service, the construction of an econometric demand model, the selection of optimal implementation methods, the simulation of the economic impact, and the analysis of the potential customer reaction. This study led to the conclusion that charging would be beneficial and pointed out the particular charging plan that would be best.

As of March 30, 1976, charging has been approved in 14 states, and regulatory decisions were pending in eight others. In areas where charging has been implemented, customers have significantly reduced their dependence upon directory assistance and are making increased use of local telephone directories, personal number lists, and other sources of telephone number information. They have expressed little dissatisfaction with the plan.

INDUSTRY STRUCTURE

The Bell System, in cooperation with approximately 1,600 non-Bell companies, called Independent telephone companies, provides telephone service throughout the continental United States. The term "Bell System" refers to the American Telephone and Telegraph Company (AT&T), its

J. McDonald is Manager, Corporate Planning Studies, American Telephone and Telegraph Company.

The work reported in this article could not have been completed without the thoughtful advice and assistance of M. A. Chaudry, R. G. Dare, B. E. Davis, J. H. Hann, W. S. Hinkley, P. N. Johnstone, W. G. Kyle, G. D. Morlan, N. B. Rathfelder, W. B. Tunstall, J. E. Yingling, Jr., and countless others. The author thanks them for their contributions and congratulates them on a job well done.

associated Operating Telephone Companies, Western Electric and Bell Laboratories. The Independent telephone companies are privately or publicly owned corporations or cooperatives. The Bell System companies serve eighty-two percent of the telephones in the United States, with the remainder served by the Independent companies.

All telecommunications services provided by the industry are regulated by federal or state regulatory bodies. These are the Federal Communications Commission (FCC) and the state Public Utilities Commissions (PUCs). These bodies have the authority to approve, reject, or revise the rates to be charged for services provided by the industry. The FCC has responsibility for interstate services, and state PUCs have responsibility for intrastate services.

DIRECTORY ASSISTANCE SERVICE

Directory Assistance Service is the system by which a telephone operator provides telephone number information to customers on a real-time basis. It is intended to be used as a last resort when customers need a number not shown in their telephone directory. Most of these directory assistance requests are handled by operators who look up the number in an up-to-date paper or microfilm version of the local telephone directory, called the operator reprint, or on a frequently called number list (FCNL) that is maintained within view of the operator. These operators work on directory assistance calls in teams ranging from groups of 2 or 3 in some remote rural locations to teams of several hundred in large metropolitan areas, where incoming requests are automatically routed to team members on a random basis.

Directory assistance service is a very labor intensive operation. Through advertising and requests by the operator that customers look up the number in their local telephone directory, the industry was successful during the early 1940s in reducing the number of times that customers used directory assistance as their first choice when looking for a telephone number. Similar control techniques were used throughout the 1950s and 1960s. However, in the late 1950s these methods started to become less effective. Advertising in recent years has not been cost effective in reducing the volume of directory assistance calls. Customer reactions to recorded announcements and operators suggesting that customers look up the number in their local telephone directory have been somewhat negative in many locations.

In recent years the volume of directory assistance requests has increased steadily at almost 7 percent per year —significantly higher than the rate of growth of demand for telephone service. By 1974 the Bell System employed forty thousand directory assistance operators who handled about 16 million directory assistance calls on an average business day. Directory assistance calls constituted about 3 percent of all telephone traffic.

Coincident with a rapid growth in directory assistance volumes in the 1960s, the national economy was also booming, creating alternative job opportunities for many directory assistance operators. This, in turn, caused high attrition rates among directory assistance operators and made it extremely difficult for the Bell System to retain enough qualified operators to handle the work load. Another concern had also arisen by the early 1970s. Due to inflation it had become apparent that Bell System companies would have to engage in a series of rate cases in which local Bell telephone companies would be requesting approval for increases in basic service rates. Customers have always paid for the cost of directory assistance as part of the charges for other telephone services and have never seen explicit charges for directory assistance on their bills. In recent years directory assistance cost has become a significant and escalating component of telephone service charges—approximately fifty cents per customer per month in 1974. Increased usage of directory assistance, as well as inflation, was causing additional pressures for increases in basic service rates.

An additional directory assistance volume control technique that had been discussed for several years, by both Bell and Independent telephone company management, but that had not been implemented, was direct charging for use of local directory assistance. It was anticipated that charging would reduce volume and produce some additional revenue. The primary reason that charging has not been implemented, even on a trial basis, was because of the difficulty expected in convincing regulatory bodies and the public that charging would be in the public interest. In order to convince regulators, indeed even for AT&T to recommend to its Operating Companies that they request approval from their PUCs, would require that the objectives of charging be clearly specified, that the "optimal" charging plan be determined, that the economic and social impact be known, and that customer reactions be anticipated.

MANAGEMENT SCIENCE INVOLVEMENT

In 1972 the AT&T Corporate Planning Organization was asked by top AT&T management to examine the need for changes in the methods used for providing telephone number information to customers. That organization, which employs several management science people, is charged with conducting studies of selected interdepartmental policy issues in areas of the business where alternative policy choices could result in significantly different futures for the corporation. The team that was assigned to work on this issue began by studying the matter of charging for local directory assistance. The subsequent analysis, decision, and results are the subject of this paper.

Charging for directory assistance has three primary objectives:

1. reducing the need for directory assistance operators so they can be made available for handling other tasks that require large amounts of labor,
2. reducing pressures for increases in basic telephone rates by reducing operating costs, and

3. introducing a more equitable and efficient pricing structure by making each customer's telephone bill more sensitive to the costs generated by that customer's use of the service.

In order to establish the appropriateness of these objectives and the effectiveness of directory assistance charging in achieving them it was necessary that a study be undertaken to answer the following questions:

1. How do customers currently use directory assistance service?
2. How would they modify their usage if a charging plan were implemented?
3. What particular charging plan should be recommended and how should it be implemented operationally?
4. What would be the economic impact on the company and the customers?
5. How would customers feel about charging and do they have a preference among charging plans?

STUDY TECHNIQUES

To answer these questions, statistics were compiled on how customers currently use directory assistance; an econometric model was developed to estimate the volume reduction that could be anticipated as a result of charging; a series of computer models to estimate the economic impact of charging was developed; and studies of customer attitudes toward directory assistance were analyzed.

USAGE STATISTICS

Estimates were made of the proportion of directory assistance requests originated from each major class of telephone line, i.e., residential, business, and coin, and the proportion of times requests seeking each of these types of numbers were made. Requests reaching the operator were classified in terms of source in which the number could be found: the calling customer's telephone book, some other telephone book that was not regularly distributed to that customer, the operator's reprint, or whether it was a request for a nonpublished or nonexistent number. These estimates are shown in Exhibit 1. The distribution of frequency of use of the service by business and residence customers was also estimated. These distributions are shown in Exhibit 2. All of these estimates were based on statistical samples taken at a number of directory assistance bureaus and central offices throughout the United States. They are estimates of national averages. The original data showed that there was wide variability in usage among geographic locations, so these results cannot be assumed to be typical of any specific location.

The major conclusion drawn from the statistics were that a relatively high percentage (60 percent) of the numbers that were requested from the directory assistance operator could have been found by the customer in his own telephone book, and that usage by both residential and business customers was very skewed, with about 30 percent of customers making no use of the service in any given month and 10 percent of the customers making over half of the requests.

ECONOMETRIC MODEL

An econometric model was developed to estimate the impact that charging might have on the volume of customer demand for the service. This was a difficult task, since almost no historical price/volume data were available for directory assistance service. The model assumed that directory assistance demand would be a function of the number of telephones in service, the basic telephone service rate, customer habits, disposable income, the consumer price index, and the price to be charged for directory assistance. It was a hybrid model in that some coefficients were based upon historical demand for directory assistance service in the Bell System and some were based upon historical data from a small Canadian telephone company that had instituted a charge plan in a rural area of Quebec in 1972.

Straightforward application of the model to directory assistance service in the United States indicated that volume would drop about 30 percent upon initiation of a charge and then would continue to grow at about the historical rate of 7 percent if the charge per call remained at a fixed level. This estimate was dissatisfying because it was a somewhat smaller reduction than team members who were familiar with customers' use of telephone service had intuitively expected, and was considerably smaller than reductions that have resulted when water companies moved from flat rate to measured billing for water. Intuitive estimates of volume reduction were in the 40 to 50 percent range. Water companies have experienced 50 to 60 percent volume reductions. Because of these discrepancies it was decided that no single estimate of volume reduction could be used, but that volume reduction would have to be treated parametrically. Throughout the remainder of the analysis a range of volume reduction from 20 to 70 percent was used.

IMPACT ANALYSIS

In order to determine which charge plan would best meet the objectives and which combination of billing equipment and operating methods would minimize costs, a series of computer models, as shown in Exhibit 3, was developed. They consisted of the following main parts:

1. *Revenue Model.* Usage statistics from Exhibits 1 and 2, as well as descriptions of various charge plans, were input to this model, which calculated expected revenues from various charging plans. The model was based on numerous reasonable assumptions about how individual customers would modify their usage in response to each charging plan. In the aggregate, these assumptions produced changes in the usage distribution quite similar to those encountered upon implementation of charging.
2. *Work Time Model.* A distribution of operator work time, by type of request (found in reprint, found in FCNL, nonpublished, or not found), was estimated from time-study data (Exhibit 4). It was anticipated that a large portion of the calls the operator would have found on the FCNL, i.e., short work time calls, would disappear since these were generally requests for numbers which could be found quite easily by the customer from other sources. The result would be an increase in mean work time (Exhibit 5). This model estimates the increase in operator work time that can be expected

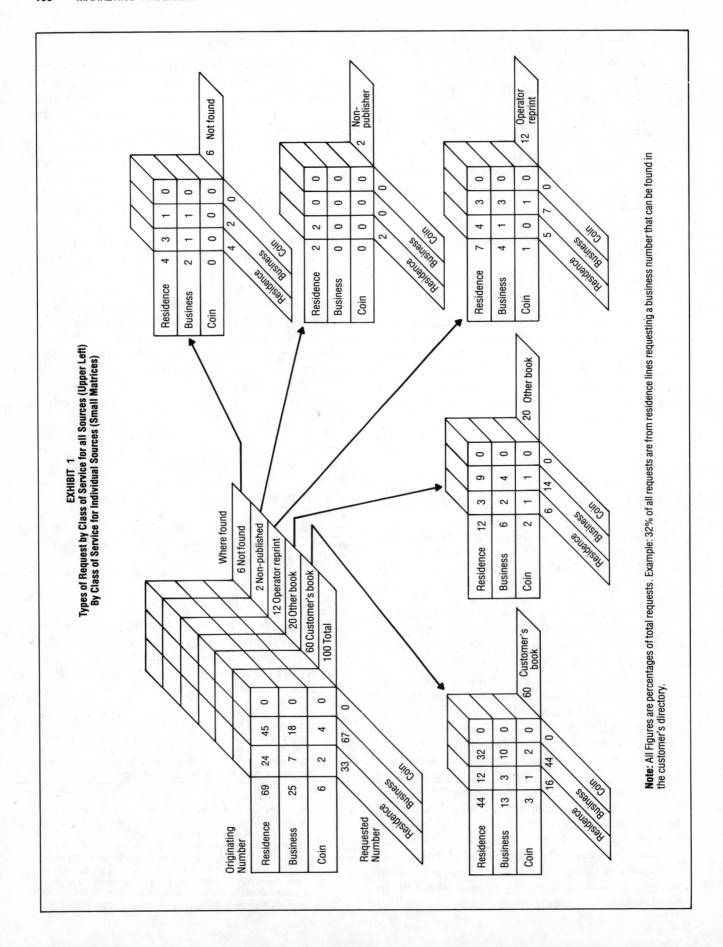

EXHIBIT 1
Types of Request by Class of Service for all Sources (Upper Left)
By Class of Service for Individual Sources (Small Matrices)

Note: All Figures are percentages of total requests. Example: 32% of all requests are from residence lines requesting a business number that can be found in the customer's directory.

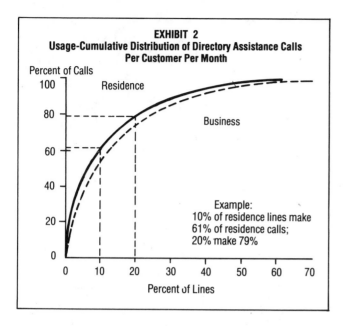

EXHIBIT 2
Usage-Cumulative Distribution of Directory Assistance Calls Per Customer Per Month

Percent of Calls

Residence

Business

Example:
10% of residence lines make
61% of residence calls;
20% make 79%

Percent of Lines

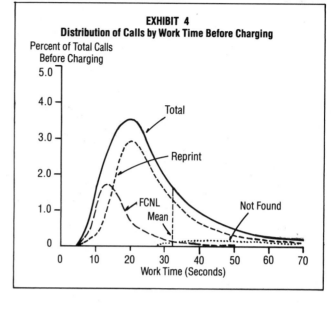

EXHIBIT 4
Distribution of Calls by Work Time Before Charging

Percent of Total Calls Before Charging

Total

Reprint

FCNL
Mean

Not Found

Work Time (Seconds)

when the mix of calls changes over a reasonable range of assumptions, shown by the upper and lower bounds in Exhibit 6. The best estimate curve was used for the remainder of the analysis.

3. *Cost Model*. Estimates of change in operator work time from the work time model and the details of various charging plans were input to a cost model that determined an optimal, i.e., minimum cost, implementation method for that plan and computed capital, operator, and expense impact. This model was concerned primarily with balancing operator work time, equipment cost, and billing operations that would be required to record and bill directory assistance calls.

4. *Economic Impact Model*. The results obtained from the revenue model and the cost model were fed into an economic model which deterministically simulated the corporated accounting system and calculated present worth of net costs over a seven-year time horizon.

CHARGING PLANS

Directory assistance charging plans can be characterized by five parameters: selectivity, the amount of rate reduction, breakpoint, the charge for each call up to and including the breakpoint, and the charge for all calls above the breakpoint. These parameters may be defined as follows:

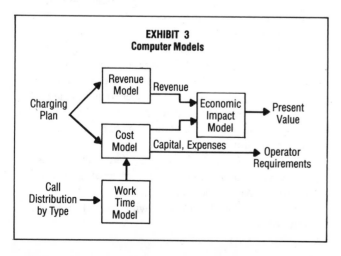

EXHIBIT 3
Computer Models

Charging Plan

Revenue Model → Revenue

Cost Model → Capital, Expenses

Call Distribution by Type → Work Time Model

Economic Impact Model → Present Value

Operator Requirements

The charge plans that were studied ranged from fully selective (charging only for requests for numbers available in the customer's local directory) to nonselective (charging for all requests regardless of whether the listing requested exists in the customer's local directory or is available from any other source).

Since a significant portion of telephone service rates consists of the cost of directory assistance service, it was thought that it might be necessary to reduce basic telephone service rates in order to receive approval for directory assistance charging. Some charge plans that were studied had a stated, per customer per month rate reduction. The rate reductions associated with the plans studied ranged from zero to fifty cents—about the cost of directory assistance service in 1974.

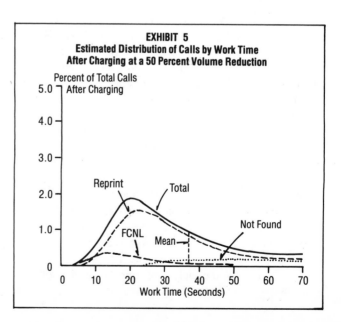

EXHIBIT 5
Estimated Distribution of Calls by Work Time After Charging at a 50 Percent Volume Reduction

Percent of Total Calls After Charging

Reprint

Total

FCNL
Mean

Not Found

Work Time (Seconds)

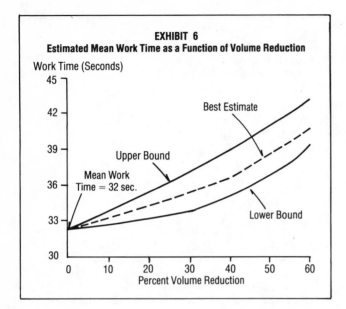

EXHIBIT 6
Estimated Mean Work Time as a Function of Volume Reduction

Work Time (Seconds)

- Best Estimate
- Upper Bound
- Mean Work Time = 32 sec.
- Lower Bound

Percent Volume Reduction

EXHIBIT 7
Definition of Charge Plans

Plan	Selectivity	Amount of Rate Reduction	Breakpoint (Allowance)	Charge up to Breakpoint	Charge above Breakpoint
1	Non	50¢	5	10¢	15¢
2	Non	30¢	3	10¢	15¢
3	Non	30¢	3	0	10¢
4	Non	0	3	0	20¢
5	Non	0	3	0	15¢
6	Non	0	5	0	20¢
7	Fully	0	0	0	25¢

The breakpoint is the point at which the per call charge for requests changes from a reduced rate (perhaps zero) to some other rate. Plans studied had breakpoints ranging from zero to five calls per line per month; thus an ''allowance of free calls'' describes the situation when the charge per call below the breakpoint is zero. This may be required because it is recognized that customers sometimes have need for numbers for which they have no alternative source. On the average, customers make about 2.4 calls per month to directory assistance for numbers for which they have no alternative telephone company-provided source.

The charge per call for calls up to the breakpoint in the various study plans ranged from zero to twenty-five cents. The charge per call for calls above the breakpoint ranged from ten to twenty-five cents, a range which included the current average cost of handling a call.

Of the many charge plans studied, seven were found to best illustrate the effects of changing each charge plan parameter (see Exhibit 7). Plan 1 is nonselective, has a fifty cent per customer per month rate reduction, a ten cent call charge up to five calls, and a fifteen cent charge for each call over five. Plan 2 is also nonselective, but the rate reduction is changed to thirty cents and the breakpoint is three calls. Plan 3 is nonselective, has a thirty cent per customer rate reduction, allows three calls with no charge, and charges ten cents per call above three. Plan 4 has no rate reduction, an allowance of three free calls, and a twenty cent charge for each call above three. Plans 5 and 6 are the same as Plan 4 except that Plan 5 has a lower charge per call (fifteen cents) above the breakpoint, while Plan 6 has a higher breakpoint (5). Plan 7 is fully selective, has a twenty-five cent charge for each chargeable call, and has no rate reduction.

Throughout the analysis of charge plans that follows, it was assumed that charging was instituted in all Bell Sys-

tem Companies simultaneously in 1974. In reality charging would probably be introduced in one state at a time with the implementation spread over several years. However, comparisons among plans would not be affected by the rate of implementation.

OPERATOR REQUIREMENTS

One of the objectives of charging was to reduce the required number of directory assistance operators. As shown in Exhibit 8, nonselective plans are more effective in reducing the number of required operators than fully selective plans. The reason for the difference at a given level of call reduction is that fully selective plans require additional operator time to record the requested number so that in the billing process the calling customer's number can be compared with the requested number to determine if a charge should be applied. This additional information is not required for nonselective plans. At a 50 percent reduction in the number of calls, the reduction in the required number of operators immediately after implementation under nonselective plans is approximately 17,100 compared with 13,000 under fully selective plans.

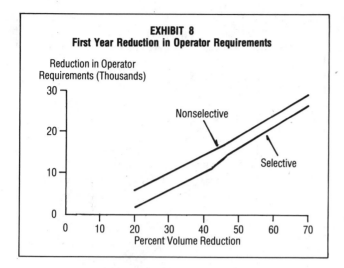

EXHIBIT 8
First Year Reduction in Operator Requirements

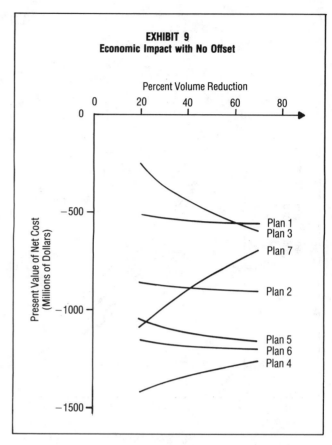

EXHIBIT 9
Economic Impact with No Offset

ECONOMIC IMPACT

Since it was uncertain what response PUCs would make to requests for approval of directory assistance charging, the present value of the impact of charging on net costs was estimated using three different assumptions. First, it was assumed that any revenues collected as a result of charging for directory assistance would be collected in addition to total revenues that would have been collected without charging, resulting in a net increase in revenues and a net reduction in costs. Second, it was assumed that no increase in net company-wide revenues would be allowed in the year charging was implemented. This would be equivalent to reducing rates on other telephone services to levels that were lower than they would otherwise be. Finally, the economic impact was examined assuming that rates for other services were lowered below the levels at which they would otherwise be by an amount equal to the revenues that would be collected by charging for directory assistance plus the operator expense savings that would accrue in the first year after charging began. In the analysis that follows, negative values for economic impact are more favorable than positive values since the plans are being compared on the basis of their impact on net costs.

In Exhibit 9 the impact on net costs, with an assumption of no offset, shows that among the nonselective plans, Plan 4 contributes most favorably to reductions in net costs. Plans 1 and 3 have the smallest impact on net cost, and the other nonselective plans fall in between. Plans 4, 5 and 6, which have an allowance of free calls but no rate reduction, perform more favorably than the nonselective approaches offering a rate reduction. The relationship of the selective plan (Plan 7) to the other plans is highly dependent upon the volume reduction that is actually achieved.

Exhibit 10 compares the plans assuming a revenue offset. Plan 7 is clearly less favorable than the others under these conditions. The nonselective plans are grouped fairly closely. Particularly, Plans 4, 5 and 6 differ only slightly.

Thus, varying the allowance level or the charge per call does not significantly alter the economic impact when a revenue offset is included. Plans 1, 2 and 3, which are based on a rate reduction, perform somewhat better than those modeled after Plan 4. The relationship among the plans remains the same at all levels of volume reduction with only the magnitude of the differences changing at different levels of volume.

Exhibit 11 shows that with an assumption of both a revenue and an operator savings offset the relationship among the plans is almost the same as when only a revenue offset was assumed with Plans 1, 2 and 3 exhibiting less sensitivity to volume reductions than Plans 4, 5 and 6. The obvious difference is that the economic impact of all the plans is generally less favorable than under the previous assumption, with Plan 7 breaking even only at relatively high levels of volume reduction.

The three assumptions made in this analysis may not actually be observed in practice. They were hypothesized as practical and reasonable assumptions for a comparison of the various plans over a wide range of very uncertain economic conditions. If and when requests are made by local telephone companies to their PUCs for approval of directory assistance charging, they will usually propose such a charge as part of a general rate case in order to reduce the need for increases in rates for other telephone services that would otherwise be required.

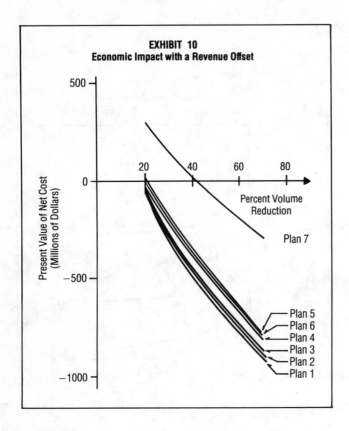

EXHIBIT 10
Economic Impact with a Revenue Offset

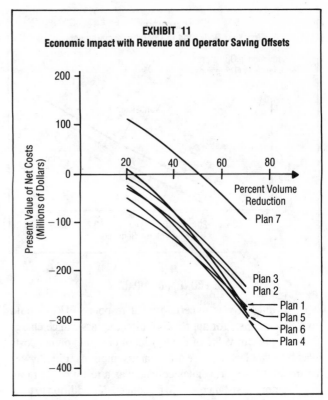

EXHIBIT 11
Economic Impact with Revenue and Operator Saving Offsets

USAGE SENSITIVITY

The introduction of more equitable usage-sensitive pricing was the third objective of charging. The purpose of usage-sensitive pricing is to make individual customer's costs more proportional to their individual usage. Nonselective plans with no free calling allowance are best in this regard with 100 percent of the calls being potentially chargeable. Nonselective plans with three to five free calls per month subject 82 to 89 percent of all present requests to a potential charge. Fully selective plans are the poorest with respect to usage sensitivity. They subject only 60 percent of the present volume of requests to a potential charge.

CUSTOMER ATTITUDE

One of the important variables in the analysis of charging plans is public acceptance of the plan and how it might differ among plans. Some information about customer attitude was available from focus interviews and public opinion surveys. Most studies of customer reaction had two common findings: Customers prefer not being charged for directory assistance. However, they can accept the concept when the rationale is explained, particularly when they realize that all customers pay for the high directory assistance usage of a few customers.

In one series of customer attitude studies, each group of customers was presented with only one charge plan. The results for the series of tests, in which a fully selective plan was compared with a nonselective plan, show no statistically significant difference in customer acceptance of these plans. Other studies measured public reaction in circumstances when, first, people are asked to discuss their reactions to charging, and second, they are asked to compare different charging plans. Under these circumstances, customers prefer selective plans to nonselective plans and clearly prefer nonselective plans with a free calling allowance to those without a free calling allowance.

CONCLUSIONS

Based upon an expanded version of the foregoing analysis, the following conclusions were presented to the Bell System's top management in the middle of 1974.

First, charging for directory assistance service could have definite benefits. Certain charge plans can serve to reduce pressures for other rate increases. At the same time charging can relieve the pressure on a labor-intensive service and introduce a more equitable and efficient pricing structure. Second, nonselectivity is the most important feature of desirable charge plans. The nonselective approach best meets the objectives for charging by having the most favorable economic impact, by reducing operator requirements more than selective plans and by making most calls potentially chargeable. Third, the economic benefits of charging increase with time for all plans. Therefore, prompt requests to local PUCs are important to begin the process of reducing costs and reducing pressure on other telephone rates. Fourth, other than selectivity, the parameters of the various charge plans make relatively little difference in economic impact at a given level of volume reduction. And, fifth, available studies of customer attitudes do not support any one charge plan as clearly best for gaining customer acceptance.

Based upon these conclusions, a decision was made by AT&T management to recommend that the Bell System's Operating Telephone Companies request approval of a non-selective charging plan for local directory assistance service, with three free calls per month and a charge of twenty cents per call beyond that point. Handicapped customers, who cannot use the directory, and customers calling from coin telephones, hotels, motels, hospitals and nursing homes would be exempt from all charges. There would be no charge for interstate directory assistance requests.

As of March 30, 1976, charging had been authorized in fourteen states and regulatory decisions were pending in eight others. In the locations where charging was in effect, customer use of the service had been reduced by approximately 60 percent, somewhat greater than the study team's subjective estimate (about 40 to 50 percent) and considerably greater than estimates developed with the econometric model (about 30 percent). Operator work time had increased from thirty-two seconds to about forty seconds, exactly the increase that was predicted by the holding time model. Only 5 percent of all customers were seeing charges on their bill in any given month. The other 95 percent did not exceed the free calling allowance. Public hearings at which the public is invited to express its opinions over this proposal have, in some cases, become quite raucous, and in some states, the charging proposal has become a cause for legislative debate. However, in locations where a charge has been implemented, there has been minimal adverse customer reaction.

It is not intended that operators be laid off as a result of reductions in operator requirements. It was intended that excess employees who were on the payroll at the time charging was implemented would be transferred to other jobs. In most areas where charging has been implemented, local management has been successful in avoiding the layoff of permanent employees.

The analysis reported in this paper and similar ones developed at the local level have been quite effective in convincing local regulatory bodies that charging for directory assistance service is equitable, efficient, and in the public interest.

23

ARTS PLAN: A Model Based System for Use in Planning a Performing Arts Series

Charles B. Weinberg
Kenneth M. Shachmut

This article is concerned with the application of marketing and management science to problems involved in managing a series of performing arts presentations. Although some of the decisions are largely "artistic," many others can be aided by model-based analytic procedures. The ARTS PLAN model uses historical data to predict attendance at future performances. This prediction can be overriden by the manager if he or she disagrees with the forecast. The forecast is then embedded in an interactive model that can be used for planning the mix of performances in a season or for deciding which events to promote in a season already planned.

This article is concerned with the application of marketing and management science to some of the problems in managing a series of performing arts presentations. Among the problems faced by managers of such series are the following: (a) selection of performers to book, (b) scheduling of performances over the year, and (c) choice of booked performances to promote.

These decisions are often made on an intuitive basis, with relatively little systematic analysis. Although some of these decisions are largely "artistic" and not subject to formal analytic procedures, many other decisions made by the management can be aided by model-based procedures. This article describes some of the procedures used by the management of one performing arts series. Although this one application is described in some detail, the program and the problems encountered by the arts manager are analogous to those of other managers who are responsible for presenting a series of events or activities over a period of time.

Charles B. Weinberg is Associate Professor of Marketing, Stanford University.

Kenneth M. Shachmut is with McKinsey and Company, London.

The authors gratefully acknowledge the assistance and cooperation of Thomas Bacchetti and Lynn Bonde, who in succession served as Director of the Office of Public Events at Stanford University while the work described in this article was completed.

This paper is divided into the following sections: (1) Problem Description, (2) Forecasting Model, (3) Planning Model, (4) Usage Example, (5) Implementation Experience, and (6) Conclusions.

PROBLEM DESCRIPTION

The "Lively Arts at Stanford" (LAS) annually presents approximately 30 performances of classical music, theater, and dance. The manager has exclusive responsibility for artist selection and scheduling. The manager has a number of major goals for LAS: (1) to establish LAS as a major source of first-rate performing arts events throughout the academic year across a broad variety of classical fields; (2) to run the series on a close to break-even basis, incurring only a minimal deficit as approved by the university; and (3) to make performances widely accessible by keeping prices low. As is typical in public sector management problems, the goals conflict to a certain extent. For example, by maintaining a varied program, the manager includes in each season a number of performance types that do not seem to draw large audiences. Classical guitar draws very well, but dance, in general, fares poorly. A conflict exists to some extent between the second (low deficit) and third (low price) goal; however, price elasticity may ameliorate this conflict under certain conditions. A similar conflict arises because the manager has only a limited budget for promotion and for staff, so that these resources are scarce. The manager has to choose to which performances to allocate promotional dollars and staff time beyond the minimum amount required as part of the operational plan. Attendance does appear to be sensitive to marketing changes. The manager has increased the marketing effort in the past three years. Subsequently, attendance as a percentage of capacity has increased to 68 percent in the past three years from 54 percent in the previous three years.

The analytic work described in this paper is designed to help the manager in two main areas: (1) for a season that is already scheduled, to identify those performances to which above-normal promotional efforts should be allocated; and (2) for a season being scheduled, to assess the impact on attendance of including different performances.

Seasons are scheduled approximately a year in advance. The choice of performances is constrained by the availability of touring groups and auditoriums on campus. Although the manager can quickly choose a core group that the program "must have" because of its overwhelming merit or some other quality, there remains considerable choice in completing the schedule. The analytic work in scheduling a season is concerned primarily with the "discretionary" choices.

FORECASTING MODEL

A number of factors beyond the distinctive appeal of an individual performer can influence the attendance at any given performance. The first step was to determine these factors and to measure their importance via the use of regression analysis. The resulting model forms a preliminary base case forecast for the planning model. The manager can override the forecast, if necessary, because of factors not captured in the model.

Data were available on attendance by performance for 93 performances over the past three years. Preliminary analyses of these data revealed that there were seasonal effects in attendance. An average performance drew 85 percent of capacity in the fall, whereas attendance declined to 60 percent of capacity in the winter, and to 50 percent in the spring. Similarly, there were effects by type of performance. Chamber music performances drew 80 percent of capacity, dance 60 percent, guitar 105 percent, and jazz 75 percent. Performers classified as Young Concert Artists (YCA) drew 50 percent of capacity. These five performance types accounted for 81 of the 93 performances. The remaining 12 averaged 60 percent of capacity. It was also believed, although not specifically tabulated, that performances on Friday nights drew better than performances during the week. There were few Saturday night or Sunday performances to examine other weekend nights.

Approximately 15 percent of the performers who were booked appeared for more than one performance. There were a number of reasons for multi-performance bookings. Some groups had a varied repertoire and fairly broad appeal. Dance groups were generally booked for multiple performances because of the fixed costs involved in bringing such a group to campus. The number of performances for some groups was determined by their availability or the availability of auditoriums on campus. Because of the various reasons for having multiple performances, the effect on attendance was problematical. Multiple performances could spread out a limited audience over several days, provide opportunities for word-of-mouth to build second or third day audiences, and allow devotees to attend several times.

Examination of the data revealed that there was only one group that appeared more than five times over the three years. A specific variable was set up to represent this group. Although no dance group appeared more than five times, there appeared to be a subset of dance groups that were particularly well known. A specific variable was also established for dance groups belonging to this subset.

The performances were held (with three exceptions in 93 performances) in three different halls on campus with 3 different capacities: 350 seats, 700 seats, and 1,700 seats. Thus, the capacity of the hall would be a factor in the actual attendance obtained, especially since about a third of the performances had attendance over 95 percent of capacity.[1] However, the hall chosen was dictated by the musical and

---

[1] About half of the "sold-out" performances occurred in halls with more than 700 seats; the others were in the 700 seat hall. Capacity in the 700 seat hall could be increased by as much as 15 percent by the use of on-stage seats, for performances by chamber music groups and soloists.

technical requirements of the performance type and not by an estimate of attendance. Thus, for example, chamber music concerts usually are held in a 700 seat hall, and dance groups always perform in a 1,700 seat hall. Because of the collinearity between capacity of hall and type of performance, it was not possible to separate the effect of capacity from performance type. Thus the performance type "dance" actually refers to dance held in a 1,700 seat auditorium, and if a dance performance were to be held in a 2,000 seat auditorium, some extrapolation would be required.[2]

Data on several other potentially important factors (such as competing events being held on the same night and different weather conditions) were not readily available in LAS records. For example, attendance might suffer if a basketball game were being played that night. Also, the effect of any special promotion was not included. However, to account for any temporal shift, variables to represent year were included. Both a linear and multiplicative model were tested; however, since both achieved similar results, only the linear model is reported.

The model tested was the following:

$$Y = a_o + a_{S1}S_1 + a_{S2}S_2 + a_{T1}T_1 + a_{T2}T_2 + a_{T3}T_3 + a_{T4}T_4$$
$$+ a_{T5}T_5 + a_{F1}F + a_{M1}M + a_{G1}G_1 + a_{G2}G_2 + a_{Y1}Y_1$$
$$+ a_{Y2}Y_2,$$

Where

Y = attendance,

S_1 = 1, if held in winter, 0 otherwise,

S_2 = 1, if held in spring, 0 otherwise,

T_1 = 1, if chamber music, 0 otherwise,

T_2 = 1, if dance, 0 otherwise,

T_3 = 1, if guitar, 0 otherwise,

T_4 = 1, if jazz, 0 otherwise,

T_5 = 1, if young concert artists, 0 otherwise,

F = 1, if held on Friday, 0 otherwise,

M = 1, if part of a series of multiple performances, 0 otherwise

G_1 = 1, if by group performing more than five times, 0 otherwise,

G_2 = 1, if by well known dance group, 0 otherwise,

Y_1 = 1, if held during year 1, 0 otherwise,

Y_2 = 1, if held during year 2, 0 otherwise.

The independent variables are all 0, 1 dummy variables in order to represent different effects and, as is usual, are defined to omit one class in order to preserve the nonsingularity of the independent variables.

When a forward step-wise regression was run, all variables except Y_1 for year 1 entered with a t value greater than 1. The four variables, M for multiple performances, F for Friday, S_I, for winter, and T for chamber music were the last four to enter and were not significant at the 0.05 level. When these variables were deleted, all the remaining variables were significant. The regression results are shown in Exhibit 1.[3] The adjusted R^2 in the original and reduced model were 0.81 and 0.79, respectively. The Durbin Watson statistic of 2 indicates no serial correlation. When a split-half double cross over validation was run, the R^2 turned out to be 0.70. These results are considered to be very good and are superior to what had been expected. All the significant effects were in the expected direction.

EXHIBIT 1
Regression Results for Predicting Attendance

Variable	Coefficient	Beta Weight	Standard Error (B)	F^*
S_2(Spring)	−127.2	−0.12	54.4	5.5
T_2(Dance)	230.7	0.22	65.7	12.3
T_3(Guitar)	480.9	0.26	92.6	27.0
T_4(Jazz)	732.2	0.46	82.0	79.6
T_5(YCA)	−399.7	−0.30	69.5	33.0
G_1	177.9	0.10	87.4	4.1
G_2	804.3	0.50	93.4	74.1
Y_2(Year 2)	−112.8	−0.12	46.2	6.0
Constant	647.0			

F = 43.7.
Adjusted R^2 = 0.79.
n = 90.

---

* $F_{0.05(1, 90)} = 4.0$, $F_{0.01(1, 90)} = 6.9$. As discussed in the text, all coefficients are significant at the 0.05 level or above.

Some of the results of the regression were surprising and deserve additional comment. As a result of the regression analysis, it is now believed that the historical drop off in winter attendance is primarily due to performance selection rather than to a seasonal effect; however, the spring decline is considered to be real and due to such factors as the relative attractiveness of the weather and the need to complete academic year projects. Upon discussion of the winter effect results with the manager, he suggested that because he tended

---

[2] One alternative is to divide attendance by capacity and to try to forecast percentage of capacity sold. This, of course, does not resolve the problem of interdependence of performance type and capacity. When attendance as a percentage of capacity is used as a dependent variable, the regression results are similar to those reported below. (In the planning model, forecasts are reported as a percentage of capacity in keeping with the manager's usual approach to the problem.) Note that when percentage of capacity is used as the dependent variable, an error of 10 percent on the 700 seat hall is treated the same as a 10 percent error on the 1,700 seat hall in the regression model.

[3] Three performances that drew less than 25 percent of capacity were not included in the sample for the regression. These three performances all occurred during the winter. If they were included, the effect was to decrease the value of the coefficient of S_1 (winter) so that it became statistically significant. This effect is believed to be due to the particular characteristics of these performances, rather than to a seasonal effect for winter. The effect on R^2 is less than 0.02.

to schedule the fall season first, he may have placed the more well-known groups in the fall. Examination of the data confirms this observation. Because the manager has some flexibility in influencing when groups tour in the area, one result of this analysis has been for the manager to try to persuade some groups that usually tour in the fall, to appear later in the year. Thus, the manager hopes to counter-balance the spring drop-off with unusually appealing groups and to decrease the concentration of these groups in the fall term.

There was a clear effect for performance type, four of the five dummy variables for performance type were significant and, in addition, were significantly different from each other. Although the dummy variable for chamber music did not achieve significance, this only implies that its attendance is not significantly different from that for the 13 nonclassified performances. Its attendance is significantly different from the other four performance types. Further, the variable G_1, which represents a particularly well-known chamber music group, was statistically significant.

Year 3 was the base case for the annual effects. No particular explanation for the comparative drop-off in year 2 attendance, but not in year 1, has been developed. In the absence of an apparent trend, it was decided to assume $Y_2 = 0$ in the forecasting model.

The model explained a substantial portion of the variation in attendance. Although the results contained some surprises, the outcome was largely in accordance with the manager's prior beliefs. The surprising results for seasonality have been explained and appear to be resulting in some potential changes in the booking of performers. The regression model serves as the basis for the planning model discussed in the following sections.

PLANNING MODEL

The planning model is designed to help the manager determine whether a tentative or planned schedule will meet his attendance objectives for the year and what the impact of promoting certain events would be on the attendance predictions.

A target of 70 percent of capacity attendance was used as a measure of the program's success. Because the total capacity varied from season to season, depending on the number of performances booked and the size of facilities used, the manager had found this percentage acceptable over time.

Instead of using attendance data as measures, financial criteria could be used. The talent fee is known, the manager can make a very close estimate of the operating costs of staging a performance, and attendance data can be translated into gross revenues. However, financial criteria were not used for this planning model for several reasons. First, in a deficit operation, it is not pleasant or helpful to plan a season where the objective is expressed as "minimize the deficit." It does not capture the optimism and spirit of the

management, nor does it focus efforts to achieve the objective. Second, the more expensive performance types generally are held in the larger auditorium—so that as percentage capacity increases, the deficit declines. Third, for a season already established, the decision is not how much money to spend on personal selling and advertising, but, rather, how to allocate a budgeted amount of time and money. Management felt that, at most, three events could be heavily promoted. The question was: Which three? And finally, the notion of percentage capacity better reflected management's approach to the problem.[4] It is the authors' judgment, in light of the newness of both marketing and analytic approaches to arts management problems, that the most appropriate model structure is one that reflects the manager's viewpoint. The inclusion of financial information is technically straightforward.

The model has three main stages. The first stage establishes a base case forecast for the season being planned, using the forecasting model discussed in the previous section. The second stage allows the manager to override the regression forecast because of unique factors of which the manager is aware. For example, although jazz groups booked in the spring generally draw 74 percent of capacity, one group may be expected to do particularly well on a campus because of its reputation or a previous successful appearance. The manger may wish to test alternative estimates for groups falling in the "other" category. When this stage is completed, a forecast of attendance by performance, by quarter (or semester) and for the season is available.

In the third stage, the manager can then test the impact of alternative strategies. The strategic options are to make scheduling changes (add, omit, or substitute a performance) and to promote particular performances. For example, if the manager wants to schedule a dance company instead of a guitarist as the second performance of the season, he can assess the impact of this scheduling change.

A routine for suggesting performances to promote has also been developed. As discussed above, the manager's choice is primarily whether to promote a given performance, rather than the level of promotional effort. Not all performances are equally responsive to promotion. For example, the young concert artist series presents relatively unknown classical soloists who appeal primarily to dedicated music lovers. This segment is believed to seek information about performances without the benefit of extensive promotion. On the other hand, some groups can be extensively promoted to a large potential audience. For each performance, using the regression forecast (possibly adjusted) as a base, the manager estimates the percentage attendance with promotion. After the estimate is given for all performances, an optimizing routine then calculates the impact of promotion on attendance and produces an ordered list of performances in which the sequencing variable is increase in attendance due

---

[4] In other work (not reported here), a computer program that allows the manager to explore the relationship between percentage capacity, pricing, revenues, and talent costs has been developed.

to promotion of a performance. The manager then chooses the performances to promote. The model substitutes the forecast of percentage attendance with promotion for the previously utilized attendance forecast and then develops a projection of attendance for the season.

More elaborate systems for making promotion decisions were considered. For example, using the manager's estimates of promotion responsiveness, the model could assign promotional effort to those events whose attendance would be increased above a prespecified level or to the three performances with the largest indicated attendance increase. If the manager would specify multiple levels of promotional effort and consequent attendance response, allocation schemes across events would also be developed. However, the manager viewed his decision as whether to promote or not, and for this decision the ordered list was very helpful. Most importantly, the manager retained the decision as to what performances to promote.

SAMPLE APPLICATION OF USAGE

Exhibit 2 is an illustration of the usage of the ARTS PLAN system. The number of options considered is relatively small because of space limitations, but, in an actual application, can be considerably increased. Exhibit 2 is largely self-explanatory, and only limited supplementary comments will be made here. Input can be done either from files or directly at the terminal.

After identifying the time period to be examined and setting the number of performances, the program prints out the historical record. The program then requests the user to identify each performance by name and type, give the capacity of the hall it is held in, and indicate any special effects that may exist. If the performance is not one of the five types, the user has the immediate option to override the attendance forecast. This is because the "other" category includes a wide mix of performance types. When all the required information has been submitted, the program then provides a forecast of attendance by performance and for the quarter.

An option is then provided to override the base case projections because of additional information that the manager has available. For example, the jazz group Sari may be particularly well known and consequently may be expected to do better than the average jazz group, even without special promotion. The adjustment may either be upwards or downwards. The manager can also examine the impact of adding, deleting, or replacing a performance with another. When all the adjustments are completed, a planning base forecast for the quarter is established. If desired, the forecast can be saved in a file.

The manager has the opportunity in the next phase of the program to investigate the impact of allocating promotional effort to one or more performances. First, the manager is asked what would be the impact of promotion on the percentage of capacity sold for each performance. The per-

formances are then ranked in order of increase in attendance. This ranking reflects the promotion responsiveness of a performance, capacity of the hall, and attendance without promotion.

The user then selects the performances to be promoted in light of the above results and any other information available. An attendance projection by performance and by quarter, including the effect of promotion and a variety of summary statistics, are then output. The user has the option to revise estimates or make programming changes before terminating the program.

IMPLEMENTATION EXPERIENCE

The ARTS PLAN system has been used as an aid in the management of an on-going season and in the planning of a future season. Before the start of the 1976–77 season, attendance forecasts were made for the 26 performance schedule. Adjustments were made to the regression analysis forecast to account for the several chamber music concerts that were to be given in a 1,300 seat capacity hall and to reflect other factors that the manager thought were important. Selected performances in the winter and spring were scheduled for intensive promotion. At the end of the 1976–77 season, the actual and predicted attendances were compared. An R^2 of 0.80 between actual and predicted was obtained.[5] Further, the total attendance prediction of 20,875 was virtually identical to the actual attendance of 20,882.

Stimulated by the availability of a quantitative attendance forecast, the manager developed an information system, a "spread sheet," composed of the following kinds of information for each performance:

1. Forecast of attendance.
2. Mail order sales prior to commencement of over-the-counter sales.
3. Series ticket sales.
4. Sales prior to commencement of either normal or intensive promotion.
5. Sales prior to performance.
6. Sales at the door.
7. Actual attendance.
8. Reasons for deviation of actual attendance from forecast.

The last item was included to help discover if there were any systematic reasons for the variance of actual from estimated attendance and to help the manager learn about other factors that might affect attendance.

At the end of the fall quarter, the results were reviewed. Reassuringly to the manager (and the model builders), the forecast had been accurate. The only large deviation from the forecast was the unexpected sellout of a performance that had received rave notices when it played the week

---

[5] It should be noted that this is not an entirely "pure" validation because, as explained in the paragraphs directly following, ARTS PLAN was used as a control system in which some marketing changes were made when sales to date differed sharply from forecast. However, at the end of the fall quarter, before any such changes were made, an R^2 of 0.84 was obtained between actual and forecast.

EXHIBIT 2
Excerpts from a Sample Run

```
ARTS PLANNING MODEL
DO YOU WISH TO INVESTIGATE AN ENTIRE SEASON, OR A
SINGLE QUARTER?  (S = SEASON;  Q = QUARTER)?Q
WHICH QUARTER DO YOU WITH TO INVESTIGATE
    (FALL = 1, WINTER = 2, SPRING = 3)      ?3
WILL DATA COME FROM KEYBOARD (K) OR FILE (F)?K
NO. OF PERFORMANCES PLANNED FOR QUARTER (MAX = 17)?  4
THE FOLLOWING TABLE PRESENTS THE BASE-CASE ATTENDANCE
PERCENTAGES WHICH WILL BE USED IN GENERATING THE
FIRST-ROUND ATTENDANDE PROJECTION

                      ESTIMATED ATTENDANCE PERCENTAGES (HISTORICAL)
*                 FALL          WINTER          SPRING
(1)   CHAMB MUS    87            87              70
(2)   DANCE        52            52              44
(3)   GUITAR       104           104             92
(4)   JAZZ         81            81              74
(5)   YCA          71            71              34
(6)   OTHER-(700)  90            90              72
(7)   OTHER-(1700) 38            38              31
*IN ADDITION THE FOLLOWING SUPPLEMENTARY EFFECTS HAVE BEEN OBSERVED
    (G)   GALA QUARTET          25
    (P)   POPULAR DANCE GROUP   47
AT THIS STEP YOU ARE ASKED TO PROVIDE SPECIFIC INFORMATION ON
THE PROGRAM YOU ARE PLANNING.

*********************************************************************
PERFORMANCE NUMBER 1
ENTER PERFORMANCE NAME (MAXIMUM 12 CHARACTERS)?BETH
ENTER PERFORMANCE TYPE (USE CODE NUMBER:)
        1=CHAMBER MUSIC  3=GUITAR  5=YOUNG CONCERT ARTISTS(YCA)
        2=DANCE          4=JAZZ    6=OTHER-(700)  7=OTHER- (1700)
?2

ENTER CAPACITY OF HALL?1700
    POPULAR DANCE GROUP  (Y=YES, N=NO)?Y

*********************************************************************

  * (Remainder of initial input deleted)

ATTENDANCE PREDICTIONS FOR SPRING QUARTER

PERFORMANCE    PERFORMANCE      PERCENTAGE       CAPACITY
NUMBER         NAME             ATTENDANCE       OF HALL       ATTENDANCE
  1            BETH         P    91              1700          1547
  2            SARI              74              1700          1258
  3            AMY               34              350           119
  4            MICHELLE          45              1300          585
-----------------------------------------------------------------------
TOTALS         *                 69              5050          3509

*********************************************************************
DO YOU WANT TO SAVE TABLE ON A FILE (Y OR N)? N
DO YOU WISH TO MAKE ANY CHANGES? (Y=YES, N=NO)?Y
ENTER NUMBER OF PERFORMANCE YOU WISH TO CHANGE?2
CURRENT STATUS OF PERFORMANCE NUMBER 2
    NAME       SARI
    TYPE       (4) JAZZ
  PCT ATTEND   74
  CAPACITY     1700
  ATTENDANCE   1258
INDICATE BY CODE NUMBER THE PARAMETER YOU WISH TO CHANGE
ENTER ONE ONLY  1=PERFORMANCE NAME  3=PERCENTAGE  ATTENDANCE EXPECTED
                2=PERFORMANCE TYPE  4=CAPACITY OF HALL
?3
OLD PERCENTAGE ATTENDANCE IS:        74
NEW PERCENTAGE ATTENDANCE EXPECTED? 85
ANY OTHER CHANGES TO THIS PERFORMANCE  (Y=YES, N=NO)?N
```

EXHIBIT 2 (Continued)

ATTENDANCE PREDICTIONS FOR SPRING QUARTER

PERFORMANCE NUMBER	PERFORMANCE NAME		PERCENTAGE ATTENDANCE	CAPACITY OF HALL	ATTENDANCE
1	BETH	P	91	1700	1547
2	SARI	RV	85	1700	1445
3	AMY		34	350	119
4	MICHELLE		45	1300	585
TOTALS	*		73	5050	3696

```
****************************************************************************
```

DO YOU WISH TO MAKE ANY MODIFICATIONS TO THE PLANNED
SEASON?   (Y = YES, N = NO)   ?Y

INPUT TYPE OF CHANGE DESIRED.   (ONE ONLY)

    1 - ADD A NEW PERFORMANCE
    2 - DELETE AN OLD PERFORMANCE
    3 - REPLACE AN EXISTING PERFORMANCE WITH ANOTHER
    4 - MAKE CHANGES TO AN EXISTING PERFORMANCE
?2

WHICH PERFORMANCE DO YOU WISH TO DELETE?
    (ENTER PERFORMANCE NUMBER)   ?2

DO YOU WISH TO EXAMINE PROMOTIONAL IMPACT (Y=YES, N=NO)?Y

AT THIS STAGE YOU ARE ASKED TO ESTIMATE THE IMPACT OF DEVOTING
CONSIDERABLE PROMOTIONAL EFFORT TO A PARTICULAR PERFORMANCE.

PERFORMANCE NAME		PROJECTED % ATTENDANCE	ESTIMATED % ATTENDANCE WITH PROMOTION
BETH	P	91	?95
AMY		34	?34
MICHELLE		45	?75

THE FOLLOWING TABLE LISTS PERFORMANCE BY ORDER OF INCREASE
IN ATTENDANCE DUE TO PROMOTION

PERFORMANCE NUMBER	PERFORMANCE NAME		PROJECTED ATTENDANCE	INCREASE FROM PROMO	ATTENDANCE WITH PROMOTION
3	MICHELLE		585	390	975
1	BETH	P	1547	68	1615
2	AMY		119	0	119

WHICH PERFORMANCE, IF ANY, DO YOU WANT TO PROMOTE. INDICATE BY
  PERFORMANCE NUMBER. IF NONE, ENTER ZERO. . . .?3
PERFORMANCE NUMBER OR ZERO IF NO MORE . . . . .?0
ATTENDANCE WITH PROMOTIONS CHOSEN IS NOW ESTIMATED

```
****************************************************************************
```

ATTENDANCE PREDICTIONS FOR SPRING QUARTER

PERFORMANCE NUMBER	PERFORMANCE NAME		PERCENTAGE ATTENDANCE	CAPACITY OF HALL	ATTENDANCE
1	BETH	P	91	1700	1547
2	AMY		34	350	119
3	MICHELLE	*	75	1300	975
TOTALS	*		79	3350	2641

```
****************************************************************************
```

before at a nearby university. The review, using the information described above, indicated that some winter and spring performances would achieve their attendance goals without normal promotion, but that the performances selected for intensive promotion truly needed that effort. The model was fundamental in focusing management attention on this issue. Towards the end of the winter season, sales to date and predicted attendance for the spring quarter were compared by the manager. At this time, it was found that one event, which was budgeted for normal promotion, had unexpectedly low sales. The manager was then able to take appropriate corrective action.

The system has also been used to help plan a forthcoming season's schedule. Three 2 to 3 hour computer terminal sessions were employed in this process. Prior to each session, the manager prepared a schedule and a set of changes to that schedule. The manager evaluated the alternatives and generated new ones in response to the forecasted results. It appears that the questions the manager was asking were: (1) does a schedule meet attendance goals with or without promotion; (2) is the effort required to manage a season within the resources of the organization (e.g., not too many different performers) and (3) does the schedule meet the artistic goals of the manager? The quantitative forecasts, however, have not replaced the manager's qualitative goals. For example, while evaluating one schedule, it appeared that booking a well-known but mediocre group would help the manager solve a seasonal attendance problem. The manager, however, said, ''What am I trying to do?''—and rejected that group. The system has become an aid to the manager's planning, but does not dominate it.

The model-based system has become an integral part of the management process. The manager has reversed an anticomputer bias and become an enthusiast of at least some computer systems. Future research plans focus on trying to develop means to adapt the forecasting model to trends (''fads'') in preferences for performance types and the manager's desire to add new performance types to the programs.

It is worthwhile to speculate on possible reasons why the ARTS PLAN system has been utilized by management. Before the start of this project, one of the authors had worked with LAS on several audience surveys and student projects over a five year period. Although not all the collaborations had been successful, a relationship of some trust had been built. Thus, the management was willing to discuss problems openly, to specify needs, and to indicate when analytical approaches were inappropriate. This relationship greatly facilitated the process of model building and model using.

There were four other factors that seem to have been important in the adoption process. The first stage of the project was to develop a system to predict attendance accurately without knowing the names of the individual performers. There was considerable skepticism that good results could be achieved. However, when the results were presented, the manager was able to understand the model as well as be satisfied with the results.

The second critical factor was to develop a system that the manager would feel he or she had control over. An important means of providing this control was to include a very visible method for overriding the regression forecast by the manager. Although the override feature was seldom used, its availability was important in dealing with the manager's questions about the relationship between the arts and the computer. (As can be seen, other aspects of the system are also designed to preserve the manager's control of the system.)

A third critical factor was the problem itself. The ARTS PLAN system was deliberately designed to help the manager with a limited, but important, component of the process of planning a season. In particular, attendance forecasts for even one performance previously involved consideration of many possible factors and was a difficult, time consuming, and somewhat unpleasant task. At one terminal session, the manager wanted to see what the attendance effect of adding a certain group to the winter season would be. The manager said, after seeing the forecast, that previously she would have spent portions of several days thinking about the problem, but now she could just accept the forecast and make a decision.

Finally, the ability of the regression forecast to perform accurately at the end of the fall season was important in building managerial confidence in the overall system.

CONCLUSIONS

The product or performance mix decision is a problem of major concern to managers of performing arts series. There are more than 400 organizations in the United States that present at least ten different classical performing artists a year. The decisions as to whom to book ultimately depend upon a number of factors beyond the current capability of analytic procedures; however, marketing models can be of considerable assistance in planning such series while still allowing for artistic integrity. Playing to a small audience is extremely disappointing to an artist; using scarce resources of time and money where they are not needed or will be of no effect is demoralizing to a performing arts manager who is, at best, operating at a breakeven level. The use of marketing and analytic procedures such as those embodied in the ARTS PLAN system can help to reduce such frustrations.

It should be noted that the approach described in this article, although not the specific analytic procedure, should be applicable to organizations having to schedule a mix of activities over time. For example, YM/YWCAs, community centers, adult education schools, athletic departments, and recreation programs, all of which schedule a season of activities, would seem to be amenable to similar types of analysis. In particular, it would be extremely useful to know what factors account for attendance at activities or usage of services.

Considerable questions remain as to how to best compose a season of events that must meet a variety of criteria.

Until recently, marketing techniques have not been used in nonbusiness organizations unless the organization is under some sort of stress from such factors as falling usage (such as that experienced by some mass transit organization) or general public displeasure. However, this does not have to be the case. The ARTS PLAN system was designed and implemented at a time when the program was doing extremely well and, moreover, is only part of a set of marketing activities being carried out by management to help foster continued success.

24

Pricing a Ticket to Ride

Roger Ford

In recent years, British Rail has abandoned the widely used railway practice of setting fares in proportion to the distance traveled. Instead, it has adopted a much more flexible approach to pricing, reflecting such marketing variables as product quality, market strength, and degree of competition.

In the beginning railways charged passengers in proportion to the distance traveled. It is a logical approach to pricing which nearly every railway in the world still follows today. In the Swiss railway timetable, for example, the rate per kilometer is given and passenger fares can be worked out from the distance column of each table. Up to 1968 scale charges were British practice too. But in that year British Rail (BR) applied to the erstwhile Prices & Incomes Board for a further price increase, based, as had always been the case previously, on an across-the-board rise in fares. But the Board told BR that while it could raise the total extra cash required, it would have to do so by making selective increases. For its time, this was a mildly revolutionary idea—and BR grasped the opportunity presented with enthusiasm because it offered scope for deeper market penetration and improved earnings. Not universal enthusiasm though—critics of the idea saw two major problems. One was administrative: much more work would be involved and the fares structure would never be as simple again. The other was more philosophical: the concept of a "fair fare" would disappear—no longer would the cost per mile for each ticket type be the same for everyone. Indeed, it was correspondence to *Modern Railways* on this very topic which led to the preparation of the present article.

Roger Ford is Contributing Editor, *Modern Railways*.

PRICING INPUTS

Clearly, selective pricing requires considerably more effort and skill than a scale system. It is no longer a case of basing fares documents on four columns for each ticket type —originating station, destination, distance, fare. Instead, the third column is replaced by a complexity of inter-related factors. The starting point is the basic Inter-City grid of 236 principal locations. Between these points are the key fares on which the whole fares structure (except for those in the politically-sensitive London & Southeast area) is based. These fares are under constant review by a committee made up of the fares experts of the Railways Board and the five Regions. Each key fare is reviewed in the light of three main factors:

· Quality of product.
· Strength of market.
· Degree of competition.

In the last round of increases quality of product was an important factor. The introduction of Inter-City 125 services meant that fares to South Wales and the West were increased more than those to the West of England. Similarly, the new fares levels on the Great Northern suburban services were influenced by the advent of the inner-suburban electrification—prior to the introduction of the new service fares had reflected the effects of construction delays on the product.

The strength of the market is basically determined by the type of industry in the catchment area, its prosperity, employment levels and similar factors. Finally, there is the degree of competition. The best example of this is the considerable impact of the British Airways' Scottish Shuttles, which is being reflected in the pricing and promotional activities on BR's Anglo-Scottish services.

All these factors are weighed by the committee for the key routes and eventually agreement is reached. It is a complex but now routine procedure, to a rigid timescale. According to BR's Chief Passenger Marketing Manager, Doug Ellison, there are no serious disagreements because the facts are there and speak for themselves. However, in addition to the science and the collective experience, there is also a measure of seat-of-the-pants commercial judgement. But in the end it comes down to the appearance in print of that basic tool of ticket offices and travel centers—the *Selective Prices Manual*. The watchword of the fares committee is "coherence." A fares structure has to be coherent within itself or else anomalies can distort traffic patterns and flows—perhaps driving passengers off one route onto another which does not have the capacity to support its new popularity. And it also has to be coherent to those who use it—railway staff and public. To the traveling public, a coherent fares structure is one under which passengers know what they are going to pay. Without this knowledge the transport user cannot plan to travel by rail. In other words, train travel has to be equated with other purchasing situations where the consumer looks in the shop window and considers prices before making the decision whether or not to buy or go to another shop or even buy something else—a concept of free will ignored by many transport activists. The whole aim of selective pricing is to balance price with demand at a level which maximizes revenue.

DISCOUNT FARES

However, the basic full fare is only the starting point in the selective-pricing process. There is also the armory of reduced fares used to get more people traveling. And the structure of these is also based on selective pricing. Many would agree that BR has some way to go before the word "coherence" would be justified in this area. But matters improved greatly with the introduction of the National Reduced Fares Plan (NRFP) in 1973 since when reduced fares have come under increasingly tight control. Setting levels for short-term promotional fares is another complex exercise. Having arrived at a full fare which the market will bear, the introduction of a reduced fare (to generate more business) will inevitably reduce the ranks of full-fare payers. There will be travelers arriving at ticket offices prepared to pay £5 for a ticket and finding that they are eligible for a £3.50 reduced fare. The traveler goes happily on his way, but BR has just lost £1.50. And restrictions to prevent that happening can only go so far before they make the scheme incoherent to

the traveler. This is what is called the "abstractive phase," present in any reduced-fare plan. Ensuring that the gains in new business outweigh the abstractions is an interesting exercise in elasticity. The NRFP reduced a jungle of promotional fares to four. In order of discount they are:

- Midweek Economy return (up to 50%).
- Awayday (up to 45%).
- Weekend return (up to 35%).
- Monthly return (up to 25%).

Under the NRFP selective pricing extends within each of the promotional fares. Thus the percentage saving on Awaydays (advertised as up to 35%) can be as high as 45%. The reason for these variations lies in judgments of what the market will bear. A frequent criticism of the reduced-fares structure is its complexity to the potential user. A simplified graduated scheme, starting with the period return at 20% discount and increasing in 10% steps to the Economy return at 50% off, might be more coherent. However BR policy is to set out its stall to quote the potential customer the price for the particular journey he has in mind in the belief that this is all that interests him.

One result of such a fares structure is that a fares increase of $x\%$ does not necessarily bring in $x\%$ more revenue—even if the volume of traffic is undiminished. What happens is that people trade down—first class to second class, full fare to reduced fares. Thus over the entire traveling public on a particular route there is an average fare and the movement of this is perhaps the best indicator of how a particular BR passenger service is performing. On the Western Region, for example, the average fare was falling until the introduction of Inter-City 125[1] when the trend was reversed; moreover in addition to the rapid increase in traffic over the first six months of the new services by about 15%, the average fare has risen too, by 7½%, as first-class custom returned. In such a fast-moving situation, one experienced passenger manager sees the need for a faster reaction time than that possible with the procedure described at the start of this article. With the availability of computers it should now be possible to have the prices for all routes stored on magnetic tape and continually up-dated to allow for changes in the travel pattern. These increases (or decreases) would be solely concerned with selective pricing. Increases to cater to rising costs or inflation would be calculated separately and would be a flat across-the-board percentage addition as at present. Thus when it became necessary generally to increase fares, the chosen figure would be fed into the computer which would add it to the percentage changes already introduced during the routine up-dating and the new fare would be printed out automatically. The effect would be to ensure that each time a new fares level was introduced it reflected as accurately as possible the current state of affairs in the passenger market.

---

[1] New diesel trains capable of speeds of 125 mph.

Recent years have seen the emergence of what is virtually a two-part tariff reduced fares structure. This has resulted from the introduction of the Senior Citizen and Student Railcards which entitle the user to "buy" tickets at a 50% discount. While it undoubtedly does endow a social benefit in terms of greater mobility for the elderly, the Senior Citizen Railcard was introduced for the purest commercial reasons. A market had been identified with the time, inclination and money to travel. Clearly it was the last factor which was critical and even BR was surprised when a demand emerged for the Railcard to cover first-class travel. The introduction of the Railcard was another example of nice commercial judgement. Clearly there would be an abstractive element (the Midweek return was largely aimed at the same market) and tickets were frequently bought on behalf of elderly parents. However the results in the second year of the scheme show that the decision was justified. Around 500,000 Railcards were sold representing an income of nearly £3million before a single seat was filled. Additional revenue generated is estimated at £2million, a figure which will no doubt increase as the Railcard becomes more widely known and easier to use—for example now that the 1 April starting date is replaced by a year's validity from date of purchase. A similar scheme is the Student Railcard. Here the potential abstractive effect was much stronger. Use of the pass would halve BR's income from the journeys to and from college each term. Once again a commercial judgement was made and has proved sound. Students did have the time, money and inclination to travel to the tune of another extra £2million revenue a year.

The final level of pricing is the local short-term promotion which, despite the guidelines of the NRFP, had shown signs of getting out of hand in 1975 and 1976, when deliberate efforts were made to exploit the technique to counter the reduction in demand stemming from the state of the national economy. As a result local promotions were brought under "rigorous control" early this year. Such schemes—generally originating at Divisional level—are now measured by standard success criteria and have a limited life of six months.

MONITORING THE MARKET

Central to the concept of selective pricing is the ability to detect the reaction of the consumer to the tunes BR is playing on its three variables. Ellison and his committee watch the passenger traffic statistics and the National Computing System permits them to see details of tickets issued in a particular area within four weeks. Where a drop in sales is noted, it is first checked against national or local economic forces. If there is no apparent reason for the fall BR turns to its three factors to see what has changed. It may be that the last price increase was over-optimistic as to the resilience of the market, in which case the short-term remedy may be a course of stepped-up promotional activity. Alternatively, the product may be in need of improvement to justify the price

asked. Action here can take the form of a new timetable with an earlier start or shorter journey-times or the introduction of a better standard of rolling stock.

A classic example of this technique in action can be seen at present as BR tries to stave off the threat to its Anglo-Scottish services of the British Airways' Shuttle to Glasgow and Edinburgh. Scotland's North Sea oil-fuelled prosperity has provided one of the strongest markets in Britain. At 400 miles range and journey times of 5 hours-plus BR has a weakened product in terms of the day-return business traveler while the hourly (or two-hourly) Shuttle with a guaranteed seat is highly competitive. The result has been a turnaround from loss to profit on the two routes from which British Airways has "creamed off" a sizeable part of BR's traffic. How sizeable, BR prefers not to say—but the loss is substantial. BR's reaction to the Shuttle has been complex. For a start, in the last round of fares increases the Anglo-Scottish services were favorably treated and some first-class fares actually reduced. True to character, the Scottish Region introduced a promotion—the Executive package offering a combination of sleeper berths, meals and first-class travel for less than the Shuttle return fare. [New, high speed equipment has also been earmarked for these routes and more promotions are planned].

Clearly commercial security (and political prudence) makes BR unwilling to discuss areas where market resistance to over-pricing is currently a problem. BR points out that despite the recession, the fall in disposable income and a series of fares increases needed to catch up after the period of price restraint, the railways carried only 3% fewer people in 1976 than in 1975 and since the last quarter of 1976 passenger traffic has been growing strongly. Perhaps the example of Leeds traffic about five years ago might be quoted here —perhaps more typical than the Shuttle competition. Traffic between Leeds and London fell off sharply. The experience was clearly not part of a national phenomenon as traffic to a similar catchment area (Manchester) was holding up. The trouble was traced to the emergence of Leeds as the Motorway City, the M1 [motorway] not only running into Leeds but all round it so giving excellent access from the surrounding dormitory areas. No spectacular corrective action was taken, but fares increases were held back slightly, schedules improved and new equipment introduced. Even so, road might have made even greater inroads into BR's traffic had it not been for the long-running (and continuing) chaos at the London end of the M1 at Hendon. But that London-Leeds remains a vulnerable route is instanced by its choice for the first of the National Bus Company's proposed new generation of inter-city express coach routes designed to compete directly with rail.

SELECTIVE PRICING: AN EVALUATION

As noted by critics, the rate per mile charged to passengers on BR now varies considerably. But analyzing fares in this way serves no practical purpose—other than to indicate BR's relative commercial judgment of the value to the customer in BR's many markets of the service offered in the light of the prosperity of the places concerned and the strength of the competition on the route. Nor is fairness—the other criterion of critics of selective pricing—a valid yardstick in BR's commercial position. Ellison freely admits that with selective pricing minor anomalies are bound to occur. But these are accepted as the price for getting the fares right between the principal markets. And the cherished railway tradition of not letting passengers buy into a cheaper fare has been abandoned. Thus, it is sometimes possible to buy a cheaper journey by rebooking en route. If there is an acceptable market price for fast non-stop travel between A and D, then there is no reason why one should not pay less for a slower inconvenient journey, buying new tickets at B and C —not that such an idea would occur to 99% of travelers.

Selective pricing has one aim in mind—to generate as much revenue as possible from the railway system as a whole. And Doug Ellison believes that the policy is working. He estimates that the passenger business is producing an extra £30-50 million a year as a result of charging what each market will bear compared with a mileage-based scale. Selective pricing also explains why suggestions for an across-the-board fare cut gets such a dusty response. After eight years of market pricing BR must have a shrewd idea of cause and effect—and not just on a global scale but on the key Inter-City routes between the nodes of its basic grid. Whatever one's personal views on selective pricing, there can be no denying that a scheme which claims to make more money in today's tough economic conditions, is more responsive to the customer and, at the same time, lessens the burden on the taxpayer, is quite an achievement—even if it isn't "fair"!

Part VI
Introducing New Services and Behavior Patterns

Thus far, most of the chapters in this book have been concerned with doing a better job of marketing existing products. In Part VI, the spotlight is on developing marketing programs for introducing new services and for encouraging people to adopt new behavior patterns.

The articles selected for inclusion in this part of the book cover a fascinating array of application areas. They range from programs as basic as encouraging water-boiling for health purposes in a Latin American village to the complexities of introducing the metric system in highly industrialized nations. They include successes such as Sweden's switch from driving on the left-hand side of the road to driving on the right, and failures such as the attempt to introduce a new $2 bill into circulation in the United States. Among the other "new products" discussed here are preventive health programs, computerized library information services, agricultural innovations, and introduction of a new decimal currency in Britain.

The first chapter, "Diffusion of Innovations," is a specially prepared excerpt from Rogers and Shoemaker's classic book, *Communication of Innovations*. This selection provides a brilliant conceptual framework for looking at innovations and at how, over time, they gain, or fail to gain, acceptance in a particular social system. Drawing from the findings of numerous research projects, in both developed and developing nations, the authors show what factors are likely to facilitate or impede the spread of an innovation. They discuss the process by which new ideas are communicated, evaluated, and either adopted or rejected, identifying the roles played in this process by change agents and opinion leaders. They look at how individuals' personal characteristics both affect communications flow and influence decisions on whether or not to accept specific new ideas and behavior patterns.

Douglas Ferguson's article, "Marketing Online Services in the University," raises the question of how university libraries should go about encouraging use of new computer-based information services. It illustrates the importance of thinking carefully about the characteristics of an innovation and the benefits it can offer different segments of the potential user market. By identifying possible barriers to adoption, such as resistance to change or misperceptions of the new service, marketing strategies can be developed for overcoming these problems and winning new users. These strategies are very much influenced by the framework proposed in the previous readings.

Robertson and Wortzel's article, "Consumer Behavior and Health-Care Change: The Role of Mass Media," is concerned primarily with the role of marketing communication in bringing about desired changes in consumer behavior. It emphasizes the difficulties involved in getting people to adopt new and healthier lifestyles. Based upon careful evaluation of a number of unsuccessful health-related campaigns—including anti-smoking, seat-belt usage, water fluoridation and enrollment in health maintenance organizations—it proposes a series of guidelines for preparing communication campaigns desiged to *change* current behavior rather than just to reinforce it.

The larger the market and the greater the risks (and consequences) of failure, the more intensive the planning needed to ensure successful introduction of a major innovation. Christopher H. Lovelock's chapter, "Marketing National Change: Decimalization in Britain," focuses on the five-year program undertaken in Britain to replace shillings and pence with a new decimal currency. Here was a program where the consequences of failure could have been disastrous, potentially resulting in chaos in the daily financial transactions of the country's entire population. This chapter highlights the role of a government agency in planning and coordinating a major changeover, and in leveraging its activities through the efforts of intermediary organizations in closer touch with consumers than itself. It looks at the program from a marketing perspective, identifying the role of each element of the marketing mix, and demonstrating the importance of basing strategic decisions on detailed up-to-date market information.

Michael B. Amspaugh's article, "Americans Continue to Ignore the $2 Bill," provides an interesting contrast to the British decimalization program. Introducing a new denomination banknote is a much simpler task than changing an entire currency, yet at the time of this writing the $2 bill represents an innovation which has yet to gain broad public acceptance. This chapter identifies some of the reasons behind the $2 bill's failure. Among the lessons of this experience is that of avoiding excessive reliance on public relations as an element in new product introductions. A brief appendix highlights some of the research findings that could have been used to develop a market-oriented introduction strategy; unfortunately these went largely ignored.

Finally comes Anders Englund's article, "Changing Behavior Patterns: Sweden's Traffic Switch." This describes the extremely thorough research and planning underlying the 1967 changeover from driving on left to driving on the right in Sweden. An important goal of the Swedish program was to reinforce the desired new behavior patterns so that people did not revert unconsciously to old and subsequently dangerous habits. Also discussed here is the issue of how to prepare people in advance for a major change.

Introducing new products is an extremely risky proposition with relatively high failure rates. Some of the articles in Part VI illustrate how both large-scale and small-scale innovations can be sucessfully marketed when careful and thorough management is applied; but other articles show that without proper planning and effective management, failure is likely to ensue.

25
Diffusion of Innovations

Everett M. Rogers
F. Floyd Shoemaker

Much of the change which takes place in society nowadays is planned and directed.
Often a government agency or nonprofit organization is responsible for trying to encourage the development
and acceptance of new ideas and new behavior patterns. In planning and managing change programs,
it is important to understand how innovations affect (or fail to affect) existing social systems.

Although it is true that we live more than ever before in an era of change, prevailing social structures often serve to hamper the diffusion of innovations. Our activities in education, agriculture, medicine, industry, and the like are often without the benefit of the most current research knowledge. The gap between what is known and what is effectively put to use needs to be closed. To bridge this gap we must understand how new ideas spread from their source to potential receivers and understand the factors affecting the adoption of such innovations. We need to learn why, if 100 different innovations are conceived simultaneously, ten will spread while ninety will be forgotten.

WATER-BOILING IN A PERUVIAN VILLAGE:
AN EXAMPLE OF INNOVATION THAT FAILED

The public health service in Peru attempts to introduce innovations to villagers to improve their health and lengthen their lives. The change agency enjoys a reputation throughout Latin America as efficient. It encourages people to install pit latrines, burn garbage daily, control house flies, report suspected cases of communicable disease, and boil drinking water. These innovations involve major changes in thinking and behavior for Peruvian villagers, who have little knowledge of the relationship between sanitation and illness.

A two-year water-boiling campaign conducted in Los Molinos, a peasant village of 200 families in the coastal region of Peru, persuaded only eleven housewives, who are the key decision makers in the family, to boil water. From the viewpoint of the health agency, the local hygiene worker, Nelida, had a simple task: To persuade the housewives of Los Molinos to add water-boiling to their pattern of existing behavior. Even with the aid of a medical doctor, who gave public talks on water-boiling, and fifteen village housewives who were already boiling water before the campaign, Nelida's program of directed change failed. To understand why, we need to take a closer look at the culture, the local environment, and the individuals.

Most residents of Los Molinos are peasants who work as field hands on local plantations. Water is carried directly from stream or well by can, pail, gourd, or cask. The three sources of water include a seasonal irrigation ditch close by the village, a spring more than a mile from the village, and

---

Everett M. Rogers is Professor of Communication, Stanford University.

F. Floyd Shoemaker is an official in the Michigan Department of Education.

a public well whose water the villagers dislike. All three are subject to pollution at all times and show contamination whenever tested.

Although it is not feasible for the village to install a sanitary water system, the incidence of typhoid and other water-borne diseases could be reduced by boiling the water before consumption. During her two-year residence in Los Molinos, Nelida paid several visits to every home in the village but devoted especially intensive efforts to twenty-one families. She visited each of these selected families between fifteen and twenty-five times; eleven of these families now boil their water regularly.

What kinds of persons do these numbers represent? By describing three village housewives—one who boils water to obey custom, one who was persuaded to boil water by the health worker, and one of the many who rejected the innovation—we may add further insight into the process of planned diffusion.

Mrs. A: Custom-Oriented. Mrs. A is about forty and suffers from sinus infection. She is labeled by the Los Molinos villagers as a "sickly one." Each morning, Mrs. A boils a potful of water and uses it throughout the day. She has no understanding of germ theory, as explained by Nelida; her motivation for water-boiling is a complex local custom of hot and cold distinctions. The basic principle of this belief system is that all foods, liquids, medicines, and other objects are inherently hot or cold, quite apart from their actual temperature. In essence hot–cold distinctions serve as a series of avoidances and approaches in such behavior as pregnancy and child rearing, food habits, and the entire health–illness system.

Boiled water and illness are closely linked in the folkways of Los Molinos; by custom, only the ill use cooked, or "hot" water. Once an individual becomes ill, it is unthinkable for him to eat pork (very cold) or to drink brandy (very hot). Extremes of hot and cold must be avoided by the sick; therefore, raw water, which is perceived to be very cold, must be boiled to overcome the extreme temperature.

Villagers learn from childhood to dislike boiled water. Most can tolerate cooked water only if flavoring, such as sugar, cinnamon, lemon, or herbs, is added. At no point in the village belief system is the notion of bacteriological contamination of water involved. Mrs. A drinks boiled water in obedience to local custom; she is ill.

Mrs. B: Persuaded. The B family came to Los Molinos a generation ago, but they are still strongly oriented toward their birthplace, located among the peaks of the high Andes. Mrs. B worries about lowland diseases which she feels infest the village. It is partly because of this anxiety that the change agent, Nelida, was able to convince Mrs. B to boil water.

Nelida is a friendly authority to Mrs. B (rather than a "dirt inspector," as she is seen by most housewives), who imparts knowledge and brings protection. Mrs. B not only boils water but also has installed a latrine and has sent her youngest child to the health center for an inspection.

Mrs. B is marked as an outsider in the community by her highland hairdo and stumbling Spanish. She will never achieve more than marginal social acceptance in the village. Because the community is not an important reference group to her, Mrs. B deviates from group norms on innovation. Having nothing to lose socially, Mrs. B gains in personal security by heeding Nelida's friendly advice. Mrs. B's practice of boiling water has no effect on her marginal status. She is grateful to Nelida for teaching her how to neutralize the danger of contaminated water, a lowland peril.

Mrs. C: Rejector. This housewife represents the majority of Los Molinos families who were not persuaded by the efforts of the change agent during the two-year health campaign. Mrs. C does not understand germ theory. How, she argues, can microbes survive in water which would drown people? Are they fish? If germs are so small that they cannot be seen or felt, how can they hurt a grown person? There are enough real threats in the world to worry about—poverty and hunger—without bothering with tiny animals one cannot see, hear, touch, or smell. Mrs. C's allegiance to traditional customs are at odds with the boiling of water. A firm believer in the hot–cold superstition, she feels that only the sick must drink boiled water.

Several housewives, particularly those of the lower social class, are rejectors because they have neither the time nor the means to boil water, even if they were convinced of its value. These women lack time to gather firewood and to boil water. The poor cannot afford the cost of fuel for water-boiling and the wives often work as field laborers beside their husbands, leaving them less time to boil water for their families.

Understanding Why Water-Boiling Failed. This intensive two-year campaign by a public health worker in a Peruvian village was largely unsuccessful. Nelida was able to encourage only about 5 percent of the population to adopt the innovation. In contrast, change agents in other Peruvian villages were able to convince 15 to 20 percent of the housewives. Reasons for the relative failure of the campaign in Los Molinos can be traced partly to the cultural beliefs of the villagers. Local tradition links hot foods with illness. Boiling water makes it less "cold," and hence, appropriate only for the sick. But if a person is not ill, he is prohibited by cultural norms from drinking boiled water. Only the least integrated individuals risk defying community norms on water-boiling. An important factor affecting the adoption rate of any innovation is its compatibility with the cultural beliefs of the social system.

Nelida worked with the wrong housewives if she wanted to launch a self-generating diffusion process in Los Molinos. She concentrated her efforts on village women like Mrs. A and Mrs. B. Unfortunately, they were perceived as a sickly one and a social outsider and were not respected as models of water-boiling behavior by the other women. The village opinion leaders, who could have been a handle to prime the pump of change, were ignored by Nelida.

The way that potential adopters view the change agent affects their willingness to adopt his ideas. In Los Molinos Nelida was seen differently by lower and middle status housewives. Most poor families saw the health worker as a ''snooper'' sent to Los Molinos to pry for dirt and to press already harassed housewives into keeping cleaner homes. Because the lower status housewives had less free time, they were not likely to initiate visits with Nelida about water-boiling. Their contacts outside the community were limited, and as a result, they saw the cosmopolite Nelida with eyes bound by the social horizons and cultural beliefs of Los Molinos. They distrusted this outsider, whom they perceived as a social stranger. Further, Nelida, who was middle class by Los Molinos standards, was able to secure more positive results from housewives whose socioeconomic level and cultural background were more similar to hers. This tendency for effective communication to occur with those who are more similar is a common experience of change agents in most diffusion campaigns.

In general Nelida was much more ''innovation-oriented'' than ''client-oriented.'' Unable to put herself in the role of the village housewives, her attempts at persuasion failed to reach her clients because the message was not suited to their needs. Nelida did not begin where the villagers were; instead she talked to them about germ theory, which they could not, and did not need to, understand.

SOCIAL CHANGE

The theme to be developed throughout is: *Communication is essential for social change.* The process of social change consists of three sequential steps: (1) invention, (2) diffusion, and (3) consequences. *Invention* is the process by which new ideas are created or developed. *Diffusion* is the process by which these new ideas are communicated to the members of a social system. *Consequences* are the changes that occur within a social system as a result of the adoption or rejection of the innovation. Change occurs when a new idea's use or rejection has an effect. Social change is therefore an effect of communication.

What Is Social Change? *Social change* is the process by which alteration occurs in the structure and function of a social system. National revolution, invention of a new manufacturing technique, founding of a village improvement council, adoption of birth control methods by a family—all are examples of social change. Alteration in both the structure and function of a social system occurs as a result of such actions.

One of the more useful ways of viewing social change is to focus on the source of change.

1. *Immanent change* occurs when members of a social system with little or no external influence create and develop a new idea (that is,

invent it), which then spreads within the system. A farmer in the senior author's home community in Iowa invented a simple hand tool to clear cornpickers that were plugged with damp cornstalks. The invention was easy to make and a great time-saver. In a short time, most of the inventor's neighbors were using it. Immanent change, then, is a ''within-system'' phenomenon.

2. *Contact change,* the other type of social change, occurs when sources external to the social system introduce a new idea. Contact change is a ''between-system'' phenomenon. It may be either *selective* or *directed,* depending on whether the recognition of the need for change is internal or external.

Selective contact change results when members of a social system are exposed to external influences and adopt or reject a new idea from that source on the basis of their needs. The exposure to innovations is spontaneous or accidental; the receivers are left to choose, interpret, and adopt or reject the new ideas. An illustration of selective contact change occurs when school teachers visit a neighboring school that is especially innovative. They may return to their own classrooms with a new teaching method, but with no pressure from school administrators to seek and adopt such innovations.

Directed contact change, or planned change, is caused by outsiders who, on their own or as representatives of change agencies, intentionally seek to introduce new ideas in order to achieve goals they have defined. The water-boiling compaign in Peru is an example of directed contact change. The innovation, as well as the recognition of the need for change, originates outside the social system in the case of directed change. The many government-sponsored development programs designed to introduce technological innovations in agriculture, education, health, and industry are examples of contemporary directed change. Programs of planned change are largely the result of dissatisfaction with the rate of change that results from immanent and selective contact change.

The prevailing enthusiasm for planned change has not always been matched by overwhelming success. As communication research is conducted on the spread of new ideas and as the results are accumulated in a meaningful way, we shall be able to use these findings to design more effective programs of planned change.

Individual and Social System Change: Levels at Which Change Occurs. We have been looking at social change from the viewpoint of the innovation's origin. Another perspective is provided by the nature of the *unit* that adopts or rejects the new ideas.

1. Many changes occur at the *individual* level; that is, the individual is the adopter or rejector of the innovation. Change at this level has variously been referred to as diffusion, adoption, modernization, acculturation, learning, or socialization. We might term this the microanalytic approach to change analysis in that it focuses on an individual's change behavior.

2. Change also occurs at the *social system* level where it has been diversely termed development, specialization, integration, or adaptation. Here our attention is centered on the change process at the social system level and is thus macroanalytic in approach.

Of course, change at these two levels is closely inter-related. If we regard a school as a social system, then the school system's adoption of team teaching will lead to individual teachers' decisions to change their teaching methods.

Communication and Social Change. *Communication* is the process by which messages are transferred from a source to a receiver. We might think of the communication process in terms of the oversimplified but useful S–M–C–R model. A *source* (S) sends a *message* (M) via certain *channels* (C) to the *receiving* individual (R). One can easily see how communication factors are vitally involved in many aspects of the decision processes which together make up social change: A farmer's decision to move to the city or to participate in a government program, an industrialist's adoption of a new manufacturing technique, or the decision of a husband and wife to engage in family planning. In each of these instances, a message (M) is conveyed to individuals (R) via communication channels (C) from a source individual (S), which causes the receivers to change an existing behavior pattern.

Although communication and social change are not synonymous, communication is an important element throughout the social change process. Essentially, the concept of social change includes, in addition to the communication process, the societal and individual consequences that result from the adoption or rejection of an innovation. When examining social change, our concern is with alteration in the structure and function of a social system, as well as the process through which such alteration occurs. Thus to the S–M–R–C model, we might add (E) the effects of communication. (See Exhibit 1).

Communication and Diffusion. Diffusion is a special type of communication. *Diffusion* is the process by which innovations spread to the members of a social system. Diffusion studies are concerned with messages that are new ideas, whereas communication studies encompass all types of messages. As the messages are new in the case of diffusion, a degree of risk for the receivers is present. This leads to somewhat different behavior on their part in the case of innova-

tions than if they were receiving messages about routine ideas.

There is often a further difference between the nature of diffusion research versus other types of communication research. In the latter, we often focus on attempts to bring about changes in knowledge or attitudes by altering the makeup of the source, message, channels, or receivers in the communication process. But in diffusion research we usually focus on bringing about *overt behavior change,* that is, adoption or rejection of new ideas, rather than just changes in knowledge or attitudes. The knowledge and persuasion effects of diffusion campaigns are considered mainly as intermediate steps in an individual's decision-making process leading eventually to overt behavior change.

The focus on new ideas by diffusion researchers has led to a more thorough understanding of the communication process. The conception of the flow of communication as a multi-step process lacked clear conceptual development until it was probed by researchers studying the diffusion of innovations. They found that new ideas usually spread from a source to an audience of receivers via a series of sequential transmissions, rather than in the oversimplified two steps that had been originally postulated. By tracing communication patterns over time, diffusion researchers expanded the conceptual repertoire of communication researchers. Until students of diffusion began studying the flow of communication, consideration of the role of different communication channels at various stages in the innovation-decision process was masked. Specifically, it was learned that mass media channels are often more important at creating awareness-knowledge of a new idea, whereas interpersonal channels are more important in changing attitudes toward innovations.

Heterophily and Diffusion. One of the obvious principles of human communication is that the transfer of ideas occurs most frequently between a source and a receiver who are alike, similar, homophilous. *Homophily* is the degree to which pairs of individuals who interact are similar in certain

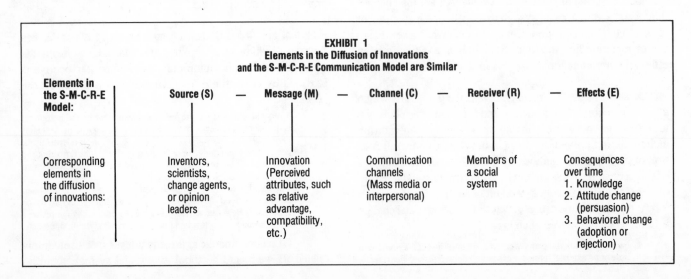

EXHIBIT 1
Elements in the Diffusion of Innovations
and the S-M-C-R-E Communication Model are Similar

Elements in the S-M-C-R-E Model:	Source (S) —	Message (M) —	Channel (C) —	Receiver (R) —	Effects (E)
Corresponding elements in the diffusion of innovations:	Inventors, scientists, change agents, or opinion leaders	Innovation (Perceived attributes, such as relative advantage, compatibility, etc.)	Communication channels (Mass media or interpersonal)	Members of a social system	Consequences over time 1. Knowledge 2. Attitude change (persuasion) 3. Behavioral change (adoption or rejection)

attributes, such as beliefs, values, education, social status, and the like. In a free-choice situation, when a source can interact with any one of a number of receivers, there is a strong tendency for him to select a receiver who is most like himself. Similar individuals are likely to belong to the same groups, to live near each other, to be drawn by the same interests.

But in many situations, propinquity explains only a part of homophilous tendencies. *More effective communication occurs when source and receiver are homophilous.* When they share common meanings, a mutual subcultural language, and are alike in personal and social characteristics, the communication of ideas is likely to have greater effects in terms of knowledge gain, attitude formation and change, and overt behavior change.

Many examples could be cited to support the proposition about homophily and effective communication. In everyday life most of us interact with others who are quite similar in social status, education, and beliefs. And when we occasionally seek to communicate with those of a much lower social status, many problems of ineffective communication arise. Consider the middle class teacher who seeks to communicate with slum children, the social worker who tries to change the behavior of her lower class or foreign born clients, the technical assistance worker overseas who attempts to introduce innovations to peasants.

One of the most distinctive problems in the communication of innovations is that the source is usually quite heterophilous to the receiver. The extension agent, for instance, is much more technically competent than his peasant clients. This frequently leads to ineffective communication. The very nature of diffusion demands that at least some degree of heterophily be present between source and receiver. Ideally, they are homophilous on all other variables (education, social status, and the like) even though heterophilous regarding the innovation. In actuality, source and receiver are usually heterophilous on all of these variables because competence, education, social status, and so on are highly interrelated.

Time Lags in Diffusion. Evidence that diffusion is not a simple, easy process is the time that it requires. Change takes time, much time. Despite generally favorable attitudes toward change in nations like the United States, a considerable time lag exists from the introduction of a new idea to its widespread adoption. This is true even when the economic benefits of the innovation are obvious.

1. A forty-year time lag existed between the first success of the tunnel oven in the English pottery industry and its general use (Carter and Williams, 1957).
2. More than fourteen years were required for hybrid seed corn to reach complete adoption in Iowa (Ryan and Gross, 1943).
3. U.S. public schools required fifty years to adopt the idea of the kindergarten in the 1930s and 1940s (Ross, 1958), and more recently, about five or six years to adopt modern math in the 1960s (Carlson, 1965).

One of the goals of diffusion research is to shorten this time lag. It is clear that research alone is not enough to solve most problems; the results of the research must be diffused and utilized before their advantages can be realized. Even diffusion research findings must be diffused before their benefits can be derived.

In spite of the fact that the communication of most innovations involves a considerable time lag, there is a certain inevitability in their diffusion. Most attempts to prevent innovation diffusion over an extended period of time have failed. For instance, the Chinese were unsuccessful in their attempt to maintain sole knowledge of gunpowder. And today, a growing number of nations share the secret of the nuclear bomb with the United States. Similar are university administration and campus police attempts to prevent the widespread adoption of marijuana smoking among students.

Consequences of Innovations. The consequences of innovations are a third part of the social change process, following invention and diffusion. Consequences have an obvious interface with diffusion (for example, the selection of diffusion strategies affects the consequences that accrue).

Consequences are the changes that occur within a social system as a result of the adoption or rejection of an innovation. There are at least three classifications of consequences:

1. *Functional* versus *dysfunctional* consequences, depending on whether the effects of an innovation in a social system are desirable or undesirable.
2. *Direct* versus *indirect* consequences, depending on whether the changes in a social system occur in immediate response to an innovation or as a result of the direct consequences of an innovation.
3. *Manifest* versus *latent* consequences, depending on whether the changes are recognized and intended by the members of a social system or not.

Change agents usually introduce into a client system innovations that they expect will be functional, direct, and manifest. But often such innovations result in at least some latent consequences that are indirect and dysfunctional for the system's members. An illustration is the case of the steel ax introduced by missionaries to an Australian aborigine tribe. The change agents intended that the new tool should raise levels of living and material comfort for the tribe. But the new technology also led to breakdown of the family structure, the rise of prostitution, and "misuse" of the innovation itself. Change agents can often anticipate and predict the innovation's *form,* the directly observable physical appearance of the innovation, and perhaps its *function,* the contribution of the idea to the way of life of the system's members. But seldom are change agents able to predict another aspect of an innovation's consequences, its *meaning,* the subjective perception of the innovation by the clients.

ELEMENTS IN THE DIFFUSION OF INNOVATIONS

Crucial elements in the diffusion of new ideas are (1) the *innovation* (2) which is *communicated* through certain *channels* (3) over *time* (4) among the members of a *social system*. The four elements of diffusion differ only in nomenclature from the essential elements of most general communication models. For example, Aristotle proposed a very simple model of oral communication consisting of the speaker, the speech, and the listener. Laswell described all communication as dealing with *"who* says *what,* through *what channels* of communication, to *whom* with what . . . *results."*

The Innovation. An *innovation* is an idea, practice, or object perceived as new by an individual. It matters little, so far as human behavior is concerned, whether or not an idea is "objectively" new as measured by the lapse of time since its first use or discovery. It is the perceived or subjective newness of the idea for the individual that determines his reaction to it. If the idea seems new to the individual, it is an innovation.

"New" in an innovative idea need not be simply new knowledge. An innovation might be known by an individual for some time (that is, he is aware of the idea), but he has not yet developed a favorable or unfavorable attitude toward it, not has he adopted or rejected it. The "newness" aspect of an innovation may be expressed in knowledge, in attitude, or regarding a decision to use it.

Every idea has been an innovation sometime. Any list of innovations must change with the times. Black Panthers, computers, micro-teaching, birth control pills, chemical weed sprays, LSD, heart transplants, and laser beams might still be considered innovative ideas at this writing, but the reader in North America will probably find many of these items adopted or even discontinued at the time of reading.

The diffusion and adoption of all innovations is not necessarily desirable. In fact, some are harmful and uneconomical for either the individual or his social system.

It should not be assumed that all innovations are equivalent units of analysis. The several characteristics of innovations, as sensed by the receivers, contribute to their different rate of adoption.

1. *Relative advantage* is the degree to which an innovation is perceived as better than the idea it supersedes. The degree of relative advantage may be measured in economic terms, but often social prestige factors, convenience, and satisfaction are also important components. It matters little whether the innovation has a great deal of "objective" advantage. What does matter is whether the individual *perceives* the innovation as being advantageous. The greater the perceived relative advantage of an innovation, the more rapid its rate of adoption.
2. *Compatibility* is the degree to which an innovation is perceived as being consistent with the existing values, past experiences, and needs of the receivers. An idea that is not compatible with the prevalent values and norms of the social system will not be adopted as rapidly as an innovation that is compatible. The adoption of an incompatible innovation often requires the prior adoption of a new value system. An example of an incompatible innovation is the use of the IUCD (intra-uterine contraceptive device) in countries where religious beliefs discourage use of birth control techniques.
3. *Complexity* is the degree to which an innovation is perceived as difficult to understand and use. Some innovations are readily understood by most members of a social system; others are not and will be adopted more slowly. For example, the rhythm method of

family planning is relatively complex for most peasant housewives to comprehend because it requires understanding human reproduction and the monthly cycle of ovulation. For this reason, attempts to introduce the rhythm method in village India have been much less successful than campaigns to diffuse the loop, a type of IUCD, which is a much less complex idea in the eyes of the receiver. In general those new ideas requiring little additional learning investment on the part of the receiver will be adopted more rapidly than innovations requiring the adopter to develop new skills and understandings.
4. *Trialability* is the degree to which an innovation may be experimented with on a limited basis. New ideas which can be tried on the installment plan will generally be adopted more quickly than innovations which are not divisible. Ryan and Gross (1943) found that not one of their Iowa farmer respondents adopted hybrid seed corn without first trying it on a partial basis. If the new seed could not have been sampled experimentally, its rate of adoption would have been much slower. Essentially, an innovation that is trialable represents less risk to the individual who is considering it.
5. *Observability* is the degree to which the results of an innovation are visible to others. The easier it is for an individual to see the results of an innovation, the more likely he is to adopt. For example, a technical assistance agency in Bolivia introduced a new corn variety in one town. Within two years the local demand for the seed far exceeded the supply. The farmers were mostly illiterate, but they could easily observe the spectacular results achieved with the new corn and were thus persuaded to adopt. In the United States a rat poison that killed rats in their holes diffused very slowly among farmers because its results were not visible.

The five attributes just described are not a complete list, but they are the most important characteristics of innovations, past research indicates, in explaining rate of adoption.

Component elements in an innovation are often modified, adapted, and changed when the innovation is implemented by various adopters, as they fit the innovation to the distinctive conditions of their own situations.

Re-invention is the degree to which an innovation is changed by an adopter in the process of implementing its use. The amount of re-invention that occurs depends on the nature of the innovation, the similarity among the adopters' situations, and the policies of the change agency promoting the innovation.

When a high degree of re-invention occurs, it raises certain methodological questions about research on the diffusion of innovations. For example, how does one interpret a study of the rate of adoption if each adopter is selecting a slightly different innovation?

Given that an innovation exists and that it has certain attributes, communication between the source and the receivers must take place if the innovation is to spread beyond its inventor. Now we turn our attention to this second element in diffusion.

Communication Channels. *Communication* is the process by which messages are transmitted from a source to a receiver. In other words communication is the transfer of ideas from a source with a viewpoint of modifying the behavior of receivers. A communication *channel* is the means by which the message gets from the source to the receiver.

The essence of the diffusion process is the human interaction by which one person communicates a new idea to one or several other persons. At its most elementary level, the diffusion process consists of (1) a new idea, (2) individual A who has knowledge of the innovation, (3) individual B who is not yet aware of the new idea, and (4) some sort of communication channel connecting the two individuals. The nature of the social relationships between A and B determines the conditions under which A will or will not tell B about the innovation, and further, it influences the effect that the telling has on individual B.

The communication channel by which the new idea reached B is also important in determining B's decision to adopt or reject the innovation. Usually the choice of communication channel lies with A, the source, and should be made in light of (1) the purpose of the communication act, and (2) the audience to whom the message is being sent. If A wishes simply to inform B about the innovation, *mass media channels* are often the most rapid and efficient, especially if the number of Bs in the audience is large. On the other hand, if A's objective is to persuade B to form a favorable attitude toward the innovation, an *interpersonal channel,* involving face-to-face interchanges, is more effective.

Over Time. Time is an important consideration in the process of diffusion. The time dimension is involved (1) in the innovation-decision process by which an individual passes from first knowledge of the innovation through its adoption or rejection, (2) in the innovativeness of the individual, that is, the relative earliness-lateness with which an individual adopts an innovation when compared with other members of his social system, and (3) in the innovation's rate of adoption in a social system, usually measured as the number of members of the system that adopt the innovation in a given time period.

The Innovation-Decision Process. The *innovation-decision process* is the mental process through which an individual passes from first knowledge of an innovation to a decision to adopt or reject and to confirmation of this decision. Many diffusion researchers have conceptualized a cumulative series of five stages in the process: (1) from awareness (first knowledge of the new idea), (2) to interest (gaining further knowledge about the innovation), (3) to evaluation (gaining a favorable or unfavorable attitude toward the innovation), (4) to small-scale trial, (5) to an adoption or rejection decision. We prefer to conceptualize four main functions or steps in the process: (1) knowledge, (2) persuasion, (3) decision, and (4) confirmation. The *knowledge function* occurs when the individual is exposed to the innovation's existence and gains some understanding of how it functions. The *persuasion function* occurs when the individual forms a favorable or unfavorable attitude toward the innovation. The *decision function* occurs when the individual engages in activities which lead to a choice to adopt or reject the innovation. The *confirmation function* occurs when the individual seeks reinforcement for the innovation-decision he has made, but he may reverse his previous decision if exposed to conflicting messages about the innovation.

An example should clarify the meaning of the innovation-decision process and to show the importance of the time dimension. Mr. Skeptic, an Iowa farmer, first learned of hybrid seed corn from an agricultural extension agent in 1935 (the knowledge function). However, he was not convinced to plant hybrid corn on his own farm until 1937, after he had discussed the innovation with several neighbors (the persuasion function). Skeptic purchased a small sack of hybrid seed in 1937 and by 1939 was planting 100 percent of his corn acreage in hybrids. When did he adopt hybrid corn?

Skeptic adopted in 1939 when he decided to continue full scale use of the innovation (decision function). *Adoption* is a decision to make full use of a new idea as the best course of action available. The *innovation-decision period* is the length of time required to pass through the innovation-decision process; in the present instance it lasted four years. The innovation decision can also take a negative turn; that is, the final decision can be *rejection,* a decision not to adopt an innovation.

The last function in the innovation-decision process is confirmation, a stage at which the receiver seeks reinforcement for the adoption or rejection decision he has made. Occasionally, however, conflicting and contradictory messages reach the receiver about the innovation, and this may lead to discontinuance on one hand or later adoption (after rejection) on the other. In the case of Mr. Skeptic, a decision was made to *discontinue* use of the innovation after previously adopting it. Farmer Skeptic became dissatisfied with hybrid seed and discontinued its use in 1941, when he again planted all of his corn acreage in open-pollinated seed. Discontinuances occur for many other reasons, including replacement of the innovation with an improved idea. Discontinuances occur only after the individual has fully adopted the idea.

Innovativeness and Adopter Categories. If Skeptic adopted hybrid seed in 1939 and the average farmer in his community adopted in 1936, Skeptic is less innovative than the average member of his system. *Innovativeness* is the degree to which an individual is relatively earlier in adopting new ideas than the other members of his system. *Adopter categories* are the classifications of members of a social system on the basis of innovativeness. The five adopter categories used here are: (1) innovators, (2) early adopters, (3) early majority, (4) late majority, and (5) laggards. Mr. Skeptic is in the "late majority" adopter category. Diffusion research shows clearly that each of the adopter categories has a great deal in common. If Skeptic is like most others in the late majority category, he is below average in social status, makes little use of mass media channels, and secures most of his new ideas from peers via interpersonal channels.

Rate of Adoption. There is a third specific way in which the time dimension is involved in the diffusion of innovations. *Rate of adoption* is the relative speed with which an innovation is adopted by members of a social system. This rate of adoption is usually measured by the length of time required for a certain percentage of the members of a system to adopt an innovation. Therefore, we see that rate of adoption is measured using an innovation or a system, rather than an individual, as the unit of analysis. Innovations that are perceived by receivers as possessing greater relative advantage, compatibility, and the like have a more rapid rate of adoption (as we pointed out in a previous section of this chapter).

There are also differences in the rate of adoption for the same innovation in different social systems. Generally, diffusion research shows that systems typified by modern, rather than traditional, norms will have a faster rate of adoption.

Among Members of a Social System. A *social system* is defined as a collectivity of units which are functionally differentiated and engaged in joint problem solving with respect to a common goal. The members or units of a social system may be individuals, informal groups, complex organizations, or subsystems. The social system analyzed in a diffusion study may consists of all the peasants in a Latin American village, students at a university, high schools in Thailand, medical doctors in a large city, or members of an aborigine tribe. Each unit in a social system can be functionally differentiated from every other member. All members cooperate at least to the extent of seeking to solve a common problem or to reach a mutual goal. It is this sharing of a common objective that binds the system together.

In this section we shall deal with the following topics: How the social structure affects diffusion, the effect of traditional and modern norms on diffusion, the roles of opinion leaders and change agents, and types of innovation-decisions. All these issues involve interfaces between the social system and the diffusion process that occurs within it.

Social Structure and Diffusion. Both formal and informal social structures have an effect on human behavior and how it changes in response to communication stimuli.

Diffusion and social structure are complexly interrelated.

> 1. *The social structure acts to impede or facilitate the rate of diffusion and adoption of new ideas through what are called "system effects."*

The basic notion of system effects is that the norms, social statuses, hierarchy, and so on of a social system influence the behavior of individual members of that system. *System effects* are the influences of the system's social structure on the behavior of the individual members of the social system.

In the case of innovation diffusion, one can conceptualize an individual's innovation behavior as explained by two types of variables: (1) the *individual's* personality, communication behavior, attitudes, and so on, and (2) the nature of his *social system.*

Van den Ban (1960) studied the effects of traditional and modern norms (for a sample of Wisconsin townships) on the innovativeness of farmers. Although such individual characteristics as a farmer's education, size of farm, and net worth were positively related to his innovativeness, the township norms were even better predictors of farmer innovativeness. Van den Ban concluded that a farmer with a high level of education, on a large farm, and with a high net worth, but residing in a township with traditional norms, adopted fewer farm innovations than if he had a lower level of education and a smaller farm in a township where the norms were modern.

System effects (such as system norms, the composite educational level of one's peers, and the like) *may be as important in explaining individual innovativeness as such individual characteristics as education, cosmopoliteness, and so on.*

> 2. *Diffusion may also change the social structure of a system.*

Some new ideas are "restructuring" innovations in that they change the structure of the social system itself. The adoption of a village development council changes the village social structure by adding a new set of statuses. The initiation of a research and development unit within an industrial firm and the departmentalization of a public school are also restructuring innovations. In many instances the restructuring affects the rate of future innovation diffusion within the system.

System Norms and diffusion. We have just pointed out that a system's norms affect an individual's innovation-adoption behavior. *Norms* are the established behavior patterns for the members of a given social system. They define a range of tolerable behavior and serve as a guide or a standard for the members of a social system.

A system's norms can be a barrier to change, as was shown in our example of water-boiling in a Peruvian community. Such resistance to new ideas is often found in norms relating to food. In India, for example, sacred cows roam the countryside while millions of people are undernourished. Polished rice is eaten in most of Asia and the United States, even though whole rice is more nutritious.

We conceptualize system norms that are most relevant for innovation diffusion as either traditional or modern.

Individuals in social systems with modern norms view change favorably, predisposing them to adopt new ideas more rapidly than individuals in traditional systems. Traditional social systems can be characterized by:

1. Lack of favorable orientation to change.
2. A less developed or "simpler" technology.
3. A relatively low level of literacy, education, and understanding of the scientific method.
4. A social enforcement of the status quo in the social system, facilitated by affective personal relationships, such as friendliness and hospitality, which are highly valued as ends in themselves.
5. Little communication by members of the social system with outsiders. Lack of transportation facilities and communication with the larger society reinforces the tendency of individuals in a traditional system to remain relatively isolated.
6. Lack of ability to empathize or to see oneself in others' roles, particularly the roles of outsiders to the system. An individual member in a system with traditional norms is not likely to recognize or

learn new social relationships involving himself; he usually plays only one role and never learns others.

A social system with modern norms is more change oriented, technologically developed, scientific, rational, cosmopolite, and empathic.

There is one danger in attempting to fit our thinking into the framework of idea types: There is a tendency to overemphasize the extent of the differences. Traditional and modern ideal types are actually the end points of a continuum on which actual social system norms may range. We should not forget that the norms of most systems are distributed between the extremes that we have described.

One should not conclude that traditional norms are necessarily undesirable. In many cases, tradition lends stability to a social system that is undergoing rapid change and is in danger of disorganization. Modern systems have their own unique drawbacks, including slums, pollution of water and air, alienation, neuroses, and an almost endless list of social problems rooted in the consequences of "progress."

An individual may be a member of more than one social system. If the norms of the systems to which the individual belongs are widely divergent, he is likely to experience cross-pressures in making innovation decisions. For instance, a school teacher who is continuing his part-time graduate education in a university where new ideas are constantly discussed is likely to experience conflict when he attempts to introduce these innovations into the traditional school system where he teaches.

The *commitment* of the individual to the social system affects his conformity to its norms. An innovative teacher in a traditional school may be relatively unaffected by the norms because the local school is not important as a reference group to him. Thus, an individual's integration into a social system, as well as the nature of the system's norms, need to be studied in order to fully explain his adoption behavior.

Opinion Leaders and Change Agents. Now we turn to the different roles that individuals play in a social system and the effect of these roles on diffusion patterns. Specifically, we shall look at two roles: Opinion leaders and change agents.

Very often the most innovative member of a system is perceived as a deviant from the social system, and he is accorded a somewhat dubious status of low credibility by the average members of the system. His role in diffusion (especially in persuading others about the innovation) is therefore likely to be limited. On the other hand there are members of the system who function in the role of opinion leader. They provide information and advice about innovations to many others in the system.

Opinion leadership is the degree to which an individual is able to informally influence other individuals' attitudes or overt behavior in a desired way with relative frequency. It is a type of informal leadership, rather than being a function of the individual's formal position or status in the system. Opinion leadership is earned and maintained by the individ-

ual's technical competence, social accessibility, and conformity to the system's norms. Several researches indicate that when the social system is modern, the opinion leaders are quite innovative; but when the norms are traditional, the leaders also reflect this norm in their behavior.

In any system, naturally, there may be both innovative and also more traditional opinion leaders. These influential persons can lead in the promotion of new ideas, or they can head an active opposition. In general, when opinion leaders are compared with their followers, we find that they (1) are more exposed to all forms of external communication, (2) are more cosmopolite, (3) have higher social status, and (4) are more innovative (although the exact degree of innovativeness depends, in part, on the system's norms).

Opinion leaders are usually members of the social system in which they exert their influence. In some instances individuals with influence in the social system are professionals representing change agencies external to the system. A *change agent* is a professional who influences innovation-decisions in a direction deemed desirable by a change agency. He usually seeks to obtain the adoption of new ideas, but he may also attempt to slow down diffusion and prevent the adoption of what he believes are undesirable innovations. Change agents often use opinion leaders within a given social system as lieutenants in their campaigns of planned change. There is research evidence that opinion leaders can be "worn out" by change agents who overuse them. Opinion leaders may be perceived by their peers as too much like the change agents; thus, the opinion leaders lose their credibility with their former followers.

Types of Innovation-Decisions. The social system has yet another important kind of influence on the diffusion of new ideas. Innovations can be adopted or rejected by individual members of a system or by the entire social system. The relationship between the social system and the decision to adopt innovations may be described in the following manner:

1. *Optional decisions* are made by an individual regardless of the decisions of other members of the system. Even in this case, the individual's decision is undoubtedly influenced by the norms of his social system and his need to conform to group pressures. The decision of an individual to begin wearing contact lenses instead of glasses, an Iowa farmer's decision to adopt hybrid corn, and a housewife's adoption of birth control pills are examples of optional decisions.
2. *Collective decisions* are those which individuals in the social system agree to make by consensus. All must conform to the system's decision once it is made. An example is fluoridation of a city's drinking water. Once the community decision is made, the individual has little practical choice but to adopt fluoridated water.
3. *Authority decisions* are those forced upon an individual by someone in a superordinate power position, such as a supervisor in a bureaucratic organization. The individual's attitude toward the innovation is not the prime factor in his adoption or rejection; he is simply told of and expected to comply with the innovation-decision which was made by an authority. Few research studies have yet been conducted of this type of innovation-decision, which must be very common in an organizational society such as the U.S. today. In all authority decisions we must distinguish between (1) the decision maker, who is one (or more) individual(s), and (2) the

adopter or adopters, who carry out the decision. In the case of optional and collective decisions these two roles (of deciding and adopting) are performed by the same individual(s).

These three types of innovation-decisions range on a continuum from optional decisions (where the adopting individual has almost complete responsibility for the decision), through collective decisions (where the adopter has some influence in the decision), to authority decisions (where the adopting individual has no influence in the innovation decision). Collective and authority decisions are probably much more common than optional decisions in formal organizations, such as factories, public schools, or labor unions, in comparison with other fields like agriculture and medicine where innovation-decisions are usually optional.

Generally, the faster rate of adoption of innovations results from authority decisions (depending, of course, on whether the authorities are traditional or modern). In turn, optional decisions can be made more rapidly than the collective type. Although made most rapidly, authority decisions are more likely to be circumvented and may eventually lead to a high rate of discontinuance of the innovation. Where change depends upon compliance under public surveillance, it is not likely to continue once the surveillance is removed.

The type of innovation-decision for a given idea may change or be changed over time. Automobile seat belts, during the early years of their use, were installed in private autos largely as optional decisions. Then in the 1960s many states began to require by law installation of seat belts in all new cars. In 1968 a federal law was passed to this effect. An optional innovation-decision then became a collective decision.

There is yet a fourth type of innovation-decision which is essentially a sequential combination of two or more of the three types we have just discussed. *Contingent deci-*

sions are a choice to adopt or reject which can be made only after a prior innovation-decision. An individual member of a social system is free to adopt or not to adopt a new idea only after his system's innovation-decision. A teacher cannot adopt or reject the use of an overhead projector in his classroom until the school system has decided to purchase one; at that point the teacher can decide to use or reject the overhead projector. In the Punjab State of India hybrid corn adoption is a contingent decision because hybrid corn requires a growing season two weeks longer than open-pollinated varieties, and villagers release their cattle to roam for forage across the unfenced fields once their corn is harvested. One can readily imagine the difficulty of making an optional decision to adopt hybrid corn in the Punjab without a prior collective decision by the entire village.

In recent years, several important studies have explored the innovation process in organizations, where the innovation decision is collective or authoritative in nature.

The innovation process begins with an individual, or a set of individuals, recognizing that their organization is facing a "performance gap" between expectations and reality. This problem recognition sets off a search for alternatives, one of which may be an innovation. The new idea usually comes from outside of the organization and often must be modified somewhat as it is implemented to fit the organization's conditions.

Thus, the innovation process in organizations consists of problem recognition, searching for alternative solutions, matching the innovation with the organization's problem, and implementation of the innovation. This leads eventually to its institutionalization, when it is no longer recognized as a separate element.

26
Marketing Online Services in the University

Douglas Ferguson

Business, scientific, and social information is increasingly becoming available for search and retrieval through online computer networks. However, as the technical capability to search and retrieve information expands, librarians and information specialists face a marketing challenge in making bibliographic and statistical data bases serve the needs of decisionmakers and researchers. This article discusses how applications of marketing concepts can transform the intangibility of information into tangible benefits and make this public good serve the personal needs of people.

Marketing is a new buzzword around the information world. I first heard of marketing information services at a University of Maryland seminar in 1971. Since then, the National Science Foundation's Division of Science Information has supported several marketing studies.

Marketing was a major concern of the Denver Research Institute's study of scientific information in 1975 and marketing was extensively discussed at recent meetings of the National Forum for Scientific and Technical Communication. The 1978 volume of the *Annual Review of Information Science and Technology* will have a chapter on marketing information. What is marketing and what does it have to offer information professionals serving the University Community?

Douglas Ferguson is Head, Data Services, Stanford University Libraries.

FIRST—WHAT MARKETING IS NOT

One thing marketing is *not* is a panacea for under funding, under staffing, and under competence in information service. It is not a substitute for knowing databases; for knowing what they do and do not offer; for knowing effective search techniques; for knowing the interests and concerns of potential as well as actual users and for effective personal service to your clientele. Marketing is not just selling what you have through a publicity blitz. Marketing represents an organized way of offering online services that includes user interests, databases, communication methods, imaginative design of services and products and feedback that improves what you are doing.

A Marketing Perspective. A marketing perspective asks five questions of information services: (1) Who am I trying to reach? (2) What are their interests? (3) What can I create to serve these interests? (4) Under what conditions can I offer services and products? and (5) How can I communicate with my natural audiences, and how can they communicate their needs to me?

Learning From an Early Failure. In 1973 online searching was introduced at one university in the following way. One librarian was trained to search three databases containing engineering information. Announcements were sent to all Engineering faculty at the beginning of the academic year, and another announcement was placed in the library newsletter. A flat fee was charged for each search. Signs were posted in the Engineering library. Searching was done on a terminal in a building two blocks from the library. Almost no provision was made for allocating the librarian's time to work with the service other than doing searching. At the end of each academic term only a handful of faculty and students had used the service. At the end of the academic year the service was discontinued.

What went wrong? Probably many things, but primarily this can be viewed as a failure to ask and answer basic marketing-type questions. Was the service for faculty, for graduate students, for faculty with research grant money, for graduate students preparing to write a dissertation, or for graduate students with access to funding?

How would faculty know about the service without digging out the initial announcement just at the time they were doing work that could benefit from online information? How would anyone know about the service if they didn't come to the library and notice the signs? Did the remoteness of the terminal and the limited personnel time make a potentially fast online service into a slow service in real-time and therefore defeat a major advantage? Did the pricing have any real relationship to the different uses made of the services and the different requirements of various user groups? You can probably think of more questions to ask, but the point is clear. As someone remarked about computer services in general, a badly designed information system just means you get useless information printed faster than you can read it, on tons of printouts that you have no place to store while you are not reading them.

The University is Really a Multiversity. Planning online services is 90% thinking and 10% acting. The place to begin thinking is with your natural clientele. "Selling focuses on the needs of the seller; marketing focuses on the needs of the buyer," says Theodore Levitt, one of the most respected names in marketing theory. No group you are trying to reach is homogeneous; it is composed of smaller, often overlapping, groups that have certain characteristics in common. Marketing specialists call this "market segmentation," but don't think this means attacking your customers with knives. The *common characteristics* of groups within your clientele can be translated into ways of reaching them and into benefits that you can provide.

Librarians in university libraries have been grouping users for years, and it just takes a little refinement to also do it in marketing online services. Traditional groupings are by status (faculty, staff, students) or by department or by academic discipline. Another way to cut the audience pie is by dominant activity, such as research, teaching, administration, or course work. Yet another classification is by task, such as preparing a research grant proposal, preparing a term paper, preparing a doctoral dissertation proposal, or writing a review article. Another grouping might be by access to research or other university funds or presumed ability to pay from personal funds.

A useful basis for segmenting the university market is by purposes for gathering information. Harry Back in a 1972 *Journal of the American Society for Information Science* article derived the list in Exhibit 1 from studies of information usage. These purposes are statements of need, which are benefits to the information seeker when they are met. Almost all of them can be met with some form of online database service. What do these classifications of users and uses suggest when compared to the resources of online databases?

EXHIBIT 1
Purposes for Gathering Information

1. Acquiring ideas for new work

2. Supporting work in progress
   a. Gaining theoretical information
   b. Developing alternative approaches to problems
   c. Results of related work performed by others
   d. Finding answers to specific questions
   e. Recommending procedures, apparatus or methodology
   f. Evaluating an approach or result

3. Keeping current
   a. Being aware of workers in specific areas or problems
   b. Being aware of developments in one's field
   c. Being aware of developments in related fields

4. Developing competence
   a. Brushing up on an old specialty
   b. Learning a new specialty

5. Preparing educational material

Source: (Back, *JASIS,* May–June 1972).

WHAT DO YOU HAVE TO OFFER?

A Nobel prize winner's research grant proposal and a freshman's term paper have one requirement in common. There is a definite and fast approaching deadline. A scholar's review paper and a doctoral student's dissertation have at least one requirement in common; they must comprehensively survey the literature. A humanities scholar and a physics researcher may have one big difference—the physicist has a research grant and the historian doesn't. In the same way, engineering students may have access to department research funds that undergraduate psychology majors do not. These requirements and circumstances, when compared with online capabilities, suggest a wide range of benefits for various groups in your university market.

Analyze Online's Benefits.   Can you deliver a search in a few days that would take weeks to do with laborious copying of citations and photocopying of abstracts? Can you deliver abstracts of recently funded research, of unpublished technical reports, of fugitive conference papers? Can you search interdisciplinary databases that might contain material outside of the researcher's normal reading scope? Can online services be charged to academic department or research accounts? Can you locate a vital reference in minutes that might take days of manual searching to find? Can you identify the "invisible college" working on a new research topic by doing citation searches? Can you dispel the myth of expensive online searching by working out a way to provide undergraduates with computer-produced citation lists for around $10? These are just a few of the benefits that can be translated into services to your clientele. How can you deliver these benefits to the people who want them?

Product and Service Design Scenarios.   Linking people with services doesn't begin with flashy, expensive and time-consuming publicity. It begins with preparing service packages with separate groups in your audience in mind. Once again, the marketing specialists are able to clothe common sense in technical phrases. They call it "product design" and "product differentiation." Most discussions of marketing information focus exclusively on promotion, *but the heart of marketing is designing products for the requirements of separate groups*. This is virtually unexplored territory in university libraries, and offers the possibility of imaginative service and rewarding results. But isn't a database just its contents (citations, statistics or abstracts) printed out and sold or given to someone? That's one way to think about it but not a very productive way.

TRY SEARCH PACKAGES

What about a Dissertation Search Package designed for the weary doctoral candidate struggling to get a proposal accepted by a faculty committee? What about a Research Monitoring Package that offers regular searches during the span of a research grant; so when the final report is ready to be written, the relevant literature is at hand? What about a Proposal Writing Package for the Assistant Professor looking for outside support that will bring a research breakthrough, and tenure, a little bit closer? And what about calling your products by various names that appeal to different groups: *Research Monitoring, The Term Paper Helper, Research Locators, Custom Bibliographies, Computer Assisted Searches*.

There are other benefits you can talk about that are a vital part of online service. Very few searchers can be done without interviewing your customer. This is part of

your service, and it should be made explicit in the package you design. Very few topics submitted for online searching can be searched only in terms of computer sources. If you offer advice on printed sources, include this in your package. Will you help your customers get material that is not at your library or information center? Why hide your interlibrary loan capability under a basket? Say that you will give document delivery assistance. It's one of a library's strongest points. Exhibit 2 gives suggested content and presentation formats for information products you can derive from just a few of the many databases available.

Designing and Delivering Your Message.   The best advertisement is something that does a good job for the people who use it. There are many ways to communicate with your audiences in addition to delivering the online goods. The most common devices are brochures, posters, one-page flyers and use of campus news media. Each university needs to decide how much effort and money it can give to preparing printed material and to personal sales efforts. For printed material you can borrow freely from universities that have already done it. No one copyrights in-house publicity ideas, and most of us are flattered when someone else "steals" a publicity idea from us. Attractive printed items have been prepared by libraries at the University of Kentucky, Oregon State University, Massachusetts Institute of Technology, and the University of California's Computerized Information Services to name just a few.

Consider User Needs First.   In designing printed material be sure the central message starts from what the potential user needs, not from what you happen to have. "Last year 1 million quarter-inch drills were sold," observes Theodore Levitt in *The Marketing Mode,* "not because people wanted quarter-inch drills, but because they wanted quarter-inch holes." Don't offer drills, offer holes. "ORBIT databases available" or "Library offers computer searching" are unlikely to light fires in your audiences. Talk about what ORBIT databases have to offer—"Congress is Online At Your Nearest Library." "Would a bibliography of 15,000,000 Citations Push You Through the Research Barrier?" "Will a Computer Search Help You Get That Paper Done On Time?" If these sound like medicine show signs, no doubt you can improve them. What the customer gets out of online services should be the focus of your message. Well phrased questions often attract attention.

GOOD PLACEMENT IS VITAL

Once you have designed effective brochures and signs what do you do with them? Marketing specialists talk about point-of-*traffic* advertising (e.g. billboard signs on a busy street), point-of-*service* advertising (counter signs in a drug store), and point-of-*need* advertising (water signs at the end of a hiking trail).

EXHIBIT 2
Selected Information Products

Dissertation Proposal Package

This is what you get on convenient 8½ × 11 printed pages:

1. *Previous Dissertations.* A search of American dissertations 1861 to the present in your research area. Often containing literature surveys and bibliographies that can save you weeks of background searching.
2. *Research Reports.* Reports that may never have been published in books or articles. Often containing data and details of methodology that can strengthen your research design.
3. *Journal Articles.* Not just in your own field but research relevant to your topic in related fields and disciplines.
4. *Books and Conference Proceedings.* An interdisciplinary search of recently published books and conference proceedings and references to book reviews.

—*Plus consultation on supplementary searches of printed indexes.*

—*Plus advice on how to locate documents at this library and at libraries throughout the country.*

Grant Proposal Package

To strengthen your request for research support:

1. *Sources of Research Funds.* Listings of foundations and government agencies with names, addresses, funding interest, funds available and more.
2. *Recently Funded Projects.* Search of the only national registry of recent and ongoing projects with information on the researcher, project funds and time periods and often a description of the project.
3. *Reports of Completed Research.* Research reports that may not yet be part of the journal or book literature, including conference papers.
4. *Published Articles and Books.* A comprehensive and multidisciplinary search of recent journal articles, books and published conference proceedings.

—*Delivered to you in a standard, easy to scan, report format in time to meet your proposal deadline.*

Course Support Bibliographies

Custom bibliographies on each major topic in your course: Computer-produced from multidisciplinary databases of journal articles, books, research reports, and conference proceedings.

1. Produced in consultation with a computer search specialist.
2. To complement your reading and course preparation.
3. To assist in updating your lecture material.
4. To prepare recommended lists of readings for students.
5. To check availability in the library and request purchases.
6. May be placed on reserve to help students with papers and projects.

—*A course package can be prepared for you and charged to your authorized department account.*

At Stanford University we used the point-of-need concept by placing signs at printed indexes. "This Index Can Be Computer Searched. Ask At the Desk." A point-of-service sign was placed at most library circulation or reference desks: "Ask Us About Computerized Literature Searching." Small signs tastefully designed went on appropriate department bulletin boards and student lounges: "Computer-

ized Literature Searching Is As Near As Your Library." These are background advertisements that usually stay up indefinitely if they are nicely printed and reasonably small.

Brochures were placed in clear plastic holders in libraries, department lounges, and other department locations.

POSTERS AND BROCHURES DO HALF THE JOB

When we asked a sample of our users how they learned about the library's computer search service, almost half said from posters or brochures. The other half heard about it from librarians or friends. Of course stories in campus newspapers (both official and student) and library and computer center newsletters are helpful, but they need to be done *regularly* because of the changes in the student, faculty and staff populations. Human interest stories that stress successful use of a service by a typical user, including quoted statements can have solid impact. My favorite comment came in a note from a Professor of Education: "It's a great service. I wish the literature were as good as the retrieval."

PERSONALIZED APPROACHES

Mass mailings, personalized letters, telephone solicitations, and free searches for prominent faculty or "opinion leaders" can be successful in achieving a strong response to online services. This is what a well designed library marketing study at Ohio State University showed. However, this is costly in people-time and in material costs. Most universities will want to experiment with small mailings to targeted audiences or to single departments. "Well done demonstrations make the greatest impact," says Peter Watson of California State University at Chico, author of *Computer-Based Reference Service*.

PACE YOUR EFFORTS

Demonstrations can best be done for departments where there are relevant databases and few active users. Don't exhaust yourself and your budget by doing all your personal sales efforts in the first few months of service. Do a small personal mailing or a demonstration, see what the results are, then plan your next promotional move.

Behind Every Desk: A Referral Person. At Stanford, we began with the notion that every person who sits at a public service desk in any library is a potential referral person. With brochures and signs throughout the campus, there were bound to be questions directed to anyone. To make the staff feel comfortable in fielding inquiries and to expand our "sales force" we planned a 30 minute orientation for over 100 librarians and library assistants. We expected that some librarians would do initial screening and select people who could best use printed sources. The staff seemed satisfied to learn about what the new computer search service was.

The effectiveness of this staff referral capability is unclear. The screening process has worked to a limited degree. However, there is still a tendency to immediately refer a person who asks about a computer search to a search specialist. This suggests the need for continuing training and repeat orientations for the library staff.

Personalized Approach Best. A study done at MIT under a National Science Foundation grant compared a variety of direct sales approaches such as an Information Booth at a heavy traffic point, class talks, seminars for departments, mini-searches given free to faculty, and an all-day Information Bazaar. Few libraries have the resources to conduct such an all out effort, but the conclusion came out with a plus for the personal approach: ''People respond best to publicity which is individualized and personally relevant.'' The mechanics of doing a demonstration are very well described in ''Promoting Online Service'' in the January issue of *Online*. Additional personal approaches might be to get a regular list of newly funded grants and contracts from your campus research office and to send the principal investigator an information package. Or arrange with a few departments to get a list of graduate students in the proposal preparation stage and send them an information package. Identifying typical times of need and having standard packages of material and a standard covering letter that can be individually typed can reach a ready audience with a minimum of effort.

MANAGEMENT ISSUES IN MARKETING

Who should plan and execute a library marketing effort? Where do you find the time to do it? How can it be paid for? If there is such a thing as a sales or marketing personality, this is the kind of librarian who should organize and carry out your online service effort. Recruit staff with this in mind as one important factor. You don't have to hire a marketing specialist. Often you can consult with one on the faculty of your business school. Many marketing faculties are cultivating public or nonprofit marketing as a specialty. This is the person to find. At a minimum, read Philip Kotler's book, *Marketing for Nonprofit Organizations*.

Energy From Users. Where do you get the time? You make the time. You squeeze it out of your overcommitments, then when it pays off, argue for a formal allocation of time for personal sales efforts. Don't expect library managers to know how much time and effort it takes. They are usually too busy with budgets, policies, and various crises. You have to do some upward educating based on results you have produced. You will get some energy and uplifted spirits from satisfied customers. ''Librarians report online searching gives them recognition as competent information specialists,'' reports Professor Pauline Atherton of Syracuse University's School of Information Studies after a nationwide tour of research libraries. A short evaluation form with each search package

will give you statistics to buttress your budget requests and, in our experience, produces personally gratifying expressions of satisfaction.

Systems Development Corporation's pioneering study, *Impact of Online Retrieval Services: A Survey of Users, 1974–75*, contained some interesting management views on marketing. Exhibit 3 (from the SDC study) shows the responses of managers in educational organizations to the question, ''Is a SPECIAL 'marketing' program needed to promote your online search services?''

EXHIBIT 3
Managers Views of Need For Marketing

Yes, a full program is needed	27.6%
Yes, a limited program is needed	37.2%
No, word of mouth is sufficient	6.9%
No, normal announcement methods are sufficient	22.1%
No, we do no promote the service	1.4%
No response	4.8%

Industry and Government Responses Similar. Responses of library and information managers in government agencies and corporations were very much the same. These figures mean many things, but at least it shows a majority of managers have a positive view of marketing, although less than a third are fully committed to it. Some of the reasons given for skepticism, such as too few databases, are rapidly disappearing. However, the real costs of marketing as a planning, budgeting, and execution effort can not be discounted.

Pricing: An Important Part of Marketing. Pricing online services is a complex topic that can be touched on only briefly. It is part of marketing, since various pricing schemes can be used to attract customers, and price is one of the major determinants of use—but not the most important one for many potential users. There are at least four ways to price your services:

1. *Token pricing,* in which you set a fixed fee, usually low to encourage maximum use, but enough to discourage frivolous use, such as $5 per search.
2. *Partial cost pricing* allows you to cover some of your costs, typically direct or out-of-pocket expenses. Many university libraries charge only for connect-time and print charges made by service suppliers.
3. *Full cost pricing* allows you to recover all of your direct and indirect costs. With full cost pricing, you can cover all marketing costs.
4. *Loss leader pricing* means giving a search for free or for very little cost with the expectation that individuals will be repeat customers and tell other people about the service.

There is a need for more experimentation with various pricing schemes to establish price elasticity for certain groups (such as undergraduates) and for certain types of service, such as ''rush'' searches.

Results Are a Two Way Street. There are no hard and fast guidelines yet on what works in what situations. We are in an era where we can try the approaches that *might* work and then retain those that *do* work. Marketing research, using the sophisticated tools of sample surveys and semantic differentials, may have a place in the future of online services. The resources are not now available at most universities. For some time, marketing may remain essentially a pragmatic discipline, like diagnostic medicine. This leaves scope for innovation and outstanding individual effort.

The Limiting Factor—Our Own Minds.   Some libraries have a brief evaluation form that helps them improve the service and also asks how the individual learned about the service and if they would use it again. Online services are a new level of customized information service for unversity libraries, who typically do not do literature searches for faculty and students. Online searching takes longer than most reference questions. Decisions will have to be made about use of professional time and how important online services are in relation to other services.

No doubt there will be different mixes of service that will be established, and it will take years to fully integrate online services into the university's information repertoire. Josh Smith of Herner and Herner once remarked that libraries are good at serving their users, but not at serving their markets. A striking result reported by some libraries who have introduced online services is that people who never used library services before are now active users. Online services can be a natural part of a full range of information services offered by libraries, information centers, and information entrepreneurs. Right now, most of the limits may be in our own minds and not in the minds of our users.

27

Consumer Behavior and Health Care Change: The Role of Mass Media

Thomas S. Robertson
Lawrence H. Wortzel

Mass media have considerable potential for affecting health behavior. The pervasiveness of mass media and the exposure levels of broad segments of society suggest that mass media may be an important *information source* regarding health and a relevant *socialization force* regarding health attitudes and behavior. Nevertheless, research evidence indicates that most mass media campaigns oriented toward changing health care habits fail. The objectives of this paper are to analyze *why* health care campaigns fail and to derive generalizations for more effective use of mass media by health care professionals.

The role of mass media in affecting knowledge, attitudes, and behavior toward health care may be thought of in terms of the following two dimensions.

1. Mass media may impact health knowledge, attitudes and behavior both in a *deliberate* sense through "campaigns" that are specifically designed for such impact, and in an *unintended* or "incidental learning" sense through material that contains health-related information, but which is not specifically intended to impact health knowledge, attitudes or behavior.
2. In both cases, mass media may act either as a "change agent" or as a "reinforcing agent"—that is, media may function in such a way as to *change* knowledge, attitudes and behavior or to *confirm* existing behavior patterns. In these respects, the role of mass

Thomas S. Robertson is Professor of Marketing, The Wharton School, University of Pennsylvania.

Lawrence H. Wortzel is Professor of Marketing, Boston University.

media in affecting health care is similar to their role in affecting knowledge, attitudes and behavior toward other products and services.

CAMPAIGN VERSUS UNINTENDED EFFECTS

Mass media *campaigns* are intended to communicate certain health care information with a view toward change in health habits. Examples include anti-smoking, seat belt usage, lower cholesterol, and hypertension identification campaigns.

Mass media may also have unintended effects in the sense that the average viewer is exposed to a regular diet of "medical" shows on television and also to large numbers of commercials for proprietary medicines. The learning from such programming and commercials may be in the form of "misinformation" and may not be compatible with good health habits. A national study by the Louis Harris Organization (1973), for example, concluded that mass media were second only to the individual's physician as a source of health information. Furthermore, much of the health information absorbed from television is likely to be under low involvement conditions and, therefore, processed without evaluation.

A logical question then is whether mass media depict an accurate profile of health, illness, and the value of medical services, drug products, or medical treatment. Some social critics suggest that mass media depict a distorted and stereotyped view of these topics with consequences for people's health beliefs, attitudes and behavior and for their probabilities of accessing the medical system under specified conditions. For example, to what extent does advertising for proprietary drugs convince people to search for simplistic solutions to medical symptoms that may be indicative of more serious problems? To what extent does cigarette advertising help people to deny or sublimate the medically dangerous effects of smoking?

The extent to which mass media either positively or negatively impact health is an important empirical question requiring systematic evidence to resolve. One study of television programming found that 30 percent of the health-related information was "useful" while the remaining 70 percent was inaccurate or misleading or both (Smith, 1972). This may suggest the magnitude of the potential problem, although this study is only one isolated piece of research evidence. Another study (Frazier et al., 1974) of dental health avertisements concluded that 43 percent of the information is inaccurate, misleading, or fallacious. The hypothesis may well be that mass media act more to misinform than to educate people about health and appropriate health habits.

CHANGE AGENT OR REINFORCING AGENT

The potential of mass media communications in the health care arena is generally phrased in terms of their promise for *changing* habits and life styles. However, the history of communication research indicates that the most persistent finding is that mass media act mainly to *reinforce* existing attitudes and behavior.

The ability of mass media to effect change is actually a function of a number of factors and requires certain conditions which we will develop later in this paper. Basically, however, the probability of *change* tends to be a function of how much commitment people have to existing behavior patterns. Under high commitment conditions, as is frequently the case in health care, bringing about change may indeed be a difficult undertaking. This is likely to be the case since health behavior is frequently rooted both in long term reinforcement patterns and in support by the individual's social environment. (In some special cases physical and psychological addiction patterns may also be a factor with which to

contend.) A look at the evidence on health care campaigns supports the statement that most health care campaigns do not succeed among large numbers of intended subjects. The literature is replete with discouraging case studies.

1. *Obesity.* In summarizing the evidence on obesity Stunkard (1975), sets forth five propositions: (1) most obese people do not enter treatment, (2) of those who do, most drop-out, (3) of those who remain, most do not lose much weight, (4) of those who lose weight most will regain it, and (5) many of those entering treatment pay a high emotional price. Nevertheless, Stunkard registers considerable hope based on behavior modification programs, which recently have improved the treatment of obesity. He implicitly rejects mass media as an important force in changing behavior.

2. *Smoking.* Anti-smoking campaigns have had limited success, at best. Cigarette consumption has not declined, despite communication campaigns and public policy initiatives protecting non-smokers. In fact, it is increasing among teenagers, especially among girls. However, there has been a change toward consumption of lower tar and nicotine cigarettes. Perhaps the consequence of messages about lower tar and nicotine cigarettes has been to convince smokers that smoking is becoming safer.

On the other hand, one potentially successful anti-smoking campaign was initiated, when counter-advertising messages were shown on television under the equal time provision of the Federal Communications Commission. Possibly the combination of smoking and counter-smoking commercials presented together acted similarly to a two-sided communication; however, it is unlikely that mass media counter-advertising alone accomplished the job.

3. *Seat Belts.* In a review of research on seat belt usage campaigns, Leon Robertson (1974) *et al.*, report a general lack of positive results. These authors then initiated a well controlled experimental study using split-cable television whereby one audience received messages advocating seat belt use and a matched audience on the other half of the cable did not receive messages. After a nine month period tracking actual seat belt usage behavior, the authors could only conclude that: "The campaign had no measured effect whatsoever on safety belt use" (p. 1077).

4. *Community Fluoridation Programs.* Despite endorsement by the U.S. Public Health Service and the Surgeon General, controlled fluoridation of community water supplies has more often been rejected than accepted by voters. Between 1950 and 1969, 1,139 communities voted on fluoridation; the issue lost in 666 communities and won in 473 (HEW, 1970). One part of the difficulty is the complexity of the fluoridation issue and another part is voters' susceptibility to the fear appeals used by opponents.

5. *Health Maintenance Organizations.* Despite the advantages claimed for the HMO concept, enrollment campaigns have met with limited success—with a few notable exceptions (primarily the Kaiser plan). Perhaps the HMO concept is not as desirable as its advocates claim (Glasgow, 1972) or perhaps the benefits to consumers are not readily apparent and communication campaigns have underestimated the difficulties of changing medical behavior patterns.

6. *Heart Disease.* The most encouraging results on a mass media campaign are from the Stanford study conducting a program to reduce susceptibility to heart disease among residents of three communities. Instructional programs used in conjunction with mass media have documented attitudinal and behavioral changes in diet and cigarette smoking. The role of mass media alone in one community on a delayed continuity basis is almost as effective as the personal instruction-mass media combination (Maccoby and Farquhar, 1975). The cost-effectiveness of this campaign, however, is very much in question.

WHY HEALTH CAMPAIGNS FAIL, AND HOW TO HELP THEM SUCCEED

Analysis of the foregoing and other campaigns indicates that there are some basic reasons why most health care campaigns fail. These reasons may be summarized as follows:

1. Most health care campaigns operate without explicit objectives or with inappropriate or unrealistic objectives, probably because they are based on an inadequate understanding of the way mass communications work, and on an inadequate understanding of the marketing requirements of the ''product'' being promoted.
2. Most health care campaigns are non-programmatic; they are short-run, one-time efforts, while the behavior change they are designed to induce must continue in the long run.
3. The beneficial effects of the recommended behavior change are not immediately apparent to the consumer, and perhaps never will be.
4. Most health care campaigns fail to identify market segments within the total audience who require different communication approaches in line with their specific needs.

SETTING OBJECTIVES AND ASSIGNING A ROLE TO THE MASS MEDIA

It is not sufficient to seek knowledge change or attitude change without a mechanism for also achieving behavior change and it is difficult for the mass media to achieve behavior change. For example: most smokers have *knowledge* of the ill effects of smoking and may have a negative *attitude* toward smoking. Therefore, presenting them with more knowledge as to the negative effects of smoking is unlikely to have much impact. Instead, a communication campaign must be linked to a behavior change mechanism other than mass communications (such as behavior modification group enrollment) if the campaign is to be successful. But behavior change even so induced is unlikely to persist in the long run unless its beneficial effects are continuously reinforced, since the beneficial results from the behavior change are not apparent in the short run and since there may also be some gratifications attached to the previous behavior.

Although non-smoking is a regularly repurchased ''product,'' this is a different marketing situation from the usual consumer packaged goods situation in which advertising is used to achieve trial, and in which reinforcement from use of the product is a significant force is accomplishing continuing use of the product. An important function of mass communications in changing health behavior must be to *reinforce* new behavior, since use of the ''product'' is insufficient reinforcement in itself. Fortunately, this is a role which mass media have continually demonstrated an ability to perform well. Nevertheless, behavior change must be accomplished first, and by means other than mass media.

As we have noted, most health campaigns are short-run, start and stop efforts, with little long-term systematic and programmatic planning. Yet, changing health is likely to involve both multiple channels of persuasion and regular long term reinforcement. In summary, people must be moved through a decision sequence which is likely to take some significant amount of time and different means of persuasion may have complementary and cumulative impact, and may be necessary to achieve persistent behavior change.

SEGMENTATION

Most health care campaigns try to reach everyone. Yet, not all segments of the market are as likely to change and different segments may require different incentives for change. It is incumbent on the change agent to specify the market segments likely to be receptive to change and to expect that different messages focused on different needs may be effective with different demographic and psychographic segments.

Examination of needs by segment may be mandatory. For example: smoking provides gratification for smokers; it fulfills certain needs. These needs may relate to anxiety patterns or may be tied to social interaction patterns (Wortzel and Clarke, 1977). Programs to help reduce smoking, we might argue, should help find alternatives for the continued satisfaction of these needs. Basically, if we are to change health we must do so in line with people's needs. It does little good to scare people, insult people, etc., except under certain extreme conditions. Changed health patterns must be shown to be in line with the audience's self-perceived needs.

Segmentation is also critical if mass media are used to support a campaign in which behavior change has been accomplished by other means. Reaching the yet unchanged will be wasteful, if not counter-productive in light of possible future efforts. It is essential to reach the changed in order to reinforce the behavior changing mechanism.

CONCLUSION

Following is a set of tentative propositions for the successful design and implementation of health care campaigns.

1. Mass media communication by itself may be effective in initiating change, but generally only if the change sought is minor and consumers have low information needs. This is seldom the case in health care.
2. Mass media communication will generally be most effective at an early point in the health decision change process whereas personal sources will generally be most effective later in the decision change process.
   a. Mass media communication objectives, therefore, must be tied toward encouraging people to access the professional health care system, or to sensitize them to other sources of communication.
   b. The peer and professional system will constitute the subsequent supporting mechanism necessary to bring about actual change.
3. It is the cumulative effect of a communication campaign that eventually results in behavior change.
   a. This indicates the need for repetition and reinforcement over time. Reinforcement of health change is a particularly important role for mass media.
   b. This indicates the need for multiple information sources which play complementary roles—including advertising, personal selling, peer support, and professional intervention.
4. Peer sources (personal influence) will be a particularly important source of legitimation and ''reality testing'' when the benefits of change are not obvious or cannot be demonstrated in the short run. This is likely to be the case in much of health care.
5. Communication campaigns for health care—even when they make use of donated public media time and space—are not free. The real cost is the opportunity cost if the communication campaign could have been more successful.
6. A health care communication campaign must explicity recognize the problem of selective perception—that those who see the message may be those who are already concerned about the issue and engaging in recommended change activities.
7. A communication campaign may have to provide support for change within a family or peer group context. Obesity, for ex-

ample, may be tied to family diet habits and change may depend on family involvement.

8. Communication messages must be keyed to the needs of the market segment being reached. It is necessary to offer positive alternatives and not simply to denigrate the individual's existing health habits.

9. Low returns should be expected in a communication campaign. Most advertising and persuasion seeks small levels of change—in the range of 3 to 5 percent of the audience per year. Mass conversion in the short-run is indeed a rare phenomenon.

REFERENCES

Frazier, P. Jean; Jenny, Joanna; Ostman, Ron, and Frenick, Charles. "Quality of Information in Mass Media: A Barrier to the Dental Health Education of the Public." *Journal of Public Health Dentistry* 34 (Fall 1974) 244–57.

Glasgow, John M. "Prepaid Group Practice as a National Health Policy: Problems and Perspectives." *Inquiry,* 9 (September 1972) 3–15.

Harris Organization, Louis. A study cited in *The Report of the President's Committee on Health Education*, New York, 1973.

HEW. *Fluoridation Census 1969,* Bethesda, MD: U.S. Dept. of HEW, 1970.

Maccoby, Nathan, and Farquhar, John W. "Bringing the California Health Report Up to Date." *Journal of Communication* 26 (Winter 1976) 56–67.

———. "Communication for Health: Unselling Heart Disease." *Jurnal of Communication* 25 (Summer 1975) 114–26.

Robertson, Leon S.; Kelley, Albert B.; O'Neill, Brian; Wixom, Charles W.; Eiswirth, Richard S., and Haddon, William. "A Controlled Study of the Effect of Television Messages on Safety Belt Use." *American Journal of Public Health* 64 (November 1974) 1071–80.

Smith, Frank A.; Trivaz, Goeffrey; Zuehlke, David A.; Lowinger, Paul, and Nghiem, Thieu L. "Health Information During a Week of Television." *New England Journal of Medicine* 286 (March 2, 1972) 516–20.

Stunkard, Albert J. "Presidential Address—1974: From Explanation to Action in Psychosomatic Medicine: The Case of Obesity. *Psychosomatic Medicine.* 37 (May–June 1975) 195–236.

Wortzel, Lawrence H., and Clarke, Roberta. "Environmental Protection for the Non-Smoker: Consumer Behavior Aspects of Encouraging Non-Smoking." *Advances in Consumer Research*, Vol. V, Association for Consumer Research, 1978.

28

Marketing National Change: Decimalization in Britain

Christopher H. Lovelock

What happens when an entire country has to change its way of doing things? An analysis of the 1966–1971 program for decimalizing the British currency provides valuable insights into the role of the different elements of the marketing mix in helping to facilitate a major societal change. It also highlights the tasks facing an official change agency in managing and coordinating such a program. Parallels are drawn to current programs for the metrication of weights and measures.

Government organizations are increasingly finding themselves cast in the role of change agencies. In order to achieve social, economic, or environmental objectives, it is sometimes necessary for large numbers of citizens to modify or discard old ways of doing things and to adopt new ones.

Recent examples of dramatic national changes in industrialized countries include the 1967 Swedish switch from driving on the left to driving on the right [3, 6]; the adoption of decimal currencies by Australia, New Zealand, and the United Kingdom between 1966 and 1971 [1, 7, 10]; and current programs in Australia, Britain, Canada, the United States, and elsewhere to replace customary systems of measurement with the metric system [9].

However, even more modest programs may require careful coordination by a central agency to be successful.

Christopher H. Lovelock is Associate Professor of Business Administration, Harvard University.

The assistance of the Central Office of Information and the J. Walter Thompson Company is gratefully acknowledged. Unless otherwise specified, the views expressed are those of the author.

In 1976, the United States Treasury Department attempted to reintroduce the two-dollar bill into general circulation [8]. By replacing half the 1.6 billion one-dollar bills printed annually with an equivalent value of "twos," it hoped to save $35 million in printing costs over a five year period. Yet the two-dollar bill has so far failed to find acceptance in the U.S. This failure reflects the apparent inability of the Treasury and the Federal Reserve System to develop and fund a coordinated marketing strategy for reintroduction, although they had the results of a detailed study of consumers, retailers, and bankers available to guide them [2].

In this article, we shall examine a much more complex task—namely, the replacement of an existing currency system with an entirely new one. Apart from its intrinsic interest, an evaluation of the successful British decimalization program of 1966–71 provides some valuable insights into the planning and management of large-scale changes in established practices. It also highlights the role of an official change agency in facilitating such changes through judicious use of marketing.

THE PROBLEM IN PERSPECTIVE

On February 15, 1971, the United Kingdom officially went decimal. In a program described as "the biggest monetary operation in the history of the world," the old currency of 12 pence to a shilling and 20 shillings to a pound was abandoned for a new decimal currency of 100 new pence to a pound.[1]

Since money is used by almost everyone, this dramatic change affected the daily lives of practically everybody in a nation of over fifty million people. Almost overnight, it seemed, a coinage with a twelve-hundred-year background was replaced with some five billion units of a new one that had a different value and appearance but a similar name. And yet, this seemingly momentous switch came to be referred to as the "non-event of 1971"—confounding the many critics who had predicted chaos.

How was such a smooth and successful operation achieved in the face of significant public antipathy? Many factors contributed, but the key element in facilitating the changeover was undoubtedly the marketing strategy adopted by the official Decimal Currency Board and its advisers.

Most major marketing programs are directed at specific segments within the population, and their originators are generally satisfied to achieve desired changes in attitudes, behavior, or purchasing patterns among only a fraction of the target audience. Consumer goods marketers are often contented with seeing their products purchased by only a small percentage of potential consumers; a politician may be glad to obtain 50.1% of all votes cast in a two-way election race. But for the decimalization campaign to be successful, it had to encourage virtually an entire population to change its behavior. In the long run, there could be no personal choice about whether to work in decimals *or* in the old currency. Everyone had to change sooner or later, since the old coins— and the calculations based on them—were to be phased out. The challenge was to see that the desired adaptation to the new currency took place as quickly as possible, with minimum public confusion or dislocation of business.

THE DECISION TO DECIMALIZE

A feature in the conservative *Sunday Telegraph* on January 3, 1971, just six weeks before "D Day" ("Decimal Day"), reflected the bemusement felt by many citizens concerning the way in which decimalization had finally caught up with them:

---

[1] Under the old system £1 = 20 shillings = 240 pence, and 1 shilling = 12 pence; under the new system £1 = 100 new pence (the pound remained unchanged). At the time of decimalization in 1971, the Pound Sterling was worth $2.40 in U.S. currency. Thus one (old) penny was exactly equivalent to 1¢ and one shilling to 12¢. Under the new system, one new penny was equal in value to 2.4¢. The abbreviation £sd was widely used to denote pounds, shillings and pence and was for years referred to in colloquial speech as "LSD." The use of the £ sign, a fanciful "L," was derived from the Latin "libra" (a pound), while the "d" for penny came from the Latin "denarius," a small Roman coin. With the advent of decimal currency, new pence were designated "p."

There remains to this day a certain mystery about how a nation so [unkindly] disposed to [decimals], a nation moreover habitually accused of excessive attachment to historic institutions such as its own venerable currency, came to acquiesce with apparent calm in the abandonment of pounds, shillings and pence in favour of the decimal system which will invade its life on February 15. . . .

Needless to say, there had been no perceptible demand from the general public for the change. However, the idea took root [in government circles] in a way that it had signally failed to do hitherto, in spite of the efforts of interested minorities during upwards of two centuries to plant it there.

In practice there were several forces at work. In the early 1960s, three major trends combined to bring about decimalization in Britain. Since the Second World War, a growing number of other Commonwealth countries had successfully abandoned pounds, shillings, and pence (£sd) for new decimal currencies, or else had announced their intention of doing so. Another significant development was Britain's growing trade and tourist links with already decimalized countries, particularly in Europe. Tourists especially found the British currency hard to use and to understand. The third major incentive for change concerned the rapid mechanization of accounting and cash handling procedures, which could not be used to their full advantage with a £sd system.

A Marketing Framework for Decimalization. How should one go about introducing a new currency in an economically stable, highly industrialized democracy of some fifty million people? Several major considerations faced the British Government in developing and implementing an appropriate program for change.

The key problem was the need to design a new decimal currency. In a three-tier currency system, where twelve pence equaled one shilling, and twenty shillings equaled one pound, decimalization necessarily involved the disappearance of at least two of the existing units. The unresolved question in the past had always been, which? Once the basis of decimalization had been selected, there were what might be termed "packaging" decisions to be made, relating to the names selected for the new monetary units, the denominations in which coins and bills were to be issued, and the physical appearance of the new currency.

Conversion to decimals would involve financial costs for business and a certain amount of effort and inconvenience for individual citizens. The Government had to decide whether it should pay compensation to businesses and how it could minimize the time and psychic costs to individuals. In part, the answer would lie in judicious use of advertising, personal selling, publicity, and sales promotion. The problem was to design an appropriate campaign, directed at all types of businesses, cash handlers and the public, that would explain the rationale for the changeover and provide each target segment with the information needed to make the change to decimals smoothly and at the appropriate time.

Since money is used so widely, there would be a significant distribution problem in getting the new coins rapidly into circulation wherever money changed hands. A related problem was to ensure that all coin-operated and accounting machines were quickly converted to decimals. Clearly, market research would be needed to provide insights into these problems and to facilitate evaluation of alternative strategies designed to resolve them.

PRODUCT DECISIONS: DESIGNING THE NEW DECIMAL CURRENCY

In December 1961, the Government announced the appointment of a Committee of Inquiry under the Earl of Halsbury, a distinguished scientist and administrator, to advise on the method, timing, and cost of decimalization. In a very real sense, the Halsbury Committee's principal task was one of product design. As can be seen from Exhibit 1, there are a variety of alternative ways of transforming a £sd

system into a decimal one, and some important considerations involved. The question was, which approach would yield the most enduring benefits, while minimizing the problems of changeover? The table lists the eight most plausible alternatives. In September 1963, by a majority of four to two, the Committee recommended adoption of the £-cent-½ system [11]. The minority recommended a 10s-cent system (as adopted in Australia, New Zealand, and South Africa).

A lengthy delay ensued, due in part to a change of government. Finally, on March 1, 1966, two weeks after successful introduction of a decimal currency in Australia [1], the British Government formally announced its decision to adopt a decimal currency, with the official changeover scheduled for February 1971. The pound was to be retained as the major unit, and divided into 100 "new pence." (The name "new penny" (p) was chosen for the minor unit instead of "cent," since it was felt that the latter would be unpopular because of its foreign associations.) The coins and notes selected for the new system—designated as £p—are listed in Exhibit 2 with their £sd predecessors.

The final product-related decision was taken the following year and concerned the size, shape, and metal of the new coins, as well as their design. Bronze was selected for the new 2p, 1p, and ½p coins, continuing the tradition of the

---

EXHIBIT 1
Some Decimalization Problems

1. Basis of Decimalization

(a) Old System:
12 pennies (d) = 1 shilling(s); 20 shillings = 1 pound (£)

(b)

Principal decimal alternatives	Terminology	Previous adopters
1 major unit of 200 subunits	£-cent-½	
1 major unit of 1,000 subunits	£-mil	Cyprus
10s major unit of 100 subunits	10s-cent	Australia, New Zealand, South Africa Ghana
8s 4d major unit of 100 pence	100-penny	
5s major unit of 100 subunits	Crown-cent	
4s 2d major unit of 100 half-pence	100-ha'penny	British West Indies
2s major unit of 100 subunits	Florin-cent	
1s major unit of 100 subunits	Shilling-cent	

(c) Some Considerations

Retention of old upper unit (pound)
Retention of old lower unit (penny or halfpenny)
Easy conversion of old middle unit (shilling) to new system (1s = 10¢ in 10s-cent system)
Extent to which present coins and/or notes can be used
Impact of any change on inflation (size of smallest monetary unit)
Preservation of confidence in the currency
Continuity of record-keeping
Two spaces vs. three spaces after decimal point/avoidance of fractions
Integration of old and new currencies during changeover period

2. Naming the New Currency

Need for public acceptance
Preservation of tradition vs. creation of new tradition
Avoidance of confusion, both domestically and internationally

3. Design of New Coinage

Choice of denominations
Size/shape/design/metal for new coins (identification, handling, acceptance)

EXHIBIT 2
The Old and New Currencies

		New (£p)	Old (£sd)	Name
Notes		£20[1]	—	
		£10	£10	
		£ 5	£ 5	
		£ 1	£ 1	
Circulating Coins:		50p (= 10s)	10s (= 50p)	
		10p (= 2s)	2s6d (= 12½p)	Half-crown
			2s (= 10p)	Two shillings (or florin)
		5p (= 1s)	1s (= 5p)	Shilling
			6d (= 2½p)	Sixpence
		2p[2] (= 4.8d)	3d[3] (= 1.25p)	Threepence
		1p[2] (= 2.4d)		
		½p[2] (= 1.2d)		
			1d[3] (= 0.42p)	Penny
			½d[3] (= 0.21p)	Ha'penny

---

[1] This new note was not part of the decimalization program. Its introduction simply reflected the need for a higher denomination banknote.

[2] No exact £sd equivalent.

[3] No exact £p equivalent.

old penny and halfpenny. One innovation was to adopt a weight-to-value relationship for these coins, such that 1p weighed twice as much as ½p and 2p weighed four times as much. In this way, cash handlers could simply weigh a bag of mixed bronze coinage to determine its value. The cupronickel ("silver") 5p and 10p coins were to retain the same weight, size and metal specifications as the equal value 1s and 2s coins they replaced, while a new seven-sided 50p coin was announced in 1968 to replace the equal value 10s note. Higher value notes were unaffected by decimalization and remained unchanged. Like current American coins, the old British coins displayed their face values in words. To simplify identification, especially for foreign visitors, the designs of the new coins incorporated their values in prominent numerals.

FORMATION OF THE DECIMAL CURRENCY BOARD

In 1966, the government established a Decimal Currency Board (DCB) to plan and coordinate the decimalization program. The Board's function was to "examine in detail, with the institutions concerned, the problems of the changeover, to organize a programme of guidance to the public, and to do everything necessary to promote a speedy and efficient transition." [10, p. 60].

The concerns of the Decimal Currency Board were broadly threefold: the logistics of the changeover, the education of people and organizations concerning the switch to decimal currency, and the resolution of any resulting problems. Underlying its work was a continuing program of investigation, consultation, and research.

Named as Chairman of the DCB was Lord Fiske of Brent, a former Leader of the Greater London Council. Lord Fiske's personality, experience and appearance were all well suited to the increasingly exposed role he was to fill. A big, bearlike, avuncular man with a long record of public service, he projected an image of good humor and unflappability.

THE STRATEGY OF CHANGEOVER

The five-year preparatory period prior to D Day emphasized the amount of work that had to be done. The biggest physical task—and one requiring early action by manufacturers—was conversion or replacement of machines. Some 2.3 million business machines and cash registers and 2.7 million coin-operated machines were affected by decimalization. In addition, five billion new coins had to be minted, and some existing coins had to be withdrawn from circulation.

The DCB's strategy was to spread the publicity effort over a three year period, 1968 to 1971. It concentrated first on informing business management about decimalization and encouraging early and systematic planning for the changeover. Then it turned its attention to retail and other cash-handling organizations, emphasizing the need for full and detailed preparations. Finally, it explained the new system

and coinage to the general public, so that people could go shopping with confidence from February 15, 1971, onwards.

In its *First Annual Report* the Board outlined the role it expected to play in the communications effort, noting that

> Many other organisations besides the Board will be issuing publicity and educational material about decimal currency. We welcome this because we cannot alone persuade over 50 million people in Britain to change the money habits of a lifetime. We are always willing to help organisations to prepare publicity and training material. . . . The publicity campaign is a team effort but we are glad to act as coordinators [4, pp. 1–2].

In late 1967 the Decimal Currency Board appointed the London office of the J. Walter Thompson Company (JWT) to handle its advertising account. JWT was to work closely with the Central Office of Information—a Government office which exercised a centralized, coordinating function for all Government advertising—and with the DCB's own Publicity Group.

The advertising agency's main tasks were creation of advertisements and media selection and buying; in addition, its market research subsidiary undertook consumer surveys at various stages in the campaign. The DCB handled its own, very extensive, public relations activity. Looking back some years later, the former secretary of the DCB reflected:

> The early appointment of an agency was important for, although it soon became established policy that the main advertising campaign should be reserved until the final weeks, a good deal of careful forward planning had to be done; there were also general advertising campaigns on several aspects of the Board's campaign for businessmen; and a programme of regular research surveys was carried out so that the Board would be aware of what people knew of and thought about the changeover. The early appointment also ensured that the Board and agency staff . . . were able to build up a close and informal working relationship which was conducive to the interchange of ideas [10, p. 182].

Encouraging Early Planning by Business. The Board moved quickly to establish some priorities:

> The immediate need is to convince management, in the widest sense of that word, that they face problems which they should be seeking to solve now rather than in 1970—not because these problems are great but because, if they are tackled early, they can be solved with comparative ease [4, p. 15].

For decimalization to go smoothly, businesses had to plan well in advance for conversion or replacement of the machines they operated, to draw up new accounting conventions, to develop revised cash-handling procedures, and to retrain certain personnel.

In what was termed the Management Campaign, the DCB emphasized use of publications, particularly reference booklets and newsletters. In all, 11 reference booklets were published between 1968–1970. All booklets had an initial free distribution of about 60,000 copies through trade associations, with additional copies thereafter being sold through government bookstores and retail booksellers. Some 3.75 million booklets were distributed in this way. The DCB *Newsletter* was issued at approximately six—week intervals and by

1970 had a print run of some 275,000 copies, with around 140,000 being distributed to trade and other associations for circulation to their members and the balance going to a subscription list, sent out in response to inquiries, or distributed at meetings.

The Board's most direct contact with the business community was through its extensive program of speaking engagements. These were often reported in local newspapers, which greatly widened their audience. The DCB also participated in many exhibitions and issued news releases with information of interest to business managers.

Marketing Decimals to Cash-Handling Organizations. A second major thrust of the Board's educational and promotional work was directed at retailers, transport operators, and other cash handlers, with 1969–70 being promoted as the "Year of the Retailer." The Board developed close links with trade and professional associations in order to ensure a frank, two-way flow of ideas and suggestions. Formal surveys of management and retailers provided periodic feedback on levels of preparedness for decimalization and indications of problem areas.

Recognizing the problem of reaching small shopkeepers, many of whom were not members of trade associations, a variety of media were employed to convey the Board's message to retailers. Press advertising was done in national and provincial papers and in 52 trade publications; postal franking messages were used to get the attention of those operating small businesses; and 1.6 million copies of a popularly written booklet entitled *New Money in Your Shop* were distributed free through banks to all businesspeople having cash transactions with the general public. A special film about retailing aspects of the decimal changeover was produced for free loan to Chambers of Commerce, trade associations, clubs, and other business groups: it proved very successful. Other audiovisual messages appeared over BBC (the government-owned British Broadcasting Corporation) television. These consisted of four short public-service films of interest to retailers, plus a series of five BBC-TV programs entitled *Decimal Shop*, aimed at helping retailers prepare for D Day. Rounding out the Board's communications with re-tailers was a series of 12 syndicated articles for the trade press which appeared in about 350 journals. In addition, trade pub-lications ran many articles of their own on issues relating to decimalization, and several books were published on the topic.

Preparing the General Public for the Changeover. In spite of this early managerial focus, the general public was not being neglected in the years preceeding D Day. For both logistical and educational reasons, the DCB had decided on a phased withdrawal of £sd coins and notes and introduction of new decimal coins over a period of several years, as follows:

April 1968—Introduce 5p and 10p coins (exactly equivalent in size, metal and value to the existing one-shilling and two-shilling coins).

Aug. 1969—Withdraw the old ½d (halfpenny) coin.
Oct. 1969— Introduce the 50p coin—equivalent in value to the ten shilling note—and withdraw all 10s notes.
Dec. 1969—Withdraw the half-crown (2s6d) coin.
Feb. 1971— Introduce ½p, 1p and 2p coins, and begin withdrawal, over a period of up to 18 months, of 1d, 3d and 6d coins.

The Board insisted that:

Each coinage change must be carefully presented to the public, through Press advertising and other means, and its relevance to the general operation explained. By adopting this approach, we hope people can accustom themselves to decimal currency in easy stages [4, p. 15].

The general publicity campaign began on February 15, 1968, with the announcement that D Day would be in exactly three years' time (February being selected as a month of low retail sales activity, with a Monday being chosen so the weekend could be used for final preparations). That same day, the Royal Mint released the designs of all decimal coins but the 50p piece. From then on, the Board planned to maintain a steady flow of news, building to a peak in early 1971.

Half-page newspaper advertisements introduced the 5p and 10p coins in April 1968. Special copy was produced for use in children's periodicals. These initial advertisements set the style (described by the Board as "reassuring and authoritative but with a light touch of friendly informality" and by a journalist critic as "faintly patronising") for subsequent Board advertising to the general public. One of these initial advertisements was chosen by the Gallup Field Readership Index as "Ad of the Month," achieving higher reading and noting scores than any other half-page newspaper advertisement in the Index's 21-year history. Similar but smaller advertisements in 1969 announced the introduction of the 50p coin, the withdrawal of the ten-shilling note, and the demonetization of the half-crown.

Two of these changes resulted in public outcries, which the press covered with enthusiasm. The new seven-sided 50p coin was initially very controversial; a newspaper survey reported that 75% of respondents were opposed to what was, for them, a strange-looking coin with a very high value ($1.20). But the government resisted demand for withdrawal of the new coin; after nine months, surveys showed 53% of respondents favoring the new coin and only 7% preferring the old 10s note. Another controversy later arose over the DCB's proposal to withdraw the sixpence, a popular and widely used little coin which converted to 2½p in decimals. Faced with emotional campaigns to "Save the Sixpence" and polls with loaded research questions "proving" that 80% of the population wanted to retain this coin, the government finally overruled the DCB and allowed the coin to stay.

From February 1968 onwards, the DCB made regular use of the British Market Research Bureau's continuous consumer survey. Questions on decimalization were added to the survey every two to four months, revealing long-term trends in public awareness and attitudes. Individual questions were added as needed to investigate specific problem areas.

The Preparatory Campaign. This research confirmed the need for a preparatory advertising campaign to provide basic facts on decimalization and to dispel misconceptions and anxiety. The findings showed that the elderly and less well educated were the least informed segments of the population. It also showed that many women were concerned about prices and shopping.

So between July and November 1970, informative and reassuring advertisements were placed in a wide range of women's magazines, social and welfare publications, and selected religious periodicals. The campaign was supplemented by distribution to local authorities and citizens' advice bureaus of 300,000 posters in four different designs, and of ten million single-page leaflets. Additionally, 500,000 booklets entitled *Decimal Money: Some Questions and Answers* were prepared as a reference source for workers in local welfare departments, women's groups, and welfare-oriented voluntary organizations.

During 1970, a modest level of advertising and publicity was also directed at the general public. A 25-minute color film, *Granny Gets the Point,* prepared by the Central Office of Information, received thousands of showings across the country during the months to D Day, and was also widely shown on television.

THE FINAL CAMPAIGN

The main task of educating the general public on the specifics of the decimal changeover was confined to the period December 30, 1970, to February 24, 1971—beginning less than seven weeks prior to D Day and ending a week and a half after it. The advertising campaign was believed to have been the most concentrated ever directed at the general public in the United Kingdom. There were three good reasons why this final campaign was compressed into a relatively short period.

First, in contrast to machine suppliers and businesses, which needed a lengthy planning horizon, there was no need for the general public to have *detailed* information on decimalization years in advance of the date. Second, it was desirable to reduce the risk that people might forget much of the information contained in the advertising before they had had a chance to put it into practice. And, third, it was important to reach people when they were more likely to be attentive—and therefore receptive—to detailed information about an event which was shortly to affect them, instead of preoccupied with Christmas.

JWT defined the objectives of the campaign as follows:

1. To convey all the information, some elementary and some more complicated, that the general public must have if the switch is to go smoothly.
2. To make the DCB be seen to be giving the lead, to be an authoritative, responsible, sympathetic body providing all the information necessary to complete a smooth changeover.

Advertising's task was primarily one of educating the public, helping them to eradicate the money habits of a life-time, to learn new habits, and to put these into practice. Since money played such a central role in people's lives, it was vital to maintain public confidence in the new decimal currency throughout the changeover period and thereafter; it was especially necessary to reassure people that decimalization was not a major cause of inflation as many feared. Above all, the changeover had to go smoothly on the first attempt.

Surveys showed a continuing level of significant public resistance to decimalization. As D Day drew nearer, public concern appeared to increase; the percentage of respondents not in favor of the change rose from 39% in July 1969 to 45% in November 1970. Attitudes seemed to be closely related to socio-economic class (Exhibit 3). Worries about confusion over conversion and anxiety over prices and shopping were the major concerns.

The cornerstone of the educational campaign was a free, 24-page color booklet, *Your Guide to Decimal Money,* intended for distribution to every household in the country. This contained all the information necessary for an understanding of decimalization, but its disadvantage as an educational text was that its authors had no control over when it was read, or how much was read at a time, in what order, how often, and so forth.

EXHIBIT 3
Public Attitudes Towards Decimalization

	Favor	Against	Don't Know
(A) All Respondents			
July 1969	48%	39%	13%
November 1969	50%	38%	12%
March 1970	47%	41%	12%
May 1970	51%	39%	10%
July 1970	44%	48%	8%
September 1970	45%	46%	9%
November 1970	44%	45%	11%
January 1971[1]	49%	45%	6%
(B) By Socio-Economic Class			
(1) AB: Professional/Higher Managerial			
July 1969	60%	34%	6%
November 1969	69%	25%	6%
March 1970	64%	28%	8%
(2) C1: Lower Managerial			
July 1969	54%	37%	9%
November 1969	59%	30%	11%
March 1970	54%	37%	9%
(3) C2: Skilled Working Class			
July 1969	49%	37%	14%
November 1969	51%	36%	13%
March 1970	47%	41%	11%
(4) DE: Unskilled Working Class/Pensioners			
July 1969	36%	46%	19%
November 1969	35%	50%	15%
March 1970	36%	50%	14%

(Numbers may not add to 100% due to rounding)

---

[1] National Opinion Poll Survey (all other surveys made by British Market Research Bureau for Decimal Currency Board).

Source: Decimal Currency Board.

To make the learning task as logical and coherent as possible, without confusing the audience with too much information at once, the balance of the campaign was structured into three sequential "lessons."

1. The effect of decimalization on coins.
2. The effect of decimalization on shops and prices.
3. How to handle mixed money (i.e., low denomination old and new coins).

The advertising media employed for the campaign were local and national newspapers, magazines, television, and billboards.[2] The coverage of this total campaign was estimated at 99% of the adult population.

Newspapers carried the basic information about decimalization, with all three elements of the educational program outlined above being dealt with in a series of nine large advertisements commencing in late December. These used a countdown approach, with headlines reading "D Day —7 Weeks to Go," "D Day—6 Weeks to Go" and so on down to "D Day Starts at Midnight" and "Today is D Day." An example appears in Exhibit 4.

Magazines carried full-page advertisements giving practical advice on shopping and cash-handling. Five such advertisements, in continuity form, appeared between January 11 and D Day, February 15, in large circulation magazines. Exhibit 5 shows an example.

Television was used to demonstrate shopping situations and to accustom the eye and ear to the sight and sound of decimal prices and change giving. From the week commencing January 18, a series of six 30-second commercials appeared at both peak and off-peak hours on the Independent Television Network. Altogether, 1,444 30-second spots were shown on TV, one of the most concentrated television campaigns ever undertaken in the U.K. Meantime, the noncommercial BBC television and radio networks broadcast a large number of TV and radio programs and short announcements devoted to decimalization.

Billboards (known as "posters" in Britain) were used on some 10,000 high-visibility urban sites to reiterate key points about the decimal system.

Since research had shown that the elderly and less well educated groups might need additional help, a special advertisement was run in selected social welfare and religious publications—encouraging readers and their families to study the booklet *Your Guide to Decimal Money* and then pass on their knowledge to those who might find some of the points a bit confusing. The Board also supplied information directly to organizations working with these groups.

Weekly surveys were conducted from January 26 to February 22. The objective was to pinpoint any major areas of difficulty so that the content of later advertising could be adjusted accordingly. Speed was essential and a nationally representative sample of 800 adults was interviewed on the Tuesday and Wednesday of each week, with the results being processed and tabulated for a Friday presentation.

A contingency plan had to be brought into operation when delivery of the booklet was halted by a lengthy postal strike, with an estimated 25% of all British households still to receive a copy. More press advertising was placed, reproducing as much as possible of the information in the booklet.

As the DCB had anticipated, numerous other organizations provided publicity concerning the changeover to decimals.

> The Board were not alone shouldering the task of preparing Britain for D Day. Children were given decimal lessons at school; those who handled money in their everyday work received training courses from their employers; many shops provided information for their customers; there was a growing volume of articles in the general and specialist press, many of them prepared after consultation with the Board or based on Board material; and the broadcasting authorities were very active [5, p. 16].

The banks produced leaflets for all their account holders and bank speakers addressed more than 18,500 meetings with a total audience of nearly 800,000 people. In addition, there were a large number of commercial promotions with a decimal theme, such as decimal games, dishcloth and dress materials with a decimal pattern, and so forth. The DCB itself spent a total of £2 million ($4.8 million) on publicity (including advertising) over a 3½ year period, of which 75% was spent on the final, two-month campaign.[3]

Press Coverage. The editorial role of the press during the decimalization period was viewed with mixed feelings by some of those responsible for the changeover. One J. Walter Thompson executive stated that women's magazines had done an "outstanding" job in preparing their readers for decimalization, but that most of the press had approached D Day with an attitude which he described as "eagerly anticipating disaster."

Newspaper articles in the "popular" national dailies reported the results of their own opinion polls, which showed often sharply different findings from those of the DCB concerning people's preparedness for the changeover. For instance, an article in the *Sun* (a popular daily), on February 1, 1971, began in this discouraging vein:

4 Out of Every 10 Still Don't Quite Get the Point

> Four out of every 10 people are still totally confused about decimal money.
> This startling fact has emerged from a nationwide SUN survey to find out if Britain is ready for the switch to the new decimal currency a fortnight today.
> It means that only a dramatic increase in the public's decimal knowledge will avert chaos in the High Street on D Day, February 15.[4]

---

[2] There were no commercial radio stations in Britain at the time of decimalization. Neither BBC radio nor television carried commercial advertising.

[3] Total advertising expenditures in the U.K., by all advertisers, in all media, were £591 million ($1.3 billion) in 1971.

[4] "The High Street" is Britain's version of "Main Street."

DECIMAL CURRENCY BOARD

D DAY- ONE WEEK TO GO

When you go shopping on Monday week, you'll find this information useful

On 15th February, we change to decimal currency. Three new 'copper' coins—the 1 new penny (1p), the 2 new pence (2p) and the new halfpenny (½p)—will join the money we are already using. Some public transport and most shops will switch on that day and the rest will do so as they change their cash registers and other machines to decimal working.

There will be £sd shops and decimal (£p) shops and this is what the new prices will look like

Most shops will start trading in decimal money at once but for a time some will continue as £sd shops. £p shops will mark prices in £p, and the top illustration is how decimal prices under £1 will look. £sd shops will continue to show their prices in £sd. To help you, some shops will show their prices in both £p and £sd for a time. This is called dual pricing. An example is shown in the centre illustration. The selling price is shown in large figures; the £sd amount is a guide to value only. The lower illustration gives an example of how decimal prices over £1 will look.

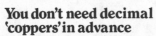

You don't need decimal 'coppers' in advance

You will be able to go shopping on D Day with your existing money. £p shops will have stocked their tills with the new decimal 'coppers' and you will get them in your change. The shopkeeper can give the right change if you give him a note or silver coins. You can spend old pennies and 3d bits in decimal shops, in lots totalling 6d, which exactly equals 2½p. The shopkeeper can then give you the right change in decimal 'coppers.'

Two ways to simplify shopping

First, as far as you can, use decimal 'coppers' in decimal shops, and old pennies and 3d bits in £sd shops. You may find, at first, that it helps if you keep these coins separate.

Second, if you do not have the exact money handy, do just as you do now—*give more and get change.*

Some examples of shopping after D Day

In a decimal shop. You want to buy a small tin of soup marked 4p.

1. You can pay exactly with decimal coins—for example, with two 2p coins.

2. Or you can hand the shopkeeper a 5p coin (or an old shilling) and get 1p change.

3. Or you can pay with £sd coins by giving, say, two threepenny bits and a sixpence. That equals 1/-, of course, and is the same as 5p. So you'll get 1p change.

In an £sd shop. You want to buy a packet of sweets marked at 1s 2d.

1. You can pay exactly with an old shilling (or a 5p coin) and two old pennies.

2. Or you can also hand the shopkeeper a 5p coin, a 2p coin and a ½p coin. That equals 7½p. And since 7½p is 1s 6d in the old money, you'll get 4d change.

Check with 'Your Guide to Decimal Money'

If you are doubtful about anything, refer to the official booklet, "Your Guide to Decimal Money," which has been sent to every home. Remember, too, that it contains two pull-out copies of the Shoppers' Table to help you check £p prices against £sd prices.

If you need another copy of the booklet, you can get one this month from any Post Office.

Dial-a-Disc

In all towns and cities where the Post Office Dial-a-Disc service is available, you can hear a recorded message about the change to decimal currency by Lord Fiske, the Chairman of the Decimal Currency Board. This message can be heard during the week before D Day and for two weeks after it. Just dial the normal Dial-a-Disc code between 8 am and 6 pm on weekdays.

POINTS TO REMEMBER

From D Day:

- The £ stays the same, but is made up of 100 new pence.
- There will be decimal (£p) shops and £sd shops.
- You can use both old and new coins in either kind of shop.
- In decimal shops, use 3d bits and old pennies in amounts totalling 6d (2½p).
- If in doubt, give more and get change.

From 15th February-think decimal

Cut this out and keep it.

EXHIBIT 5
Magazine Advertising, Final Campaign, January 1971

Mum gets the message

On Monday, 15th February, we change to decimal currency. Let's follow Betty Fisher as she takes her old (and rather crotchety) mother with her to the shops on D (for Decimal) Day.

A free copy of 'Your Guide to Decimal Money' is now being delivered to every home. It tells you all about shopping with the new money. Read it carefully and keep it by you for reference.

DECIMAL CURRENCY BOARD

The "quality" press was, as always, more restrained, but still voiced fears that things could not possibly go as smoothly as the DCB seemed to be anticipating.

D DAY AND AFTER

The normal financial workings of the U.K. came to a halt on Thursday, February 11, four days before D Day. The banks, Stock Exchange, and Foreign Exchange were all closed for four days to allow a breathing space for the necessary changeover. The banks faced the biggest task, since they could not convert their machines and accounts to decimal until all outstanding £sd items had been brought to account; a massive clearing operation, "Operation Checkpoint," was launched to clear all checks and credits on schedule and then to convert each account to its decimal equivalent. Retailers obtained supplies of decimal bronze coins (½p, 1p, 2p) in advance, so as to have decimal change ready for customers on D Day, but remained open during normal working hours.

British Rail and the London Underground had decided to go decimal a day early, since Sunday was obviously a quieter day for travel than Monday. This went over smoothly, and on D Day the morning newspapers were expressing cautious optimism, already having one decimal success story to report.

Early indications on February 15 were that members of the public seemed to have learned their lessons well. Among retailers, the DCB later reported,

> The general consensus was that customers, although unpracticed, had a good understanding of basic principles . . . elderly customers tended to be slower. Customers appreciated the efforts which retailers had made to help them—for example, by providing special decimal advisers or enquiry points—even though their services were in practice not often called upon. . . . Many people had used up their low-value £sd coins the previous week and others deliberately disposed of them on D Day. . . . There was a general air of calm acceptance and good humour amongst the shopping public; and shop staff on the whole enjoyed the exercise [5, p. 38].

During the morning of D Day a special survey was taken of a representative sample of 1,040 shoppers across the country, with responses being telephoned to London, quickly processed, and released to the press that afternoon. The results showed that 67 percent of those interviewed found shopping easy, 25 percent had difficulty and 8 percent had no definite feelings. When asked whether, once they had got used to the new money, they felt it would be easier, harder, or about the same as shopping in the old money, 73 percent said easier, 6 percent harder and 17 percent about the same. The evening papers reported D Day as a success story, with headlines such as the London *Evening News'* "You're Getting the Point."

Two guidelines which the DCB had sought to put across to the general public were, wherever possible, to give old coins in "6d lots" (since this was the smallest amount converting exactly into decimals, namely 2½p), and when in doubt, to "give more and get change." Many people resorted extensively to the latter approach, often tendering one-pound notes for quite small purchases; this helped them avoid having to work in decimals at all, while also serving to get large supplies of decimal coins quickly into circulation. Over 90 percent of all retailers and other traders went decimal during the first week of the changeover, thus quickly driving out the old coins and reducing to a minimum the confusion which inevitably arose from having old and new currency systems in operation together. Compared with other countries that had switched to decimals, Britain came nearer to an overnight change.

Perhaps the most remarkable feature of the press coverage on the morning after D Day was that only two of the ten national newspapers made decimalization their lead story. Although one paper claimed that prices had been rounded up by pubs and restaurants, most papers stressed the smoothness of the changeover. Some coverage was given to last-ditch efforts to persuade the public to resist decimals by a small organization called the Anti-Decimal Group. Most newspapers reported that a London housewife had made her own contribution to putting the new money into circulation by swallowing a 2p coin in the early morning. Perhaps the most telling observation of all appeared in the February 20 edition of *The Economist*. "Lord Fiske [the DCB Chairman] was right," they said, "and the politicians who told Mr. Wilson [the former Prime Minister] not to risk a spring election after decimalization were wrong. It was a non-event."

Within six weeks of D Day, virtually all business in the U.K. was being transacted in decimal currency. Although the duration of the changeover had originally been set at 18 months, it was decided to end the changeover period a year sooner, on August 31, 1971. One month later, the Decimal Currency Board was dissolved, its early dissolution a tribute to its success as a change agency.

AN EVALUATION OF THE CHANGEOVER

Few people would disagree with the contention that the decimal changeover was a remarkable achievement. What was the key to its success? Perhaps a major advantage in Britain's favor was the fact that it was virtually the last country to decimalize its currency. Consequently, it was able to profit from a detailed study of the South African, Australian, and New Zealand experiences, avoiding any mistakes these countries had made and improving upon approaches which had already proven successful.

Several aspects of the Decimal Currency Board's work may be credited for the success of the operation.

1. The very well organized planning of the logistics of the changeover;
2. The carefully researched and sequenced nature of the Board's publicity strategy, concentrating first on business, then on retailing and trading organizations, and finally on the general public;
3. The decision to concentrate the main public communications campaign in the weeks immediately preceding the changeover;
4. The use of regular surveys to monitor progress, followed by appropriate corrective action where needed;
5. The use of each medium of communication to its best advantage, complementing, rather than duplicating, messages in other media;

6. The leveraging effect which DCB publicity efforts obtained through close coordination with businesses and other organizations, so that much of the publicity and educational effort surrounding the change came to people in the course of their day-to-day dealings with retailers, banks, post offices, and transport undertakings;
7. The personality of the DCB's Chairman and chief ''salesman,'' Lord Fiske, who seems to have conveyed throughout an impression of calm, reassuring competence, coupled with good-humored confidence and a pleasing common touch;
8. Early selection of an advertising agency. By involving the agency very early in the planning process, rather than leaving selection until the time came for mass media advertising, the DCB was able to coordinate its marketing communications activities more closely than might otherwise have been the case. The agency's wealth of expertise (its clients included banks, retailers, and marketers of a wide range of consumer and industrial goods and services) provided skills which are not normally found in government agencies.
9. The firm commitment of successive governments to the decimalization program from 1966 onwards.

As a change agency, the DCB and its personnel seem to have possessed most of the characteristics necessary for a change agent's success in securing adoption of an innovation [12, 14]. In particular, the Board was highly ''client-oriented''; it developed a program compatible with the needs of both intermediary organizations and the general public; it commanded the support of organizations which might be thought of as opinion leaders in their fields; and, despite periodic carping from critics, it succeeded in maintaining considerable credibility.

What, if anything should have been done differently? The answer is, probably very little. It is possible that additional consumer research concerning the 50p coin might have resulted in a design and an introductory campaign which would have generated less controversy. The argument over whether the £-newpenny-½ system should have been selected over the ten shilling-cent system can still occasionally be heard. A major advantage of the latter was supposedly its easy conversion against the old currency, but this is one area in which consumer input was not sought.

Although the press did not, in some people's view, play a particularly helpful role with its widely voiced fears of ''Chaos in the High Street,'' it was basically supportive of decimalization once the decision had been made. One of the media's problems in this instance was that good news may be no news. After all, there is little journalistic challenge or excitement in reporting the fact that a major change is proceeding so smoothly as to be a ''non-event.'' However, the press may well have contributed to the final success of the changeover by verbalizing people's fears and doubts in the preceding weeks and making it clear to their readers that these fears were being made known to the DCB and the Government. At the same time, the press performed a very useful task with their various ''price-watching'' services; these watched out for any attempts to cheat the public with fraudulent price conversions or surreptitious price hikes.

As an exercise in change, decimalization was clearly a brilliant success, especially when one considers the extent of opposition among ordinary citizens. But was it worth the effort and expense? Within a matter of weeks, business interests—including banks, retailers, and the accounting profession—were reporting that significant benefits were already being derived from working in the new system. Formal and informal research showed steady gains in acceptance of decimal currency as people accustomed themselves to using it. The following editorial comment in the March 24, 1971, edition of the popular *Daily Mirror* is probably a fairly accurate reflection of public opinion some six weeks after D Day:

> Nobody wanted decimal currency. . . . But now it's here we don't know how we managed so long without it.

INSIGHTS FOR OTHER CHANGE PROGRAMS

For students of marketing and communications, the decimalization campaign in Britain represents what may come to be seen as a classic example of utilizing the tools and strategies of marketing and research to facilitate a major, but initially unpopular, societal change. The nature of the task, persuading the entire population to change the habits of a lifetime, required a sophisticated understanding of communications theory and the potential and limitations of each available medium. It also required the presence of a change agency capable of implementing a marketing program in both industrial and consumer markets.

The coordinating role of the Decimal Currency Board illustrates clearly the leveraging powers possessed by this type of change agency. By far the greater part of the communications and promotional effort was actually carried out by groups such as machine manufacturers, banks, transport organizations, and retailers. These were obviously in much more direct contact with small businesses and the general public than the Board itself. By coordinating such efforts (although it could not *control* them), the DCB succeeded in ensuring that these other communications were both accurate in content and reasonably consistent with its own work.

While it is rare that an entire country faces such sweeping innovations as decimalization, social and technological change will periodically require adoption of new ways of doing things at national or local levels or among specific segments of the population. A clear understanding of the marketing tasks involved is central to facilitating such changes, and it is evident that official change agencies can play important coordinating roles. However, their task is likely to be more difficult in situations where businesses, the mass media, and/or other intermediary organizations are antagonistic towards the change program.

Metrication Programs. One program of national change, which is of current interest in several countries and which poses a number of problems somewhat similar to decimalization, is metrication of weights and measures. Several major industrial nations—including Britain, Canada, Australia, and the United States—are currently engaged in metricating their weights and measures.

Although there are some obvious parallels (including that of unpopularity), metrication differs from decimalization in at least two important respects. First, there is no need for a universal "M Day" comparable to D Day, since metrication can proceed on a sector by sector basis. Second, compulsory use of metric measures by consumers is limited to legislative areas such as highway speed limits, although it may become increasingly inconvenient to "speak" in and use traditional measures. In the case of decimalization, by contrast, the old currency units literally disappeared.

Curiously enough, the success of the decimalization program in Britain has made the task of metrication there harder rather than easier. Many people blamed decimalization for inflation, a claim largely unsupported by economic studies. The fact that inflation accelerated sharply in the United Kingdom from 1970 onwards is a good example of "correlation not causation" where decimalization is concerned, but many Britons became afraid lest metrication should "also" prove inflationary. Concerned, in part, about electoral popularity, successive British governments have been reluctant to take firm stands on metrication with the result that the program is now several years behind schedule. The work of the Metrication Board has been made much harder by the lack of strong Government support and it has been somewhat difficult for this Board to maintain an ongoing, coordinated marketing effort.

Australia and Canada started their metrication programs some years later than Britain, but both are now ahead. By 1978 Australia's program, begun in 1970, was almost 75 percent complete. In part, this success may be ascribed to strong government support for the metrication program, cooperation by the news media in quickly ceasing to use the old units as each metric change was initiated, and a series of legislated cut-off dates after which use of the old units in industry or trade became illegal.

How much has the United States learned from national change programs in other countries? The evidence to date is not encouraging. The Department of the Treasury and the Federal Reserve Board ignored the insights provided by the British decimalization program when they came to implement the much simpler two-dollar bill reintroduction. The result was an embarrassing flop. Although one can argue the merits of the decision to reintroduce the two-dollar bill, once that decision had been made, a serious effort should have been made to ensure success.

In the case of metrication, there is a very real danger that America may be ignoring the lessons of the successful Australian experience and instead drifting into a poorly coordinated program lacking government support and legislated cut-off dates. If public confusion and deceptive practices are to be avoided, then stronger powers will have to be given to the U.S. Metric Board. The Administration's current philosophy, as expressed by President Carter in a recent message to the American National Metric Council, is that,

> It is the intent of the Metric Act that the rate of metrication be governed by the market place, with the U.S. Metric Board playing but a facilitating part in the process [13].

But for metrication to be completed in a reasonable time frame will require a strong, centrally coordinated marketing effort. Reacting simply to the forces of the market place could easily result in a haphazard conversion program lasting fifty years.

REFERENCES

1. *Australia and New Zealand Bank Quarterly Review,* "Decimals—Change After the Changeover." Vol. XVII (October 1967), 12–15.
2. Axelrod, Joseph *et al. The Feasibility of Reintroducing the Two Dollar Bill: A Marketing Approach.* A Report to the Board of Governors of the Federal Reserve System. Boston, MA: Graduate School of Business Administration, Harvard University, 1975.
3. Bjorkman, Johan. *Kortsiktiga Effekter Av Trafikinformation.* Stockholm, Sweden: EFI, 1971.
4. Decimal Currency Board. *First Annual Report, 1967/8.* London: Her Majesty's Stationery Office, 1968.
5. Decimal Currency Board. *Fourth Annual Report, 1970/71.* London: Her Majesty's Stationery Office, 1971.
6. Englund, Anders. "Changing Behaviour Patterns: Sweden's Traffic Switch." *Progress* (The Unilever Quarterly), No. 3, 1968, 26–32.
7. Lovelock, Christopher H. "Decimalization of the Currency in Great Britain," 9-575-101. Boston, MA: Intercollegiate Case Clearing House, 1975.
8. Lovelock, Christopher H. "Department of the Treasury: Reissue of the $2 Bill" (A), 9-576-102, and (B), 9-578-168. Boston, MA: Intercollegiate Case Clearing House, 1975, 1978.
9. Lovelock, Christopher H. "Marketing the Metric System—1978," 9-578-167. Boston, MA: Intercollegiate Case Clearing House, 1978.
10. Moore, N. E. A. *The Decimalisation of Britain's Currency.* London: Her Majesty's Stationery Office, 1973.
11. *Report of the Committee of Inquiry on Decimal Currency.* London: Her Majesty's Stationery Office, Cmnd. 2145, 1963.
12. Rogers, Everett M. and F. Floyd Shoemaker. "The Change Agent," Chapter 7 in *Communication of Innovations.* New York: The Free Press, 1971.
13. *The Wall Street Journal.* "U.S. Metric Board's First Meeting Hears Wide Discord on Outlook for Conversion." April 5, 1978.
14. Zaltman, Gerald and Robert Duncan. "The Change Agent," Chapter 9 in *Strategies for Planned Change.* New York: Wiley, 1977, 185–224.

29
Americans Continue to Ignore the $2 Bill

Michael B. Amspaugh

Introducing a new denomination of banknote might seem a relatively simple task, yet people are surprisingly conservative about money matters and may resist change unless they have been properly prepared for it. In addition to educating consumers, efforts must also be made to gain the cooperation of bankers and retailers who serve as channels of distribution for currency. This article demonstrates the problems that befell the $2 bill in the United States, as a result of the authorities' failure to take a marketing approach when "relaunching" the bill into general circulation.

Customers who use the drive-up window of one Michigan bank are likely to find a $2 bill among the change from their transactions. But if the customers go into the bank to conduct their business, they are unlikely to receive one of the bills. "Customers at the drive-up window are less likely to return the bills," a bank official explained.

The bank's reluctance to give customers $2 bills is indicative of the failure of the bill nationally.

The U.S. Treasury Department reintroduced the bill in April 1976 to save on costs of printing and transporting $1 bills, which make up 60 percent of the nation's currency. Treasury officials estimated that if one-half of the 1.6 billion $1 bills in circulation were replaced with $2 bills, $35 million in printing costs could be saved over five years.

The U.S. Bureau of Engraving and Printing planned to print 400 million $2 bills a year. But the Bureau has not printed the bill since January 1977 because about 200 million of them have accumulated in the 37 Federal Reserve System (FRS) banks and branch banks around the country.

Michael B. Amspaugh is a staff writer for *The Flint Journal*.

As one FRS official has said, "We ordered a lot of the bills because we wanted to avoid a scarcity when the banks came in to get them. We've sure done that. We'd be overjoyed if we could get more bills in circulation and out of our vaults."

REASONS FOR FAILURE

Treasury and FRS officials have attributed the bill's lack of success to the failure of merchants to use it. But John E. Sheehan, a former member of the FRS Board of Governors, said, "The Federal Reserve has dropped the ball in the execution of the program." Sheehan said the FRS "should have gotten someone from Procter & Gamble, General Mills and General Foods to decide how to market the bill." A government program exists for borrowing middle management employees from private industry for such purposes. "Then they could have test-marketed the bill in two big cities for a year, found out the problems and applied the information to marketing the bill in the rest of the country," he said. "They would give back tenfold in savings to the Federal Reserve what they spent on marketing," Sheehan said of the executives. He said that even now the test-marketing program could be applied and the bill successfully marketed in the three-year period.

But the FRS official contacted by *The Journal* disagreed. "Jack (Sheehan) has always favored marketing," he said. "But I and a lot of other people wonder if there is anything to market. There is no real advantage to the $2 bill to the customer."

Before the bill was reintroduced, Sheehan commissioned a survey for the FRS by graduate students at Harvard Business School working under Professor Christopher H. Lovelock. That marketing survey found that 51 percent of the public was against reintroduction of the bill mainly because the public thought it would cost the government extra money to print. But the survey said the public would get to like the bill if the government would spend about $1 million in advertising.[1]

The Treasury department considered spending $300,000 in advertising both before the bill was reintroduced and last spring after the Treasury stopped printing it. But in both cases, the idea was dropped because of the expense and because Treasury officials said they were uncertain the advertising campaign would be effective.

The FRS has never considered handling marketing for the bill because agency officials have neither considered it their duty nor have they had the expertise, the FRS official said. Instead, it has been left to the Treasury department.

But one former FRS official said the agency should handle the marketing because it ultimately pays the cost of printing and transporting currency, and therefore stands to gain from the bill's success. He suggested that the FRS ignore requests from commercial banks for just $1 bills, and instead send them half $2 bills to get more of the bills in circulation. Suggesting that the FRS allows itself to be abused and does not use its power, he said, "Commercial banks would request $1 bills, and then send them back to us because they were new." "They wanted used bills because they said their customers didn't like new bills because they stick together. They'd pull this because the Federal Reserve pays all the cost to transport and provide security for the bills."

PROMOTION ATTEMPTS

The Treasury department has made three attempts to promote the bill. The first involved only a few thousand dollars and was built around the announcement of then Secretary of the Treasury William E. Simon that the bill was being reintroduced. Unfortunately, it came on the same day that Vice President Nelson A. Rockefeller announced that he would not be running on the ticket with President Gerald R. Ford in the 1976 election, and it received little attention.

The second attempt came late last year when Simon, by then a lame duck, sent letters to large retail chains around the nation asking them to use the bill more in their stores. Treasury department officials admit that that effort failed.

The third came early last spring when officials at the FRS branch bank in Portland, Oregon, asked retail grocery chains in the area to use the bill in making change in their stores. Peter H. Daly, assistant director of the Bureau of Engraving and Printing, said the program increased circulation of the bill 4,000 percent in the Portland area. But that increase in circulation was not reflected in figures on the bill's circulation nationally, which Daly supplied *The Journal*. This indicates the increase was not significant in terms of numbers.

Daly said a similar effort was being made by FRS officials in the Salt Lake City area, and would be occurring in the next several months in the Los Angeles, Washington, D.C., and Boston areas. But the FRS official who spoke with *The Journal* said he knew nothing of the plans Daly mentioned, even though he was the official who had been handling the $2 bill situation for the FRS. Asked if the Treasury department has contacted Lovelock since the bill ran into trouble, Daly answered, "No, the Harvard report was a marketing survey."

Lovelock told *The Journal* that the government missed a big opportunity by not promoting the bill before it went into circulation, rather than after it had done poorly. "It is harder to promote in an atmosphere of cynicism," he said. Promotion must be aimed at both the merchant and the consumer. The merchant must be convinced not to place the bills under the till in the cash register drawer, but to use them and thus keep them in circulation, Lovelock said.

Five Flint area store officials said they use the bill when their cashiers remember to do so if they receive them from customers. But they do not order the bill from banks when ordering low denomination currency for cash registers. They said this was because they stuck to old habits in ordering bills and because there isn't a slot in cash drawers for the bill.

But cash register manufacturers have said the $2 bill can replace the $20 bill in the till, with the $20 bill going underneath. They said $20 bills are seldom used [for change-giving] because cashiers seldom have to change $50 and $100 bills. They said this procedure is used all the time in Canada, where the same type of cash drawers are used and the $2 bill has been in widespread use for years.

Officials of two of five area banks surveyed said they do not normally give the bill to customers, and officials at two others said it is left up to the tellers whether the bill is used. The banks said they follow this policy because customers are reluctant to accept them and the tellers are unfamiliar with them.

But government officials argue that it is just a matter of getting the bills into widespread circulation so that consumers and cash handlers will use them.

---

[1] Editors' note: For more details of this survey, see the Appendix following this article.

Lovelock and Sheehan agreed that the bill will have a much better chance of gaining acceptance if a proposal to replace $1 bills and silver dollars with a $1 coin slightly larger than a quarter is implemented.

But regardless of whether the bill gains acceptance, it is unlikely that it will be withdrawn from circulation soon. Daly said the Treasury expects the bill to take five to eight years to gain acceptance. The FRS official said, "It would be ridiculous to withdraw the bill when we have vaults filled with ones we have already paid to have printed."

So customers at the Michigan area bank can expect to see the bill for several years to come—at least if they use the drive-in window.

APPENDIX
The Harvard Survey[1]

In May 1975, the Board of Governors of the Federal Reserve System received a 261 page research report they had commissioned from a team of graduate students working under faculty supervision at the Harvard Business School. Entitled *The Feasibility of Reissuing the $2 Bill* [1], this report detailed the findings of extensive consumer research—including 1,600 personal interviews conducted nationwide by the Harris Poll—plus surveys and interviews among large retailers, commercial banks, retail trade associations, trade publications, cash register manufacturers, and other organizations.

Key findings of the research included the following:

- When consumers were asked if they would like the Government to start printing $2 bills again, 35% of those surveyed said yes, 51% said no, and 14% were undecided. However, 95% of respondents indicated that if $2 bills were reissued they would "willingly accept" them from a retail store clerk.
- Reasons for favoring reintroduction included convenience, a dislike of carrying many $1 bills, and the declining purchasing power of the $1 bill. Those opposed to the $2 bill saw no need for it, were afraid the new bill would be confusing, and thought it would result in extra costs for the Government.
- Banks and retailers agreed that accommodating the $2 bill would be operationally feasible; their attitudes towards reintroduction ranged from mildly positive to strongly negative. Estimates of the lead time required for planning ranged from a week to six months. Concerns were expressed by some organizations relative to increased cash handling expenses, equipment limitations, staff retraining, and customer behavior.
- Cash register industry executives anticipated no significant problems for retailers. They emphasized that in Canada (where the $2 bill circulated widely) most merchants used registers identical with those in the United States.

The researchers concluded that reintroduction of the $2 bill was "entirely feasible," but that success would require a determined commitment by the Treasury and the Federal Reserve System. "The probability of a successful reintroduction," said the report, "could be enhanced by a carefully developed marketing program."

Possible reluctance on the part of the retail and banking communities, concluded the report, might be minimized by adopting marketing strategies designed to give them sufficient lead time and assistance in making operating adjustments, and by development of educational programs designed to correct misconceptions and to promote the advantages of the $2 denomination to the general public. It was recommended that promotional literature and trade advertising aimed at the banking and retail communities be educational in nature, with the intent being:

1. To make the transition as smooth as possible;
2. To provide reassurance of the Government's commitment to the success and permanence of the reintroduction; and
3. To encourage bankers, retailers, and other cash handlers to provide consistent and accurate information about the bill to their customers, especially at locations where cash transactions took place.

The report also urged the Treasury and the Federal Reserve to seek professional marketing counsel in developing the reintroduction program, in the event that it was decided to reissue the $2 bill. Although the report made no attempt to calculate the cost to these organizations of the suggested marketing program, it was subsequently estimated at around one million dollars, assuming full advantage were taken of opportunities for public service advertising.

On November 3, 1975, five months after receipt of this research report, the Secretary of the Treasury announced the decision to reintroduce the $2 bill.

REFERENCE

1. Axelrod, Joseph *et al. The Feasibility of Reintroducing the Two Dollar Bill: A Marketing Approach*. A Report to the Board of Governors of the Federal Reserve System. Boston, MA: Graduate School of Business Administration, Harvard University, 1975.

---

[1] This appendix was prepared by the editors.

30

Changing Behavior Patterns: Sweden's Traffic Switch

Anders Englund

Anyone who has ever traveled abroad to a country where traffic travels on the opposite side of the road knows how disconcerting this can be at first. We are taught the "rules of the road" at an early age and, as adults, driving a vehicle on the correct side of the road quickly becomes second nature. This article reports on the dramatic marketing challenge posed by Sweden's 1967 switch from left to right hand driving. Marketing efforts have been widely used in many countries for highway safety programs designed to encourage and reinforce desired behavior patterns; but in this instance the task for marketing was to help Swedes unlearn a deeply ingrained behavior pattern and replace it by a new one.

At five o'clock in the morning of September 3, 1967, Sweden changed her rule of the road from driving on the left to driving on the right. For the people of Sweden—almost 8,000,000 of them—this meant that an old and extremely well learned pattern of behavior would have to be changed. From that time, 2,000,000 motor vehicles and 1,000,000 other vehicles would have to be driven on the right instead of on the left, and people would have to pass each other on the left instead of on the right. In addition they would have to learn how to find their way about in the large towns, where traffic engineers were taking the opportunity to make a thorough reorganization of traffic and to introduce, for example, many new one-way streets.

Anders Englund served as director of research, Right-Hand Traffic Commission (Sweden).

GREATEST EVER TRAFFIC SAFETY CAMPAIGN

The reorganization meant that the whole population —and of course those who happened to be visiting Sweden at the time—would have to be supplied with information telling them that traffic was to be reorganized, when and how the reorganization was to be effected, what traffic rules would be in force afterwards, and what local changes had been made for the regulation of traffic. For two weeks before September 3, therefore, and after that date until the end of the year, an information campaign of seldom-experienced dimensions was put into action. All conceivable media were used in the campaign—between three and four TV programs a day; an average of two daily radio programs and more than ten trailers; a 32-page brochure of which 7,900,000 copies were printed and which was distributed to every household in Sweden. The brochure was translated into nine languages and was directly distributed to aliens resident in Sweden. It was also issued in editions for the deaf, the blind, and other special groups.

Every pupil in Sweden's schools received study materials adapted to the various stages of education from kindergartens to higher secondary schools and other advanced types of schools. Special printed matter was also produced for other public institutions such as pensioners' homes, hospitals and prisons. For weeks after the changeover, practically every poster site in the country was used, and along the highways reminder signs were set up every three to five kilometers.

An advertising campaign was carried on in all the 130 daily newspapers and in weeklies and trade papers, from the last weeks in August until November. Even comics of the "Donald Duck" type carried advertising with traffic information adapted to their readers. In addition radio, TV and newspapers gave information about the changeover in their news. On September 4, facts about right-hand traffic took up one-third of column space in the dailies.

Advertising films were shown before the main feature in movie houses and a sound track reminded audiences of right-hand traffic before they left at the end of the show. Spectators were given similar reminders at sports contests and other events. Traffic information and notices of various kinds were also given on, for example, milk cartons, soft drinks, plastic cups, coffee cans, and department stores' carrier-bags. Private enterprise produced right-hand traffic games, men's underpants suitably marked with admonitions, and warning devices of the most diversified kinds for car drivers.

ARGUMENTS FOR AND AGAINST

With the traffic change-over, Sweden started driving on the right—again. We had in fact had right-hand driving before 1734, but an ordinance dated that year contained a rule about left-hand driving which stayed in force for 233 years. As long ago as the 1920s, the question whether to change from left-hand to right-hand driving was reventilated, and several official inquiries on the subject were made in the 1930s, 1940s and 1950s. At the same time many people took sides energetically in the debate for and against a changeover.

A major factor in support of a change was the rapid growth in transport across Sweden's frontiers to countries with a right-hand rule of the road. The difficulties arising out of varying systems of traffic rules were manifest in accidents to Swedes abroad and to foreigners in Sweden—the number of such accidents involving motor vehicles rose from 1,850 in 1957 to 7,788 in 1966.

The difficulties that the actual changeover would bring in its train were argued against it; those who recommended the retention of left-hand driving gave warning of the massacre that a changeover would bring about. The cost, to, was an important argument against a change, and it rose

rapidly the longer the alteration was delayed: a changeover in 1943 would have cost Sw.Kr. 16 million compared with Sw.Kr. 600 million ($120 million) in 1967. In the spring of 1963, Parliament decided that the change to right-hand driving would be made in 1967, and the National Commission for Right-Hand Traffic was appointed to plan and direct the work.

In the beginning, the Right-Hand Traffic Commission concentrated its work on the rebuilding of roads and streets and the reconstruction of buses and tramcars. This work naturally involved many technical and administrative problems, not least for the reason that the transport mechanism would have to function on a basis of left-hand driving until the night of September 2nd-3rd during which it would switch over and would have to work equally well on the following day when right-hand driving was the rule.

A corresponding instantaneous changeover would be required from road users also. There is no doubt that precisely this requirement for an immediate change in the individual's behavior involved some of the more difficult fundamental problems that would have to be solved when the changeover was made. There are innumerable examples to show that a change in behavior does not occur at once; it needs a certain amount of time. Much experience has also been acquired to show that it is difficult—not to say impossible—to supply *everyone* in a country with the information they must have if they are to be able to cope with a reorganization of this kind.

Gradually, a group of people in the Commission and the advisory delegations gained a hearing for the idea that the problems concerning man and his readjustment would have to be subjected to special inquiries and investigations. Accordingly, a Scientific Working Group was formed, including experts in the psychology of learning, education and mass communication.

CHANGING BEHAVIOR PATTERNS

One of the first problems the Right-Hand Traffic Commission's Scientific Working Group had to deal with was the question of training for right-hand traffic before the change-over. There were many who even at that early date—in the spring of 1964—wanted the public to be provided with facilities for practicing on special driving-grounds. The results of the Working Group's inquiries were published in a report which objected to such training in advance, as it was felt that it might lead directly to wrong actions—or to delayed reactions—in left-hand traffic. We know from several experiments concerned with learning-processes that if two reactions are learned simultaneously, or consecutively, and the reactions are such that they may compete with each other, "interference" can occur. Translated into terms of traffic conditions, this means that after training in right-hand traffic, right-hand traffic reactions—or delayed left-hand traffic reactions—may appear when the person concerned is driving in left-hand traffic. For these and other reasons mentioned in the report, the Commission decided that training in right-hand driving would not be given before the changeover.

However, some kinds of behavior could of course safely be learned in advance—for example, teaching car drivers to look for information on road signs placed on the right-hand side of the road as well as on the left. Most of the more than 360,000 road signs existing before the changeover were placed along the left-hand side of the road. As it could not be expected that it would be possible to change all these signs during one night in September, the road signs were doubled—a duplicate sign was already set up on the right-hand side of the road during the six months immediately preceding the changeover. The Working Group supported this measure for two reasons; road users would thus get an opportunity to learn to register information from signs placed along the right-hand side of the road, before the changeover to right-hand traffic, and they would also learn the new signs and new symbols that the authorities were taking the opportunity to introduce since in any case road signs would have to be set up on the right.

Another example concerned pedestrians; efforts were made during the information campaigns in 1966 and 1967, before the changeover, to teach them to look both ways before they crossed a roadway—a habit which works equally well in left-hand and right-hand traffic.

The investigations carried out before the changeover also included a series of simulator experiments. The aim of these was to make a closer study of the course taken by the process of learning right-hand traffic behavior, and, for example, how different amounts and types of training affected learning. One of the results of the simulator experiments showed that training after a change from left-hand to right-hand driving certainly leads to increased learning, but that the frequency of wrong actions—in the form of relapses to left-hand traffic behavior—falls relatively slowly, in spite of intensive training. Especially in panic situations, the frequency of these wrong actions seemed to diminish slowly. It was also found that if a car driver changed his traffic environment—that is, traveled by new and unfamiliar routes on his way to and from his work—the frequency of wrong actions was comparatively lower after a change from left-hand to right-hand driving. It proved, however, that as soon as the driver returned to the familiar route the frequency of wrong actions rose again.

The Working Group also tried to make a survey of the kinds of traffic situations in which there were grounds for expecting that road users would commit such wrong actions—that is, relapses to their former and extremely well learned left-hand traffic behavior. The Working Group first carried out a theoretical analysis of this, followed by two empirical studies, in which among others several hundred Swedish drivers who had recently driven in right-hand traffic abroad were interviewed. The results of these investigations were compiled

in a list of what were called "critical traffic-situations," which were afterwards simulated in the simulator experiments.

By systematically investigating in this way a series of different problems, the Scientific Working Group could supply the Right-Hand Traffic Commission with a factual basis of information, on which it was possible to base the various steps to be taken. The information might concern, for example, the particular kind of police supervision, or reminders along streets and roads in the form of a special sign. This mark—the sloping "H"—which is set up at different spots to remind road users of right-hand traffic, was experimentally produced with the aim of obtaining a mark that would be observable from a long distance and which would give clear and unmistakable information. The results of all these inquiries and investigations were of course also used as a basis for the structure of the Commission's information campaigns.

INFORMATION FOR EVERYONE

It was, of course, essential if the reform was to function properly that everyone in Sweden should be told that there was to be a changeover to right-hand traffic, when and how the change would be made, and what new traffic regulations, roadside signs and other instructions would thereafter have to be observed in traffic. In itself this was not a very easy task; and it was further complicated by the fact that many people were opposed to the changeover.

In October 1955 a national referendum was held in which about 53 percent of those entitled to vote did so; 82.9 percent of these voted in favor of the retention of left-hand traffic. A public opinion survey made at the same time showed that 67 percent were for left-hand traffic. In October 1964 the Scientific Working Group made an attitude study which showed that 36 percent thought that the changeover would be a good thing, while 50 percent regarded it as undesirable. The Working Group thereafter followed the situation with respect to public opinion by making repeated inquiries. The results showed a relatively steady increase, until the changeover, in the number of those who had a positive attitude, but as late as two days before it was made, about 30 percent were still against it.

Such a negative attitude complicates the possibilities of supplying the individual with information, and it naturally also affects the individual's way of interpreting the information he receives. This was an important factor to be taken into account in the planning and composition of the information campaigns. Yet another factor of importance concerned the public's media contacts. The Working Group therefore carried out inquiries for the purpose of surveying the ways in which the public was obtaining information in matters concerning traffic—that is, the extent to which people looked at traffic programs on TV, listened to them on the radio, read about traffic in the newspapers or took part in the activities of the different motorists' organizations. One of the results of these inquiries was to show that it would be essential to find new forms of traffic information if the public was to be reached at all.

The data supplied by the Right-Hand Traffic Commission would, accordingly, during the period until the changeover, have to be directed primarily towards providing information about the work the changeover involved, but also towards the creation of basic materials that would favor the changeover—towards building up interest in traffic questions among the public and getting people to accept traffic information. Special efforts were also made to try to improve the public's traffic knowledge in some important respects, for example, behavior in turning, rules of priority, and behavior during overtaking. Defective knowledge in these and other fields was revealed in a survey of traffic knowledge among adults; the inquiry was carried out on a nationally representative selection of more than 2,500 persons aged between 15 and 80 years.

In order to reach these people, the Commission carried out during 1965, 1966 and the spring of 1967 three information campaigns and also two traffic safety campaigns of a more extensive kind. These activities also fulfilled the important aim of co-ordinating the training of all the different authorities, organizations, enterprises, undertakings, groups and individuals who would finally be jointly responsible for information and training immediately before and after the changeover. In all the campaigns, the Commission also made use of a systematic model based on research in behavioral science. Using as a starting point the inquiries and investigations that had been carried out, it was possible precisely to specify the purpose and significance as well as the timing and use of different media in order to reach different target-groups. During the production of various media items such as advertisements, film strips, radio and TV programs, use was also made of the possibility of pretesting these in different respects. Finally, the steps taken were followed up *via* effect measurements in which studies were made of the extent to which information had been successfully supplied to the individuals, and what effect had been achieved as regards attitudes, knowledge or behavior.

FOLLOW-UP METHODS

The Right-Hand Traffic Commission's aim for the changeover was stated as follows in the detailed plan for the reorganization stage:

> The aim is for information supply and training, as well as other steps, to help to ensure that traffic after the changeover will flow without unnecessary disturbances, and that every category of road users will be assured of the same degree of safety in traffic after the changeover as before. Within the scope of this objective, the activity shall be given a structure and intensity of such a kind that in the long run it will result in a reduction in the number of victims of traffic accidents.

To achieve this aim, practically all available media for information and training were used—and these media were also supplemented by a large number of "tutors" who visited people living alone and others who it was known could not be reached *via* press, radio and TV or *via* organizations of various kinds. Speed limits were also enforced from September 3 onward—in towns and densely populated regions the maximum permitted speed was reduced from 50 km.p.h. to 40 km.p.h., and on other roads a speed limit of 60 km.p.h. was enforced during the first three days, and thereafter 70 km.p.h. Police supervision was intensified—with the aid of the military, the force at work could be made seven times larger than usual—and pedestrians in the towns received the aid of "road guides" at more than 19,000 crossings during the first ten days.

But the target aimed at also demanded a careful following-up of the adaptation of road users to the new conditions prevailing with right-hand traffic. The purpose of this follow-up was to provide a basis for evaluating the situation with regard to traffic safety, and for the selection and formation of further traffic safety measures in the event of its becoming evident that the situation with regard to traffic safety might diverge from the objective. The follow-up therefore included not only a continuous analysis of the road traffic accidents that had occurred but also investigations for the purpose of, so to speak, trying to forestall the accidents. The course of reasoning pursued was briefly that the degree of adaptation between man and his traffic environment primarily depends on—and can be measured in terms of—the behavior of road users; if they behave wrongly, this must sooner or later lead to accidents. Suitable behavior, again, requires the road user to have the necessary knowledge, but depends also on the attitudes of the road user to, for instance, the prevailing traffic rules and other road users.

As regards the attitudes of road users, we have been able to ascertain that their opinion of the changeover to right-hand traffic became much more positive after the reform—in November 1967 fewer than 10 percent still regard it as undesirable. Inquiries also show that people estimate the risk of making mistakes themselves in right-hand traffic to be considerably less than it is actually, and than the risk that other people will make mistakes; the subjective sense of safety increases more quickly than the safety for which a real basis is provided by the behavioral adaptation. A continuous follow-up has also been made of the public's demand for traffic information and of its attitude towards this and other measures, such as, for example, police supervision and speed limits.

With regard to traffic knowledge, it could be ascertained that road users immediately before and after the changeover knew much better how to behave in traffic than they did while left-hand traffic prevailed. In certain respects, for example, which side of the road to go on, how to turn when meeting oncoming traffic, and knowledge of the meanings of many road signs, the measurements showed a reply frequency that was higher by between 20 percent and 30 percent. But in some cases these investigations gave results which led to the fact that certain informative steps that had already been taken before the changeover—advertisements as well as radio and TV programs—were directed towards effecting further improvement in knowledge of, for example, the rules of priority and some of the new road markings.

The behavior of car drivers on overtaking, adaptation to speed limits in force, and signalling on turning, are continuously studied during the follow-up. Also included are of course repeated investigations with respect to relapses to left-hand traffic behavior. In this respect, the forecasts from the inquiries made before the changeover prove to agree very well with the actual course of development. Relapses occurred—and still occur—most frequently when left-hand turns are made and in selecting which side to take when there is an obstacle in the road. The probability of such relapses fell fairly rapidly during the autumn, but then slowed. In May, 5 percent of a nationally representative selection still reported that as vehicle drivers they had almost relapsed, or had actually relapsed, into left-hand traffic behavior once or more often during a period of two weeks immediately before the occasion of the inquiry.

The behavior of pedestrians is also studied; for example, how pedestrians acquire information about surrounding traffic before they cross a road. In October 1967, the level of adaptation was almost 65 percent of complete adaptation to right-hand traffic conditions. At present it is fully 70 percent —in other words, the advance in adaptation is proceeding fairly slowly in this respect also.

The final criterion of the adaptation of road users in traffic and to the new right-hand traffic rules is, of course, the number of traffic accidents. A reduced total frequency of accidents could be noted during the period immediately after the changeover, in spite of the fact that the traffic intensity did not measurably fall. The number of persons killed in traffic accidents was 555 in the second six months of 1967, which means that we must return to the year 1957 to find a lower figure. As a background to this it may be mentioned that the number of motor vehicles has more than doubled during the same period of ten years. This relatively good situation with respect to traffic safety prevailed also during the first months of the present year, but during April, May and June it has gradually worsened, first in the built-up areas and, in June, outside them as well. The accident figures for June are of almost the same magnitude as for this month during the past few years.

During the autumn of 1967, detailed analyses of the accident statistics showed that bicycle and moped accidents were at a relatively high figure during the first two weeks after the changeover, and also that head-on collisions were two to three times more than ''normal'' during the period September–November. In both these cases, preventive measures were taken and these should have helped to ensure that the frequency of these types of accidents returned to the ''normal'' figure. During the spring this year, accidents in connection with turning have been at a relatively high figure —here too various counter-measures have been taken.

The conclusion that can be drawn from the course of developments after the changeover must reasonably be that it is possible to change the public's attitudes in traffic matters, that it is possible considerably to increase road users' traffic knowledge, and that it is possible to make a radical change in people's behavior in traffic. It has shown that the essential requirements exist, even with the present traffic system—with present standards as regards roads and vehicles—for creating safer traffic, but also what this requires in the form of resources, of preliminary work—not least in the field of the behavioral sciences—and co-ordinated contributions.

Part VII
Keeping Existing
Organizations Responsive

Previous parts of this book have emphasized the market and consumer analysis that underlies program development. Part VII focuses on the institutional perspective, emphasizing the need for organizations to remain responsive to their markets over time if they are to remain healthy. In particular, it raises issues concerning the "product mix," including the addition of new services and discontinuation of existing ones that no longer appeal to the marketplace.

The areas of application discussed here cover services offered by a broad range of public and nonprofit institutions, including libraries, hospitals, colleges, churches, transit systems, and municipal electrical utilities.

Charles B. Weinberg's chapter, "The University Library: Analysis and Proposals," reviews trends in the field of information services and examines how these relate to university library operations. It demonstrates how an organization's overall mission may need to be redefined as the environment changes. In the case of libraries, these changes include the availability of new technologies (see Chapter 26), dramatic increases in consumer demand, new patterns of usage behavior due to increasing specialization, and an exponential increase in the number of volumes published. Yet by clinging to strategic goals which emphasize being an independent storehouse of books, many libraries have failed to respond to such changes, and service has consequently declined. This chapter shows how consumer research coupled with a good understanding of the components of library operations can help generate strategic guidelines for acquiring, maintaining, and discarding volumes in the library collection.

The next chapter, "Hospital Revises Role, Reaches Out to Cultivate and Capture Markets," is concerned with redefinition of a hospital's mission in response to declining utilization of its services. Douglass J. Seaver shows how one hospital's product mix was revised in response to changing patterns of demand and competition. In common with many fixed-site service operations (such as schools, theaters, museums, and sports facilities), the demand for hospital services is very susceptible to population movements. Some services can "follow the market" by moving physically. But that is difficult for operations housed in expensive, specialized facilities. This chapter shows the steps taken by one hospital to reverse its declining situation. These involved eliminating some traditional services, improving or adding others, emphasizing outreach efforts, and developing cooperative referral programs with other neighboring hospitals.

A different situation is portrayed in Roger Ricklef's article, "New York New School Rides on Rising Wave of Adult Education." Here, strategy is less constrained by existing physical facilities or specific technical skills. As a result, it is much simpler to make significant changes in the product line. However, this chapter raises a dilemma: just how far should an organization go in trying to be responsive to current market demands? Continued short-term changes may lead to a lack of consistency and purpose in the institution, as well as raising doubts as to whether it has any central purpose or mission.

From education and health care, the focus changes to religion. "The Baptists Want You!" is a journalistic article by William Martin describing development of a marketing campaign which seeks to win new members for the Baptist Church in Texas. Although this campaign places heavy emphasis on communications, the article suggests the importance of also being concerned with other elements. For instance, lay people and ministers must be made aware of their own role in making newcomers feel at home in the church. Marketing of religion is a contentious subject, but there is nothing new to this concern, as shown by the excerpt at the end of the chapter. This is extracted from a speech delivered at the Church Advertising Convention at New Haven, Connecticut, and published more than 60 years ago in the November 1916 issue of *Advertising and Selling*.

Marketing in the public sector is just as important at the local level as it is on a national level. Linda Lewis' article, "Local Government Agencies Try Advertising," describes the approaches used by five different public institutions or municipal departments in Seattle, Washington. It is interesting to compare and contrast the five programs developed respectively by the transit authority, the electric utility, the state university, and the city's engineering and community relations departments. In each instance, the factors motivating use of marketing were different: the objectives ranged from highly measureable behaviors (such as using public transportation more or electricity less) to more intangible attitudinal changes, and the programs adopted reflected the different financial resources available.

31

The University Library: Analysis and Proposals

Charles B. Weinberg

University libraries should attempt to maximize the amount of information they supply. within certain financial and operational constraints. Yet, despite an increase in the size of such libraries, service standards have been tending to decline in many instances. This article suggests reasons for this decline and attempts to redefine strategic goals for the university library. It develops an approach for determining the information value of library resources for prospective users, highlighting the implications for acquisition, shelving and retention policies.

The past few decades have been an era of rapid growth and expansion for university and research libraries. For example, while it took 192 years (1754–1946) for Columbia University to acquire its first 2 million volumes, it took only fourteen years for Columbia to acquire its second 2 million volumes [7, p. 10]. Unfortunately, despite this increase in resources, library service has declined because of the increased and changing nature of demand. Specifically, more people more often cannot get the information they seek from the library.

Three main factors are the cause of this decline in service. The first is that the increase in the number of books, journals, periodicals, government publications, working papers, conferences, speeches, and other sources of information (henceforth referred to collectively as volumes) and the

increase in number of users have overwhelmed the increase in library resources. As shown in Exhibit 1, the number of published books has doubled and the number of potential users has increased at a greater rate than that for volumes in the university library. Thus, a university library has a decreasing fraction of total volume published, and it has to serve a growing population.

A second factor in the declining library service is the increased specialization of fields. Kemeny [5, p. 90] dramatically describes the situation.

> Specialization is the order of the day. To make a contribution to a field, the researcher must have reached the frontiers of knowledge. It is very hard to do this, unless one is willing to focus one's attention on a narrow segment of the field. Nonmathematicians have long ago given up trying to understand current mathematical research. It is becoming increasingly difficult to attempt communication between mathematicians.

Thus, as researchers develop narrower and narrower ranges of interests, the number of works that can be shared with

Charles B. Weinberg is Associate Professor of Marketing, Stanford University.

EXHIBIT 1
Doubling Times for Volumes and Users[1]

	Time to Double	Annual Growth Rate (Assuming Exponential)
Number of volumes produced [14]	10–15 years	6%
Number of volumes in Columbia libraries [7]	21–24 years	3%
Number of scientists [14]	10–15 years	6%
Number of university students in U.S. [3]	15–20 years	4%
Number of university faculty in U.S. [3]	15–20 years	4%

[1] Data inferred from the references listed.

other researchers declines. In order to provide the same amount of information per user, a greater number of volumes per user is required.

A third factor is a result of the "discipline-mission duality" [13]. Traditional disciplines (such as physics, biology, and mathematics) are being complemented by interdisciplinary fields (such as operations research and American civilization) and mission oriented fields (such as space research). It is no longer easy to identify a volume with a particular user. Thus, a researcher may have to search in many libraries before finding the volume he seeks. As specialized collections become located in different physical locations, the cost to the researcher becomes higher in terms of time lost. One solution is to buy copies of the volume for each of the specialized collections. This, however, sacrifices funds that could otherwise be spent to keep up with the increase in the literature. Another problem that the interdisciplinary studies introduces is in the selection of volumes to be purchased. For example, how should a book in sociology—which may have use in American studies, business schools, comparative religions, and sociology—be evalutated? Thus, the discipline-mission duality increases the difficulty of volume selection and location.

In summary, both the increase in the demand and the change in the type of demand have led to a decline in service from libraries. An approach to reversing this trend is developed in the following sections of this article.

GOALS AND OBJECTIVES OF LIBRARY SERVICES

In order to analyze the library and develop a framework of methodology for improving library services, we must define the proper strategy for libraries. By strategy we mean "the determination of the basic long-term goals and objectives of an enterprise, and the adoption of courses of action and the allocation of resources necessary for carrying out these goals" [2, p. 16]. The concept of strategy is vital to an organization; it provides a means of channelling resources in an orderly structured manner in such a way as to achieve objectives.[1]

Libraries currently conduct their operations as if their strategy were *to store and provide access to books, periodicals, papers, and other materials*. The reason for this strategy is most likely historical. Libraries were originally book collections and, while they now contain other materials, no major effort seems to have been made to reevaluate this strategy. Their current strategy should be *to supply information*. This new strategy is not merely a change of words. We will demonstrate the significance of the difference between the two strategies.

The first difference is "to store and provide access to" versus "supply." A library places heavy emphasis on its storing function, to the detriment of its ability to provide access. The policies followed for the binding together of a year's journals demonstrate this phenomenon. At the end of the year, the library gathers together all of the year's issues and sends them to the bindery. This is done to prevent the loss of single issues, which are often difficult to replace, and to protect and preserve the individual issues. The binding process usually takes at least three months. However, it is during the period just after its issue that a journal is most in demand. Thus, journals are taken out of circulation in their most demanded period to allow for use when they will not be as heavily demanded.[2]

The second difference is "to provide access to books, periodicals" versus "to supply information." Libraries place heavy emphasis on the physical characteristics of objects. Separate housing is often maintained for microfilms, current and bound periodicals, and other items. They are not stored with other physical objectives that bear on the same topic. Furthermore, comparatively little attention is paid to nonprinted materials. Finally, the criteria for the listing of items in card catalogs are based on physical characteristics. For example, books are listed in card catalogs, but articles are not. Certainly, there are many articles that should be listed individually because of their significance, and there are many books that could be removed from the card catalog or demoted to a *Reader's Guide* type of listing. As another example, if emphasis were placed on supplying information, then we might expect libraries to duplicate (with copyright permission) sections of books that are useful or in much demand. Under this system, the best way to meet the demand for such a book as William Feller's *Probability Theory and Its Applications* might be to divide it into chapters, since the demand is often for particular sections rather than the entire book. In marketing terms, we must design the product to fit the needs of the customer.

---

[1] The following analysis is based on the author's experience in several large libraries in American universities.

[2] In fact, some libraries do recognize this problem and practice delayed binding in which, for example, 1971 journals are not bound until the end of 1972.

For the remainder of this paper we will consider a library as an enterprise designed *to supply information*. For emphasis, we shall call the commodities that a library deals in to carry out its strategy by the name *Information Message Units,* abbreviated I.M.U.

OBJECTIVES OF A LIBRARY

In order to define more fully the objectives of a library, we must introduce two concepts: (1) the value of information maintained and provided, and (2) the cost of service to provide this information.

The value of information can only be defined in terms of its worth to its potential users, the members of the university community. Thus, there cannot be an objective measure of an item's value—the measure must be subjective. Furthermore, because a library maintains items in anticipation of their future usefulness, the value must be probabilistic. Let us discuss this more fully. A library purchases and retains I.M.U.'s that it feels have sufficient potential usefulness for the university community. Once a particular individual uses an I.M.U., she can then make a better estimate of its value to herself or to others. Her evaluation (see discussion of measurement below) will apply to the future use of this I.M.U., for the same purpose as hers or for other related purposes. In Bayesian terms, she is updating prior probabilities to obtain posterior probabilities. In other words, the following system is developed:

Prior.

P_i . . . probability that user group i will use the item (note, the sum of the P_i's is $\gtreqless 1$),

$R_{j|i}$ . . . probability that the information obtained will have value j if used by user group i,

$E_i = \int jR_{j|i}$ . . . expected value of this information to user group i if it uses it at all,

$C = \int P_iE_i$ . . . expected worth to entire community.

Posterior. Upon a user's experience, the values of P_i and $R_{j|i}$ can be updated to obtain

$$E_i' = \int jR_{j|i}',$$
$$C' = \int P_i'E_i'.$$

This system's usefulness depends upon the ability to measure and update the parameters P, R, and j. In the following paragraphs we will attempt to show that this determination is currently being done on an individual-by-individual basis. What is needed is a standard scale for j. It is suggested that such a scale is obtainable.

The approach suggested here is in contrast to that in [8] and [12], where the emphasis is on utilizing circulation data alone to decide stocking and storage questions. Circulation based approaches necessarily do not deal with the origi-

nal purchase decision and put infrequently used but high value volumes at a disadvantage. On the other hand, these approaches eliminate the need for a user evaluation system. The approach developed here, however, can lead to integration of the purchase and retention decisions on the basis of a value versus cost comparison.

To the members of a university community, time is an important constraint. Because of the exponential increase in the quantity of literature produced, a person no longer has time to read all that is written in his own and associated fields. Thus, the decision on what to read is not made lightly; it is of serious concern to the individual and is usually well thought out, at least implicitly. Thus, a person does not read at random, but reads what appears to be most useful to him. In other words, he calculates the expected value of books, journals, and other reading materials to his purposes and then chooses what he will read. This expected value is based on reading book titles, previous experience with an author, recommendations, and other factors. The purposes may differ for reviewing different items. Some are read to remain current in one's own speciality and to know what one's colleagues are doing, others are read to maintain a general knowledge of the field, others are read to provide material for lectures, and so on. The important points are these: One, prior to reading the item, a conscious decision is made as to its expected value. In other words, a person is calculating his E_i. He may calculate the E_i directly or by thinking in terms of $R_{j|i}$ and j. Two, after reading an item, he can made a new estimate of E_i. In addition, the specialist library staff who are trained in both academic fields and librarianship can help to operate this evaluation scheme. Such staff help to discover potential sources of I.M.U.'s as well as to set the E_i's.

The problem now is that people might not be able to think of E_i or j in quantitative terms; and that if they do, they will all be using different scales. Let us attack the second case first. One can infer from [13] that all branches of science have followed rather closely the same growth pattern, especially with respect to the development of the literature (see p. 10 especially). Now it would seem likely that the probability distribution of the quality of literature would be the same in any field. As a hypothetical example, we might see the following distribution:

Probability	Value
5%	Very High
10%	High
30%	Medium
40%	Low
15%	None

After developing the shape of this distribution, we could then promulgate it as the scale to use in assigning values. That is, when reviewing current literature, evaluate it in terms of a long run frequency distribution. Short run deviations would, of course, be expected. If the probability distribution is to be accepted, then the range each individual uses—once specified—could be adjusted later for overall conformity. Again, if we consider those people who do not think quantitatively, we must at least be able to convince them of the validity of the probability distribution for the quality discussed above. If they can then develop qualitative evaluations that fit key points on the curve, it would then be possible to interpolate for the quantitative values to a sufficient degree of accuracy.

The user evaluation system may possibly operate in the following manner. On a periodic basis, users are given a list of I.M.U.'s the library is considering acquiring. Alongside each item is, for example, a five-point scale on which the user checks his evaluation or gives his probability of the I.M.U. being in that category. In order to conserve user time, a specialist librarian can edit the list so that all I.M.U.'s that have a high probability of being at the extremes may be omitted or placed in a separate category in which the librarian's evaluation is given. Thus, the user needs to evaluate only those I.M.U.'s that the librarian thinks are likely to have an E_i in the middle of the range.

Thus, it seems reasonable that the expected value of information to an individual or to a group of individuals in the same field can be obtained. In other words, we can derive the parameter E_i. In order to evaluate a volume, however, we need to aggregate over all the different groups in the university. Furthermore, as we discussed earlier, the value of E_i changes as a result of experience. That is, it must be updated. Later, we will describe a procedure for carrying out this aggregating and updating of the information value. For the present, let us assume that a current value of C can be obtained. The objective of a library can now be defined operationally as "to maximize the amount of information supplied to its users."

This maximization is subject to at least two constraints. The first is a service criterion that includes the time a user must wait before a request is fulfilled and the percentage of time that a request cannot be filled. It is essential to realize that a library cannot meet every request; and for those that it can meet, it cannot always supply the necessary I.M.U. immediately.[3] The concepts of inventory management as related to the flow of information are valid here. Probabilistic assessments of stock outs, lost sales, and order cycle times must be made. In business inventory management an attempt is made to convert these assessments into dollar figures, so that operating policies can be set which maximize profits. For libraries, no method of converting information values and service standards into a single measure appears to be at hand. A framework for setting service standards, however, can be developed.

We have already developed a measure of value for I.M.U.'s. It would seem that the greater the value of informa-

tion, the more stringent the service standard we would set.[4] Thus, we could divide all I.M.U.'s into some arbitrary number of ranks, and for each rank set a standard for service.[5] A summary control system report might appear as follows:

Rank	Value of Information Provided	Average Time to Provide Information	Value of Information Not Provided
1			
2			
.			
.			
.			

As experience is gained with the system, reasonable objectives for "Average Time to Provide Information" and "Value of Information Not Provided" can be developed.

A second constraint is financial. The library must work within a budgetary limitation. However, the present method of allocating funds to book buying, buildings, salaries, and capital equipment and facilities is improper because it is arbitrary with respect to the objective of supplying information. In the next section, we will show how the application of this strategy requires a library to rethink its policies on the storage and retention of I.M.U.'s.

APPLICATION

A library is an enterprise that attempts to maximize the amount of information it supplies within financial and service constraints. To achieve this objective, it carries out five main operations—the procurement, processing, storage, dissemination, and disposal of I.M.U.'s. The first four are standard functions of a library; the last is not often thought of as being a means to achieve a library's objectives. The costs of these operations are substantial. For example, for serial publications the average initial cost of acquiring and cataloguing a new title was found to be $60.60, in a survey of four university libraries [12]. Storage costs consist of annual recurring costs of actually caring for the items held in storage and a fixed one-time charge for building and equipping the storage facilities. The service standards that are set have a large effect on storage costs for two reasons. First, lower priority items can be stored more compactly so that less storage space is required per item. Second, the storage location for lower priority items can be moved to less valuable land

---

[3] See [10] for a methodology for testing delivery time in a library and an analysis of results. See [4] for a description of a market research procedure to determine customer reactions to different service policies.

[4] One device to prevent people from placing high values on all items would be to have a longer borrowing period for lower valued items.

[5] A lower standard of service can result when a library saves money by assigning a lower level of personal resources, employing a less expensive bibliographic format, and storing the I.M.U. in a less expensive storage area.

than that on which the main library is located. From an economic standpoint, this cost is significant.

The fifth operation—disposal of I.M.U.'s—at first seems contradictory to how a library should function. However, it is not. The principle behind this operation is that the funds freed by disposing of I.M.U.'s can be used to purchase other I.M.U.'s that have a higher expected information value. This principle is operational because of the rapid decline in frequency of usage of most I.M.U.'s ten to fifteen years after their publication, as Exhibit 2 illustrates for the books in the Yale Medical Library. Although the number of books published in 1960 (15,012) is 2.3 times the number published in 1945 (6,548), the Yale data show about 13 times as many *uses* of 1960 books versus 1945 books. (This topic is pursued in depth in [12].) Our conclusion is not that all old books should be thrown out, but that many of them should be stored in a more remote location or in a regional or national archive. This decision depends upon the expected value of the books as opposed to the cost saved, and possibly the salvage value of the old books. Since the decision is based on the expected value of the I.M.U., old but high value I.M.U.'s will be retained. In other words, we can derive a number representing Expected Value per Dollar. (Note that by placing an item in a lower storage category, we increase the Expected Value per Dollar. Thus, most books would go through a series of storage locations before being disposed.) The other side of the decision is whether to buy a new book. The relevant costs here are procurement, processing, and storage costs. Thus, for new books, we can also calculate an Expected Value per Dollar. The library then allocates its funds between storage of old volumes and purchase of new volumes so as to maximize the expected value of its collection.

EXHIBIT 2
Recorded Use of Books in the Yale Medical Library by Age of Book[1]

Age of book (years)	1	2	3	4	5	10	15	20	25	30
Uses of books	157	121	118	86	90	54	12	4	10	3

[1] Derived from data in [6].

One argument against the disposal of old works is that invaluable but as yet unrecognized discoveries are possibly contained in them. There are two counterarguments. The first is that the discovery will be made later by someone else and that, therefore, the information will not be lost to humanity for ever. For example, although Gregor Mendel made his famous studies of garden peas to develop the theory of dominant and recessive genes in 1865, it was not until 35 years later "that his paper was 'discovered' by three biologists. All three were working independently on the same kind of problem that Mendel had investigated. These men . . . obtained results that agreed with those of Mendel" [1, p.

527]. Thus, we may surmise that even if Mendel's work had never been found, the same principles would have been discovered. The second counterargument is that the amount of time saved in research by eliminating all the inconsequential works from reading lists by making them no longer available more than offsets the time lost because a particular discovery was not known.

Finally, the system need not go so far as to destroy all copies of a volume. We can envisage a series of interrelated libraries on a hierarchical basis. When there is insufficient demand at a single library to buy or retain an I.M.U., the I.M.U. can be evaluated at the next level of the system. Because the higher level will cover a larger population, the value of the I.M.U. will be increased relative to its value at the more local level. Further, presumably the higher the level the lower the storage and holding costs. The ultimate level, which would have the lowest storage cost, would then buy or retain all I.M.U.'s that were not elsewhere in the system. Because only I.M.U.'s that fail to meet the standards at one level go on to the next higher level, the final library will not be a collection of all I.M.U.'s, but rather of those that were not sufficiently valued to be retained at more accessible levels.

SELECTION AND MAINTENANCE OF INVENTORY INFORMATION

Exhibits 3 describes a procedure for libraries to select and maintain volumes in their inventory of information in accordance with the expected values of the potential users. This procedure is best illustrated by a flow chart (see Exhibit 3).

This procedure can be extended to journal articles in a way to determine whether an article should be listed in the card catalog. As long as an article maintains a high enough expected value of information it can be maintained in the card catalog listing.

Through this procedure, a library can maintain its collection so that it functions to maximize the information it supplies to the entire university community.

RELATIONSHIP BETWEEN UNIVERSITY LIBRARIES

This article has confined itself to the design and operation of a university library system, viewed primarily as an entity in itself. However, most university libraries have developed interrelationships with other universities in order to share the burden of keeping up with the vast growth of I.M.U.'s. These relationships are of two types. In one type, libraries form agreements among themselves in which each library agrees to specialize its collections in some areas and essentially serve as a resource library to other libraries in the agreement. In terms of the framework developed in this article, the library is expanding the number of user groups *i* that it includes in its calculation for an I.M.U. decision in the areas in which the library will specialize. Operationally, rather than attempt to develop ratings from a geographically

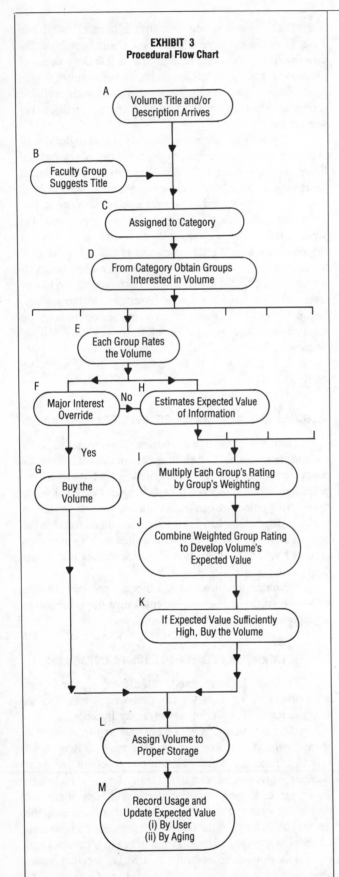

EXHIBIT 3
Procedural Flow Chart

A — Volume Title and/or Description Arrives

B — Faculty Group Suggests Title

C — Assigned to Category

D — From Category Obtain Groups Interested in Volume

E — Each Group Rates the Volume

F — Major Interest Override

H — Estimates Expected Value of Information (No)

G — Buy the Volume (Yes)

I — Multiply Each Group's Rating by Group's Weighting

J — Combine Weighted Group Rating to Develop Volume's Expected Value

K — If Expected Value Sufficiently High, Buy the Volume

L — Assign Volume to Proper Storage

M — Record Usage and Update Expected Value
(i) By User
(ii) By Aging

KEY

Steps A and B. New titles for possible acquisition are brought to the attention of the library either through conventional channels or by faculty recommendation.

Steps C and D. In the first section of this article, we described the discipline-mission duality. Volumes no longer are of interest to a single group in a university community, but, instead, work in one subject may be of concern to many groups. Steps C and D deal with this duality. In step C, volumes are classified into their subject "category." In step D, the faculty is classified into "groups." The categories and groups may or may not be identical. The important point is that each faculty group indicates in which categories of volumes they are interested. For example, the international affairs group may be interested in volumes on economics, political science, and history. Steps C and D operate as follows: after a volume title and description comes to the attention of the library, it is classified as to category and then sent to the interested groups for evaluation.

Steps E, F, G, and H. As indicated earlier, each group (with the help of specialist library staff, if available) rates a volume as to its expected value for that group (E and H). As discussed previously, the specialist librarian may edit the list presented to the user so that only the "borderline" evaluations need to be obtained from the user. This rating must then be combined wth others in order to determine its overall expected value to the community. In some cases, a book may be of interest to a particular group even if no other groups wish to utilize this volume. In such a case, steps F and G provide a means for purchasing this volume. (By placing limits on the quantity that each group can order for its own interests, a control can be placed on the use of step F. If a group has an excess of volumes that it wishes to purchase via step F, it can superimpose this entire system for its own subgroups.)

Steps I and J. In a previous section, we indicated that an E_i value could be obtained. The development of the measure P_i was postponed. P_i was described as the probability that the ith group would read a particular volume. This probability cannot be easily obtained for each volume. However, a reasonable substitute is each group's probability of utilizing an item from a particular category. (The circulation system can be designed to provide these usage probabilities. For example, the computerized circulation system at Ohio State University provides this information as a byproduct of its circulation control function [9].) These probabilities weigh each group's expected value to yield an expected value of the volume for the community. Furthermore, these weights can be modified so that groups that the university wants to emphasize can have a more significant influence in the valuation of volumes. (This is also done directly by the controls set on step F.) In summary the category assignment of a volume determines which groups will review it and the influence of their judgments.

Step K. The expected value of a volume is compared to other possible uses of library funds; if the value is sufficiently high, the volume is purchased. A volume that is not originally purchased may later be acquired because of changes in other opportunities.

Step L. Upon receipt, the volume is assigned to its proper storage location.

Step M. An important function of the library system is to maintain the expected value of its possessions on a current basis. This is especially important in view of the arguments made earlier concerning disposition of volumes and alternation of their storage location.

Two processes operate to carry this out. The first is automatic and depends upon the age of the volume. In accordance with data similar to that used in Exhibit 2, a deterioration factor is applied to the expected value of volumes as they grow older. The second process depends upon usage. Each time a person uses a volume, he would be required to submit a new estimate of its expected value; in other words, the prior probabilities are revised on the basis of sample information. The structure of the system is designed so that it is to his advantage to reevaluate the volume whether he found it useful or not. If he found it useful and does not indicate that this is so, then the automatic deterioration process will lower the volume's expected value and he may not be able to obtain it again. If the user did not find the book informative, then failure to downgrade it allows it to deteriorate less rapidly than it should and thus prevents its replacement by new materials.

dispersed set of users, the system could be designed so that probabilities of usage in certain groups could be modified as suggested in the description of Steps I and J.

In the type of network agreement described in the previous paragraph, decisions about I.M.U. availability are made prior to specific user requests. (In such cases, it would be logical to list I.M.U.'s in card catalogues of all the libraries in the specialization agreement.) The other type of network arangement applies to instances when a user requests an I.M.U. that the library does not have. Through the use of the Union catalog and interlibrary loan agreements, the library can find out where the I.M.U. is located and borrow it for the user. Thus, one effect of the network system is to transform a library's decision not to acquire or to continue to maintain an I.M.U. from one of nonavailability to the researcher to one involving the time to gain access to an I.M.U. However, currently, the time to acquire an I.M.U. on an interlibrary loan is considerably longer than the time required if the I.M.U. is presently in the user's own library system.[6]

The approach described in this paper for an individual university library system can be applied to networks of library systems. For example, we may view each university library as a user of a regional system, and each regional system as a user of a still larger system, and so on. Then according to the value and probability of use of I.M.U.'s in particular communities, the locations of I.M.U.'s could be set. By balancing costs and potential usage, sizes of different libraries in an overall system could be developed. As in an individual library, the key point is the accurate assessment of a library system's strategy and objectives and the development of effective actions to reach these goals.

---

[6] Data on time from when a user requests a volume to the time at which the user receives it are not generally kept by libraries. However, Orr and Schless [11] report, in a study of biomedical libraries, that in a test the median time period from library initiation of a request to its receipt was 8.7 days.

REFERENCES

1. Biology Curriculum Study Committee. *Biological Science: An Inquiry Into Life*. New York: Harcourt, Brace, and World, 1963.
2. Chandler, A. D. *Strategy and Structure*. New York: Anchor Books, 1962, p. 16.
3. *Historical Statistics of the United States and Continuation*. Washington, D.C.: Government Printing Office, 1960 and 1962.
4. Hutchinson, W. M., and Stolle, J. F. "How to Manage Customer Service," *Harvard Business Review* (November–December, 1968):85–96.
5. Kemeny, J. G. "The Knowledge Explosion: A Mathematician's Point of View." In *The Knowledge Explosion* edited by F. Sweeny, Farrar, Straus, and Giroux, New York, 1966.
6. Kilgour, F. G. "Recorded Use of Books in the Yale Medical Library." *American Documentation* (October 1961).
7. Logsdon, R. *The Vast Library Resources of New York City*. New York: Columbia University Press, 1965.
8. Morse, P. M. *Library Effectiveness, A Systems Approach*. Cambridge, MA: M.I.T. Press, 1968.
9. IBM Corporation. "On Line Remote Catalog Access and Circulation Control System, Part I: Functional Specifications." Data Processing Division, Available as ERIC Document No. ED-050792.
10. Orr, R. H. *et al.* "Development of Methodologic Tools for Planning and Managing Library Services: II. Measuring a Library's Capability for Providing Documents." *Medical Library Bulletin* 56 (July 1968): 241–67.
11. Orr, R. H., and Schless, A. P. "Document Delivery Capabilities of Major Biomedical Libraries in 1968: Results of a National Survey Employing Standardized Tests." *Bulletin of the Medical Library Association* 60 (July 1972):383–422.
12. Palmour, V. E., and Wiederkehr, R. R. "A Decision Model for Library Policies on Serial Publications." Paper presented at TIMS International Conference, July 1, 1970.
13. President's Science Advisory Committee. *Science, Government, and Information*. Government Printing Office, Washington, DC, 1963.
14. Price, D. J. *Little Science Big Science*. New York: Columbia University Press, 1963.

32

Hospital Revises Role, Reaches Out to Cultivate and Capture Markets

Douglass J. Seaver

The Methodist Hospital of Indiana conducted a marketing study to identify actions it might take to reverse a decline in utilization of the hospital. Starting with the product line, the study suggested that the hospital deemphasize its primary care services in such areas as obstretics and build its capability as source of specialized services for doctors and other hospitals in the regional area it served. A marketing communication program was implemented to support these changes. In addition, Methodist Hospital developed a marketing information system to help it identify problems and make decisions.

From June to December 1974, immediately following the Economic Stabilization Program (ESP), Methodist Hospital of Indiana, Indianapolis, Marion County, was a troubled institution. It had just avoided bankruptcy, it had no capital, and it was operating in a still unhealthy economy. Furthermore, the hospital faced continuing stringent price controls as third-party payers strongly represented their subscribers, who remained concerned about hospital costs. The hospital also faced a serious population shift and the concomitant growth or relocation of other local hospitals.

When the hospital's inpatient census did not climb back above 80 percent by the second week of January 1975,

following the traditional Christmas decrease, the hospital's management decided to shift its strategy from restricting its operations because of reduced revenues to aggressively reaching out. With the end of the ESP restrictions, the hospital had the freedom to undertake new directions of development; however, it had to answer serious public and institutional questions.

The public issue was how to best use the hospital's existing resources, considering that the population it traditionally served was moving away and that hospitals closer to growing population areas were expanding. The answer was to emphasize the hospital's development as a sophisticated referral center—a trend that had actually begun 10 years earlier. The institutional concern was how to maintain a viable hospital that had a tertiary care role and the necessary referral

Douglass J. Seaver is vice-president for planning and operations, Methodist Hospital of Indiana, Indianapolis.

patterns. The answer was to market the hospital, that is, its image and its services. However, the hospital was in the worst possible marketing position. It had virtually no capital, no developmental funds, no usable marketing information, no continuing marketing research, and no trained or disciplined sales force.

MARKETING PLAN BROACHED

In January 1975, the hospital held a two-day marketing retreat. For the first time, it seriously broached the idea of marketing the hospital. Even in its capital fund-raising activities, the hospital had worked through the United Hospital Fund of Indianapolis. The participants in the retreat included the president of the hospital; the vice-presidents; the president and other officers of the medical staff; and the directors of the hospital's major revenue-producing departments, such as the laboratory, radiology, and emergency departments.

The retreat generated three significant results. First, the developing role of the hospital as a tertiary referral center was recognized. The potential for building this role by emphasizing the hospital's sophisticated services in seeking markets from which to draw referrals became the basic marketing thrust.

Second, the framework of the hospital's marketing plan emerged. The hospital had been almost strictly in the "retail business" of selling services through "salesmen," the medical staff members, to "customers," the patients. At the retreat, the hospital planned to develop a "wholesale market" in which other hospitals would buy services from Methodist Hospital and would sell them to their own patients. It soon became obvious that the hospital needed a full-time marketing director to work with outlying institutions in order to develop this "wholesale business."

Third, a long list of miscellaneous suggestions for generating better publicity regarding the hospital's services, for developing new services, and for building the medical staff as a "sales force" was made.

One of the ideas that first was explored at the marketing retreat was the development of the admitting department's outreach to private physicians' offices. This outreach was intended to build rapport with the physicians' office staffs and to make it as convenient as possible for the physicians and their office staffs to admit patients to the hospital. It took about one year to fully implement this program. The hospital now has one full-time admitting employee who is responsible strictly for visiting physicians' offices to explain the hospital's admissions procedures, to provide preadmission information, to provide preprinted physician orders, and to perform other similar services.

A number of new programs were discussed at the retreat. For example, it was agreed that a pediatric pulmonary center should be developed to provide a needed service and stabilize the census of Children's Pavilion, a 112-bed component of the hospital. Developing a training program for county ambulance service paramedics was recognized as

a way to establish rapport with the community, to educate it about the hospital's services, and to cultivate potential sources of patients. A special van to transport critically ill newborns to the hospital's special care nursery also was discussed. The hospital management believed that this service was needed in the community, that it would offer tremendous visibility, and that it would offer the potential for publicity through the news media.

The importance of recruiting physicians, particularly specialists, and the importance of the hospital's medical education programs, especially its residency programs, also were discussed. Medical education builds the hospital's medical staff directly and increases the number of physicians who are familiar with the hospital, some of whom may settle in other parts of Indiana to practice, but who may refer their more complicated cases to their former teachers at the hospital.

Each of these suggestions from the marketing retreat was acted on or implemented. It took two years to implement some of them, such as the pediatric pulmonary center. However, the marketing retreat definitely provided a new focus and perspective for the hospital.

During the six months after the retreat, a study written by Marc Voyvodich, the hospital's administrative resident, provided a framework for a comprehensive, detailed marketing plan for the hospital. It assembled a tremendous amount of data regarding the hospital's services, its markets, and its medical staff. The study concluded with recommendations on where to market, on which services to market, and on how to reach the markets.

Where to market. First, the study recommended that, in order to best compete for Marion County patients, the hospital market its emergency department services. The hospital has the largest and most comprehensive emergency department in the state, it is the most centrally located hospital in relation to all of the major interstate highways, and it has the largest and most sophisticated intensive care unit. Moreover, emergency patients contributed heavily to inpatient days. For these reasons, the development of the emergency department as a trauma center was undertaken. In addition, the hospital developed specific emergency department links with local industries through means such as direct telephone hookups for immediate consultation.

Second, the study recommended that the hospital market inpatient services to patients outside Marion County by emphasizing the hospital's sophisticated specialty services and the availability of specialists located close to the hospital. Reaching the outlying markets was deemed worthwhile, because their expanding populations needed to be served and because their hospitals were small, ranging from 83 to 184 beds. The interstate highway system also provides very convenient access to the hospital from all of the contiguous counties.

Which services to market. The study's recommendations emphasized the hospital's highly specialized services and deemphasized its primary care services. It seemed logical that patients should receive care at their local hospitals whenever possible. Consequently, the hospital chose not to aggressively market routine services, such as obstetrics, even though it had a declining obstetrical volume.

Another issue raised concerning which services to market was whether to build on the hospital's strengths or to shore up its weaknesses. Emphasizing and building on its strengths proved to be the more successful approach. The marketing study suggested that the hospital develop "centers" for various specialized types of care, such as a neurosurgical center, a cardiovascular center, a renal disease center, a newborn center, and a diabetic management center.

How to reach the market. The study recommended building rapport with the outlying hospitals through shared service programs. These programs would help develop the relationships between hospitals and between medical staffs that would be necessary to groom these markets for patient referrals.

REGULAR MARKETING REPORTS

As a result of the marketing study, it became clear that the hospital needed to routinely gather patient information in order to assess the results of its marketing efforts and to identify new areas for future growth. The hospital management considered it important to have a marketing information system that was as complete as possible and that could track changes in patient volumes on a monthly basis. It was decided to design a computerized information system that would collect information from all patients and provide monthly reports. The hospital's computerized billing tapes were selected as an accurate, convenient source of information.

The system is designed to examine the hospital's inpatient market, emergency department market, and referred outpatient market. Five reports are generated. The first report, a physician utilization report, lists each physician's name, age, office address, specialty, credentials, and number of patients admitted in any particular month. These patients are grouped according to discharge diagnosis. The average length of stay for each diagnostic group is indicated, and each group is divided further according to sex and age.

The focus of the physician utilization report is on the admitting physicians, because the hospital is interested in knowing which of them are most active in admitting patients. An annual summary of this report can be shared with individual physicians, who can be asked then to indicate how their hospital practice of medicine will change in the next year. The hospital can use this information in its annual planning.

The second report focuses on the geographic markets from which inpatients are drawn. It analyzes them by individual medical services. For each medical service, it lists the names of all of the physicians in that service and the number of patients and their lengths of stay for 13 zip code groupings. This report quickly shows the geographic markets from

which each service draws, the physicians who draw from each area, and each physician's volume for each area.

The third report is a summary of the geographic origin of all inpatients according to the hospital's five primary-secondary services and eight secondary-tertiary services. According to geographic area, the number of patients receiving primary-secondary services and the number receiving secondary-tertiary services are totaled. The relationship between the two totals tracks the changing mix of patients as the hospital becomes more specialized.

The fourth report is a zip code analysis of emergency department patients according to age and sex. The fifth report is a zip code analysis of referred outpatients according to the medical service used. The difference between these two outpatient markets is studied. In addition, the outpatient markets and the primary-secondary care inpatient markets are compared.

The information from these reports is analyzed, charted, graphed, and summarized in an overall monthly report. The hospital has developed demographic data, such as average family income and racial composition, according to zip code. When the hospital undertakes a new marketing program such as the sponsorship of a neighborhood health center, it can examine what happens to its outpatient and inpatient utilization from the zip code area in which the new program is located. In addition, the Indiana Hospital Association and the former Comprehensive Health Planning Agency have provided the hospital with the number of all hospital admissions per 1,000 population according to zip code. The hospital can compare its number of admissions per 1,000 population from each zip code area with the total number to determine the percentage of the market that it has captured.

SELLING SERVICES "WHOLESALE"

In May 1976, the hospital established the corporate position of vice-president for shared services. This vice-president is the hospital's marketing officer. The title "vice-president for shared services" was selected because the main thrust of the job is the "wholesale marketing" of the hospital's services to other hospitals and health care providers. Creating this full-time position was an important decision, because, by doing so, the hospital committed specific manpower and provided a corporate structure for its marketing program. Because the "wholesale" marketing involved selling services to small rural hospitals, the former administrator of a 100-bed Indiana hospital was selected for the position of vice-president for shared services. The hospital believed that knowing the needs of small hospitals and having a reputation among administrators of small and rural institutions were important qualifications. In essence, the hospital selected this vice-president on the basis of his ability to relate and sell to that market.

The hospital sells two types of services—administrative services, such as purchasing and management consultation, and clinical services, such as respiratory therapy and pathology. The purpose of selling administrative services is to increase the hospital's revenue and ultimately stabilize its financial condition through unrelated business income. These services are priced at full cost plus a net margin. Shared clinical services are sold to effect better distribution of scarce health care resources within Indiana and to build relationships between hospitals and between medical staffs in order to increase referrals, when appropriate, from primary-secondary hospitals to Methodist Hospital as a specialty referral center. Clinical services are priced at full cost only.

Under this kind of arrangement, a hospital buys the available services that it wants. The arrangement can be ended easily. A small hospital may have little to say about the makeup of the services, usually having to take what is offered. However, in its community, the small hospital can be proud of being a prudent buyer and of offering services that are comparable in quality to services available in large, sophisticated hospitals.

Selling clinical services to small hospitals presents one very threatening problem. Small hospitals are wary that a large one from which it buys services may draw its patients away. This fear must be overcome. One of the basic tenets of Methodist Hospital's marketing program is that the provision of shared services be designed to keep patients at their local hospitals whenever possible.

PROGRAM IMPACT

What has been the impact of the marketing program at Methodist Hospital? New revenue programs have been developed, and new clinical shared services have been implemented. The hospital has significantly changed the population it serves, while it has maintained its traditionally high occupancy rate and stabilized its financial position.

Some of the shared service programs that have been developed include a respiratory therapy service in a rural hospital, remote cardiac monitoring for a small institution, a total management contract with another hospital, and joint purchasing agreements with two neighborhood health centers.

The remote cardiac monitoring shows how these shared services meet the criteria of the marketing program. A dedicated telephone hookup links Methodist Hospital with Decatur County Memorial Hospital, a 100-bed institution located 45 miles away in Greensburg. Cardiac monitors in Decatur Hospital's cardiac care unit transmit patients' signals to Methodist Hospital's heart station, where specially trained nurses monitor the signals 24 hours per day, seven days per week. Internal medicine residents, cardiology fellows, and some of the leading cardiologists in the state are available at Methodist Hospital for consultation. Computerized electrocardiography over telephone lines also is provided to Decatur Hospital. The computer at Methodist Hospital reads the ECG, a cardiologist then reviews it, and his reading is sent through the computer and the telephone line to Decatur Hospital. ECG scanning equipment also is provided to Decatur Hospital. Because of the cardiac monitoring program, patients now can remain at Decatur Hospital, which does not have a cardiologist. The quality of patient care is improved through the monitoring, and physician rapport is enhanced through the consultations. For patients who need open-heart surgery, the link is established for referral to Methodist Hospital.

From 1974 to 1976, the average inpatient occupancy rate at Methodist Hospital remained about the same. However, the hospital's market changed significantly. The percentage of patients from Marion County dropped from 72 percent to 67 percent, whereas the percentage of patients from other counties rose from 28 percent to 33 percent. The decrease in the percentage of Marion County patients resulted from a population shift and from increased utilization of other Marion County hospitals. The increase in the percentage of referrals from other counties resulted from Methodist Hospital's emphasis on more sophisticated services; it reflects clearly the hospital's trend away from primary-secondary services toward secondary-tertiary ones.

The hospital's outpatient volume increased, and the market from which these patients were drawn also changed significantly. In 1974, the hospital served 13.3 percent of Marion County's outpatients; by 1976, it served only 11.4 percent. The percentage of emergency department visits and clinic visits remained about the same, but the percentage of referred outpatient visits for sophisticated laboratory and radiology procedures increased significantly, by six percent.

SUMMARY AND OUTLOOK

Methodist Hospital aggressively and successfully has marketed its tertiary care services, maintained its patient volume and financial viability, and faced population shifts and the growth of other hospitals. The hospital's marketing approach has been to develop more specialized services, to seek broader markets from which to draw patients, to recruit physician-specialists, and to build relationships between hospitals and between medical staffs through shared services programs. The hospital is confident that these efforts will continue to sell its growing tertiary care services to new markets.

33

New York New School Rides on Rising Wave of Adult Education

Roger Ricklefs

The New School for Social Research is a recognized pioneer and leader in the field of adult education. It has succeeded in this increasingly competitive marketplace by appealing to the wide range of reasons that prompt Americans to take such courses and by using sophisticated approaches for selecting, pricing, and advertising the courses it offers. In determining its continuing education offerings, the New School must also be concerned with their appropriateness in a university which offers numerous demanding academic courses.

Plenty of universities have courses in Shakespeare or Shelley. But what if you're more interested in Porky Pig?

The New School for Social Research has the course for you: "That's NOT All Folks: A Look Behind the Scenes of America's Great Cartoons." One evening a week, some 70 students may watch reruns of Porky's first appearances and follow his development. Or they contemplate the technical milestone of Daffy Duck's incredible expanding eyes. They learn that Woody Woodpecker's characteristic laugh first belonged to Bugs Bunny, and that irreverent filmmakers sprinkled profanities only evident to lip readers in some of the early cartoons.

"It's great to learn what went on behind the scenes. I just love Bugs Bunny," says Jerry Beck, a computer operator who enrolled.

Such courses make educational purists wince, but they are routine fare at the New School, a recognized pioneer and leader in the booming field of adult education. While

Roger Ricklefs is a staff reporter for *The Wall Street Journal*.

many institutions have expanded adult course offerings as a sideline, the New School has viewed them as its main business for nearly 60 years. Teaching everything from "Medieval Thought and Culture" to "Creative Knitting," the school attracts 17,000 students a semester, nearly triple the figure of 15 years ago. For many New Yorkers, taking courses at the New School has become a way of life.

KNOWLEDGE-THIRSTY ADULTS

Indeed, "taking courses" is a growing part of American life in general. Enrollment in adult education programs of all sorts soared to more than 17 million in 1975 (the latest figures available) from 13 million only six years earlier and still is rising, the Department of Health, Education and Welfare says.

As traditional enrollments stagnate, many colleges hope evening courses for adults will save the day. But many of the offerings are embroiled in the growing national controversy over possibly frivolous college courses. While enthusiasts say the adult education boom brings "life-long learning" to millions, others say it merely opens classroom doors to Porky Pig.

Whatever the case, competition for adult enrollments is leading higher education ever more conspicuously into the marketplace, and a look at the New School shows how the process works. The New School advertises on television. It lets students enroll by telephone and charge tuition on their Master Charge or Visa cards. It distributes nearly 130,000 catalogs a semester. It even buys mailing lists.

As it concentrates on adult education, the New School lacks a captive audience of traditional students who will suffer required courses to obtain degrees. Thus, it must sell its offerings course-by-course to people who take them solely by choice. It succeeds by appealing to the wide range of reasons that prompt millions of Americans to take such courses.

READING AND ROMANCE

"I found I wasn't doing as much reading as I wanted to, and I knew I wouldn't do it on my own," says Dr. Kenneth Rosenbaum, a young anesthesiologist who enrolled in a Greek literature course. Anne Kahn, a middle-aged legal secretary who has taken several New School courses, says, "I just like to get out—to get away from the TV, actually." She says she seeks courses that are "noncommittal—the ones that don't have any homework." (Few New School continuing education students take courses for credit, and many courses don't carry credit anyway.)

Many students want to learn business skills. Some also would like to find love. Marsha Slucker, who has taken numerous courses, says, "In some classes, you can see people change seats if things don't look promising."

Thus, the New School's modern, nine-story building in Greenwich Village attracts just about any variety of New Yorker who can pay the $115 fee for an average semester course. In the bustling lobby lined with modern art, striped suits headed for "Technical Factors in Stock Market Analysis" brush past denim jackets bound for "Folk-Rock Guitar Techniques."

The New School today seems far removed from the tiny experimental institution that opened its doors in 1919, offering only seven courses. Philosopher John Dewey, historian Charles A. Beard and a few other celebrated scholars founded the New School to help educate adults "interested in the grave social, political, economic and educational problems of the day."

EARLY BLACK STUDIES

The school soon offered pioneering courses in black culture taught by W. E. B. DuBois and in modern dance taught by Martha Graham. The famous social scientist Thorstein Veblen also taught there—and was fired, partly for mumbling his lectures.

The New School founded the University in Exile as a haven for scholars fleeing Nazi Europe. Later called the Graduate Faculty, it claimed such famous professors as the late philosopher Hannah Arendt. Economist Robert L. Heilbroner, political scientist Hans J. Morgenthau and other well-known figures teach there today.

While the Graduate Faculty teaches subjects like "Neural Mechanisms of Psychological Processes," the thriving Adult Division often appeals to less cerebral interests. The course "Antique Flea Markets" teaches how to buy and sell in such markets. ("You can often get good prices on breakables at the end of the day because dealers hate to pack these things," advises instructor Margorie Friedman, a college teacher and veteran flea-market enthusiast.) Students visit several flea markets and finally operate one of their own for a day.

The course was packed with 70 students last fall—often with people who would like to sell the piles of merchandise they have bought at flea markets over the years. Julian Marwell, a businessman who has accumulated 150 antique typewriters, says he wants "to learn the tricks of the trade" so that he can sell as well as buy. "Besides, I'm spreading out into buying other junk," he adds.

Tapping a market that colleges have largely neglected, the intensive one-day foreign language courses attract 600 students a year, mostly people who want to learn basic expressions prior to a trip abroad, but don't want to take a semester-long course.

The popularity of such courses contributes handsomely to the hefty profit potential of adult education. Though recent figures aren't available, New York University said four years ago that its adult program was earning a 25 percent profit on revenue. The New School says profits from the Adult Division essentially offset the deficit of the prestigious Graduate Faculty. (The other two New School divisions, the Center for New York City Affairs and the Parsons School of Design, approximately break even, officials say.)

Adult programs can be profitable partly because they sell instruction only; the salary dollar goes a long way. New School faculty members are part-timers who do their research elsewhere. Many have primary occupations outside teaching; a marketing executive, for instance, may teach a course in his field. The school pays most instructors less than $700 (although some get more) for a normal course of one 90-minute session a week for 15 weeks.

Officials say a course usually can break even with about 12 students. If too few students enroll, a course usually is canceled. Of 1,300 Adult Division courses offered each term, 18 percent to 20 percent are canceled, the school says. But low enrollments aren't the only reason that courses are killed. A course in "Wilderness Survival" was dropped this fall because the instructor broke his leg hiking in the wilderness.

THE ME GENERATION

New School officials say the courses that sell briskly increasingly revolve around the big interest of many people these days: themselves. Many seek courses that help the student understand himself or do something useful for himself, officials add. They say students often approach even traditional subjects in terms of the self. "They'll still study religion, but the question they ask is, 'what's in it for me? Does Zen Buddhism have something that I need?'" observes John R. Everett, the New School's hearty and outspoken president.

Following demand, the New School offers scores of practical courses. Assorted courses show students how to choose a New York private school (with guest appearances by various headmasters), build a solar hot-water heater or a dollhouse, plan an estate, grow herbs or cope with depression. Business and investment courses enrolled 1,300 students this fall, compared with only 350 five years earlier. "These days, people are taking courses where they can see a direct relationship with dollars and cents," says Claire B. Benenson, head of the business department.

The New School also prides itself on catching trends. "We were early in death studies," says President Everett. With interest in the subject rising in recent years, the catalog carries both "Coping with Death" and "The Philosophy and Psychology of Death," as well as a course or so that merely touches on growing old gracefully.

The school also sells courses by making them convenient. An "Early Risers" program offers 14 courses—and free coffee—at 7:45 a.m. Early evening courses in fashion design and merchandising are conducted in the city's garment district. A suburban New School branch operates in Westchester County. As older people often dislike leaving home at night, a special program for retired professionals and executives generally meets during the day. Taking an active part in one another's continuing education, participants plan and conduct their own courses.

The New School also relies on heavy promotion. "For 15 years, we've been the pacesetter in educational marketing," says Albert W. Landa, vice president for development, who supervises promotion. Other institutions once criticized the New School for aggressive marketing. "But now they're all doing it," he adds.

Mr. Landa says the New School spends over $250,000 a year on radio, television and newspaper advertising. During registration periods, radio listeners and TV viewers can call special numbers 24 hours a day to obtain copies of the catalog. To compare the impact of commercials on competing stations, the school uses a separate answering service telephone number for each station and tabulates the calls.

But the key sales tool is the catalog, which is filled with zippy course titles and descriptions. ("The Incredible Houdini! The Man . . . The Myth . . . The Magic.") A whole section is entitled "Courses You Always Wanted to Take, but Didn't Know Where to Find." These include "Learning to Entertain with Magic," "Dynamics of Hatha Yoga," "How to Play the Races Successfully" and "Karate for Women."

New School officials say big names sell courses. "Cultural Patterning of Human Development," taught by anthropologist Margaret Mead, attracted over 400 students this fall. A course on movies that has featured guest appearances by Robert Redford, Shirley MacLaine and other stars regularly sells out with over 500 students.

Several movie courses are packaged to reach specialized markets. For instance, "Chillers . . . The Cinema of Terror" promises a horror or mystery movie plus a discussion every Monday for 14 weeks. One evening's topic was vampirism, featuring "Dracula's Daughter." Succeeding whole evenings are devoted to movies about mad doctors, houses of horror, werewolves and so on.

"SINGLES AND MARRIEDS"

Many courses sell because they help students understand themselves and cope with their problems. "Writing as a Means of Self-Discovery" concentrates on "freeing yourself to record your thoughts and feelings, to find out who you are" through diaries and similar work. A popular course called "Singles in New York" deals with "creating a more satisfying singles life style"—everything from designing a pleasant place to live to meeting other people. Should students tire of the more satisfying singles life style and get married, the New School is ready with course 5002, "Predictable Crises in Marriage."

Even traditional courses tend to focus on what students want to learn rather than what is traditionally taught. David Randolph, a conductor and musicologist who teaches two popular music appreciation courses, says: "I started with the questions that people have asked me over the years." One course considers such questions as what music can and cannot do, whether it is the language of emotions and what influence composers have on one another.

Many students effusively praise such courses for letting them pursue interests they developed years after leaving school or college. "At the New School, I discovered skills and interests that I didn't even know existed for me," says Toni Montenegro, a middle-aged housewife. But even enthusiasts say the quality of New School courses varies dramatically. One student says the instructor of a beginning painting course made such a point of insulting everybody's work that attendance shrank from 15 to two. "Of course, the New School got its money anyway," he adds angrily.

THE RELAXED APPROACH

One problem is that most students are under no pressure to work hard. A New Yorker who enrolled in a drama writing course says he was the only one of 20 students who completed the course's basic writing assignment, even though the instructor was extremely capable. A woman who spent a year in the school's small undergraduate program found the courses "a lot easier" than her regular courses at prestigious Sarah Lawrence College. "A lack of expectation pervades the place," she says.

Others contend that courses in dog grooming and the art of lightweight camping simply don't belong in an academic program. But the New School's Mr. Everett argues that such critics don't see the difference between formal and continuing education. As over 70 percent of New School students "have already done the formal stuff" in college, there is little reason to restrict the curriculum to what universities traditionally teach, he contends.

As Mr. Everett points out, the New School does offer numerous demanding academic courses. Nobody claims that "Dense, Subtle and Complex Poetry" panders to frivolous tastes. But the New School official concedes that the temptation to meet the demand for "any sort of course" is a real problem for adult education. "We're always in danger of slipping into something easy," he says. "It would be crazy to think we didn't live on that razor's edge all the time."

34
The Baptists Want You!

William Martin

In 1976–1977, the Baptist General Convention of Texas developed an extensive marketing program to increase the membership in their church. This program included consumer research to help determine the creative strategy for the advertising campaign, a marketing budget of more than $1.5 million dollars, and coordination of the efforts of 4,200 Baptist churches, their ministers, and members.

God, as is His custom, has once again confounded the wise. After listening to a generation of theologians speak bravely of His death, the Almighty has established Himself as the odds-on choice for Comeback of the Decade. Conservative churches are growing, evangelical Christianity has been declared mainstream American religion, and a Southern Baptist Sunday school teacher has become Leader of the Free World. And now, as if that were not enough, the Baptist General Convention of Texas is about to launch a media blitz designed to share the good news of God's love with every man, woman, and child in the state an average of forty times apiece during a four-week period in February and March. The $1.5 million campaign, to be called Good News Texas, will feature commercials for Christ on television and radio, ads in newspapers and other print media, booster spots on billboards, pins on lapels, and an extensive personal visitation program to be run by the local churches. It is going to be pure Baptist. Well, almost pure. To help them do it right, the Baptists have hired one of the largest and most successful advertising firms in the country, the Bloom Advertising Agency of Dallas. Neither Sam nor Bob Bloom has roots in the Christian branch of the Judeo-Christian tradition.

I have mixed feelings about all this. Some of my best friends are Baptists, always have been. Still, I have never been able to shake completely the conviction that Baptists are the Aggies of religion. That in itself is not enough to damn them, but it does sort of set them apart. Part of my problem with Baptists stems from the fact that I grew up in the Church of Christ (Romans 16:16). As you may know, Church of Christ people believe the circle of the saved is rather small, and not many of them would care to sound too certain about their place in it. Baptists, on the other hand, never seem to tire of telling how sure they are they are saved and how good this blessed assurance feels. I thought their "once saved, always saved" doctrine of salvation was unsound—too easy; cheap grace; why, that would mean you could do anything you wanted to—but at least they had some doctrine, which was more than you could say for the Methodists, and at least we all agreed that nothing could send you to Hell faster than kissing the Pope's toe. No, the main problem wasn't doctrine. It was style. No matter what I believed, I could no more have been a Baptist when I was growing up than I could spend every Thursday night at the bowling alley or wear a seafoam-green leisure suit today.

William Martin is Associate Professor of Sociology, Rice University.

For one thing, Baptists were so *organized* about inviting people to church. Once I was in the barbershop getting my weekly haircut when Mr. Joy Tilley, who was a big Baptist—I think it says something that the counterpart of "staunch Presbyterian," "devout Catholic," and "pillar in the Methodist Church" is "big Baptist"—stuck his head in and invited the barber to come sit in his pew at a revival then in progress. That astonished me. We had a few elderly members who sort of had squatter's rights to pews they had occupied for years, but we would never have dreamed of assigning somebody a particular pew and then sending them out to drum up people to pack it.

The contrast carried over to the revivals themselves. The mark of a successful Church of Christ revivalist was his ability to drive the nail of terror into slumbering souls. Though some Baptist revivalists made use of hellfire and brimstone, I always felt that the mark of a successful Baptist preacher was his ability to make you laugh and feel good. That didn't seem much like religion to me.

This difference was further reflected in the Sunday schools, where we gave our classes sensible, functional names—"Preschool," "Elementary," "Junior High," and "Young People"—and encouraged attendance by quoting scriptures, especially Hebrews 10:25 ("Forsake not the assembling of yourselves together"), and threatening slackers with hellfire. Baptists called their classes things like "Sunbeams" and "Pioneers" and "Aviators" and drew crowds by having the youth minister bounce over the church bus from a trampoline.

I used to marvel at what they would do to appeal to young people. Our high school assembly programs fell into two primary categories: magicians, myna birds, and trickshot artists sent out from the Southern School Assemblies organization and—this was before Ms. O'Hair took God out of the schools—preachers holding revivals over at the Baptist church. They would juggle and tell a few jokes and then talk to us earnestly about taking care of our bodies, which are temples of the Holy Spirit (I Corinthians 6:19). Once a revival team from Baylor entertained us with several hymns and gospel tunes arranged for trumpet trio. Then the leader, a young man with the unforgettable name of Horace Oliver Bilderback, placed a trombone mouthpiece in his trumpet and played "Let the Lower Lights Be Burning," while one of his fellow clerics moved an imaginary trombone slide out in front. That, to me, was the pure essence of the Southern Baptist Church.

At times, to be sure, I envied my Baptist friends and made some effort to be one of them. I went to the Baptist Vacation Bible School several years and made bookends and potholders and whatnot shelves, and did right well at a Bible game called Sword Drill—"Attention! Draw swords! (No thumbs over the edges, now.) John 3:16! Charge!"—and I thought it was keen that their pastor, Brother Rose, illustrated his devotional lessons with magic tricks and showed us slides of his trip to the Holy Land. Once, I joined the Royal Ambassadors (and got elected Ambassador-in-Chief) just to have a chance to go to the summer encampment at Alta Frio, but I lost my nerve before the bus left and stayed home. Later, I longed to go on hayrides and swimming parties with the Training Union and even wished I could go into San Antonio and hear Angel Martinez preach in a white suit. But it was just no use. I was like a lonely traveler watching a group of Shriners cutting up in a hotel lobby: it might be fun for a day or two to wear a fez and ride a little motor scooter down Main Street, but you wouldn't want to go home and still have to be one.

Before all the Baptists walk out on me, I have a confession to make. About four or five years ago, I became sort of a Baptist myself. After spending the better part of the sixties studying religion at Harvard, I grew a bit weak on matters of doctrine and decided I would do more harm than good by sticking with the Church of Christ. When I came back to Texas, I cast around a bit and finally wound up at a church that I suppose could be described as liberal and ecumenical, though even now I find it difficult to identify myself as a theological liberal, so strongly was I taught to believe that few states of being are more pernicious. Still, at least half the people in this church grew up as Baptists, a good handful of them are former Baptist preachers, and even though the Union Baptist Association of Houston threw them out for accepting members from other denominations without rebaptizing them, they still persist in calling themselves Baptists. I have had some trouble with it. I am embarrassed when they look at me in amazement because I have never heard of Lottie Moon, and I get a little squirmy when they sing "Do Lord" at the annual retreat up in the woods, and I admit it doesn't make a dime's worth of difference to me whether Baylor wins or loses a football game. Still, we don't have revivals and if we did we wouldn't have trumpets or trombones or jugglers, and nobody checks to see why you haven't been coming to Sunday school and, as far as I can tell, nobody much cares about the details of your belief, so long as you are kind and try to help folk when they need it. It doesn't have anything like the zip of a straight-out evangelical church, but ex-Fundamentalists are some of the best people you'll find anywhere, so I expect I'll keep my letter in a while longer. Besides, if Good News Texas works, we may all be Baptists by summer.

Baptists, of course, have always been aggressive. They sought "A Million More in Fifty-four" and they have sponsored Billy Graham Crusades and hold "Win Clinics" to instruct people in the techniques of personal evangelism. But this is bigger, better, grander than anything they have ever done before.

My immersion in the project came in Dallas at a regional meeting of the Baptist General Convention of Texas (BGCT). The Good News Texas portion of the program was co-chaired by Drs. L. L. Morriss and Lloyd Elder. Morriss, with his smooth gray hair, metal glasses, and high-quality fall woolens, could easily pass for a corporation executive. His speech and manner befit his appearance—one senses he does little by accident. Lloyd Elder's obvious intelligence, warmth, and gentle wit are engaging, but his slightly more rumpled look and apparent unconcern for slickness make it easier to believe he is a seminary professor or church executive.

Morriss declared he was as excited as "an auctioneer at an auction of used furniture," a metaphor I thought fell somewhat short of the mark. He was excited, he said, about what God had done for Texas in the past and about what He is doing now. He introduced Elder, who was also excited. Good News Texas, Elder said, would have three major targets: (1) the 4.7 million Texans—one third of the state's population—who do not belong to any Christian group, persons "who are completely uninvolved in the things of Christ," (2) inactive and apathetic church members, including 700,000 Baptists, and (3) the active membership of local Baptist churches. He summarized what the Bloom Agency had done so far and sketched out the main lines the media campaign would follow. Then he reminded the assembly that Good News Texas "is not a goodwill campaign for the convention. It is not church advertising. It is going with the best product we have, and that is the gospel of Jesus Christ."

Elder then called on Dr. Jimmy Allen, the pastor of San Antonio's First Baptist Church. Allen is a big man who wears his graying hair rather long for a Baptist preacher and gives off an unmistakable impression of high energy. Working from a few notes scribbled on the back of an envelope, he spoke of "the rhythm in the way God moves in His world, in the tide, in our heartbeat, in the very energy levels of our lives." "There are times," he said, "when God moves in great force and power in our lives, and then there are times of wandering in the wilderness when we begin to appreciate the fact that we cannot live in ecstasy all the time. There must be a hunger before there is filling. There must be thirst before there can be a slaking of thirst. I am convinced we are at the edge of a spiritual awakening in our nation and that some of us are in places where we can already sense the tide of God coming in."

Allen noted that *Newsweek* had carried Charles Colson's testimonial, that the *Fort Worth Star-Telegram* had printed an editorial that told how to be saved, and that CBS had interviewed members of his church for an hour-long documentary on the meaning of salvation. He went on for about twenty minutes, talking about how much we needed revival and how much he hoped God might choose Baptists to be part of the central apparatus by which He moved. Then, in a hushed voice that visibly moved the audience with its intensity, he concluded: "I find myself saying, 'God, could this be the time? Lord, could you be ready now? Is it something that will take our breath away?' I find myself saying, 'O Lord, let it be good news, not just for Texas, not just for Texas Baptists, but for a nation and a world that desperately needs to find out that, indeed, there is good news.'"

Later that afternoon, I sat down with Morriss, Elder, and BGCT executive director Dr. James Landes. Though he was quick to note he is a chemical engineer by training, Dr. Landes' beneficent countenance and rather sermonic manner make it clear he has been around a lot of preachers.

"The rationale of Good News Texas," Landes said, "is the commandment 'Go ye into all the world.' I have seen the heartbreaking conditions so many people are experiencing throughout this state. I had no alternative but to study how to spread the message that there are people in the world who *care,* who are interested in persons just because they are human beings, regardless of race or color or creed, and that the reason these people care is because they believe God *is,* and Christ *is,* and the Scriptures are a mirror of Christ's mind. I realized also that many of our leaders were reaching out for some undergirding arm that could strengthen and help them in their ministry in the local church. So, as I thought and prayed and did a bit of meditating in between fly fishing on the riverbanks of Colorado, I said, 'Lord, if this great big denomination with two million people and forty-two hundred churches and missions will make up its mind to do one thing across a period of a couple of years, there is no telling what good could come of that.' And I thought if we could just plant a seed, maybe it could grow, maybe it could bless a whole state and the nation. I shared that dream with my associates here on the administrative staff and they asked me to share it with the executive board. I came away somewhat shocked but deeply gratified, because men who do not normally react enthusiastically to another evangelistic thrust got to their feet and said, 'This sounds different, get with it!'"

As we talked, Landes and his colleagues echoed what Jimmy Allen had said about the soon-coming revival. Exciting things are happening among our laymen, they said. Signs of awakening are blowing across our nation. But if revival was coming with or without their help, as they seemed to be saying, why didn't Baptists take their $1.5 million and spend it some other way? "Somebody has to be the agent," Landes replied. "God always works through an Abraham, a Moses, an Isaac, a Joseph, a John the Baptist. He doesn't work without working through people. If Texas Baptists have the favorable image the research for this project shows we have, then we've got a *responsibility* commensurate with it. If God wants to use us, we have a responsibility to be available."

I brought up something that had struck me from the moment I saw the first piece of promotional literature about Good News Texas. The logo for the campaign is the Christian fish symbol, with the state of Texas stuffed inside it like Jonah. To accommodate both Amarillo and Laredo, the fish is drawn a bit fat, so that it looks something like a football with a tail or perhaps a Gospel Blimp. Several years ago a mild satire, widely circulated in evangelical circles, described the misadventures of a Christian group that hired a blimp to broadcast sermons and drop leaflets on the hapless community below. Though it attracted great attention, the townspeople were irritated and offended, and the initial spirit and purpose of the enterprise were lost and perverted. I was curious about whether these men had considered the possibility that Good News Texas might be a Baptist version of the Gospel Blimp.

Elder was aware of the perils. "If we just saturated the media with the gospel message," he said, "and expected something to happen automatically, that would be the Gospel Blimp approach. Just pay your money and send up the blimp. But we are making a real effort to keep that from happening. We are trying to equip ministers and lay people in the local churches to be *witnesses,* so that they don't just let the blimp fly over, but can knock on doors and present the gospel to people as caring, sharing neighbors."

Jimmy Allen had said Baptists would need to remember that "when God comes to town, He doesn't always stay in our house. He moves where He chooses to move and leaps over all kinds of barriers." How would they feel if the Methodists or Presbyterians or Church of Christ picked up some new members on Baptist nickels? The prospect did not seem to dismay them. They were, in fact, informing other denominations in the state about their plans so that if the awakening comes, they can also be ready for it. There is, of course, some confidence that their 4,200 outlets will give Baptists a healthy share of whatever market develops.

This ecumenical talk emboldened me to raise a point I regarded as of at least mild interest. Why had they chosen the Bloom Agency? Granted, it was recognized as one of the best agencies in the country and its Dallas location provided the advantage of close and frequent contact, but was there no sense of incongruity in hiring a Jewish-owned agency to conceive and produce an evangelistic campaign for Southern Baptists? Apparently not. The Baptists chose their agency the same way Procter and Gamble or Exxon might, with a steering committee of seventeen people and a much larger consultation group from across the state that heard presentations by a number of respected firms.

"Bob Bloom is a good salesman," said James Landes. "When he was through, I heard a Baptist preacher from East Texas say, 'I don't need to hear anybody else. The man knows where he is going.' When that group voted, they did so with a great feeling of confidence in the ability and desire of the Bloom Agency to help us do what we wanted to do. It was almost unanimous. It was an overwhelming decision." Landes admitted to some early personal reservations but insisted things had worked out "more beautifully and fantastically than we had expected." Then he suggested I check out the backgrounds of the men at the agency with primary responsibility for the account.

The Bloom Agency occupies several floors of the Zale Building, which sits alongside Stemmons Freeway like a giant homemaker's misplaced toaster. Instead of the customary rooms and hallways, the agency uses "action offices," work spaces defined by movable partitions about five and a half feet high, which can be shaped to fit needs that change with each new client or campaign. Flexible white hoses bring electrical and telephonic nourishment to each of the modules, so that one can tote up the number of offices currently in use by counting the accordion-pleated umbilici. The occupants of these spaces decorate them as if they are planning to stay for years, so I presume one has a fair chance of hanging onto one's own partitions, but I was told reshuffling is not uncommon.

The furnishings run heavily to chrome, glass, and plastic, with plenty of plants and bright colors. Most of the offices are densely decorated in pop-artifactual chic, with tapestries and macrame hangings and inspirational posters framed in Lucite and fire-alarm boxes and street signs and—everywhere—reminders and remnants of past campaigns. Shelves in the reception area hold symbols of the agency's various clients: Bekins, Southwest Airlines, Owens Sausage, Amalie Motor Oil, Rainbo Bread, Lubriderm Cream, Whataburger, and a score of others. I looked in vain for a New Testament or a Broadman Hymnal, but I guess the display had not yet been brought that far up to date.

Bob Bloom showed me around and talked about the Baptist account. "We are in the consumer advertising business," he explained. "Our job is to communicate with the general public and get a response from them. That is what we do best. We try to generate retail purchases, to get people to buy motor oil, or a home, or seats on an airplane. We have never been involved in anything like this before, but the thing that stimulated us was the feeling that the BGCT could give us what we want in a partnership role, a sharing of responsibilities as opposed simply to doing what we tell them. They know how to listen, how to guide, how to tell us when we are off base, and they know how to stroke, so we are pleased to have the association from that standpoint. I was impressed that they could not only accept but embrace aspects of our craft that we have difficulty getting business people, including some Harvard MBAs, to accept."

How did he account for this? "I'm not really sure," Bloom said. "I guess they are just smart. I had expected a sharp drop-off in intelligence between the leaders of the organization and the men in lower positions. In a business organization like a bank, for example, once you get past the president and a few directors to some of the department heads, you find some terrible prejudices about certain things, a lack of understanding about advertising and research, and an unwillingness to bend. I expected that with the Baptists, but frankly, I found a lot of sharp men at all levels. And they are very flexible. When we got out with the pastors, I expected to confront some prejudice, both from my being Jewish and in their willingness to marry our craft with their pulpit responsibilities. I just didn't find any of that. I found a high degree of comprehension when we went through the various alternatives with them. I kind of expected someone to get up and make an appeal to 'throw all that stuff away and just give people the simple gospel.' It didn't happen. They had smart, agile minds and they really embraced what we were trying to do. If I could get forty rabbis together to do that, I would be terribly surprised. They are also very sincere about the undertaking. It is great to have a client who believes in what he is doing, as opposed to someone who is just grinding out a product.''

Did he have any misgivings about mounting a campaign whose basic premise he, as a Jew, did not believe? ''I never felt any real sensitivity on that issue, except in regard to the terminology, which was very alien to me. Once I became confident they were willing to accept me as a spokesman for the agency and as a craftsman with some expertise, I became very comfortable with it. My role has been much the same as with any client. I feel I am particularly good at organizational work and strategic thinking. I am not concerned with the technological aspects of a motor oil—what it will or won't do for an engine—and I can't comment on the religious aspects of this project. What I am interested in is how we can communicate the selling points to the customer.''

Bob introduced me to his father, Sam Bloom, the agency's founder, who professed an interest in the project that went beyond craftsmanship. He was concerned ''about both the standards and ethics which appear to be declining in politics and business.'' The Baptists, he thought, were on the right track on these matters. Their willingness to lay $1.5 million on the line to bolster the ethics and morality of the state was a courageous act and he was ''terribly enthused'' to have a part in it.

I visited with most of the key personnel working on the account in the agency's new think tank, a tiered and carpeted room with no furniture except for ashtrays and huge pillows covered in plaid, madras, batik, and Marimekko. A tray on one of the lower tiers held coffee, Styrofoam cups, little packets of Cremora, Imperial Sugar, Sweet 'n' Low, and a box of those red-and-white plastic sticks that are too skinny to stir anything. On the assumption, I presume, that ideas generated in the room would be too dramatic to jot down on 3×5 cards with a ball-point pen, jumbo pads of paper and Magic Markers lay within easy reach. While a person in Faded Glory jeans with stars on the pockets went out to get Frescas and Tabs and Cokes for the non-coffee drinkers, we took our positions, shifted around a bit to look properly relaxed, and began to talk.

Dick Yob, research director for the project, explained that ''the days of doing what we *think* will work are becoming extinct because of the amount of money that is involved. We have to go out and find what really does communicate. Our approach has been to come at this like we would any package goods account, since that is basically what we know how to do.'' The first step had been to see what problems were bothering Texans these days. To accomplish this, Yob hired the Dallas marketing research firm of Louis, Bowles and Grove, Inc., to show a list of problems to approximately 300 Dallas and Austin citizens—divided evenly between active Baptists, inactive Christians, and non-Christians—

and ask which most accurately mirrored their own feelings and which were the problems they heard other people discuss. On both counts, all three groups ranked hypocrisy as the number one problem, by agreeing with such statements as ''It's getting harder to trust anybody or anything'' and ''People are not what they pretend to be. They say one thing and do another.''

Survey participants were then offered three possible solutions: (1) reading the Bible, (2) joining a group of active Christians, and (3) entering into a personal relationship with Jesus Christ and following his teachings. All three groups agreed that of the three answers, Christ was the best—though only 27 percent of the inactive Christians and 14 percent of the non-Christians actually felt it was an appropriate solution for them. More than two-thirds of the non-Christians chose none of the three options. In short, despite evidence of considerable spiritual and emotional malaise among backslidden and secular Texans, the field appeared to be something less than white unto harvest. Still, the Baptists and the agency agreed that a personal relation with Jesus was the most commercial of the products they had to offer. The next step was to decide how to package it for wholesale distribution.

At this point, the burden shifted to Bill Hill, the agency's creative director. He did not find the yoke an easy one. What could they say that would communicate effectively to all three target groups? And what vehicle would they use to say it: testimonial? dramatizations? slice-of-life vignettes? cartoons? jingles? During our first conversation, Hill had a discernible case of advertiser's anxiety. ''We are trying to avoid coming across as too churchy,'' he said, ''and we want to avoid clichés. The men working with us from BGCT are theologians. When they say 'Christ died for you,' there is a lifetime of knowledge behind it and all sorts of subtleties ripple out of it, but to the people they have singled out as the primary audience—non-Christians—that is a cliché and it may be a turnoff. We want to save the Jesus message to the very end of the TV spots, so we can get people nodding and saying, 'Yes, that is a problem. Yes, I would like to have a solution to that problem.' Then, at the end, we want to say, 'That solution is available to you through Jesus Christ.' We are trying to say, in the simplest form possible, that 'something that happened two thousand years ago is a real force that is relevant to your own individual problems right here and right now. If you are really concerned about your own problems and about what is going on in the world, and you have tried everything else, what have you got to lose?' We are not really trying to say *how* Christ is the answer, but simply *that* he is. We may go into *how* a little more in the other media.'' The problem of doing justice to the gospel in a brief commercial is tough, Hill admitted: ''I keep writing forty-two-second commercials because I just can't boil it all down into thirty seconds. In a thirty-second spot, about all we can say is, 'This aspirin contains more pain relievers than all the others combined.' ''

Guy Marble outlined the key public relations aspects of the campaign. His main task would be to bombard local churches throughout the state with newsletters, articles, speechs, posters, lapel buttons, and other communiqués to allow them to take full advantage of the media campaign when it hit their area. The agency people and Baptists both agreed that the word would be barren, like seed on stony ground, unless the local churches were ready not only to urge personal evangelism, but also to accept and nurture those who might be converted. As Jim Goodnight, who has overall responsibility for the account, put it, "We are going to give people the opportunity to respond, but when a guy walks in the back door of a Baptist church some Sunday morning to find what he has been looking for—what happens then will be up to the members of that church. If they are not ready for people who may not share any of their values, then it won't work. If they are ready to accept people 'just as I am,' I believe there will be a tremendous awakening of visible growth in both numbers and spirit." Another promotion task will be to make sure the local churches understand the strategy that will govern the campaign. "When we buy time for these commercials," Goodnight explained, "we are not going to be buying the Sunday Morning Revival Hour. We are going to be buying *Mary Hartman, Mary Hartman* and *All in the Family* and *Sonny and Cher*. You can anticipate the kinds of reactions thousands and thousands of Texas Baptists are going to have —'What are we doing supporting that kind of program?' Of course, our purpose is not to support the program. It's where we have to go to reach the people we want to reach."

Despite the frequent comparison of selling the gospel to selling aspirin or motor oil, it seemed clear these men were taking the matter more seriously than that. I recalled what Dr. Landes had said about checking their backgrounds, so I asked each of them to characterize his religious position. The agency didn't exactly turn out to be a collection of Madison Avenue cynics. Dick Yob is a graduate of Catholic University at Marquette, sends his oldest son to parochial school, and is active in the Church. Bill Hill is the son of a Baptist preacher in Amarillo but became so disillusioned with evangelical Christianity by the time he reached high school that for several years he dabbled in Zen, studied Rosicrucian literature, and considered going to live with the Dalai Lama in Tibet. Instead, he got married and became an Episcopalian. For the past seven years, he has participated in a Bible class taught by conservative Biblicist Mal Couch, a graduate of fundamentalist Dallas Theological Seminary who specializes in the interpretation of Biblical prophecy. Public relations advisor Guy Marble describes himself as "a lapsed Methodist," but his colleague Frank Demarest is a member of the Northwest Bible Church in Dallas (also aligned with the Dallas Theological Seminary) and admits he stands a bit to the right of Southern Baptists in his theology. Jim Goodnight grew up in the Park Cities Baptist Church in Dallas but switched to the Church of Christ after he married the granddaughter of G. H. P. Showalter, a Church of Christ patriarch

and former editor of one of its most conservative papers, the *Firm Foundation*. Though he locates himself in "the liberal, ecumenical wing of the Church of Christ" (a figure of speech like "virile impotence"), he is still active in the Preston Crest congregation in Dallas and has taught classes in C. S. Lewis' *Mere Christianity*, hardly a radical treatise.

These men, it turns out, are not the only Christians in the Bloom Agency. "You would be amazed," Goodnight said, "at the number of people within the agency who wanted to work on this account. Not only have a number of these closet Christians surfaced, but about twenty-five of us now meet each Wednesday at noon to pray and share our concerns and testimonials." "It's really neat," Demarest said. "All our working lives we have had this separation between our Christian faith and what we do on our jobs. For me, this is the first time to bring the two together."

"There is a terrible intensity among the people on the team," Hill said. "This is not just another piece of package goods. This is something that is going to affect people's lives. I really feel what I am doing. I keep thinking, 'We are going to save Texas!' and that gets to be a bit of a hang-up and causes a mental block." Another problem, Goodnight observed, is that "each of us gets his own theology and beliefs, his own personal slant woven into it. One of the hardest thing to do in any advertising is to wash yourself out of it and consider only the people you are trying to write for and what their needs are."

"With most products," Yob pointed out, "you are selling to people who are already users. It is a matter of getting them to switch brands or buy more of your product. But in this campaign, non-users are the number one target."

That afternoon I attended a meeting between members of the Bloom team and key staff members at the Baptist Building. Mainly, they were catching each other up on how things were going in their sections of the ball park. Jim Goodnight read the strategy statement that had emerged from their research. "What we are trying to do," he said, "is communicate to people that the frustrations they experience with the hypocrisy and lack of integrity in today's world is the result of misplaced priorities, and that the solution is to place their trust in Jesus Christ who will never fail them, rather than on the imperfect things of the world." The Baptists liked that a lot.

Demarest, Marble, and Mary Colias Carter reviewed PR plans. A steady stream of articles would appear in the *Baptist Standard* to "soften up the terrain," and a piece would appear in the next issue of the *Helper*, BGCT's women's magazine. Pastors would be supplied with information they could use to raise money for the program. Every church would receive material explaining the nature and scope of the project. Marble reported that he and his associates had done "much agonizing posterwise," but promised the first in a series of posters would be ready in "six weeks max."

They also talked a bit about honorary chairmen. Billy Graham had agreed to serve as national honorary chairman, but both the Baptists and the Bloom representatives wanted to make sure the campaign did not become a Graham affair. "We are not going to be able to use him much in a public way," Marble said. "If he is flying from coast to coast, we may be able to get him to stop off at DFW airport for a press conference and say how great Good News Texas is. We can do little things like that without much financial or time commitment, but that will be about the extent of it. Right now, we just want to get half a day with him at his place in North Carolina to produce several short items that could be used to stir up enthusiasm in the local churches." In addition to Graham, two state chairmen would be chosen—people who could generate prestige and interest in Jesus just by their association with the campaign. After all, one Baptist executive observed, "Public relations is the name of the game."

Over the next several weeks, Bill Hill and his associates developed four proto-commercials in "animatic" form—a series of still drawings with voice-overs rather than the live action or true animation that would be used in the final product. Each of the four took a different slant and would be tested to see which, if any, might appeal most to the Texas contingent of a lost and dying world. If none clicked, it would be, quite literally, back to the drawing board. If one seemed clearly better than the others, it would become the model for the actual spots to be used in the campaign. On three successive evenings in early October, representatives of Louis, Bowles and Grove showed the spots to "focus groups" drawn from the three target populations. Active Baptists met the first night in three churches scattered around Dallas.

I am not supposed to identify either the church or the people I observed, so I won't, but I promise you it was a real Baptist church, with a poster thermometer in the foyer that showed how the fund drive was going.

Judy Briggs, a market researcher for Louis, Bowles and Grove, told the group they were to give their reactions to some commercials being prepared for television. She did not say they were Baptist commercials or mention Good News Texas. She then showed the commercials on a videotape machine and asked the group to fill out a questionnaire after they viewed each one.

The first commercial, identified as "Promises," offered shots of politicians, automobile dealers, and various businessmen making familiar promises—"You've got my word on it.' "It's a sure thing." "You can depend on it." It ended with a note to the effect that Jesus is the only one whose promises can be trusted and "Isn't it time we listened?" The positive responses to "Promises" indicated the Christians held a disillusioned view of humanity: "Everybody is trying to put something over on us." "People will let you down, but if you trust in God, He won't let you down." "You have to put your faith in the Lord and not in other people." I got the message, but I felt sad, and the stark ceiling light illumined other, almost forgotten rooms in my soul, rooms not fur-

nished with warm and reassuring memories, rooms abandoned because the heat had been shut off and the broken panes let in too much damp and cold.

The next example showed a man arising to the sound of a strident alarm and struggling to meet the day as he listened to the depressing litany of the morning news. Then a voice-over announcer asked, "Wouldn't it be a change to wake up on morning without anxiety over what the day might bring? To know that whatever the world throws at you, you'll make it? If that kind of change would be welcome, then get with the one person who can do the changing—Jesus Christ. For a change." This, too, seemed to confirm the experience of the group: "We can't depend on the news being good," they said, "but if we have Jesus Christ with us, it makes no difference. You have to have Him because what problems can you face without Christ?"

The third effort did not lend itself so easily to clichéd response. In this one, a black man told of how he had been a revolutionary, seeking social change by whatever means seemed expedient. But not long ago, he said, he had run across another revolutionary and it had changed his life completely. He can change yours, too, the man promised. Then he said, "My name is Eldridge Cleaver. I'm Living Proof."

Bill Hill had told me one of the commercials would be a testimonial, and I would not have been surprised to have seen Charles Colson or Johnny Cash telling about what God had wrought in their lives. I try to keep up with the box scores on notable conversions, but I had somehow missed the news that the icy soul of Eldridge Cleaver had been warmed with fire from above. I was impressed that Texas Baptists would consider pumping hundreds of thousands of dollars into publicizing the testimony of a man who might still be regarded with skepticism and caution by some of the new white brothers. And I was especially curious about how the members of this largely working-class church might react.

I studied the lone black member of the group, a man about 45. Was he an Uncle Tom who would fear that the sight and sound of this panther in lamb's clothing might stir resentment left over from the sixties and jeopardize his perhaps lately won and still tenuous place in a predominantly white congregation? Would he say of Cleaver, as Peter had said of Christ, "I never knew him"? No, he wouldn't. "This is very beautiful," he said. "It comes from a controversial person a lot of us can identify with. We know Eldridge Cleaver was searching for something he could not find in the world, but only in Jesus Christ. I had much the same problems in my life at one time. It was very hard for me to accept certain things, but now I am able to face these things and accept them." That is not exactly revolution, but it isn't "white folks always been nice to me" either.

A middle-aged woman who had taken much longer than anyone else to fill out her questionnaire spoke next. I sensed she was about to vent a little of the racist spleen we often associate with working-class fundamentalists. "This was also my favorite," she said. "It shows that Christ is a

Man for all men. He is not a white man's savior or a black man's savior or a Jew's savior. He is for everyone. I think every minority feels pressures and I think there are times in everybody's life when they feel like they are a minority, even though nobody else may look upon them that way. When you are low man on the totem pole in your office and everybody says, 'You do this' and 'You do that,' and it seems like you do everything for everybody, then you can identify with the feeling of being a little bit left out."

The final commercial depicted a child learning to ice skate with the loving help of a parent-figure in a unisex outfit like the Olympic speed skaters wear. The narrator told how important it is to have someone you can depend on when the going gets a bit hazardous and concluded with the slogan, "Learn to live with Jesus Christ." I liked it best of the four. Its symbolism was aesthetically appealing and I liked the way it avoided both the negative connotations about human nature (though I am not especially sanguine about the natural goodness of our kind) and the spurious overgeneralization implicit in any case based on a single testimony. The nine focus groups agreed more strongly than on any other point that "Ice Rink" was clearly the poorest of the four commercials. "It was boring," they said. "It just beat around the bush and didn't really say anything." "I can't ice skate, so I don't identify with that one at all." "A waste of film." I decided not to become a consultant on mass evangelism.

Ms. Briggs asked who they thought might sponsor commercials like these. Oh, the Catholics or SMU or maybe the Dallas Council of Churches. Not one named the Baptists. Baptists have W. A. Criswell; they don't need Eldridge Cleaver.

The meetings with the Baptist groups were designed to see if any of the commercials were likely to run into the kind of opposition that might make funding or other forms of cooperation difficult. But the real test, everyone agreed, would be with those who described themselves as nominal or inactive Christians and those who openly acknowledged they were not religious in any conventional sense. A pool of such people had been obtained by distributing questionnaires in Dallas office buildings; groups representing both sexes and a broad range of ages had been selected from this pool. In keeping with the piety of the groups, we met at a neutral site, the Marriott Inn. Curtiss Grove, a partner in Louis, Bowles and Grove, was moderator for the evening. As we waited for people to assemble, he lamented having to pass up a cocktail party down the hall.

The group looked pretty representative of backsliders I have known: a workingman in his thirties; an overweight balding man who talked knowledgeably about the video equipment; a tall, thin older man who wore a tie with a leisure suit and looked as though he smoked a lot and was perhaps familiar with the taste of liquor; a woman who was pretty in the way that Southwest Airlines stewardesses are pretty, and a thin, serious man who appeared to be with her; a young woman about twenty who wore blue eye shadow and orthodontic braces; a neat woman in her thirties who looked

like she was probably in charge of several people where she worked and had a reputation for getting things done on time; one of those ubiquitous, interchangeable young men with a moustache and styled hair and a preference for shiny shirts with sailboats or jockeys on them; a foxy brunette in a suede jacket and lots of bracelets and rings and dark fingernail polish who seemed a poor conversion prospect; and several others I knew then I wouldn't be able to remember. For the most part, they represented a bit higher socioeconomic status than the Baptists I had visited the night before.

Grove is good at his job and easily elicited comments from the group. Interestingly, their reactions were not remarkably different from those of the active Baptists, except that none of them rated the Cleaver commercial highest and four of the twelve designated it their least favorite. (As it turned out, this response was something of an anomaly; the other two groups meeting at the same time felt strongly that the Cleaver spot was the best.) When asked what the commercial sought to accomplish, one man guessed it was trying to stir up pity for Cleaver. Another thought it too controversial even for minority-group people and felt its appeal would be limited to revolutionaries or people "with awful problems."

Each of the other spots got three or four votes as the best of the lot, but what one felt was pungent, another would judge pedantic. The 28-year-old in the shiny shirt said he didn't think any was much better than the others, since they were all about God and the church. A young man about nineteen seemed rather bemused by the whole business, as though he thought his sainted mother had somehow arranged to get him invited to a subtle soulwinning campaign, maybe even paid his way. But all things considered, I think this group uttered more pious clichés than the dedicated Baptists. Since they did not know they had been chosen because of their shared lukewarmness, they seemed to feel some need to let their colleagues know they were believers. In spite of what may have been a bit of overcompensation, however, I sensed almost none of the assurance I had seen and heard the night before. Several people got sad looks on their faces and lit up cigarettes. I believe they were pretty serious about it all. I had agreed not to ask any questions and I may have misread their reaction, but I had not expected what I sensed and it seemed unmistakable. I wouldn't be surprised to learn that the older man in the leisure suit had started going back to church with his wife.

As before, almost no one perceived the commercials as Baptist in origin. The President's Council on Physical Fitness, the Cerebral Palsy Association, an ice rink, the Department of Health, Education, and Welfare, Channel 39, and Sominex all seemed as likely as the Southern Baptists to sponsor such spots.

On the third night, self-designated unbelievers viewed the spots. This was the crucial test, the people at whom the main thrust of the campaign was aimed, but their preferences turned out to differ little from their more pious predecessors. Neither "Morning News" nor "Promises" struck a responsive chord. One man who at first thought "Morning News" was touting CBS news was irritated when it proved to have a religious theme. Another picked up the religious slant earlier but just thought, "Here we go again." A woman complained that "it doesn't tell me what to do with my problems, except give them to someone else. A little information about how Jesus is going to handle my problems would be helpful."

"Promises" caused even stronger negative reactions —one woman characterized it as "hateful" and said, "It made me want to lock myself in a room and shoot anybody that makes promises"—and "Ice Rink" once again came in as the unanimous last choice. One woman described it as "childish the way they wanted you to put yourself in Jesus' hands with no mention of adult choices." Another took issue with the whole ice-skating metaphor; she didn't feel at all like an ice skater, but rather "a yo-yo, every day I feel like a yo-yo." A man about thirty said he felt a better metaphor would be someone playing poker, or perhaps even solitaire. I doubt seriously the Southern Baptists will pick up on that.

Once again the Cleaver commercial was picked as the best—unanimously by one caucus. A man who freely called himself an agnostic said, "I know what Cleaver's life has been, and if this guy says he can pull it out with Christ, well, I may think there is something to it." He admitted to some doubts whether Cleaver might just be trying to escape a prison sentence by publicly embracing religion, but rejected them: "I have not agreed with Cleaver in the past, but I have respected his integrity." Others did question Cleaver's sincerity, but what carried the day was the feeling that "it gave me a choice. It told me what his opinion was, but it didn't say, 'You take my opinion, buddy, because it is good for you too.' "

The success of the Cleaver spot naturally raised the question of whose testimonials people could accept. The subject shouldn't be an ordinary person, someone from the viewer's own neighborhood ("I would figure someone was just trying to get on television and get some publicity"); it certainly shouldn't be Richard Nixon or Patty Hearst ("It is still to close. With Cleaver you can almost feel the guy has paid his debt and now has a whole new slant on life"). The ideal person, one man thought, would be a noncriminal figure who still had room for notable repentance—the two names mentioned were Billy Graham and Earl Scheib, the $29.95 auto paint job man.

Interestingly, the non-Christians had no difficulty accepting the idea that Southern Baptists might be behind the commercials. The us of testimonials seemed "more Baptist" than any of the other approaches, even though Eldridge Cleaver seemed like an unlikely star. One woman suggested that if Baptists were indeed the sponsors, they would do well to hide the fact, since "many people are turned off by their extremist actions."

If the consultants were looking for useful criticism, the non-Christians gave them plenty of that, but if they were looking for some signs that Good News Texas was going to send unbelievers flocking to church, the meeting provided little basis for hope. One man quickly deduced that his group contained no practicing Christians and said, "I think people like us tend to rely on ourselves rather than look outside for some kind of placebo. I don't care whether people believe in Jesus or Muhammad or Darrell Royal; just because they believe it and get out and preach it doesn't mean it's true. I just don't buy the idea that you can blindly put your faith and trust in any person, including Jesus."

The bad news for Good News Texas was that the non-Christians didn't like the whole idea of religious commercials. "I am turned off by commercials of this sort," said one. "It cheapens religion to sell it like toothpaste." "There is nothing in these commercials that appeals to me in any way or makes me feel I should investigate Christianity," another said. They make it sound like Jesus is going to open up a used-car lot." But one man who also had a negative reaction to selling Jesus on TV conceded that "television is such a powerful communications medium that if they use it right, it can help. There are some people whose only way of touching anything outside their home is television."

It is Bloom's job, then, to see that TV is used right. The hope that any single commercial might provide Baptists with an offer lost Texans could not refuse seemed pretty well dashed. Still, the response to news that the sins of the apostle of Black Power had been washed away had proven sufficiently promising to convince Bloom and the BGCT that testimonials were the route to take. At the state convention in San Antonio two weeks later, L. L. Morriss proclaimed that the theme of Good News Texas would be "Living Proof" and would concentrate on "presenting the testimony of people who have experienced the saving grace of our Lord." Dr. Landes announced that Baylor football coach Grant Teaff and actress Jeannette Clift George had agreed to serve as honorary co-chairmen and played a tape from Billy Graham, who said the world was hungry for good news and he was pleased to have a part in the boldest evangelistic venture in the history of Texas Baptists.

By the first of December, some of the top converts in the country had been lined up to add their testimony to Cleaver's. There had been minor problems. Some Christian entertainers had been discouraged from participating by their agents, who feared it might hurt their image with the public. Others had been screened out when their faith was adjudged not yet solid enough to guarantee against an embarrassing relapse during the campaign; no one, for example, would want to take a chance on Jerry Lee Lewis if he were suddenly to go into one of his periodic conversion phases. The final list included country singers Jeannie C. Riley and Connie Smith, Mexican musician Paulino Bernal, Consul-General of Honduras Rosargentina Pinel-Cordova, Houston Oiler Billy "White Shoes" Johnson, and Allan Mayer of Oscar Mayer and Company. A couple of big ones had gotten away. For some reason, Charles Colson had backed out and had to be replaced by Dean Jones, and a former Hell's Angel who conducts a bike ministry on the West Coast didn't leave a forwarding address when he set out on his latest missionary journey. But all the others were ready to go and film crews were heading for Nashville and L.A. to record their stories. We'll see the results soon.

As I wait, I am aware of poignant feelings. I have watched and listened as good, sincere, intelligent men and women groped for a way of making that which stands at the center of their lives plausible and attractive to those who live outside the sacred canopy. Perhaps it will work. I think I could accept that in good grace. I generally feel pretty comfortable around people who take their religion seriously, especially if it is one of the leading brands. But I confess I do not believe historians will remember 1977 as the year the Great Awakening came to Texas. I expect Baptist churches may be stirred up considerably and some wayward Christians may return home like the prodigal. These are the groups that have always responded best to the call of revival. The main work of evangelism in American history—with, it should be noted, some exceptions—has been to keep believers plugged into their systems. That in itself is a significant accomplishment and may well justify the cost and effort involved. Of course, here and there a real scoundrel or a true skeptic may be turned around and set on the Glory Road, but I expect Good News Texas will come and go without making a great deal of difference in the lives of the 4,700,000 sinners at whom it is primarily aimed. That will no doubt discourage a lot of folks, but maybe it shouldn't. After all, even though He knew how to use a bit of dash and sparkle to draw a crowd, Jesus never got anything like a majority, and if the Word of God is anything to go by, He never expected to (Matthew 7:13–14).

APPENDIX

Dignity in Church Advertising [1916]

O. C. Harn

The church has discovered in advertising, a new force which it believes it can use in furthering its work. There is danger that, in its enthusiasm over its discovery, mistakes may be made. . . .

Dignity is an attribute which should be possessed by all advertising which advertises dignified things. Some advertising men believe that dignity is a handicap to forceful, resultful publicity; but that is because they do not know what dignity is. They confound it with dryness, dullness—old-fogyness.

This is a wrong conception. A dignified man may be the most intensely interesting man in your circle. He may be the best business-getter. He may be the man above all others to whom to look to get things done.

Contrast the dignified methods of . . . advertising success with this sickly attempt found in a collection of church advertisements.

"Don't be a lemon! Tie on to the happy Sunday-nighters."

O. C. Harn was Advertising Manager, National Lead Co., at the time this article was written.

Excerpt from *Advertising and Selling*, Nov. 1916, p. 15.

Or this: A paper wrapper was folded about a piece of pasteboard to imitate chewing gum and the label was printed thus:

Chew	Dr. White's	The
this	Compound	Flavor
over!	for human ills	lasts.

This, if you will believe it, was used to advertise the service a church has to offer for the benefit of men!

But, you say, flippant and even vulgar preachers seem to have success in getting serious results. Why will not advertising work similarly?

I would say first that, as it is the exception in the commercial world for trivial advertising to bring the results desired, so is it the exception in the pulpit. . . .

A final caution, do not get the idea that dignity precludes warmth, earnestness, appeal to the emotions, startling effects, and force (or punch, if you like the overworked word—I don't).

The great orator knows well how to use all these means of moving his audience—knows it better than does the clown.

35
Local Government Agencies Try Advertising

Linda Lewis

The use of marketing in the public sector is not confined to major national organizations. As this article about Seattle shows, many local government agencies are adopting a marketing orientation. Described here are paid and public service advertising campaigns designed to encourage transit riding and carpooling, demarket electricity consumption, promote a state university, and build citizen pride in Seattle.

Seattle's Metro Transit is David with $300,000 to buy slingshots. The automobile industry is Goliath with $30 million worth of heavy artillery.

Larry Coffman is the person making this analogy. As manager of marketing for Metro Transit, he is using advertising to try to get people out of their cars and into buses. This year he will spend $30,000 for research and $270,000 for production and media placement of commercial messages.

"We're competing for business with the automobile," Coffman says. He estimates that his competitor will spend at least $30 million this year on advertising in the Seattle-King County area of Washington State.

Metro, which gets one-third of its revenues from transit fares and the other two-thirds from taxpayers in King County, has been putting more and more money into advertising since its first campaign—"Take Me, I'm Yours"—was launched in the fall of 1975 for $70,000. Advertising is necessary for this government agency, Coffman says, be-

cause Metro has a product to sell and needs a way of letting people know the advantages of that product.

But Metro is not alone. Several other public agencies in Seattle have also begun to use slickly-produced, smoothly-orchestrated ad campaigns to try to sway public opinion. If advertising can successfully be used to sell soap, cornflakes and station wagons, so the theory goes, it might also be useful in giving the public a better feeling about its governmental agencies.

This, too, has raised questions—however mild—about the propriety of governmental agencies using public money to promote themselves, as well as a number of other issues regarding the financing of such ads.

Seattle City Light is in the first phase of a $235,000 television, radio and newspaper advertising campaign to sell the idea of energy conservation and to promote its own image.

The University of Washington used $47,000 donated from corporations to produce seven television commercials letting people know that what goes on at the University affects their lives.

Linda Lewis is a staff writer for *The Seattle Post-Intelligencer.*

The City of Seattle, through the Department of Community Development, has spent $2,500 on six television spots promoting the advantages of living in the city.

And the Commuterpool, in the city's Engineering Department, has invested $2,500 in four television commercials selling the concept of carpooling.

All of these agencies, because they are public, theoretically have greater access to the media in news stories than profit-oriented private businesses. The people who run these agencies, however, have become dissatisfied with news coverage of their activities. In some cases they felt that the coverage was not telling the whole story of what they were about, that it was giving the public a negative view of the various agencies.

Jean Withers, citizens information officer for the Department of Community Development, says: "We were concerned that news coverage dealt primarily with conflicts. We wanted to turn the public on to some of the positive things going on in the city. The Madrona picnic is not news; the Madrona rapist is."

Consequently, in April 1976, the director of the Department of Community Development came up with the idea to produce a series of 30-second television spots that would portray the good things going on in Seattle.

When the spots were ready, they were shown to station managers and public service directors of TV stations KING, KOMO and KIRO. All three stations, under the terms of their licenses granted by the Federal Communications Commission, are required to give a certain amount of air time free to the messages of non-profit organizations. The Department of Community Development wanted to take advantage of this free time to put the idea of in-city living across.

Not all of the agencies producing commercial messages use free public service time. Metro and City Light are paying for their advertising campaigns. The people in those agencies say that public service time is too unpredictable for a coordinated campaign. Public service advertisers do not have control over when, or even if, their messages appear on the air. Those decisions are made by the television stations.

SELLING PEOPLE ON TRANSIT

Metro's "model citizens"—the three plaster of paris, wire and wood figures that appear to be upset by the inconvenience and cost of driving a car to work—are appearing on television because Metro is buying the time. Its aim is to get commuters to leave their cars at home and to ride the bus.

"We're trying to have fun with our advertising and also to catch people's attention," Coffman says. "The thing we want to hit them first with is the cost of driving a car."

Metro hired an advertising agency to come up with the concept.

Soon, Metro's commute-by-bus campaign will shift its emphasis from the unpleasantness of driving to the advantages of bus riding. A half-dozen new model citizens—these happy and smiling because they are bus riders—will be introduced. The tag line for the second phase of the campaign will be "I'm no dummy; I ride the bus."

According to Coffman, Metro does not make its decisions about advertising haphazardly. This year's campaign grew out of three months of planning and two research projects, one a $15,000 county-wide survey of bus riders and non-riders. The survey determined that people found the transit system confusing; did not consider the service fast, direct or convenient enough and, generally, had a "less than great" image of the bus. It also showed that commuters, who make up 35 percent of all bus riders, do 78 percent of the bus riding.

Using these results, Coffman decided to aim his advertising campaign at commuters, trying to convince them that taking the bus is smart, convenient and easy.

A study done for $5,000 showed where most of the commuters live. "We found that people are in fact living closer to where they work than had previously been thought," Coffman says.

These results enabled Coffman to identify target groups among the population for his advertising message. "Now we can convey specific messages to specific audiences," he says.

Besides pushing the idea that it is smart to ride the bus, Metro this year will be promoting its monthly passes and spending $90,000 to do so. Coffman's staff has arranged to have the passes available in 200 banks throughout the area.

Also this year Metro will be promoting its effort to make the transit system more easily understood by the rider. Beginning in April Metro will install 7,000 new bus stop signs, which will be coordinated with the roller signs on the buses. At 3,000 stops schedule information will list the times each bus arrives.

Metro plans to spend about $35,000 in advertising to tell people about these changes. The budget for this part of the campaign is lower than for the other two because most of the information, Metro assumes, will be given free media news coverage.

Coffman used focus groups, gatherings of about 20 people, to measure reaction to various pitches before those pitches went on the air. The focus groups liked the model citizens concept, and Metro went ahead with it. However, focus group reaction canceled an earlier campaign.

Coffman had planned as part of the "Take Me, I'm Yours" push to sell T-shirts with that message written across them. A focus group thought the whole idea was in bad taste, and Coffman canceled the campaign.

Coffman says that the goals for his advertising campaign this year are to increase the number of riders by 7 percent, to get at least one rider in 20,000 more households, to increase the use of bus passes and to neutralize the fare increases that went into effect at the first of the year.

DEMARKETING ELECTRICITY USE

City Light, the other public agency using paid advertising to get its message across, is trying to discourage the use of its product. The utility has given its advertising agency $235,000 to produce and place radio and television spots and newspaper ads that ask people not to use so much electricity. (See Exhibits 1 and 2).

Public utilities have traditionally advertised for people to use more of their products, but City Light's campaign may be the first to encourage conservation. The budget for the campaign was approved by the Seattle City Council last winter.

Joan Whiley, coordinator of community relations for City Light, worked closely with the agency in the production of four 60-second radio spots, four 30-second television spots and four newspaper ads.

Whiley, who moved to City Light from an ad agency, says, "You just can't go out and talk to people in a dull way about conservation. You have to put on a show.

"You have to do something unusual and different. People are inundated with 1,500 advertising impressions a day. They remember only three or four. We wanted to cut through the barrage of sameness."

The radio spots, which began running mid-February, seem to have gotten people's attention.

One spot in particular has gotten a considerable amount of attention. In this a woman's voice invites the listener to enter the shower with her so that she can demonstrate how to take a shower in 60 seconds, thus saving energy. Commentators and columnists have said that this message encourages showering together. The agency claims that this was not the intention at all.

According to Whiley: "It depends on how your mind works whether you think that shower spot is lascivious or not."

She says that the people at KIRO radio initially refused to run it because it offended their moral standards.

EXHIBIT 1

THERE'S A FOUR LETTER WORD TO DESCRIBE PEOPLE WHO WASTE ELECTRICITY.

EXHIBIT 2

ARE YOU A POWER JUNKY?

"When they refused to run that one spot, I cancelled the whole schedule," she says. "Then they rethought their position and decided they could run the spot, after all."

According to Whiley, the first week that the radio spots ran, City Light got 125 calls on its special conservation line from people asking for the booklet on energy saving tips advertised or offering their own tips.

One City Light subscriber in Monroe wrote that the ads were, indeed, encouraging him to save energy because he turned off his radio whenever one of the spots came on. A woman called and objected to the ads' use of the line "the light of your life" to identify City Light. She said such a reference was appropriate only for God.

The television spots will run for eight weeks, one week on and one week off, now—and will reappear for a second cycle in October.

Said the advertising executive who developed this strategy: "If you don't have a lot of money to compete with major advertisers, you compress your messages into a short period of time so that you look just about as big and impressive as they do. Then you drop out and come back again later."

Whiley says that for the fall phase of the conservation campaign City Light would like to use public service air time in addition to its paid spots. The utility tried for free air time for the first phase, but only one station, KING-TV, agreed to cooperate.

"Because of the crunch we had to start the campaign about three weeks earlier than we had planned, and we didn't have the time to negotiate with the stations about public service," Whiley says. "Maybe when things simmer down this fall, we'll have to use some leverage with the stations."

PROMOTING THE UNIVERSITY

The University of Washington (UW) is using television to promote itself, but the campaign—which tells people that they get something out of the University whether they go there or not—is not costing the UW anything.

The seven 30-second spots, which have been distributed to 13 television stations throughout the state, were paid for by money raised by the Seattle Chamber of Commerce and are being aired on public service time.

Margaret Chisholm, vice president for university relations and development, talks about the "remarkable cooperation" from the television stations in airing the spots. "They have been enthusiastic, and they have commented on the quality of the spots."

Executives from the Seattle area stations attended a preview at the Washington Athletic Club. University and Chamber officials encouraged them to give the spots air time.

The idea that the University and the Chamber should cooperate in creating a better image for the UW came more than two years ago, when the Chamber president met with the president of the university. They agreed to use the Seattle Chamber of Commerce University Committee to find a way to inform citizens what impact the school has on the state.

An advertising agency donated its time to provide creative direction of the project. More than $47,000 was raised from 12 Seattle area businesses to pay for production of seven television spots showing different examples of how the University touches people's lives.

The spots are being sent two at a time to TV stations, and they should be on the air for between 16 and 18 months. Reaction has been positive and other universities have called the UW to ask about the process in producing and airing them.

One public service director for a Seattle station says that he was slightly reluctant to air the spots because he felt the University was using them to influence the legislature. A committee spokesperson denied this intention, saying that the idea originated before all the publicity about University funding.

"We have an obligation to tell people how the UW touches everyone at some point in his or her life," he said. "The point is to raise citizens' awareness of the University of Washington's contributions."

The University is supposed to return the favor to the Seattle Chamber of Commerce. The Chamber's University Committee will be beginning soon on the second part of its mission—agreed upon more than two years ago—for the UW to help the business community be better understood.

BUILDING PRIDE IN SEATTLE

At the Department of Community Development, which in October 1976 began promoting living in Seattle through television spots, Jean Withers and Paul Schell say they were surprised at the amount of reaction the television messages have gotten.

"It was apparently a very innovative idea," Withers says. "We've gotten a great deal of national coverage."

Stories about the advertising program have been carried in *The New York Times*, the *Los Angeles Times*, and *Advertising Age*, and have been featured on all three television networks and the British Broadcasting Corp.

According to Schell, the ads are aimed at people who live in the city. Their purpose is to instill a sense of responsibility and to promote pride in the city.

"It's private decision-making that's going to determine the future of the city. That's the basic premise behind the spots; we wanted to promote the idea of self-help.

"We used TV because the way people get most of their ideas is through TV advertising. It's a format that people are used to getting information through. We wanted the spots to be subtle and humorous, with no smiling politicians or bureaucrats."

Six spots were produced. One shows attractions like the Pike Place Market and Seattle Center, another talks about traffic diverters in the Stevens neighborhood. The spots are 30 seconds long and cost the city a total of $2,500.

Withers says that "because there are serious questions about city government spending a lot of money on TV," the Department of Community Development was concerned about keeping the cost down.

She and Schell spent some time creating the ads, but most of the work was undertaken by the public information director for a Seattle TV station and a local filmmaker who admit that they did the spots "ridiculously cheap."

After the program had been planned and production of the advertising had started, a consulting group contacted the Department and offered to do the same job for $60,000. This figure included a study to determine where the spots should be aimed and the creation and production of the advertising.

According to Schell, the Department of Community Development ultimately would like to turn the entire project of promoting the city over to a television station.

"We'd like to get the stations involved, have them do this kind of thing on their own," he says.

The television spots did prompt one radio station to produce a similar series for radio. KJR paid a free-lance script-writer who came up with the theme: "Seattle's a nice place to visit, but I'd rather live here."

Then the station interviewed several people (not professional performers) who enjoyed living in the city and talked about why. The interviews were edited down to 30- and 60-second spots, which were taped and sent to five radio stations and have been playing since January.

The KJR news director said that the radio station wanted to do something "to respond to the potential disaster that could occur in this city if people keep leaving at the rate they have been."

ENCOURAGING CARPOOLING

Thirty-second television spots promoting carpooling will begin running in public service slots sometime this month. These ads are brought to you by the Commuterpool in the city's Engineering Department. Manager Bill Roach and marketing coordinator Janet Thomas worked on the project. The four spots cost $2,500 of city and county funds.

"We're trying to get across to people the idea that carpooling can be fun," Roach says. "The ads are aimed at getting people's attention. The image of carpooling could take some sprucing up."

One shows a chauffeur picking up three well-dressed men who drink champagne on the way to work and are smug about being so thrifty by having to pay only 10 cents to cross the Evergreen Point Floating Bridge.

Two others show before and after shots of people who stopped driving to work by themselves and joined a carpool.

"National research showed us that the reason people carpool is companionship," Roach says. "We tried to keep that in mind. We realized that we were talking to a suburban driver and that cost is an issue and becoming more of one."

A fourth spot gives figures showing that a commuter could pay for a trip for two to Hawaii by a year of carpooling.

"Being the bureaucrat that I am, I insisted on using one straight spot to get information across," says the department manager.

Thomas says: "With the other spots, we're having some fun with sterotyped situations. We also show the various carpooling incentives that we offer, and we're trying to let people know that they can take—and have to take—individual steps to do something that can make a difference. Government isn't going to be coming up with any great grand solutions."

Roach says that he believes his agency should use the same sort of "living lightly" approach in putting its messages before the public that it is trying to convince the public to use.

"We shouldn't spend a great deal of money on media campaigns; we should find an opening and use what's available," he says. "We need to get more mileage out of public space. The issue is whether the policy makers want to put money into advertising for a change of lifestlye."

USING PUBLIC SERVICE ADVERTISING

The advertising executive who did the production for Commuterpool and the Department of Community Development believes that more public agencies should be taking advantage of free television time. "For good or bad," he says, "television has become the main medium of public information. It seems right now like a wasted medium to me; it could be a more effective medium for social change."

He and two other people have recently formed Summit Productions, a company for public service advertising. "We're trying to get agencies past the idea that they can't afford advertising." They are seeking out clients in government and among foundations.

KING-TV's public affairs director agrees that public agencies could make better use of the air time his stations is required to provide.

The public service spots that we run in a year's time are worth in excess of $1 million," he says. "It's the most valuable resource that we have to offer. It's a resource that could be used more effectively."

He says that he has been encouraged by the Department of Community Development's and Commuterpool's efforts in using public service time.

"The spots are effective, well-produced, aimed at a broad constituency and are tremendously important for the welfare of this area."

Part VIII
Analyzing the Environment and Evaluating Marketing Efforts

As shown by many of the previous chapters, developing a marketing program is often a difficult and time-consuming process. To do an effective job, managers must ensure that their programs are based upon sound information—about consumer needs, preferences, and behavior patterns; about trends in the external environment; about the structure of the marketplace; and about competitive offerings and how they are being marketed.

But the marketing manager's responsibilities do not end with the development and implementation of a program. To ensure that marketing activities are meeting their objectives, it is necessary to undertake careful evaluations. In the light of such evaluations, which should be conducted on an ongoing basis, existing programs may have to be redirected or even discontinued. Part VIII looks at several aspects of evaluation, including development of a marketing audit, problems with data systems in nonbusiness organizations, and the role of test-marketing. It concludes with two chapters on the role of marketing research in development of energy conservation programs. One of these, based on the situation in the United States, focuses on the type of information that is useful in understanding the dimensions of the energy consumption problem. The second, based on the British situation, reports on an actual campaign and shows how periodic marketing research reports can be used to evaluate progress and make changes in an ongoing program, as was also seen previously in Chapter 28.

The concept of a formalized marketing audit is introduced in Douglas Herron's contribution, "Developing a Marketing Audit for Social Service Organizations." The context discussed here is evaluation of social service agency programs, but the general approach is applicable to other types of programs. A comprehensive set of questions is provided to serve as a "check list" in undertaking a thorough audit of the organization's marketing operations.

In order to undertake a formal evaluation of a program, a manager needs data that are relevant, timely, and accurate. In "Why Data Systems in Nonprofit Organizations Fail," Regina Herzlinger argues forcefully that the state of control and information systems in most public and nonprofit organizations is dismal. This is not a matter of lack of data, but of systematically provided information. She suggests some guidelines for managers to improve the design, installation, and operation of information systems.

Evaluation is not confined to ongoing programs. The next chapter, "A Negative Income Tax Experiment," is concerned with data-gathering through the conduct of a "social experiment," or what marketers call a "test market." David Kershaw discusses the testing of alternate forms of a proposed program for making payments to families with incomes below a specified level. Test marketing is sometimes the only realstic way of evaluating how a new program will perform in the marketplace. A controlled experiment, involving delivery of several variations of a particular marketing program to matched samples, can provide valuable insights into how consumers respond to different features, pricing and distribution strategies, or communication efforts.

The last two chapters in the book are concerned with the contributions of research to one of the most pressing marketing challenges of our time, the marketing of energy conservation. Jeffrey S. Milstein's article, "Consumer Behavior and Energy Conservation," provides a detailed evaluation of energy consumption patterns, conserving behavior, and attitudes towards conservation in the United States. From these, guidelines for governmental policy and actions are drawn. These data could have formed the basis for a carefully developed, consumer-oriented conservation program. However, at the time of writing, political pressures have prevented the U.S. Department of Energy from introducing such a program.

The situation in the United Kingdom, as demonstrated by Phillips and Nelson in "Energy Savings in Private Households: An Integrated Research Program," is sharply different. Building on the same type of consumer research data presented in the preceding chapter, Britain's Department of Energy has developed a 12-point energy conservation program, involving marketing communication as one of its key elements. Most importantly, detailed research activities have been conducted to monitor progress and evaluate the effectiveness of the campaign. As shown in this chapter, measures of performance need not be confined to end results but can also focus on important "intermediate indicators," such as purchase of insulation materials. The advantage of such measures is that they provide faster feedback and often allow for greater precision in evaluating specific components of a comprehensive marketing campaign.

Most managers would agree that they do not suffer from a lack of data, but from a lack of relevant, timely, meaningful information. The chapters in Part VIII show that the type of information required varies according to the nature of the problem. But they also indicate that resourceful managers can develop both continuing information systems and special reports to help them as they seek to identify problems, to test the impact of alternative courses of action, and to select the most appropriate strategies.

36

Developing a Marketing Audit for Social Service Organizations

Douglas B. Herron

Performance appraisal is one of the most difficult tasks in social service marketing. Services, like people, are not standardized and it is difficult to compare one service objectively with another. Undertaking a comprehensive marketing audit can help social service agencies (and other types of public and nonprofit organizations) to determine the appropriateness of present marketing objectives, strategies, and organizational structures, as well as identifying any needed changes across the entire array of their marketing activities.

Besides reading letters to the editor and hearing complaining or praising phone calls, how does a social agency manager measure success? Business organizations can declare that success has been achieved when they produce a certain profit or return on invested funds. That is not an acceptable criterion for nonprofit institutions, however. Donors, unlike investors, do not expect to get their money back. Staff members do not expect to build up any equity in the organization through their efforts. Even the Board of Directors does not get too upset if revenue does not quite meet the expenses at the end of the year—"After all, it was for a good cause."

There is a growing cry for more rational kinds of measurement. Currently, the objectives of programs are being spelled out much more concisely than in the past. Governmental agencies and many United Ways are now purchasing services, so there is a need for measurement of service effectiveness. In the old days we would say, you just cannot measure the impact of that program; it was a mountain-top experience. Now the funders want proof.

CUSTOMER SATISFACTION

In addition to internal, staff-generated measures of program effectiveness, regular appraisals of consumer satisfaction should also be taken. Some agencies have systematized this so that participant evaluation forms are automatically sent to everyone immediately following the last session. In this case the evaluation is not a staff discretionary item. Using a standardized feedback form for every program, comparisions can more easily be made between different programs and different time periods for the same service.

Events can cause dramatic changes in consumer satisfaction to take place. The hiring or firing of a popular staff

Douglas B. Herron is Executive Director, Northwest Branch YMCA in Minneapolis, Minnesota.

person, for example, can either stimulate or depress partici-pant response to a sustaining membership or capital funds drive. So it is best to measure consumer satisfaction on a regular basis, not just once a year. Other events can then be more sensitively timed to take maximum advantage of the prevalent feelings.

You cannot please everyone all the time, but you can come close to pleasing no one most of the time. Some say it is a matter of costs. How much are you willing to pay for greater consumer satisfaction? If you gave them more staff time, better facilities, and more individualized services they would probably be a lot happier, but no agency can afford it. Fair exchange rates have to be established. "For this I can give you that." "Is it worth the price?"

There are different values that usually cannot be ap-preciated by all consumer segments of an agency. A multi-service agency is particularly vulnerable to this problem. The basketball players want more gym time; so do the gymnasts. The senior citizens do not sympathize with our doing some pregnancy counseling with unwed women. The pregnant women do not understand why the talented staff members are wasting their energies with the old folks. And so it goes! Attaining the right levels of consumer satisfaction is a man-agement task that must be monitored by the top leadership.

At least three techniques of measuring consumer sat-isfaction are popularly employed. Suggestion boxes, com-ment cards, and grievance committees produce unsolicited responses which are easy to get, but not reliable because they are unrepresentative. Questionnaires can be used for the sec-ond evaluative technique. They give a direct report of satis-faction from a representative group—that is, if the question-naires are worded correctly and the consumers know how to fill them out properly. A third evaluative method com-monly employed is observation. From just listening and watching, a manager can infer some things about the pro-gram's effectiveness. This method is vulnerable to the ob-server's biases, and the sample is warped by the times the observations take place.

Several benefits can be expected when the level of consumer satisfaction is raised. First, there should be less staff and consumer turnover. The organization should gain greater stability (unless the service is a one-shot thing like U.S.O. services for visiting sailors in port). There should also be an increase in pride, more consumers, and greater community good will.

Good will is important because of its strong relation-ship with an organization's ability to attract financial re-sources. If a sizable amount of donations can be acquired from program consumers, that is a good indication of their satisfaction.

But sizable donations from the public do not neces-sarily provide any real proof that an agency is working hard enough on the right things. Occasionally some organiza-tions, like Father Flanagan's Boys Town, master the art of fund raising. Critics claim that in those cases their generated revenue far exceeded their benefit to the community. Indi-vidual donors did not see the agency's books. For them, value was received in the transaction when they responded to the mail canvass or television ads. Giving that money made the donors feel good, or perhaps relieved some sense of guilt, but the gift had no relationship to proof that Father Flanagan's Boys Town was effective.

One of the problems is that agencies that have been offering a set of services for a number of years are reluctant to drop them in favor of something else. Perhaps a division or even the whole agency has outlived its usefulness, but it is reluctant to die. Because there is no profit motive, and in-dividual program service costs are not generally known, there is little motivation in a nonprofit agency to drop the losers. Sentiment often lasts longer than consumer demand. Watch out for the sacred cows!

MARKETING AUDIT

The best way to find out how an agency is doing with its marketing program is to have an outsider conduct an in-dependent marketing audit. This can be defined as follows:

> A marketing audit is an independent examination of the entire marketing effort of an organization covering objectives, programs, implementation, organization, and control for the purpose of de-termining and appraising what is being done and recommending what should be done in the future [1].

Unfortunately, organizations do not usually request a marketing audit until they feel some pain: goals are not being met consistently, resources are not sufficient, planning has little relationship to execution, or there is criticism of the agency. A more positive and equally effective time to get an audit is when a new director assumes control of an agency and adopts as a goal the use of marketing management tech-niques for the more effective and efficient delivery of social services.

One good way to begin a marketing audit is to list the different viewpoints of the service providers and the sevice users. What is the agency selling? How does the staff feel about the services and the consumers? How do the consum-ers feel about the quality of the service, its economy and ef-fectiveness? What discrepancies exist between what the staff say the end results of their actions are and what the consum-ers feel are the real benefits?

An internal marketing audit of the agency is con-ducted to see what it is doing. The internal audit consists of inquiries into phases of the agency's business, including its public relations, community organization, staff grievances, reward systems, and financial affairs.

An external audit is normally made to study the service from the viewpoint of the consumers, donors, and others on the outside who contribute to the well-being of the organization.

Information obtained from both the internal and ex-ternal audits can be used effectively to guide a strategy for solving some of the organization's problems or to seize more opportunities that exist.

QUESTIONS FOR A MARKETING AUDIT[1]

The questions which follow are intended as a guide. The precise set of questions to be asked of any organization should be developed with it specifically in mind. The list shown here suggests the major areas to be covered and illustrates the detailed questions that might be used. For additional insights in preparing a marketing audit, the reader is referred to [1], [2], and [3].

A. *The environment*

1. What are the significant, relevant, short- and long-run developments and trends in the organization's external environments (political, regulatory, economic, social, cultural, technical, others)?

2. What are the likely impacts of these factors on the organization?

B. *Users, funders, and other constituencies*[2]

1. Describe—size, growth rate, national and regional trends, etc.—each of the organization's major constituencies: users, donors, and volunteers. In each constituency, where do the major growth opportunities seem to be?

2. In each constituency what are the major segments? How can these segments be characterized and how are these segments changing over time? Which segments have the most potential?

3. Who are the organization's direct and indirect competitors?

4. What benefits does the organization offer to each segment? How does this compare to the benefits offered by competitors to users? To private and public benefactors? To volunteers?

5. How much of the consumer volume is repeat versus new business? What percent of consumers can be classified as light users? Heavy users?

6. How do users find out about and decide to try and/or use the organization's services? When and where? (Similarly for funders and volunteers.)

7. Describe other important constituencies (e.g., suppliers) and their present and future interaction with the organization.

C. *The organization*

1. What is the mission of the agency? What business is it in? How well is its mission understood throughout the organization? What business does it wish to be in five years from now?

2. Describe any plans for major changes in the organization in the next five years (e.g., new central facility, divestment).

3. What are the organization's major strengths and weaknesses?

4. What are the stated objectives of the organization? Do they lead logically to clearly stated marketing objectives?

5. Are the organization's marketing objectives stated in a hierarchical order? Are they quantified so that progress toward achievement can be measured? Are the objectives reasonable in light of the organization's resources?

6. What is the organization's marketing philosophy? (a) Is it formalized in writing? (b) Is it well thought out and internally consistent? (c) Who determines the philosophy and how is it changed?

7. Are the objectives and roles of each element of the marketing mix clearly specified?

8. What is the corporate structure? Is it designed for better service to customers or for internal convenience? Is there a senior marketing officer? Who in the organization works on marketing problems?

9. Does the organization have a marketing planning and control system? Are annual marketing plans developed, implemented, and used as the basis for a control system?

10. Does the organization carry out periodic reviews of the efficacy of its operations and evaluations of its resource allocation decisions? How and with what results?

11. Do marketing resource allocations reflect the importance of different segments, services, and territories, and different marketing activities as specified in the marketing philosophy and plan?

12. How is marketing research being used? What information does the organization have about its markets and other publics?

13. How much and what kind of outside opinion and training in marketing does the staff get?

14. What benefits and services does the organization receive as a result of its affiliation with other groups?

D. *Services offered by the organization*

1. What are the major services offered by the organization? Do they complement each other or is there unnecessary duplication?

2. For each service, what are the volume, past trend, and future expectations in terms of (a) dollars (number and share of market); (b) units, e.g., number of class sessions, treatments, visits; (c) participants (number and share of market).

3. If the organization has multiple facilities or branches, answer the previous question for each of the major subdivisions.

4. What are the market and nonmarket pressures to increase or decrease service volume? Service quality?

5. For each service, what are the weaknesses? (a) What goes wrong most often? (b) What are the major complaints?

---

[1] This section has been specially revised by the editors for inclusion in this book of readings.

[2] Some authors use the term "publics" instead of "constituencies."

(c) How vulnerable is it to competitive alternatives? Financial pressures?

6. What quality control procedures does the organization have?

7. In what ways should services be improved?

8. Are there any new services planned or that appear to be worth adding?

9. What services are being or apparently should be phased out?

10. For the last three questions, how does the organization determine what services are to be altered, added, or dropped? Does this lead to a product line which is attuned to community needs and organizational resources?

11. How does the organization choose where and when to promote and offer particular services?

E. *Enrollment* (if the organization has members)

1. Who enrolls or becomes a member of the agency? How does a potential enrollee find out about the organization? When and how does a user or non-user become a member?

2. What is the agency's biggest enrollment problem with consumers? What are the typical objections given by consumers as to why they do not enroll?

3. Who has the responsibility for enrolling service users? Have they had any sales training?

4. Are there regularly scheduled and held reporting meetings where results are measured and suggestions for improvement are made?

5. How much professional staff time is spent on encouraging people to enroll? What incentive does the staff have to enroll more people?

6. How much of a typical program director's time is spent promoting more enrollments as compared to serving those already enrolled?

7. How is it determined which new prospects will be called on by whom? How is the frequency of contacts determined?

F. *Pricing* (if fees are charged for services)

1. What are the procedures for establishing and reviewing pricing policy?

2. Is pricing demand-oriented? Are there variations by market segments, time of use, number of services used?

3. What methods of payment are accepted (e.g., credit cards, credit accounts, and checks).

4. What discounts to the basic fee structure are offered and with what rationale?

5. Are there any guarantees of program quality?

6. What are the refund agreements?

7. What short-term promotional pricing policies are used and with what effect?

G. *Distribution: Time and Place of Service Delivery*

1. What geographical areas are now served?

2. How does the agency rank its various geographic service areas in terms of priority of need and best return on investment of resources?

3. Is service delivery decentralized (out-reach)? Are information, reservation, and payment for services decentralized?

4. How are the service delivery centers identified by the public? Are the centers easy to find? Easy to give directions to? How good is public transportation access, parking for bicycles and cars? What is the access for the physically handicapped?

5. When are services made available to users? (a) season of year; (b) day of week; (c) time of day.

6. How frequently are services offered? Are there multiple offerings?

7. Are the timing decisions made in the two previous questions based on analysis of users' preferences? To what extent do the choices made reflect staff and/or volunteer convenience? Inertia from the past?

H. *Communication—Advertising, Personal Selling, Direct Mail, Promotion, and Public Relations*

1. Are there clear objectives for each element of the communication mix? How are the activities related to these objectives?

2. How is the budget for each element determined? Does it appear to be at the appropriate level? How does the organization decide on which programs or markets to concentrate promotion?

3. Are the advertising themes and copy effective? What do users, funders, volunteers, and organizational members think about the advertising?

4. What media is currently being used? (a) newspapers and magazines: (b) radio and TV; (c) church bulletins, United Way newsletters, business house organs, school catalogs; (d) telephone directories; (e) exhibitions, billboards, posters; (f) direct mail.

5. Does the organization have a paid or volunteer advertising agency? What functions does the ad agency perform for the organization?

6. What system is used to handle consumer inquiries resulting from advertising and promotion? What follow-up is done?

7. Is there a paid or volunteer personal selling force for either fund-raising or increasing service utilization? If so, how is this sales force organized and managed?

8. On what basis does the organization measure the effectiveness of its various communication programs (e.g., number of people aware of its services, knowledge about the services, attitudes toward the organization, program enrollment, financial contributions).

9. How are public relations activities normally handled? By whom?

10. How is promotion designed for and directed to different markets?

11. What do the annual meeting and annual report say about the agency and its services? Who is being effectively reached by those two vehicles? Do the benefits of these publications justify the costs?

12. Are news clippings kept? Do they show proof of the agency's ability to get accurate and favorable press coverage?

I. *Consumerism*

1. What is the agency's general reputation in the community (e.g., significant response to community needs, high quality of services, ability to get the job done)?

2. How are consumer interests represented in the decision making process about services?

3. What is done about negative feedback from consumers about agency staff? How are complaints handled?

4. What research findings about consumers' needs and interest are utilized by the service staff? How up to date is the staff with recent research findings?

5. Are catalogs and instruction booklets easy to read and understand (without being patronizing)? Might a prospective user find the wording ambiguous or misleading? Are graphics effectively used to facilitate understanding?

6. Does the agency newsletter provide needed, useful information to consumers, or is it just an ego boosting sheet for the staff?

REFERENCES

1. Kotler, Philip. "Marketing Method," Chapter 4 in *Marketing for Nonprofit Organizations*. Englewood Cliffs, NJ: Prentice-Hall, 1975, pp. 55–75.
2. Kotler, Philip, Gregor, William, and Rodgers, William, "The Marketing Audit Comes of Age," *Sloan Management Review,* Winter 1977, pp. 25–43.
3. Tirmann, Ernst, "Should Your Marketing Be Audited?" *European Business,* August 1971, pp. 49–56.

37

Why Data Systems in Nonprofit Organizations Fail

Regina Herzlinger

Nonprofit institutions have as much need for efficient information and control systems as for-profit organizations do; after all, top management in the "nonprofits" are similarly burdened with acute budgeting problems and policy issues whose resolution depends on the availability and sensible exploitation of accurate, current data. But the slovenly, unbusinesslike accounting practices that characterize many government agencies and the seat-of-the-pants managerial style of many private agency executives result in neglect and poor handling of the in-house information systems. This article examines this phenomenon and offers guidelines—as well as some hope—for improvement.

The director of a large social service agency in a New England state was told at fiscal midyear that unexpectedly lower tax revenues had forced a 5 percent reduction in his budget (or about $100 million). The distribution of the cut among the different programs was left to his judgment, but he couldn't respond to the order in a reasonable manner because he lacked the resources that would have given him the needed information. The state's use of a line-item, object-of-expense budgeting and accounting system frustrated his efforts to learn how much money had been committed to different programs; the statistical system that was supposed to tell him how many people were served and how many services were delivered wasn't working; and, to boot, the most recent cost data were four months out of date.

Regina Herzlinger is Associate Professor of Business Administration, Harvard University.

Lacking relevant information, he had to make a judgment solely on the basis of political considerations. He chose to cut the budgets of those programs affecting people with the least political influence—abandoned children and the mentally retarded.

The state of control and information systems in most nonprofit organizations is dismal. Despite billions of dollars spent to provide relevant, accurate, and timely data, few nonprofit organizations possess systems whose quality equals those found in large, profit-oriented corporations. Nonprofit organizations do not lack data; if anything, they enjoy an overabundance of numbers and statistics. Rather, they lack *systematically* provided information to help management do its job. Without good information, it is obviously difficult for managers to make reasoned and informed decisions, evaluate performance, motivate their employees, and protect the institution against fraud.

This problem is by no means confined to public agencies; it also crops up in private, nonprofit organizations.

Consider the case of one voluntary agency that delivered services ranging from medical care to adult education classes. Once boasting a healthy endowment and a substantial yield on its endowment, the agency had suffered through three consecutive years of increasing deficits and was suspended on the brink of bankruptcy.

Its director was a controversial person who had converted it from a stodgy, upper-class "charity" to a vital, existing organization. Or so her supporters said. Her detractors, convinced that she was responsible for the precarious financial position, accused her of wasting money on frivolous, faddish activities that benefited neither their participants nor the organization's reputation.

Was she a superlative manager or an incompetent? The answer to that question was vital to the organization's future. But it couldn't be answered objectively; the agency's board simply had too little information with which to evaluate the quality of her management. The agency had no budget, no output data, and such a poor system of internal controls that even the number of members was in doubt.

Many nonprofit organizations are deficient in the routinized internal control that ensures the integrity of the accounting for expenditures and services. The welfare error rate is a familiar subject of newspaper stores. Often as high as 40 percent, the error rate consists of seemingly random underpayments and overpayments to welfare recipients. It is vivid evidence of a poor system of internal control.

A similar case is the Guaranteed Student Loan Program, administered by the Office of Education of HEW. Every one of the program's annual financial statements has received an "adverse" opinion from the General Accounting Office. This opinion is rendered, in part, because the program's managers do not know the magnitude of the loans they have insured and therefore can accurately account for neither the contingent reserves account on their balance sheet nor the loss expense account on their income statement. The loan volume outstanding is estimated at $7 billion to $8 billion —with an unknown amount in the range of $1 billion for which there are no proper accounting records. The possibilities for fraud in these cases are staggering.

The presence of a management information system does not guarantee its proper use, of course. Many hospitals, for example, identify their outpatient departments as "money losers," while in fact the outpatient department frequently substantially offsets the total operating costs of the hospital and may even contribute to covering the direct costs of its inpatient side.

The losing position of the outpatient department is merely an artifact of some states' medical aid systems, in which a ceiling is placed on the reimbursement a hospital receives per inpatient day, while reimbursement for the outpatient department is handled on a "cost or charges, whichever is lower" basis. To maximize reimbursement, a hospital will allocate as many "joint costs" as possible to the outpatient department and thereby create an accounting "loser." This system of cost accounting is perfectly sensible for purposes of reimbursement, but it creates an unfair basis for the evaluation of the manager of an outpatient department.

More serious are situations in which the data network leads to a totally inappropriate course of action. In the mid-1960s, the U.S. Department of Labor designed an elaborate information system for programs to train the hard-core unemployed and place them in useful employment. While the system measured many aspects of cost and output, one measure was of paramount importance: number of people placed in jobs. When Labor Department supervisors visited a local manpower office, they particularly wanted to know the number of placements the director had generated.

The directors of the local programs got the message. Soon they were ensuring a high placement rate through a practice known as "creaming"—that is, they skimmed the cream of the unemployed and accepted only persons who were temporarily unemployed and who had a high probability of appropriate placement. This strategy was obviously antithetical to the purpose of the national program.

In some far-removed location in a public agency or a private nonprofit organization, computing equipment frequently stands idle, away from prying eyes—another symptom of the problem. It is idle because the computer has not "worked out" for its intended purpose. Its intended purpose may have been based on a totally unrealistic notion of what an information system can do. When the inevitable failure occurs, the computer gets the blame, anthropomorphically, and ignominiously disappears.

Computer graveyards are most often found in large hospitals and welfare departments. They have mammoth data-processing requirements that supposedly can be met by buying large computers and "integrated" management information system packages. The systems will somehow solve all the organizations' information needs, from record keeping to planning and control reports. Since the human mechanisms for obtaining and "inputting" the data are weak, however, an integrated system never quite succeeds. Moreover, the technical problems of programming and operating such a system are sometimes beyond the capability of the organization and its system contractor.

AT THE ROOT OF THE PROBLEM

A major cause of the problem is the method of financing such organizations. Funding in block grants, which vary with neither volume nor quality of service and which are made before the work is done, does not reward effective and efficient performance and gives managers little incentive to encumber themselves with tighter controls.

The best way to change this attitude is to make the form of funding more like the financing mechanism used in the private sector. Financing the *consumers* of services—rather than the *suppliers* of services—would impose the discipline of the marketplace on the organizations. Consumers, armed with purchasing power, could pick and choose among them.

Such a policy change, however, is unlikely to occur. Proposals for it have been aired since early in the twentieth century; the most recent one is Milton Friedman's plan for the use of vouchers in education. Although the federal government has experimented with vouchers in education and housing, it shows little sense of urgency about adopting these mechanisms. Even the laudable negative income tax idea—a voucher-like device which, among other benefits, would eliminate much of the paper pushing in welfare departments—is now languishing in academic journals.

Admittedly, nonprofit organizations are beset by demands for data from financial supporters and other parties. A typical hospital files financial and statistical reports with a number of insurance companies, the state in which it is located, the federal government, the planning agencies in its area, the licensing authorities, the certificate-of-need agency personnel, and the quality and utilization review administration—not to mention the financial statement it prepares, on a fund-accounting basis, for its own board of trustees. None of these statements duplicates another in content or format. School systems use an accounting system recommended by the U.S. Office of Education that has more than one million possible entries!

Obviously, many factors inhibiting improved information handling are beyond the control of a nonprofit organization. Yet the one factor accounting for most failures of information systems lies directly within the control of the organization: the characteristics and attitudes of top management.

Rarely does one hear the executives of a nonprofit organization described as being "good with numbers." More frequently, the acolades are "creative," "innovative," "caring," or "great scholars." Being good with numbers may actually do the managerial image a disservice, for it implies the absence of such qualitative skills as creativity, courage, and humanitarianism. Indeed, some managers of nonprofits view their lack of quantitative skills as a rather endearing imperfection—like having freckles.

Many of these managers were initially professionals who carry with them the culture and attitudes of the professional, including strong resistance to quantitative measures of their organizations' activities. They argue, sometimes persuasively, that professional work is too complex and diffuse in its impact to be easily accounted for and that naive attempts to account for its outcome might undermine the credibility and integrity of the work itself.

A case in point is the experience of the state of Michigan, which in 1969 began a program to collect data on the resources and achievements of its school systems. The purpose of the assessment was to link expenditures with results and presumably to hold school personnel responsible for their performance.

The project was greeted with such hostility that the department of education retreated from its original goals. The report on the third year of the project stressed that the assessment "is not to be viewed as an evaluation of Michigan schools. Instead it is to provide information on . . . student needs." The next year the department expanded its cautionary position, explaining that the program "does not indicate which schools or districts are most effective or efficient." [1]

Many professionals-turned-managers do not command the technical skills required for the design and implementation of a good information system. When I have taught accounting to top executives of large nonprofit organizations, they have often told me that until then they had never been able to understand their own financial statements.

A lack of technical skills and an institutionalized aversion to measurement, when combined with the traditional definition of the role of manager in these organizations, lead many managers of nonprofit institutions to abdicate the task of designing and implementing a sound information system to their staffs, particularly to their accountants. A manager will say, "I don't know much about these numbers, but my accountant is a genius." It is doubtful that the manager has the capability to judge an accountant's genius.

SOME SOLUTIONS

The problem of the multiplicity of external demand for data could be partly reduced through coordination of the agencies that fund a particular organizational entity in the design of the data system for monitoring the program. The many federal agencies that finance community health centers could, for example, design a single system that would meet not only their data needs but also those of the insurance companies and the state welfare departments involved.

We should not, however, be overly sanguine about the likelihood of this solution. Under the present structure of federal and most other government units, the different groups have no reason to coordinate. Moreover, organizations and benefactors fund programs for different reasons, and they are unlikely to agree on a common data set that meets all their needs. Finally, even if federal and state agencies could cooperate on information system design, their actions would still be subject to legislative review, which is not always intelligent or objective.

An approach different from most has been taken by the National Centers for health Statistics and for health Services Research and Development. They have designed a data

[1] Jerome T. Murphy and David K. Cohen, "Accountability in Education—the Michigan Experience," *The Public Interest,* Summer 1974, p. 62.

system for planning and evaluating purposes. The network, now in its early stages of implementation, involves these steps:

> The federal level specifies a very small amount of information for each program to generate.
>
> State and local programs receive funding for experimentation with the installation of systems that meet their internal needs.
>
> The federal government reimburses the state and local bodies for providing the required data.

This approach has several admirable aspects: (a) the requirements for external data are kept to a minimum; (b) the operational programs are given the opportunity, and funding, to integrate the external data into a system that meets their needs; and (c) the users must pay for the data. The user payment feature is important and unusual because the payment is direct and thus tends to make agencies asking for the data more sensitive to the financial impact of their requests.

Until the necessity and feasibility of approaches like that of the National Centers are recognized, nonprofit organizations must limp along individually as best they can. Much depends on the quality of their managers, who, as I pointed out earlier, are often long on professional training and experience but short on administrative skills and experience. The management component of most professional training is usually completely absent, limited to office practices such as billing, or covered through a quick survey course of administrative techniques—a week on accounting, a week on interpersonal behavior, and so on. This level of education is unlikely to develop people with the skills and attitudes of professional managers. Many professional schools, however, are beginning to offer their students appropriate managerial training courses.

GUIDELINES FOR MANAGERS

Of course, the impact of that trend will not be felt for a while, so the main thrust of the improvement of information systems must lie with present managers. Here are some suggestions for improvement of the design, installation, and operation of information systems:

System Design. The top manager who remains uninvolved in the design of the content of the system negates the reason for its existence. Participation in the system design process ensures that the system is relevant and responsive to management's needs.

It is also important to recognize that information systems must meet different needs (also, some questions can be answered on a totally ad hoc basis). The framework developed by Robert N. Anthony is very useful for classifying different types of information systems.[2] He distinguishes

---

[2] See Robert N. Anthony, *Planning and Control Systems: A Framework for Analysis* (Boston: division of Research, Harvard Business School, 1965), particularly the first three chapters.

three managerial functions and delineates the characteristics of the different kinds of information systems needed to support these functions.

Measurement of output and efficiency in most nonprofit institutions is a big problem. The output is usually a service, with a host of measurable attributes. Furthermore, since the output is generally not sold, it is impossible to measure it in financial terms by assigning it a market value. Some system designers go overboard in an attempt to solve the problem. A small nursing agency, for example, drew up a list of 103 finely grained output measures and 21 efficiency measures per nurse. To get an overall measure of effectiveness, the agency then adjusted and weighted these criteria in some arcane manner. Such efforts result in data of dubious validity. A balanced solution sets a standard of measurement without excessive elaboration.

An important component of the design phase is the stipulation of the means for implementing the system, including estimates of time required, cost involved, and milestones to be achieved. This step is frequently omitted or neglected because managers justify information systems on a "cost-saving" basis and fear that documentation of the costs of installing the system will belie their initial estimates.

Since most nonprofit organizations seriously underfund their information system activities, it is unrealistic and unnecessary to justify installation of a new design on a cost-saving basis. Rather, they should be justified on benefit/cost reasoning—that is, that the benefits of the system will exceed its cost. And the design phase should include meticulous documentation of these costs.

The design phase should also include designation of the organizational unit that will install and/or operate the system. Otherwise, such responsibility is diffused along the breadth of the organization. This leads to difficulties in assigning responsibility and authority.

Installation. An important and frequently neglected precondition to success is adequate pretesting of the form and content of the system. The organization should not stint in the planning and financing of the pretesting phase.

Extensive training of those who will use and operate the system is a worthwhile investment. Because of the high rate of turnover at the top level of most nonprofit organizations, it is important to "institutionalize" the system through training.

Thorough documentation of all aspects of the form and content of the system is an essential part of the installation process, especially the preparation of manuals explaining how every item of input or output is to be measured. At a minimum, the organization should draw up a chart of the accounts used for reporting purposes and give a detailed explanation of how and when they are to be recognized. This is a tedious job, often neglected. Furthermore some designers gain power from the absence of documentation, making them the only ones who know how to run the system.

Operation. An information system used regularly by top management for making such key decisions as budget allocation will eventually overcome any initial flaws of design and installation. At the same time, it is important to designate an appropriate organizational unit for the routinized production of the information. If this unit is different from the one that designed the system, the people in the former unit will be less reluctant to modify the system. This policy of separation, however, may cost the organization much more money than having one unit responsible for the operation of the system as well as its design.

Most of the issues in the design and implementation of these information systems in nonprofit institutions are similar to those in profit-oriented organizations. If the condition of such systems in these two types of organizations were also the same, we would enjoy a much more efficient economic environment.

38

A Negative Income Tax Experiment

David N. Kershaw

A test market, conducted prior to the wide-scale introduction of a new product or service, can help a manager assess market reaction to the innovation. By running several test markets and varying key attributes of the innovation, the manager can make better decisions as to the most appropriate product or service configuration to introduce. In 1967, a test market, or experiment, was carried out in six cities to help determine the effect of negative-income-tax on the incentive to work of potential recipients. In different cities the size of the cash payments was varied.

The welfare-reform proposals of both President Nixon and Senator McGovern embody the concept of the negative income tax: a downward extension of the income-tax system that would pay out cash (negative taxes) to families at the low end of the income scale. An essential feature of the concept is that as a family's income rises above the poverty level the tax payments are reduced by an amount less than the earnings, so that the family is always better off the higher its own earnings are. The concept was first presented to a broad public in 1962 by Milton Friedman of the University of Chicago, who argued that the negative income tax would strengthen the market economy and individual initiative by enabling poor people to make their own decisions on spending and saving and would cut back on the large and growing apparatus of social-welfare programs.

David N. Kershaw is Vice President, Mathematica, Inc.

It is difficult to predict what the impact of a negative-income-tax plan would be on the people covered and on the economy. The word "experiment" is often applied to new social programs, but it is not used in the normal scientific sense. For the past four years, however, my colleagues and I at Mathematica Incorporated, working with a group at the Institute for Research on Poverty of the University of Wisconsin, have been conducting a more rigorous kind of social experiment to test the effects of a negative income tax. Money for the experiment was provided by the U.S. Office of Economic Opportunity. The main objective of the work has been to explore the key question about the negative tax, namely the extent to which it would reduce the incentive of the recipients to work. The extent of such a work reduction will determine both the actual cost of a new program and whether or not it is acceptable to the taxpayers. Our preliminary findings indicate that a negative income tax does not significantly reduce the earnings of the recipients. We think the findings also point to the value of social experimentation as a tool for policy makers.

The need for some such technique arises from the large sums that the Government regularly commits to the eradication of one social ill or another: additional housing for the poor, health facilities for the elderly, medical care for the indigent, school lunches for poor children and so on. Since the supply of skills and money for these activities is limited, the legislative process becomes essentially a system of bargaining or of trading off one set of programs for another. On what basis do Government officials recommend one set of programs rather than another? What criteria do legislators employ to measure the probable effectiveness of one idea as opposed to another? The fact is that there have been few effective ways for determining the effectiveness of a social program before it is started; indeed, in most cases it is impossible even to forecast the cost of a new social program until it has been in operation for some time.

Clearly this situation is not conducive to sound and effective decision making. Moreover, it results in such unforeseen disasters as the Medicaid scandals, empty public-housing projects and relentlessly increasing costs for welfare programs. Social experimentation of the kind I am discussing is a tool that has been developed and tested in the past five years for avoiding unanticipated developments in new social programs and for measuring in advance what the programs will cost.

What is usually unforeseen in a new program is how the people affected by it will behave. What they do, of course, is likely to have a profound effect on the program. For example, in the Medicaid program unexpectedly high fees charged by physicians and hospitals and unexpectedly high use of the services took policy makers by surprise. Various behavioral changes induced in the recipients similarly determine the cost and effectiveness of new income-transfer programs. Since most major social programs will induce changes in behavior, which in turn will affect the program, it is clearly vital for policy makers to understand the magnitude and direction of such changes in behavior in advance in order to make the most rational choices among new programs.

A social experiment as we view it has the same general design as an experiment in the natural sciences. One undertakes to identify the experimental population, then to change one of the variables affecting its behavior and finally to compare its subsequent behavior with that of a control population in which the variable has not been changed. If the experiment is well designed, the investigator can attribute any difference in the behavior of the experimental population to the stimulus. The question we faced was whether or not this approach would work when the population consisted of human beings, when the laboratory was the community and when the stimulus was a complex new social program.

Our experiment was the first attempt to answer the question. The experiment has been conducted as the New Jersey Negative Income Tax Experiment because its first operations were in Trenton, although it was later extended to Scranton, Pa., as well as to three other cities in New Jersey: Paterson, Passaic and Jersey City. Negative-income-tax payments were begun in Trenton in August, 1968, and were ended in Scranton September 1972. The only part of the experiment now in progress is the analysis of the data.

The welfare-reform proposals of the two presidential candidates are among a number of negative-tax plans that have been advanced in recent years. Although the various plans differ in many ways, all of them are defined by two common variables: the guarantee level and the rate of reduction (sometimes called the tax rate) applied to the guarantee.

The guarantee is the amount paid to a family or an individual with no other income. In a negative-income-tax system the guarantee would be in effect a floor under incomes, providing a basic level of income for everyone. Various guarantee levels have been proposed, ranging from $2,400 annually for a family of four (the amount in H.R. 1, a House of Representatives bill incorporating the Administration's proposals for welfare reform) to $6,600 per year (advocated by the National Welfare Rights Organization).

The rate of reduction is the rate at which the negative-tax payments are reduced as the family's other income rises. The reduction is always less than the amount of the rise in other income. That is to say, for each dollar of other income the family receives, the negative-tax payment is reduced somewhat, but not dollar for dollar. A dollar-for-dollar reduction formerly applied in welfare programs, and the rate in such programs remains high today.

The guarantee and the rate of reduction can be combined in many ways. Suppose the guarantee is $3,000 and the rate of reduction is 50 percent. A family with no earned income receives the full $3,000, and the reduction is not applied. If in the next year the family's earned income is $1,000, the rate of reduction of 50 percent means that the negative-tax payment to the family is reduced by $500. The family now receives $2,500 in negative-tax payments and $1,000 of its own income for a total of $3,500. The reduction works just as the positive income tax works; in this example the family is effectively in a 50 percent marginal tax bracket.

The key point is that the family's total income continues to rise as its earned income rises, notwithstanding the reduction in negative-tax payments. Just as in the positive-tax program, the family is always better off with a higher earned income. The point is important because it shows that the negative-income-tax system is designed to minimize the disincentive to work that has often been associated with welfare programs. People who are able to work keep a portion of their earnings just as people in the positive-tax system do.

In the example I have given, the family would continue to receive negative-tax payments until its own income reached $6,000. At that level the family would become a taxpayer rather than a tax recipient. As long as the level remained above $6,000 the family would receive no payments. If the income dropped below $6,000, the payments would be resumed.

Choosing the "best" combination of guarantee level and rate of reduction is a difficult problem. The two things one is most concerned with in a welfare system are (1) how much it will cost and (2) whether or not it will have a strong tendency to make the recipients disinclined to work. Unfortunately the objectives of low cost and minimum work disincentive are in direct conflict.

The problem is evident if one envisions plans applying rates of reduction of 30, 50 and 70 percent respectively to a guarantee of $3,000. At 30 percent a family would continue to receive payments until its earned income reached $10,000, which is close to the median income in the U.S. for a family of four. Under this plan half of the families in the nation would be recipients of negative-tax payments. Although the low rate of reduction would presumably keep the work disincentive low, the cost would be very high. On the other hand, a rate of reduction of 70 percent would keep the cost of the system down but could severely limit the incentive to work.

The problem of establishing an appropriate guarantee level and rate of reduction, of ascertaining the effect of various combinations on work behavior and of estimating the cost of a national program led to a decision by the Office of Economic Opportunity that a field experiment should be undertaken as a way of obtaining evidence. In 1967 the office gave money for the experiment to the Institute for Research on Poverty and to Mathematica, which has its headquarters in Princeton, N.J. These organizations shared the responsibility of designing the experiment and of analysing the data, and Mathematica set up the administrative system.

The design of the experiment was focused on the work-response issue. Given a guaranteed annual income, how much, if any, would recipients reduce their work effort? The designers of the experiment decided that the population of most interest consisted of intact families among the working poor. The work response of single-parent families and of the aged and disabled were of less interest. Data on the work response of single-parent families were partly available through the program of aid to families with dependent children, and it appeared that the cost of a guaranteed income for the aged and the disabled could be estimated without a field test since the variability of their response to negative-tax payments was limited. For these reasons the designers decided that the sample for the experiment should consist of intact families with ablebodied males between the ages of 18 and 58 who were either in the labor force or physically capable of entering it.

A second major decision concerned the method of choosing the participants. The designers considered a national sample, which would consist of families chosen on a random basis from places in every region of the country; a "saturation" experiment, consisting of all the eligible families in a given area, and a "test-boring" approach involving a limited number of families from several geographic areas. It appeared that a national sample would cost too much and would be risky administratively in view of how little was known about conducting a social experiment of this kind. The saturation approach was rejected both for its cost and because it was difficult to see how data from a single area would be helpful in making generalizations about a national negative-tax program. We decided on the test-boring approach.

Choosing the site involved several considerations. The first decision was to concentrate on an urban area, since most of the working poor live in cities. Second, we focused on the Northeast because it is densely populated and is close to Washington, so that the Office of Economic Opportunity could more easily participate in the decision making. In the end we settled on New Jersey because it is densely populated and has a substantial number of poor people. Moreover, the state government was interested in the experiment. Trenton was chosen as the pilot site because it is close to Princeton (and so to Mathematica) and because as the capital of New Jersey it facilitated liaison with state officials. Paterson, Passaic and Jersey City were added later because they are fairly large cities, and Scranton was added because its preponderance of white residents would bring an ethnic balance to a sample that was otherwise largely black or Puerto Rican.

The selection of families was based on two preliminary interviews: a 44-question screening survey administered to about 30,000 families in the five cities and a 340-question "pre-enrollment" interview administered to 2,300 families. Both interviews obtained information on the composition of the family and on income. In addition the pre-enrollment interview provided baseline measurements of certain other sociological and economic variables.

The designers decided to test three rates of reduction: 30, 50 and 70 percent. The reasoning was that this group of rates covered the relevant policy range, inasmuch as a national program would never be designed with a reduction rate lower than 30 percent (on cost grounds) or higher than 70 percent (on work-disincentive grounds). Four guarantee levels were established, ranging from $1,650 (half of the official poverty level for a family of four in 1967) to $4,125 (125 percent of the poverty level). Eight combinations of reduction rate and guarantee level were established, and each one was designated as a "plan."

More than 1,300 families have been involved in the program, although some have dropped out and are not reflected in our data. Somewhat more than half of the 1,300 families were assigned to one or another of the eight negative-tax plans. The other families constituted a control group that received no negative-tax payments, although they were interviewed periodically just as the experimental families were. A control group is necessary in order to be able to compare the families receiving payments with families of similar situation who are not. In this way the experimenter can be sure that random events in the cities are not responsible for the results he is measuring.

In order to participate in the experiment the families in the group receiving payments were required only to report their correct income and any changes in family composition. The reports, which we verified through various auditing procedures, were made every four weeks to the Council for Grants to Families, a corporate body set up by Mathematica and the Institute for Research on Poverty to process and disburse payments. On the basis of income reported to the council, families were paid every two weeks by check sent by mail from Princeton. The council also had an office in each of the experimental cities to answer questions from the families and from Princeton.

Families were free to do whatever they wished with the payments. They also could move anywhere in the U.S. If a member left the original family unit, he or she still received a share of the family grant. Payments were excluded from taxable income under a ruling obtained from the Internal Revenue Service.

In addition to the income data on the forms mailed in by the experimental families every four weeks, information on the work response and other characteristics of the sample was obtained from interviews administered every three months by the Urban Opinion Surveys Division of Mathematica to both the experimental and the control families. The questionnaires sought information on such matters as participation in the labor force, financial status, medical and educational histories, family structure and political and social integration. Twelve such interviews were made, and a 13th quarterly interview was undertaken to ascertain what understanding the families had of the experiment.

We have now obtained a great deal of information about the 1,300 families. We shall be analyzing the results for another year. Unanalyzed portions of the data will be made available, under controlled conditions, to investigators over the next few years. Even though the analysis is not complete, we have reached a stage where it is possible to describe the principal results in a preliminary way.

The most important results, of course, are those that bear on the work response. The question to be asked here is: How did the work behavior of the families in the experimental group compare with the work behavior of the families in the control group? The preliminary results give no evidence indicating a significant decline in weekly earnings as a result of the introduction of the payments. About 31 percent of the families in the experimental group showed earning increases of more than $25 per week, compared with about 33 percent of the controls. About 25 percent of the experimental families showed earning declines of more than $25 per week, compared with 23 percent of the controls. These differences are too small to be regarded as statistically significant. That is a most encouraging finding.

A second finding in terms of work response was identified when improvements in the computer system enabled us to analyze indicators other than earnings. One such indicator was the number of hours worked. An analysis primarily made by Harold Watts of the University of Wisconsin, who is the principal investigator in the experiment, showed that the hours worked by families in the experimental group are about 12 percent fewer than the hours worked by families in the control group. The difference is statistically significant.

Close examination reveals that about 40 percent of the difference is attributable to primary earners in the experimental group who worked less than primary earners in the control group. The reasons appear to be small differences in overtime pay, in periods of unemployment and in time spent on a second job. The remaining 60 percent is attributable to spouses and other adult workers in the family. Interestingly enough, it does not appear that these people are leaving the labor force in comparison to the control group; instead it seems that they are entering the labor force less rapidly. This observation suggests that the reason for the lower number of hours worked in the experimental group may be that people in those families take longer to look for better jobs. The availability of the negative-income-tax payment enables the worker to do that instead of having to accept the first job he finds.

The possibility that recipients spend more time looking for better jobs is a hypothesis; it may not be the actual reason for the reduction in hours worked. Attributing precise causes is a complicated process. Further analysis may provide answers. In any case a reduction of only 12 percent suggests that the introduction of a national negative-income-tax program will not give rise to a tidal wave of voluntary idleness. It certainly would be encouraging if people are reducing their work hours in order to look for better jobs.

We have also obtained information on the attitudes of the people in our experimental and control populations toward work. There would appear to be little reason for low-income workers to adhere to the "Protestant ethic." Why should they consider work a good thing? In the labor market they have met discrimination, low wages, poor working conditions and arbitrary layoffs. For some reason, however, the people we interviewed generally supported the idea of work. This attitude could prove significant if the nation undertakes to develop an income-maintenance system that provides a smooth transition from poverty to reasonable affluence.

It is conceivable that the most important and lasting result of the New Jersey experiment will be the support it provides for the idea of social experimentation. Although the experiment encountered a number of serious unforeseen problems, in general it worked: families were chosen and assigned to experimental or control groups, money was paid, interviews were conducted, data were assembled, analysis was done and results were sent to Washington, where policy makers used them. A more rigorous question is whether social experimentation is a cost-effective way of obtaining answers to policy questions.

The weaknesses of the method are fairly clear: it is an expensive way of gathering information (the cost of the New Jersey experiment will be almost $10 million in the end); it takes a long time to get results, since measuring human behavior with confidence requires at least several years, and it is difficult to control the environment of the experiment. The strengths of social experimentation as a policy tool are also rather clear: it is the only way to obtain information on some kinds of behavioral change before a new program is introduced; it is the best way to collect precise information on specific issues because it is carefully structured and controlled, and it can help to focus the attention of able and imaginative scholars and professionals on new issues. On balance, social experimentation has thus far proved to be an effective new tool.

The New Jersey experiment has given rise to, or at least encouraged, a number of other social experiments. The rural negative-income-tax experiment, sponsored by the Office of Economic Opportunity and conducted by the Institute for Research on Poverty, covers 800 rural families in Iowa and North Carolina. The Department of Health, Education, and Welfare has provided money for income-main-tenance experiments in Seattle, Gary, Ind., and Denver and also for the Vermont family-assistance-planning study, which was designed to explore the more important administrative issues in the Family Assistance Plan. The experiments in housing allowance, sponsored by the Department of Housing and Urban Development, give housing vouchers to poor families in several cities with the aim of studying the response of families and landlords, the demand and supply of housing and how a national housing-allowance program might be administered. The Office of Economic Opportunity is sponsoring an education-voucher demonstration and a health-insurance experiment. The education-voucher program seeks to measure the effect on communities and students of giving all parents in a particular area vouchers good for education at a school of their choice. In the health-insurance experiment about 2,000 families will be placed on various health-insurance plans to measure how the utilization of medical services changes in response to differences in the cost of medical care.

Other social experiments are under consideration. They involve such issues as child care, problems of income measurement and administrative techniques in cash-assistance programs. One can anticipate that an increasing number of policy decisions on major social programs will be made with the assistance of information obtained through social experiments undertaken to explore these issues and others yet unforeseen.

39
Consumer Behavior and Energy Conservation

Jeffrey S. Milstein

American consumers, who use one-third of our energy, favor energy conservation, but generally do not practice it. This article presents empirical data and analyses of psychological, cultural, economic, and political reasons for this; indicates effective incentives and motivations for conservation; and spells out the implications for governmental policy and action.

THE CONSUMER AND AMERICA'S ENERGY PROBLEMS

In balancing American energy demands with available supplies and thereby reducing American dependence on foreign oil imports, which proved unreliable during the embargo, American consumers play an important role. Almost a third of the energy used in the United States is consumed by people in their homes (20 percent) and automobiles (12 percent). Another 15 percent is used in the commercial sector, 41 percent in the industrial sector, and an additional 12 percent in the non-automobile transportation sector.

There is specific behavior in homes and in cars that consume the greatest amount of energy. City driving accounts for 55 percent of all miles driven by consumers. Within the home, an average 53 percent of the energy is used for space heating, 15 percent for water heating, 6 percent for air-conditioning, 7 percent for refrigeration, 5 percent for cooking, and 11 percent for lighting, clothes drying, and other uses.

If consumers are to conserve energy effectively, they must choose and use their purchases much more wisely. They must buy more insulation and more efficient cars and appliances. And they must *use* their cars more efficiently: carpooling, driving at slower speeds, etc. They must use their appliances more efficiently, in off-peak hours. Consumers must set their heating thermostats lower and their air-conditioning thermostats higher.

But American consumers are reluctant to change their behavior to save energy. This paper seeks to explain why, by analyzing and interpreting empirical data gathered by FEA. It will also explain how these answers can be used in designing effective governmental policy.[1]

Jeffrey S. Milstein is Director of Marketing Research, Office of Conservation and Solar Applications, U.S. Department of Energy.

The author wishes to thank Joanne Bakos and Jill Lady for their help in preparing and editing this document.

[1] The findings and interpretations in this document should not be interpreted as necessarily representing the official policies, either expressed or implied, of the Federal Energy Administration or the U.S. Government. For additional information, contact the author.

DATA SOURCES[2]

The Office of Energy Conservation and Environment of the Federal Energy Administration directed contractors to do research on consumer attitudes, knowledge, preferences, motivations, and behavior regarding energy conservation. The research is of two types: national probability sample surveys and focused group discussions. Surveys of 1,000 to 1,200 people each were made monthly from August 1974 to April 1976 in the forty-eight contiguous states. Each respondent was interviewed by telephone for twelve to twenty minutes. A total of eighteen focused group discussions were held in Denver, Trenton, Hartford, Seattle, Chicago, and Nashville. In each case, trained leaders led ten to twelve people in discussions that lasted from an hour and a half to two hours.

AWARENESS OF THE ENERGY PROBLEM

A majority of the public is aware of the Nation's energy problems. In April 1976, those surveyed responded fairly knowledgeably to the question, "In general, what is your understanding of what the energy problem is all about?". (See Exhibit 1). People are aware that the demand for energy exceeds the supply and that it is important to conserve. But note that only 5 percent of the public mentioned U.S. dependence on foreign supplies; yet the Arab oil embargo is what precipitated the energy crisis three years ago.

EXHIBIT 1
Consumers' Understanding of the Energy Problem

Response	Percent
Demand is greater than supply	29
Natural resources are being used up	15
Need to conserve	11
Energy is being used wastefully	9
High cost of energy	9
U.S. dependence on foreign supply	5
Haven't developed alternative fuels	3
No real problem	13
Other answers	8
Don't know	17

Note also that 30 percent of the public still does not understand what the energy problem is or that there is an energy problem. Among those who have not completed high school the percentage is 41. The trend, however, is toward a greater public understanding that the energy problem is real. Just after the embargo ended, fewer than one-third of the people thought that the energy shortage was real.

[2] The references to specific data contained in the body of this article can be found in the reference section at the end. Survey data can be found in the Opinion Research Corporation studies. Information from focused group discussions can be found in the Bee Angell and Associates and Gallup Organization studies.

We must be concerned with the public's understanding of the energy problem because consumers will not conserve unless they know how and why they should. Americans do not realize how dependent they are on foreign imports or that the amount imported has actually increased from 38 percent at the time of the embargo to 43 percent today. Consequently it will be difficult to induce the public to accept any foreign policy decisions that are designed to reduce our imports. Perhaps even more important, such unawareness relieves the consumer of a compelling reason for saving energy.

ATTITUDES AND BEHAVIOR

Energy conservation is now an "apple pie" concept —virtually everyone is for it, but in the abstract. In February 1976, when asked in a national survey, "How serious is the need to save energy?", 45 percent said very serious, 39 percent said somewhat serious, 5 percent had no opinion, and only 11 percent said not at all serious. Moreover, 74 percent of the people queried in September 1975 thought that personal conservation efforts have a real effect on the total amount of energy used.

People are saving some energy in their homes and cars. Actual consumption in these areas is about one-tenth lower than the amount predicted if Americans had continued their energy consumption growth rate in the decade prior to the Arab oil embargo of 1973–74. But there is a great discrepancy between lip service and action. In April 1976, 76 percent of the people surveyed said they *prefer* to cut down on their car's fuel consumption by sharing a ride to and from work, but in December 1975 only 10 percent said they *do* share rides. Forty-seven percent said they prefer to use a bus or train rather than a car, but only 8 percent said they took a bus or train to work. And 76 percent say they prefer to drive no faster than 55 mph on an open highway. We can judge from our own experience the actual speed most people drive.

A similarly large majority (53–91 percent) say that they prefer to walk rather than drive to places within a half-mile from where they are, to tune their engines, to buy radial tires, to install weatherstripping and caulking, to buy insulation for their attics and storm windows and doors, to use cold water detergent, to service their furnaces, to set their thermostats lower than 68° in the day and 60° at night, and to set their air-conditioning thermostats no lower than 78° in the summer. But we must question how much these statements of preference are translated into actual behavior.

That American consumers have a long way to go in developing specific energy conserving behavior can be seen from Exhibit 2, which is based on surveys made in December 1975 and January 1976. The true percentages may be even lower than the table indicates; evidence shows that people may not report their own behavior accurately.

People like to think that they are contributing to energy conservation, so they take the energy-saving steps that involve little inconvenience. They turn off lights when they

EXHIBIT 2
Energy-Conserving Behaviors of Consumers

Behavior	Percent of People
Turning out lights when they leave a room	55%
Turning heating thermostats to 68° F or below during the day	48%[1]
Turning thermostats down at night to 68°	61%
Turning thermostats to 64° or less at night	22%[2]
Turning thermostats to 60° or less at night	15%
Waiting until clothes dryer is full before running	77%[3]
Waiting until dishwasher is full before running	89%[4]
Carpooling to work	10%
Taking public transportation to work	8%
Walking to work	5%
[Compare, driving car alone to work	69%]

[1] Of the 82% of the total who have thermostat controls.

[2] FEA recommends 60° F or less.

[3] Of the 63% who have a clothes dryer.

[4] Of the 34% who have an automatic dishwasher.

leave a room. This ritual leaves their consciences free to drive alone to work (it's so much more convenient) or heat their homes to higher temperatures (it's so comfortable).

People are apparently taking a middle position on energy efficiency in their automobiles. Measuring car purchasing behavior, Exhibit 3 shows new car sales.[3] The trend in actual purchasing is clearly towards intermediate and compact size cars with sub-compact and full-size cars becoming the minority.

EXHIBIT 3
Trend in Purchases of New Cars

Size	September 1–10 1975	1976
Subcompact	17%	17%
Compact	25%	30%
Intermediate	32%	34%
Full-size	25%	18%
Vans	2%	1%

WHY PEOPLE ARE NOT SAVING ENERGY

Lack of Knowledge. Many consumers do not really know how to save energy. For example, 36 percent of the people surveyed in January 1976 do not even know that lower-wattage light bulbs use less electricity (even though turning out lights is the one energy-conservation action that a majority of people perform). Fifty-nine percent of the people incorrectly think that keeping a light bulb on uses less energy than turn-

[3] "Ward's Automotive Statistics," September 1976.

ing it off several times an hour. Forty-six percent do not know that over the year the water heater uses more energy than any other appliance in the home. Forty-two percent of the people do not know where their water heater control is, and 42 percent of the people whose water heaters have controls do not know their setting. Fifty percent of the people do not know that it takes less gasoline to restart a car than to let it idle for a few minutes. Only 13 percent think their insulation is inadequate, although by objective standards the actual inadequacy is much higher.

The Comfortable, Convenient Affluent Society. The focused-group research done for FEA suggests that Americans have cultural norms that militate against reducing their use of energy. Americans place a high value on indulging their comforts and conveniences, living for today rather than for the future, materialism, and success defined in terms of conspicuous consumption. People work and save in order to become rich. But once rich, they want to publicize their success with energy-consuming material goods and activities. People resent being told that they must forgo the success symbols that, according to American mores, is the reward for their work.

The materialistic American dream, while dominant, is not universal. Young adults show a concern for the quality of life as well as material success. They would like to see a restructuring of social values so as to stress simplicity, independence of technology, and conservation in a larger sense. But, they do not see energy conservation itself as being particularly constructive.

Teenagers, though angry at the adult world for handing them the energy problem while the adult world goes about doing its own thing, are themselves primarily interested in doing their own thing—having a good time—and feel that the responsibility for solving the energy problem is not theirs but that of adults.

Children (7–12 years old) also feel that adults have the major responsibility for energy conservation—not themselves. They see adults as indulgent, but do not reject this behavioral model. They are already socialized to the American dream. Their primary concern is their ability to enjoy their own future.

Skepticism and Cynicism. Contributing to a diminished energy conservation effort on the part of the American public is their skepticism and cynicism regarding the nature of the energy problem. People in focused groups in the fall of 1975 perceived politicians as struggling to use the energy problem to enhance their own power and prestige, rather than acting to cope with the problem itself, and oil companies and utilities as using the energy crisis to enrich themselves. About one-third of the surveyed public think that the consumers' own demands caused the energy problem. But, another third think it is caused by big business, particularly the oil companies; and another third, politicians and the government—including both Congress and the Administration. As of September

1975, only 3 percent of the public thought that the energy shortage was caused by the foreign oil producing countries. Consequently, people do not feel that information about energy is credible if it comes from either government or industry. (They place much more trust in information that comes from consumer groups.)

Moreover, people are frustrated because their fuel, electricity, and gasoline bills have risen despite their attempts to save energy. People are thus unwilling to make personal sacrifices because they are not sure that the need is genuine; that the burden of sacrifices will be carried equitably by industry, the government, and consumers; and, that others will not profit economically or politically from their attempts to conserve. Since the end of the embargo, about one-third of the public has continued to believe that the energy crisis and subsequent energy problems are contrived.

WHOM PEOPLE BELIEVE

Consumers get most of their information about the energy problem from television (42 percent of the public) and newspapers (45 percent) and believe the information given by consumer organizations more than that of business or the government. (See Exhibit 4.)

Given this background of indulgence, skepticism, and the incredibility of the major institutions of Government and business, we must ask what is it that will lead and motivate people to save energy.

INCENTIVES FOR SAVING ENERGY

We cannot instill in Americans an energy conservation ethic as such because people are not interested in saving energy for its own sake. Nor will they save out of patriotism or concern about their progeny. The chance to save money is the most effective incentive in inducing a consumer to conserve energy. In the focused group discussions, homeowners said that they do turn down their thermostats and that they have their homes insulated—but only in order to reduce their bills. People who carpool cite the parking savings as the reason.

In February 1975, people who said that they or their family were making a little effort to save energy (95 percent of the total) were asked why. In response to this open-ended question, *59 percent of the people cited cost,* 17 percent cited

shortages of energy and the Nation's running out of resources, 11 percent cited their responsibilities as citizens, 6 percent said it would help the economy, 10 percent cited other reasons, and 5 percent did not know or had no answer. Thus, people conserve energy mainly to save money.

In February 1975, respondents were asked the psychologically projective question of why people do not try to save energy. The answers reflect consumers' indifference, skepticism, and indulgence. Forty-four percent said that people do not care or are selfish. Thirty-seven percent said there really is no shortage and saving is not necessary. Fourteen percent said it was too hard or causes inconvenience. Five percent said people do not know what to do. Two percent said individuals' actions do not have much impact. Nine percent gave other answers and 8 percent did not know.

Note that the financial motivation has nothing to do with a conservation ethic as such. Rather, it's a pragmatic response to economic pressure. If lowering the thermostat or carpooling helps one to save money, so that one can continue to be indulgent in other ways, then saving energy is rewarding and gratifying. Otherwise, it causes discomfort, inconvenience, or other deprivations. The amount of money saved is the only meaningful measure of energy conservation to those whose motive is financial. Information and tips on how to save energy are meaningful to those people only if they have a dollar sign attached to them.

EXPERIMENTAL BEHAVIOR ANALYSIS OF ENERGY CONSERVATION

Many research groups other than FEA have done experimental analyses of energy conservation. These studies show that the most effective means of modifying energy-using behavior is financial *reward,* the second most effective is *feedback* of behavioral performance, the third most effective is *exhortation,* and the least effective is *information* on how to save energy.

Rewards or incentives in the form of cash payments have reduced driving 20 percent [Foxx and Hakke], and electrical use 29 percent [Hayes and Cone]. In general, the greater the cash incentives, the more energy is saved.

Feedback, the second most effective means of getting people to save energy, has reduced electricity consumption in house-

	Federal Government	Business	Gas Companies	Consumer Groups	Media	None	No Opinion
To Save Energy in the Home (Feb. 1975)	21%	9%	—	36%	23%	8%	7%
To Save Natural Gas in the Home (Sept. 1975)	18%	—	24%	30%	36%	9%	4%
To Save Energy Using One's Car (Feb. 1975)	14%	9%	—	40%	14%	15%	11%

EXHIBIT 4
Groups People Rely On For Energy Conservation Information

holds by as much as 18 percent [Palmer, Lloyd, and Lloyd; Hayes and Cone]. Feedback is accomplished by telling a consumer how much energy he has been using and how much it will cost him if he continues to use it at the same rate. A combination of cash incentives and feedback has reduced electrical use during peak hours [Kohlenberg, Phillips, and Proctor].

Exhortation or prompting was found to be less effective than either incentives or feedback. Prompting in the form of social commendation was found to be effective in reducing fuel oil consumption [Seaver and Patterson] and almost as effective as feedback in getting people to reduce their use of electricity [Palmer, Lloyd and Lloyd].

Information on energy saving or environmental consequences is the least effective means of inducing energy conservation [Cass]. Neither information nor feedback enhances the results that are obtained when payments are used to induce people to save energy.

While many of these studies have been economically unrealistic (paying people to save energy), they do validate the importance of using the desire to save money to induce people to save energy.

IMPLICATIONS FOR GOVERNMENTAL POLICY AND ACTIONS

What are the implications for governmental policy and action of these research findings on American attitudes, knowledge, and behavior regarding energy conservation?

The government should use incentives, feedback, exhortation, and information to influence peoples' energy-using behavior. Despite the fact that these four methods vary in their effectiveness, they are all acceptable to the public.

Effective exhortation by the government requires it to increase its credibility with the people. It must use as its spokesmen men and women who have no vested economic or political interest in energy, men and women who are perceived by the public as being expert in and knowledgeable about the energy problems that the country faces. These spokespersons should urge people to save our dwindling supplies of energy, reminding them that they can use tomorrow what they save today, and save themselves money in the process.

To further bolster its credibility, the government must lead by example and publicize how impressive its own energy conservation has been. Because people are reluctant to sacrifice unless they see others sacrificing, government should also publicize the conservation achievements of all classes of consumers and industry.

The government must accept the challenge of making people understand the energy problem. People must be made to realize that despite the lack of gasoline lines we are dangerously dependent on undependable foreign sources of oil. They must realize that we do not produce enough of our own

oil and gas, that the supplies of oil and gas are finite, and that the world may run out of these resources in the not-too-distant future. These lessons can and should be taught in terms that are meaningful to Americans. If Americans place convenience and comfort ahead of energy conservation, they must be told how uncomfortable and inconvenienced they will be if the country is embargoed again or if our supplies fail to meet our demand. Then they must be told how to make our demand meet our supplies: the necessity of doing that which saves the most energy (insulating, carpooling, and setting thermostats down in winter and up in summer, for example).

The Federal, State, and local governments must make use of the finding that a chief incentive for saving energy is the desire to save money. They can do this in a variety of ways, They can, and in some areas do, offer tax credits, low-interest loans, or loan guarantees to those who buy energy conserving household equipment such as insulation, storm windows, heat pumps, and solar energy systems. Federal, State, and local governments that own or lease parking lots can allot free parking to those who carpool, and expensive parking to those who do not, and tax parking in commercial lots in a way that encourages carpooling. Governments can also tax cars in ways that reward those who drive energy-efficient vehicles. They can tax fuel and offset the burden placed on poorer people by granting them a special tax rebate. They can use tax incentives as a means of rewarding those who manufacture cars and appliance and who construct buildings that consume less energy. And State and local governments could strictly enforce the 55 mph speed limit law and impose heavy fines for its violation.

Government must, however, balance many factors in making use of financial incentives. Participants in an April 1976 survey were asked how they felt about different kinds of actions the government could take to encourage conservation: "There are a number of things the government can do to get people to cut down on how much gas, oil, and electricity they use. Would you tell me which of the government actions in Exhibit 5 that you favor and which you oppose?"

It is clear from Exhibit 5 that the idea of government using its powers to make energy more expensive or less available is unpopular. It is this very distaste for higher prices, and consequently the political reluctance to raise them, that has been a major cause of the slow pace of energy conservation in the United States as compared to that in Japan and Western Europe.

Exhibit 5 also demonstrates that people prefer policies and actions that are personally rewarding to those that are penalizing. People also prefer policies that require manufacturers and builders of appliances, cars, and buildings to help consumers save energy.

The use of higher prices as an incentive to conserve energy has a built-in limitation and may generate serious social and political problems. Many people will be able to afford all the energy they want no matter how high the prices

EXHIBIT 5
**Popularity of Possible Governmental Actions
to Stimulate Energy Conservation**

	Favor	Oppose
Provide information on how to cut down on gas, oil, and electricity	96%	3%
Require that new cars, air conditioners, refrigerators, heaters, etc., have labels indicating what the yearly cost for energy to run them will be	91%	6%
Set energy conservation standards for buildings, cars, air conditioners, and other equipment that all builders and manufacturers are required to follow	85%	8%
Point out to people why it is their patriotic duty to cut down on their use of gas, oil, and electricity.	80%	16%
Offer tax rebates to people who install extra insulation in their homes, buy storm windows, and other things that cut down on energy use	75%	21%
Remove price regulations and rely on free competition to determine what the price of energy will be	47%	39%
Ration the amount of gas, oil, and electricity each family can use and let people decide for themselves where they will cut down	39%	57%
Limit the available supply of gas, oil, and electricity and let people work out for themselves how to meet their needs	38%	56%
Adding a special tax that would make it more expensive to use energy	22%	71%

are likely to go. Those who will not be able to afford enough energy will not only sacrifice unfairly, they will probably resent the oil companies and utilities for raising their prices, the government for allowing the prices to rise, and the well-to-do for being able to afford the extra expense.

The government must make use of the finding that people respond to feedback, both because feedback is effective and because, as Exhibit 5 suggests, the people see this as a proper role for government. The feedback must allow people to see how much money and energy they are spending, and how much they have saved or could save compared to their previous consumption rates. It can require new homes and apartments to have a kind of utility meter that shows how much energy is being used and how much it will cost if the consumer continues to use energy at the same rate. It can require utility bills to project the monthly consumption to an annual cost. It can use television and newspapers much more than it has to keep people informed about how much energy the country is using, importing, and saving.

The government should continue to require the labeling of new cars and appliances so that people can know before they buy how many miles they will get from a gallon and how much they will have to pay per year for the energy needed to run a car or an appliance. FEA's April 1976 survey shows that such information does affect a consumer's choice: 82 percent of the people surveyed say they prefer a refrigerator priced at $400 that uses $40 worth of electricity a year to a refrigerator priced at $300 that uses $65 worth of electricity a year. The miles-per-gallon figures about cars that EPA and FEA publish are also effective. Of the people surveyed, half

of those who had heard of the figures said that the figures would influence their choice of a new car.

The government can fund research to help develop new and more energy-saving devices that consumers can use. It can pass and enforce laws that require manufacturers to make more efficient appliances and cars and builders to construct buildings that are more energy efficient.

The final point that Government should consider in designing and implementing energy conservation policies is that, in the end, a major part of energy conservation comes down to what the individual consumer does. And this squares with what consumers themselves think. In June 1975, when people were asked who could do the most to ease the energy crisis, 36 percent cited the individual, whereas only 21 percent cited the federal government, and only 8 percent cited business, industry, or the oil companies. Public feeling on this point has not changed since then. American consumers believe that a part of the solution to this Nation's energy problem lies in their own hands. They are right. The government can help by providing the incentives and information that will lead more people to conserve energy.

REFERENCES

Dueker, Kenneth J. and Levine, Irwin P. "Carpooling: Attitudes and Participation." University of Iowa, Center for Urban Transportation Studies, Institute of Urban and Regional Research. Technical Report No. 81. (Unpublished). July 1976.

Federal Energy Administration. "A Qualitative Study of Consumer Attitudes Toward Energy Conservation." Prepared for FEA by Bee Angell & Associates, Inc.: Chicago, IL. (November 1975).

———. "Group Discussions Regarding Consumer Energy Conservation." Prepared for FEA by the Gallup Organization, Inc.: Princeton, NJ (March 1976).

———. "General Public Attitudes and Behavior Toward Energy Saving." Highlight Report, vol. 1. Prepared for FEA by Opinion Research Corporation, Princeton, New Jersey. (National Technical Information Service: Springfield, VA, September 1974). (PB 944 979/AS).

———. "General Public Attitudes and Behavior Toward Energy Saving." Highlight Report, vol. 2. Prepared for FEA by Opinion Research Corporation, Princeton, NJ. (National Technical Information Service: Springfield, VA, October 1974). (PB 244 980/AS).

———. "Attitudes and Behavior of Residents in All-Electric Homes." Highlight Report, vol. 3. Prepared for FEA by Opinion Research Corporation, Princeton, NJ. (National Technical Information Service: Springfield, VA). (PB 244 981/AS).

———. "Energy Consumption and Attitudes Toward the Energy Shortage." Highlight Report, vol. 4. Prepared for FEA by Opinion Research Corporation, Princeton, NJ. (National Technical Information Service: Springfield, VA, November 1974). (PB 244 982/AS).

———. "Trends in Energy Consumption and Attitudes Toward the Energy Shortage." Hightlight Report, vol. 5. Prepared for FEA by Opinion Research Corporation, Princeton, NJ. (National Technical Information Service: Springfield, VA, December 1974). (PB 244 983/AS).

———. "Consumer Attitudes Toward Gasoline Prices, Shortages, and Their Relationships to Inflation." Highlight Report, vol. 6. Prepared for FEA by Opinion Research Corporation, Princeton, NJ. (National Technical Information Service: Springfield, VA, January 1975). (PB 244 984/AS).

———. "Consumer Attitudes and Behavior Resulting from Issues Surrounding the Energy Shortage." Highlight Report, vol. 7. Prepared for FEA by Opinion Research Corporation, Princeton, NJ.

(National Technical Information Service: Springfield, VA, February 1975). (PB 244 985/AS).

———. "Consumer Behavior and Attitudes Toward Energy-Related Issues." Highlight Report, vol. 8. Prepared for FEA by Opinion Research Corporation, Princeton, NJ. (National Technical Information Service: Springfield, VA, March 1975). (PB 244 986/AS).

———. "General Public Attitudes and Behavior Regarding Energy Saving." Highlight Report, vol. 9. Prepared for FEA by Opinion Research Corporation, Princeton, NJ. (National Technical Information Service: Springfield, VA, April 1975). (PB 244 989/AS).

———. "General Public Attitudes and Behavior Regarding Energy Saving." Highlight Report, vol. 10. Prepared for FEA by Opinion Research Corporation, Princeton, NJ. (National Technical Information Service: Springfield, VA, May 1975). (PB 244 988/AS).

———. "The Public's Attitudes Toward and Knowledge of Energy-Related Issues." Highlight Report, vol. 11. Prepared for FEA by Opinion Research Corporation, Princeton, NJ. (National Technical Information Service: Springfield, VA, June 1975). (PB 244 987/AS).

———. "General Public Behavior and Attitudes Regarding Vacation and Business Travel, Beverage Containers, Reasons for Using Mass Transit." Highlight Report, vol. 12. Prepared by Opinion Research Corporation, Princeton, NJ. (National Technical Information Service: Springfield, VA, July 1975). (PB 244 969/AS).

———. "Energy-Related Attitudes and Behavior of the Poor and the Elderly." Highlight Report, vol. 13. Prepared for FEA by Opinion Research Corporation, Princeton, New Jersey. (National Technical Information Service: Springfield, VA, August 1975). (PB 244 990/AS).

———. "Automobile Usage Patterns." Highlight Report, vol. 14. Prepared for FEA by Opinion Research Corporation, Princeton, NJ. (National Technical Information Service: Springfield, VA, September 1975). (PB 246 076/AS).

———. "How the Public Views the Nation's Dependence on Oil Imports; A Possible Natural Gas Shortage This Winter; The Overall Need to Save Energy." Highlight Report, vol. 15. Prepared for FEA by Opinion Research Corporation, Princeton, NJ. (National Technical Information Service: Springfield, VA, October 1975). (PB 245 828/AS).

———. "A Public Opinion Survey on Energy and Economic Considerations and Air Pollution Controls." Highlight Report, vol. 16. Prepared for FEA by Opinion Research Corporation, Princeton, NJ. (National Technical Information Service: Springfield, VA, January 1976).

———. "Conservation of Energy in the Home." Highlight Report, vol. 17. Prepared for FEA by Opinion Research Corporation, Princeton, NJ. (National Technical Information Service: Springfield, VA, February 1976). (PB 254 628/AS).

———. "Consumption and Conservation of Natural Gas." Highlight Report, vol. 18. Prepared for FEA by Opinion Research Corporation: Princeton, NJ. (National Technical Information Service, Springfield, VA, February 1976). (PB 254 629/AS).

———. "Private Individual's Willingness to Make Energy-Saving Efforts and Their Perception of the Likelihood of Others' Doing the Same." Highlight Report, vol. 19. Prepared for FEA by Opinion Research Corporation, Princeton, NJ. (National Technical Information Service: Springfield, VA, February 1976).

———. "Public Knowledge, Attitudes, and Behavior Relating to Natural Gas Issues." Highlight Report, vol. 20. Prepared for FEA by Opinion Research Corporation, Princeton, NJ. (National Technical Information Service: Springfield, VA, February, 1976).

———. "Driving and Energy Conservation." Highlight Report vol. 21. Prepared for FEA by Opinion Research Corporation, Princeton, NJ. (National Technical Information Service: Springfield, VA, March 1976).

———. "Energy Saving Behavior Around the Home." Highlight Report, vol. 22. Prepared for FEA by Opinion Research Corporation, Princeton, NJ. (National Technical Information Service: Springfield, VA, April 1976).

———. "Parents' Perceptions of Their Children's Sources of Energy Information and Energy-Related Activities." Highlight Report, vol. 23. Prepared for FEA by Opinion Research Corporation, Princeton, NJ. (National Technical Information Service: Springfield, VA, April 1976).

———. "Understanding of the Energy Situation and Evaluations of Alternative Actions." Highlight Report, vol. 24. Prepared for FEA by Opinion Research Corporation, Princeton, NJ. (National Technical Information Service: Springfield, VA, May 1976).

Foxx, R. M., and Hake, D. F. "Gasoline Conservation: A Procedure for Measuring and Reducing the Driving of College Students," University of Maryland Baltimore County (Unpublished report).

Hayes, Steven C., and Cone, John D. "Reducing Residential Electrical Energy Use: Payments, Information, and Feedback." West Virginia University (Unpublished report).

Kohlenberg, Robert; Phillips, Thomas, and Proctor, William. "A Behavioral Analysis of Peaking in Residential Electrical-Energy Consumers." *Journal of Applied Behavior Analysis,* 1 (Spring, 1976): 13–18.

Palmer, Michael H.; Lloyd, Margaret E., and Lloyd, Kenneth E. "An Experimental Analysis of Electricity Conservation Procedures." Drake University (Unpublished report).

Seaver, W. Burleigh, and Patterson, Arthur H. "Decreasing Fuel-Oil Consumption Through Feedback and Social Commendation," *Journal of Applied Behavior Analysis,* 2 (Summer, 1976): 147–52.

40
Energy Savings in Private Households: An Integrated Research Program

Nicolas Phillips
Elizabeth Nelson

How should energy conservation be marketed? And how does one measure the effectiveness of conservation marketing programs? This article evaluates British experience in promoting energy savings, and shows how research methods such as attitude surveys, depth research, reinterviews, consumer panels, and surveys of the retail trade have been used to monitor movements in relevant "intermediate indicators" of successful energy saving.

The substantial increase in the price of energy, particularly of imported oil, since the Arab/Israeli war of Autumn 1973 has led a number of countries to develop energy conservation programs as a matter of national priority.[1]

A number of energy conservation measures were introduced in the United Kingdom in 1974, particularly in the 12-point program announced by the Secretary of State for Energy on 9 December, 1974. The program involved some

legal compulsion, incentives, and the economic pricing of energy. It also included as one of its main points "a government backed publicity campaign to inform and advise consumers on how they can help themselves and the nation by using energy more carefully and efficiently."

The campaign was launched on 20 January 1975 and has come to be known, as a result of its slogan, as the *Save It* campaign. Its objectives are to promote economy and efficiency in the use of all forms of energy—oil, petrol, coal, gas, and electricity and to cut out waste. It seeks to secure short term reductions in the use of energy, and longer term changes in public attitudes and habits which will produce a permanent and continuing economy. Industrially the aim is to reduce the amount of energy required for a given level of

---

[1] The background to energy conservation in the United Kingdom is discussed elsewhere, particularly in reports produced by the National Economic Development Office (1974) and the Central Policy Review Staff (1974).

Nicolas Phillips, is with the Central Office of Information.

Elizabeth Nelson, is with Taylor, Nelson & Associates Ltd.

output; domestically it is to encourage thrift without reducing comfort and more especially to raise the low level of thermal insulation in United Kingdom homes. The campaign has been developed over a number of phases and has used a variety of media—press and television advertising, leaflets, posters, displays and exhibitions, radio broadcasts, syndicated newspaper articles and—the fuel industries' own publicity campaigns.

This paper is concerned with just one aspect of an energy conservation program and the publicity campaign, that is the part directed to the private householder. There are some 19 million homes in the United Kingdom that together account for between 25% and 30% of national energy consumption; they therefore represent an important target, and one which was considered susceptible to a publicity campaign.

DOMESTIC CONSUMPTION OF ENERGY

The priority of the domestic sector in energy conservation programs varies from country to country, but it has ranked high in the United Kingdom particularly because of the general poor standard of insulation of the housing stock. Apart from thermal insulation the greatest potential savings lie in greater efficiency in space heating (which accounts for some two-thirds of household energy consumption) and water heating (which accounts for a fifth); the third greatest use of energy is in cooking followed by appliances of various kinds, and lighting.[2]

In the monitoring of a domestic energy conservation program the ultimate objective to be borne in mind is of course a net saving in consumption—and the estimate should make allowance for any secular trend, changes in temperature etc. It may be possible, with some difficulty, to obtain estimates on a global basis from national consumption figures. This paper, however, concentrates on the monitoring of *intermediate* objectives which are either known or assumed to be associated with the ultimate objective. This approach is shared by a number of countries in their energy conservation programs, particularly the Federal Energy Agency of the USA. It is also in accord with the practice of research on other Central Office of Information campaigns, where measurements are sought of the achievement of intermediate objectives.[3] Particularly important "intermediate indicators" in the United Kingdom have been the rate and specification of acquisition of certain energy-saving devices such as loft insulation and hot water tank lagging.

---

[2] The pattern of domestic energy consumption, which is applicable to a number of countries, and the potential for energy saving is discussed elsewhere, particularly in work by the Building Research Establishment. (1975, 1976).

[3] This is discussed by Phillips in an earlier article (1975) which includes references to research on other United Kingdom government campaigns previously presented to ESOMAR Conferences.

THE RESEARCH PROGRAM

The research program from August 1974 to January 1976 is listed in full in Exhibit 1. Eleven surveys have been carried out by Taylor, Nelson and Associates, Audits of Great Britain Ltd., and Retail Audits Ltd.[4] The surveys have all been commissioned by the Central Office of Information on behalf of the Department of Energy. In order satisfactorily to explain and monitor the various intermed'te indicators we have found it necessary to employ a number of complementary research techniques—depth interviews; structured attitude surveys; re-interviews to establish association between attitudes and behavior; consumer panels and trade surveys.

This paper may, to some extent, be regarded as complementary to that presented by Lowe Watson at the 1975 ESOMAR Conference. His paper which was concerned with reactions of motorists to the oil crisis made use of a number of data sources. In it he showed,

> How these different types of information were combined in an endeavour to understand and interpret the behaviour of motorists and to attempt to predict how they would react to expected future event. . . .
>
> I shall try to draw some general conclusions from the analysis, including a tentative contribution to the well-known problem area of the relationship between information, experience, attitudes and behaviour. The analysis of a real life situation is never simple. The situation is often confused, and events and their consequences cannot easily be isolated as in a controlled experiment. Ideally, one would wish for a tidy mathematical model to help identify and isolate the effects of individual factors. But in a rapidly changing and unprecedented situation such a model is almost impossible to construct and validate . . . it has therefore been necessary to rely on the traditional methods of inference and deduction with admittedly a degree of subjective judgment and insight.

Our experience has been close to this. As with his paper we have attempted to build a coherent picture with the jigsaw of surveys; we have learned something of the role of the price mechanism; and we have brought some of the key factors in the successful saving of household energy into a (non-mathematical) model which while based on United Kingdom experience is likely to be applicable to a number of other countries.

Timing of the Research. Between Summer 1974 and January 1976 five quantitative attitude surveys were undertaken. The first (1,238 respondents, comprising as did all the subsequent ones, one half heads of household and one half housewives) took place in August 1974. Its aim was to collect information on householders' current behavior and attitudes related to the use of energy and to assess the level of interest in conservation prior to a possible campaign. The second survey (1,491 respondents) took place in the first half of January 1975 *immediately before* the launch of the *Save It* campaign, but after considerable comment in the media on energy

---

[4] The authors are grateful to the latter two companies for agreement to illustrate some of their findings in the context of this paper.

EXHIBIT 1
The Research Program

	Research	Date of Fieldwork	Sample
1. Before the Campaign			
(i) 1st quantitative attitude survey	Taylor Nelson & Assoc.	August 1974	1,238
(ii) 2nd quantitative attitude survey (fieldwork period chosen immediately prior to campaign)	Taylor Nelson & Assoc.	January 1975	1,491
(iii) Study of motivations to save	Taylor Nelson & Assoc.	January 1975	50
2. After Phase I of Campaign			
(iv) 3rd quantitative attitude survey (fieldwork period chosen 8 weeks after campaign launch)	Taylor Nelson & Assoc.	March 1975	1,094
3. After Phase II of Campaign (which culminated in pull-out Supplement)			
(v) 4th quantitative attitude survey (one year after first survey)	Taylor Nelson & Assoc.	July 1975	1,498
(vi) Survey of hardware and DIY stores and builders' merchants	Retail Audits Ltd.	July 1975	1,230
4. During Phase III			
(vii) Merchandising test and evaluation in 4 towns	Retail Audits Ltd.	Aug./Oct. 1975	120
(viii) Depth survey into the planning and acquisition of certain energy saving devices (re-interviews)	Taylor Nelson & Assoc.	November 1975	158
(ix) 2nd builders' merchants survey (re-interviews)	Retail Audits Ltd.	December 1975	160
(x) 5th quantitative attitude survey (one year after 2nd survey)	Taylor Nelson & Assoc.	January 1976	1,501
5. Continuous from early 1974			
(xi) Home audit of ownership and acquisition of certain energy-saving services	Audits of Great Britain Ltd.	from January 1974	35,000

---

conservation. At the same time as the second survey a small-scale study (50 interviews held jointly with husbands and wives) was carried out into people's motivation to save. The third survey (1,034 respondents) was conducted only some eight weeks after the second was completed, after the first phase of the *Save It* campaign had been running for two months. The fourth survey (1,498 respondents) took place in July 1975. It was so timed to follow immediately the second phase of the *Save It* campaign which culminated in the issue of a pullout supplement on home insulation in all the main national newspapers; the timing also allowed year-over-year comparisons to be made with the first survey. The timing of the fifth survey (1,501 respondents) in January 1976 enabled year-over-year comparisons to be made with the second survey, and to establish the situation one year after the launch of the *Save It* campaign.

Because a main aim of the *Save It* campaign has been to persuade householders to improve their standard of thermal insulation, other behavioral data has been purchased in addition to the surveys undertaken by Taylor Nelson and Associates. Information on the rate of acquisition of certain energy-saving devices (loft insulation, tank lagging, cavity wall insulation and double glazing) has been purchased from Audits of Great Britain Ltd, who operate the Home Audit which has a sample size of 35,000. Surveys of the retail trade (including insulation products stocked and displayed in hardware stores, do-it-yourself shops and builders' merchants) have been purchased from Retail Audits Ltd.

Objectives of the Research. Broadly the research program has sought to assess on a quantitative basis:

· awareness among domestic consumers of the need for using energy economically and efficiently;
· the awareness of the means of doing this;
· the extent to which domestic consumers are taking positive action to save energy;
· the extent to which they are prepared or intend to take positive action to save energy.

Throughout the research program we have attempted to measure the extent to which observed changes in attitudes and behavior of domestic consumers, over the 18 month period August 1974 to January 1976, could be attributed to advertising and could be related to the price mechanism.

THE MEASUREMENTS

Within the quantitative attitude surveys the measures have been manifold. They have included:

· recall of energy-saving messages;
· source of energy-saving messages;
· expected sources of advice on energy-saving;
· claimed behavior with regard to energy-saving;
· perceived relative cost of different uses of energy within the household;
· reasons given for starting to save energy;
· perceived price rises in energy compared with other goods and services;
· how people will cope with price rises;
· ownership of energy-saving installations;
· planning of energy-saving installations;
· attitudes to energy-saving installations;

· consumers' perception of the importance of energy-saving;
· reasons why energy-saving is important;
· detailed recall of advertising and claimed action following;
· deterrents to installations of energy-saving devices;
· thickness of owned and planned installations.

There is not the space in this paper to indicate more than some highlights of movements in these indicators. At this stage we should only wish to emphasize that a campaign on domestic energy saving does not have a straightforward homogeneous task. The communication may work at a number of levels in order to achieve different elements of behavioral change. We are seeking to persuade people to undertake a large number of actions such as turning down thermostats, only heating rooms in use, draft-proofing and so on—many of these actions being trivial individually but having a substantial additive effect; we are also seeking to influence purchase of major energy-saving devices.

Two points are relevant here. The first is the precept of Fishbein (1967) that in seeking to measure attitudes we must know what behavior we are trying to predict; certainly this was in danger of being lost in the first survey in the ultimate but remote objective of "saving energy." The second is the conclusion of King (1975) that we should not "try to produce advertisements or evaluate their effect without having some theory on how they are to work." King postulates a number of links of different complexity between the advertisement and the derived action where sometimes an attitudinal shift is seen as an important intermediary. In the case of the *Save It* campaign the individual advertisements have covered a number in King's typology (e.g., some designed to modify attitudes, some to reinforce attitudes, some to get the consumer to seek further information, some to pass on direct information). It is not possible to know, a priori, which attitudes are associated with behavior and this has been investigated in the research program by means of re-interviews which yielded information on attitudes and actual installation behavior by the same respondents.

The "behavioral" measures of achievement include claimed good housekeeping; validated claims where possible, including interviewers inspecting thickness of tank lagging and loft insulation, draft excluders and alterations to time clocks and thermostat; plans to install energy-saving devices, and actual installations, by thickness.

SOME RESULTS OF THE RESEARCH PROGRAM

Pre-campaign. From the baseline study of summer 1974 three main conclusions were drawn. While most people believed that energy saving was important there was no apparent crisis —no shortage of petrol or coal and no power cuts. Secondly, government and industry were criticized for wasting energy. People were quick to suggest ways in which energy could be saved—by reducing street lighting, cutting out public floodlighting, by less overheated offices and public buildings for example. Yet they could not believe that their contribution in terms of saving in their own homes could make any differ-

ence to the country or that energy-saving was mainly their responsibility.

Thirdly, there was another barrier to overcome.

There was a lack of public knowledge on *how* to save energy. People tended to think in terms of "switching off"— lights and appliances in particular. There was little awareness of the need for insulation in the home and those few who knew about it had mistaken ideas of what mattered most.

The advertising campaign, developed by the advertising agents, Young and Rubicam, in conjunction with the Central Office of Information, therefore sought to persuade householders (and others) of the necessity to save and to demonstrate to them *how* to save.

The motivation study conducted in January 1975 concluded that respondents needed to be made more aware of the seriousness of the energy problem, its effect on the country and its relevance to themselves. They had to be convinced that small savings they and others made would be a significant help. They needed information about ways of saving energy which were within their means and which would not seriously lower their standard of comfort. They needed to be reassured that the government, public bodies, and industry were also trying to conserve energy in a co-ordinated manner. These findings reinforced some of those of the first two quantitative surveys particularly in highlighting the problem of relevance among people who already owned certain energy-saving devices and among council tenants. They were also remarkable similar, in tone and content, to the findings of qualitative research carried out in the United States on behalf of the Federal Energy Agency—particularly the necessity of combating the problem of "why me?" and of emphasizing the collective contribution of all the sectors of the economy and of society.

The conclusion of the motivation study was that while the consumers' prime interest in energy-saving was to save money, no one was prepared to sacrifice their standards of comfort. Thus, for some consumers financial savings are more likely to be savings on luxuries. This is confirmed by reaction to prospective rises in the price of energy given in the quantitative surveys. The motivations to save on household energy are put in diagrammatic form in Exhibit 2.

Some motivating factors other than the desire to save money have been identified in the surveys. These include background rationalizations such as the problem of limited resources, the balance of payments, and the desire to help the country. Other countries' campaigns have been based on a very similar spectrum of motivations; perhaps the neatest use of patriotic appeal has been the Danish campaign which has used, as a symbol, the national flag in the shape of an oil drop.

The Third Quantitative Survey (March 1975). The measured changes between January 1975 and March 1975 (eight weeks) included a very high level of advertising recall; overwhelmingly favorable attitudes to the advertising; encouraging levels of claimed good housekeeping; a marginal but

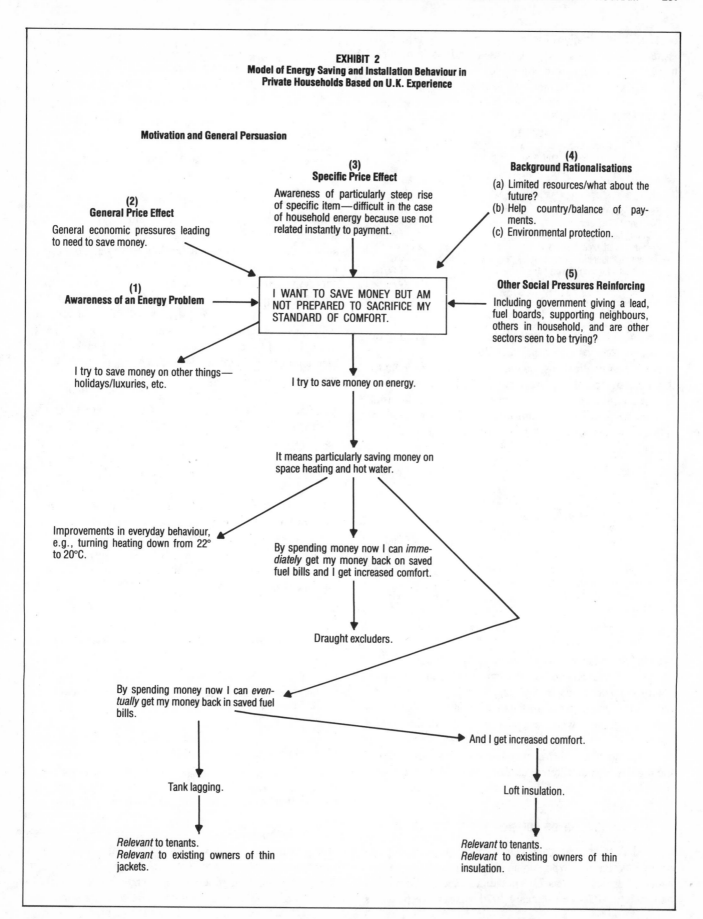

EXHIBIT 2
Model of Energy Saving and Installation Behaviour in
Private Households Based on U.K. Experience

Motivation and General Persuasion

(3)
Specific Price Effect

Awareness of particularly steep rise of specific item—difficult in the case of household energy because use not related instantly to payment.

(4)
Background Rationalisations

(a) Limited resources/what about the future?
(b) Help country/balance of payments.
(c) Environmental protection.

(2)
General Price Effect

General economic pressures leading to need to save money.

(1)
Awareness of an Energy Problem

(5)
Other Social Pressures Reinforcing

Including government giving a lead, fuel boards, supporting neighbours, others in household, and are other sectors seen to be trying?

I WANT TO SAVE MONEY BUT AM NOT PREPARED TO SACRIFICE MY STANDARD OF COMFORT.

I try to save money on other things—holidays/luxuries, etc.

I try to save money on energy.

It means particularly saving money on space heating and hot water.

Improvements in everyday behaviour, e.g., turning heating down from 22° to 20°C.

By spending money now I can *immediately* get my money back on saved fuel bills and I get increased comfort.

Draught excluders.

By spending money now I can *eventually* get my money back in saved fuel bills.

And I get increased comfort.

Tank lagging.

Loft insulation.

Relevant to tenants.
Relevant to existing owners of thin jackets.

Relevant to tenants.
Relevant to existing owners of thin insulation.

consistent shift in plans for installations; favorable shifts in attitude to loft insulation, tank lagging, and draft excluders; movements in attitudes to household energy not reflected (in that short period) in the motoring field. (Exhibit 3).

EXHIBIT 3
Some Changes January 1975–March 1975
(Based On All Households)

	Jan. 1975	March 1975
Recall of some energy saving message	75%	90%
Planning loft insulation	7%	9%
Planning tank lagging	3%	5%
Planning draft excluders	9%	10%
Believe loft insulation is worth it	62%	73%
Believe tank lagging is worth it	66%	80%
Believe draft excluders are worth it	62%	75%

The Fourth Quantitative Survey (July 1975). In considering the measured changes between March 1975 and July 1975 the effect of seasonality must be noted. The measures included the maintenance of the encouraging level of claimed good housekeeping and substantial movements in plans to install various devices and the number of homes claiming to be acting on a basis of the pull-out supplement on home insulation. (Exhibit 4).

EXHIBIT 4
Some Changes March 1975–July 1975
(Based On All Households)

	March 1975	July 1975
Claiming to be doing something to save energy	71%	71%
Claiming to be doing this to save energy:		
Saving on hot water	17%	21%
Insulating	7%	17%

The Fifth Quantitative Survey (January 1976). By January 1976 the level of claimed good housekeeping had risen still further. Claimed installations in the last year also increased. Although the deterrents to installation remained as strong as ever among those who were planning to install there was a continuing trend towards greater thickness. (Exhibit 5). Respondents in this fifth survey also had an accurate idea of the relative cost of different uses of energy within the household.

DISCUSSION OF SOME OF THE MEASURES

Claimed Good-housekeeping. The proportion of survey respondents claiming to be "doing something particular to save energy these days" was 71% in the third and fourth surveys and rose to 81% in the January 1976 surveys. Respondents

---

EXHIBIT 5
Some Changes July 1975–January 1976
(Based On All Households)

	July 1975	Jan. 1976
Claiming to be doing something to save energy	71%	81%
Claiming to have started to save recently	42%	55%
Loft insulation	11%	16%
Tank lagging (Installed in last year)	8%	14%
Draft excluders	21%	35%

---

were also asked whether they had started particular measures "recently" (defined as the last three months in the March survey, the last six months in the July survey and the last 12 months in the January 1976 survey). In the third and fourth surveys three out of five of these people (or just over 50% of the total sample) said that they had started some particular measure *recently*. This rose to over two-thirds of those claiming to save, or 55% of the total sample by January 1976. In the content of the claims "lighting" still enjoyed the highest mention in 1976, but there were increasing mentions of saving on heating and hot water.

Sub Groups of the Population Who Are More Energy Saving-conscious. By January 1976 over half of the population were claiming to have started to save energy recently. Consistently throughout this research program a higher proportion of certain sub-groups claimed to be doing something to conserve energy. Consistently these sub-groups were owner occupiers, those in middle class occupational groups, those in more modern houses, those with central heating (see Exhibit 6). These segments became important target groups for the *Save It* campaign, in the same way as those who were less energy saving conscious became important target groups for different aspects of the campaign.

EXHIBIT 6
What Sub Groups Started to Save Energy Recently

		Jan. 1976
Total		55%
ABC1 (professional, managerial)		64%
C2DE (working class, pensioners)		50%
Owner occupiers		61%
Council tenants		49%
Others		52%
Age of accommodation	pre 1939	51%
	1939–65	57%
	1966–76	67%
Detached house		68%
Central heating owners		65%

We concluded that the market for energy saving is segmented in a number of different ways. The primary segmentation relates to the *home itself,* i.e. the presence of central heating, type of tenure, age, and type of property in relation to building specifications. The secondary segmentation relates to *household composition,* e.g. presence of children. The third segmentation relates to *household circumstances,* e.g. the income, social grade, occupational grouping, age of housewife.

Perceived Price Rises In Energy Compared With Other Goods and Services.

During 1975 domestic consumers were aware of the increase in energy prices. They did not think, however, that energy prices had gone up or were likely to go up more than the general level of inflation. It was not until January 1976 that the increase in the *relative* level of inflation of energy prices was apparent to consumers; those who had recently received bills had a markedly higher tendency to claimed good housekeeping. (Exhibit 7).

EXHIBIT 7
The Relationship Between Having Received A Fuel Bill And Claiming To Be Saving Energy
(Received in Last Month)

	Total	Electricity Bill	Gas Bill
Claiming to be doing something to save energy	81%	94%	96%

"Plans" to Install.

"Plans" to install showed a steady growth until summer 1975 for four out of five energy-saving devices (loft insulation, tank lagging, draft excluders and double glazing) though the growth appeared to plateau by January 1976. The one device not to share in this general growth trend was cavity wall insulation; this is borne out by acquisitions of this installation, as measured by the AGB Home Audit, which reached their peak in the first quarter of 1975. (Exhibit 8). These "plans to install" should perhaps be regarded as no more than a measure of attitude, a conditional forecast by the consumer of his subjective probability to purchase. Their potential predictive value is further weakened because until the January 1976 survey we did not include a scale of probability of installation against specified time horizons.

EXHIBIT 8
Plans For Energy-Saving Installations
(Based On All Households; Potential Households In Brackets)

	Aug. 1974	Jan. 1975	March 1975	July 1975	Jan. 1976
Loft insulation	3%	7%	9%	11[16]%	13[17]%
Tank lagging	3%	3%	5%	10[12]%	10[12]%
Draft excluders	4%	9%	10%	23%	19%
Wall insulation	2%	5%	2%	3[7]%	2[5]%
Double glazing	5%	6%	7%	11%	10%

Many authors have commented on the problems of using intention statements to predict purchase of consumer

durables. A particularly useful paper with detailed references to over 60 earlier findings of Juster and Katona in the United States and of UK authors was given at the 1975 ESOMAR seminar by De Jonge and Oppedijk Van Veen. Their paper builds up a model which includes "situational variables," "anticipatory variables" and "change variables" as the predictors of a consumer durable purchase. Two other recent authors, Pickering and Isherwood, have been quite optimistic on the predictiveness of intention question. In reporting on an investigation of the role of purchase probability statements as predictors of individual household purchases of consumer durables they found that, for most durables, respondents stating higher purchase probabilities were more likely to have made a purchase of the specified item within the following four or fourteen months than those with lower purchase probabilities (1974).

We have so far tested the predictive value of "plans to install" each of three energy saving devices (loft insulation, tank lagging and draft excluders) by means of personal reinterviews in November 1975 with 158 respondents who in the first four quantitative surveys were either planners or non-planners matched demographically with planners (Exhibit 9). The original planning question was found to be predictive of behavior, particularly in the case of tank lagging but also with loft insulation and draft excluders. We believe that the explanation for greater predictiveness in the case of tank lagging lies in the fact that those "planning" tended to be thinking of a reasonably short period of three months and that the overwhelming motivation was to save money. For both these reasons there are fewer opportunities for the consumers' anticipation to be upset than is the case with loft insulation, where the planning period is longer, the capital outlay higher and the perceived benefits include comfort—all factors leading to competition with other priorities; at the other extreme draft excluders, which are installed mainly for comfort and are very inexpensive, perhaps do not rank as a "planned purchase" consumer durable at all. About *one-third* of those planning to install tank lagging during the first four surveys had done so by November 1975, against less than *one-tenth* of matched non-planners. However, the total sample (158) was quite small and we hope to undertake more work on the predictiveness of these questions by means of postal surveys of larger samples of re-interviewed respondents.

EXHIBIT 9
Percentage Increase In Acquisition Since Original Interview
(Based On 158 Households Reinterviewed)

	Draft Excluders	Tank Lagging	Loft Insulation
Original			
Planners/owners	20%	38%	17%
Planners/non-owners	39%	31%	22%
Non-planners/owners	23%	7%	17%
Non-planners/non-owners	24%	10%	5%

One other point must be made about these re-interviews. When the results are weighted back to include the proper proportion of owner occupiers there is no evidence that the sample as a whole were conditioned by their having been interviewed previously. Ownership among the 158 figures re-interviewed November 1975 are very similar to those based on the national Survey V.

Deterrents to Installing Energy-saving Devices.   One of the most important, if pessimistic, findings of the research program up to January 1976 is that the natural market for energy-saving devices is very limited and that there are substantial deterrents to installation. Quite apart from concerns on the capital cost of major items, council tenants tend to give as their reason for not planning installations as "not owning the property;" or the other major reason for not planning loft insulation and tank lagging was that respondents already had these items *albeit less than 3 inches (75mm) thick*. This finding of a limited natural market being mainly owner-occupiers who do not necessarily already own installations is confirmed by the AGB Home Audit data. Considering the three items on which the campaign has specifically concentrated, draft excluders are seen as reasonably applicable to all households; tank lagging is biased towards owner-occupiers though there is a growth in plans on the part of council tenants; and loft insulation is still heavily skewed towards owner-occupiers, like cavity wall insulation and double glazing. A segmented approach has had to be used in the advertising—different messages to different audiences for the different energy-saving devices.

Thickness of Insulation.   Part of the message of the *Save It* campaign was to persuade householders to buy thicker insulation for their lofts and tanks. The attitude surveys show a steady trend in this direction in terms of items planned. The findings of the Home Audit and retail trade surveys are discussed later. (Exhibit 10).

EXHIBIT 10
Thickness of Insulation Planned
(Based on Households Planning)

	Loft Insulation		Tank Lagging	
	July 1975	Jan. 1976	July 1975	Jan. 1976
1" (25mm)	7%	2%	3%	2%
2" (50mm)	18%	12%	17%	14%
3" (75mm)	24% } 32%	31% } 45%	29% } 35%	42% } 56%
4" (100mm)	8%	14%	6%	14%
Don't know	42%	40%	45%	29%

Knowledge of Relative Costs of Different Uses of Energy Within the Household.   In the January 1975 study the order of importance was found to be space heating, cooking, water heating, lighting, all other appliances. It was concluded that consumers

were fairly sensible, prior to any advertising campaign about what items take up most energy. They did, however, tend to over-estimate cooking relative to water heating and lighting relative to all other appliances. A year later respondents placed the different energy uses in the correct order, i.e. space heating, water heating, cooking, other appliances, lighting.

EXHIBIT 11
Knowledge of Relative Costs of
Different Uses of Energy Within the Household
(Based on an Importance Rating Made by All Households)

	Jan. 1975 (scored 5–1)	Jan. 1976 (scored 7–1)
Room space heating	4.55	6.44
Cooking	3.23	4.93
Water heating	3.11	5.51
Lighting	2.09	3.57
All other appliances	2.05	2.31
TV/radiogram	—	2.54
Laundry appliances	—	3.73

Model of Installation Behavior.   The motivations to install energy-saving devices are presented in diagrammatic form, following on from the general model of motivations to save (Exhibit 2). Provided that the householder translates his general desire to save money to saving specifically on energy he needs to be persuaded that the most efficient means of doing so is to raise the standard of thermal insulation and that this applies to *his* household. The re-interview survey of November 1975 highlighted different motivations for acquiring the various devices (e.g., tank lagging, just to save money; draft excluders, predominantly for comfort; loft insulation, to save money *and* to add to comfort). The findings confirmed many of the deterrents (e.g., for loft insulation the problem of perceived relevance to council tenants and to owners of existing [thin] insulation; credibility of the savings to be achieved and understanding of the pay-back period).

DATA ON ACQUISITION AND TRADE SURVEYS

Of households with an accessible loft only around one-half are insulated. Of these around four in ten have insulation to a depth of 3 inches or more and six in ten are below this figure. The potential market thus consists of some 50% of relevant households which are *uninsulated* and 30% which are *under* insulated. Acquisition will be accounted for by some initial purchasers and some households "topping up." Against this market background acquisitions of loft insulation among existing houses were 24% up in the first three quarters of 1975 over 1974. To these numbers may be added the builders' installations in new houses which from February 1975 had a stipulated minimum thickness of 2 inches (50mm) in place of the previous 1 inch (25mm) thickness.

On thickness of loft insulation the AGB figures for the third quarter of 1975 for "total thickness following acquisition" are very encouraging. Eight out of ten acquisitions were claimed to add up to 3 inches or more. This is consistent with the attitude survey figures shown in Exhibit 10 insofar as "don't knows" would rely on retailers' advice—which changed dramatically during 1975 according to the two surveys by Retail Audits Ltd, among the same sample of 160 builders' merchants. In July 1975 some 56% of them said that they would recommend a thickness of 3 inches or more and by December this figure had increased to 80%. This advice, in turn, reflected a substantial change in the pattern of stock among the same builders' merchants with a decline in the proportion stocking 1 inch and 2 inch material and a corresponding increase in those stocking 3 inch.

Cylinder Jackets. Of those homes with a hot water tank some three-quarters have a cylinder jacket. Of these, however, only around one quarter are 3 inches thick or more. The potential market therefore, among existing households lies particularly in persuading present owners to trade up to 3 inch as well as getting non-owners to buy for the first time. Against this market background, AGB are not so far showing a growth in numbers, which reflects the difficulty of convincing existing owners to change in a market which is near-saturation in terms of ownership level.

The picture is much more encouraging however in terms of thickness of cylinder jackets acquired. Substantially at the instigation of the Department of Energy the cylinder jacket manufacturers have been making only 3 inch jackets from August 1975. Once current stocks are exhausted this will automatically upgrade the thickness of acquisitions. The extent to which this movement is happening is reflected in both the AGB and the RAL data. According to AGB estimates some 20% of installed cylinder jackets are at least 3 inches thick; the proportion of *acquisitions* of this thickness was 23% in the 18 months to June 1975, but rose to 33% in the third quarter of 1975.

The retail surveys by Retail Audits Ltd, of the same 160 builders' merchants confirm this movement to 3 inch jackets. In July 1975 some 36% of them said that they would recommend a thickness of 3 inches or more and by December the figure had increased to 72%. Again, this advice reflected a very substantial change in the pattern of stock among the same builders' merchants, with 32% stocking 3 inch jackets in July and 63% in December.

Cavity Wall Insulation. According to AGB acquisitions doubled in the first three quarters of 1975 over the equivalent period of 1974 (from 46,000 to 91,000) but the first quarter of 1975 was very much more buoyant than the second or third. There were a number of marketing factors causing an erratic market performance, for instance, bad reports of instances of wall insulation and the timing of local authority approvals.

Double Glazing. According to AGB acquisitions were up 27% in the first three quarters of 1975 over the equivalent period of 1974 (154,000 to 195,000). This market has received substantial commercial publicity over the years and branded advertising in the year to September 1975 was in excess of £1m ($2.3m), so that market performance (as with cavity wall insulation) cannot be attributed primarily to the *Save It* campaign, which for thermal insulation has concentrated particularly on loft insulation, tank lagging and draft excluders.

ACHIEVEMENTS OF THE
DOMESTIC ENERGY CONSERVATION PROGRAM TO DATE

Reference has been made to movements in certain indicators and the obstinacy of others. In this connection our experience has been close to that of Greyser (1975):

> One must understand the difficulty of achieving one's goals. In this regard, Professor Philip Kotler of Northwestern University has offered a 'hierarchy' of four kinds of measureable change at which social marketing can be directed. They are:
> · *cognitive change* (e.g. awareness or knowledge regarding a campaign and for its substantive message; and attitudes towards the organisation/cause/idea);
> · *action change* (e.g. a specific action during period such as donation to a charity);
> · *behavioural change* (e.g. people giving up smoking);
> · *value change* (altering a deeply held belief, such as modifying racial or sexist prejudice, views on abortion, etc.).
>   Each of these successively is a step up the ladder of difficulty for the social marketer to achieve. It is important to delineate them, and to know the degree of difficulty at which one's communications and overall programme is directed.

In the UK domestic energy conservation program we have witnessed a variety of "cognitive" changes in the period under review. We have also seen changes in claimed behavior and some simple "actions" like turning heating or thermostat down. We have had some success in instigating more major "behavioral" changes such as the installation of loft insulation; but here the surveys have been as useful in highlighting the problem areas as the achievements. We are aware that a behavioral change may lead to a value change, that is, acquiring an energy-saving device may affect the importance one places on energy conservation. There is, however, *no* evidence to date of any "value" changes either with regard to how important householders rate energy-saving or who they think would expect them to cut down on energy; all the pressure to date is seen to come from the government and the Department of Energy rather than the community at large or even other members of the household.

Behind all the changes in the indicators has been the combined effect of economic pricing, the *Save It* advertising and other promotional support. The latter has included free media activity by the Department of Energy, the encouragement of conservation advertising on the part of the fuel industry and direct contact with the insulation industry which has led, for instance, to the manufacture of cylinder jackets being solely 3 inches or more.

The attitude research indicates that the general desire to save money is the prime motivator of the consumer to save energy. It is impossible to extricate the price and income effects from the advertising effects or to quantify the contribution made by each (a) in the absence of a controlled experiment, with and without advertising support and (b) because creatively the main promise of the *Save It* campaign has been the saving of money, i.e. one has reinforced the other. However the results of the attitude surveys, related to their timing (the third survey after only eight weeks of the *Save It* campaign and the fourth immediately after the pull-out supplement) do indicate the cumulative effect of the *Save It* campaign.

Although the saving of money is the prime motivator to save energy, the price-mechanism *by itself* appears to be a blunt instrument in achieving efficient savings in household energy. There are a number of reasons why the price message needs to be reinforced. As far as motivations to save energy are concerned it should be remembered:

· The use of most household energy is not related clearly or instantly to payment (and for some tenants, not at all);
· Up to summer 1975 the perceived *specific* price effect was weak. Past and prospective increases in energy prices were seen as no different from the general rate of inflation;
· While the consumers' prime interest in energy saving is to save money, no one is prepared to sacrifice their standards of comfort. As prices of energy increase and as consumers feel under greater economic pressure, they are likely to make savings on items other than energy. They have yet to be convinced that they should invest in order to save;
· Some motivating factors other than the desire to save money have been identified in the research surveys;
· The desire to save money on energy is not directly translated into investments in energy-saving devices unless the householder is aware of the benefits of good insulation. The problem of relevance to certain householders (e.g. tenants or existing owners of devices) is critical. Furthermore, the general economic pressures (the "income effect") which lead to a need to save money also act *against* investment expenditure on energy-saving devices unless the consumer is convinced of a clear, and not too lengthy, pay-back period.

CONCLUSIONS

After undertaking the market research program on UK domestic energy conservation, we should like to offer some broad conclusions which we believe are likely to apply, to a greater or lesser extent, to other countries' domestic conservation programs.

Marketing Conclusions.

· Economic pricing is a prerequisite of a credible conservation policy, but price *alone* will not lead directly to efficient energy saving;
· Paid advertising needs to be supported by other publicity activity;
· For a program to achieve credibility the support and co-operation in publicity by the fuel industries is essential;
· The campaign needs to be followed through to the point-of-sale if one of the objectives is to stimulate purchase of energy-saving durables;
· Different households will have different priorities in interpreting the energy-saving message. These differences will be partly subjective (such as council tenants rejection of the relevance of loft

insulation) and partly objective according to type of property, space heating needs etc. These factors may lead to a very segmented approach in the communication, along the lines of the Swedish household booklet.

Research Conclusions.

· In monitoring domestic conservation programs researchers should focus on a *number of relevant intermediate* indicators—in the UK this has particularly meant the rate of acquisition and thickness of certain energy-saving devices;
· Where the intermediate indicators are attitudinal their relevance may be uncertain a priori and should be checked;
· A research program may include a number of different jigsaw surveys which together build up a coherent picture;
· Both quantitative and qualitative techniques of attitude research are recommended; the latter add valuable insight to more structured surveys;
· Where the researcher seeks to monitor movements in behavior, panels should be used; however where cognitive changes are likely to be substantial, separate *ad hoc* surveys should be employed for measuring attitudes. If some re-interviews are undertaken in addition to these separate surveys it is possible to gain understanding of links between attitudes and behavior;
· If there are dangers of conditioning as well, then *ad hoc* surveys based on independent samples are better than panels; there is however, no evidence of conditioning in the small scale re-interviewing which forms a part of this research program;
· In the case of certain energy-saving devices (particularly tank lagging) statements of behavioral intention are likely to be more predictive than in many consumer durable markets;
· The market for energy-saving is segmented in a number of ways. The segmentation relates the home itself to *household composition*—and to *household circumstances*. Energy saving is highest among owner occupiers, owners of central heating, those in detached houses and newish property, the higher social grades and younger households. The more attitudinal differences are reflected in different *objective* priorities for different households in energy-saving, the greater need for a segmented approach to the marketing and research of energy-saving;
· The model of motivations to save energy and of installation behaviour, while based on UK experience, is likely to have general applicability to other countries.

REFERENCES

Building Research Establishment Working Party Report, (1975) *Energy conservation: a study of energy consumption in buildings and possible means of saving energy in housing*, Watford.
Building Research Establishment, (1976) *International symposium on energy conservation in the built environment*, Watford.
Central Policy Review Staff, (1974) *Energy Consumption*, London: HMSO.
De Jonge, L., and Oppedijk Van Veen, W. M. (1975) ESOMAR seminar on market modelling.
Fishbein, M. (1967) "Attitude and the prediction of behaviour" in Fishbein, M. *Readings in attitude theory and measurement*, Wiley & Sons.
King, S. (1975) "Towards a theory of advertisements." Market Research Society Conference, Bournemouth.
Kotler, P. (1975) *Marketing for nonprofit organizations*. Prentice Hall 1975, Chapter 15 quoted by Greyser, S. A. "Social marketing, the need for planning," *Advertising Quarterly* 45, Autumn, pp. 33–35.
Lowe Watson, D. (1975) "The British motorist and the oil crisis." ESOMAR Conference, Montreux.
National Economic Development Office, (1974) *Energy conservation in the United Kingdom*. London: HMSO.
Phillips, N. H. (1975) "The work of the Central Office of Information Research Unit." *Statistical News,* 31, November.
Pickering, J. F. and Isherwood, B. C. (1974) "Purchase probabilities and consumer durable buying behaviour." *Journal of Market Research Society* 16, 3, p. 203.

For Further Study

The readings in this book provide a broad perspective on marketing in public and nonprofit organizations. The early chapters, in particular, give an overview of theory and practice, while later ones focus on issues and applications in specific areas. But we hope that this book will also spur many readers to explore specific issues in greater depth.

USEFUL BIBLIOGRAPHIC REFERENCES

Managers or students interested in pursuing areas of interest in more depth might usefully start by seeking out and reviewing some of the approximately 500 bibliographic references included in the book's 40 chapters.

Another source of information for those wishing to undertake further study of public and nonprofit marketing is the useful, but modestly titled, *Incomplete Bibliography of Works Relating to Marketing for Public Sector and Nonprofit Institutions (Revised Edition-1977)* compiled by Michael Rothschild [1]. This listing of more than 600 items is subdivided by marketing topic (e.g., product, price, consumer behavior) and by area of application (e.g., health care, education, the arts). A more specialized reference is *Sources of Marketing Information for Educational Managers* by Michael Sales and Christopher Lovelock [2], which describes how to go about getting information pertinent to the management of educational institutions. Many of the reference sources cited in this document may also prove useful to managers of other types of nonbusiness organizations. Finally, there is Lorna Daniells's book, *Business Information Sources* [3], which has an entire chapter devoted to references on nonprofit organizations, as well as detailed guides to U.S. government statistical sources.

CONDUCTING AN INFORMATION SEARCH

A good library represents a veritable powerhouse of information for the public or nonprofit manager seeking information on such issues as market and environmental trends, competitive activity, new management techniques and strategies, recent research findings, and insights into consumer needs and behavior. But users unfamiliar with the collection of a large library often find it a problem to identify and locate relevant books, articles, statistics, and research reports. Professional librarians are, of course, trained to help users satisfy specific information needs. In addition, a search of the card catalogue under specific topics, even where one does not know names of authors or volume titles, may yield valuable results.

To identify relevant periodical articles—in major newspapers, magazines, and trade or professional journals—a variety of indexing and abstracting services are available. In printed form, those widely available in the United States include:

> *Readers' Guide to Periodical Literature*
> *Business Periodicals Index*
> *F&S Index*
> *F&S International Index*
> *New York Times Index*
> *Wall Street Journal Index*

Each of these guides is published annually, with cumulative updates at regular intervals throughout the year. By searching under a particular topic, the reader can find listed the titles of all relevant articles published in the periodicals referenced during the period in question, including publication name, date, and page reference.

Another approach to discovering published materials on public and nonprofit marketing, especially with regard to a specific area of application, is to conduct a computerized literature search. (As a matter of interest, Chapter 26 in this book, "Marketing Online Services in the University," by Douglas Ferguson, discusses the marketing of computerized literature searching in a university community.) More than 300 computer readable data bases—consisting of titles, abstracts, and/or key words from articles, books, government documents, and other sources—are available for search at many private and public libraries. In 1975, the number of computerized literature searches exceeded one million, a hundred-fold increase in utilization over a ten-year period.

The assistance of a knowledgeable librarian or information specialist is usually required to conduct a successful online literature search. In contrast to manual searches of card catalogs and reference indices in which a researcher is primarily concerned with overlooking or missing critical references, a person carrying out a computerized search is more likely to be concerned with casting the net too wide and acquiring numerous references that prove unrelated to the topic of interest. Thus, a careful specification of what to include and exclude is required. For example, in May 1978, a computerized search in *Dissertation Abstracts International* of titles that contained the words "marketing" and either "social" or "nonbusiness" or "public" or "nonprofit" produced a list of 25 dissertations. Although many of the references were useful, the list included ones with titles such as "The Social Organization of Marketing in a Southern Ghanaian Town." Of the 25 titles, 18 were given by "social marketing," six by "public marketing," one by "nonprofit marketing," and none by "nonbusiness marketing."

Computerized literature searches may represent a very productive use of the researcher's time. In preparing this book, more than one million citations were searched in less than one day of the authors' and a skilled information specialist's time. The computer charges for this search were less than $100. There is another important benefit, too. Since the data bases are usually updated at monthly or at most quarterly intervals, the user is assured that the information is current at the time of conducting the search.

CONCLUDING NOTE

The field of public and nonprofit marketing is attracting a great deal of attention from both researchers and practitioners at the present time. New research findings are regularly being reported, and many managers are sharing their insights and experiences in speeches and in published articles. This leads to better understanding of consumer needs and motivations, as well as providing new insights into how to manage different types of nonbusiness organizations more effectively.

We urge readers to try to stay abreast of current developments in areas of particular interest to them, since the state of the art is constantly moving ahead. The many different periodicals cited in this book of readings provide an ongoing source of new information. Another way of keeping up-to-date is to participate in conferences and workshops (and/or to read any subsequent published "proceedings."). Those interested in a particular organization may wish to request copies of its recent annual reports as well as examples of any consumer-oriented publications that it has produced.

As editors, we hope that the content of this book will prove both useful and stimulating. We welcome any feedback that you may wish to offer us.

REFERENCES

1. Rothschild, Michael L. *An Incomplete Bibliography of Works Relating to Public and Nonprofit Institutions (Revised Edition, 1977)*, 9-577-771, Boston, MA: Intercollegiate Case Clearing House, 1977, $4.30[1]
2. Sales, Michael J., and Lovelock, Christopher H. *Sources of Marketing Information for Educational Managers*, 9-578-140, Boston, MA: Interlegiate Case Clearing House, 1978, $1.00.[1]
3. Daniells, Lorna M. *Business Information Sources*, Berkeley, CA: University of California Press, 1976, $14.95.

---

[1] May be ordered from Intercollegiate Case Clearing House, Soldiers Field Post Office, Boston, MA 02163.